DO NOT REMOVE
CARDS FROM POCKET

FOLKLORE AND FOLKLIFE

GARLAND FOLKLORE BIBLIOGRAPHIES
(General Editor: Alan Dundes)
Vol. 16

GARLAND REFERENCE LIBRARY
OF THE HUMANITIES
Vol. 1429

Garland Folklore Bibliographies

Alan Dundes, *General Editor*
University of California, Berkeley

FOLKLORE AND FOLKLIFE
A Guide to English-Language Reference Sources

Volume II

Susan Steinfirst

GARLAND PUBLISHING, INC. • NEW YORK & LONDON
1992

Library of Congress Cataloging-in-Publication Data

Steinfirst, Susan.
　　Folklore and folklife : a guide to English-language reference sources / by Susan Steinfirst.
　　　　p.　cm. — (Garland folklore bibliographies ; vol. 16) (Garland reference library of the humanities ; vol. 1429)
　　Includes indexes.
　　ISBN 0-8153-0068-9
　　1. Folklore—Bibliography. I. Title. II. Series. III. Series: Garland folklore bibliographies ; v. 16.
Z5981.S74　1992
[GN66]
016.398—dc20　　　　　　　　　　　　　　　　　92-13594
　　　　　　　　　　　　　　　　　　　　　　　　　　CIP

Printed on acid-free, 250-year-life paper
Manufactured in the United States of America

For Gene

CONTENTS

Volume I

Folklore and Folklife

Chapter V

FOLK BELIEF SYSTEMS

It is very difficult to catalog and subdivide **folk beliefs**, which overlap into general works of folklore and folk ritual. This chapter includes reference works on customs, beliefs and superstitions, supernatural beliefs--magic, ghosts, fairies and little folk--and folk beliefs concerning animals, birds, trees, flowers, and the sea. Further, it includes works on folk religious beliefs and religious and secular symbols. And it concludes with a section on the works dealing with folk medicine, folk healing, and herbals.

A good place to begin research on folk customs is part III, "Customary Folklore," of Jan Harold Brunvand's *The Study of American Folklore* (3rd ed., pp. 300-397), in which he covers superstitions, customs, and festivals, folk dances and dramas, folk gestures, and folk games. (Folk festivals, dances and dramas, and games are covered in this work in Chapter 6.) In *Folklore and Folklife: An Introduction*, edited by Richard M. Dorson, a section on "Social Folk Custom" (pp. 159-232) has separate chapters on folk medicine, folk religion, festivals and celebrations, and recreations and games, among others.

FOLK BELIEF SYSTEMS
Customs, Beliefs, and Superstitions

This section is really concerned with *general* works on customs, folk beliefs, and superstitions. Works on the supernatural (witches, magic, ghosts, the occult, etc.), fairies and little people, mythic animals and mythic places, birdlore, and plantlore are treated separately below. Customs dealing with rites (death, birth, marriage) and rituals are included in the Chapter 6 as are calendar and holiday customs. Many comprehensive references and collections on folklore include beliefs, customs, superstitions, etc., so consult Chapter 1 also.

Consult Brunvand's two chapters on customs (pp. 328-349) and superstitions (pp. 300-327), in his *The Study of American Folklore* (3rd ed.) for an excellent overview of these subjects. For a good introduction to the collecting of superstitions, see Kenneth Goldstein's "The Collecting of Superstitious Beliefs" in (*Keystone Folklore Quarterly* 9 [1964]: 13-22). See also Alan Dundes' "The Structure of Superstition" (*Midwest Folklore* 11 [1961]: 25-56; reprinted in *Analytic Essays in Folklore* (The Hague: Mouton, 1975, pp. 83-94) and Wayland Hand's "Folk Beliefs and Superstition: A Crucial Field" in *Folklore Today: A Festschrift for Richard Dorson*, edited by Linda Dégh et al. (Bloomington: Indiana University Research Center for Language and Semiotic Studies, 1976, pp. 209-220) which details the need for more investigation into the function of folk beliefs and superstitions, for a structural study of beliefs, and for a body of theory. Also useful is Karl E. Scheibe's and Theodore R. Sarbin's "Towards a Theoretical Conceptualization of Superstition" (*British Journal for the Philosophy of Science* 16 [1965]: 143-158).

An interesting study of custom and belief is Patrick Mullen's *I Heard the Old Fishermen Say: Folklore of the Texas Gulf Coast* (Austin: University of Texas Press, 1978) which has a chapter on **occupational folklore**, covering magic beliefs, magic belief legends, and empirical beliefs, the forms, transmission, and changes of folk beliefs, and folk beliefs of ethnic groups, and another chapter on **regional folklore** which deals with local beliefs, character anecdotes, tall tales, and legends; appendixes include a list of magic and folk beliefs and a list of empirical folk beliefs.

As to the confusion of the terms **folk belief, custom, superstition**, etc., I offer this paragraph from Don Yoder's "Toward a Definition of Folk Religion":

> The term "superstition," as we all know, has its defenders. It was even used in it its German form, *Aberglaube*, in the title of the best work on folk beliefs produced in Europe, the *Handwörterbuch des deutschen Aberglaubens* [see no. 1454], all ten volumes, although it was minimally used in the text itself. European scholars who oppose *Aberglaube* as a value judgment, understandable solely in relation to a system of hard orthodoxy which sees truth only in its own terms, have, of course, proposed the neutral substitute term *VOLKSGLAUBE*, which is now also widely current in its English form "folk belief." (*Western Folklore* 33 [1974], p. 9)

Unfortunately the terminology is very vague, and folklorists use the terms differently. It has been suggested that **the belief** provides the philosophy or rationale, and **the custom**, the corresponding action or manifestation. Of course, one does not require the other; there are beliefs without any accompanying custom and vice versa. Jan Brunvand, who separates custom and superstition, says that although they are closely associated and both involve "both verbal and nonverbal elements that are traditionally applied in specific circumstances," they differ in that customs, unlike superstitions, "do not usually involve faith in the magical results of application. Thus the 'customs' that incorporate traditional belief in the supernatural are usually classified as superstitions." (*Study of American Folklore*, pp. 328-329) And Alan Dundes even suggests using the term **folk ideas** to mean any of the simple statements of popular misconceptions that appear in folklorists' collections of superstitions ("The Structure of Superstition" cited above).

Bibliography--Customs, Beliefs, and Superstitions

1445.   Cannon, Anthon S. "Selected Bibliography," in *Popular Beliefs and Superstitions from Utah*. Salt Lake City: University of Utah Press, 1984, pp. 415-422. LC 84- 5286; ISBN 0-87480-236-9.

This bibliography includes a very complete listing of titles on folk belief and superstition as well as articles and books on folk medicine, witchcraft, and ghostlore, and works on "other kinds of folk legends strongly underlain by folk belief."

1446. Danaher, Kevin D. [Ó Danachair, Caoimhín]. *A Bibliography of Irish Ethnology and Folk Tradition.* Dublin: The Mercier Press, 1978. 95p. LC 79-311272; ISBN 0-85342-490-x.

Cited previously (no. 90), this is a major bibliographic source of works on Irish folk customs and beliefs. Cites 3,000 books and articles, using the same format as *Handbook of Irish Folklore* (see no. 120). Updated by Danaher and Patricia Lysaght's "Supplement to a Bibliography of Irish Ethnology and Folklore" in *Béaloideas* (1980): 48-49; (1981): 206-207.

1447. Pitrè, Giuseppe. *Bibliografia delle Tradizioni Popolari d'Italia.* Torino-Palermo: Carlo Clausen, 1894. 603p. Reprinted: New York: Franklin Reprints, 1974. LC 72-82380; ISBN 0-8337-2775-3.

Not in English but a standard work. This is a massive work, covering 6,080 articles and books grouped in broad subject areas: *novelline, raconti, leggende, indovinelli, formole, proverbi,* etc. Covers all aspects of Italian popular tradition. Within each genre, the listing is alphabetical by author. The annotations, in Italian, are brief and descriptive. See as well Paolo Toschi's *Guida allo Studio delle Tradizione Popolari* (Turin: P. Boringhiere, 1962 [1945]) and his *Bibliografia delle Tradizioni Popolari d'Italia dal 1916 al 1940* (Florence: Barbera, 1964) which updates Pitrè's work. Regional bibliographies of Italian traditions include Giovanni Crocioni's *Bibliografia delle Tradizione Popolari de San Marino* (San Marino: F. della Balda, 1947), Crocioni's *Bibliografia delle Tradizioni Popolari Marchigiane* (Florence: Leo Olschki, 1953), with citations, some briefly annotated, to 1,503 books and journal articles, divided into sections: general writings, morals, superstitions, literature, vulgarisms and dialects, and arts, and Giuseppe Profeta's *Bibliografia delle Tradizioni Abruzzesi* (Rome: Aleneo, 1964).

1448. Ramsell, Jean E. "A Bibliography of Superstition." *RQ* 10 (Fall 1970): 45-48.

The author lists separately dictionaries, encyclopedias, and treatises or essays. Of particular interest is a list of problems associated with reference works on superstitions.

Classification--Customs, Beliefs, and Superstitions

Note: almost all collections are based and classified according to the one devised by Wayland Hand, in his work on "Superstitions" for the *Frank C. Brown Collection of North Carolina Folklore* (see no. 1470).

Dictionaries and Encyclopedias--Customs, Beliefs, and Superstitions

1449. Bonnerjea, Biren. *A Dictionary of Superstitions and Mythology.* London: Folk Press, 1927. Reissued: Detroit, MI: Singing Tree, 1969. 314p. LC 69-17755.

Very short definitions for each entry are given, and each is identified as a myth or superstition. The book includes people, places, and phrases (e.g., **"accidental upsetting of a cup**: In Japan, if a cup of medicine...be accidentally upset, it is a sure sign of speedy recovery." Sources are given if known). There is a bibliography of sources used in the text but no index.

1450. Daniels, Cora Linn, and C.M. Stevens, eds. *Encyclopaedia of Superstitions, Folklore, and the Occult Sciences of the World.* Chicago, IL, and Milwaukee, WI: J.H. Yewdale, 1903. Reprinted: Detroit, MI: Gale, 1971. 3 vols. 1,751p. LC 70-141151; ISBN 0-8103-2186-8.

This older work is divided into 27 chapters, dealing with birth and child life, love and marriage, death, the human body, etc., and subdivided, in a dictionary format, into smaller topics (i.e, death:

apparitions, bed, burial, etc.), within which many international superstitions are listed and origins given. The index in the last volume is inadequate and lacking in cross references.

1451. Donner, Cécile, and Jean-Luc Caradeau. *Dictionary of Superstitions.* Trans. Richard LeFanu. New York: Henry Holt, 1987 [1985]. 162p. LC 86-32008; ISBN 0-8050-0366-5.

This is not easy to use. Arranged alphabetically by one word or phrase, there are subsections for each entry. For example, for **aeroplane** or first word of a phrase, the authors give "**advice**: before setting off for the airport, put on one of your amulets and touch wood. As you step from the plane, 1. Cross your fingers, 2. make the sign of the cross, 3. spit. **If you're flying**: Don't use any word which might conjure up an air disaster. **Flowers are forbidden on the plane.** All flowers are forbidden, but the most ill-omened are **white**, etc." There is no bibliography and, worse, no index. Also no sources are given.

1452. Demetrio, Francisco R., et al., comps. *Dictionary of Philippine Folk Beliefs and Customs.* Cagayan de Oro City: Xavier University, 1970. 4 vols. 992p. LC 78-150504. (Museum and archives publication, 2)

This four-volume dictionary has broad subject entries: actions, amulets and talismans, animals, *aswangs* (or witches), birth, death, diseases and sickness, directions, feasts and celebrations, folk medicine, games and pastimes, houses, household utensils and objects, human persons, marriage, natural phenomena, numbers and numerals, omens, plants, prayers, sacrifices and rituals, transport, weaponry, which are then subdivided. Vol. 4 contains a distribution of folk beliefs according to province and an index to all four volumes.

1453. Hazlitt, William Carew. *Faiths and Folklore of the British Isles; A Descriptive and Historical Dictionary of the Superstitions, Beliefs and Popular Customs of England, Scotland, Wales, and Ireland, from Norman Times to the End of the Nineteenth*

Century, with Classical and Foreign Analogues. 2 vols. London: Reeves and Turner, 1905. 672p. Reprinted: New York: Benjamin Blom, 1965. LC 64-18758; ISBN 0-405-08604-0. Note: This work has several variant titles and has been published in one and two volumes throughout the years.

This work is based on John Brand's *Popular Antiquities of Great Britain*, only the second and expanded version of which was in alphabetic format (see Brand, no. 1495). However, Hazlitt's work is a major expansion and a complete reorganization, and he adds his own comments and uses illustrative examples not used by Brand. Definitions in this dictionary vary from short to quite long. It covers beliefs, superstitions, and customs as well as holidays and calendar customs.

1454.   von Hoffmann-Krayer, Eduard, and Hanns Bächtold-Stäubli, comps. *Handwörterbuch des Deutschen Aberglaubens.* 10 vols. Berlin and Leipzig: Walter de Gruyter, 1927-42. LC 31-20138.

Considered the most complete collection of European traditions and customs, this massive work has signed articles, many of great length, each with a bibliography. Vol. I contains a lengthy general bibliography.

1455.   Lasne, Sophie, and André Pascal Gaultier. *Dictionnaire des Superstitions.* Paris: Tchou, 1980. 317p. LC 80-155416; ISBN 2-7107-0233-9. Translated as *A Dictionary of Superstitions* by Amy Reynolds (Englewood Cliffs, NJ: Prentice-Hall, 1984).

Listed as just one example of many dictionaries of French-language beliefs. This work is arranged topically (e.g., minerals, objects, animals, calendar, human body, objects, the house, etc.), and then subdivided into a classified dictionary. Under each entry, several beliefs/superstitions are given. General introductions precede each chapter; there are many black and white illustrations. The work is indexed and there is a bibliography of other works, especially early French dictionaries and encyclopedias. See also, among others, Pierre Canavaggio's *Dictionnaire Raisonné de Superstitions et des Croyances Populaires* (Paris: Jean-Claude Simoën, 1977) and Robert Morel's and Suzanne

Walter's *Dictionnaire des Superstitions* (Verviers [Belgium]: Gerard, 1972 [1967]) which emphasizes the origins of the superstitions listed.

1456. Opie, Iona, and Moira Tatem, eds. *A Dictionary of Superstitions.* Oxford: Oxford University Press, 1989. 494p. LC 89-32327; ISBN 0-19-211597-9.

The editors say in the preface (v), that "the vast subject of 'superstition', taken by us to include divination, spells, cures, charms, signs and omens, rituals, and taboos, has never before been systematically organized." Included are superstitions from Great Britain and Ireland surviving into the nineteenth and twentieth centuries. Arranged alphabetically by subject (e.g., **adulterer cures wart**), with superstitions following chronologically. Sources are given. There is a select bibliography and an analytic index with 1) cross references to entries or to the index itself and 2) thematic entries.

1457. Radford, Edwin, and Mona Radford. *Encyclopaedia of Superstitions.* Ed. and rev. by Christina Hole. Chester Springs, PA: Dufour Editions, 1969 [1961]. 384p. LC 69-20013.

"The superstitions listed in this book have all been found to exist in one part or another of the British Isles." The entries given for each superstition provide an origin and definition. There is an attempt to distinguish superstition from custom and to exclude the latter. Included are a selected bibliography and general index.

1458. Wedeck, H.E., and Wade Baskin. *Dictionary of Gypsy Life and Lore.* New York: Philosophical Library, 1973. 518p. LC 72-75317; ISBN 0-8022-2094-0.

This includes an odd assortment of entries, arranged alphabetically by name or key word, such as **Abraham** ("there is a gypsy legend that when Abraham left Ur and traveled into Canaan, the Gypsies accompanied him"), **academic course**, **affinity with Rumania**, etc.

Gazetteer--Customs, Beliefs, and Superstitions

1459.   MacFadyen, David, and Christina Hole. *Folk Customs of Britain: A Gazetteer and Travellers' Companion.* London: Hutchinson, 1983. 112p. ISBN 0-09-151540-8.

Contemporary customs and rituals from England, Wales, and Scotland are arranged by country and town. Also included are a brief bibliography, an index, and a list of useful addresses.

Handbooks and Guides--Customs, Beliefs, and Superstitions

Note: See the citation to Phyllis H. Williams' *South Italian Folkways in Europe and America; A Handbook for School Workers, Visiting Nurses, School Teachers, and Physicians* (no. 1492).

Annotated Collections--Customs, Beliefs, and Superstitions

Note: This is a select list of published collections of customs and superstitions, arranged geographically, following a section of worldwide works. There are innumerable books with verbatim printed texts of oral and printed customs. Included here are those which are usable for comparative purposes and are easily referenced. There are many collections of beliefs printed in the folklore journals, such as T.J. Farr's "Riddles and Superstitions of Middle-Tennessee" (*Journal of American Folklore* 48 [1935]: 318-326), which have been generally omitted here. Consult also the dictionaries and encyclopedias listed above, as they also contain customs, superstitions, and beliefs.

Worldwide/Multicultural

1460.   Ackermann, A.S.E. *Popular Fallacies: A Book of Common Errors, Explained and Corrected, with Copious References to Authorities.* 4th ed. London: Old Westminster Press, 1950. 843p.

Reprinted: Detroit, MI: Gale, 1970. LC 79-121184; ISBN 0-8103-3295-7.

General beliefs and superstitions, arranged in broad subject areas, are listed and then debunked "by authorities." Similar works include: Philip Ward's *A Dictionary of Common Fallacies* (2nd ed., 2 vols., Cambridge, MA: Oleander Press, 1978, 1980), an alphabetic listing by key word of commonly held beliefs; Ashley Montagu's and Edward Darling's *The Prevalence of Nonsense* (New York: Harper, 1967), arranged also within broad subject areas (i.e., beliefs about the human body, misconceptions about the human mind, etc.); Ronald Duncan's and Miranda Weston-Smith's *Lying Truths: A Critical Scrutiny of Current Beliefs and Conventions* (New York: Pergamon, 1979); and Guy Bechtel's and Jean-Claude Carriere's *Dictionnaire de la Betise et des Erreurs de Jugement* (rev. ed., Paris: Laffont, 1983 [1965]).

1461. Ashley, Leonard R. N. *The Wonderful World of Superstition, Prophecy, and Luck.* New York: Dembner Books, 1984. 182p. LC 83-23182; ISBN 0-934878-33-1 (p).

Part I deals with Superstition and Part II covers "The Future." Each is subdivided into topics and, somewhat haphazardly, further subdivided into smaller topics (i.e., Superstition: People: shadows, ladders, lightning, etc.). There is an index of authors, titles, and subjects mentioned. Ashley also wrote *The Wonderful World of Magic and Witchcraft* (New York: Dembner, 1986).

The Americas
North America

Note: See also no. 1492.

1462. Ainsworth, Catherine Harris. *Superstitions from Seven Towns of the United States.* Buffalo, NY: University Press, State University of New York at Buffalo, 1973. 58p. LC 73-163892.

These superstitions were collected in small towns--Seward, Alaska, Winslow, Arizona, Newington, Connecticut, etc.--and arranged and numbered within these geographical units. There is no cross referencing with other standard collections or bibliography.

1463. Brewster, Paul G., ed. "Beliefs and Customs," in *The Frank C. Brown Collection of North Carolina Folklore.* Vol. 1. Durham, NC: Duke University Press, 1952. pp. 221-282.

Customs and beliefs from North Carolina are arranged within the following topics: childhood, folk toys, courtship and marriage, holidays and "get togethers," household superstitions, plants and animals, death and burial, miscellaneous, quilt patterns, dyeing, cooking and preserving, and beverage making. The source of each custom is given. A bibliography is also included. See Hand (no. 1470) for further lists of customs in this collection of North Carolina folklore, and Clark (no. 1467) for more North Carolina beliefs.

1464. Browne, Ray B. *Popular Beliefs and Practices from Alabama.* Los Angeles and Berkeley: University of California Press, 1958. 271p. LC 58-9290. (Folklore studies, 9)

There are 4,340 customs listed within broad subject areas--birth, infancy, and childhood; folk medicine and the human body; domestic and household; travel and communication; economic and social relationships; love, courtship, and marriage; death and funeral customs; the supernatural; cosmic, time and months; weather; animals and animal husbandry; fishing and hunting; plants and plant husbandry; and miscellaneous. The list of 104 contributors is included in the back of the book, and each custom is assigned to its informant. There is a bibliography but no index.

1465. Cannell, Margaret. "Signs, Omens, and Portents in Nebraska Folklore." *University of Nebraska Studies in Language, Literature, and Criticism* 13 (1933): 3-50.

611

Listed separately are weather signs, portents and omens about marriage and courtship (e.g., if someone meets you and tells you that he did not know you, it is a sign that you are going to be married), death, bad and good luck, animals, etc., with an introduction for each section. There is a bibliography but no index.

1466.   Cannon, Anthon S. *Popular Beliefs and Superstitions from Utah*, ed. Wayland D. Hand and Jeannine E. Talley. Salt Lake City: University of Utah Press, 1984. 491p. LC 84-5286; ISBN 0-87480-236-9.

This is a huge collection of 13,207 items, collected mostly between 1954-1960. There is a long introduction, unsigned but presumably by Cannon who died in 1976. The customs are arranged within 13 sections, covering birth, infancy, childhood; the human body; physical ailments and diseases; love, courtship, marriage; domestic pursuits; economic and business affairs; travel and communication; social relationships, recreation; death and funeral customs; religion, lower mythology, witchcraft, magic; divination; ghostlore; weather, cosmic phenomena, time and the universe; and animal and plant husbandry. The material is endlessly subdivided. Each custom listed includes the gender of the informant, the place, and the date taken, and each is cross listed with both of the above collections. There is an index.

1467.   Clark, Joseph D. "North Carolina Superstitions." *North Carolina Folklore* 14 (1966): 3-40.

Almost 1,500 superstitions are listed topically--birth, infancy, childhood, the human body, folk medicine, home, domestic pursuits, economies, social relationships, travel, etc.

1468.   Fogel, Edwin Miller. *Beliefs and Superstitions of the Pennsylvania Germans*. Philadelphia, PA: American Germanica Press, 1915. 387p. LC 15-132289. (American Germanica; new ser., 18)

There are 2,083 separate superstitions given in English.

1469. Frankel, Barbara. *Childbirth in the Ghetto: Folk Beliefs of Negro Women in a North Philadelphia Hospital Ward.* San Francisco, CA: R & E Research Associates, 1977. 123p. LC 76-27000; ISBN 0-88247-418-9.

This is based on interviews with 59 American black women between the ages of 15 and 42. Frankel arranges 285 customs and superstitions into three categories: signs (of pregnancy, sex, etc.), causes (of pregnancy, of harm to babies, etc.), and controls (over conception of unwanted pregnancy, etc.). There is an excellent introduction and bibliography.

1470. Hand, Wayland, ed. *Popular Beliefs and Superstitions from North Carolina.* Vols. 6 and 7 of *The Frank C. Brown Collection of North Carolina Folklore.* Durham, NC: Duke University Press. Vol. 6, 1961, 664p.; Vol 7, 1964, 677p.

This is a comprehensive collection of 8,569 popular beliefs and superstitions arranged according to topic. Vol. 6 (nos. 1-4873) covers birth, infancy and childhood; the human body, folk medicine; home, domestic pursuits; economic, social relations; travel, communication; and love, courtship, and marriage. Vol. 7 (nos. 4874-8569) covers death and funeral customs; witchcraft, ghosts, magical practices; cosmic phenomena: times, numbers, seasons; weather; animals, animal husbandry; fishing and hunting; and plants, plant husbandry. These fourteen categories constitute the basic classification and indexing scheme used in most collections of folk belief. For each custom listed, Hand gives the sources, place, date, and name of the informant. Vol. 7 has an index to both volumes and a list of informants and collections. See also Brewster's collection of North Carolina beliefs (no. 1463) and Clarke's collection (no. 1467).

1471. Howell, Benita. *A Survey of Folklife Along the Big South Fork of the Cumberland River.* Knoxville: Department of

Anthropology, University of Tennessee, 1981. 431p. LC 83-620672; ISBN 0-8704-0350-7. (Report of investigation, 30)

This collection of folklore, based on fieldwork done in 1979 and 1980, includes examples of plant and weatherlore and beliefs about tools, shelters, food, railroads, family, and the church.

1472.   Hyatt, Harry Middleton. *Folk-Lore from Adams County, Illinois.* 2nd rev. ed. New York: Memoirs of the Alma Egan Hyatt Foundation, 1965 [1935]. 920p. LC 66-6468.

Over 16,500 beliefs are listed and arranged by topic and subtopic. No information is given about the informant, place, or time of collection.

1473.   Hyatt, Harry Middleton. *Hoodoo--Conjuration--Witchcraft--Rootwork; Beliefs Accepted by Many Negroes and White Persons....* 5 vols. Printed for Harry M. Hyatt by Western Publishing Company (Hannibal, MO) and distributed by the American University Bookstore, Washington, DC, 1970-1978. 4,754p. LC 71-12434. (Memoirs of the Alma Egan Hyatt Foundation)

The subtitle of this massive collection is "Beliefs Accepted by Many Negroes and White Persons. These Being Orally Recorded among Blacks and Whites." This collection is a chaotic compilation of beliefs collected entirely through interviews, covering folk beliefs, religious beliefs, and folk medicine (Vol. 2, for example, is entirely interviews with "doctors"). Vol. 6 was planned as a much-needed index to the other volumes. Without it, this fascinating collection is mighty hard to use.

1474.   Johnson, Jerry Mack. *Country Scrapbook.* New York: Simon and Schuster, 1977. 320p. LC 77-24912; ISBN 0-671-22848-X (c); ISBN 0-671-22895-1 (p).

Described by the author as "a collection of nature facts and rural lore," this wonderful book includes weather wisdom, hunting and fishing lore, animal and plant lore, with separate sections on farm foods, recipes, homemade household items, cleaning methods, pest purges, and country cures (listed alphabetically by ailment), and country pastimes (also arranged in alphabetical order). There is an index.

1475. Klein, Barbro Sklute. *Legends and Folk Beliefs in a Swedish American Community: A Study in Folklore and Acculturation.* 2 vols. New York: Arno, 1980. LC 80-730; ISBN 0-405-13317-0 (vol. 1); 0-405-13342-1 (vol. 2).

Vol. 1 is a study, but Vol. 2 contains texts of folk beliefs taken from 139 interviews with immigrants, second generation Swedish-Americans, and subsequent generations of adults and children. There is a long bibliography in Vol. 1.

1476. Koch, William E., ed. *Folklore from Kansas: Customs, Beliefs, and Superstitions.* Lawrence: Regents Press of Kansas, 1980. 467p. LC 79-20197; ISBN 0-7006-01929.

Over 5,000 items, collected by 45 students, are listed under 12 topics (including courtship and marriage, prevention and cure of illnesses and injuries, luck, making wishes, etc.). Each section has a brief introduction; the listings include the year collected, age, and gender of the person, etc. The appendixes include maps, a profile of contributors, and a statistical tabulation of the frequencies of items tabulated. There is no index. Mr. Koch also included a collection of 266 beliefs and sayings, topically arranged, in *Kansas Folklore,* edited by Samuel J. Sackett and Koch (Lincoln: University of Nebraska Press, 1961).

1477. Parler, Mary Celestia, ed. *Folk Beliefs from Arkansas.* 15 vols. [Fayetteville, AK: The author], 1962. 4,996p.

This work, in typescript, is available from the University of Arkansas, Fayetteville. All 11,788 entries, the author states in the preface, were "gathered from oral sources--from family, friends, and acquaintances--by students in my course in Arkansas folklore during the years 1955-1961." Parler uses Hand's system of classification (see no. 1470), citing by whom and where each belief was collected.

1478. Puckett, Newbell Niles. *Folk Beliefs of the Southern Negro.* Chapel Hill: University of North Carolina Press, 1926. 644p. Reprinted: New York: Negro Universities Presses, 1968. LC 68-55912. Reprinted: New York: Dover, with the title *The Magic and Folk Beliefs of the Southern Negro*, 1969. LC 72-92389; ISBN 0-4862-2460-0.

The customs are arranged within the following chapters: practical and emotional background (slave England, African stories, riddles, etc.); burial customs, ghosts, and witches; voodooism and conjuration; minor charms and cures; taboos; prophetic signs or omens; and Christianity and superstition. Although given in text format, a 40-page detailed index is helpful for accessing customs and beliefs. Information about informants is also given.

1479. Puckett, Newbell Niles. *Popular Beliefs and Superstitions: A Compendium of American Folklore: From the Ohio Collection of Newbell Niles Puckett*, ed. Wayland D. Hand et al. Boston, MA: G.K. Hall, 1981. 3 vols. 1,829p. LC 81-6687; ISBN 0-8161-8585-9 (set).

Hand and two other editors, Anna Casetta and Sondra B. Thiederman, have edited the written catalog of manuscript material compiled by Puckett, who died in 1967. There are 36,209 classified beliefs listed (from the over 72,000 items collected by Puckett) in the first two volumes, each with the initial of the informant, sex, age, occupation, ethnic heritage, date of response, and geographical data. The third volume contains an introduction, a chapter on the background of the "settlement and peoples of Ohio," an ethnic finding list, a 200-page index, and appendixes, which include the collecting questionnaire, sample entries, and list of nationalities.

1480. Randolph, Vance. *Ozark Superstitions*. New York: Columbia University Press, 1947. 367p. Reprinted: New York: Dover, 1964. LC 64-18649; ISBN 0-486-21181-9.

This is not really a classified listing of beliefs, but Randolph's collection of superstitions, which are embedded in chapters about the weather signs, mountain medicine, water witches, Ozark witchcraft, etc., is important for comparative purposes. There is an index and a good bibliography. See also Randolph's "Folk Beliefs in the Ozark Mountains" (*Journal of American Folklore* 40 [1927]: 78-93), in which he used basically the same groupings of beliefs.

1481. Snapp, Emma Louise. *Proverbial Lore in Nebraska*. Lincoln: University of Nebraska, 1933. pp. 53-112. (Studies in language, literature, and criticism, 13)

This lists beliefs in proverb format about animals, nature, weather, women/love/marriage, vice and folly, virtue and wisdom, money, home life, professions and trades, sports and games. Each section is briefly introduced, followed by the beliefs, listed, and numbered. There is a brief bibliography but no index.

1482. Stout, Earl J., ed. *Folklore from Iowa*. New York: G.E. Steckert for American Folk-Lore Society, 1936. 228p. LC 37-19297. (Memoirs of the American Folk-Lore Society; v. 29)

Part I includes ballads and folk songs, and Part II includes current beliefs from Iowa, pp. 141-204, listed in subject areas. Sources are given; there is an index to both parts.

1483. Thomas, Daniel Lindsey, and Lucy Blayney Thomas. *Kentucky Superstitions*. Princeton, NJ: Princeton University Press, 1920. 334p. LC 20-18391.

The authors list 3,954 superstitions, arranged in 32 subject areas (birth and child life, family relationship, etc.). Broad sources are given for each (e.g., Western Kentucky, Louisville Negroes, etc.). The subject index is complete and will provide access.

Canada

1484.   Creighton, Helen, ed. *Bluenose Magic; Popular Beliefs and Superstitions in Nova Scotia.* Toronto: Ryerson Press, 1968. 297p. LC 68-143142.

These beliefs and superstitions are grouped within the following subject areas: the supernatural, witchcraft, and enchantment, treasure, Micmac Indians, fairies, dreams, superstitions, good luck and bad, divination, home remedies, weather, crops, and animals, and birds. Numbering is consecutive within each section. Sources are given for each, and there is a motif index. A bibliography and a general index are also included.

1485.   Halpert, Herbert, ed. *A Folklore Sampler from the Maritimes: With a Bibliographical Essay on the Folktale in England.* St. John's [Newfoundland]: Memorial University of Newfoundland, 1982. 273p. LC 83-181599; ISBN 0-88901-086-2. (Published for the Center for Canadian Studies, Mt. Allison University, by Memorial University of Newfoundland folklore and language publications; bibliographical and special series, 8)

Aside from the narratives, there is a substantial collection of folk beliefs about the weather, Christmas, etc., divided, subdivided, and numbered, with sources given. There is a complete bibliography but no index.

Asia

1486.   Massé, Henri. *Persian Beliefs and Customs.* Trans. Charles A. Messner. New Haven, CT: HRAF, 1954. 526p. LC 55-3661.

Published originally as *Croyances et Coutumes Persanes, suivi de Contes et Chansons Populaires*. 2 vol. Paris: Librarie Orientale & Americaine, 1938.

This book discusses customs of pregnancy, childbirth, and childhood; marriage; death and funeral rites; periodic ceremonies; popular meteorology; customs surrounding plants and water; divination, signs and pressages; magical procedures; popular medicine; and supernatural beings. Legends, games, and folk poetry are also included. Notes, additions, and a bibliography conclude the work. There is no index.

Europe
France

1487.   van Gennep, Arnold. *Coutumes et Croyances Populaires en France*. Paris: Chemin Vert, 1980. 322p. LC 81-109692; ISBN 2-903533-01-6. (Le temps et le memoire)

This is a mishmash of history, sayings, beliefs, legends, etc., taken from van Gennep's earlier writings, primarily from his first work, *Le Folklore* (Paris: Stock, 1924), and from his *Manuel de Folklore Français Contemporain* (4 vols. in 10. Paris: A. Picard, 1943-1958 [1937]), which covers ritual beliefs (see no. 1762). Includes French popular beliefs and traditions, legends, songs, games, as well as a questionnaire used to collect folk traditions compiled by Armand Landrin and Paul Sébillot (1896). See also Paul Sébillot's *Le Folk-lore de France* (4 vols. Paris: Guimolto, 1904-1907; reprinted in 8 vols.: Paris: Imago, 1982): Vol. 1 covers beliefs about the sky and the land; Vol. 2, beliefs about the sea and water creatures; Vol. 3 covers flora and fauna-lore; and Vol. 4 is about French people and history.

Germany

Note: See the citation to *Handwörterbuch des Deutschen Aberglaubens*, ed. Eduard von Hoffmann-Krayer and Hanns Bächtold-Stäubli (10 vols., Berlin: Walter de Gruyter,

1927-1942), possibly the greatest compilation of beliefs and superstitions in print (no. 1454).

Ireland

1488.   Danaher, Kevin. *Irish Country People*. Cork: Mercier Press, 1966. 127p. LC 72-411.

Discusses the beliefs of the Irish widow, the tailor, mason, cooper, basket maker, the blacksmith, working people as well as the beliefs about ships and horses. See also Danaher's *Gentle Places and Simple Things* (Cork: Mercier Press, 1964), dealing with the beliefs about wandering people and wee people, ghosts, and places, and *"That's How It Was!"* (Cork: Mercier Press, 1984) which covers all aspects of Irish traditional life--proverbs, children's games, the healing arts as well as folk beliefs and customs.

1489.   Evans, Emyr Estyn. *Irish Folk Ways*. New York: Devin-Adair, 1957. 324p. LC 57-14898.

Covers customs, rites, festivals as well as descriptions of farms, homes, and homemade artifacts.

1490.   Ó Súilleaháin, Seán. *Irish Folk Custom and Belief.* 2nd ed. Cork: Mercier Press for the Cultural Relations Committee of Ireland, 1977 (1962). 99p. LC 79-302343; ISBN 0-85342-146-3. (Irish life and culture, 15)

Stating that there is "a very rich variety of Irish folk customs" (p. 15), the compiler discusses the nature of folklore, folk custom and belief in general, and then includes, in chapter format, customs and beliefs of 1) house and home, 2) the farmer, fisher, and craftsman, 3) travel, trade, and communication, 4) the community, 5) human life, and 6) healing the sick; there are further chapters dealing with festivals, magic and other powers, and the world outside us. A bibliography is appended.

1491.   Pitrè, Giuseppe. *Biblioteca Delle Tradizioni Popolari Siciliane*. 25 vols. Palermo: L. Pedone-Lauriel, 1872-1913. Reprinted: Bologna: Forni, 1968-1969.

These volumes cover the full range of Sicilian traditions: Vols. 1 and 2 cover songs; Vol. 3 covers poetry; Vols. 4-7 cover fables, stories, and legends; Vols. 8-11 and 23 are on proverbs; Vols. 12 and 21 are on festivals; Vols. 14-17 are on costume, beliefs, and prejudices; Vol. 19 covers folk medicine; Vol. 20 is on riddles,; Vol 22 is on the study of legend; and Vol. 25 is on the family, the house, and the life of the people. Each book has a different format.

1492.   Williams, Phyllis H. *South Italian Folkways in Europe and America; A Handbook for Social Workers, Visiting Nurses, School Teachers, and Physicians*. New Haven, CT: Published for the Institute for Human Relations by Yale University Press, 1938. Reprinted: 1969. LC 69-16768; ISBN 0-8462-1322-2.

This work attempts to introduce helping professionals to the cultural problems faced by Italian immigrants when adjusting to life in America. **Culture** is defined by Williams as "the method worked out by human groups to solve their life problems...the folkways, mores, and institutions that define their mode of life." (pref.) Williams deals with customs of the homeland, employment, housing, diet and household economy, dress, marriage and the family, recreation and hospitality, education, religion and superstition, health and hospitals, care of the aged and of other dependents, and death and mortuary practices. The work is often cited as being a model for field workers. The index will aid users to locate specific customs.

Europe--Great Britain

Note: There is an abundance of books on English customs and folklore, such as John Glyde's *Folklore and Customs of Norfolk* (New York: E.P. Dutton, 1973 [1872]), John Symonds Udal's

Dorsetshire Folk-Lore (Hertford: Stephen Austin, 1975 [1922]), and I.F. Grant's *Highland Folkways* (London: Routledge & Kegan Paul, 1961). Most of these are in chapter format and are excluded from this work.

1493.   Baker, Margaret. *Folklore and Customs of Rural England.* Newton Abbot [ENG] and Totowa, NJ: David & Charles and Rowman & Littlefield, 1974. 208p. LC 74-7065; ISBN 0-87471-549-0.

The customs and beliefs are grouped around farm customs, house and garden customs, the country calendar, customs "from cradle to grave," beliefs of the country church, and country cures and remedies. There are notes and references, and indexes and bibliographies are included.

1494.   Bergen, Fanny D., ed. and annot. *Current Superstitions: Collected from the Oral Traditions of English Speaking Folk.* Boston and New York: Published for the American Folk-Lore Society by Houghton, Mifflin, 1896, 161p. LC 4-4052. (Memoirs of the American Folk-Lore Society; v. 7). Reprinted: New York: Kraus, 1969.

Almost 1,500 brief superstitions are listed within the following categories: "babyhood," childhood, physical characteristics, projects, Halloween and other festivals, love and marriage, wishes, dreams, luck, money, visitors, cures, warts, the weather, moon, sun, death omens, mortuary customs, and miscellaneous superstitions. The regional sources of the beliefs are given in most instances, and there is an extensive notes section. The lack of an index will hamper use.

1495.   Brand, John. *Observations on the Popular Antiquities of Great Britain: Chiefly Illustrating the Origin of Our Vulgar and Provincial Customs, Ceremonies, and Superstitions.* 3 vols. London: Henry G. Bohn, 1848. Variant title: *Popular Antiquities of Great Britain, with Notices of the Movable and Immovable Feasts.*

Vol. 1 covers holidays and feasts; Vol. 2 includes all kinds of customs and rites--cock fighting, marriage customs, funeral rites, and games; Vol. 3 covers witchcraft, omens, charms, divinations and "vulgar errors." The index to all three volumes is in Vol. 3. Customs are rather loosely presented. It is from this set of books that Hazlitt prepared his dictionary of national beliefs, superstitions, and popular customs. (See also no. 1453.)

1496. Ditchfield, P.H. *Old English Customs Extant at the Present Time; An Account of Local Observances, Festival Customs and Ancient Ceremonies Yet Surviving in Great Britain.* London: Methuen, 1896. 343p. Reprinted: Detroit, MI: Singing Tree, 1968. LC 68-21765.

Aside from calendar and holiday customs, this older source contains lists of rural and local customs, superstitions, marriage customs, legal, civic, Parliamentary and court customs, bell-ringing customs, and army customs. There is an index.

1497. Hole, Christina. *Traditions and Customs of Cheshire.* London: Williams and Norgate, 1937. 214p. Reprinted: Norwood, PA: Norwood Editions, 1975. LC 73-12972; ISBN 0-8830-5260-1.

Beliefs and customs are grouped around the following subjects: life's occasions; farming; birds and beasts and living things; wells and water; the spring of the year; wakes and fairs; dark winter; trouble and disgrace; ghosts and boggarts; admirable curiosities; tales; and traditions. There is a brief bibliography and an index.

1498. Kirkwood, James. *A Collection of Highland Rites and Customs, Copied by Edward Lhuyd from the Manuscript of the Rev. James Kirkwood (1650-1790) and Annotated by Him....* London: Published for the Folklore Society by D.S. Brewer; Totowa, NJ: Rowman & Littlefield, 1975. 117p. LC 75-1308; ISBN 0-87471-676-4.

The customs are arranged in 47 sections (e.g., "Observations upon their computation of tyme," "their habits and ornaments," etc.). The beliefs are not numbered but are listed with Scottish Gaelic words and English with editor's notes appended at the end of each section. The appendix includes a bibliography and a glossarial index by Scottish Gaelic word and Scots word.

1499.   Lean, Vincent Stuckey. *Lean's Collectanea; Collections... of Proverbs..., Folklore, and Superstitions....* 4 vols. in 5. Bristol: V.H. Arrowsmith, 1902-1904. 940p. Reprinted: Detroit, MI: Gale, 1969. LC 68-26583; ISBN 0-8102-3203-5.

Vol. 2 covers "folklore, superstitions, omens, and popular customs." The scope, though basically British, is international; the source is given for each listing.

1500.   McPherson, J.M. *Primitive Beliefs in the North-East of Scotland.* London: Longmans, Green, 1929. 310p. Reprinted: New York: Arno, 1977. LC 77-70605; ISBN 0-405-10109-0. (International folklore series)

Part I is concerned with nature worship and includes fire festival customs, a section on holy wells, river spirits, locks and oceans, tree spirits, stones, fairies, devil worship, etc. Part II is about "the black arts" and covers ritual, divination, etc. There is an index of place names and a subject index.

1501.   Newall, Venetia J., general editor. *Folklore of the British Isles.* London: Batsford, 1973--.

This is a series of books about the customs of Great Britain. Included are separate works on the folklore of Cornwall (by T. Deane and T. Shaw, 1975), of the Cotswolds (by K. Briggs, 1974), of Devon (by R. Whitlock, 1977), of East Anglia (by E. Porter, 1974), of Hampshire and the Isle of Wight (by W. Boase, 1976), of Ireland (by S. O'Sullivan, 1974), of the Isle of Man (by M. Kilip, 1975), of the Lake District (by M.

Rowling, 1976), of Orkney and the Shetlands (by E. W. Marwick, 1975), of the Scottish Highlands (by A. Ross, 1976), of Somerset (by K. Palmer, 1976), of Staffordshire (by J. Raven, 1978), of Sussex (by J. Simpson, 1973), of Warwickshire (by R. Palmer, 1976), of the Welsh border (by J. Simpson, 1973), and of Wiltshire (by R. Whitlock, 1976). Each volume has sections on different customs, a section of notes, a select bibliography, an index of tale types, a motif-index, and a general index.

1502.   Porter, Enid. *Cambridgeshire Customs and Folklore.* London: Routledge & Kegan Paul, 1969. 419p. LC 70-397354; ISBN 0-7100-6201-x.

This is one of a series of collections of British county folk customs published for the English Folklore Society. Of this series, Jan Brunvand has said that it carries on the tradition of publishing such collections of customs, but that this particular series does it "in a much more sophisticated comparative approach than most earlier works. In American folklore we have nothing comparable to these English products." *(Folklore: A Study and Research Guide*, p. 74)

FOLK BELIEF SYSTEMS: SUPERNATURAL BELIEFS
Witchcraft, Magic, Ghosts, and the Occult

There is an enormous amount of literature on these subjects, much of which is neither folklore nor reference.

There are several classic texts on magic and the supernatural, one of which is Kurt Seligmann's *Magic, Supernaturalism, and Religion* (New York: Pantheon, 1973 [1948]) which covers magic in the ancient worlds and in the Middle Ages and discusses the concept of the devil as well as witchcraft, the magic arts, and diabolic rites. There are also several serious histories of magic: Lynn Thorndike's *History of Magic and Experimental Science*, 8 vols. (New York: Macmillan, 1923-1958) is the standard history, but there are newer ones such as the work by Richard Cavendish--*A History of Magic* (New York: Taplinger, 1977). Also, of course, there is Sir James Frazer's *The Golden Bough; a Study in Magic and Religion* (12 vols. and supplement, London: Macmillan, 1907-1915, 1936; the abridgement, *The New Golden Bough*, published by Macmillan in 1959), which, though not really a reference, is still a goldmine of information on the magic arts and primitive religion.

Several works deal with the relationship between folklore and magic, such as Margaret Stutley's *Ancient Indian Magic and Folklore* (Boulder, CO: Great Eastern, 1980) which discusses medical charms and rites and charms to protect royalty, priests, and their possessions and ensure prosperity, etc.

There are also a great many books dealing with witchcraft. Many of them are written by "practitioners"; however, there are many scholarly works on witchcraft, the most famous of which is probably George Lyman Kittredge's *Witchcraft in Old and New England* (Cambridge, MA: Harvard University Press, 1929) which studies many aspects of early witchcraft; a newer scholarly work is *Witchcraft*, edited by Charles Alva Hoyt (2nd ed., Carbondale: Southern Illinois University Press, 1989 [1981]) which looks at Satan, the origins, development, orthodox and anthropological positions on witchcraft as well as the psychological and pharmacological schools of witchcraft. Of particular interest to folklorists is *The Witch Figure; Folklore Essays by a Group of Scholars in England honoring the 75th Birthday of Katharine M. Briggs*, edited by Venetia Newall (London: Routledge & Kegan Paul, 1973), with eleven essays on various aspects of witches and witchcraft, an appreciation of Katharine Briggs, and a bibliography of her publications. David J. Hufford's *The Terror that Comes in the Night: An Experience-centered Study of Supernatural Assault Traditions* (Philadelphia: University of Pennsylvania; Publication of the American Folklore Society, new series, 7, 1982) is concerned with witch-riding.

There are many, many studies of witchcraft as practiced in other countries, both in the past and today: Gabriel Bannerman-Richter's *The Practice of Witchcraft in Ghana* (Winona, MN: Apollo Books, 1982), Sir Henry Bell's *Obeah; Witchcraft in the West Indies* (Westport, CT: Negro Universities Press, 1970 [1889]), Barrie Reynolds' *Magic, Divination, and Witchcraft among the Barotse of Northern Rhodesia* (Berkeley: University of California Press, 1963), and *Witchcraft in Western India* (Bombay: Orient Longman, 1983) by Sohaila Kapur, among many others. Marion

Lochhead's *Magic and Witchcraft of the Borders* (London: Robert Hale, 1984) covers witches and warlocks, dragons, ghosts and hauntings, and elves, and trickery. And John Middleton's book of essays, *Magic, Witchcraft, and Curing* (Austin: University of Texas Press, 1977 [1967]), places magical belief and behavior in primitive societies, and discusses specifically the function of magic, the concept of "bewitching," sorcery, shamanistic behavior, divination, and spirit possession in terms of these societies.

And finally, there are several scholarly texts on ghosts and haunted places and the tales and lore of haunted places. One of the best might well be Christina Hole's *Haunted England: A Survey of English Ghost-lore* (2nd ed. London: B.T. Batsford, 1950 [1941]). An excellent introduction to ghostlore is *The Folklore of Ghosts*, edited by Hilda R. Ellis Davidson and W.M.S. Russell (Cambridge [ENG]: Brewer for the Folklore Society, 1981), which is especially helpful because the authors differentiate the works useful for the folklorist. The authors' aim is "to examine a number of ghost traditions and to attempt to analyze them and to see what characteristics emerge when the various studies are made." Less scholarly, but typical of many books, is James Reynolds' *Ghosts in Irish Houses* (New York: Bonanza Books, 1947).

The reference works listed below deal with all aspects of magic, though some works on magic and religion are included in the section on folk religion. There are also works on the occult and ghosts. As far as possible books on witchcraft were confined to those that deal with the magic of witchcraft or prophecies and superstitions concerning witches. I have tried very hard to exclude works on demonic possession, theological and legal disputations concerning witches, witchcraft trials, and torture, etc., although there are many good sources for this material, such as Rossell Hope Robbins' "Witchcraft: An Introduction to the Literature of Witchcraft" which serves as an introduction to the Cornell University Library's *Catalogue of the Witchcraft Collection in the Cornell University Library* (Millwood, NY: KTO Press, 1977), a collection of 2,900 printed works and manuscripts on demon possession, sorcery, heresy, witchcraft trials, etc.

1503.   Galbreath, Robert. "The History of Modern Occultism: A Bibliographical Survey." *Journal of Popular Culture* 5 (1971): 727-754.

This is a bibliographic essay covering 300 works arranged by type of work: bibliography, reference work, general history of magic and occultism, occult sciences and themes, and occultism from Romanticism to the present.

1504.   Goss, Michael, comp. *Poltergeists: An Annotated Bibliography of Works in English, circa 1880-1975.* Metuchen, NJ: Scarecrow, 1979. 351p. LC 78-11492; ISBN 0-8108-1181-2.

This is a briefly annotated bibliography of over 1,100 books and journal articles about poltergeists, i.e., noisy ghosts, hobgoblins, racketing spirits, etc. There is a general index and a geographical index.

1505.   Hall, Trevor H. *Old Conjuring Books: A Bibliographical and Historical Study with a Supplementary Check-list.* New York: St. Martin's Press, 1973. 228p. LC 72-93469.

This is a series of bibliographical essays on different aspects of conjuring. The supplemental checklist is of books on conjuring in England that were published up to the year 1850. Also included are indexes of names, places, and publications.

1506.   Kies, Cosette N. *The Occult in the Western World: An Annotated Bibliography.* Hamden, CT: Library Professional Publications, 1986. 233p. LC 86-7256; ISBN 0-208-02113-2.

This work includes 889 annotated entries, grouped in the following sections: general works on the occult; traditional witchcraft and satanism; modern witchcraft and satanism; magic and the hermetic arts; secret societies, exotic religions, and mysticism; psychics; ghosts, poltergeists, and hauntings; primitive magic and belief; myths, legends, and folklore; ancient astronauts, disappearance, and UFOs; prophecy and fortune tellers; astrology; and skeptics and debunkers. There is a glossary and separate name and title indexes. This bibliography makes fascinating browsing.

1507. Melton, J. Gordon. *Magic, Witchcraft, and Paganism in America: A Bibliography.* New York: Garland, 1982. 231p. LC 81-43343; ISBN 0-8240-93771. (Garland bibliographies on sects and cults; v. 1; Garland reference library of social science; v. 105)

This superb bibliography is intended to survey "the literature produced by and about the American magical community... from Colonial times to the present." (p.3-4) The bibliography includes an unannotated listing of 1,439 items within the following subject areas: background materials, ritual magic, witchcraft, neo-paganism, Afro-American magical religions, Kahuna, and Bruja. There is an author and periodical index. An appendix includes "List of Works in the New York Public Library related to Witchcraft in the United States" by George Black.

1508. Nugent, Donald. "Witchcraft Studies, 1959-1971: A Bibliographical Survey." *Journal of Popular Culture* 5 (1971): 710-725.

This work, which covers "the entire Western experience of witchcraft," is a bibliographical essay that provides "critical comment or elucidation of the works under consideration." (p. 711)

1509. Olschki, Leo S., ed. *Bibliotheca Magica: Dalle Opere a Stampa della Biblioteca Casanatense di Roma.* Florence: L.S. Olschki, 1985. 225p. LC 85-181812; ISBN 8-8222-3310-7. (Biblioteca di bibliografia Italiana, 102)

Included here because it includes books and articles in all languages, including English. A long introduction precedes the text which is a dictionary listing by author of 1,266 books and articles. There are several indexes: second author, commentator, translator, geographical, chronological (from 1469-1796), and broad subject indexes--astrology, astronomy, magic amulets, talismans, exorcisms, superstitions, etc.

1510.   Toole-Stott, Raymond. *A Bibliography of English Conjuring, 1581-1876.* 2 vols. Derby: Harpur and Sons, 1976-1978. Vol. 1, 288p.; Vol. 2, 143p. LC 77-362191.

This comprises a total listing of 1,414 items, most of which are rare books. The author gives the bibliographic collation and locates the work in collections and libraries. The index to both volumes is in Vol. 2.

1511.   Zaretsky, Irving I., and Cynthia Shambaugh. *Spirit Possession and Spirit Mediumship in Africa and Afro- America: An Annotated Bibliography.* New York: Garland, 1978 [1966, under title *Bibliography on Spirit Possession and Spirit Mediumship*]. 443p. LC 78-4181; ISBN 0-8240-9823-4. (Garland reference library of social science; v. 56)

There are over 2,000 articles and books cited by the authors, most with annotations. Problematic for the beginning researcher is the lack of a general index; however, there are 18 indexes for those who have a handle on the material, some of which are: Africa: ethnic groups; Africa: ethnic groups in political units; Africa: ethnic groups in major religions; Africa: general sources; Afro-America: regions, political units, religious movements and ethnic groups; Afro-America: general sources; world areas outside Africa and Afro-America; theoretical sources on spirit possession and spirit mediumship; altered states of consciousness; art; music; religious movements, etc. Also included are lists of journals, newsletters, and periodicals.

Dictionaries and Encyclopedias--Witchcraft, Magic, Ghosts, and the Occult

1512. Butler, Bill. *Dictionary of the Tarot.* New York: Schocken, 1975. 253p. LC 74-9230; ISBN 0-8052-0559-4.

Though called a dictionary, this one is not for the uninitiated as it is arranged like the Tarot deck. Chapter 1 is on the Minor Arcana (pentacles, wands, cups, swords), Chapter 2 is on the Major Arcana (the Fool, the Magician, the High Priestess, etc.). Another chapter is on the method of divination, with another on systems design. There is a long glossary, pp. 213-250 ("some of the basic meanings or attributions behind symbols and terms used in the Tarot system"). There are several books on the Tarot, some of which are: *The Tarot* by Richard Cavendish (New York: Harper and Row, 1975), *A Complete Guide to the Tarot* by Eden Gray (New York: Crown, 1972), A.E. Thierens' *The General Book of the Tarot* (San Bernardino, CA: Borgo, 1975 [1930]), and Arthur Edward Waite's *The Pictorial Key to the Tarot (Being Fragments of a Secret Tradition under the Veil of Divination)* (Blauvelt, NY: Rudolf Steiner, 1971 [1959]), a classic work on the Tarot which includes an annotated bibliography of 29 works.

1513. Cavendish, Richard. *Man, Myth & Magic: The Illustrated Encyclopedia of Mythology, Religion and the Unknown.* New ed., edited and compiled by Yvonne Deutch. 12 vols. New York: Marshall Cavendish, 1983. LC 82-13041; ISBN 0-86307-041-8 (set).

The encyclopedia has many signed longer articles on aspects of magic and supernaturalism (e.g., **alchemy, witchcraft**) as well as on religious movements. Vol. 12 contains an index. This is a revised edition of a longer (24-volume work), published in 1970, and is abridged in *The Encyclopedia of the Unexplained: Magic, Occultism, and Parapsychology* (New York: McGraw-Hill, 1974), an alphabetical listing of 521 "mysteries of life" (e.g., **abominable snowman**). Both works are lavishly illustrated.

1514. Cohen, Daniel. *The Encyclopedia of Ghosts.* New York: Dodd Mead, 1984. 307p. LC 84-10172; ISBN 0-396-08308-0.

Entries are listed alphabetically by key word (e.g., **Commander Potter's Vision, Death Foreseen, The Evil Returns**), within broad subject areas: famous ghosts and ghosts of the famous, classic cases, hauntings, animal ghosts, poltergeists, revenge, warnings, crisis apparitions, ghostly phenomena, and ghostly legends. There is an introduction and an annotated bibliography.

1515. Collin de Plancy, Jacques Albin-Simon. *Dictionary of Demonology.* Ed. and trans. by Wade Baskin. New York: Philosophical Library, 1965. 177p. LC 65-11952.

Written by Collin de Plancy in the nineteenth century, this dictionary formed a basis of the Romantic period. It includes words (e.g., **abracadabra, apparitions,** and **ashes**) as well as persons who engaged in and wrote about demonology.

1516. Gettings, Fred. *Encyclopedia of the Occult: A Guide to Every Aspect of Occult Lore, Belief, and Practice.* London: Rider, 1986. 256p. LC 87-113357; ISBN 0-7126-1262-9.

This is an alphabetical listing of 2,000 entries of varying lengths, some quite long and some quite short. A bibliography is included.

1517. Haining, Peter. *A Dictionary of Ghosts.* London: Robert Hale, 1982. 271p. LC 82-190523; ISBN 0-7091-9622-9.

Haining defines ghosts as "disembodied figures believed to be the spirits of people who have died." (p.7) The definitions are fairly short and sometimes lighthearted (e.g., **Actors:** the group of people with the strongest belief in--and most healthy respect for--ghosts and superstitions). There is an index, but no bibliography. The work is illustrated with photographs and drawings.

1518. Newall, Venetia. *The Encyclopedia of Witchcraft & Magic.* New York: The Dial Press, 1974. 191p. LC 73-17944; ISBN 0-8037-2343-1.

In his introduction to this work, Richard Dorson says, "this encyclopedia is a convenient and readable introduction to specific ideas and themes in witchcraft and magic," providing "succinct and authoritative entries that serve as a trustworthy and readable guide to the complex and perennially intriguing subjects of magic and witchcraft." (pp. 8, 11) There are 179 entries, some quite long, ranging from **abracadabra** to **zombie.** There is also a bibliography and a complete index, and the work is exquisitely illustrated.

1519. Robbins, Rossell Hope. *The Encyclopedia of Witchcraft and Demonology.* New York: Crown, 1959. 571p. LC 59-9155.

In the long introduction and preface, the author defines witches and witchcraft, traces the concepts historically, considers them from a religious point of view, differentiates witchcraft from sorcery, and discusses trials of witches and torture. This alphabetical listing goes from **Aberdeen witches** to **witnesses.** Some entries are quite long. There is a bibliography of 1,140 items as well as a classified subject bibliography.

1520. Shepard, Leslie, ed. *Encyclopedia of Occultism & Parapsychology.* 3rd ed. 2 vols. Detroit, MI: Gale Research, 1991 [1978]. ISBN 0-8103-4907-8 (p) (set).

The subtitle of this is: "A compendium of information on the occult sciences, magic, demonology, superstitions, spiritism, mysticism, metaphysics, psychical science, and parapsychology, with biographical and bibliographical notes and comprehensive indexes." This work is based on "substantially revised material" from *The Encyclopaedia of Psychic Science* by Nandor Fodor (London: Arthur Press, 1934) and *The Encyclopedia of Occultism* by Spence Lewis (New York: Strathmore, 1920; reprinted: Hyde Park, NY: University Books, 1969). There are 3,000 entries, in alphabetical order, and although there is more occult material than folklore, there are entries on mythic and heroic materials and superstitions (e.g., **Cuchulain, evil eye,** etc.). There is a general index and topical indexes on animals/birds/beasts, demons, geographical places and phenomena, gods, paranormal phenomena, and periodicals.

1521.   Wedeck, Harry E. *Dictionary of Magic*. New York: Philosophical Library, 1956. 105p. LC 56-13757.

This is a popularized work, though it might be useful as a beginning reference tool. The entries are brief and wide ranging, and the work ends with a brief, selective bibliography; it is lacking an index.

Gazetteers--Witchcraft, Magic, Ghosts, and the Occult

1522.   Summers, Montague. *The Geography of Witchcraft*. London: Routledge & Kegan Paul, 1978 [1927]. 623p. LC 78-40094; ISBN 0-7100-7617-7.

This work is usable as a reference with the aid of its good index. Includes large chapters on witchcraft in various countries: Greece and Rome, England, Scotland, New England, France, Germany, Italy, and Spain. Unfortunately, there is no attempt to contrast and compare.

1523.   Underwood, Peter. *A Gazetteer of Scottish and Irish Ghosts*. London: Souvenir Press, 1973. 252p. LC 73-173622; ISBN 0-285-62089-4.

Divided into Scotland and Ireland and subdivided by city, town, etc., the author discusses the ghostlore of that particular area. The book is illustrated with photographs and includes a fairly comprehensive bibliography. The author also wrote *A Gazetteer of British Ghosts* (New York: Walker, 1975) and *A Gazetteer of British, Scottish, and Irish Ghosts* (New York: Bell, 1985), both in the same format.

Handbooks--Witchcraft, Magic, Ghosts, and the Occult

1524.   Marlbrough, Ray T. *Charms, Spells, and Formulas for the Making and Use of Gris-Gris, Herb Candles, Doll Magick, Incenses, Oils, and Powders--To Gain Love, Protection, Prosperity, Luck, and Prophetic Dreams.* St. Paul, MN: Llewellyn Publications, 1986. 171p. LC 85-45286; ISBN 0-87542-501-1 (p).

Intended for "the practitioner," this lists charms to invoke, magic to make, and evil eyes to fashion. Formulas, rituals, prayers, etc., are given in full.

1525.   Skelton, Robin. *Spellcraft: A Handbook of Invocations, Blessings, Protections, Healing Spells, Binding and Bidding.* Toronto: McClelland and Stewart, 1978. 206p. ISBN 0-7710-8208-8 (c); 0-7710-8177-4 (p)

A spell is defined in the introduction as "the science and art of causing change to occur with the will." The author includes separate sections on invocations, incantations, blessings and protections, binding and bidding, love spells, healing spells, and ways and means. An appendix includes twentieth-century spells and the names of some contemporary spellmakers. There are notes and a brief bibliography but no index.

Annotated Collections--Witchcraft, Magic, Magic, Ghosts, and the Occult

Note: many supernatural beliefs are included in general collections of customs and beliefs listed above (see nos. 1460-1502) and in the dictionary collection (nos. 1312-1521). Those listed here are primarily collections of beliefs concerned with magic, ghosts, witches, and other elements of the supernatural.

1526.   Cannell, Margaret. "Signs, Omens, and Portents in Nebraska Folklore." *University of Nebraska Studies in Language, Literature, and Criticism* 13 (1933): 3-50.

The superstitions are listed under several subjects: weather signs, marriage and courtship signs, death and bad luck signs, plants and crops, domestic signs, wishes, exorcisms, and charms. Each section is preceded by an introduction. A bibliography is included.

1527.   Stewart, William Grant. *The Popular Superstitions and Festive Amusements of the Highlanders of Scotland.* London: Alyott and Jones, 1851. Reprinted: Norwood, PA: Norwood Eds., 1974. 203p. LC 74-34350; ISBN 0-88305-631-3.

Although the title says "popular superstitions," the bulk of this work deals with ghosts, fairies, and witchcraft. One section, however, covers calendar customs and rites. There is no index.

1528.   Wedeck, Harry E. *Treasury of Witchcraft.* New York: Philosophical Library, 1961. 271p. LC 60-15949.

A popularized compendium of magic, charms and innovations, beliefs, talismans, concoctions, etc., listed within 11 subject areas. Some sources are given, there is a brief bibliography and no index, though the table of contents is very detailed.

SUPERNATURAL BELIEFS
Fairylore

In the preface to her *An Encyclopedia of Fairies...* (no. 1530), Katharine Briggs, who was, before her death in 1980, responsible for most of the scholarly work on fairies and little people, refers to fairylore as "that whole area of the supernatural which is not claimed by angels, devils, or ghosts."

There are several introductory texts on fairylore, many by Mrs. Briggs. These include *The Vanishing People: Fairy Lore and Legends* (New York: Pantheon, 1978) which includes fairy beliefs, a discussion on their origins, and descriptions of the various types of fairies, *The Personnel of Fairyland; A Short Account of the Fairy People of Great Britain for Those Who Tell Stories to Children* (Oxford: Alden, 1953; reprinted: Detroit, MI: Singing Tree, 1971 [1953]), and *The Fairies in English Tradition and Literature* (Chicago, IL: University of Chicago Press, 1967). Two older standard works on fairies are Robert Kirk's *The Secret Commonwealth of Elves, Fauns and Fairies* (London: D. Nutt, 1893; reprinted, with variant titles, in 1939 and 1976) and Thomas Crofton Croker's *Fairy Legends and Traditions of the South of Ireland* (Delmar, NY: Scholars' Facsimiles and Reprints, 1983 [1825]). Another excellent introduction is Lewis Spence's *The Fairy Tradition in Britain* (London: Rider, 1948), with chapters on nomenclature and the description, appearance, and costume of fairies, fairy life, fairy changelings, the relationship between fairies and mankind, fairyland, and fairy cults and ritual. Also useful is Diarmuid MacManus' *The Middle Kingdom; The Faerie World of Ireland* (London: Parish, 1959), with chapters on fairy folk, fairy trees, the pooka, pranks and mischief, fairy grounds and paths, and hostile spirits and hurtful spells. *A History of Irish Fairies* by Carolyn White (Dublin: Mercier Press, 1976) is available for an historical approach. And W.Y. Evans-Wentz' book, *The Fairy-Faith in Celtic Countries* (London: Henry Frowde, 1911; reprinted Lemma Publishing Co., 1973), is a fascinating collection of testimonies of early twentieth century fairy faith in Great Britain. Patricia Lysaght's *The Banshee: The Irish Supernatural Death-Messenger* (Dublin: The Glendale Press, 1986) is a full-length scholarly study, including legends and beliefs concerning the Irish banshee, and a 25-page bibliography. Other studies of banshees include Karen Ackerman's *The Banshee* (New York: Philomel, 1990), Dan Barton's *Banshee* (Toronto: Worldwide, 1988), and Margaret Millar's *Banshee* (New York: Morrow, 1983).

There are also quite a few lavishly illustrated, coffee-table volumes on the little people, including Leonard Baskin's *Imps, Demons, Hobgoblins, Witches, Fairies & Elves* (New York: Pantheon, 1984), with Baskin's wonderful paintings, Wil Huygens' *Gnomes* (New York: Abrams, 1976), Brian Froud's and Alan Lee's *Faeries* (New York: Abrams, 1978), and

Time-Life Books' *The Enchanted World of Fairies and Elves* (Alexandria, VA: Time-Life Books, 1984), to name just a few.

Classification--Fairylore

Note: See Briggs' *An Encyclopedia of Fairies...* (no. 1530) for a motif- and type-index of fairy tales.

Dictionaries and Encyclopedias--Fairylore

1529. Briggs, Katharine Mary. *Abbey Lubbers, Banshees, & Boggarts: An Illustrated Encyclopedia of Fairies.* New York: Pantheon Books (a division of Random House), 1979. 158p. LC 79-1897; ISBN 0-394-50806-8.

This work, derived from *An Encyclopedia of Fairies...* (no. 1530), is intended for children. The entries are more straightforward and shorter. There is a great amount of cross referencing as in the larger work as well as many illustrations and references. Included also is a bibliography.

1530. Briggs, Katharine Mary. *An Encyclopedia of Fairies: Hobgoblins, Brownies, Bogies, and Other Supernatural Creatures.* New York: Pantheon Books, 1976. 481p. LC 76-12939; ISBN 0-394-40918-3.

Briggs has arranged entries for primarily British little folk from the last 1,000 years. The dictionary arrangement, ranging from **Abbey Lubbey** to **Young Tam Lin, or Tamlane,** includes wonderfully written and informative entries. Each entry is generously cross referenced, and the work is illustrated by the classic illustrators. Motif- and/or type-numbers are given, when appropriate. There is an index of types and motifs at the end of the book and a selected bibliography though no general index. Some entries include whole tales, for example in the entry for "Tom Tit Tot." This is the standard work on fairylore.

1531. Haining, Peter. *The Leprechaun's Kingdom.* New York: Harmony Books, 1980. 128p. LC 79-23714; ISBN 0-517-540797 (c); 0-517-540800 (p).

The entries are arranged alphabetically within large subject areas: banshees, cave fairies, changelings, *cluricaunes, daoine sidh,* demons, *dullahans,* etc. The illustrations are from older works. There is no bibliography and no index.

Guides and Handbooks--Fairylore

1532. Arrowsmith, Nancy. *A Field Guide to the Little People.* New York: Hill and Wang, a division of Farrar, Straus, and Giroux, 1977. 296p. LC 77-13706; ISBN 0-8090-4450-1.

The author groups the little people under three categories: light elves, dark elves, and dusky elves, the most numerous, which are "tied to their environment," with their lives being "defined by laws of time, space and place." There are 79 entries, randomly listed within the three categories. For each, there is a definition and a paragraph on identification and habitat. Appended is a section of black-and-white illustrations, notes, bibliography, and an index of names.

1533. Keightley, Thomas. *World Guide to Gnomes, Fairies, Elves, and Other Little People.* New York: Avenel Books, distributed by Crown, 1978 [1878, under the title *The Fairy Mythology*]. 560p. LC 78-12628; ISBN 0-517-26313-0.

This mishmash of a book is arranged by type of lore and place; there are entries for eddas and sagas and other entries listed under Scandinavia which is subdivided by type of little person (elf, dwarf, etc.). Keightley covers all of Great Britain, Switzerland, Southern Europe, Eastern Europe, and Africa. The content of the entries varies, including for the most part a description of the fairy, a legend, and any superstitions or legends about that particular fairy. It has an index but no bibliography.

SUPERNATURAL BELIEFS
Animals and Mythic Beasts

The best introductory work on mythic creatures might well be J.R. Porter's and William M. S. Russell's *Animals in Folklore* (London: D.S. Brewer for the Folklore Society, 1978), essays on animal ethics, regional studies, shape-changing animals, and animal images. Each chapter has a bibliography, and the introduction is by Katharine Briggs. Peter Costello's *The Magic Zoo: The Natural History of Fabulous Animals* (New York: St. Martin's Press, 1979) covers the full range of mythic beasts but in narrative format. And Willy Ley's *Exotic Zoology* (New York: Viking, 1962 [1941]) is a study of mythological animals, oceanic creatures, and mythical islands.

There are many coffee-table books on different kinds of mythic beasts, all richly and lavishly illustrated, such as Nancy Hathaway's *The Unicorn* (New York: Viking/A Studio Book, 1980) and Time-Life's *Magical Beasts* (Alexandria, VA: Time-Life Books, 1985). A popular topic for these oversized books is dragons. See Ernest Ingersoll's *Dragons and Dragon Lore* (New York: Payson and Clarke, 1928; reprinted, Detroit, MI: Singing Tree, 1968), Paul Newman's *The Hill of the Dragon: An Enquiry into the Nature of Dragon Legends* (Bath [ENG]: Kingsmead, Press, 1979) as well as Paul and Karin Johnsgard's *Dragons and Unicorns: A Natural History* (New York: St. Martin's Press, 1982), Peter Hogarth's *Dragons* (New York: Viking, 1979), Tao Tao Liu Sanders' *Dragons, Gods, & Spirits from Chinese Mythology* (New York: Schocken, 1983 [1980]), and Peter Dickinson's *The Flight of Dragons* (New York: Harper and Row, 1979).

There are also texts on nonmythic animals such as Maria Leach's *God Had a Dog; Folklore of the Dog* (New Brunswick, NJ: Rutgers University Press, 1961); Patricia Dale-Green's *Lore of the Dog* (London: Rupert Hart, 1960; Boston, MA: Houghton, 1967) is concerned only with dogs and has a section on phantom dogs. Dale-Green also wrote *The Cult of Cats* (Boston, MA: Houghton, 1963). Other works on nonmythic animals include H.W. Janson's *Apes and Ape Lore in the Middle Ages and the Renaissance* (London: University of London Press, 1952) and *A Treasury of Snake Lore, From the Garden of Eden to Snakes Today, in Mythology, Fables, Stories...*, ed. Brandt Aymar (New York: Greenberg, 1956).

This section includes works about **animals and mythic beasts** in general. A subsection on **birdlore** follows this larger section.

Bibliographies--Animals and Mythic Beasts

1534.   Eberhart, George M. *Monsters, A Guide to Information on Unaccounted for Creatures, Including Bigfoot, Many Water Monsters, and Other Irregular Animals.* New York: Garland, 1983. 344p. LC 82-49029; ISBN 0-8240-9213-9. (The unexplained, the mysterious, and the supernatural; v. 1; Garland reference library of social science; v. 131)

The author defines monsters as "living animals uncaught and uncatalogued by scientists." (ix) There are 4,500 entries, from English language books, pamphlets, and journal articles, from earliest times through 1982, from the fields of science, folklore, literature, and from travelogues. The unannotated entries are in twenty categories (e.g., **Africa dinosaur**, *dragons, flying humanoids, sea monsters*). Basic sources are marked. There is a separate section of books for children and young adults. There are separate periodical and author indexes, but the lack of a subject index may be a problem.

1535.   Robinson, Margaret W. *Fictitious Beasts: A Bibliography.* London: Library Association, 1961. 76p. LC 67-124667. (Library Association bibliographies, 1)

This work is restricted to European beliefs and confined to English-language printed books, and, for the most part, it omits deliberate inventions and traditional beasts in fiction. The introduction is concise and useful. There are 349 entries, mostly annotated, listed under general works, books of the Classical period, the Middle Ages, and the Renaissance, and beasts: barnacle-goose, basilisk, dragon, phoenix, unicorn, mermaid, etc. Includes an index of authors and subjects.

1536.   Borges, Jorge Luis, with Margarita Guerrero. *The Book of Imaginary Beings*. Rev., enl., and trans. by Norman Thomas di Giovanni in collaboration with the author. New York: E.P. Dutton, 1969 [1957]. 256p. LC 76-87180; ISBN 0-525-47538-9 (p).

This bestiary, ranging from **Bao A Qu** ("a being sensitive to the many shades of the human soul") to **Zaratan** ("a whale that looks like an island"), is really a hodgepodge, with some real oddities included (e.g., the animal imagined by Kafka, the animal imagined by C.S. Lewis, antelope with six legs, as well as the fairy folk: brownies, banshee, centaur, etc.). Each entry covers one or two pages. There is an index but no bibliography.

1537.   Cohen, Daniel. *The Encyclopedia of Monsters*. New York: Dodd, Mead, 1982. 287p. LC 82-4574; ISBN 0-396-08102-9.

Cohen defines "monster" as "an animal of strange and terrifying shape." The work is divided into eight sections: humanoids, land monsters, monster birds and bats, phantoms, river and sea monsters, visitors from strange places, and weird creatures in folklore (e.g., basilisks, dragons, fairies, giants, griffin, etc.). There is a bibliographic essay at the end of the work but it lacks an index.

1538.   Fetros, John G. *A Dictionary of Factual and Fictional Riders and their Horses*. Hicksville, NY: Exposition Press, 1979. 200p. LC 79-51665; ISBN 0-682-49417-8.

There are over 600 entries, arranged alphabetically by the names of the riders rather than the animals which are mythic, literary and historical, as well as contemporary (from the media). An index is useful for locating riders and horses.

1539.   Lloyd-Jones, Hugh. *Mythical Beasts*. London: Gerald Duckworth, 1980. 70p. LC 81-466245; ISBN 0-7156-1439-8 (c); 0-7156-1503-3 (p).

This is an alphabetical listing of ten animals from **amphisbaena** to **tutor**. Each animal is described, and literary sources are given. There is no index and no bibliography.

1540.   McGowen, Tom. *Encyclopedia of Legendary Creatures*. Chicago, IL: Rand, McNally, 1981. 64p. LC 81-10529; ISBN 0-528-82402-3.

There are 116 entries, arranged in alphabetical order, of animal creatures from all over--Greece, Africa, Europe, the Pacific Islands, etc. Unfortunately, lacks index, cross references, and bibliography.

1541.   Page, Michael, and Robert Ingpen. *Encyclopedia of Things That Never Were: Creatures, Places, and People*. New York: Viking Penguin, 1987. 240p. LC 86-40356; ISBN 0-670-81607-8.

Divided into six sections (**of the Cosmos, of Ground and Underground, of Wonderland, of Magic, Science and Invention, of Water, Sky, and Air, and of the Night**), the 400 plus entries, varying in length, are arranged alphabetically within these divisions. Handsomely printed and lavishly illustrated. Index and bibliography are included.

1542.   Rowland, Beryl. *Animals with Human Faces; A Guide to Animal Symbolism*. Knoxville: University of Tennessee Press, 1973. 192p. LC 70-173657; ISBN 0-87049-136-9.

The entries are arranged alphabetically from **amphisbaena** to **venomous serpent** and **wolf**. The author gives literary sources, proverbs, and other beliefs as well as a description of each animal. There is a selected bibliography and index.

Gazetteer--Animals and Mythic Beasts

1543. Whitlock, Ralph. *Here Be Dragons*. London: George Allen & Unwin, 1983. 165p. ISBN 0-04-398007-4.

The bulk of this work is a gazetteer which lists 194 dragon sitings by county. An introduction covers the origins of dragons and discusses dragon lore. There is also an index and a bibliography.

Guides--Animals and Mythic Beasts

1544. Dorson, Richard M. *Man and Beast in American Comic Legend*. Bloomington: Indiana University Press, 1982. 184p. LC 81-48622; ISBN 0-253-33665-1 (c); 0-253-20296-5 (p).

Published posthumously, this covers, in chapter format, several legendary creatures: the Windham frogs, the Hugag, the Hodg, the Jackalope, the Sea Serpent, and Big Foot, etc. There are notes but no index or bibliography.

1545. de Gubernatis, Angelo. *Zoological Mythology; Or, The Legends of Animals*. 2 vols. London: Trübner; New York: Macmillan, 1872. Reprinted: 2 vol. in 1: New York: Arno, New York Times, 1978. LC 77-79129; ISBN 0-405-10540-1.

Vol. 1 covers animals of the earth, cows and bulls, horses, asses, dogs, cats, etc. Vol. 2 continues describing animals of the earth and also includes animals of the air and animals of water. Though really a text, the work is usable as a reference. The index to both volumes is at the end of the current work.

1546. Lehner, Ernst, and Johanna Lehner. *A Fantastic Bestiary; Beasts and Monsters in Myth and Folklore*. New York: Tudor, 1969. 192p. LC 68-9487.

This work is divided into eleven sections: dragons, Oriental dragons, serpent monsters, aquatic monsters, etc. Each animal is described and there are lavish pictures from older books and manuscripts. There is a bibliography, glossary, and index.

1547.   Lum, Peter. *Fabulous Beasts*. London: Thames and Hudson, 1952. 256p. LC 52-36311.

In chapter format, this guide covers the cockatrice or basilisk, the gryphon, the unicorn, the salamander, dragons, mermaids, sea-monsters, the sphinx, etc. An excellent introduction includes an essay on the beast in fable and another on the fabulous beast. Bibliography and index included.

1548.   Mercatante, Anthony S. *Zoo of the Gods: Animals in Myth, Legend, & Fable*. New York: Harper and Row, 1974. 240p. LC 74-4618; ISBN 0-06-065561-5.

The author says this work "represents a world mythological view of its animal subjects." Part I covers animals of the water (goose, duck, pelican, swan, etc.); Part II covers animals of the earth (serpent, ape and monkey, cat, tiger, leopard, and panther). The author relates each animal to literature, old and new, mythology, legends, music and dance. There is a bibliographic essay at the end of the book and indexes--general, author, composer, painter, and an index to works of multiple or anonymous authorship cited in the text.

1549.   South, Malcolm. ed. *Mythical and Fabulous Creatures: A Source Book and Research Guide*. New York: Greenwood, 1987. 393p. LC 86-14964; ISBN 0-313-24338-7.

In the Preface, the author says "this work is designed primarily as a reference and research guide that describes fabulous creatures and their appearances in history, literature and art." However, since it is not in dictionary/encyclopedia format, it may be hard for the beginner to use. Part I covers "Twenty Fabulous Creatures," grouped under birds and beasts, human-animal composites, creatures of darkness, and giants and fairies. Each essay is written by a different person and there is a general bibliography. Part II is a "Miscellany and Taxonomy." South uses five major groupings to classify most of the 20 main beings: 1) human-animal combinations, 2) fabulous animals, 3) fabulous people and fabulous creatures with a human or humanlike appearance, 4) creatures with a makeup different from that in previous groupings, and 5) fabulous creatures with a variety of forms. The work concludes with a glossary and a section of illustrations with sources.

1550. Wyman, Walker D. *Mythical Creatures of the U.S.A. and Canada: A Roundup of the Mythical Snakes and Worms, Insects, Birds, Fish, Serpents, and Mermaids, Animals and Monsters that Have Roamed the American Land.* Park Falls, WI: University of Wisconsin, River Falls Press, 1978 [1969]. 105p. LC 80-6053.

The author describes mythical snakes and worms, insects, birds, fish, serpents and mermaids, and mythical animals and monsters alphabetically within those sections as well as the Sasquatch and other ape-like creatures.

Lexicons--Animals and Mythic Beasts

1551. Hendrickson, Robert. *Animal Crackers: A Bestial Lexicon.* New York: Viking, 1983. 239p. 81-23973; ISBN 0-670-12697-7 (c); 0-14-006487-7 (p).

This is a listing of words or phrases pertaining to animals, with popular superstitions appended (e.g., **albatross**, subject of more legends than any other sea bird...). There is no bibliography.

1552. Lyman, Darryl. *The Animal Things We Say.* Middle Village, NY: J. David, 1983. 258p. LC 82-10026; ISBN 0-8246-0291-9.

This is an alphabetical listing, but the book's entries are subdivided, and it is, therefore, easier to use (e.g., **cock**--then, cock and bull story, cockney, cock of the wall, cock pit, cockscomb, cocksure, weathercock). There is a bibliography and index.

Annotated Collections--Animal and Mythic Beast Lore

1553.   Bergen, Fanny D., ed. *Animal and Plant Lore; Collected from the Oral Tradition of English Speaking Folk.* Boston, MA, and New York: Published for the American Folk-Lore Society by Houghton, Mifflin, 1899. 180p. LC 99-4363 (Memoirs of the American Folklore Society; v. 7). Reprinted: New York: Kraus, 1969.

   The book is divided into two parts--animal lore and plantlore. The animal section covers amulets and charms, omens, weather signs, incantations and formulae, folk names of animals, and the folklore of ectodenial structures. In all, there are almost 1,400 listed beliefs, each with a source. There is an extensive notes section and a brief bibliography of items cited more than once. Also included is an index.

1554.   Clark, Joseph D. *Beastly Folklore.* Metuchen, NJ: Scarecrow, 1968. 326p. LC 68-12617.

   Includes stories and superstitions about various types of mythical animals as well as derivative names, proverbs, and proverbial phrases. Lacking an index, this is hard to use.

1555.   Rolland, Eugène. *Faune Populaire de la France: Noms, Vulgaires, Dictons, Proverbes, Légendes, Contes et Superstitions.* 13 vols. in 7. Paris: Edition G.-P. Maisonneuve et Larose, 1967 [1877-1911].

   In French but included here as it is always cited in terms of animal lore. This massive work, in narrative format, covers the lore of wild animals and birds, reptiles and fish, and insects, domestic animals and birds. Rolland gives sources freely. Each of the volumes has an index.

Birdlore

The book by Edward Allworthy Armstrong, *The Folklore of Birds; An Enquiry into the Origin & Distribution of Some Magico-Religious Traditions*, listed as a guide below (no. 1558), is the most comprehensive work on birdlore. Jessie M.E. Saxby's *Birds of Omen in Shetland, with Notes on the Folk-Lore of the Raven, by W.A. Clouston* (privately printed, 1893; reprinted: New York: AMS, 1972), contains essays on birdlore. Evert Ingersoll's *Birds in Legend, Fable, and Folklore* (New York: Longmans, Green, 1923; reprinted: Detroit, MI: Singing Tree, 1968) is a treatise on birds as national emblems, on the folklore of bird migration, on birds in Christian tradition, on birds as symbols and badges, on bird legends in a historical setting, etc.

There are works in other languages, such as Ismael Moya's *Aves Magicas: Mitos, Supersticiones, y Legendas en el Folklore Argentino y Americano* (Buenos Aires: La Plata, 1958) and Guiseppe Pitrè's *La Rondinella nelle Tradizione Popolari* (Rome: Societè Editrice del Libro Italiano, 1941), a collection of beliefs grouped around generalities on birds, legends, birds in popular poetry, proverbs, riddles, and beliefs.

There are several works on Native American birdlore such as Hamilton Tyler's *Pueblo Birds and Myths* (Norman: University of Oklahoma Press, 1979) as well as a few books on the folklore of specific kinds of birds, such as Krystyna Weinstein's *Owl, Owls, Fantastical Fowls* (New York: Arco, 1985), Lucienne Portier's *Le Pélican: Histoire d'un Symbole* (Paris: Cerf, 1984), and L. Arnould de Grémilly's *Le Coq* (Paris: Flammarion, 1958).

Bibliographies--Birdlore

1556.   Ó Ruadháin, Micheál. *Birds in Irish Folklore*.... Basel: 1955. Reprinted from Acta XI Congresssus Internationalis Ornithologici, Basel, 1954. pp. 667-676.

This is a bibliographic essay that outlines Irish birdlore.

Dictionaries and Encyclopedias--Birdlore

1557. Rowland, Beryl. *Birds with Human Souls: A Guide to Bird Symbolism.* Knoxville: University of Tennessee Press, 1978. 213p. LC 77-4230; ISBN 0-87049-215-2.

This dictionary, ranging from **albatross** to **wren**, with extensive entries, gives much folkloric information and source material and includes beautiful illustrations. The bibliography is excellent, and there is a comprehensive index.

Handbooks and Guides--Birdlore

1558. Armstrong, Edward Allworthy. *The Folklore of Birds; An Enquiry into the Origin & Distribution of Some Magico-Religious Traditions.* 2nd ed., rev. and enl. New York: Dover, 1970 [1958]. 284p. LC 69-15035; ISBN 0-486-22145-8 (p).

The essays in this volume contain information about the historic background and origins of birds and the transmission of magico-religious beliefs. Essays include lore of several mythic birds (i.e., the rain goose, the bird-maiden, etc.) taken from oral sources from British folklore. Theodore Avery, Jr., in *ARBA* calls it a "highly speculative collection of essays."

1559. Newall, Venetia. *Discovering the Folklore of Birds and Beasts.* Tring: Shire Publications, 1971. 72p. LC 72-193180; ISBN 0-8526-3126-x.

Newall has put together a dictionary of mythic birds and beasts from **adder** to **zebra**. Definitions are long with traditions and legends given and variant forms of the animals and birds and variant stories as well.

1560. Nigg, Joe. *A Guide to the Imaginary Birds of the World*. Cambridge, MA: Apple-wood Books, 1984. 160p. LC 85-160617; ISBN 0-918222-55-9.

A beautiful but difficult book to use. Arrangement is in broad categories, based on the origin of each of the 30 mythic bird's stories, which is given along with a brief description of the bird and an exquisite full-page woodcut. A list of 35 "More Imaginary Birds" is appended. Notes, sources, and commentaries are all given at the end with a bibliography and a comprehensive index.

Lexicons--Birdlore

1561. Swainson, Charles. *The Folklore and Provincial Names of British Birds*. London: Published for the Folk-Lore Society by Elliot Stock, 1886. 243p. LC 43-10352. (Folk-Lore Society of Great Britain publications; v. 17)

The name of the bird is given in English, along with its Latin name, its order, suborder, section, family, subfamily, and genus. Then the regional name is given and lore is appended. There is an index of Latin names and an index of common and provincial names.

1562. Thompson, D'Arcy W. *A Glossary of Greek Birds*. Oxford: Clarendon, 1895. 343p. Reprinted: Hildesheim: Georg Olms, 1966. LC 67-99155.

Birds are listed in alphabetical order by Greek name. Also given is the habitat, English name, derivation of the word as well as epithets, myths and legends, proverbs and fables concerning that bird. There is an index of English names, so the work is easy to use. There is no bibliography, but it contains liberal literary sources given throughout the text. This work can be very useful for the folklorist. See also John Pollard's *Birds in Greek Life and Myth* (London: Thames and Hudson, 1977), in narrative format, this is a guide to birds that live in Greece and are part of their literary heritage: Part III is especially useful, covering birds in Greek myths, sacred birds, gods in bird form, men in bird form, bird cults, birds in folklore and fable, and soul birds. It also has a bibliography and index.

SUPERNATURAL BELIEFS
Mythical Places

Dictionaries--Mythical Places

1563. Manguel, Alberto, and Gianni Guadalupi. *The Dictionary of Imaginary Places.* New York: Harcourt Brace Jovanovich, 1987 [1980, Macmillan]. 454p. LC 86-26063; ISBN 0-15-6260549 (p).

Restricted to "places that a traveller could expect to visit, leaving out heaven and hell and places of the future, and including only those on our planet," the author lists mythic places from **Abaton** ("a town of changing location. Though not inaccessible, no one has ever reached it, and visitors headed for Abaton have been known to wander for many years without every catching a glimpse of the town") to **Zuy** ("a prosperous Elfinkingdom in the Netherlands"). There is an index of authors and titles.

1564. Palmer, Robin. *A Dictionary of Mythical Places.* New York: H.Z. Walck, 1975. 118p. LC 75-6018; ISBN 0-8098-2431-0.

Not seen.

Gazetteer--Mythical Places

1565. Morris, Ruth, and Frank Morris. *Scottish Healing Wells: Healing, Holy, Wishing, and Fairy Wells of the Mainland of Scotland.* Sandy: The Alethea Press, 1982. 211p. ISBN 0-907859-00-3.

Following an introduction on the origins of well worship among the Celts, there is a gazetteer, alphabetically arranged by county, then by town, each with a listing of the sites of the wells, with beliefs about them. Concludes with a bibliography and index.

SUPERNATURAL BELIEFS
Plantlore and Flowerlore

Probably the most authoritative and often-cited works on plantlore are the two books listed below by de Gubernatis and Rolland (see nos. 1573 and 1586), neither of which have been translated into English. Two nineteenth-century books might well serve as introductions to this area: T.F. Thiselton-Dyer's *The Folk-Lore of Plants* (London: Chatto & Windus, 1889; reprinted: Detroit, MI: Singing Tree, 1968) which focuses on primitive and savage notions about plant worship, plants in witchcraft, fairylore, and plants, plant names, plant proverbs, sacred plants, plant superstitions, plants and the calendar, plants in folk medicine and "mystic plants" and Hilderic Friend's *Flowers and Flower Lore* (London: Allen & Unwin, 1884), covering fairy garlands, bridal wreaths, superstitions, the seasons, the language of flowers, plant names, witches and plant lore, etc. There are narratives just on forestlore and treelore, such as Alexander Porteous' *Forest Folklore, Mythology, and Romance* (London: Macmillan 1928; reprinted: Detroit, MI: Singing Tree, 1968) which discusses primeval, traditional, and fabulous forests as well as mythical denizens of the forest and myths and legends about trees and forests. There are also several studies of the mythical mandrake, the mysterious plant associated with mysterious rites, customs, and secret ceremonies. See especially C.J.S Thompson's *The Mystic Mandrake* (London: Rider, 1934; reprinted, Detroit, MI: Gale, 1975).

Of special interest is Rita Zorn Moonsammy et al.'s *Pinelands Folklife* (New Brunswick, NJ: Rutgers University Press, 1987), a Project of the New Jersey Council of the Arts, the N.J. Historical Commission, the N.J. State Museum, and the American Folklife Center at the Library of Congress. This work details folklore taken from the Pinelands region of southern New Jersey, which deals mostly with the environment and the landscape.

This section includes works on flowerlore and plantlore. It excludes works that deal with herbal healing; those works are found below in the section on Folk Medicine (nos. 1675-1758). It also omits popular books such as Euell Gibbons' *Stalking the Healthful Herbs* (New York: McKay, 1966), one of a series of books that deals with "living the natural life," this one, in particular, dealing with the use of sage, comfrey, wild lettuce, etc., for medicinal and other purposes.

Bibliography--Plantlore and Flowerlore

1566.   Langman, Ida Kaplan. *A Selected Guide to the Literature on the Flowering Plants of Mexico*. Philadelphia: University of Pennsylvania Press, 1964. 1,015p. LC 64-10897.

This is a gigantic alphabetical listing of works about flowering plants, some of which are folkloric. A detailed index will help ferret out that material.

Dictionaries and Encyclopedias--Plantlore and Flowerlore

1567.   Baker, Margaret. *Discovering the Folklore of Plants*. Rev. ed. Aylesbury [ENG]: Shire Publications, 1971 [1969]. 72p. ISBN 0-85263-080-8.

This book is in two sections; the first section covers general beliefs, but the second section is a plant folklore alphabet from **achillea** (used to heal all wounds) to **yew** (a life symbol).

1568.   Coon, Nelson. *The Dictionary of Useful Plants*. Emmaus, PA: Rodale Press, 1974. 290p. LC 74-14947; ISBN 0-87857-090-x.

The introduction includes a short chapter on American Indians and their use of plant life, American plants useful for food, medicinal plants and their uses, poisonous plants of the United States, plant uses for crafts, and dye plants of the U.S., each section with a bibliography. There is also a separate bibliography of botanical reference books and a bibliography of regional plant life materials. The dictionary proper (pp. 47-279) lists plants alphabetically by family, but common names are given (e.g., under The Maple Family-**aceraceae**; the Water-Plantain Family-**alis mataceae**, etc.); plants in each family are discussed, Latin and common names are given, and the origin and history of each plant are told, along with recipes for medicinal or craft use. This is a particularly useful and easy-to-use book that gives a lot of basic information. There is an index.

1569. Gupta, Shakti M. *Plant Myths and Traditions in India*. Leiden: E.J. Brill, 1971. 117p.+33p. plates.

A 17-page introduction talks about the importance of plants to Indians for ritual use. The listing is alphabetical by Latin name; also given are family names and the name in Sanskrit, Hindi, and English. Many myths, legends, and meanings are given for each entry. In addition, there is a bibliography, a glossary of mythological names and religious sects, and a section of photographs of statues that have plants as part of them.

1570. MacFadyen, David. *A Cottage Flora*. Exeter [ENG]: Webb & Bower, 1982. 112 p. LC 82-197751; ISBN 0-906671-64-7.

Flowers are listed alphabetically by common name (e.g., **anemone**). Also given are Latin name, location found, description, and blooming period as well as lore and poems. The format is one page of text for each flower with one picture. There is a select bibliography.

1571. Powell, Claire. *The Meaning of Flowers: A Garland of Plant Lore and Symbolism from Popular Custom & Literature*. London: Jupiter Books, 1977. 181p. LC 78-313555; ISBN 0-904041-87-5.

This beautifully designed dictionary is arranged by the common name (e.g., **American cowslip, anemone**). A short entry contains the meaning of each flower and a note on its use and traditional lore. There is a glossary of plants and their meaning (e.g., **abatina**. Fickleness) and sentiments and the plants which express those sentiments (e.g., **absence.** Wormwood).

1572. Richardson, P. Mick. *Flowering Plants: Magic in Bloom.* New York: Chelsea House, 1986.121p. LC 86-950; ISBN 0-87754-757-2. *(Encyclopedia of psychoactive drugs)*

The plants are listed by type: nutmeg family, canabis, cactus, morning glory, etc. The emphasis in each description is on the role of the hallucinogenic plant in religious rites and ceremonies of primitive cultures. There is a glossary, index, and bibliography.

1573. Rolland, Eugène. *Flore Populaire; ou, Histoire Naturelle des Plantes dans leurs Rapports avec la Linguistique et le Folklore.* 11 vols. in 6+index. Paris: Librairie Rolland, 1896-1914. Reprinted: Paris: G.-P. Maisonneuve et Larose, 1967.

In French, but a standard and seminal work, Vols. 1-3 include a systematic alphabetic listing of plants with their vernacular names in various languages; Vols. 4-11 include mostly a French language list. For each plant listed, Rolland gives Latin and French (or other) name, synonyms, usages, genres, species, etc., places found and "folklore." There is a bibliography of Vols. 1-7 in Vol. 7, and in each subsequent volume, with a bibliography of cited authors in each volume but no index. (The set I saw had a typed separate index in French and Latin, which appears to have been unique.)

Guides and Handbooks--Plantlore and Flowerlore

1574. Emboden, William A. *Bizarre Plants: Magical, Monstrous, Mythical.* New York: Macmillan, 1974. 214p. LC 73-2749.

This book covers useful herbs, herbs of black magic, plants that eat animals and insects, monstrous plants, orchids used for magic and witchcraft, and specialized plants such as ginseng, and mandagora. There is a bibliography and index. A description and lore are given.

1575.   Lehner, Ernst, and Johanna Lehner. *Folklore and Symbolism of Flowers, Plants and Trees.* New York: Tudor, 1960. 128p. LC 60-15038.

This work is divided into several sections: sacred plants, flowerlore and legend, strange and wondrous plants, the flower calendar, and the language of flowers. Within each section, the flowers and plants are arranged alphabetically for the most part. A short paragraph for each includes information on the sources, place of growth, flavor, taste, and use of each plant; also given are legends and myths associated with each plant. The material is gleaned from all religions and many cultures. There is no index or bibliography. But it is lavishly illustrated with drawings taken from old texts and herbals.

1576.   Miller, Richard Alan. *The Magical & Ritual Use of Herbs.* New York: Destiny Books, 1983. 143p. LC 83-7457; ISBN 0-89281-047-5.

This work is divided into stimulants, depressants, narcotics, and hallucinogens. For each herb described, the common name, family, botanical name, synonym, geographical location, physical description, history, chemical makeup, primary effect, preparation, and ritual use are given, with a note of caution appended for each. A quick reference chart, a variety of indexes (chemical, geographical, etc.), and a bibliography complete this book.

Lexicons--Plants and Flowers

1577.   Bergen, Fanny. "Popular American Plant Names." *Journal of American Folklore* 11 (1899): 221-230; 273-283.

Lists Latin genus and Latin names of plant with common names and places used and found.

1578.   Cunningham, John James, and Rosalie J. Cote. *Common Plants: Botanical and Colloquial Nomenclature*. New York: Garland, 1977. 120p. LC 76-24393; ISBN 0-8240-9906-0. (Garland reference library of science and technology; v. 3)

In two parts, Part I lists botanical nomenclature of common names, an alphabetical listing of common names, higher plants, algae, and fungi. Part II is an alphabetical listing of colloquial names, from **addis tongue** to **zinnia**, with "the history and folklore of the common names of selected plants" given. There is a general bibliography.

1579.   Durant, Mary B. *Who Named the Daisy? Who Named the Rose?: A Roving Dictionary of North American Wildflowers*. Boston, MA: G.K. Hall, 1976. 440p. LC 77-601; ISBN 0-8161-6460-6.

This is concerned with the common names for the wild plants in America, "some of which are evident from the flower itself (sunflower, cattail), some of which are described by their medical properties--real or imagined (feverfew, speedwell), those named by where they grow (bogberry) and by what it does (lamb-kill, sneezeweed), and those thought to be used by Indians (Indian pipe)."

1580.   Lick, David E., and Rev. Thomas R. Brendle. *Plant Names and Plant Lore Among the Pennsylvania Germans*. Lancaster, PA: Published by the Pennsylvania German Society, 1923. pp. 21-300. LC 34-21941. (*Proceedings and Addresses*, 1922; v. 33)

This is an alphabetical listing by Pennsylvania-German name. For each plant, the authors give origins, emigration history, and an overview of customs. Also listed is English name, Latin name, county collected, translation of the Pennsylvania German name, comparative study of the name, and lots of folklore that has been accumulated about each plant. There is a 37-item annotated bibliography, addenda items, and a dictionary of the non-English words of the Pennsylvania-German dialect. No index.

Note: See also annotated collections of herbal lore (see nos. 1690-1758).

1581.   Baker, Margaret. *Gardener's Magic and Folklore.* New York: Universe Books, 1978. 181p. LC 77-73799; ISBN 0-87663-299-1.

This work of "garden folklore" is a collection of "garden beliefs," that discusses the effect of the moon, sun and stars on the garden, the use of magic, the seasons, garden witchcraft, the supernatural, and the folklore of companion planting. There are references, a bibliography, and an index.

1582.   Bergen, Fanny D., ed. *Animal and Plant Lore; Collected from the Oral Tradition of English Speaking Folk.* Boston, MA, and New York: Published for the American Folk-Lore Society by Houghton, Mifflin, 1899. 180p. (Memoirs of the American Folk-Lore Society; v. 7). Reprinted: New York: Kraus, 1969.

The section on plantlore covers amulets, charms, and divinations; omens; weather signs; and medicinal flowerlore. In all, 1,397 beliefs are listed, each with a source. There is an extensive section of notes and a brief bibliography of items cited more than once. An index is also included. (See also no. 1553.)

1583.   Beyerl, Paul. *The Master Book of Herbalism.* Custer, WA: Phoenix Publications, 1984. 415p. LC 85-115769; ISBN 0-919345-53-0 (p).

This work is devoted to plantlore and plant remedies. Introductory material includes information about the remedial herb, a dosage guide, material on herbs and astrology, herbs and Tarot, the use of amulets, herbs and gemstones, and the ritual use of plants. A large section of the book is an herbal (pp. 51-170), the herbs listed alphabetically with their lore and remedial powers. An abundance of appendix material includes herbal/planetary correspondences, planetary/herbal correspondences, mythological/herbal correspondences, remedial herbal classification, magical herbal classification, a listing of alternate common names for herbs, a bibliography, index, notes, and a section of resources. This reference is very complete and relatively easy to use.

1584. Crowell, Robert L. *The Lore & Legends of Flowers.* New York: Crowell, 1982. 80p. LC 79-7829; ISBN 0-690-04035-0.

This work is divided into big units on types of flowers: tulips, narcissi, crocuses, irises, carnations, roses, nasturtiums, dandelions, marigolds, and dahlias. In each section, the author gives the history of flowers, variants, roots, etc., and a great deal of mythology and folk-related materials. There is also a section on plant use, especially medicinal, and an index.

1585. Gordon, Lesley. *Green Magic: Flowers, Plants, & Herbs in Lore & Legend.* New York: Viking, 1977. 200p. LC 77-6338; ISBN 0-670-354279.

In chapter format and stressing lore, this work covers Christian flower legends, herbals, love plants, plants of hate and blood, flowers in Shakespeare, and political and historical flowers. Cross references plants and the sentiments expressed. An index and bibliography are included.

1586. de Gubernatis, Angelo. *La Mythologie des Plantes; ou, les Légendes du Règne Végétal.* 2 vols. Paris: C. Reinwald, 1879-82. LC 4-13583.

This is a classic work on plantlore as yet untranslated. Includes both general botany and specialized botany (herbs, pines, etc.), with arrangement alphabetical by common name. The entries are long and include much legendary material.

1587.   Martin, Laura C. *Garden Flower Folklore*. Chester, CT: Globe
        Pequot Press, 1987. 273p. LC 87-17394; ISBN 0-87106-766-8.

The flowers are arranged alphabetically by common names
within appropriate blooming seasons, each with a full-page drawing.
Much folkloric information is given for each, legends, superstitions,
sources, uses, etc., as well as where and when the flower is grown. There
is an index of common and scientific names and some appendix material
on the Victorian language of flowers, a short history of flowers, and a
section on the use of flowers today.

1588.   Martin, Laura C. *Wildflower Folklore*. Charlotte, NC: East
        Woods Press, 1984. 256p. LC 84-48039; ISBN 0-88742-016-8.

This work is arranged by color within blooming seasons: blue
and violet flowers, white flowers, yellow flowers, pink flowers, orange
and red flowers, etc.; it is subdivided alphabetically by the common name
of the flower, with folk legends, superstitions, uses, etc., given for each
one.

1589.   Mercatante, Anthony S. *The Magic Garden: The Myth and
        Folklore of Flowers, Plants, Trees, and Herbs*. New York:
        Harper and Row, 1976. 185p. LC 76-9992; ISBN 0-06-065562-3
        (p).

This is divided into three main parts: the enchanted forest,
nature's bounty, and potions and herbs, and then subdivided into smaller
subjects (e.g., **nature's bounty**--apple, pomegranate, figs and apricots,
etc.). Each item is described and defined, and beliefs are given from
myths and legends. Part IV, Cornucopia, includes "Victorian language of
flowers," flowers and their sentiments and meanings, a listing of flowers
that bloom each month, the astrological signs and their relationship to
plants, the signs of the zodiac, and an herb list with culinary uses. There
is an annotated bibliography and an index.

SUPERNATURAL BELIEFS
Sealore

There are several narratives on sealore available, of which Wilbur Bassett's *Wander-Ships: Folk Stories of the Sea, with Notes Upon Their Origin* (Chicago, IL: Open Court, 1917; reprinted: Folcroft, PA: Folcroft Eds., 1978) is probably one of the most well known, along with Horace Beck's *Folklore and the Sea* (no. 1593). Another beginning point is Angelo Solomon Rappoport's *Superstitions of Sailors* (London: St. Paul's, 1928; reprinted: Ann Arbor, MI: Gryphon, 1971) which covers the origins of the sea, folktales of winds and storms, enchanted islands, the denizens of the deep (mermaids, mermen, kelpies, and watersprites), sea monsters, phantom ships and apparitions, omens and ceremonies, and superstitions of English sailors. There are several more specialized narratives: one of the best is Janet C. Gilmore's *The World of the Oregon Fishboat: A Study in Maritime Folklore* (Ann Arbor, MI: UMI Research, 1986), a full-length study of the fishermen of Charleston, Oregon, and the fisheries, commercial fishing, maintenance, and repair of fishing boats, and craftsmen who make the boats and equipment; Peter F. Anson's *Fishermen and Fishing Ways* (London: Harrap, 1932; reprinted: Totowa, NJ: Rowman & Littlefield, 1975), is concerned with the birth, childhood, marriages, festivals, witches and witchcraft, taboos, and superstitions, and diseases of sailors. And, Timothy Charles Lloyd's and Patrick B. Mullen's *Lake Erie Fishermen: Work, Identity, and Tradition* (Urbana: University of Illinois Press, 1990) is really a study of occupational folklore, however, there is some material on traditions. *Sea Enchantress*, by Gwen Benwell and Arthur Waugh (New York: Citadel, 1965 [1961]), deals only with mermaids "and her kin." Benoit Lacroix's *Folklore de la Mer et Religion* (Montreal: Leméac, 1980) looks at the religion of French Canadian-fishermen, their beliefs in God and the saints and angels, and non-religious rites; and Serge Bertino's *Miti e Leggende del Mare* (Milan: Bompiani, 1977) is an international collection of tales and sayings about the creation of the sea, fantastic navigation, magic islands, magic fish, sea monsters, and sea horses.

Directory/Index--Sealore

1590.   Bartis, Peter, and Mary Hufford. *Maritime Folklife Resources: A Directory and Index*. Washington, DC: Library of Congress, American Folklife Center, 1980. 129p. LC 80-602335. (Publications of the American Folklife Center, 5)

   This is a directory of museums and other institutions that collect maritime folklore and folklife material. The arrangement is alphabetical by institution; information given includes address, dates and hours open, a description of the collection and its special features. The second half of this work is an index to key holdings in such areas as watercraft, larger and smaller vessels, model watercraft, scrimshaw, figureheads, ropework, folk songs (e.g., sea shanties and forecastle songs), tales, legends, stories, belief systems and rituals, logs, recipes, etc. Includes also a listing of masters' theses and Ph.D. dissertations, a state index, and a glossary of vessel types.

Annotated Collections--Sealore

1591.   Baker, Margaret. *Folklore of the Sea*. Newton Abbot [ENG]: David & Charles, 1979. 192p. LC 80-455982; ISBN 0-7153-7568-7.

   Although in narrative format, easy division makes this usable as a reference book. Baker covers the ship, phantom ships and sailors, talismans and taboos, customs, the perennial sea-serpent, the weather-gods, and sea-words: the sailor's language. Appended are a section of sources used for material in the text, a two-page bibliography, and an index.

1592.   Bassett, Fletcher S. *Legends and Superstitions of the Sea and of Sailors in All Lands and at All Times*. Chicago, IL: Belford, Clark and Co., 1885. Reprinted: Detroit, MI: Singing Tree, 1971. 505p. LC 70-119444.

This is "an attempt at collecting the folklore of the sea and its belongings." (p.5) In narrative format, this work covers sea dangers; gods, saints, and demons of the sea; wind-makers and storm-raisers; water sprites and mermaids; sea monsters and sea serpents; spectres of the sea; the Flying Dutchman; sacrifice, offerings, and oblations; ceremonies and festivals; and luck, omens, images, and charms.

1593. Beck, Horace. *Folklore and the Sea.* Middletown, CT: published by Wesleyan University Press for the Marine Historical Association, Mystic Seaport, 1973. 463p. LC 73-6011; ISBN 0-8195-4062-5. (The North American maritime library; v. 6)

In narrative format, this work covers language, weatherlore, songs, art of the sea, mermaids, sea serpents, legends and tales, and sceptre ships. Wonderful photographs serve as illustrations. There is an index and notes. The bibliographic listing on pp. 436-453 is noteworthy.

1594. Shay, Frank. *A Sailor's Treasury.* New York: W.W. Norton, 1951. 196p. LC 51-7454.

This is a collection of sealore, divided into chapters on myths, superstitions, omens and weatherlore; customs, traditions, legends and yarns; cries, epithets, gripes and maxims. There is a bibliography, but no index.

SUPERNATURAL BELIEFS
Stonelore

Dictionaries and Encyclopedias--Stonelore

1595. Kunz, George Frederick. *The Curious Lore of Precious Stones; Being a Description of Their Sentiments and Folk Lore, Superstitions, Symbolism....* Philadelphia, PA: Lippincott, 1913. 406p. Reprinted: New York: Bell, 1989. LC 88-7910; ISBN 0-517-67944-3.

Although primarily a narrative study of stones used as talismans and amulets and for religious purposes, the section, "On Talismanic Use of Special Stones" (pp. 54-114), lists stones and gems alphabetically and gives much folklore about them. There is an index. See also Gaspar de Morales' *De las Virtudes y Propiedades Maravillos de las Piedras Preciosas* (Madrid: Editora Nacional, 1977), Campbell Bonner's *Studies in Magical Amulets: Chiefly Graeco-Egyptian* (Ann Arbor: University of Michigan Press, 1950), and Léonard Rosenthal's *Au Jardin des Gemmes* (Paris: Payot & Cie, 1975 [1924]) which discusses superstitions and legends of diamonds, emeralds, etc.

Annotated Collection--Stonelore

1596. Clark, Joseph D. "Madstones in North Carolina." *North Carolina Folklore Journal* 24 (March, 1976). Special Monograph Issue. 40p.

This is a survey of madstones in North Carolina and a series of madstone lore. Madstones are opal-like gems, usually retrieved from an open field or river bed, that have magical powers, some of which are medical (applied to wounds they can absorb the venom), some not. This is a collection of 46 "digests," told by madstone owners, fascinating accounts of madstone lore. The author introduces the stories, discusses the origins of madstones, has a concluding statement or two, asks some pertinent questions, and provides some references.

SUPERNATURAL BELIEFS
Weatherlore

There are a few narrative accounts of weatherlore. Paul John Goldsack's *Weatherwise: Practical Weather Lore for Sailors and Outdoor People* (Newton Abbot [ENG]: David & Charles, 1986) discusses sunrise and sunset, the complexion of the sky, clouds, winds, night owlers, countryside lore, and lore about barometer readings; Sankar Sen Gupta's *Rain in Indian Life and Lore* (Calcutta: Indian Publications, 1963) includes essays on rain ceremonies, popular beliefs about the wind, folk cults and magical rites relating to rain, rain-invoking songs, and superstitions about rain.

Almanac--Weatherlore

1597. *Old Farmer's Almanac*. Dublin, NH: Yankee Publications. Annual.

The 1992 *Farmer's Almanac* is the 200th edition. There are two pages for each month with a daily record of feasts, fasts, aspects, and high tides and weather. There is a farmer's calendar with proverbs and astronomical calculations, with changes for New England, New York, New Jersey, North Atlantic, Piedmont and Southeast Coast, Florida, Upstate New York, Toronto, Montreal, the Greater Ohio Valley, etc. There is also a compilation from the *Farmer's Almanac*, ed. Edward Dolan, *The Old Farmer's Almanac Book of Weather Lore: The Fact and Fancy Behind Weather Predictions, Superstitions, Old-Time Saying, and Traditions* (Dublin, NH: Yankee Books, 1988).

Dictionary--Weatherlore

1598. Sloane, Eric. *Folklore of American Weather*. New York: Duell, Sloan and Pearce, 1963. 63p. LC 63-10342.

The bulk of this work is a "Dictionary of American Weather Folklore," with true/false possibilities. (Example: **Ants**: when ants travel in a straight line, expect rain; when they scatter, expect fair weather. True or False? This is false, and Sloane tells why.) Sloane's lovely illustrations are also included. Sloane has written many books on weatherlore, all of which are popular and light. Among the titles are: *Look at the Sky and Know the Weather* (New York: Hawthorn, 1961, *Eric Sloane's Almanac and Weather Forecaster* (New York: Hawthorn, 1955), *Eric Sloane's Weather Book* (New York: Duell, 1952), and *Clouds, Air, and Wind* (New York: Devin-Adair, 1942).

1599.   Garriott, Edward B. *Weather Folk-Lore and Local Weather Signs.* Washington: GPO, 1903. 153 pp. (U.S. Department of the Agriculture Bulletin, 33)

Weather folklore is listed under the following divisions: winds, clouds, the barometer, unseasonable weather due to abnormal barometric conditions, the physical effect on animal life of changes in atmospheric pressure, temperature, humidity, animals, birds, fish, insects, plants, the sun, the moon, the stars, long-range weather forecasts, sun spots, the moon and the weather, the stars and the weather, etc. There is also a section on local weather signs arranged by city.

1600.   Inwards, Richard. *Weather Lore; The Unique Bedside Book. Taken from the World's Literature and the Age-Old Wisdom of Farmers, Marines, Bird Watchers.* 4th ed. London: Rider, 1950 [1893 as *Weather Lore; A Collection of Proverbs, Sayings, and Rules Concerning the Weather*]. 251p. LC 50-11755.

These proverbs, sayings, and customs are listed under topical sections: times and seasons, proverbs related to various movable feasts, proverbs related to the months and days of the week, sun, moon, stars, clouds, tide, rain, rainbows, hail, snow, mists, dew, air, sky, etc. For each listing, there is a source given. Also included is an index.

1601.   Swainson, Charles. *A Handbook of Weather Folk-Lore; Being a Collection of Proverbial Sayings in Various Languages Relating to the Weather.* Edinburgh: William Blackwood, 1873. 275p. LC 4-13073.

Proverbs relate weather to the year, leap year, the seasons, the months, and the week, to the sun, and moon. Prognostications based on the weather are also given in proverbial form for animals, birds, fish, etc. There is no index or bibliography.

FOLK BELIEF SYSTEMS
Folk Religion/Religious Beliefs

Don Yoder, in "Toward a Definition of Folk Religion" (*Western Folklore* 33 [1974]: 2-15), says that there are two strands of definitions of folk religion: 1) "the religion dimension of folk-culture, or the folk-cultural dimension of religion" (such as, he says, Joshua Trachtenberg's *Jewish Magic and Superstition*), and 2) "anthropological study of syncretisms between two forms of religion on different levels of civilization (e.g., African primitivism plus Roman Catholicism equals Haitian Voodoo)." (pp. 2, 3)

An excellent introduction to the study of the folk religion is the issue of *Western Folklore* cited above, the proceedings of a Symposium on Folk Religion, at the annual meeting of the American Folklore Society in 1971, edited by Don Yoder. Another special folklore journal issue is "The Folklorist and Belief," a special issue of *New York Folklore* 8 (Winter 1982), edited by Lydia Fish, with articles on the folklore of Mormon missionaries, urban witchcraft beliefs, traditions of disbelief, religious folk art, ethnicity and Catholicism, Catholic folklore, and folk Catholicism.

There are three essays in Dorson's *Handbook of American Folklore* on this subject: William M. Clements' "The Folk Church: Institution, Event, Performance" (pp. 136-144), William H. Wiggins, Jr.'s "The Black Folk Church" (pp. 145-154), and William A. Wilson's "Mormon Folklore" (pp. 155-161). Richard M. Dorson's *Folklore and Folklife* has an essay also, "Folk Religion" by John C. Messenger, (pp. 217-232). And Elliott Oring's *Folklore Groups and Folklore Genres: An Introduction* has a chapter on "Religious Folklore" by Larry Danielson (pp. 45-69). William M. Clement's "The American Folk Church in Northeast Arkansas" (*Journal of the Folklore Institute* 15 [1978]: 161-180), his dissertation, "The American Folk Church, A Characterization of American Folk Religion Based on Field Research Among White Protestants in a Community in the South Central United States" (Indiana University, 1974), and his essay on "The Folk Church: Institution, Event, Performance," in Dorson's *Handbook of American Folklore* (cited above), discuss several traits of the regional American folk church. Also useful are two essays in the *Encyclopedia of the American Religious Experience* (no. 1643) "Folklore and the Study of American Religion" by Donald

Byrne Jr. (pp. 85-100) and "Ethnicity and Religion" by Laura L. Becker (pp. 1477-1492).

There are several excellent basic anthropological texts on this subject. Charles M. Leslie's *Anthropology of Folk Religion* (New York: Knopf, Vintage Books, 1960), with articles on folk cultures and religions, with special emphasis on religions in Africa, India, the South Pacific, and the New World, and a selected bibliography (pp. 449-452), provides a basic list of books on this subject. William A. Lessa's and Evon Z. Vogt's *Reader in Comparative Religion* (4th ed., New York: Harper, 1979 [1958]) is a basic reader with over 80 essays on comparative religions. Edward Norbeck's *Religion in Primitive Society* (New York: Harper, 1961) deals with primitive religions; Norbeck also wrote *Religion in Human Life: Anthropological Views* (New York: Holt, Rinehart and Winston, 1974). The proceedings of the *Symposium on New Approaches to the Study of Religion*, chaired by Melford A. Spiro (Seattle: University of Washington Press, 1966), has ten essays, including a classification scheme. Sir James G. Frazer's work, *The Golden Bough: A Study of Magic and Religion* (12 vols., London: Macmillan, 1911-1915) is an earlier study of magic and religion, "linking primitive concepts and modes of thought to the many institutions and folk customs they underlie." James Messenger, in his essay on "Folk Religion" (cited above), calls Mircea Eliade's *Patterns in Comparative Religion* (New York: New American Library, 1987 [1949]) "a modern, compressed *The Golden Bough*, with its wealth of comparative materials," though it "eschews evolutionary theory, and its sources are more dependable" (*Folklore and Folklife*, p. 229).

There are also texts which deal with specific folk religions, such as Austin and Alta Fife's *Saints of Sage & Saddle: Folklore Among the Mormons* (Bloomington: Indiana University Press, 1956; reprinted: Salt Lake City: University of Utah Press, 1980), Daniel Overmayer's *Folk Buddhist Religion: Dissenting Sects in Late Traditional China* (Cambridge, MA: Harvard University Press, 1976) which, aside from a description of the various sects, has several chapters on patterns of folk Buddhist religious beliefs, myths, and rituals, Martin P. Nilsson's *Greek Folk Religion* (New York: Columbia University Press, 1940; reprinted: New York: Harper Torchbooks, 1966), with chapters on rural customs and festivals, the house and the family, superstitions, seers, and oracles, and

Ichori Hori's *Japanese Religion: A Survey* (Palo Alto, CA: Kodansha International, 1972) which is concerned with the origins of Japanese religion and its practice today.

A classic older text is Sir James Frazer's *Folk-Lore in the Old Testament; Studies in Comparative Religion, Legend and Law* (New York: Avenel, 1988 [1918]), with legends and studies of religious parallel customs and rites in the Old Testament. A newer work is Hermann Gunkel's *The Folktale in the Old Testament*, translated by Michael D. Rutter (Sheffield [ENG]: The Almond Press, University of Sheffield, 1987), a textual study of stories and legends in the Old Testament, with a discussion of the nature of fables and folktales, folktale motifs handed down from nature, folk tales about fools, tales of spirits, demons, scepters, tales about giants, tales of magic and primitive beliefs, Old Testament folktales about children, etc. A particularly useful concluding chapter, "Review of the Material According to Form and Content," looks specifically at folktale characteristics and the Israeli folktale in particular.

There is a fair amount of work being done currently on folk religion. Don Yoder has recently published *Discovering American Folklife: Studies in Ethnic, Religious, and Regional Culture* (Ann Arbor, MI: UMI, 1990). Another contemporary work is *The American Quest for the Primitive Church*, edited by Richard T. Hughes (Urbana: University of Illinois Press, 1988). *Diversities of Gifts: Field Studies in Southern Religion* by Ruel Tyson et al. (Urbana: University of Illinois, 1988) and Jeff Titon's *Powerhouse for God: Speech, Chant, and Song in an Appalachian Baptist Church* (Austin: University of Texas Press, 1988) are both studies of southern religion. Bruce A. Rosenberg's *Can These Bones Live?: The Art of the American Folk Preacher* (rev. ed., Urbana: University of Illinois Press, 1988) and William H. Pipes' *Say Amen, Brother! Old-Time Negro Preaching: A Study in American Frustration* (New York: William Frederick, 1951; reprinted: Westport, CT: Negro Universities Press, 1970) are both studies of black folk preaching style.

Although there is little work done on the folklore of Catholicism, there are many compilations of the legends of saints' lives (and often deaths), such as Christina Hole's *Saints in Folklore* (New York: M. Barrow, 1965), Lady Gregory's *A Book of Saints and Wonders* (3rd ed., New York: Oxford, 1971 [1906, 1907]), Klaus Speck's *Medieval Saints and*

Legends (Tubingen: Messenger, 1970), Gilbert Hunter Doble's *Lives of Welsh Saints* (Cardiff: University of Wales Press, 1971), Charles Plummer's 3-volume *Lives of Irish Saints* (Oxford: Clarendon, 1968 [1922]), João Ameal's *Santos Portugueses* (Porto: Tavares Martins, 1957), and Kim Chang-seok Thaddeus' *The Lives of 103 Martyr Saints of Korea* (Seoul: Catholic Publishing House, 1984).

There are, in contrast, many, many studies of Jewish folklore. Joshua Trachtenberg's *Jewish Magic and Superstition: A Study in Folk Religion* (New York: Atheneum, 1984 [1939]) includes chapters on sorcery, evil powers, demons, spirits of the dead, magic, amulets, medicine, divination, and legends of the Jews. Others include: Immanuel Löw's *Studien zur Jüdischen Folklore* (Hildesheim: Georg Olms, 1975); Raphael Patai's *On Jewish Folklore* (Detroit, MI: Wayne State University Press, 1983), dealing with a definition of Jewish folklore, Biblical and Talmudic material, customs, rites and tales of the Marranas, Sephardic and Oriental Jewish folklore, and Jewish birth customs; Angelo Rappoport's *The Folklore of the Jews* (London: Soncino Press, 1937; reprinted: Detroit, MI: Singing Tree, 1972), concerned with sources and characteristics of Jewish folklore, magic, demonology, rites, folk medicine, tales, etc.; and *Studies in Jewish Folklore: Proceedings of a Regional Conference of the Association for Jewish Studies. 1977* (Cambridge, MA: Association for Jewish Studies, 1980), edited by Dov Noy, with a variety of essays including Noy's on "Is There a Jewish Folk Religion?" Two final background works on Jewish folklore are S.M. Lehrman's *Jewish Custom and Folklore* (3rd ed., London: Shapiro, 1964 [1949]) and Jacob Lauterbach's books of essays, *Studies in Jewish Law, Customs, and Folklore* (New York: Ktav, 1970). Also available are David Goldstein's *Jewish Folklore and Legend* (London: Hamlyn, 1980) and Haim Schwarzbaum's *Jewish Folklore Between East and West: Collected Papers* (Beer-Sheva: Ben-Gurion University of the Negev Press, 1989). See also no. 1608 for another work by Schwarzbaum.

Folk religion is closely allied with **mythology** and **folk medicine**, so both those sections should be consulted. I have tried to include only those works that focus on religious folklore and have not included works on religious ritual (which is covered in Chapter 6). For works on religious festivals, see **Jewish Festival and Calendar Rites** and **Christian Festival and Calendar Rites** also in Chapter 6.

This section is admittedly awkwardly arranged into works concerned with religion in general and then works about specific religions--Judaism, the religions of Africa, of America (the Amish, Mennonites, Mormons, Shakers), and of Asia (Hinduism and Buddhism).

Bibliographies--Folklore of Religion/Religious Belief
Worldwide/Multicultural/Multi-religious

1602. Diehl, Katharine Smith. *Religions, Mythologies, Folklores: an Annotated Bibliography.* 2nd ed. New York: Scarecrow Press, 1962 [1956]. 573p. LC 62-16003.

Listed in the section on general folklore (see no. 4), this bibliography is geared towards "the literature of faith and practice in all cultures." Chapter 1 includes a bibliography of works concerned with "universal religious knowledge," and Chapter 4 is concerned with works dealing with "religions, exclusive of Judaism and Christianity," with Chapter 5 covering material on the Judeo-Christian tradition. Diehl's annotations are brief. There is an author and title index.

1603. Turner, Harold W. *Bibliography of New Religious Movements in Primal Societies.* 4 vols. in print. Boston, MA: G.K. Hall, 1977-1991. LC 77-4732. Vol. 1: Black Africa. 277p., ISBN 0-8161-7927-1; Vol. 2: North America. 286p., ISBN 0-8161-7928-x; Vol. 3: Oceania. 347p., ISBN 0-8161-8984-6; Vol. 4: Europe and Asia. 279p., ISBN 0-8161-7930-1. Future volumes will cover Latin America and the Caribbean.

Vol. 1 supersedes, corrects, cumulates, and updates Turner's and Robert Cameron Mitchell's *A Comprehensive Bibliography of Modern African Religious Movements* (Evanston, IL: Northwestern University Press, 1966). "The religious movements with which this bibliographic series is concerned are defined as those which arise in the interaction of a primal society with another society where there is great disparity of power or sophistication." (Intro.) Vol. 1 contains almost 1,900 items, arranged geographically (West Africa, West Central Africa, Eastern Africa, South East Central Africa, South Africa). There are brief descriptive annotations, and an index of authors and sources, plus a select thematic guide (e.g., **healing**). Vol. 2 includes almost 1,600 items, arranged geographically (U.S.A., Canada/Alaska/Greenland, and North Mexico) and subdivided by topic: Apache movements, ghost dances, peyote: botanical, pharmacological, etc. Vol. 3 includes 2,205 entries arranged by country or culture area (Australia, Melanesia, Micronesia, Polynesia). Vol. 4 has almost 1,750 entries, and is arranged into two sections--Europe and Asia. Each volume has an index of authors and sources, an index of films, records and tapes, and an index of the main religious movements of the countries or culture areas covered.

1604. Wilson, John F., and Thomas P. Slavens. *Research Guide to Religious Studies.* Chicago: American Library Association, 1982. 192p. LC 81-22862; ISBN 0-8389-0330-4. (Sources of information on the humanities, 1)

Not particularly folkloric, however, there are relevant reference works cited (in the section on General Works), and useful dictionaries and encyclopedias on mysticism, and works on particular religions (various African sects, Buddhism, Hinduism, Islam, Christianity, Judaism, and Shinto). There is a subject index to guide the folklore researcher and an author and title index.

1605. Yoder, Don. "Introductory Bibliography on Folk Religion." *Western Folklore* 33 (January 1974): 16-34.

This preliminary bibliography, which serves as the bibliography for the special issue on Folk Religion, "was constructed to illustrate the extent of research in the subject areas of folk religion and folk belief," in Europe and North America. The bibliography is appended to an introduction in which Yoder, the reigning expert on folk religion, guides the reader to particularly useful books for specific interests. The bibliography of books, articles, and dissertations in all languages is a listing only, but it is long and seemingly comprehensive. Although a bit old, this is the work with which to begin a search of the literature. See also nos. 1618, 1619.

1606. Berger, Abraham. "The Literature of Jewish Folklore." *Journal of Jewish Bibliography* 1 (1938-1939): 12-20; 40-49.

This is a bibliographic essay in English and a survey of what the author considers Jewish folklore with both religious and secular material included. There are many bibliographical references mostly in English and German.

1607. Bunis, David M. *Sephardic Studies: A Research Bibliography Incorporating Judezmo Language, Literature and Folklore, and Historical Background.* New York: Garland, 1981. 234p. LC 78-68282; ISBN 0-8240-9759-9. (Garland reference library of the humanities; v. 174)

This very comprehensive work has one entire section on Judaic Folklore and Folklife (Ch. 4, pp. 99-168, items 850-1570) which includes, like the whole work, listings (no annotations) of materials, arranged by subject: folk song, folk poetry, and folk music; ballads; folktales; proverbs and proverbial phrases; humor; riddles, folk dramas; games; folk medicine and magic; cookery; dress; folk art and material culture; the life cycle; the calendric cycle; and folklore and folklife of specific areas. There are three indexes to the whole work: institutions and organizations concerned with Sephardic studies, an index of authors, and an index of selected subjects. Although this is a highly specialized aspect of Judaism, there is an abundant amount of material on Sephardic folklore and folklife. The format and subject areas used are most likely based on the work below.

1608. Schwarzbaum, Haim. "Some Recent Works on Jewish Folk-Narrative Lore" and "Recent Contributions to the Study of other Genres of Jewish Folklore," in *Studies in Jewish and World Folklore*, by Schwarzbaum. Berlin: Walter de Gruyter, 1968. pp. 375-408; 409-441.

These are both bibliographical essays, the first covering only folk narrative and the second one covering Jewish proverbs and riddles, Jewish folksong, folk music, and folk dance, Jewish folk belief and practice, folk art, and material culture.

1609.   Weinreich, Uriel, and Beatrice Weinreich. *Yiddish Language and Folklore; A Selective Bibliography for Research.* 's-Gravenhage: Mouton, 1959. 66p. LC 63-1121. (Janua linguarum, 10)

The authors intend this bibliography as "an introduction to the study of the language and folklore of Ashkenazic Jewry." It includes 481 titles of Yiddish, Hebrew, Hungarian, Polish, and Russian articles and books, each with English translation. The work is divided into two parts: Part I is concerned with the Yiddish language, but Part II includes works on Yiddish Folklore with items 254-481 being divided into subject areas: general folklore, which is subdivided into general and theoretical works, works on cultural background, anthologies, and miscellaneous collections, collective volumes of studies, serials, bibliographies, and the history of Yiddish folkloristics. There are also subject divisions for folksong and folk music, folktales, proverbs and proverbial phrases, humor, riddles, folk drama, games, folk medicine and magic, cookery, dress, folk art, the life cycle, and the calendric year. No entry is annotated and there is only an author index.

1610.   Yassif, Eli. *Jewish Folklore: An Annotated Bibliography.* New York: Garland, 1986. 341p. LC 83-48282; ISBN 0-8240-9039-X. (Garland folklore bibliographies; v.10; Garland reference library of the humanities; v. 450)

In the introduction the author says that "this book constitutes the first attempt to present the fruit of the study of Jewish folklore in the form of an annotated bibliography." Covering up to 1980, and with very specific parameters of inclusion (Yassif includes "studies alone and no other kind of publication on Jewish folklore text or artifacts" and excludes studies of European Jewish culture and Judeo-Spanish culture, and most Biblical scholarship studies, except those that describe Biblical literature as folk literature), the work includes 1,356 items, and is arranged, as are most Garland bibliographies, in alphabetical order by author. Articles, books, and monographs are international in scope, the annotations are quite critical, and there is a subject index of 48p. In a prefatory note, the author lists other bibliographies covering Jewish folklore (pp. xv, xvi), but this is obviously the work to begin with when researching Jewish folklore, and most likely it supersedes all others including nos. 1607 and 1608.

Africa
Traditional Religions

1611. Ofori, Patrick E. *Black African Traditional Religions and Philosophy: A Select Bibliographic Survey of the Sources from the Earliest Times to 1974* Nendeln [Liechtenstein]: Kraus-Thomsoness, 1975. 421p. LC 75-22939.

"This bibliography covers all the major ethnic groups of black Africa."(Intro.) The work is arranged by geographic area: Africa in general, West Africa, Central Africa, East Africa, and Southern Africa) and subdivided into country and ethnic group within those countries, with some of the larger ethnic groups also subdivided into categories such as, **fetish, witchcraft, magic, ritual, superstitions, totems, myths, proverbs,** etc. Both books and articles are included in the bibliography, and some of the entries are annotated. There are separate author and ethnic indexes.

1612. Williams, Ethel L., and Clifton F. Brown. *The Howard University Bibliography of African and Afro-American Religious Studies; with Locations in American Libraries.* Wilmington, DE: Scholarly Resources, 1977. 525p. LC 76-5604; ISBN 0-8420-2080-2.

This massive work includes about 13,000 entries arranged in five sections: African heritage, Christianity and slavery in the New World, the black man and his religious life in the Americas, civil rights movement, and the contemporary religious scene. There is a section in Part II (Christianity and slavery in the New World) on spirituals, gospel songs, music, poetry, oral traditions and folklore (pp. 170-180) listing items nos. 5955-6347 which are excellent for folklorists. There are two appendixes, a selected list of manuscripts and an "autobiographical and biographical index" as well as a comprehensive index.

The Americas
North America

Note: for entries on traditional black religions in America, see nos. 1603, 1612.

The Amish, Mennonites, and Pennsylvania Germans

1613. Bender, Harold Stauffer. *Two Centuries of American Mennonite Literature: A Bibliography of Mennonitica Americana, 1727-1928.* Goshen, IN: Mennonite Historical Society, Goshen College, 1929. 181p. LC 30-3847. (Studies in Anabaptist and Mennonite history, 1)

This bibliography contains articles and books about the Mennonites and other Anabaptist groups, arranged chronologically. Some entries are annotated, and there is an author and a title index.

1614. Benjamin, Steven M. *Amish Bibliography, 1951-1977.* Morgantown: West Virginia University, Department of Foreign Languages, 1979. 35p. (Occasional papers of the Society for German-American studies)

This listing of works about the Amish, heavily folkloric, is meant to supplement the main bibliographic work on the Amish prepared by Hostetler (no. 1615).

1615. Hostetler, John A. *Annotated Bibliography on the Amish; An Annotated Bibliography of Source Materials Pertaining to the Older Order Amish Mennonites.* Scottdale, PA: Mennonite Publishing House, 1951. 100p. LC 51-6543.

This bibliography includes published and unpublished books and pamphlets, articles, masters' theses, Ph.D. dissertations, and other unpublished sources, such as undergraduate papers of "substantial nature," letters and documents. This work by the world's leading authority on the Amish concludes with an analytic subject index. A thorough work, updated through 1977 by the work above. Hostetler's *Amish Society* (3rd ed., Baltimore: Johns Hopkins Press, 1980) is the standard study of the Amish in America. See also *The Sociology of Canadian Mennonites, Hutterites and Amish: A Bibliography with Annotations*, ed. Donovan E. Smucker and Wilfred Laurier (Waterloo: University Press, 1977).

1616. Meynen, Emil. *Bibliography on German Settlements in Colonial America, Especially on the Pennsylvania Germans and Their Descendants, 1683-1933*. Leipzig: Otto Harrassowitz, 1937. 636p.

Not seen, but Yoder calls this the most basic bibliography on the Pennsylvania Germans.

1617. Springer, Nelson P., and A.J. Klassen, comps. *Mennonite Bibliography, 1631-1961*. 2 vols. Scottdale, PA: Herald Press, 1977. LC 77-9105; ISBN 0-8361-1208-3.

Vol. 1 covers the international literature on the Mennonites, and the Mennonites in Latin America, Asia and Africa. Vol. 2 includes work on the Mennonites of North America. In all, there are 28,155 unannotated items listed, primarily works dealing with Mennonite history and doctrine, and descriptive works. The indexes to both volumes (separate author and subject indexes) are in Vol. 2.

1618. Yoder, Don. "The Pennsylvania Germans: A Preliminary Reading List." *Pennsylvania Folklife* 21 (Winter 1971-72): 2-17.

This "selected list for beginners" is concerned with all aspects of the folklore and material culture of the Pennsylvania Germans. Covering general historical works, language and literature, genealogy, religion, medicine, the arts, music, costumes, cookery and foodways, and the Pennsylvania Dutchman in fiction, Yoder has prepared a bibliographic essay for each one of these topics.

1619. Yoder, Don. "What to Read on the Amish." *Pennsylvania Folklife* 18 (Summer 1969): 14-19.

This is a bibliographic essay with books and articles grouped under the following headings: general introduction to Amish life, the Amish religion and its leadership, the Amishman and the State, Amish language patterns, the Amish community and the Amish family, Amish folk-magic, the Amishman in fiction, the Amishman in art, medical aspects of the Amish life, and the journalist and the Amishman.

The Mormons

1620. Flake, Chad J., ed. *A Mormon Bibliography, 1830-1930: Books, Pamphlets, Periodicals, and Broadsides Relating to the First Century of Mormonism.* Salt Lake City: University of Utah Press, 1978. 825p. LC 74-22639; ISBN 0-87480-016-1 (Univ. of Utah Press); 0-913738-13-1 (Utah State Historical Society). Supplemented: *A Mormon Bibliography, 1830-1930*, comp. Flake and Larry Draper. Salt Lake City: University of Utah Press, 1989. 413p. LC 89-36679; ISBN 0-874803-38-1.

This is an alphabetical listing of 10,145 items plus 56 addenda items--books, periodicals, predominantly Mormon newspaper articles-- with their locations. There is a chronological index and no general index, which might hamper its use. Supplement not seen.

1621. U.S. Library of Congress. Archive of Folk Song. *A Selected Bibliography of Mormon Folklore and Folksong.* Washington, DC: Library of Congress, Archive of Folk Song, 1970. 4p.

An unannotated checklist of works about Mormon folklore and song.

1622. Wilson, William A. "A Bibliography of Studies in Mormon Folklore." *Utah Historical Quarterly* 44 (Fall 1976): 389-394.

Included are "only those works that treat folklore as folklore--that is, as material to be studied for increased cultural understanding"--and excluded are "works that use folklore to support the arguments of theological treatises." This short bibliography is an author listing of 97 articles and monographs and six recordings of Mormon folklore by subject: general works, folk speech, folksong, folk narrative, folk belief and custom, and material culture.

Shaker

Note: Books on Shaker crafts and music are to be found in Chapters 4 and 7.

1623. Richmond, Mary L. Hurt, comp. and annot. *Shaker Literature: A Bibliography*. 2 vols. Hancock, MA: Shaker Community; distributed by University Press of New England, 1977. LC 75-41908; ISBN 0-87451-117-8.

Vol. 1, which includes an introduction and brief history, covers works by the Shakers; Vol. 2 covers works about the Shakers. Both volumes have two parts: a listing of books, pamphlets and broadsides and a listing of periodical articles, arranged by author or main entry. There is a title and joint author index in Vol. 2, but the lack of a subject index might hamper use for the beginner. In all, there are 3,986 entries with brief annotations.

Other

1624. Maguire, Marsha, comp. *American Snake-Handling Sects: A Selected Bibliography*. Washington, DC: Archive of Folk Song, 1980. 4p.

This is a listing of books, articles, and films on background sources or on works about snake-handling revivalism in America.

Note: See also the works on Asian mythology, nos. 624-633.

Buddhism and Hinduism

1625. Hanayama, Shinsho. *Bibliography on Buddhism.* Tokyo: The Hokuseido Press, 1961. 869p. LC 62-5865.

This is an alphabetical arrangement by authors of articles and books--15,073 items in all--accessed by a complete index.

1626. Holland, Barron, comp. *Popular Hinduism and Hindu Mythology: An Annotated Bibliography.* Westport, CT: Greenwood, 1979. 394p. LC 79-7188; ISBN 0-313-21358-5.

This work includes almost 3,500 entries with one-line descriptive annotations. It is divided by subject: general studies, deities, ritual and worship, festivals and pilgrimages, sacred literature, symbolism and iconography, myth and legend, and religious dance and drama, among others. There is a general index and a separate subject index for easy access.

1627. Satyaprakash, comp. and ed. *Buddhism: A Select Bibliography.* 2nd ed., enl. and rev. Gurgaon, Haryana: Indian Documentation Service, 1986 [1976]. 247p. (Subject bibliography; v. 5)

This is an alphabetical listing by author, subject, and title, with some folk material, such as works on "festivals," listed. There is no general index.

1628. Vlach, John M., ed. "Islam: A Bibliography," in "Folklore and the Advent of Islam." *Folklore Forum* 9 (1972): 1-42.

This annotated bibliography, introduced by Hafizullah Baghban, is part of this special issue on Islam, edited by Vlach. It includes: works on folklore and folklife; bibliographies, dictionaries, indexes and a guide to fieldwork; works about the Islamic people, cultures and customs; Islamic folk drama; Islamic epic and romance; proverbs and riddles; magic, superstitions, and medicine; Islamic and Sufic philosophy; and Islamic folktale collections. There is an author and an area index.

Other

1629. Bowman, Mary Ann. *Western Mysticism: A Guide to the Basic Works.* Chicago, IL: American Library Association, 1978. 113p. LC 78-18311; ISBN 0-8389-0266-9.

This selective bibliography is arranged by subject: philosophy, history, practice and experience of mysticism, Oriental mysticism, mystical expressions in literature, and mystical and contemplative writings. Further, there are a few entries concerning fairy tales and several on myths. There are separate author, title, and subject indexes.

Dictionaries and Encyclopedias--Folklore of Religion/Religious Beliefs
General/Multicultural/Multi-Religious

1630. Eliade, Mircea, editor in chief. *The Encyclopedia of Religion.* 16 vols. New York: Macmillan, 1987. LC 86-5432; ISBN 0-02-909480-1 (set).

This encyclopedia, with long signed articles, each with bibliographic notes, contains many entries dealing with folk religion (e.g., entries on Chinese popular religion, folk Buddhism, folk Islam, folk Shinto, Indian rural traditions, Japanese popular religions, popular Christian religiosity, and an entry on fairies and fairy tales) as well as entries on many aspects of mythology.

1631. Gaskell, George Arthur. *Dictionary of All Scriptures and Myths.* New York: Avenel, 1981 [1960]. 846p. LC 81-3499; ISBN 0-517-34663-x.

Useful for determining religious symbolism but also for entries on religion and myth. The entries range from **Aaron**, the high priest (the symbol of the spiritual mind) to **Zoroaster** (a symbol of the soul or the son of the supreme).

1632.   Hinnells, John R., ed. *The Facts on File Dictionary of Religions.* New York: Facts on File, 1984. 550p. LC 83-20834; ISBN 0-87196-862-2.

This is a rather compact dictionary with references to folklore, mythology, and religious holidays. There are many maps, a long bibliography (divided geographically), and a synoptic index and a very long general index with entries for **folk magic, folk songs, folklore**, and **festivals and food**.

1633.   Kennedy, Richard. *The International Dictionary of Religion: A Profusely Illustrated Guide to the Beliefs of the World.* New York: Crossroad, 1984. 256p. LC 83-27209; ISBN 0-8245-0632-4 (c); 0-8245-0650-2 (p).

This is a one-volume dictionary with folklore entries and an emphasis on religious calendar rites. It has great illustrations and a good bibliography.

1634.   Wedeck, Harry E., and Wade Baskin. *Dictionary of Pagan Religions.* New York: Philosophical Library, 1971. 363p. LC 79-86508; ISBN 0-8022-2337-0.

This is a wide-ranging work, going from **aahla** ("In Egyptian religion, one of the divisions of the lower regions. The word means 'field of peace'") to **Zivimbganana** ("In African voodoo cults, a creature raised from the dead to do a witch's evil work..."). There is much folklore material in this work, covering also aspects of Classical and Norse mythology and much mysticism.

1635.   Ausubel, Nathan. *The Book of Jewish Knowledge; An Encyclopedia of Judaism and the Jewish People, Covering All Elements of Jewish Life from Biblical Times to the Present.* New York: Crown, 1964. 560p. LC 64-23807.

Ausubel, author of *A Treasury of Jewish Folklore*, set out "to examine and analyze the many traditional facets of Jewish knowledge which, collectively make up the cultural heritage of the Jewish people." (vi) This large work contains entries related to history, tradition and customs, and religious beliefs of the Jews, many of which are folkloric (e.g., **amulets, ceremonial art, marriage,** and **sex rites**). Entries are long and there is abundant cross listing. The work includes many illustrations and a comprehensive index.

1636.   *Encyclopedia Judaica.* [Edited by Cecil Roth.] 16 vols. New York: Macmillan, 1972. LC 72-90254.

This new *Encyclopedia Judaica*, in English, has in its entirety, about 25,000 signed articles, each with a bibliography. Dov Noy served as a departmental editor of the **Folklore** section, writing the entry on **Folklore** (6: 1374-1410) which covers Jewish folk narrative, folk song, folk proverbs, riddles, folk drama and visual folklore, Jewish holidays, folk dress and costume, and folk medicine, among others. There is a major bibliography for this section (1408-1410). Other aspects of folklore are included throughout the work; there are major articles on **food, costume, animal tales,** etc. The work is profusely illustrated, the Index is in Vol. 1, with a corrigenda section in Vol. 16.

1637.   *The Jewish Encyclopedia; A Descriptive Record of the History, Religion, Literature, and Customs of the Jewish People from the Earliest Times to the Present Day.* Cyrus Adler, managing ed. 12 vols. New York: Funk & Wagnalls, 1901-1906. LC 01-9359.

Although this encyclopedia is now outdated and has been superseded by the above work, some of the information is still viable and useful for historical purposes. There is a long article on **Folk-Lore** and shorter articles on such subjects as amulets, betrothal, childbirth, cookery, evil eye, folk medicine, folk songs, folktale, game, magic, marriage, proverbs, riddles, superstitions, talisman, weatherlore, and wildcraft. Each of these articles has a brief bibliography. See also *The Encyclopedia of Folklore, Customs and Tradition in Judaism*, ed. Yom-Tov Lewinsky (Tel Aviv: Devir, 1975).

1638. Werblowsky, R.J. Zwi, and Geoffrey Wigoder. *The Encyclopedia of the Jewish Religion*. New York: Adama Books, 1986 [1965, 1966]. 415p. LC 86-10932; ISBN 0-915-361-53-1.

In English, this work is intended to provide the "interested layman with concise, accurate, and nontechnical information on Jewish beliefs and practices, religious movements and doctrines." Although this encyclopedia definitely concentrates on religious material more than Ausubel (no. 1635), there are some good articles on beliefs and practices (e.g., **magic, marriage, mysticism**). There is no index and no bibliography. Wigoder also co-edited (with Cecil Roth) *The New Standard Jewish Encyclopedia* (5th ed., Garden City, NY: Doubleday, 1977) which has some short articles on folklore and allied subjects.

Christianity

1639. Metford, J.C.J. *Dictionary of Christian Lore and Legend*. London: Thames & Hudson, 1983. 272p. LC 82-50815; ISBN 0-500-11020-4.

The author defines **lore** as "the learning and background knowledge associated with Christian culture" and **legend** as "something to be read." Included are customs associated with the seasons of the Christian calendar, religious symbols, traditional symbols, etc., so there is a sprinkling of everything, like **adder, All Hallows, Androcles**, etc. The work is illustrated with black and white photos of paintings, sculptures, drawings, etc. However, there is no index and no bibliography.

1640. Demetrakopoulos, George H. *A Dictionary of Orthodox Theology: A Summary of the Beliefs, Practices and History of the Eastern Orthodox Church.* New York: Philosophical Library, 1964. 187p. LC 63-13346.

There are brief entries on rites, ceremonies, customs, symbols, demons and devils, funerary rites, etc.

1641. Langford-James, Richard Lloyd. *A Dictionary of the Eastern Orthodox Church.* London: Faith Press, 1923. 144p. Reprinted: New York: Burt Franklin, 1975. LC 72-82261; ISBN 0-8337-4210-8.

This work has more lengthy entries than the one above, although they cover about the same material: religious customs, marriage and funerary rites, information about feasts and fasts, etc. A calendar and bibliography are appended.

America

1642. Hill, Samuel S., ed. *Encyclopedia of Religion in the South.* Atlanta, GA: Mercer University Press, 1984. 878p. LC 84-8957; ISBN 0-86554117-5.

This contains long signed articles on southern religious movements, including traditional religions and traditions and beliefs.

1643. Lippy, Charles H., and Peter W. Williams, eds. *Encyclopedia of The American Religious Experience: Studies of Traditions and Movements.* 3 vols. New York: Scribner, 1988. 1,872p. LC 87-4781; ISBN 0-684-18062-6 (set).

Covers customs, traditions, material culture, and beliefs of Judeo-Christian and non-Judeo-Christian religions in America. A comprehensive index is in Vol. 3.

1644.   Melton, J. Gordon. *Encyclopedia of American Religions*. 3rd ed. Detroit, MI: Gale Research, 1989 [1978]. 1,102p. LC 88-31784; ISBN 0-8103-2841-0. A 3rd ed. supplement was published by Gale, with a 1992 publication date (93p., ISBN 0-8203-6903-6). Not seen.

Essays cover the rituals and beliefs of all American religions, and includes a long section on **Magic**. Quite a bit of the material will be of use to folklorists. There is a directory of churches in the U.S., and many indexes including a subject index. A supplementary volume to the first edition includes a cumulative index to both the first and second editions. The 3rd edition is indexed separately.

Asia
Buddhism and Hinduism

1645.   Dowson, John. *A Classical Dictionary of Hindu Mythology and Religion, Geography, History, and Literature*. 12th ed. London: Routledge & Kegan Paul, 1979 [1879]. 411p. (Trübner's oriental series)

"The main portion of this work consists of mythology, but religion is bound up with mythology, and in many points the two are quite inseparable." (pref.) This alphabetic listing of gods' names, places, subjects and expressions, contains mostly short entries (with some exceptions: **Veda**, for example, is five pages), with generous cross listings, a Sanskrit index, and a general index.

1646.   Gibb, H.A.R., et al., eds. *Encyclopaedia of Islam*. New ed. under the patronage of the International Union of Academies. 5 vols.+ Vol. 6: Index to Vols. 1-5; and Supplement. Leiden: E.J. Brill, 1960--[1911]. LC 61-4395.

Sheehy calls this "the most important reference work in English on Islamic subjects." A new edition is in process. The index to Vols. 1-3 is in French. There are entries for **festivals, folklore, food, forests**, etc. There is also a *Shorter Encyclopedia of Islam*, by H.A.R. Gibb and J.H. Kramers (Ithaca, NY: Cornell University Press, 1953).

1647.   Hughes, Thomas Patrick. *A Dictionary of Islam: Being a Cyclopaedia of the Doctrines, Rites, Ceremonies, and Customs, Together with the Technical and Theological Terms, of the Muhammadan Religion*. Clifton, NJ: Reference Books Publishers, 1965 [1885]. 750p. LC 67-116695. (Library of religious and philosophical thought)

This older work includes many Islamic beliefs, customs, rites, etc. There is an index.

1648.   Ling, T.O. *A Dictionary of Buddhism*. New York: Scribner, 1972. 277p. LC 72-37231; ISBN 0-684-12763-6.

These entries are extracted from a larger work called *A Dictionary of Comparative Religion*, ed. G.F. Brandon (London: Weidenfeld, 1970). Covered are rites, customs, beliefs about architecture, festival beliefs, and funerary rites, etc. The entries are quite complete with bibliographic notes included in each entry. This work is probably more useful for the folklorist than C. Humphrey's *A Popular Dictionary of Buddhism* (Totowa, NJ: Rowman & Littlefield, 1976 [1962]).

1649.   Malalasekera, G.P., ed. *Encyclopaedia of Buddhism*. 4 vols. Ceylon: Government Press, 1961-1988. LC 68-12145. Complete through "C" only.

This encyclopedia covers concepts of Buddhist doctrine and philosophy as well as cultural beliefs. There are, for example, some long entries on aspects of folk belief, such as a four-page entry on **charms**.

1650.   Stutley, Margaret, and James Stutley. *Harper's Dictionary of Hinduism: Its Mythology, Folklore, Philosophy, Literature, and History.* New York: Harper and Row, 1977. 372p. LC 76-9999; ISBN 0-06-067763-5.

The entries in this work are generally short and scholarly with bibliographic sources included for each. There are entries for symbol, **plants, magical apparatus**, the gods, goddesses and other mythic characters, and various beliefs. The general bibliography (pp. 353-368) is extensive. There is a glossary of English subjects and their Sanskrit equivalents but there is no index.

1651.   Walker, [George] Benjamin. *The Hindu World; An Encyclopedic Survey of Hinduism.* 2 vols. London: Allen & Unwin; New York: Praeger, 1968. 1,305p. LC 68-26182. Reprinted: New Delhi: Munshiram Manoharial, 1983.

The entries include substantial articles on aspects of religion, mythology, symbolism, beliefs, and philosophy. Bibliographical information is listed after each entry. There is a subject index.

Guides--Folklore of Religions/Religious Beliefs

1652.   Deitering, Carolyn. *Actions, Gestures & Bodily Attitudes.* Sarasota, CA: Resource Publications, 1980. 96p. LC 80-51058; ISBN 0-89390-021-4 (p)

This work deals with customs and practices of the Catholic church, mostly with traditional movement--rising, kneeling, unison group movement, etc.--as it applies to specific parts of the liturgy.

1653.   Dell, David J., et al. *Guide to Hindu Religion.* Boston, MA: G.K. Hall, 1981. 461p. LC 79-18784; ISBN 0-8161-7903-4. (The Asian philosophies and religious resource guides)

There is a large section in this book on **Popular Practices**, which includes a basic list of reference works and general discussion of folk practices. Also included are "detailed descriptive materials collected by folklorists and ethnographers" (xi) as well as a section on Hindu ritual and practice, including coverage of life and death rites and Hindu mythology. There are also annotated lists of research aids given (bibliographies, encyclopedias, dictionaries, indexes, etc.).

1654.   Whitlock, Ralph. *In Search of Lost Gods: A Guide to British Folklore*. Oxford: Phaidon, 1979. 192p. ISBN 0-7148-2026-1 (c); 0-7148-2018-0 (p)

This work covers legends, superstitions and beliefs, sacred sites, festivals, sports and games, all based on religious belief. Each of the above sections has alphabetical entries, and there is a general index.

Annotated Collections--Folklore of Religion/Religious Beliefs
Jewish

1655.   Lutske, Harvey. *The Book of Jewish Customs*. Northvale, NJ: Jason Aronson, 1986. 383p. LC 86-22362; ISBN 0-87668-916-0.

The customs are arranged topically: birth and youth, marriage, death, signs, symbols and rituals, superstitions and folklore (pp. 137-166), the word of God, holidays, holy days and special times, houses of worship, food and eating, and words, phrases, expressions, and language. Classical sources are given and there is a bibliography.

1656.   Mintz, Jerome R. *Legends of the Hasidism: An Introduction to Hasidic Culture and Oral Tradition in the New World*. Chicago, IL: University of Chicago Press, 1968. 462p. LC 68-16707.

The author says that "this work is both a study of the contemporary hasidic customs common in New York and a collection of hasidic oral tradition," collected in the field through interviews with rabbis. The first part deals with hasidic customs concerning their settlement in New York, court life, youth and marriage, "the rebbe," the Commandments, mitsves (good deeds), supernatural beings and magic, attitudes and relationships. Part II includes the legends. There is a bibliography, a glossary, an index, and a section on the storytellers. This is a fascinating book, beautifully illustrated with wonderful photos.

1657. Sperling, Abraham Isaac. *Reasons for Jewish Customs and Traditions*. Trans. Rabbi Abraham Matts. New York: Bloch, 1968. 310p. LC 68-31711. Published originally as *Taa'mei Ha Minhagim* in 1890.

There are 598 customs of daily private observances, holiday customs, blessings, mourning customs, etc., in question and answer format. The bibliographic information is included in the index.

FOLK BELIEF SYSTEMS
Symbols

For an excellent study of a folk symbol, see Venetia Newall's *An Egg at Easter: A Folklore Study* (London: Routledge & Kegan Paul, 1971), in which she discusses the egg as a ritual and religious symbol.

Dictionaries--Symbols

1658. Cirlot, Juan Eduardo. *A Dictionary of Symbols*. 2nd ed. Trans. from the Spanish by Jack Sage. New York: Philosophical Library, 1971 [1962]. 419p. LC 72-78163; ISBN 0-8022-2083-5.

There is a long, scholarly introduction by Cirlot followed by the dictionary. The entries vary in length, though most are short, and cover Western and non-Western symbols, mostly secular but some mythological. A fascinating book, with wonderfully eclectic definitions ("**window**: an aperture; ideas of penetration, or possibilities and distance; rational and terrestrial. Also symbolic of consciousness"). There is a bibliography of principal sources and an additional bibliography, plus a comprehensive index.

1659. Cooper, J.C. *An Illustrated Encyclopaedia of Traditional Symbols.* London: Thames & Hudson, 1978. 208p. LC 78-55249; ISBN 0-500-012016.

The author says in the introduction that the "symbol differs from the emblem and allegory in that it expresses, or crystallizes, some aspect or direct experiences of life and truth and thus leads beyond itself." This work is especially useful to the folklorist. Cooper gives "the generalized or universal acceptance of the interpretation of a symbol," then particularizes "its diverse applications in varying traditions, cultural and geographic" (e.g., **Christmas tree:** the evergreen tree is the Winter Solstice; the New Year and a fresh beginning. It is the tree of rebirth and immortality, the tree of Paradise of light and gifts, shining by night..."). Illustrated throughout, the book has a glossary and bibliography, but no index.

1660. Drake, Maurice, and Wilfred Drake. *Saints and Their Emblems.* London: Laurie; Philadelphia, PA: Lippincott, 1916. 235p. Reprinted: Detroit, MI: Gale Research, 1971. LC 68-18021.

This is in two parts: a dictionary of saints and a dictionary of emblems. The second part gives a symbol (emblem) and then gives the saint who is associated with it and the saint's feast day, i.e., **acolyte, abbess, agnus dei, alms,** etc. The appendix includes drawings of medieval ecclesiastical vestments and a listing of patriarchs and prophets, sibyls, and patrons of the arts, and trades and professions with their symbols. Also included is a list of patron saints (e.g., patron saint of eloquence is St. Catherine, patron saint of girls is St. Ursula) and a list of saints to be invoked for specific problems and ills (e.g., invoke the name of St. Apollonia for toothaches).

1661.   Gaskell, George Arthur. *Dictionary of All Scriptures and Myths.*
         New York: Avenel, 1980 [1960]. 846p. LC 81-3499; ISBN 0-
         517-34663-x.

Gaskell deals, he notes, with "transcendental symbolism."
Included as part of this large work (see no. 1631) is "A Dictionary of
Sacred Language" which ranges from **Aaron, the High Priest** (a symbol
of the spiritual mind) to **Zoroaster, Zarathustra, or Zartust** (a symbol
of the soul). Each of these entries contains many literary and religious
quotes, and full sources are given in each entry.

1662.   Hangen, Eva C. *Symbols: Our Universal Language.* Wichita, KS:
         McCormick-Armstrong, 1962. 308p. LC 62-20744.

This book covers both secular and religious symbols, though the
bulk is nonreligious. In two parts, the first very short section groups black
and white drawings into themes: deities, monsters of fable and fancy,
symbols from beliefs, familiar figures and forms, symbols of devotion,
symbols of ceremony, objects of symbolic significance, flowers, etc. The
main part of this book is a dictionary from **Aaron's Rod** to **Zodiac** and
Zucchetto (a close-fitting cap which, when worn by the clergy, signifies
dignity). There is a bibliography but no index.

1663.   Jobes, Gertrude. *Dictionary of Mythology, Folklore and Symbols.*
         2 vols.+Index. New York: Scarecrow, 1961. 1,759p. LC 61-860.

Jobes, who is particularly interested in symbols as they relate to
folklore, has put together "a key to conventional symbols used throughout
the ages." In all, there are 22,000 listings, some with very long entries.
She gives traditions, legends, and explanations of the symbols and motifs.
This is not a particularly easy work to use. The Index is in two parts: Part
A is an index to deities, heroes, and personalities; Part B is an index to
supernatural forms, realms, things.

1664. Lurker, Manfred. *The Gods and Symbols of Ancient Egypt: An Illustrated Dictionary.* New York and London: Thames & Hudson, 1980. 142p. LC 80-50795; ISBN 0-500-11018-2. Adapted from the German, *Götter und Symbole der Alten Ägypter* (1974) by Barbara Cummings.

This dictionary covers from **acacia** and **aegis** (a collar-like necklace regarded as a symbol of protection) to **wreath** (given to the deceased in the netherworld). The definitions are concise and there are many illustrations. A chronological table is also included as well as a selective bibliography and an index. See also Lurker's *Wörterbuch der Symbolik* (2nd ed., Stuttgart: Alfred Kröner, 1983 [1979]) which deals with symbols found in nature, popular customs, magic, religion, and philosophy.

1665. Olderr, Steven, comp. *Symbolism: A Comprehensive Dictionary.* Jefferson, NC: McFarland, 1986. 153p. LC 85-42833; ISBN 0-89950-187-7.

Listed by the symbolic letters or word (e.g., **A.M.**: stands for Ave Maria; an attribute of the Virgin Mary; associated with Annunciation; **acorn**: life, strength, viability; latent greatness or strength, etc; **zither**: the cosmos; the synthesis of heaven and earth, etc.; **zodiac**: the year; the dignity of labor). The definitions are short, the author covers a wide territory. There is no bibliography and no index.

1666. de Vries, Ad. *Dictionary of Symbols and Imagery.* Amsterdam: North-Holland, 1974. 523p. LC 73-86087; ISBN 0-7204-8021-3 (North-Holland); ISBN 0-444-10607-3 (American Elsevier).

De Vries intends to supply "associations which have been evoked by certain words, signs, etc. in Western civilization in the past, and which may float to the surface again tomorrow." (pref.) Covers mostly non-Christian and non-graphic symbols, especially allegories, metaphors, signs, and images. With emphasis mostly on the literary and mythological, religious and proverbial, there is an abundance of mythic and folkloric material in this volume.

1667.   Whittick, Arnold. *Symbols: Signs and Their Meaning and Uses in Design.* 2nd ed. London: Leonard Hill, 1971 [1960]. 383p. LC 72-177817; ISBN 0-249-44028-8.

This work is in two distinct parts: the first is a handbook with separate chapters on what the author calls "applied symbols": totems, standards, and flags; seals; civic heraldry, etc.; and on "instinctive, creative, and imaginative symbolism": religious symbolism, national and state symbolism; the dance, gestures and the ceremonies of everyday life; dress; architecture; sculpture and painting; and drama, theater, and cinema. The second part of the book is an encyclopedic dictionary (pp. 193-355) covering traditional and familiar symbols, their origins, meanings, and history, each given with historical sources. There are bibliographic notes and an index.

1668.   Williams, C.A.S. *Outlines of Chinese Symbolism; An Alphabetical Compendium of Antique Legends and Beliefs, As Reflected in the Manners and Customs of the Chinese.* 3rd rev. ed. Rutland, VT: Charles E. Tuttle, 1974 [1932, 1941]. 472p. LC 73-90237; ISBN 0-8048-1127-x.

The author discusses written symbols (arranged alphabetically), their meanings, and symbolism in general. There are many references and illustrations as well as an index. A fascinating book.

Guides and Handbooks--Symbols

1669.   Binder, Pearl. *Magic Symbols of the World.* London: Hamlyn, 1972. 127p. LC 73-154300; ISBN 0-600-02545-4.

Discusses the parameters of magic and then covers symbols of fertility, gods as symbols, the magic protection of body and dwelling, magic protection of family, and death and after-life. The work is wonderfully illustrated, and there is an index.

1670.   Child, Heather, and Dorothy Colles. *Christian Symbols, Ancient and Modern: A Handbook for Students*. London: G. Bell, 1971. 270p. LC 72-300029; ISBN 0-7135-1960-6.

The authors are concerned with the "use of the visual Christian symbols in the service of the Church." (intro.) There are separate chapters on the cross, the Trinity, images of Christ, the Virgin Mary, the nativity of Jesus Christ, living water (baptisteries), the holy spirit, the Eucharist, good and evil, forerunners and followers, the Evangelists, the church calendar and zodiac signs, liturgy, and crafts. The authors use descriptive text and line drawings as well as photographs. Although prepared in chapter format, an excellent index makes this useful as a reference tool. There is a bibliography also.

1671.   Ferguson, George Wells. *Signs & Symbols in Christian Art*. 2nd ed. New York: Oxford University Press, 1959 [1954]. 123p. LC 59-4639.

In this basic work, intended for students, the author divides the topic into several broad categories: animals, birds and insects; flowers, trees, and plants, earth and sky; the human body; the Old Testament; Jesus Christ, the Virgin Mary, the Saints, religious dress; religious objects; artifacts, etc. Each section is subdivided rationally, most in alphabetical order but not all; some "chronologically" (The Old Testament, for example, has subsections on **creation, Adam and Eve, Abraham**). There are 96 black-and-white plates and 16 color plates plus other black-and-white line illustrations (mostly from the Renaissance period). There is an index of names and subjects. This is a very thorough work and good for quick reference.

1672.   Gillespie, Angus K., and Jack Mechling, eds. *American Wildlife in Symbol and Story*. Knoxville: University of Tennessee Press, 1987. 251p. LC 86-19315; ISBN 0-87049-522-4.

This work provides an excellent introduction to the subject of symbols in folklore. It includes essays on different animals--the turkey, rattlesnake, armadillo, bear, fox, and coyote and describes and discusses their lore.

1673. Lehner, Ernst. *Symbols, Signs & Signets.* New York: Dover, 1969 [1950]. 221p. LC 69-16134; ISBN 0-486-22241-1. (Dover pictorial archive series)

This work is divided into several sections: symbolic gods and deities, astronomy and astrology, alchemy, magic and mystic, church and religion, heraldry, monsters and imaginary figures, marks and signets, cattle brands, hobo signs, etc. Each section has an introduction with pages of marks, signs, and symbols and a page that explains what each sign or symbol means. There is a bibliography and are some section indexes, but no general index. Lehner also wrote *The Picture Book of Symbols* (New York: William Penn, 1956) which discusses the symbols of arts and sciences, astronomy, astrology, mythology, Nordic symbols and runes, semitic symbols, beliefs and religions, Oriental symbols, symbols of good luck, divinations, magic, time and seasons, etc., with many graphic symbols given on each page for one idea.

1674. Smeets, René. *Signs, Symbols & Ornaments.* New York: Van Nostrand Rinehold, 1975. 176p. LC 75-2823; ISBN 0-4422-7849-7.

A guide to graphic symbols with a section on symbolic ornamentation in folk art and folk architecture and among the primitive peoples.

FOLK BELIEF SYSTEMS
Folk Medicine

Don Yoder, in his excellent essay on "Folk Medicine," in Dorson's *Folklore and Folklife* (pp. 191-215), details two varieties of folk medicine: **natural folk medicine**, which involves herbal healing, and **magico-religious folk medicine**. Aside from Yoder's essay, David J.

Hufford's "Folk Healers," in Richard M. Dorson's *Handbook of American Folklore* (pp. 306-313), provides a welcome introductory overview of the subject.

There are also several general folklore studies of folk medicine. A good place to start might be Wayland Hand's *American Folk Medicine: A Symposium* (Berkeley: University of California Press, 1976), the papers of the UCLA Conference on American Folk Medicine held in 1973. It is a series of 25 essays on such subjects as folk medicine and history, the mole in folk medicine, California Indian Shamanism and folk curing, the interrelationship of scientific and folk medicine since 1880, medical folklore in Spanish America, folk medicine in French Canada and Louisiana and as practiced among the Amish and Pennsylvania Germans, etc. Another collection of essays, edited by Wayland Hand, is *Magical Medicine: The Folkloric Component of Medicine in the Folk Belief, Custom, and Ritual of the Peoples of Europe and America* (Berkeley: University of California Press, 1980) which covers folk curing, folk healing, and many other aspects of folk medicine. Other symposia papers include *Papers on Folk Medicine Given at an Inter-Nordic Symposium at Nordiska Museet, Stockholm, 8-10 May, 1961* (Stockholm, 1963; reprinted in *ARV* [1962, 1963]: 159-362), edited by Carl Herman Tillhagen, and those from *Ethnomedizin und Medizingeschichte: Symposium 2-4 May 1980 in Hamburg* (Berlin: Mensch und Leben, 1983), edited by Joachim Sterly. One more set of proceedings on folk medicine is *Folk Medicine and Health Culture: Role of Folk Medicine in Modern Health Care: Proceedings...*, edited by Tuula Vaskilampi and Carol MacCormack (Kuopio [Finland]: University of Kuopio, 1982).

Another good place to start a study of folk medicine would be Richard P. Steiner's *Folk Medicine: The Art and the Science* (Washington, DC: American Chemical Society, 1986) with many scholarly essays on traditional medical practices: folk medicine of the Fiji, the Zuni Indians, the natives of India, Mexico, Australia, and Africa with articles about the healing properties of ginseng and garlic, Chinese anti-cancer drugs, Chinese herbal preparations, and plant therapy. Each essay has its own bibliography, and there is an author and subject index.

There is a great deal of writing about both natural and magico-religious folk medicine, although probably more is written about the latter, and, indeed, much of this writing is composed of anthropological or ethnological studies of folk medicine. There is, in fact, a whole field of medical anthropology with a journal to support it, the *Journal of Ethnopharmacology*, begun in 1979. There are several texts that are written from an anthropological point of view, *The Anthropology of Medicine: From Culture to Method* (New York: Praeger, 1983), by Lola Romanucchi-Ross, Daniel Moerman, Laurence R. Tancredi et al., and David Landy's *Culture, Disease, and Healing; Studies in Medical Anthropology* (New York: Macmillan, 1977), both collections of scholarly essays--the latter, by the way, having a 40-page bibliography. There are several works on African and Oriental folk medical methods and medicine men, such as A.T. Bryant's *Zulu Medicine and Medicine-Men* (Cape Town, SA: C. Struik, 1967 [1909]) on the status and initiation of medicine men, descriptions and preparations of medicines, and the treatment of disease. The anthropologist Victor W. Turner also studied medical practices in Africa, writing *Lunda Medicine and the Treatment of Disease* (Livingstone [N. Rhodesia]: Rhodes-Livingstone Museum, 1969) and *Chihamba, The White Spirit: A Ritual Drama of the NDembi* (New York: Humanities Press, 1962), a fascinating study and description of a medical ritual performed to eliminate *chihamba*, the "cult of affliction."

Other English-language books dealing with folk medicine are Patience Kemp's *Healing Ritual; The Technique and Tradition of the Southern Slavs* (London: Faber & Faber, 1935) and Patrick Logan's *Making the Cure; A Look at Irish Folk Medicine* (Dublin: Talbot, 1972) which deals with internal and external ailments, and mainly nonherbal methods of treatments (holy wells, spa wells, sweat houses, etc.) and veterinary folk medicine. Linda C. Rose's *Disease Beliefs in Mexican-American Communities* (San Francisco, CA: R.& E. Research Associates, 1978) is a study of the characteristics of Mexican-American disease beliefs and cures, set in a framework of traditional values about health and medicine; an older work on the same region is Margaret Clark's *Health in the Mexican-American Culture: A Community Study* (Berkeley: University of California Press, 1959).

A few other titles which might be useful for the study of folk medicine are (listed alphabetically): W. W. Bauer's *Potions, Remedies, and Old Wives' Tales* (New York: Doubleday, 1969), by a physician interested in folk medicine, has chapters on folklore, religion and medicine, witches, witchcraft and witch doctoring, medicinal properties in foods, and the return of folk medicine; William George Black's *Folk-Medicine: A Chapter in the History of Culture* (1883; reprinted: New York: Burt Franklin, 1970) covers charms, animal cures, magic writing, etc.; John M. F. Camp's *Magic, Myth and Medicine* (New York: Taplinger, 1974) examines traditional folk practices of many countries, especially aspects of fertility and birth, contraception and abortion, infancy, household cures, herbal remedies, faith and healing, sickness and superstition, spas and watering places, death and superstition, and the survival of superstitions; Howard W. Haggard's *Mystery, Magic and Medicine: The Rise of Medicine from Superstition to Science* (New York: Doubleday, Doran, 1933; reprinted: New York: Arden Library, 1987) is basically a chronological history of medicine, with much space given to "primitive" medicine and superstition, plant medicine, and herbal remedies; Clarence Meyer's *American Folk Medicine* (New York: Crowell, 1973) is a popular text; and *Black Folk Medicine: The Therapeutic Significance of Faith and Trust*, edited by Wilbur H. Watson (New Brunswick, NJ: Transaction Books, 1984), contains eight essays on such topics as aging, illness, and traditional medicine in Ghana, health care attitudes and practices among elderly blacks in isolated rural populations, pharmacists in Jamaica, folk medicine, and older blacks in the South (U.S.A.), poverty, folk remedies, and drug misuse, and Ozark mountain and European white witches.

This section begins with a general section on folk medicine, covering sources that deal with mostly nonherbal healing; this is followed by a section on herbals and other medicinal plant guides that is confined primarily to herbal (and other plant) healing. The section on **Foodways** in Chapter 7 should be consulted also.

Bibliography--Folk Medicine

1675.   Andrews, Theodora. With the assistance of William L. Corya and Donald A. Stickel, Jr. *A Bibliography on Herbs, Herbal Medicine, "Natural" Foods, and Unconventional Medical Treatment.* Littleton, CO: Libraries Unlimited, 1982. 339p. LC 82-128; ISBN 0-87287-288-2.

This excellent reference source covers 749 publications in two main parts: Part I includes general references-- bibliographies, indexes, manuals, catalogs, directories, pharmacopeias, dictionaries, encyclopedias, glossaries, histories, and periodicals. Part II is subdivided into 16 subject areas: herbals, herb growing, herb cookery, individual herbs, **folk medicine**, treatment of specific diseases, medicinal plants and their constituents, poisonous plants, magic, witchcraft, superstitions, sacred plants, patent medicines, etc. There are generous annotations for every entry and an index. This is a very thorough source of information on herbs and herbal medicine.

1676. Arber, Agnes R. *Herbals: Their Origin and Evolution: A Chapter in the History of Botany, 1470-1670.* 3rd ed. London: Cambridge University Press, 1986 [1938, 1912]. 358p. LC 86-9596; ISBN 0-5213-2879-4.

This is primarily a history of English herbals from the Renaissance on and a study of the evolution of the art of plant description, of plant classification, and of botanical illustration. Appendix I contains a chronological list of the principal herbals and botanical works printed between 1470-1670.

1677. Cosminsky, Sheila, and Ira E. Harrison. *Traditional Medicine II, 1976-81: Current Research with Implications for Ethnomedicine, Ethnopharmacology, Maternal and Child Health, Mental Health, and Public Health: An Annotated Bibliography of Africa, Latin America,....* New York: Garland, 1984. 327p. LC 82-49115; ISBN 0-8240-9181-7. (Garland reference library of social science; v. 147)

This adds 1,389 titles to the work below (no. 1681). It is arranged like its predecessor, however, it does not have an author index at the end of each section (there is a cumulative author index at the end of the work) and there is a separate section for dissertations.

1678.   De Laszlo, Henry G. *Library of Medicinal Plants*. Cambridge [ENG]: Heffer, 1958. 54p. LC 59-164.

This is an international bibliography of the compiler's own collection of about 1,500 books, articles, and pamphlets ranging in publication date from about the late eighteenth century into the 1950s. The arrangement is alphabetic by author, and books, pamphlets, and periodical articles are covered separately.

1679.   Freedman, Robert L., comp. *Human Food Uses: A Cross-Cultural, Comprehensive Annotated Bibliography*. Westport, CT: Greenwood, 1981. 552p. LC 81-469; ISBN 0-313-22901-5. Supplement: 1983. 387p. LC 82-25163; ISBN 0-313-23434-5.

Listed also in the section on Foodways (no. 2223), this work is cross listed here because it contains many books concerned with folk medicine, tribal medicine, and ethnobotany. Relevant works are easily accessed by means of a key-word index.

1680.   Hand, Wayland. "Bibliography," in *Magical Medicine: The Folkloric Component of Medicine in the Folk Belief, Custom, and Ritual of the Peoples of Europe and America*. Berkeley: University of California Press, 1980. pp. xiii-xxii. LC 80-51238; ISBN 0-520-04129-1.

This is the best bibliography on the subject of folk medicine I could find and an excellent starting place. It is a listing only, no annotations. There is no general bibliography in Wayland Hand's other book of essays, *American Folk Medicine: A Symposium* (Berkeley: University of California Press, 1976), but each essay has its own bibliography.

1681.   Harrison, Ira E., and Sheila Cosminsky. *Traditional Medicine: Implications for Ethnomedicine, Ethnopharmacology, Maternal and Child Health, Mental Health, and Public Health: An Annotated Bibliography of Africa, Latin America, and the*

Caribbean. New York: Garland, 1976. 229p. LC 75-24105; ISBN 0-8240-9970-2. (Garland reference library of social science; v. 19)

There are 1,135 journal articles, books, and other published and unpublished items within the following categories: General-ethnomedicine, ethnopharmacology, health care systems, maternal and child health, and public health; then they are arranged within these same categories by geographical area--Africa, Latin America, and the Caribbean. There is an author index in each section and an index by country. Updated by Cosminsky and Harrison (no. 1677).

1682. Hilger, Sister M. Inez, and Margaret Mondloch. "A Source List in Ethnobotany." *New York Folklore Quarterly* 28 (March 1972): 61-78.

This work lists books and articles alphabetically by author on plants that are used for several purposes, prominent among them being health restoration.

1683. Simon, James E., et al. *Herbs: An Indexed Bibliography, 1971-1980....* Hamden, CT: Archon, 1984. 770p. LC 82-24493.

Part I is a classed listing arranged by the common name of the herb, followed by the species, genus, French, German, Italian, and Spanish name, a long description and a note on its use as well as a bibliography of works relating to botany, horticulture, culinary studies, natural dyes, etc. Part II lists articles and books by subject: classification, chemistry, botany, horticulture, culinary studies, pharmacology (including medicinal plants), and natural dyes. There is also a separate listing of references and both an author and subject index.

Classification--Folk Medicine

1684. Johnson, Greg. "A Classification of Faith Healing Practices." *New York Folklore* 1 (Summer 1975): 91-96.

The author divides faith healing practices into the following classifications: primitive, emotional, charismatic, sacramental, spiritual and psychic, and hopes this might serve as a classification scheme for further studies.

Dictionaries--Folk Medicine

Note: Many of the annotated collections of folk medicine practices (nos. 1690-1717) and of herbals and healing medicines (nos. 1718-1758) are in dictionary format.

1685. Moerman, Daniel E. *American Medical Ethnobotany: A Reference Dictionary.* New York: Garland, 1977. 527p. LC 76-24771; ISBN 0-8240-9907-9. (Garland reference library of social sciences; v. 34)

This computer-generated dictionary is a guide to Native American medicinal uses of plants and a guide to the literature on the subject. Included are 1,288 different plant species from 531 different genera, from 118 families, used in 48 different cultures in 4,869 different ways (e.g., as a diuretic, to cure syphilis, etc.). The work lists first alphabetically by genus, then gives specie, botanical name, tribe used, indication and common name, notes on preparation and use, the source of the drug, and whether it is a simple or compound drug. Then it lists by indication (primary use): analgesic, anticonvulsive, etc., then by botanical family, and by tribal cultures. Included also is a 41-item bibliography, a glossary of common names, and a long supplementary bibliography.

1686. Rinzler, Carol Ann. *The Dictionary of Medical Folklore.* New York: Crowell, 1979. 243p. LC 78-69518; ISBN 0-690-01704-9.

This work tries "to demythicize, discount, or verify old wives' tales" related to health and nutrition. The arrangement is alphabetical by key word (e.g., "acne: acne is an adolescent problem; sunbathing cures acne"). A few scientific or medical sources are given. This book deals more with popular, contemporary beliefs than folkloric beliefs.

1687.   *Index Medicus*, 1879--. Washington, National Library of Medicine. Monthly. *Cumulated Index Medicus*, 1960--. Chicago: American Medical Association. Cumulates annually.

Each monthly issue is in three parts: subjects, names, and bibliography of medical reviews. Now compiled by mechanized means and forming a partial printout of the MEDLARS (Medical Literature Analysis and Retrieval System) data-base file. The annual cumulation is made up of separate cumulated author and subject indexes for the previous year. This is the most comprehensive index to the world's medical literature, and international journals in medical and health sciences are used as well as journals in botany, chemistry, physics, psychology, and sociology. There is a subject entry monthly for **Folklore**.

1688.   Jacobs, Marion Lee, and Henry M. Burlage. *Index of Plants of North Carolina with Reputed Medicinal Uses.* Chapel Hill, NC: Published by the Authors, 1958. 322p. LC 58-37834.

There is an index of almost 1,500 plants, listed alphabetically by Latin family name, followed by English common name, with a description, place of growth, and use; an index to plant families; an index to Latin names of genera and species; an index to common and generic names, and an index of reputed therapeutic and other uses (listed alphabetically by ailment--abdominal irritation, angina, etc.). There is also an alphabetical author index of references and a chronological numerical index of references from 1817 to 1940.

1689.   Penso, Giuseppe. *Index Plantarum Medicinalium Totius Mundi Eorumque Synonymorum.* Milan: OEMF, 1983. 1,026p. LC 83-214539; ISBN 8-8707-6027-8.

This work occurred because the 31st World Health Organization Assembly in 1978 adopted a resolution requesting the Director General of WHO to "compile an inventory of medicinal plants used in different countries." The index covers 91 countries, and includes the names of

21,000 medicinal plants with their synonyms. For each listing, the genus, specie, plant family, and indigenous country in which the plants are used are given. Unfortunately, there is no index.

Annotated Collections--Folk Medical Lore (Remedies and Cures)

Note: Journal articles with folk cures, such as Paul Brewster's "Folk Cures and Preventives from Southern Indiana" (*Southern Folklore Quarterly* 3 [1939]: 33-43), or Violetta Halpert's "Folk Cures from Indiana" (*Hoosier Folklore* 9 [1950]: 1-12) have been eliminated from the list below. There are many such articles which can be accessed from the indexes of individual journals. Also, be sure to consult the annotated collections of **herbals** following this one below (no. 1718-1758). Also, see the section on annotated collections of customs, beliefs, and superstitions at the beginning of this chapter (nos. 1460-1502). These collections are arranged geographically.

Worldwide/Multicultural

1690.   Kordel, Lelord. *Natural Folk Remedies*. New York: G.P. Putnam's Sons, 1974. 284p. LC 73-78591; ISBN 0-399-11205-7.

This is a collection of folk remedies and herbal recipes from several countries. Arranged in chapter format (kitchen cures, remedies, old and updated, for aches and pains, cures for the common cold, fruit remedies, natural tranquilizer, garlic: the natural antibiotic, cures from honey, water, comfrey and chamomile, medicine from the sea, sex stimulants, Chinese folk medicine, etc.), there are recipes in every section, mostly for "preventive" remedies, and an index.

Africa

1691.   Warren, Dennis M., coll. *Yoruba Medicines*. Trans. and rev. by Anthony D. Buckleyard and Akitunde Ayandokum. Legon: Institute of African Studies: University of Ghana, 1973. 93p. LC 82-160003.

The arrangement of this book is alphabetic by key Yoruban word, which, as far as I can determine, is by cure. (Ex., "**oogun afato:** medicine that draws sperm. 10 hen's [sic] eggs. Break them into spirits and sugar; drink a little every morning.") Variant recipes are given for each one and incantations for some. There are 63 entries, with many variants for each. There is an index of some of the ingredients mentioned in the text, a glossary, and a very brief bibliography.

The Americas
North America

1692. Anderson, John Q., comp. and ed. *Texas Folk Medicine: 1,333 Cures, Remedies, Preventives & Health Practices.* Austin, TX: Encino Press, 1970. 91p. LC 71-13817; ISBN 0-88426-013-5. (Paisano Book, 5)

Fieldwork for this slim volume was done by students in Anderson's folklore classes at Texas A & M. The arrangement is alphabetic by ailment, problem, disease, etc., with various folk remedies included. The geographic source is given for each item. There is a bibliography but no index.

1693. Aurand, Ammon Monroe. *Popular Home Remedies and Superstitions of the Pennsylvania Germans.* Harrisburg, PA: The Aurand Press, 1941. 32p. LC 41-9161.

These are arranged topically (e.g., childhood and its demands on man, folk medicine and old superstitions, teeth, sex, etc.). Each section has a brief introduction, then the remedies and superstitions are arranged alphabetically by key word (e.g., "**shirt**-always wash a new shirt before wearing, for if you are taken sick in an unwashed one, you will never get well").

1694. Black, Pauline Monette. *Nebraska Folk Cures.* Lincoln: University of Nebraska, 1935. LC 36-27638. 49p. (University of Nebraska studies in language, literature, and criticism, 15)

The arrangement for this older work is by ailment or problem, with cures given for aches, colds and related ailments, eye trouble, inflammation and infection, kidney and bowel trouble, rheumatism, toothache, warts, wounds, bites and stings; and then there are chapters on preventive cure-alls and cures for animal diseases. Most of the chapters are subdivided (for example, cures for aches is subdivided into headaches, earaches, etc.).

1695. Boyd, Eddie L., et al. *Home Remedies and the Black Elderly: A Reference Manual for Health Care Providers.* Ann Arbor: University of Michigan Press and Institute of Gerontology and College of Pharmacy, 1984. 26p. LC 85-118370.

These are responses to a questionnaire about what home remedies were used in the past six months and what home remedies are recommended for certain ailments. The arrangement is alphabetic by remedy: alcohol, alfalfa, etc. An appendix includes remedies reported and ailments treated (**aloe vera**: burns; **ammonia**: bites, muscle aches, etc.).

1696. Brendle, Thomas R., and Claude W. Unger. *Folk Medicine of the Pennsylvania Germans; The Non-Occult Cures.* Norristown, PA: Pennsylvania German Society, 1935. 303p. LC 36-8112. (Proceedings of the Pennsylvania-German Society; v. 45). Reprinted: New York: A.M. Kelley, 1970. LC 71-95633; ISBN 0-6780-3753-1. (Medicina classica)

This work, which cites illnesses from childhood to old age, is arranged in a loose outline format and covers food and drink, sleep, dreams, bloodletting, the heart, throat, etc. Within each division, specific ailments and cures are listed. The Pennsylvania-German name is given first, then the cause, the cures, and the sources of the information. There are several bibliographies: of recipes in manuscript books, of books containing domestic remedies of the "more rational kind," and a bibliography of almanacs.

1697.	Hand, Wayland D. *Popular Beliefs and Superstitions from North Carolina*. Vols. 6 and 7, *The Frank C. Brown Collection of North Carolina Folklore*. Durham, NC: Duke University Press, 1961, 1964. 664p. and 677p.

Previously cited in the beginning of this chapter (no. 1470), the section on **The Human Body, Folk Medicine** contains many remedies, cures, and lore.

1698.	Hyatt, Harry Middleton. *Hoodoo--Conjuration--Witchcraft--Rootwork*. 5 vols. Hannibal, MO: Western Pub., 1970-1978. 4,754p. LC 71-12434. (For full citation, see no. 1473.)

This massive, confusing work is described in its entirety in no. 1473. However, Vols. 2 and 3, and part of Vol. 4 contain interviews with "doctors" and remedies for several ailments, including sexual impotence, blood problems, urinary problems, etc. The remedies are numbered but fairly inaccessible, as an index volume was planned but not completed.

1699.	*The Inglenook Doctor Book: Choice Recipes Contributed by Sisters of the Brethren Church, Subscribers and Friends of the Inglenook Magazine*. Intro. Walter C. Alvarez. Elgin, IL: Brethren Press, 1975. 156p. LC 75-310317.

The man who wrote the introduction, a physician, calls the book "a charming and delightful look at the not-too-distant past." The book contains over 900 remedies from the nineteenth century members of the Brethren Church, German Baptists who settled originally in Pennsylvania as farmers. The chapter arrangement is by type of ailment with suggested remedies for each being numbered. Sources of the informants are given. There is an index.

1700.	Jarvis, D.C. *Folk Medicine; A Vermont Doctor's Guide to Good Health*. New York: Holt, Rinehart and Winston, 1958. 182p. LC 58-6454; ISBN 0-03-027410-9.

This book by a physician was very controversial when it was published as was a later work he published, *Arthritis and Folk Medicine* (New York: Ballantine, 1983 [1960]). Jarvis recommends folk medicine, which he says is what rural Vermonters, all healthy people, practice. The emphasis of the book is prevention which is based on a daily supplement of apple cider vinegar and honey said to be particularly effective in cases of headache, insomnia, high blood pressure, chronic fatigue, sore throat, and obesity. A precursor of the natural food phenomenon, the copy I looked at (found in the medical school library) was totally worn out with wear.

1701.   Puckett, Newbell Niles. *Popular Beliefs and Superstitions: A Compendium of American Folklore: From the Ohio Collection of Newbell Niles Puckett*, ed. Wayland D. Hand et al. Boston, MA: G.K. Hall, 1981. 3 vols. 1,829p. LC 81-6687; ISBN 0-8161-8585-9 (set)

Previously cited (no. 1479), this work includes valuable information on folk medicine; a voluminous index in Vol. 3 will help the researcher find folk remedies.

1702.   Randolph, Vance. *Ozark Superstitions*. New York: Columbia University Press, 1947. 367p. Reprinted: New York: Dover, 1964. LC 64-18649; ISBN 0-486-21181-9.

Another previously cited entry (no. 1480), this work includes a section on **mountain medicine.**

1703.   Roeder, Beatrice A. *Chicano Folk Medicine from Los Angeles, California*. Berkeley: University of California Press, 1988 [1984]. 377p. LC 88-23426; ISBN 0-520-09723-8. (University of California Publications. Folklore & mythology studies; v. 34)

These are folk medical beliefs collected from the **barrio** by five two-person research teams (one member of which was a member of the Chicano community). All information gathered is compared with materials from other Hispanic collations of folk medicine studies. Includes also **bario** remedies from rural Mexico, beliefs dealing with "new life" (pregnancy, childbirth, postpartem care, etc.), and cures of the "second generation." Appendixes include a list of information about the informants, an alphabetical list of medicinals, a glossary of medical terms, a glossary of Spanish terms, a bibliography, and an index.

1704. Solomon, Jack, and Olivia Solomon, comps. *Cracklin Bread and Asfidity: Folk Recipes and Remedies.* University: University of Alabama Press, 1979. 215p. LC 77-13065; ISBN 0-8173-8650-5.

Folk remedies (pp. 118-180) are arranged by ailment: nose bleed, stings, and bites, etc. Although the remedies are not numbered, the authors give the names and places of the informants.

1705. Tantaquidgeon, Gladys. *Folk Medicine of the Delaware and Related Algonkian Indians.* Harrisburg, PA: Pennsylvania Historical and Museum Commission, 1972. 145p. LC 73-620801. (Anthropological series, 3)

There are several subjects covered, with chapters on practitioners, prayers, love charms, food taboos, etc. A section of 84 practices and herbal remedies includes a list of curative herbs and fruits, flowers, trees, etc. (in English and Latin) and tells how they are used for curing purposes. Also included are other beliefs, such as "A tea made from roasted, charred pig-hoofs is beneficial for colds."

1706. Teaford, Ruth Romine. *Southern Homespun.* Huntsville, AL: Strode Publishers, 1980. 126p. LC 79-91431; ISBN 0-87397-158-2.

The bulk of this book is given over to folk medicine which includes a list of hints about health, a listing of chemical elements needed by the body, and an alphabetical listing of medical ailments and diseases, with cures and treatments given for each--many of which, but not all, are herbal. Also given are "old wives' tales," remedies, "colloquialisms," and superstitions from Walker Co., Alabama.

1707. Tyler, Varro E. *Hoosier Home Remedies*. West Lafayette, IN: Purdue University Press, 1985. 212p. LC 85-9515; ISBN 0-911198-77-6.

Chapters are arranged alphabetically by ailment from **arthritis and rheumatism** to **worms and wounds**. Within each section, the cures are listed alphabetically (e.g., **arthritis and rheumatism**: angleworm oil, asparagus, balsam cucumber--witch hazel, wintergreen). There is an appendix with both common and scientific botanical names and a bibliography.

1708. Weslager, C.A. *Magic Medicines of the Indians*. Somerset, NJ: Middle Atlantic Press, 1973. 161p. LC 72-91345; ISBN 0-912608-03-x.

Not seen.

South and Central America

Note: Most of the material on Central and South American folk medicine is in Spanish. Axel Ramirez' *Bibliografia Comentada de la Medicina Tradicional Mexicana (1900-1978)* (Mexico: IMEPLAM, 1978) provides access to 500 mostly Spanish-language articles and books on all aspects of Mexican folk medicine.

1709. Kelly, Isabel. *Folk Practices in North Mexico: Birth Customs, Folk Medicine, and Spiritualism in the Laguna Zone*. Austin, TX: Published for the Institute of Latin America States by the University of Texas Press, 1965. 166p. LC 64-10313. (Latin American monographs, 2)

There are 840 listed beliefs organized into sections titled pregnancy, birth, postnatal care, folk medicine, luck and magic, and relationships. Specific illnesses and cures are easily accessed through an index. There is also a long bibliography.

Asia
China

1710.   Read, Bernard E. *Chinese Medicine series*. 4 vols. Taipei: Southern Materials Center, 1976-77. Vol. 1: *Chinese Materia Medica: Vegetable Kingdom*, 1977; Vol. 2: *Chinese Materia Medica: Insect Drugs, Dragon and Snake Drugs, Fish Drugs*, 1977; Vol. 3: *Chinese Materia Medica: Turtle and Shellfish Drugs, Avian Drugs*, 1977; Vol. 4: *Chinese Materia Medica: Animal Drugs*, 1976.

There are 444 entries in all, with each volume being arranged alphabetically by animal, insect, fish, etc. The descriptions of the medicines are given in English and Chinese. Use of drug, place of use, synonyms used, and some descriptive qualities are given. Each volume includes a list of references and English and Chinese indexes. See also *Herbal Pharmacology in the People's Republic of China* (Washington, DC: National Academy of Sciences, 1975).

1711.   Wallnöfer, Heinrich, and Anna von Rottauscher. *Chinese Folk Medicine*. Trans. Marion Paimedo. New York: American Library, 1972 [1965]. 176p. LC 65-24333.

There is a long chapter on "Medicinal herbs, drugs, and love medicines" with subdivisions including medicinal herbs in old China, recipes for preparing herbal medicines, ginseng, the use of medicinal plants, and human, animal, and mineral medicines.

1712.   Kourennoff, Paul M. *Russian Folk Medicine.* Trans., ed., and arr. by George St. George. London and New York: W.H. Allen, 1970. 213 p. LC 74-863484; ISBN 0-491-00484-2.

Ailments and remedies are presented that exist in Russia, especially in Siberia. Other parts of the book cover accident care, personal body care, and herbal remedies. There is an appendix listing of medicinal herbs and plants found in Britain and Ireland.

Europe

Note: Most of the books about European folk medicine are available only in the languages of the country from which they come. Only a very few have been translated.

1713.   Pitrè, Giuseppe. *Sicilian Folk Medicine.* Trans. by Phyllis H. Williams. Lawrence, KS: Coronado Press, 1971 [1896]. 314p. ISBN 0-87291-013-x.

This is Vol. 19 of Pitrè's great work, *Biblioteca delle Tradizioni Popolari Siciliane,* originally published in 1896. There is a general discussion on folk medicine and then five chapters on popular practitioners, anatomy, general pathology, special pathology, and internal pathology. An herbal of herbs discussed by Pitrè in the text is appended as is a picture of the healing saints of the area.

Europe--Great Britain

1714.   Chamberlain, Mary. *Old Wives' Tales: Their History, Remedies, and Spells.* London: Virago, 1981. 284p. LC 81-170581; ISBN 0-86068-015-0 (c); 0-86068-016-9 (p).

Part I traces the history of healers from goddesses to sorceresses to witches to charlatans to "experts." Part II is a listing of remedies and a listing in alphabetic order by condition or disease, with a description of how, where, and when remedies were used. Dosages and sources are given for each. There is a bibliography and an index.

Oceania

1715.   Corum, Ann Kondo. *Folk Remedies from Hawaii, Or, Don't Take Bananas on a Boat.* Honolulu: Bess Press, 1985. 137p. LC 86-70672; ISBN 0-935848-31-1.

This is a lighthearted, illustrated volume divided into sections on childbirth, children, and convalescence, aches and pains, bites, stings, and other skin things, stomach problems, etc., with ailments and cures given. There is a short glossary of remedies and a brief bibliography.

1716.   Chun, Malcolm Naea, trans. *Hawaiian Medicine Book: He Buke Laau Lapaau.* Honolulu: Bess Press, 1986. 72p. LC 85-73393; ISBN 0-935848-36-3.

Includes Hawaiian text and separate English translation and covers mythical origins of Hawaiian medicine; includes also a section of chants and one on the medicines. There is also a glossary of important names, plants, animals, and marine life and a bibliography.

1717.   Wannan, Bill. *Folk Medicine; A Miscellany of Old Cures and Remedies, Superstitions, and Old Wives' Tales Having Particular Reference to Australia and the British Isles.*   Melbourne, Australia: Hill of Content Publishing Co., 1970. 190p. LC 77-586338; ISBN 0-85572-035-2.

This is a humorous account of folk remedies, arranged alphabetically under general subject sections (**abscesses, garlic, the ears,** etc.). Sources of the remedies are included within the text. There is an index.

Eleanour S. Rohde's *The Old English Herbals* (3rd ed., London: Minerva, 1974 [1922]) is an excellent overview and historical account of herbals, covering from the Anglo-Saxon period to sixteenth- and seventeenth-century English herbals and "foreign" herbals. See also Agnes Arber's history of herbals (no. 1676).

This is a highly select list of herbals, and, for the most part, only those with folkloric information are included. Also, be sure to consult the list of Annotated Collections of Remedies, listed directly above (nos. 1690-1717), as many of those works also include information on herbs.

Worldwide/international

1718.   Bianchini, Francesco, and Francesco Corbetta. *Health Plants of the World: Atlas of Medicinal Plants*. New York: Newsweek, 1977 [1975]. 242p. LC 76-46692; ISBN 0-88225-250-X.

    The emphasis in this work is on what specific plants cure what human systems--digestive, cardiovascular, respiratory, nervous, genito-urinary, endocrine, etc. And arrangement is by groupings of separate sections according to these principal areas of operation. Organization within these sections is somewhat random with text on two or three plants on one page and a facing page of illustrations. The appendix tells what plants are useful as cures for the specific systems. There is a botanical glossary, an index, and a bibliography. A lavishly illustrated, beautiful book.

1719.   Duke, James A. *CRC Handbook of Medicinal Herbs*. Boca Raton, FL: CRC Press, 1985. 677p. LC 84-12148; ISBN 0-8493-3630-9.

    This work "treats 365 folk medicinal species," listing them alphabetically by scientific name (genus). Also given are the colloquial name and the scientific name of the plant family. The author discusses the use of the plant, folk medicinal applications, the chemical makeup of the plant, and its toxicity. There are five tables and a massive index of over 75 pages. This is a very comprehensive herbal with folk medicine as its main focus.

1720.   Grieve, Maude. *A Modern Herbal; The Medicinal, Culinary, Cosmetic, and Economic Properties, Cultivation and Folk-Lore of Herbs, Grasses, Fungi, Shrubs & Trees with All Their Modern Scientific Uses.* 2 vols. 902p. New York: Harcourt, Brace, 1931. Reprinted: New York: Dover, 1982. LC 72-169784; ISBN 0-846-22798-7 (v. 1).

The arrangement of these herbs and plants, etc., is by their most familiar name (e.g., **abscessroot**). Also given are the Latin family name, synonyms, the part used for healing, and the habitat grown in. There is a description for each, with medicinal uses, and plant action. There are 96 color plates; Vol. 2 includes an index and the 1982 Dover publication adds "An Index of Scientific Names" compiled by Manya Marshall.

1721.   Lucas, Richard Melvin. *Magic Herbs for Arthritis, Rheumatism, and Related Ailments.* New York: Parker, 1981. 248p. LC 80-23346; ISBN 0-1354-3900-0.

Not seen.

1722.   Schauenberg, Paul, and Ferdinand Paris. *Guide to Medicinal Plants.* Trans. Maurice Pugh-Jones. New Canaan, CT: Keats, 1977 [*Guides des Plantes Medicinales*, Neuchatel, Switzerland, 1974]. 349p.+39p. illus. LC 76-57861; ISBN 0-87983-161-8.

There are 410 herbs and plants described within 19 separate chapters determined by most active constituents (plants containing alkaloids, plants containing vitamins, plants containing antibiotics, etc.). Within each chapter, plants, numbered consecutively throughout this very impressive book, are listed alphabetically by Latin name. Included also are German, French, and English names, habitat, descriptions of the plant, notes on the flowering season, active constituents, properties, application, parts used, and history. There is also a chapter containing recipes for tisanes and compresses, arranged by ailment, listed alphabetically (**acne, anoemia,** etc.). A description of the malady and treatments are included here. There is a glossary of therapeutic terms and a list of maladies and treatments (with plant numbers). Two indexes complete this book: indexes to vernacular names and Latin names. This work is a very comprehensive guide to herbs giving a great deal of attention to various aspects of herbal medicine.

1723.   Thomson, William A.R., ed. *Healing Plants: A Modern Herbal.* New York: McGraw Hill; London: Macmillan, 1978. 208p. ISBN 0-333-25604-2.

Although this is a narrative account of herblore, there is a reference section called "247 Most Beneficial Plants" (pp. 17-32), with an alphabetical listing of plants with their principal medicinal uses. Also included in this work is a plant lexicon, also an alphabetical listing, which gives the Latin name, English name, plant family, references to the plant's geographical distribution, plant's original place of provenance or habitat, areas to which it has been introduced, and whether it grows wild or has to be cultivated. A physical description is also included and the author tells whether the plant has a scent or not and tries to describe it. Another reference section deals with complaints and illnesses, describes the ailment, and gives the treatment with preparation information, dose, and recipe. A third reference section covers healing substances and their effectiveness, and this gives specific information about the plant--what part is used for healing, how to harvest, and how to process. Also included in this book is a short section called "the heritage of folk medicine." There is a plant index--English/Latin and Latin/English--and a bibliography.

1724.   Weiner, Michael A. *Weiner's Herbal: The Guide to Herb Medicine.* Rev. and exp. ed. Mill Valley, NY: Quantum Books, 1990 [1980]. 276p. LC 91-188327; ISBN 0-9128-4503-1.

717

The bulk of this work is an alphabetical listing of plants by common name. Also given is the Latin name, parts used, other common names, botanical description, and medicinal use with dosage. There is a long introduction, a glossary of medical terms, a therapeutic index (e.g., **abdominal pain**--anemone), plant index (English/Latin and Latin/ English), and general index, plus a short bibliography. (Only 1980 edition seen.)

Africa

Note: An excellent text on African folk curing with plants is Abayomi Sofowora's *Medicinal Plants and Traditional Medicine in Africa* (New York: Wiley, 1982). See also no. 1756.

1725.   Ayensu, Edward S. *Medicinal Plants of West Africa*. Algonac, MI: Reference Publications, 1978. 330p. LC 78-3110; ISBN 0-917256-07-7.

Dr. Ayensu is Director of the Endangered Species Program the Smithsonian Institution. This work contains information on 187 species of medicinal plants, all of which grow in West Africa. The plants are arranged alphabetically according to family, with place of growth, local name and use given along with an illustration of each plant. There is a glossary and a bibliography of 61 items, a medicinal index (listing ailments or problem and then species) as well as an index to species. There is a 61-item bibliography also.

1726.   Boulos, Loutfy. *Medicinal Plants of North Africa*. Algonac, MI: Reference Publications, 1983. 286p. LC 82-20412; ISBN 0-917256-16-6. (Medicinal plants of the world series, 3)

There are 369 species of vascular plants, alphabetically arranged according to the 97 families to which they belong. Vernacular names are given in Arabic, Berber, and English. There are drawings for 107 of the species as well as a glossary, a medicinal and common names index, and a generous bibliography.

1727.   Macfoy, Cyrus A. *Medicinal Plants of Sierra Leone.* Sierra
        Leone: University of Sierra Leone, Botany Department, Fourah
        Bay College, 1983. 54p. LC 84-115447.

Part I is a list of plants, classed according to ailments or diseases
cured; Part II is an alphabetic listing of medicinal species by local names,
giving botanical names, preparation, and treatment. There is a botanical
index (by Latin name) and references.

The Americas
North America

1728.   Bolyard, Judith L. *Medicinal Plants and Home Remedies
        of Appalachia.* Springfield, IL: Charles C. Thomas, 1981.
        187p. LC 80-24697; ISBN 0-398-04180-6.

This is a listing of plants collected in the field that are used in
home remedies, arranged in four general sections: fungi, ferns and allies,
conebearing plants, and flowering plants. For each plant, the author gives
the Latin name, place found, historical uses, biological activities, and
organic constituents. There is an appendix of medicinal plants of unknown
scientific inquiry, a list of references (tape-recorded interviews and
non-recorded interviews), a glossary, an index of diseases and remedies,
and an index of English and Latin plant names. This is a hard book to use
because the plants are listed by unfamiliar divisions and classes.

1729.   Curtin, L.S.M. *Healing Herbs of the Upper Rio Grande.* New
        York: Arno, 1976 [1947, Laboratory of Anthropology, Santa Fe,
        NM]. 281p. LC 74-1226; ISBN 0-405-09499-x. (Chicano
        heritage series)

The herbs are listed alphabetically by remedy and or herb (in
Spanish), ranging from **Aceite Mexicano** [Mexican oil] (a patent
medicine in half teaspoons in hot water, with a little sugar for pain of the
intestine) to **zarzilla** [the aster family] (a fine spreading herb of an ash
color put in tea for kidney trouble). Definitions are all as short as this.

There are 30 pages of photographs of herbs, a bibliography, and a very comprehensive index.

1730. Elmore, Francis H. *Ethnobotany of the Navajo.* New York: AMS, 1978 [1943, University of New Mexico Bulletin... Monograph series; v. 1, 392]. 136p. LC 76-43698; ISBN 0-404-15530-8.

Plants are arranged alphabetically by family name, with synonyms, other Indian names, uses, and descriptions, as well as folklore. The use of plants and herbs for various purposes--witchcraft, ceremonial, dye, beverage, basketry, and woodcraft--are presented in appended Tables. There is an 87-item bibliography and indexes of Navajo names, scientific names, and a general index.

1731. Gilmore, Melvin R. *Uses of Plants by the Indians of the Missouri River Region.* Lincoln: University of Nebraska Press, 1977. 109p. LC 77-89833; ISBN 0-8032-0935-5. (Annual report of the Bureau of American Ethnology to the Secretary of the Smithsonian Institution; v. 33)

The bulk of this work is a taxonomic list of plants used for medicinal purposes by the Native Americans of the Missouri River. Lists by genera, then Latin plant name and common name; tells what it was used for and by whom and where it was used.

1732. Grimé, William, ed. *Ethno-Botany of the Black Americans.* Algonac, MI: Reference Publications, 1979. 237p. LC 78-20356; ISBN 0-917256-10-7.

Lists 245 species of plants used by black slaves in North and South America and the Caribbean in two separate divisions: those that came with the slaves from Africa and those that are indigenous to these countries. Medicinal and food uses are given; the arrangement is alphabetical by Latin name and common names and uses are given with sources. There are indexes of scientific and common names and a bibliography.

1733.   Kavasch, Barrie. *Herbal Traditions: Medicinal Plants in American Indian Life.* Washington, DC: Smithsonian Institution, 1984. 24p. LC 84-147317.

This pamphlet accompanied an exhibition sponsored by the Smithsonian Institution's Traveling Exhibition Service called "Nature's Harvest Plants of American Indian Life." There is one plant on a page and the arrangement is alphabetic. The history and uses of each plant are given along with a drawing of the plant. See also Kavasch's *Native Harvests: Botanicals & Recipes of the American Indian* (Washington, CT: American Indian Archeological Institute, 1977).

1734.   Krochmal, Arnold, and Connie Krochmal. *A Guide to Medicinal Plants of the United States.* New York: Quadrangle, 1973. 259p. LC 72-83289; ISBN 0-8129-0261-0.

The introduction has a section on folklore and science. The herbs are listed alphabetically by Latin name with the common name given. Also included are other common names, where it grows, what and when it is harvested, and its medicinal uses. There is an appendix giving the meaning of plant names and an index. See also the Krochmals' *A Guide to Medicinal Plants of Appalachia* (Washington, DC: USDA, 1971) and *A Field Guide to Medicinal Plants* (New York: Times Books, 1984).

1735.   Miller, Amy Bess W. *Shaker Herbs: A History and a Compendium.* New York: Clarkson N. Potter, 1976. 272p. LC 76-40485; ISBN 0-517-52494-5.

The first half of the book is a history of the Shakers and their use of herbs. The second part of the book is a listing of almost 300 herbs collected, grown, and harvested by the Shakers, arranged alphabetically by common name. Also given are Latin names, colloquial names, habitat, their uses, and where they were grown. Illustrated with an index and bibliography.

1736. Millspaugh, Charles F. *American Medicinal Plants: An Illustrated and Descriptive Guide to Plants Indigenous to and Naturalized in the United States Which are Used in Medicine.* 3 vols. New York: Boeriche and Tafel, 1887. Reprint of 1892 edition in 1 vol.: New York: Dover, 1974. 806p. LC 73-91487; ISBN 0-48623034-1.

This is a classic early work, often cited. There are several large subject divisions; within each, plants are listed by common name, family name, and genus. Synonyms and all common names are given, habitat, part used and preparation, chemical makeup, and physiological action. There are beautiful illustrated plates.

1737. Mitchell, Faith. *Hoodoo Medicine: Sea Islands Herbal Remedies.* Berkeley, CA: Reed, Cannon, and Johnson, 1978. 108p. ISBN 0-918408-06-7.

The author discusses the black culture of the Sea Island natives and their traditional medical practices in the first part of this fascinating book. The second part of the book has two sections: "A Directory of Sea Island Medicinal Roots and Herbs" and "Plant Cures Used in the Sea Island," in which the plants are arranged alphabetically by common name, with a description and statement of native use as well as a note on what properties of these herbs are used by other blacks, Native Americans, or Euro-Americans.

1738. Moerman, Daniel E. *American Medical Ethnobotany: A Reference Dictionary.* New York: Garland, 1977. 527p. LC 76-24771; ISBN 0-8240-9907-9. (Garland reference library of social science; v. 34)

Cited as a dictionary (see no. 1685), this is also "a guide to Native American medical uses of plants and...to the widely scattered literature on the subject." It includes 1,288 different plant species from 531 different genera from 118 families, used in 48 different cultures in 4,869 different ways (e.g., as a diuretic or to cleanse kidneys, etc.). Listings are by genera, primary use (e.g., **analgesic**), botanical family, and by culture using the drug. See also Moerman's *Medicinal Plants of Native America* (Ann Arbor: Museum of Anthropology, University of Michigan, 1986).

1739.   Moerman, Daniel E. *Geraniums for the Iroquois: A Field Guide to American Indian Medicinal Plants*. Algonac, MI: Reference Publications, 1982. 242p. LC 81-52514; ISBN 0-917256-15-8 (c); 0-917256-17-4 (p).

Following a long introduction, there is an alphabetic listing by common name (e.g., **asters, balsam, beard tongue**, etc.), each one taking up two or three pages. The use is told, who uses it, and its purpose. There is additional material: a section on Native American groups of herbs, an alphabetic listing and discussion of various Indian tribes, a bibliography of additional reading, range maps, and an index.

1740.   Moore, Michael. *Medicinal Plants of the Mountain West: A Guide to the Identification, Preparation, and Uses of Traditional Medicinal Plants....* Santa Fe, NM: Museum of New Mexico Press, 1979. 200p. LC 79-620000; ISBN 0-89013-107-4 (c); 0-89013-104-x (p).

This is a very complete work that is an alphabetical listing by common name. Included are the Latin name, other common names, a description of the plant, habitat, collecting information and methods, and medicinal use and cultivation. There is a drawing for each plant. Also included are a glossary, therapeutic and use index, a plant classification, a bibliography, and an index.

1741.   Morton, Julia F. *Folk Remedies of the Low Country*. Miami, FL: E.A. Seemann Pub., 1974. 176p. LC 74-81529; ISBN 0-912458-46-1.

The main part of the book is called "Principal Plant Remedies," in which the medicinal plants of South Carolina are listed by family name. The common name, a description, and notes on the growing season, habitat, range, use in South Carolina now, its medical uses, and bibliographic references are all given with a color photograph. There are additional sections on "Sundry Plant Remedies" and "Other Remedies," following the same format as above. A list of all the references and a general bibliography are also included.

1742. Scully, Virginia. *A Treasury of American Indian Herbs; Their Lore and Their Use for Foods, Drugs, and Medicine.* New York: Crown Publishers, 1970. 306p. LC 75-108063.

Many herbs and plants are cross listed in the two parts of this book, "Food and Drink" and "Maladies and Medicine." Plants and herbs are arranged alphabetically by plant name. Ailments and maladies are listed alphabetically in the second section. Plants are described, habitats are mentioned, and use of the herb is given with historical information. Also included are a bibliography and index.

1743. Taylor, Lyda Averill. *Plants Used as Curatives by Certain Southeastern Tribes.* Cambridge, MA: Botanical Museum of Harvard University, 1940. 88p. Reprinted: New York: AMS, 1978. LC 76-43866; ISBN 0-404-15725-4.

One hundred eighty-five herbs, used mainly by the Choctaw and Koasati tribes, are arranged by family, genera, and species. Listed for each herb and plant is the common name, the name of the tribe that used it, the medicinal properties, what part of the plant was used, and how it was prepared and used. Also included are the author's comments on how good the remedy was.

1744. Touchstone, Samuel J. *Herbal and Folk Medicine of Louisiana and Adjacent States.* Princeton, LA: Folk-Life Books, 1983. 175p. LC 84-114197; ISBN 0-914917-12-9 (p).

The herbs of Louisiana, Mississippi, Arkansas, and Oklahoma are listed by common name. Given are the Latin name, where it is found, how it is used and prepared, and how it was used traditionally as well as a word of caution about each one. There is a list of herbal "claims" (arranged alphabetically by common name) and of complaints and herbal treatments (arranged alphabetically by the complaint). It is completed by a glossary and an index.

1745. Weiner, Michael A. *Earth Medicine--Earth Food: Plant Remedies, Drugs, and Natural Foods of the North American Indians.* 1st rev. and exp. ed. New York: Macmillan, 1980 [1972]. 230p. LC 80-430; ISBN 0-0262-5610-x (c).

There are two sections: "Earth Medicine" and "Earth Foods." In the first part, the listing is by ailment with plants pictured and described under the appropriate ailment or problem. There is an index of English and Latin names and a bibliography.

West Indies

1746. Ayensu, Edward S. *Medicinal Plants of the West Indies.* Algonac, MI: Reference Publications, 1981. 282p. LC 80-54714; ISBN 0-917256-12-3. (Medicinal plants of the world)

There are 632 species presented alphabetically by family. Local names are given, as well as locale, uses, and references. Sixty-two of them are illustrated. There is a glossary, bibliography, medicinal index (by illness), common names index, and an index of species.

South and Central America

1747. Bastien, Joseph W. *Healers of the Andes: Kallawaya Herbalists and Their Medicinal Plants.* Salt Lake City: University of Utah Press, 1987. 198p. LC 87-13351; ISBN 0-87480-278-4.

There are two parts to this work: the first is a narrative account of Kallawaya practices; the second part (pp. 95-171) is a compendium of Kallawayan medicinal plants and their uses, listed alphabetically by common local name, followed by common name in English, family and genus, and other popular names. There is a description of each, habitat information, and use. Many are illustrated. An appendix includes a chart of the medical classification of plants, their quality, therapeutic properties, and medicinal uses. A bibliography and index conclude this useful work.

1748.   Roys, Ralph L. *The Ethno-botany of the Maya*. New Orleans, LA: Tulane University, Dept. of Middle American Research, 1931. Reprinted: Philadelphia, PA: Institute for the Study of Human Issues, 1976. 380p. LC 76-29024; ISBN 0-915980-22-3. (Middle American research series, 2; Institute for the Study of Human Issues reprints on Latin America and the Caribbean)

This work is based on manuscript material, from the eighteenth century on, held at Tulane. The book is arranged by ailment or disorder and listed alphabetically in chapter form: aches and pains; asthma, colds, and diseases of the lungs and breathing passages; birth, obstetrics, and diseases peculiar to women; bites and stings of animals, etc. A chapter entitled "A Survey of the Ethno-botany of Yucatan" is a vocabulary of Mayan terms for growth, human body parts, and the environment of plants. Also included are an annotated list of Mayan plant names and a table of nomenclature. Another ending chapter is an annotated list of Mayan fauna names.

Asia
Multinational

1749.   Perry, Lily M. *Medicinal Plants of East and Southeast Asia: Attributed Properties and Uses*. Cambridge, MA: MIT Press, 1980. 620p. LC 79-25769; ISBN 0-262-16076-5.

This is a dictionary arranged by species. Information for each entry includes where the plant is from and how it is used, what part of the plant is used, etc. There is a very substantial bibliography (pp.

447-493) of books and articles and three major indexes: 1) an index to plants according to attributed therapeutic properties (**anaesthetic, anodyne,** etc.), 2) an index to suggested plant remedies according to various disorders (**abdominal disorders, anemia,** etc.), and 3) an index to scientific names. This work, in English, is a particularly thorough one.

China

1750. American Herbal Pharmacological Delegation. *Herbal Pharmacology in the People's Republic of China: A Trip Report.* Washington, DC: National Academy of Sciences, 1975. 269p. LC 75-39772; ISBN 0-309-02438-2.

This is primarily the report of 12 American scientists to the Committee on Scholarly Communication with the People's Republic of China concerning their visit in 1974 to study Chinese herbal medicine. Almost half of the book is a table of 248 plant and animal drugs used in China, listed alphabetically by botanical name with an analysis appended. A lack of index of common name may hamper its use with the lay public.

1751. Duke, James, and Edward S. Ayensu. *Medicinal Plants of China.* 2 vols. Algonac, MI: Reference Publications, 1985. 705p. LC 84-4867; ISBN 0-917256-20-4. (Medical plants of the world, 4)

There is a long introduction to Chinese herbal medicine by Ayensu and then "a selection of the most efficacious species is presented." Volume 2 has a 234-item bibliography. There are indexes to medicines, common names, and to species.

1752. Hyatt, Richard. *Chinese Herbal Medicine: An Ancient Art and Modern Healing Science.* With Therapeutic Repertory by Robert Feldman. New York: Schocken, 1978. 160p. LC 77-87891; ISBN 0-8052-3682-1. Reprinted: New York: Thorsons, 1984. LC 83-24325; ISBN 0-7225-0957-x (p)

Chapter 3 has "the therapeutic repertory," arranged by symptoms with specific conditions given. There are sections on teas and herbal preparations and on the most commonly used Chinese herbs both arranged in alphabetical order in romanized Chinese with Chinese characters given also. There are indexes and a bibliography.

1753. Li, C.P. *Chinese Herbal Medicine.* Washington, DC: U.S. Department of Health, Education, and Welfare, Public Health Service, National Institute of Health, 1974. 120p. LC 77-374517. (DHEW Publication no. [NIH]75-732); (A publication of the John E. Fogarty International Center for Advanced Study in the Health Sciences)

Parts I and II are narrative texts, an overview of traditional herbal medicine and recent experimental studies and clinical application. The book's appendix (pp. 47-120) is a "Pharmacognosy of individual herbs" discussed in the text, a listing of 44 plants arranged alphabetically according to their scientific name in Latin then Chinese (in Romanized letters); includes also a description, a note on how and where it grows, and what it looks like, what it is composed of, and how it is used in traditional medicine. There are some illustrations, a bibliography, and an index.

1754. Reid, Daniel P. *Chinese Herbal Medicine.* Boston, MA: Shambhala, 1987. 174p LC 86-17814; ISBN 0-87773-397-x (c); ISBN 0-87773-398-8 (p).

There is an introductory text and then an "Herbal Companion" (pp. 80-159), a listing of 200 herbs arranged by Chinese name (in Chinese characters). Also given are Latin name, a description of where it is grown, the parts used, what parts of the body it works on, its effect, indications, dosages, and remarks. There is a separate section on herbal prescriptions, preventatives and curatives or tonics. Herbal recipes are given. There is an index and a bibliography. Very beautifully illustrated, this is a handsome work.

1755.   Conway, David. *The Magic of Herbs.* New York: E.P. Dutton, 1973. 158p. LC 73-79539; ISBN 0-525-15025-0.

The last chapter of this work, "Herbal **Materia Medica**," covering about half the book, is an alphabetical listing of herbs and plants by common name with a description of each plant, its uses, and some folklore material about each one.

Annotated Collections--Herbal Lore

1756.   Imperato, Pascal James. *African Folk Medicine: Practices and Beliefs of the Bambara and Other Peoples.* Baltimore, MD: York Press, 1977. 251p. LC 77-5465; ISBN 0-912752-08-4.

The Bambara live in Mali, in West Africa, and this scholarly work, by a physician, is about their traditional medical beliefs and treatments. In narrative format, the author discusses the culture, social organization, religious beliefs, and folk medicine of the rural and urban Bambara, their illnesses--physical and mental, traditional surgery, and traditional dentistry. In a final chapter, the author includes a "Traditional African Pharmacopeia" and an appendix which synopsizes the main diseases in Africa. A glossary of Bambara terms, an index, and a bibliography complete this work.

1757.   Lehner, Ernst, and Johanna Lehner. *Folklore and Odysseys of Food and Medicinal Plants.* New York: Farrar, Straus and Giroux, 1973 [1962, Tudor], 128p. LC 73-76779; ISBN 0-374-15722-7.

The plant part of this mishmash of a book includes a section on "the psychic garden" and one on "the culinary herbs." For each one discussed, the authors give a brief history of the plant, discuss its uses, and always give a bit of folklore. This is copiously illustrated and there is an index.

1758.   Northcote, Lady Rosalind Lucy. *The Book of Herb Lore.* 2nd ed. London: John Lane, 1912 [1903]. 212p. Reprinted: New York: Dover, 1971. LC 75-1436766; ISBN 0-486-22694-8.

Lady Northcote, who wrote this book at the beginning of the twentieth century, before herbs and herbal healing became popular again in the 1970s, includes much folkloric material about herbs, telling how they were used historically, giving quotes about them, and telling how to grow and harvest them "today."

Chapter VI

FOLK RITUAL AND RITES

It is often difficult to distinguish between rituals, rites, and customs, although most anthropologists use the word **rite** in conjunction with birth, puberty/adolescence, marriage, and death. This first general section on rites is expanded, however, to include **calendar rites** (customs associated with the seasons or holidays). Although the *MLA International Bibliography* separates **rites** and **festivals**, I have opted to include festivals as a subsection of rites. There are additional sections on **folk drama, games,** and **play. Ritual drama** has been incorporated into the folk drama section below, and **ritual poetry** can be found in the section on poetry, in Chapter 3. And many works encompassing religious rites are found in the section on religion, in Chapter 5, but there is also a section on religious rites and religious holidays below (nos. 1825-1846).

FOLK RITUAL/RITES
General

A good basic introduction to folk ritual is a collection of essays on contemporary ritual, *Rituals and Ceremonies in Popular Culture* (Bowling Green OH: Bowling Green University Popular Press, 1980), edited by Ray Browne, on purification and healing rituals in new religious movements, ritual in architecture, American sporting rituals, yard shrines, television viewing as ritual, the minstrel show as ritual, and new and old funeral rituals. Victor Turner edited *Celebration: Studies in Festivity and Ritual* (Washington, DC: Smithsonian Institution Press, 1982) to coordinate with "Celebration: A World of Art and Ritual," an exhibition organized by the office of Folklife Programs at the Smithsonian Institution at the Renwick Gallery, 1982 (no. 1761); the essays by Ralph Rinzler, Richard M. Dorson, Barbara Kirshenblatt-Gimblett, Ronald Grimes, Marta Weigle, and Dan Patterson, among others, cover ceremonial masks, ritual drama, initiation festivals, carnivals, religious celebrations, and political celebrations. An earlier, seminal work by Turner is his *The Ritual Process: Structure and Anti-Structure* (Chicago, IL: Aldine Press, 1969). John J. MacAloon's *Rite, Drama, Festival, Spectacle: Rehearsals Toward a Theory of Cultural Performance* (Philadelphia, PA: The Institute for the Study of Human Issues, 1984) is another collection of essays covering roughly the same material. And Gilbert Lewis' *Day of Shining Red: An Essay on Understanding Ritual* (New York: Cambridge University Press, 1988 [1980]) is an anthropological study of rite.

There are many texts which focus on one aspect of ritual. One example of this is James H.S. Bossard's and Eleanor S. Boll's *Ritual in Family Living; A Contemporary Study* (Philadelphia, PA: University of Pennsylvania Press, 1950) which covers family ritual in autobiography, and historical and contemporary trends in family ritual. Edward Westermarck's *Ritual and Belief in Morocco* (2 vols., London: Macmillan, 1926) is a study of Mohammedan calendar rites, rites practiced to influence the weather, rites of passage, and general secular and religious rites practiced in Morocco.

Studies dealing with calendar and festival rites and rites of passage are listed under the appropriate sections.

Bibliography--Ritual/Rites-General

Note: Bibliographies of specific types of rites (e.g., birth rites, death rites, etc.), are found within those sections.

1759. Goodland, Roger. *A Bibliography of Sex Rites and Customs; An Annotated Record of Books, Articles, and Illustrations in All Languages.* London: George Routledge, 1931. 782p. LC 31- 34259.

There are 9,000 international books and articles entered in this alphabetical listing. A comprehensive index includes a subject index.

1760. Grimes, Ronald L. *Research in Ritual Studies: A Programmatic Essay and Bibliography.* Metuchen, NJ: Scarecrow; Chicago, IL: The American Theological Library Association, 1985. 165p. LC 84-23474; ISBN 0-8108-1762-4. (ATLA bibliography series, 14)

The author begins with an introductory essay which defines the subject and sets parameters. The second part of the work is the bibliography with about 1,600 English-language unannotated entries published between 1960-1985. Grimes then divides the bibliography of ritual which he considers an offshoot of religion, into four major divisions: **ritual components** (action, space, time, objects, symbols, etc.); **ritual types** (rites of passage, marriage rites, funerary rites, festivals, pilgrimages, civil ceremonies, ritual exchange, sacrifice, worship, magic, healing rites, interaction rites, meditation rites, ritual drama); **ritual descriptions** (rites interpreted with primary reference to specific traditions, systems, periods or geographical areas); and **works in various "field-clusters"** (religious studies, anthropology, ethnography, ethology, folklore, sociology, literature, philosophy, etc.).

Exhibition Catalog--Ritual/Rites-General

1761. Smithsonian Institution. *Celebration: A World of Art and Ritual.* Washington, DC: Office of Folklife Programs and the Renwick Gallery of the Smithsonian, Smithsonian Institution Press, 1982. 214p. LC 81-23999; ISBN 0-87474-433-4.

See the book of essays edited by Victor Turner, the guest curator of this exhibit, cited in the headnote to this chapter. Turner also wrote the introduction to this beautiful catalog and the descriptions of the 279 items in the exhibition--ritual objects used for celebration purposes: shadow puppets, quilts, spoons and bowls, baskets, spades, headdresses, masks, drums, incense burners, blankets, clubs, etc.

Handbook--Ritual/Rites-General

1762. van Gennep, Arnold. *Manuel de Folklore Français Contemporain*. 4 vols. Paris: Auguste Picard, 1937-56. LC 47-42703.

Not in English but a standard and oft-cited work. Vol. 1, in seven parts, deals with many rites (van Gennep is the creator of the theory of "rites of passage"): Part 1 covers from birth to death, Part 2 covers marriages and funerals, Part 3 covers festivals, Parts 4-6 cover periodic ceremonies, and cycles, Part 7 covers Christmas and the other holidays of that season.

Annotated Collections--Ritual/Rites-General

Note: For collections of specific types of rites (e.g., childbirth, death, etc.), see the appropriate section below.

1763. Hale, Horatio, ed. *The Iroquois Book of Rites*. 2nd ed. Philadelphia, PA: D.G. Brinton, 1883. 222p. Reprinted: Ohsweken (ONT): Iroqrafts, 1989. ISBN 0-9196-4517-8.

This contains much introductory matter but also the full text, in English and in an Indian language, of the Camenga and Onondago book of rites as collected and translated by this early Canadian linguist.

1764. Tuleja, Tad. *Curious Customs: The Stories Behind 296 Popular American Rituals*. New York: Harmony Books/A Stonesong Press Book, 1987. 210p. LC 87-4098; ISBN 0-517-56653-2 (c); 0-517-56654-0 (p).

This deals with the rites of passage and the rituals of etiquette, mating, marriage, costume, and appearance as well as with foodways, holidays, entertainments, and superstitions.

FOLK RITUAL/RITES
Calendar and Festival Rites

This section covers religious and secular holidays, national holidays and civic holidays, and celebrations and festivals, mostly arranged by country, although there is a separate section for **Christmas** and **Easter** (see nos. 1833-1844). There is a separate subsection on folk festivals at the end of this section (see nos. 1846-1863), although many of the descriptions of festival celebrations are included in this section (the distinction is very hard to make, and in most foreign countries, festivals are specific calendar rites, e.g., Mardi Gras in New Orleans, the Palio in Siena).

There is an enormous amount of material on this general subject. Excluded are texts on particular types of festivals and holiday events such as Gary Jennings' *Parades! Celebrations and Circuses on the March* (Philadelphia: Lippincott, 1966) which describes all types of parades--military, circus, political, etc.--from all over the world, and descriptions of specific festivals or carnivals, such as Alan Dundes' and Alessandro Falassi's *La Terra in Piazza* (Berkeley: University of California Press, 1975), an interpretation of the Palio in Siena, or Errol Hill's *The Trinidad Carnival* (Austin: University of Texas Press, 1972), or Myron Tassin and Gaspar "Buddy" Stall's *Mardi Gras and Bacchus* (Gretna, LA: Pelican Publications, 1984). Journal articles on celebrations have also been excluded.

A good introduction to this field is Beverly J. Stoeltje's "Festivals in America," in Richard M. Dorson's *Handbook of American Folklore* (pp. 239-246) or Jan Brunvand's chapter on "Customs and Festivals," in his *Study of American Folklore* (3rd ed., pp. 328-349), in which he differentiates among rite-of-passage customs, calendar customs, and folk festivals. Another excellent introductory work is Robert Jerome Smith's "Festivals and Celebrations," in *Folklore and Folklife: An Introduction*, edited by   Richard M. Dorson (pp. 159-172). Dorothy Spicer's *Folk*

Festivals and the Foreign Community (no. 1847) is an older study of the role of ethnic folk festivals in the U.S. Victor Turner's *Celebration, Studies in Festivity and Ritual*, mentioned in the headnote to the chapter, includes essays dealing with celebrations and rites in the U.S., Asia, the West Indies, etc. *'We Gather Together': Food & Festival in American Life*, edited by Theodore C. and Lin T. Humphrey (Ann Arbor, MI: UMI Press, 1988) includes essays on the subject of food used at ritual occasions, such as at holidays (e.g., the Passover seder, Christmas, etc.), regional events (e.g., hog-killing in Virginia), and festive performances and festivals. Sir James Frazer's *The Golden Bough: A Study of Religion and Magic* (12 vols., London: Macmillan, 1911-15) covers festivals, which can be accessed through the general index in Vol. 12 by country. A good historical overview of festivals is C.A. Burland's *Echoes of Magic: A Study of Seasonal Festivals Through the Ages* (London: Peter Davies, 1972). Alessandro Falassi has edited *Time Out of Time: Essays on the Festival* (Albuquerque: University of New Mexico Press, 1987) with a section of essays on social functions and the ritual meanings of festival. For other works about folk festivals, see the introduction to that section.

And finally, there have been several special issues of folklore journals devoted to festivals: *Western Folklore* 31 (October, 1972, pp. 229-298) has the following articles: Richard Bauman's "Belsnickling in a Nova Scotia Island Community," Venetia J. Newall's "Two English Fire Festivals in Relation to their Contemporary Setting," Roger Abrahams' "Christmas and Carnival on Saint Vincent," and Robert Jerome Smith's "Licentious Behavior in Hispanic Festivals." And *Pennsylvania Folklife* also had a special Folk Festival issue in 1972.

Bibliography--Calendar and Festival Rites

1765.   Gregory, Ruth W. *Anniversaries and Holidays*. 4th ed. Chicago, IL: American Library Association, 1983. 262p. LC 83-3784; ISBN 0-8389-0389-4.

Although the bulk of this book is a calendar, the third part of each of the four editions (1928, 1944, 1975, 1983) contains a lengthy bibliography. The bibliography for the latest edition, on pp. 184-244, includes 875 books divided into sections on religious days (including Christmas, Jewish holidays, and Easter), festivals, national and civic holidays, days of observance, historic events days, people related to the calendar, and background sources.

Guides--Calendar and Festival Rites

Note: this includes day books (calendars of events), almanacs, descriptions of various secular holidays, customs, or rites. In some cases, festivals are included. Directories to folk festivals are listed separately (nos. 1849-1863). All religious holidays are listed separately (nos. 1834-1844).

General/International

1766. Frewin, Anthony. *The Book of Days.* London: Collins, 1979; New York: Morrow, 1981. 414p. LC 80-515948; ISBN 0-00-216085-4.

This is a day book, January-December, with indications of festivals, world-wide holidays and feasts, historical anniversaries, and important births and deaths. There is a bibliography covering: the calendar, chronology, dating; Church festivals and customs; saints and their days; and popular and other festivals and customs.

1767. Gregory, Ruth W. *Anniversaries and Holidays.* 4th ed. Chicago, IL: American Library Association, 1983 [1928, 1944, 1975]. 262p. LC 83-3784; ISBN 0-8389-0389-4.

This is a day book, a chronological listing of over 2,500 entries by day as well as a calendar of fixed holidays, a calendar of movable holidays, a Christian church calendar, and a calendar of the holidays of the Islamic and Jewish religion as well as feasts, festivals, and special days. A third section includes an annotated bibliography, listed as no. 1765. There is an index.

1768.	James, E.O. *Seasonal Feasts and Festivals*. New York: Barnes and Noble, 1963 [1961]. 336p. LC 61-3828.

Not seen but often cited as a classic work describing calendrical festivals and dramas from different periods and cultures.

1769.	*Oxbridge Omnibus of Holiday Observances around the World, 1977*. New York: Oxbridge Communications, 1977. 142p. LC 76-27493.

The holidays are arranged by country (from **Aden** to **Zambia**), then by state (from **Alabama** to **Wyoming**), and by celebration name (from **Admission Day** to **Youth Day**), with indications if it is a religious holiday or not, then by day (January-December) and by definition (Allelulia Saturday--the Saturday before Easter). Only the very briefest information is given; there is no index or bibliography. One reviewer called it "a good idea badly executed" (**ARBA**, 1978). At best, it is very ambitious.

1770.	Spicer, Dorothy G. *The Book of Festivals*. Detroit, MI: Gale Research, 1969 [1937]. 429p. LC 75-92677.

Spicer covers the festivals of different peoples (Albanians-Yugoslavians), arranged by day within each country. She also gives a history of various calendars in use today (Chinese, Gregorian, Hindu, Jewish, Julian, etc.), and includes a glossary of familiar religions and festival terms, a select bibliography, and an index of festivals.

1771.	Urdang, Laurence, and Christine N. Donohue, eds. *Holidays and Anniversaries of the World: A Comprehensive Catalog....* Detroit, MI: Gale Research, 1985. 863p. LC 85-10350; ISBN 0-8103-1546-7.

Subtitle as it appears on the title page: "A Comprehensive Catalogue Containing Detailed Information on Every Month and Day of the Year, an Extensive Coverage of Holidays, Anniversaries, Fasts and

Feasts, Holy Days, Days of the Saints, the Blesseds, and Other Days of Hertological Significance, Birthdays of the Famous, Important Dates in History, and Special Events and their Sponsors, with an Introduction on the Development of Our Modern Calendar, which Includes Notes of Interest on the Egyptian, Babylonian, Hebrew, Roman, and Gregorian Calendars, a Perpetual Calendar for the Years 1753-2100, a Projection of Major Movable Feasts through 1990, As Well As a Glossary of Time Worlds, the Text Arranged in Calendar Order and Supplemented by an Index of All Listed Names and Events."

The introduction includes a perpetual calendar, history of the modern calendar, and glossary of time words. The main section of this large work includes the holidays and anniversaries of the world, arranged from January to December, by day (approximately two pages for each day). For each day, holidays, feasts and saints' days are given, as well as birth dates of important persons and historical events. The scope is international. There is an index of names, terms, and events, but no bibliography. Useful and comprehensive.

Africa

1772. Awiah, Joseph. *Tongo Festivals, Dances and Marriage Customs.* np, 197?. 20p.

This primarily discusses two main feasts, Daa and Bogran, and two important dances, Golo and Gingana. There is also a fascinating section on marriage customs of the Talensis. It is concluded with a list of months, days, dances, and festivals. There is no index and no bibliography.

1773. Opoku, A.A. *Festivals of Ghana.* Accra: Ghana Publishing Corp., 1970. 80p. LC 79-320850.

Twelve different festivals are explained in depth and accompanied with black-and-white photos. Included also is a list of festivals celebrated in Ghana but not discussed. No index and no bibliography.

1774. Ainsworth, Catherine Harris. *American Calendar Customs*. 2 vols. Buffalo, NY: Clyde Press, 1979, 1980. 208p. Vol. 1: LC 79-52827; ISBN 0-933190-06-9; Vol. 2: LC 79-55784; ISBN 0-933190-07-7.

Vol. 1 covers Easter, Labor Day, Saturday night, St. Joseph's Day, and St. Patrick's Day; Vol. 2 covers birthdays, Christmas, Hallowe'en, Mother's Day, New Year's Day, Thanksgiving, and Valentine's Day. Contains some history and observations of holidays celebrated taken from interviews. There is a bibliography at the end of each section.

1775. *American Indian Calendar*. Washington, DC: U.S. Department of the Interior. Bureau of Indian Affairs. Annual, 1965--.

This lists and describes Indian ceremonials, dances, and feasts, giving date and locale of each event.

1776. Chambers, Wicke, and Spring Asher. *The Celebration Book of Great American Traditions*. New York: Harper, 1983. 188p. LC 82-48113; ISBN 0-06-015095-5.

A wonderful compendium of birthdays, weddings, anniversaries, funerals, calendar days and holidays, religious holidays, everyday traditions, and foods. No index or bibliography.

1777. Chase, Harrison V., and William D. Chase. *Chase's Annual Events: Special Days, Weeks, and Months in------*. Chicago, IL: Contemporary Books. Annual, 1957--.

This is a day-by-day listing of the events in the U.S. and Canada of one year as well as birthdays and national days. There is an index. It's a wonderful hodgepodge of information.

1778.   Cohen, Hennig, and Tristram Potter Coffin, eds. *The Folklore of American Holidays*. 2nd ed. Detroit, MI: Gale Research, 1991 [1987]. 509p. LC 91-014994; ISBN 0-8103-7602-4. Only first edition seen.

The subtitle of the 2nd ed. is: "A Compilation of More than 500 Beliefs, Legends, Superstitions, Proverbs, Riddles, Poems, Songs, Dances, Games, Plays, Pageants, Fairs, Foods, and Processions Associated with Over 120 American Calendar Customs and Festivals." The work, says Cohen and Coffin, aims to provide "in one convenient location a listing of American holidays and the lore and legends associated with the event." Events were included if they continued "to be celebrated even if there were no legal or commercial reason to celebrate it" and if the event creates, "or has in the past created, its own set of traditions, with associated legends, anecdotes, superstitions, foods and the like." Arrangement is chronological (Jan. 1-Dec. 31) by holiday (New Year's Day, Epiphany, etc.), not daily. The compilers cover movable and calendar holidays and present many beliefs, customs, etc., all with sources. This is a book of great charm as well as a very useful work. The introduction covers agricultural communities and the seasonal cycle, the development of formal calendars, the Chinese lunar calendar, the solar Gregorian calendar, and the establishment of festival dates, the pagan influence on Christian holidays, the durability of folk festivals, customs, calendar customs, and festivals--genuine and revived--and fabricated folk festivals, ethnic roots of American festivals, etc. There is a subject index, ethnic and geographical index, collections, informants,' and translators' indexes, song title and first significant line index, and a motif- and tale-type index.

1779.   Hatch, Jane M., comp. and ed. *The American Book of Days*. 3rd ed. New York: H.W. Wilson, 1978. 1,214p. LC 78-16239; ISBN 0-8242-0593-6.

This is a continuation of George W. Douglas' *The American Book of Days*, published in 1937, revised by his daughter in 1948. The work is arranged chronologically, Jan. through Dec. and covers public and legal holidays and movable holidays as well as historical events that were part of the development and founding of the United States (the states' individual dates of admission to the Union, for example). Access is provided through a very detailed contents section as well as a comprehensive index. The appendix material includes information on the history and definitions for **calendar, era** ("a lengthy period of time commencing from a fixed point which serves to order all subsequent years in relation to one another"), the days of the week, and the signs of the zodiac.

1780. Kurath, Gertrude Prokosch. *Michigan Indian Festivals.* Ann Arbor, MI: Ann Arbor Publishers, 1966. 132p. LC-67-15329.

The author discusses native American religious beliefs, customs, songs and dances, and feasts. There is a calendar of summer programs by state and a bibliography of books and A-V materials. Illustrated with photographs. No index.

1781. *Old Farmer's Almanac.* Dublin, NH: Yankee Publications. Annual.

This is a very popular and familiar annual publication, listed in **Weatherlore** (no. 1597). There are two pages for each month, which includes a daily record of feasts and fasts as well as weather and tide information.

1782. Schaun, George, and Virginia Schaun. *American Holidays and Special Days.* Lanham, MD: Maryland Historical Press, 1986. 194p. LC 85-063179; ISBN 0-917882-19-9.

Holidays and special days are arranged chronologically with folk customs listed for each. There is a select bibliography and an index.

South and Central America

1783.   *Calendar of Folklore Festivals of Argentina*. [Argentina], np,
        1967. 94p. LC 73-350290.

        This is a chronological and geographical index to festivals as
well as a lengthy description of major festivals. For each, date, place,
name derivation, traditional beliefs about the festival and/or origins of the
festival are given with any accompanying folklore and literary sources.
Some special observed festivities, and ceremonies are also discussed.
Included also are a list of feasts by locale, a glossary, and bibliography.

1784.   Fay, George Emory. *Fiesta Days of Mexico*. Greeley: University
        of Northern Colorado, Museum of Anthropology, 1970. 25p.
        (Museum of Anthropology, Miscellaneous Series, 17 [July
        1970])

        This is a chronological list of festivities and ceremonies, arranged
by day. Gives town, name of holiday, and a description of the event.
There is no bibliography and no index.

1785.   Milne, Jean. *Fiesta Time in Latin America*. Los Angeles, CA:
        Ward Ritchie, 1965. 236p. LC 65-24170.

        Arranged by month, this covers religious, civic and tribal
festivals in all of the Spanish-speaking Americas (Argentina, Bolivia,
Chile, Colombia, Costa Rica, etc.).

Asia
Multinational

1786.   Scanlon, Phil, Jr. *Southeast Asia: A Cultural Study Through
        Celebration*. DeKalb: Northern Illinois University, Center for
        Southeast Asian Studies, 1985.   189p. LC 86-622390. (Special
        report, 23)

        This is really a "guide to the festive life and major public
holidays of the nations of Southeast Asia" (Singapore, Indonesia,

Malaysia, Thailand, Burma, the Philippines, Kampuchea, Laos, and Vietnam). Arranged by country, the book includes religious ceremonies, cultural celebrations, political observances, traditional celebrations, and festivals. An appendix includes a list of fixed-date holidays by country, a list of references, and an index.

China

1787.   Bodde, Derk, trans. and annot. *Annual Customs and Festivals in Peking as Recorded in the Yen-ching Sui-shih-chi.* By Tun Li-Ch'en. 2nd ed., rev. Hong Kong: Hong Kong University Press, 1965 [1936]. 147p. LC 65-8424.

Yen-ching Sui-shih-chi means **Record of a Year's Time at Yen-ching [Peking].** This then is a "record, day by day and month by month, beginning with Chinese New Year's Day and taking us throughout the year of what used to take place in Peking: its festivals, temple pilgrimages, fairs, customs, and the clothing, foods, and animals of the seasons." Appendixes include a Chinese calendar, a list of principal animals the Chinese use in festivals, a list of the firecrackers, popular forms of entertainment, sweet melons, crickets, chrysanthemums, etc., mentioned in the text as well as a list of Chinese weights, measures, and currency, principal Chinese dynasties and some of the emperors and their reigning dates and titles as well as a concordance of lunar and Western calendars from 1957-1984. Also included in this fascinating and excellent work are a bibliography and an index. See also Bodde's historical work, *Festivals in Classical China: New Year and Other Annual Observances During the Han Dynasty, 206 B.C.--A.D. 220* (Princeton, NJ: Princeton University Press, 1975).

1788.   Eberhard, Wolfram. *Chinese Festivals.* London: Abelard; New York: Schuman, 1958 [1952]. 152p. LC 52-3720. (Great religious festivals series)

In text format, this work describes the New Year's festival, Dragon-boat Festival, Mid-Autumn festival, the Ch'in-ming, the Spring Festival, and the Feast of Souls. Notes and index are included.

1789.　Wong, C.S. *A Cycle of Chinese Festivities*. Singapore: Malaysia Publishing House, Ltd., 1967. 204p. LC 76-268709.

Covers mainly New Year's celebrations but also traditional secular festivals. The introduction has an interesting discussion of the 12 animal symbols that figure so predominantly in Chinese festivals, their significance, and beliefs about them. There is also a bibliography and an index.

India and Nepal

1790.　Anderson, Mary M. *The Festivals of Nepal*. London: George Allen & Unwin, 1971. 288p. LC 72-179172; ISBN 0-04-394001-3. Reprinted: Calcutta: Rupa, 1977.

Religious and secular festivals are described as they appear throughout the calendar year. There is a bibliography and index.

1791.　Thomas, Paul. *Festivals and Holidays of India*. Bombay: D.B. Taraporevala Sons, 1971. 115p. LC 70-924967.

This very thorough book lists the principal Hindu holidays, temple feasts and fairs, tribal celebrations, and Hindu pilgrimages, Muslim festivals and holidays, Christian holy days, Sikh festivals and holy places, Buddhist feasts, Jain festivals, Jewish festivals, the national festivals, and holidays of modern India, including the New Year's festival and other secular holidays. There is a list of annual festivals and holidays and a list of shrines and places of pilgrimage (arranged alphabetically). Concludes with a glossary and index.

Japan

Note: See also no. 1823.

1792. Bauer, Helen, and Sherwin Carlquist. *Japanese Festivals*. Tokyo and Rutland, VT: Charles E. Tuttle, 1974 [1965]. 231p. LC 65-19899.

Includes community celebrations, religious festivals, national festivals, and seasonal festivals, as well as a monthly calendar of all Japanese festivals. Also included is a pronunciation guide to Japanese words, an historical overview of Japanese festivals, a map of Japan, an index, and many black-and-white photos.

1793. Casal, U.A. *The Five Sacred Festivals of Ancient Japan; Their Symbolism & Historical Development*. Tokyo and Rutland, VT: Sophia University in cooperation with Charles E. Tuttle, 1967. 114p. LC 67-20954.

Lengthy descriptions are given of the following five holidays: Oshogatsu, the New Year's Festival; Hinamat Suri, the Girls' Festival; Tango no Sekku, the Boys' Festival; Tanabata, the Star Festival; Gugoya, the Chrysanthemum Festival. The index is in English and Japanese.

1794. Erskine, William Hugh. *Japanese Festival and Calendar Lore*. Tokyo: Kyo-bun Kwan, 1933. 209p. LC 34-5817.

This is a month-by-month almanac with an explanation of each festival. At the beginning of each month, there is an outline of holidays and omens of each day. There is also a section on the oracles and one on festivals as well as a calendar of birth years and stars from 1844-1933. The index is in English and Japanese. Although old and somewhat disordered, this seems to be a complete look at Japanese festival and calendar events set within a Japanese cultural framework.

1795. Haga, Hideo. *Japanese Folk Festivals Illustrated*. Trans. Fanny Hagin Mayer. Tokyo: Miura Printing Co., 1970. 187p. LC 79-138419.

This work covers Japanese folk faiths and ceremonies at festivals, the festivals of the four seasons, characteristics of Japanese festivals, the folk performing arts in Japan, festivals of other peoples celebrated in Japan, and modern festivals. The appended Japanese folk festival calendar is arranged by sections of Japan, then by city. Probably outdated somewhat now. See also Haga's *Japanese Festivals* (Osaka: Hoikusha, 1986).

Korea

1796.   Chóe, Sang-su. *Annual Customs of Korea: Notes on the Rites and Ceremonies of the Year.* Seoul: Seomun-dang, 1983. 168p. LC 84-191062.

Arranged by **moons** (there are 12 moons), calendar customs are told for each traditional holiday and ritual (e.g., New Year's ritual, New Year's visit and greetings, New Year's food and wine, etc.). The book is clearly written and easy to use. An index of English titles and Korean titles is included.

Malaysia

1797.   Lo, Dorothy, and Leon Comber. *Chinese Festivals in Malaya.* Singapore: Eastern Universities Press, 1963 [1958]. 66p. LC 59-37549. (Malayan peoples & customs series)

This work covers the Chinese New Year's festivities, Ch'ing Ming Festival, Dragon boat festival, Feast of the Seven Sisters, Feast of the Hungry Ghosts, Mid-Autumn Festival, Double Ninth Festival, and the Winter Solstice Festival. There is a Chinese index, a general index, and a bibliography.

Philippines

1798.   Aluit, Alphonso J. *The Galleon Guide to Philippine Festivals.* Manila: Galleon Publishers, 1969. 176p. LC 72-12157.

Discussed are the following: the festival of the Holy Child, Lent, Maytime, the Marian festivals, festivals of Muslim Philippines, festivals of the mountain provinces, fluvial festivals in the Philippines, feasts for the dead, and Christmas in the Philippines. There is a calendar of traditional events and a bibliography.

Europe

Note: There were a lot of works written about the festivals and calendar customs of Europe in the 1940s and 1950s; for the most part, I have eliminated those, but they are still available on the library shelves of most universities and public libraries.

General/International

1799.   Spicer, Dorothy Gladys. *Festivals of Western Europe*. New York: Wilson, 1958. 275p. LC 58-7291.

The work covers religious feasts and folk festivals with origins in the church. Holidays are arranged by country: Belgium, Denmark, France, Germany, Italy, Luxembourg, the Netherlands, Norway, Portugal, Spain, Sweden, and Switzerland. Includes also a table of Easter dates and movable feasts dependent upon Easter up to 1988. There is a glossary, a bibliography (arranged by country), an index of festivals (arranged by country), and an alphabetical index of festivals.

France

Note: Books on French calendar customs, such as Jean-Paul Clebert's *Les Fêtes en Provence* (Avignon: Aubanel, 1982), are mostly available in French. Noteworthy, however, is Nicole Vielfaure's and Anne-Christine Beauviala's *Fêtes, Coutumes et Gâteaux* (Paris: Chutre Bonneton, 1984), arranged by holiday (regionally) and by rite (e.g., Baptism, first communion), with discussions of origins, preparations, myths, and traditional foods (with recipes). Fantastique!

Germany

Note: A recent study of German festivals is Ingeborg Weber-Kellermann's *Saure Wochen, Frohe Feste: Fest und Alltag in der Sprach der Bräuche* (Munich: C.J. Bucher, 1985). Most guides to German holidays, such as Leander Petzoldt's *Volkstümliche Feste: Ein Führer zu Volksfesten, Märkten und Messen in Deutschland* (Munich: C.H. Beck, 1983), and many regional guides are in German.

1800.　Russ, Jennifer M. *German Festivals & Customs*. London: Oswald Wolff, 1983. 166p. LC 83-209773; ISBN 0-854963650.

Festivals are listed as they appear throughout the year, followed by a listing of carnivals, local festivals, and pageants (e.g., Obergammerau). Holiday customs (e.g., beer and wine drinking customs) are also presented along with some "customs through life." A bibliography, subject index in German and English, and an index of names and places conclude this work.

Greece

1801.　Megas, Georgios A. *Greek Calendar Customs*. 2nd ed. Athens: Press and Information Department. Prime Minister's Office, 1963 [1958]. 159p. LC 79-317961.

Carnivals, religious holidays, and feasts are arranged by season (winter--autumn). There is no index or bibliography.

Ireland

1802.　Danaher, Kevin. *The Year in Ireland*. Cork: Mercier Press, 1972. 274p. LC 74-158329; ISBN 0-85342-280-x.

This is a book that explains the Irish holidays from Jan. 1-Dec. 31--St. Brigid's day, Shrove Tuesday, Chalk Sunday, Ash Wednesday, Lent, St. Patrick's Day, Lady Day, Palm Sunday, Easter, April Fool's

Day, May Day, Ascension Day, etc., through Christmas. There is a select bibliography and an index.

Italy

Note: Books dealing with Italian holiday rites, such as Toni Capuozzo's and Michele Neri's recent *Feste e Sagre dei Paesi Italiani* (Milan: Arnoldo Mondadori, 1985), are available in Italian. Noteworthy are Giuseppe Pitrè's two volumes of calendar rites, *Sepattacoli e Feste Popolari Siciliane* (Vol. 12 of *Biblioteca delle Tradizioni Popolari Siciliane)* and *Feste Patronali in Sicilia* (Vol. 21).

Spain

Note: Books on Spanish festivals, such as Julio Cara Baroja's *El Estio Festivo: Fiestas Populares del Verano* (Madrid: Taurus, 1984), are primarily in Spanish.

Europe--Great Britain

1803.   Banks, Mary Macleod. *British Calendar Customs: Orkney and Shetland.* London: Folk-Lore Society, W. Glaisher, 1946. 110p. LC 48-1216. (Publications of the Folk-Lore Society; v. 112).

Banks' theory is that the peasants from Norway settled "in the western isles before the visits of Vikings" and that this is, in part, the folklore of the area. "In the end," she says, "the inhabitants of all these islands are primarily Norse in origin." This work includes a classified listing of customs about wells, fairs, the seasons, and the movable festivals, with a daybook arranged by month, with more information on festivals' names, sayings and proverbs, rhymes, omens, observances, beliefs, fasts, processions, dances, etc. There is an index.

1804. Banks, Mary Macleod. *British Calendar Customs: Scotland.* 3 vols. London: Folk-Lore Society, W. Glaisher, 1937-41. LC 38-6190. (Publications of the Folk-Lore Society; v. 100, 104, 108)

Vol. 1: Movable feasts, harvest feasts, March riding and Wapynshaws, wells and fairs; Vol. 2: the seasons, the quarters, Hogmanay, January-May; Vol. 3: June to December, Christmas, and the Yule holidays.

1805. Brand, John. *Observations on the Popular Antiquities of Great Britain;....* 3 vols. London: Henry G. Bohn, 1848. Reprinted: New York: AMS, 1970. LC 71-136368; ISBN 0-404-50005-6.

This is really a day-book of customs arranged from New Year's on. It covers all the holidays and the traditions relating to them.

1806. Chambers, Robert. *Book of Days: A Miscellany of Popular Antiquities in Connection with the Calendar;....* 2 vols. London: Chambers, 1862-64. Reprinted: Detroit, MI: Gale Research, 1967. LC 67-13009.

Arranged chronologically, January through December, and day by day. There is much information given on the history and religious origins of the popular customs, observances, and events. A general index is found in Vol. 2.

1807. Ditchfield, Peter Hampson. *Old English Customs Extant at the Present Time; An Account of Local Observances, Festival Customs, and Ancient Ceremonies Yet Surviving in Great Britain.* London: 1896. 344p. Reprinted: Detroit, MI: Singing Tree, 1968. 344p. LC 68-21765.

This work describes "the actual folk-customs yet extant, which may be witnessed to-day by the folk-lorist and lover of rural manners." (v) The customs are grouped around Christmas, New Year's Day, Lent, Easter, May Day, Midsummer Eve, and the 5th of November. Also listed are rural customs, club feasts, local customs, superstitions, marriage customs, and legal, civic, court, bell-ringing, army, and parliamentary customs.

1808. Hazlitt, W. Carew. *Faiths and Folklore of the British Isles;...* 2 vols. London: Reeves and Turner, 1905. 672p. Reprinted: New York: Benjamin Blom, 1965. 672p. LC 64-18758; ISBN 0-405-08604-0.

Vol. 1 covers the holidays and festivals, arranged from New Year's Day to Christmas in chronological order. Generally this is an alphabetical listing of all customs, including holidays and holiday objects (e.g., **maypole**).

1809. Hole, Christina. *A Dictionary of British Folk Customs.* London: Palador Grafton, 1986 [1976, as *British Folk Customs*]. 349p. LC 89-126459; ISBN 0-5860-8293-X.

This is a listing mainly of holidays, holiday traditions, places, and people associated with holidays, done in dictionary format. There is a bibliography and index.

1810. Hole, Christina. *English Traditional Customs.* 2nd ed. Totowa, NJ: Rowman & Littlefield, 1975 [1943]. 178p. LC 75-14365; ISBN 0-8741-1736-1.

By comparing two editions, written almost 40 years apart, the author says one "can chart changes, note what customs have fallen into disfavor and not used." The work describes customs within the following framework: Christmas season, opening the year, Shrovetide and Lent, Eastertide, month of May, high summer, civic customs, the land and its customs, wakes, and fairs. The index is useful; included also is a brief bibliography.

1811. Hone, William. *The Every-day Book, or, Everlasting Calendar of Popular Amusements, Sports, Pastimes, Ceremonies, Manners, Customs, and Events Incident to Each of the Three Hundred and Sixty-five Days, in Past and Present Times.* 2 vols. London: Tegg, 1826-1827. Vol.1, 860p.; Vol. 2, 856p. Reprinted: Detroit, MI: Gale Research, 1967. LC 67-12945.

The 1967 edition has an introduction by Leslie Shepard. Both volumes have chronological listings of the holidays; the second volume "contains a much greater variety of original information concerning manners and customs." Both volumes have a general index, index to Romish saints, poetical index, correspondents' index, and an index to engravings. Vol. 1 also has a floral index. Hone also wrote *The Table Book* (2 vols. London: Tegg, 1827-28; reprinted; Detroit, MI: Gale, 1966) and *The Year Book of Daily Recreation and Information Concerning Remarkable Men and Manners, Times, and Seasons* (1832; reprinted: Detroit, MI: Omnigraphics, 1991), both with the same format as *Everyday Book*. These include all sorts of information on calendric folklore.

1812. Kightly, Charles. *The Customs and Ceremonies of Britain: An Encyclopaedia of Living Traditions.* London: Thames and Hudson, 1986. 248p. LC 85-1466.

This is a collection of ceremonies and customs, many, but not all, holiday customs. There is a day calendar of customs, a regional map, and a gazetteer.

1813. Martin, Mark. *Traditional Britain.* London: Sidgwick & Jackson, 1983. 96p. LC 83-221024; ISBN 0-283-98913-0 (p). (Golden Hart guides)

The emphasis in this work is on customs and traditions still practiced today. There is a calendar of seasonal events (January-December) and also a regional guide to country customs and town traditions arranged by place. There is an index to holidays.

1814.   McNeill, Florence Marian. *The Silver Bough: A Four-Volume Study of the National and Local Festivals of Scotland.* 4 vols. Glasgow: Maclellan, 1957-70. LC 60-36082.

Vol. 1 (1957): Scottish folklore and folk belief; Vol. 2 (1959): A calendar of Scottish national festivals, Candlemas to Harvest Home; Vol. 3 (1961): A calendar of Scottish national festivals, Hallowe'en to Yule; and Vol. 4 (1970): The local festivals of Scotland. The holidays are given in calendar format. There are notes and indexes in each volume with some bibliographic material.

1815.   Owen, Trefor M. *Welsh Folk Customs.* 3rd ed. Cardiff: Welsh Folk Museum, 1987 [1968, 1959]. 258p.

This is a museum catalog divided into two parts. The first part contains chapters on Christmas and Candlemas and movable feasts, May and midsummer, Harvest and Winters' Eve, and birth, marriage, and death customs. The second part of the book is the catalog proper of 567 items used in an exhibition to illustrate Welsh folk customs. There is a brief bibliography but no index.

1816.   Palmer, Geoffrey, and Noel Lloyd. *A Year of Festivals: A Guide to British Calendar Customs.* London: Frederick Warne, 1972. 192p. LC 71-186754; ISBN 0-7232-1309-7 (c); 0-7232-1466-3 (p).

Covers specific holidays, fairs, and holiday customs that occur during the year. There is a country calendar of special events with holiday events listed and an index.

1817.   Spicer, Dorothy Gladys. *Yearbook of English Festivals.* New York: Wilson, 1954. 298p. Reprinted: Westport, CT: Greenwood, 1972. LC 74-162632; ISBN 0-8371-6132-0.

This is a chronological guide and survey of the holidays and folk festivals of Great Britain with special emphasis on the Easter cycle. There is an index of customs, counties, and regions, and a glossary of festival terms.

1818. Sykes, Homer. *Once a Year: Some Traditional British Customs.* London: Gordon Fraser, 1977. 167p. LC 77-377324; ISBN 0-9004-0668-2.

Centers on traditions that are "maintained from year to year whilst remaining entirely unknown outside the community in which they take place." Arranged from January-December, the names of the events are given with dates, places, and origins, and many traditions. Filled with marvelous photos. There is no index or bibliography.

1819. Thistleton-Dyer, T.F. *British Popular Customs, Present and Past; Illustrating the Social and Domestic Manners of the People, Arranged According to the Calendar of the Year.* London: George Bell, 1876. 520p. Reprinted: Detroit, MI: Singing Tree, 1968. LC 67-23908.

This classic work is arranged chronologically in text format from New Year's Day to New Year's Eve. Within each holiday, the arrangement of customs is by county or shire. There is a general index.

1820. Walsh, William S. *Curiosities of Popular Customs And of Rites, Ceremonies, Observances, and Miscellaneous Antiquities.* Philadelphia, PA: Lippincott, 1888. 1,018p. Reprinted: Detroit, MI: Gale, 1966. LC 66-2395.

Intended as a compendium of international customs, the entries are mostly British and mostly calendar customs and festival rituals.

1821. Whitlock, Ralph. *A Calendar of Country Customs.* London: Batsford, 1978. 168p. LC 78-325402; ISBN 0-7134-05716.

This includes agricultural rituals (ploughing, hoeing, harvesting, etc.) as well as calendar rites dealing with the cycle of farm life and its own natural seasons for festivity. There are two calendars--agricultural and pastoral, the agricultural given in quarter days (an extant system used by British farmers), the pastoral given by the old Celtic quarter days. Arranged January-December, beginning with Twelfth Night and Plough Moon and ending with Christmas and New Year's Eve. An index is included but no bibliography.

1822.   Wright, Arthur Robinson. *British Calendar Customs: England.* Ed. T. East Jones. 3 vols. London: Published for the Folk-Lore Society by W. Glaisher, 1936-40. LC 36-28983. (Publications of the Folk-Lore Society; vols. 97, 102, 106). Reprinted: Nendeln/ Liechtenstein: Kraus, 1968.

Vol. 1 contains English movable feasts: Shrovetide, Lent, Ash Wednesday, and harvest customs, and an index; Vol. 2 contains fixed festivals: January-May; Vol. 3 contains fixed festivals: June-December. New and old customs and holiday traditions are listed for each.

Oceania

1823.   De Francis, John. *Things Japanese in Hawaii.* Honolulu: University Press of Hawaii, 1973. 210p. LC 72-83489; ISBN 0-8248-0233-0.

The author has prepared this book of annual events in an attempt "to preserve the Japanese cultural heritage in Hawaii." (xi) Included are descriptions of New Year's celebrations, Girls' Day and Boys' Day, Cherry Blossom Festival, Buddha Day and Bodhi Day, Bon Festival, Shinto Thanksgiving Festival, and permanent and unscheduled attractions, including an overview of the tea ceremony, flower arranging, Japanese art, music and drama, sports, and theater. A calendar of events is on pp. 10-13. A glossary and index are also included.

CALENDAR AND FESTIVAL RITES
Religious Calendar and Festival Rites

Note: I have opted to include Christmas and Easter as part of religious calendar rites, though Christmas is not always studied as a religious event. This section is divided into works on all religious holiday rites, then by religion (Jewish before Christian), with Christmas and Easter being considered under Christian calendar rites.

Guide--Religious Calendar and Festival Rites--General

1824.   Harper, Howard V. *Days and Customs of All Faiths*. New York: Fleet, 1957. 399p. LC 57-14777. Reprinted: Detroit, MI: Omnigraphics, 1990. LC 89-63106; ISBN 0-5588-8850-0.

This is a day book (January-December) covering the religious festival rites of all religions as well as some secular events. The second part includes some Jewish customs and traditions, general holiday customs, holiday words and expressions, and a great many wedding customs. Index.

Jewish Calendar and Festival Rites

Guides--Jewish Calendar and Festival Rites

Note: This is a highly select list; there seems to be a particular abundance of books on the Jewish holidays.

1825.   Agnon, Shmuel Josef. *Days of Awe; Being a Treasury of Traditions, Legends and Learned Commentaries Concerning Rosh-ha-Shanah, Yom Kippur and the Days Between, Culled from Three Hundred Volumes*. New York: Schocken, 1965 [1948]. 279p. LC 48-8316.

This is an abridgment by Nahum N. Glatzer of Agnon's Hebrew work, *Yamim Nordim*, translated by Maurice T. Golpert and revised by

Jacob Sloan. It discusses the origins of the holidays, prayers, services and ceremonies of the ten days between Rosh ha-Shanah and Yom Kippur. There is a bibliography but no index.

1826. Gaster, Theodor Herzl. *Festivals of the Jewish Year: A Modern Interpretation and Guide.* New York: Sloane, 1953. 308p. LC 53-9341. Reprinted in paperback: New York: Morrow/Quill, 1978. LC 9431; ISBN 0-6880-6008-0 (p).

This is a description of Jewish seasonal festivals (Passover, Succoth, etc.), the "Solemn Days" (Yom Kippur, etc.), "Days of Sorrow," the minor holidays (Purim, Hanukkah), and the Sabbath. Includes a bibliography for each festival, fast, and holy day.

1827. Idelsohn, Abraham Z. *The Ceremonies of Judaism.* 2nd rev. and enl. ed. Cincinnati, OH: National Federation of Temple Brotherhoods, 1930. 134p. LC 29-11486.

Lists Sabbath customs, festivals, and daily ceremonies in the home and synagogue. Also discusses ceremonial objects in the synagogue, prayers and songs, and ceremonies for special occasions in the life of the individuals (e.g., **bar-mitzvah**). No index or bibliography is included.

1828. Schauss, Hayyim. *The Jewish Festivals, From Their Beginning to Our Own Day.* Trans. Samuel Jaffe. Cincinnati, OH: Union of American Hebrew Congregations, 1938. 316p. LC 38-11520. Reprinted in paperback as *The Jewish Festivals: History and Observance*: New York: Schocken, 1978. ISBN 0-8052-0413-x (p).

Published as *Dos Yom-Tov-buch* (1933, in Yiddish). In text format, this book covers the history, development, and contemporary celebration rites of the Sabbath, Pesach, Shavuos, Rosh Hashonah, Yom Kippur, Sukkos, Chanukkah, Purim, and the minor holidays. Includes bibliography, notes, and index.

1829. Strassfield, Michael. *The Jewish Holidays: A Guide and Commentary.* New York: Harper & Row, 1985. 248p. LC 84-48196; ISBN 0-06-015406-3 (c); 0-06-091225-1 (p).

Covers each holiday separately, explaining general presentation, what foods are eaten (or not eaten), what wine is drunk, and the traditions and customs of each holiday. Index.

Christian Calendar and Festival Rites

Christian Calendar and Festival Rites--General

Guides--Christian Calendar and Festival Rites-General

1830. Urlin, Ethel L. *Festivals, Holy Days, and Saints' Days: A Study in Origins and Survivals in Church Ceremonies and Secular Customs.* London: Simpkin, Marshall, Hamilton, Kent, 1915. 272p. Reprinted: Ann Arbor, MI: Gryphon, 1971. LC 70-89301; Detroit, MI: Omnigraphics, 1990. LC 89-43344.

This includes daily accounts of Christian festivals and holidays with customs for each given for many countries. There is an index and a brief bibliography.

1831. Weiser, Franz Xaver. *Handbook of Christian Feasts and Customs; The Year of the Lord in Liturgy and Folklore.* New York: Harcourt, 1958. 366p. LC 58-10908. Abridged edition: New York: Paulist Press, 1963. 192p.

Arranged by days (e.g., Sundays, weekdays, rogation days), Christian secular and nonsecular holidays (e.g., Advent, Christmas, Lent, Thanksgiving, etc.) and saints' days are listed. For each listing, the author includes symbols, customs, and folklore and history for each holiday. Includes a dictionary of terms and an index. A bibliography is listed in each chapter.

1832.   Weiser, Franz Xaver. *The Holyday Book*. New York: Harcourt, Brace, 1956. 217p. LC 56-9138.

This covers holidays of the Pentecost season, and feasts of saints.

Christian Calendar and Festival Rites--Christmas and Easter

Samuelson (see no. 1833) says the best general study of Christmas is James H. Barnett's *The American Christmas: A Study in National Culture* (New York: Macmillan, 1954; reprinted: New York: Arno, 1976). It covers the history of Christmas, the social role of Santa Claus, Christmas in the Church, family, and school, the exploitation of Christmas, social aspects of Christmas art, and the cult of Christmas. For another good introduction to Christmas, see Alan Dundes' "Christmas as a Reflection of American Culture" (*California Monthly* 78 [1967]: 9-15). Kenneth Hare's "Christmas Folklore" (*Quarterly Review* 263 [December, 1935]: 31-40) is a good study of the relationship between folklore and Christmas. There have been several specifically folkloric studies of Christmas, for example, A.C. Shoemaker's *Christmas in Pennsylvania, a Folk-cultural Study* (Kutztown, PA: Folklore Society, 1959) and also G.E. Nitzsche's *The Christmas Putz of the Pennsylvania Germans* (Allentown, PA: Publications of the Pennsylvania German Folklore Society; v. 6, 1941). Another interesting cultural study is David N. Plath's "The Japanese Popular Christmas: Coping with Modernity" (*Journal of American Folklore* 76 [1963]: 309-317) which compares the modern Christmas celebration in Japan to comparable American customs. Venetia Newall's *An Egg at Easter: A Folklore Study* (London: Routledge & Kegan Paul; Bloomington: Indiana University Press, 1971) is a superb folkloric study of a holiday, its customs, and symbolism.

Bibliography--Christmas

1833.   Samuelson, Sue. *Christmas: An Annotated Bibliography*. New York: Garland, 1982. 96p. LC 82-48083; ISBN 0-8240-9263-5. (Garland folklore bibliographies; v. 4; Garland reference library of humanities; v. 343)

This is a comprehensive bibliography, arranged alphabetically by author, relating to Christmas, probably the most researched holiday in the world. The author, excluding compendia of Christmas customs or comparative studies and focusing on analytic material, cites and annotates about 400 works that deal with the social, historical, economic, political, anthropological/folkloric aspects of Christmas. A review of the literature comprises the introduction. The scope is international and includes theses and dissertations as well as books, journal articles, and monographs. See particularly, "Folklore Works," xxvii-xxx. Each entry is briefly annotated.

Annotated Collections--Christmas and Easter Rites and Customs

1834.   Alter, Judy, and Joyce Gibson Roach, eds. *Texas and Christmas: A Collection of Traditions, Memories & Folklore.* Fort Worth: Texas Christian University Press, 1983. 86p. LC 83-4717; ISBN 0-912646-81-0 (p).

Includes essays mostly on traditions, some recipes, Christmas programs, etc.

1835.   Coffin, Tristram Potter. *The Book of Christmas Folklore.* New York: Seabury, 1973. 192p. LC 73-6413; ISBN 0-8164-9158-5. (A Continuum book)

Collections of Christmas customs are listed (pp. 17-47) and there are other sections on Father Christmas, mumming and other dramas (with texts), and Dickens' *Christmas Carol.* There is an index to people, places, subjects, and titles, rhymes, tales, and songs.

1836.   Cure, Karen, et al. *An Old-Fashioned Christmas: American Holiday Traditions.* New York: Harry N. Abrams, 1984. 159p. LC 84-3096; ISBN 0-8109-1816-1.

This includes an historical overview, customs of the past, regional traditions of the Creole and the South, the prairie, and the west.

There are many recipes, menus, and carol texts given, all with sources. A recipe index concludes this work.

1837.   Hartman, Tom, ed. *Guinness Book of Christmas*. Enfield [ENG]: Guinness Books, 1984. 144p. ISBN 0-85112-404-6.

A hodgepodge of a book (brought to you by the folks who bring you the *Guinness World Book of Records*) which includes information on the origins of Christmas, decorations (e.g., mistletoe, the tree), music, weather and night sky, food and drink, coins, and stamps. Full of pictures and recipes.

1838.   Hole, Christina. *Christmas and Its Customs, A Brief Study*. New York: Barrows, 1958. 95p. LC 58-10574.

A text account of the origins of the Christmas season and holiday, and some notes about garlands, gifts, givers, feasts, carols, New Years, and Twelfth Night, with a separate section on Christmas legends and superstitions.

1839.   Hole, Christina. *Easter and Its Customs, A Brief Study*. New York: Barrows, 1961. 96p. LC 68-54858.

In the same format as no. 1838, Hole covers Eastertide, Shrovetide, Palm Sunday, gifts, Good Friday, Easter Day, Easter eggs, and Easter Monday and includes some legendary information in each chapter.

1840.   Miles, Clement A. *Christmas in Ritual and Tradition, Christian and Pagan*. London: Unwin, 1912. 399p. Reprinted: Detroit, MI: Omnigraphics, 1990. LC 89-29299.

Covers Christian poetry, liturgy, drama, pagan festivals, the calendar, the Christmas tree, Christmas food, mumming, and New Year's Day.

1841.	Spicer, Dorothy G. *46 Days of Christmas: A Cycle of Old World Songs, Legends and Customs.* New York: Coward-McCann, 1960. 96p. LC 60-12497.

Arranged by day, from St. Barbara's Day (celebrated in Syria on December 4) to Somerset's (England) Old Twelfth Night (January 18).

1842.	Vaughn, Mary Ann Woloch. *Ukrainian Christmas: Traditions, Folk Customs, and Recipes.* Munster, IN: Ukrainian Heritage Co., 1983. 104p. LC 85-126854.

Includes Christmas customs and traditions of the Ukrainians as well as customs about decorating the tree and the table. Seasonal song texts and recipes are also included.

1843.	Vaughn, Mary Ann Woloch. *Ukrainian Easter: Traditions, Folk Customs, and Recipes.* Coralville, IA: Communications Printing, 1982. 96p. LC 83-210091.

Includes customs, traditions, songs, egg-decorating instructions and legends, egg designs, etc., and recipes for Easter and Lent food and many pictures.

1844.	Wernecke, Herbert H. *Celebrating Christmas Around the World.* Philadelphia, PA: Westminster, 1962. 246p. LC 62-13232.

This is a children's book. Customs are arranged alphabetically by country within Africa, Asia, Europe, North America, and South America. Descriptions are given of Christmas celebrations held in each country. Samuelson (no. 1833) pinpoints the descriptions at Annapolis and West Point as being particularly interesting.

Encyclopedia--Asian Religious Festival Rites

1845. Legge, James, trans. *Li Chi, Book of Rites; An Encyclopedia of Ancient Ceremonial Usages, Religious Creeds, and Social Institutions.* Variant title: *Li Ki, or Collection of Treatises on the Rules of Propriety or Ceremonial Usages.* Published as Vols. 27 and 28 of *The Sacred Books of the East: The Texts of Confucianism.* 2 vols. Oxford: Clarendon Press, 1885. Reprinted: Hyde Park, NY: University Books, 1967. Ed., with an introduction and a study guide by Ch-u Chai and Winberg Choi. LC 66-17934.

This Confucian classic, "a commentary on religious ceremonies, mourning rites and social etiquette which governed the moral, social and religious activities of the aristocrats," covers ceremonial usage and sacrifices in Vol. 1, and mourning rites, dress, marriage, food preparation, puberty rites, the ceremony of archery and the meaning of the banquet in Vol. 2.

FOLK RITUAL/RITES
Folk Festivals

Jan Brunvand writes:

> The term "folk festival" has been applied since the 1930s in the United States to annually sponsored public performances of folklore, generally folksongs and dances. Folklorists are increasingly attending them, planning them, and even taking part in some of them. Only on the current folk-festival stage have the folk, the folklore enthusiast, and the folklorist all met face to face and begun to try to understand one another in some depth. The oldest consecutive folk festival is the "National Folk Festival," first held in St. Louis in 1934 with strictly American performers, but eventually branching out into all manner of

immigrant and "ethnic" acts. Other festivals have sprung up (and some have died) faster than folklorists can make up their minds about how to regard them; these have ranged from glossy extravaganzas with celebrity performers to the rustic "Arkansas Folk Festival" in Mountain View, Arkansas, with its still largely home-grown talent and audience. Another development in the revivalist folk-festival field, and a very promising one, is the appearance of university-sponsored annual events (at the University of Chicago and the University of California at Los Angeles, for instance), where the enthusiastic collegiate folklore buff can rub elbows and share ideas with academic students of folklore and with practitioners of the genuine material itself. The Smithsonian Institution's "Festival of American Folklife," founded in 1967, has also successfully combined education with entertainment by employing folklorists and folklore students to locate talented folk artisans and performers who are brought to Washington, D.C., for the annual event. Jan Harold Brunvand, *The Study of American Folklore* (3rd ed., p. 343)

For an interesting look at folk festivals, see David E. Whisnant's *Folk Festival Issues: A Report from a Seminar. March 2-3, 1978* (Los Angeles, CA: John Edwards Memorial Foundation at the Folklore and Mythology Center, University of California at Los Angeles, 1979) which includes a seminar summary and analysis of such concerns as tendencies, directions, and possibilities of folk festivals with illustrations of programs for various United States folk festivals. See also Steve Johnson's and Sheldon Oberman's *The Folk Festival Book* (Manitoba [CAN]: Turnstone Press, 1983), a case study of Winnipeg's Folk Festival, a July happening since 1974, "North America's largest and most successful folk festival."

Classification--Folk Festivals

Note: See also the motif- and type-index in Cohen's and Coffin's *The Folklore of American Holidays* (no. 1778).

1846.   Moe, John F. "Folk Festivals and Community Consciousness: Categories of the Festival Genre." *Folklore Forum* 10 (1977): 33-40.

Moe proposes "a three-level classification of event to descriptively analyze the individual festival"--participatory, semi-participatory, and nonparticipatory--as levels of audience/participant involvement.

Guides and Handbooks--Folk Festivals

1847. Spicer, Dorothy Gladys. *Folk Festivals and the Foreign Community*. New York: The Womans Press, 1923. 152p. Reprinted: Detroit, MI: Omnigraphics, 1990. LC 89-43343.

Although this is old, it still contains some viable information on, among other things, the technique of folk festival production along with discussions of various different festivals which celebrate the ethnicity of various countries.

1848. Wilson, Joe, and Lee Udall. *Folk Festivals: A Handbook for Organization and Management*. Knoxville: University of Tennessee Press, 1982. 278p. LC 81-23103; ISBN 0-87049-300-0 (c); 0-87049-361-1 (p).

Covers the history, concept, and definition of the folk festival with information on its administration, programming, publicity, hospitality, and production. Also presented are examples of festivals and samples of "festival communications" to participants, staff, media, audience, etc. The bibliography by Charles L. Perdue, Jr. is not on this topic but interestingly enough is a comprehensive "Bibliography of Folklore in America" (see no. 52). There is an index. Useful.

Directories--Folk Festivals
General/International

1849. Merin, Jennifer, with Elizabeth B. Burdick. *International Directory of Theatre, Dance, and Folklore Festivals*. Westport, CT: Greenwood, 1979. 480p. LC 79-9908; ISBN 0-313-20993-6.

This is a project of the International Theatre Institute of the United States. There are 850 festivals listed and described. Arrangement is alphabetical by country, Australia to Yugoslavia, then subdivided by province, state, etc. For each listing, the address, phone, director, dates, and a brief description of the event are given. Canada is included but the U.S. is not. There are several appendixes: a calendar of festivals, arranged by country, then given chronologically (e.g., **Australia**: January: Australian Day at the Rocks, Sydney [New South Wales]; Numeralla Folk Festival [New South Wales]). There is an index of festivals and a bibliography plus a listing of the number of festivals by country. Needs to be updated.

1850.   Shemanski, Frances. *A Guide to World Fairs and Festivals.* Westport, CT: Greenwood, 1985. 309p. LC 84-12810; ISBN 0-313-20786-0.

This work covers 75 countries and Canada, from Antigua to Zambia. The arrangement is by country, subdivided by city or town, province or state. Information for each festival includes name, date (month or time of the year), information on the origin of the festival, the history of the festival, its purpose, special features, special successes and future plans, and a description of each festival or event. Includes also a calendar of fairs and festivals by country and by types of festival. There is a subject guide (includes "folkloric: folk festivals," for example) and an index of festival names and subjects.

1851.   Smith, Douglas, and Nancy Barton, eds. *International Guide to Music Festivals.* New York: Quick Fox Press, 1980. 246p. LC 79-65948; ISBN 0-8256-3165-3.

There are separate sections for classical, folk music, and jazz festivals. International in scope and including both the U.S. and Canada, the arrangement is by country within each section, then by state or province. Gives place, date, description of event, sponsor, accommodations information, ticket information, and directions on how to get there. There is an index. Also needs to be updated.

Note: For other American directories, see the following entries, listed in the section on calendar rites: *American Indian Calendar* (no. 1775) and *Michigan Indian Festivals* (no. 1780), both of which include festival calendars.

1852.   Akin, Ronald, and Bruce Fingerhut, eds. *The Book of Festivals in the Midwest, 1980 & 1981.* South Bend, IN: Icarus Press, 1980. 197p. LC 80-10971; ISBN 0-89651-052-2. A 1987 edition has supposedly been published, but was not seen.

Covers festivals in Illinois, Indiana, Michigan, Ohio, Wisconsin, Iowa, Kentucky, Minnesota, and Missouri. Festivals are listed alphabetically by place, with the dates, locations, contact persons, admission fee information, description of the event, accommodations and food concessions information given. A list of campgrounds, a calendar of events, and an index are included.

1853.   Dunn, Elizabeth, ed. *The Quarto Festival Guide to Special Events in the U.S.A.* New York: Quarto, 1965. 158p. LC 65-3326.

There are arranged by area: New England, Middle Atlantic states, Deep South, Mid-West and Plains States, South West, Mountain State (including the Pacific West), Alaska, and Hawaii. Covers all festivals, some folk festivals included, arranged rather randomly within these areas. Gives times, dates, ticket information, directions on how to get there, and accommodations information. An index lists festivals alphabetically by name.

1854.   Gilbert, Elizabeth Rees, ed. *Fairs and Festivals: A Smithsonian Guide to Celebrations in Maryland, Virginia, and Washington, D.C.* Washington, DC: Smithsonian Institution Press, 1982. 160p. LC 82-600152; ISBN 0-87474-4733 (p).

This was produced by the Smithsonian Institution's Office of Folklife Programs in conjunction with the exhibition *Celebration: A World of Art and Ritual* (see no.1761). The arrangement is by month (January-December), then by holiday and date (e.g., Epiphany [January 6]; Ukrainian New Year's Day [January 14]). Movable holidays are listed by month. For each holiday, an explanation is given with a description of the celebration, the place, directions on how to get there, and contact person. Concludes with general information on organizations to contact about specific information on events in the District of Columbia, Virginia, and Maryland.

1855. Hill, Kathleen Thompson. *Festivals U.S.A..* New York: Wiley, 1988. 242p. LC 87-3479; ISBN 0-4716-2636-8 (p).

This guide is arranged by area: Northeast, Mid-Atlantic, Mid-South, Deep South, Midwest, West, Southwest, and by state within those areas. Many folk festivals are included; all are briefly described. There is a glossary and an index.

1856. National Folk Festival Association, comp. *Calendar of Folk Festivals & Related Events.* Washington: National Folk Festival Association. Annual.

Planned as an annual (though I only saw one issue), its purpose is to list by state (and province in Canada) all folk events, to give the contact person, and to tell whether it is an indoor or outdoor event, if camping facilities are available, and if food is available on the grounds. In 1976, 600 American and Canadian festivals were listed.

1857. Rabin, Carol Price. *Music Festivals in America: Classical, Opera, Jazz, Pops, Country, Old-time Fiddlers, Folk, Bluegrass, Cajun.* 4th ed. Great Barrington, MA: Berkshire Traveller, 1990 [1979]. 271. LC 90-901; ISBN 0-9301-4501-1.

Musical events of all kinds are listed first by type of music (jazz, ragtime, dixieland, folk and traditional, bluegrass, fiddlers, and country) and then by state. There is a description of each event, with information on who to write for tickets, and accommodations information. Included is a suggested reading list and an index by title of festival.

1858.　Shemanski, Frances. *A Guide to Fairs and Festivals in the United States.* Westport, CT: Greenwood, 1984. 339p. LC 82-21080; ISBN 0-313-21437-9.

This is a guide to fairs and festivals in the U.S. and the U.S. territories, including American Samoa, Puerto Rico, and the Virgin Islands. The festivals and fairs are explained, given histories, and described. The arrangement is alphabetic by state and then city. Also included is a calendar of fairs and festivals, arranged by state and chronologically. An appendix includes a subject guide to fairs, food festivals, arts and crafts festivals, ethnic festivals, folklore festivals, etc. There is a general index. (See no. 1850 for a companion guide to world festivals.)

1859.　Wasserman, Paul, managing ed. *Festivals Sourcebook: A Reference Guide to Fairs, Festivals, and Celebrations....* 2nd ed. Detroit, MI: Gale Research, 1984 [1977]. 721p. LC 84-160130; ISBN 0-8103-0323-x.

The full subtitle is "A Reference Guide to Fairs, Festivals and Celebrations in Agriculture, Antiques, the Arts, Theater and Drama, Arts and Crafts, Community, Dance, Ethnic Events, Film, Folk, Food and Drink, History, Indians, Marine, Music, Seasons, and Wildlife." This is the most comprehensive source for festival information. Festivals and fairs are divided into type or subject matter (e.g., agriculture, the arts, arts and crafts, ethnic events, etc.). Within these topical areas, the arrangement is by state, then city. For each event, the dates, contact person, and address are given with a description of the event that ranges from one sentence to a long paragraph. There is a chronological index (by month, then state, then event), an event name index, a geographical index, and a list of subjects and subject index.

1860.	Young, Judith. *Celebrations: America's Best Festivals, Jamborees, Carnivals, & Parades.* Santa Barbara, CA: Capra, 1986. 183p. LC 85-22413; ISBN 0-88496-242-3 (p). Reprinted: San Bernardino, CA: Borgo, 1989. LC 89-735; ISBN 0-80954-007-X.

Foreword is by Ray Bradbury. Divided into geographic sections (New England, Middle-Atlantic, South, Mid-west, Southwest, Rocky Mountain, Pacific coast, Hawaii, Canada, ethnic, and Native American). Celebrations are listed within those sections by season (summer-spring); many folk festivals are included. Information for each festival happening includes a brief description with pertinent information about time, place, and tickets. There is no index or bibliography.

Canada

1861.	Chicoine, Marie, et al. *Lâchés Lousses: Les Fêtes Populaires au Quebec, en Acadie et en Louisiane.* Montreal: Societé des Festivals Populaires du Quebec, 1983.

Contemporary festivals are arranged by type of festival, with folk festivals being one option. In French, with no index; there are terrific photos.

South and Central America

Note: see the following entries, which include festival events and calendars: *Calendar of Folklore Festivals of Argentina* (no. 1783) and *Fiesta Days of Mexico* (no. 1784).

Asia

Note: See Hideo Haga's *Japanese Folk Festivals Illustrated* for a listing of festival events in Japan (no. 1795).

1862. Dunn, Elizabeth, ed. *The Quarto Festival Guide to Special Events in Europe.* New York: Quarto, 1964. 159p. LC 65-28903.

Festivals are listed by country, Austria to Yugoslavia. Needs updating.

1863. Rabin, Carol Price. *Music Festivals in Europe and Britain.* Rev. and enl. Stockbridge, MA: Berkshire Traveller, 1984 [1980]. 190p. LC 79-55709; ISBN 912944-59-5.

Arranged by country from Austria to Yugoslavia, with the new edition adding Russia, Turkey, and Japan. The emphasis is classical music festivals, but there are some folk and popular music festivals, though they are hard to find despite a comprehensive index.

Europe--Great Britain

Note: See *Music Festivals in Europe and Britain,* directly above (no. 1863), and *Festivals in Britain and Ireland* (London: Rhinegold, 1987) which has a calendar of folk festivals in those countries.

FOLK RITUAL/RITES
Rites of Passage

A good introductory work to rites of passage is Arnold van Gennep's *The Rites of Passage* (trans. Monika B. Videdom and Gabrielle L. Caffee. Chicago, IL: University of Chicago Press, 1961), in which van Gennep set forth his theory of the rites of passage. An anthropological study of rites is Martha Nemes Fried's and Morton H. Fried's *Transitions: Four Rituals in Eight Cultures* (New York: W.W. Norton, 1980) which discusses birth, puberty, marriage, and death rites among the Tlingits (Alaskan Indians), Cubans, Hausa (Africa), Chinese, Taiwanese, and

Tikopians (Polynesia), etc. Carl Seaburg's *Great Occasions: Readings for the Celebration of Birth, Coming-of-Age, Marriage, and Death* (Boston, MA: Skinner House, 1988 [1968]) is concerned with modern rites of passage.

Annotated Collections--Rites of Passage-General

1864.   Cunnington, Phillis, and Catherine Lucas. *Costumes for Births, Marriages & Deaths*. New York: Barnes & Noble, 1972. 331p. LC 72-190906; ISBN 0-06-4913376.

The main focus of this work is a discussion of the customs concerning birth, marriage, and death and the proper attire for each. Includes lots of illustrations, an index, and a bibliography.

1865.   Morgenstern, Julian. *Rites of Birth, Marriage, Death, and Kindred Occasions Among the Semites*. Cincinnati, OH: Hebrew Union College Press, 1966. 320p. LC 66-11867. Reprinted: New York: Ktav Pub., 1973. LC 16219; ISBN 0-8706-8230-X.

A fascinating compendium of all types of rites of the Jews, Christians, and Muslims: birth rites, taboos, circumcision rites, baptism rites, sacrifices, marriage rites, and death rites. Includes also extensive notes, an index, and a bibliography.

Childbirth Rites

An excellent introductory text to birth rites is Ann Warren Turner's *Ritual of Birth from Prehistory to the Present* (New York: David McKay, 1978) which describes folkloric and mythic birth customs chronologically (in prehistory, ancient times, in hunting/gathering cultures, in urban cultures, multiple births, birth in modern times, etc.). Another historical overview is Judith Walzer Leavitt's *Brought to Bed: Childbearing in America, 1750-1950* (London: Oxford University Press, 1986) which includes a superb bibliography on pp. 219-261. Marie Campbell's *Folks Do Get*

Born (New York: Rinehart, 1946; reprinted: New York: Garland, 1984) is a text of the conversational material from Georgia's "granny midwives," who "ushered into the world 26 percent of all the babies born in Georgia."

There are many anthropological and/or ethnographic studies of childbirth, such as Brigitte Jordan's *Birth in Four Cultures: A Crosscultural Investigation of Childbirth in Yucatan, Holland, Sweden, and the United States* (Montreal: Eden Press Women's Publication, 1978) and Joan Richardson Hanks' *Maternity and Its Rituals in Bang Chan* (Ithaca, NY: Southeast Asia Program, Department of Asian Studies, Cornell University, 1963) which provides setting and background information, discusses body concept, diet, illness and medicine, pregnancy and parturition, birth of a child, and birth customs (pp. 58-82), and the place of the midwife.

Annotated Collections--Childbirth Rites

> Note: See also Barbara Frankel's *Childbirth in the Ghetto: Folk Beliefs of Negro Women in a North Philadelphia Hospital Ward* (no. 1469).

1866.   Goldsmith, Judith. *Childbirth Wisdom: From the World's Oldest Societies.* London: Congdon & Weed, 1984. 291p. LC 84-7685; ISBN 0-86553-126-9.

Many childbearing customs and ceremonies from throughout the world are given. A noteworthy bibliography lists books and articles within the following categories: general works, herbal medicines, Europe, the Middle East, Asia and Australia, Africa, North America, and Central and South America. There is an index.

1867.   Hart, Donn. *Southeast Asian Birth Customs.* New Haven, CT: HRAF, 1965. 303p. LC 65-18348.

Not seen.

1868.   Kelly, Isabel. *Folk Practices in North Mexico; Birth Customs, Folk Medicine, and Spiritualism in the Laguna Zone.* Austin, TX: Published for the Institute of Latin American States by the University of Texas Press, 1965. 166p. LC 64-10313. (Latin American monographs, 2)

Customs concerning pregnancy, birth, and postnatal care are listed in this anthropological work. Includes a bibliography and index.

1869.   Meltzer, David, ed. *Birth, an Anthology of Ancient Texts, Songs, Prayers, and Stories.* San Francisco, CA: North Point Press, 1981. 247p. LC 80-82441; ISBN 0-86547-004-9 (c); 0-86547-005-7 (p).

These are stories, myths, and rites from all religions, which include conception lore, information about magic protections (songs, birth charms, amulets, invocations, etc.), birth omens, pregnancy rites (couvade, songs, remedies, taboos), birth rites (customs from all over, including delivery songs), and events after birth (naming, baptizing, lullabies). There is a bibliography.

Puberty/Coming-of-Age Rites

Almost all the writing on puberty and initiation rites is anthropological. Frank Young's *Initiation Ceremonies; A Cross-Cultural Study of Status Dramatization* (New York: Bobbs-Merrill, 1965), on both male and female sex initiation rites, hypothesizes that "dramatization of status changes in a group are most elaborate when solidarity of that group is greatest." (p. 41) Ngoma Ngambu's *Initiation dans les Sociétés Traditionnelles Africaines (Le Cas Kong)* (Kinshasa: Presses Universitaires du Zaire, 1981) discusses education and initiation rites of males and females and describes and analyzes the traditional African initiation rites. Karen and Jeffery Paige's *The Politics of Reproductive Ritual* (Berkeley: University of California Press, 1981) is also concerned with both male and female public rites and rituals enacted on attainment of sexual maturity, covering specifically theories about and ceremonies marking male circumcision and menarche, sex segregation, and birth practices. Jean Sybil La Fontaine's *Initiation: Ritual Drama and Secret Knowledge Across the World* (Middlesex [ENG]: Penguin, 1985) is about male and female secret initiation oaths and ceremonies, spiritual powers, and marriage and maternity and includes a large section on initiation rites of girls.

Studies dealing specifically with female puberty rites include Harold E. Driver's and S.H. Riesenberg's "Hoof Rattles and Girls' Puberty Rites in North and South America" (*Indiana University Publications in Anthropology and Linguistics, Memoir; 4 and 5; International Journal of Linguistics* 16 [October 1950]: 1-30), Bruce Lincoln's *Emerging from the Chrysalis: Studies in Rituals of Women's Initiations* (Cambridge: Harvard University Press, 1981), and Jean-Thierry Maertens' *Le Corps Sexionné: Essai d'Anthropologie des Inscriptions Génitales* (Paris: Aubier Montaigne, 1978) which covers female genital rites, specifically clitorectomies, a subject covered earlier by Bruno Bettelheim in his *Symbolic Wounds* (Glencoe, IL: Free Press, 1954), a Freudian analysis of castration rites in men and women. Regional studies about female puberty rites include Audrey Richards' *Chisungu: A Girl's Initiation Ceremony Among the Bemba of Northern Rhodesia* (London: Faber & Faber, 1956) which describes and interprets a cultural puberty rite and includes ritual song texts, N.N. Bhattacharyya's *Indian Puberty Rites* (New Delhi: Munshiram Mansharlal, 1980), dealing with menstrual rites, ceremonial defloration, marriage, tattooing, hair-shaving, ear-piercing, and religious ceremonies of Indian girls, and Charlotte Johnson Frisbie's *Kinaaldá: A Study of the Navaho Girl's Puberty Ceremony* (Middletown, CT: Wesleyan University Press, 1967) which details and analyzes the ceremonies and the music of this American Indian rite. *Rituals of Manhood: Male Initiation in Papua New Guinea*, edited by Gilbert H. Herdt (Berkeley: University of California Press, 1987), is a group of essays on male ritual and meaning, ritual violence, etc. And finally, H. Corey's *African Figurines; Their Ceremonial Use in Puberty Rites in Tanganyika* (London: Faber & Faber, 1957) is a fascinating study of this traditional art form used in initiation rites in Central East Africa as well as a description of four separate rites for males and females.

Guide--Puberty Rites

1870.   Moore, Mafori, et al. *Transformation: A Rite of Passage Manual for African American Girls.* New York: Star Press, 1987. 83p. LC 87-178891.

This is a guide to preparing for a rite of passage ceremony. The manual discusses the history of the ritual, its background, and the goals, talks about preparation, how to organize and plan the ceremony, and the ceremony itself. It outlines meetings, gives activities, and provides worksheets. A similar guide is Julia and Nathan Hare's *Bringing the Black Boy to Manhood: The Passage* (San Francisco, CA: The Think Black Tank, 1985).

Courting and Marriage Rites

For a good introduction to courting, see Beth Bailey's *From Front Porch to Back Seat: Courtship in Twentieth-Century America* (Baltimore, MD: Johns Hopkins Press, 1988), about changing contemporary courtship customs. Also see E.S. Turner's *A History of Courting* (New York: E.P. Dutton, 1955), a chronological history of courtship rites with many customs given. For introductory material on marriage, see Kenneth Stevenson's *Nuptial Blessing: A Study of Christian Marriage Rites* (London: Oxford University Press, 1983) and Ann Monsarrat's *And the Bride Wore...The Study of the White Wedding* (London: Gentry, 1973), an historical account of marriage customs, focusing on dress. There are also numerous anthropological texts, such as Bruce Biggs' *Maori Marriage* (Wellington [NZ]: The Polynesian Society, 1960), essays on Maori attitudes toward sex, personal and social factors determining marriage, etc., and S.A. Husain's *Marriage Customs among Muslims in India: A Sociological Study of the Shia Marriage Customs* (New Delhi: Sterling, 1976). And, Marcia Seligson's *The Eternal Bliss Machine: America's Way of Wedding* (New York: William Morrow, 1973), a wonderful read, deals with the rituals of contemporary weddings, and, particularly, with the excess of (mostly Jewish) weddings.

Annotated Collections--Courtship and Marriage Rites

Note: See also no. 1772.

1871. Baker, Margaret. *Wedding Customs and Folklore*. London: David & Charles; Totowa, NJ: Rowman & Littlefield, 1977. 144p. LC 76-1937; ISBN 0-87471-821-x.

The customs are divided into categories: approach to marriage, courting days, the marriage contract, the wedding day, married life. There is a brief bibliography, an index, and a reference section. There is more text than listings of customs, but this is usable as a reference.

1872. Emrich, Duncan. *The Folklore of Love and Courtship; The Charms and Divinations, Superstitions and Beliefs....* New York: American Heritage, 1970. 51p. LC 70-102177; ISBN 0-8281-0056-x.

_____. *The Folklore of Weddings and Marriage; The Traditional Beliefs, Customs, Superstitions....* New York: American Heritage, 1970. 51p. LC 73-102178; ISBN 0-8281-0057-8.

These are both popularized, unannotated, unindexed collections of charms, divinations, superstitions, beliefs, customs, and omens of love and marriage and the marriage ceremony.

1873. Fielding, William John. *Strange Customs of Courtship and Marriage*. London: Souvenir Press, 1961 [1942]. 322p.

Covers curious mating customs, modern survivals of ancient customs, kissing customs, bundling customs, primitive marriage practices, primitive religious marital ideas, marriage taboos, and customs and rites dealing with chastity, child marriage, matriarchy, patriarchy, multiple marriages, marriage by capture, trial marriage, divorce, and romantic marriage. A similar work is George Ripley Scott's *Curious Customs of*

Sex and Marriage; An Inquiry Relating to All Races and Nations...
(London: Torchstream, 1953).

1874.   Tally, Frances. "American Folk Customs of Courtship and
        Marriage: The Bedroom," in *Forms upon the Frontier*, eds.
        Austin and Alta Fife and Henry H. Glassie. Logan: Utah State
        University, 1969, pp. 138-158. LC 62-628747.

        Accounts of courtship beliefs and customs are given in essay
format.

1875.   Tegg, William. *The Knot Tied; Marriage Ceremonies of All
        Nations.* London: 1877. 410p. Reprinted: Detroit, MI:
        Omnigraphics, 1989. LC 89-61543.

        This is a massive mess that includes wedding customs "past and
present in many lands" and special customs dealing with the symbols in
weddings (e.g., rings, flowers, etc.). Interesting only for historical and
comparative purposes. See also, for historical reasons, H.N. Hutchinson's
Marriage Customs in Many Lands (London: Seeley, 1897; reprinted:
Detroit, MI: Gale Research, 1974).

Death Rites

There are many studies of death rites and customs, such as Richard
Huntington's and Peter Metcalf's *Celebrations of Death: The
Anthropology of Mortuary Ritual* (New York: Cambridge University
Press, 1979) which deals with the anthropology of death ritual, reactions
to death, symbols of death, and rites of passage; it also contains a section
on American "deathways." Another general comparative study is Richard
A. Kalish's *Death and Dying: Views from Many Cultures* (Farmingdale,
NY: Baywood Press, 1980) which contains essays on death rites in other
cultures. A similar work is Philippe Ariès' *Western Attitudes Toward
Death; From the Middle Ages to the Present* (trans. Patricia M. Ranun.
Baltimore: Johns Hopkins University Press, 1974) and his later *The Hour*

of Our Death (New York: Knopf, 1981) which discuss theories and beliefs about death, burial, guarantees of eternity, tombs and epitaphs, the dead body, the denial of death, etc. And, Robert Hertz' *Sociologie Religieuse et Folklore* (Paris: Presses Universitaires de France, 1970) deals, in great part, with death and death customs.

Bertram S. Puckle's *Funeral Customs; Their Origin and Development* (London: T. Werner Laurie, 1926) is an early study of burial and mourning rites, funeral feasts, cremation, embalming, etc. Another early work is E. Bendann's *Death Customs: An Analytical Study of Burial Rites* (New York: Knopf, 1930) which compares the similarities and differences of customs concerning origins of death, cause of death, disposal of the dead, dread of the spirit, general attitudes towards the corpse, mourning customs, erection of a hut on the grave, purification feasts, life after death, taboos, and totemic concepts. Louis-Vincent Thomas' *Rites de Mort: Pour la Paix des Vivants* (Paris: Fayard, 1985) deals primarily with funeral rites as does Jessica Mitford's near classic *The American Way of Death* (New York: Simon & Schuster, 1963), a biting criticism of undertakers and the funeral business.

There are also a good number of studies limited to death and dying in America: *Death in America* (Philadelphia: University of Pennsylvania Press, 1975), edited by David Stannard and Philippe Ariès, is a book of essays on death and death culture, some of which are folkloric in content, such as Fernandez Kelly's "Death in Mexican Folk Culture"; Margaret Coffin's *Death in Early America: The History and Folklore of Customs and Superstitions of Early Medicine, Funerals, Burials, and Mourning* (Nashville, TN: Nelson, 1976) is a history, with a great deal of material on the folklore of customs and early American funeral and mourning superstitions. Philippe Ariès' *Death in America* (Philadelphia: University of Pennsylvania Press, 1975) deals with death ritual and funeral rites and customs, as does Charles O. Jackson's *Passing: the Vision of Death in America* (Westport, CT: Greenwood, 1977). And James Van Der Zee et al. have written a fascinating account of death and funeral rituals in Harlem, *The Harlem Book of the Dead* (Dobbs Ferry, NY: Morgan & Morgan, 1978), with photographs of and commentary on a Harlem funeral.

Also available are many regional studies of other cultures' death rites: Niles Stora's *Burial Customs of the Skolt Lapps* (*FF Communications*; 210, 1971) which includes burial customs and rites of the Scandinavian Lapps; Loring M. Danforth's *The Death Rituals of Rural Greece* (Princeton, NJ: Princeton University Press, 1982) which examines contemporary rural Greek burial and exhumation rites; Margaret Alexiou's *The Ritual Lament in Greek Tradition* (London: Cambridge University Press, 1974), a historical study; William A. Douglass' *Death in Murelaga: Funerary Ritual in a Spanish Basque Village* (Seattle: University of Washington Press, 1969); *Death in Portugal*, ed. Rui Feijo et al. (Oxford [ENG]: JASO, 1983), essays about Portuguese death rites; Louis-Vincent Thomas' *La Mort Africaine: Idéologie Funéraire en Afrique Noire* (Paris: Payr, 1982); T.C. Lai's *To the Yellow Springs: The Chinese View of Death* (Hong Kong: Joint Publishing with Kelly Walsh, 1983); and *Death Ritual in Late Imperial and Modern China* (Berkeley: University of California Press, 1988), by James L. Watson and Evelyn S. Rawski. See also Geoffrey Gorer's *Death, Grief, and Mourning in Contemporary Britain* (London: Cresset Press, 1965), Anne Gordon's *Death is for the Living* (Edinburgh: Paul Harris, 1984), about Scottish death customs, and Graeme M. Griffin's and Des Tobin's *In the Midst of Life: Australian Response to Death* (Melbourne: Melbourne University Press, 1982).

And finally, Barbara Jones' *Design for Death* (Indianapolis, IN: Bobbs-Merrill, 1967) deals with ritual artifacts for the dead and discusses them transculturally (e.g., shrouds, hearses, undertakers' shops, corpses, flowers, cemeteries, tombs, relics, etc.).

There are two exhibition catalogs listed in Chapter 7, Martha Pike's and Janice Gray Armstrong's *A Time to Mourn: Expressions of Grief in the Nineteenth Century* (no. 2062), and Anita Schorsch's *Mourning Becomes America: Mourning Art in the New Nation* (no. 2064); they deal with death ritual paintings and artifacts.

Bibliography--Death Rites

1876.   Goody, Jack. "Death and the Interpretation of Culture: A Bibliographic Overview," in *Death in America*, ed. Philippe

Ariès and David E. Stannard. Philadelphia: University of Pennsylvania Press, 1975. pp. 1-8. LC 75-10124; ISBN 0-8122-7695-7.

This bibliographic essay discusses references that are useful in the comparative study of death customs and cultural organization.

Annotated Collections--Death Rites

1877. Enright, D.J., ed. *Oxford Book of Death*. New York: Oxford University Press, 1983. 351p. LC 82-14341; ISBN 0-19-214129-5.

Essays, narration, prose, and verse are taken from the world's best works on death and cover such topics as the hour of death, suicide, mourning, graveyards and funerals, children's deaths, epitaphs, requiems, and last words.

1878. Habenstein, Robert, and William M. Lamers. *Funeral Customs the World Over*. 2nd rev. ed. Milwaukee, WI: Bulfin Printers, 1974 [1960]. 866p. LC 63-18424.

These customs about funerals are arranged by place: Asia, Africa, Oceania, Europe, Latin America, Canada, and the U.S.

1879. Meltzer, David, ed. *Death: An Anthology of Ancient Texts, Customs, Songs, Prayers, and Stories*. San Francisco, CA: North Point Press, 1984. 322p. LC 83-61396; ISBN 0-86547-131-2.

There are 192 prose entries, divided into the following headings: entering, approaching the realm; birth of death, origin; omens, portents, warnings, protections; the moment; where the dead go, where they stay; removing the dead, funerals; the living remaining, mourning. Collected from many countries and cultures from the present and the past. Sources are given, but there is no index.

1880. Montell, William Lynwood. *Ghosts Along the Cumberland: Deathlore in the Kentucky Foothills*. Knoxville: University of Tennessee Press, 1975. 240p. LC 74- 032241; ISBN 0-87049-165-2. Note: A new edition was scheduled for 1989, but as of summer 1991 I cannot find any information on it.

Includes 489 stories and variants about death omens, the dead, and the return of the dead. There is a glossary, a select bibliography, an index of collectors, an index of tale types and motifs, and a general index.

1881. Ó Súilleabháin, Seán. *Irish Wake Amusements*. Dublin: Mercier Press, 1976 [1967]. 188p. ISBN 0-8534-2145-5 (p).

In chapter format, this covers games, mocking and tainting, story-telling, dancing, and contests of strengths. Sources are given and there is an index.

FOLK RITUAL
Folk Drama

A definition of **folk drama** is elusive. See Thomas A. Green's "Toward a Definition of Folk Drama" (*Journal of American Folklore* 91 [1978]: 843-850) for a discussion. Often linked to festival activities, specific holidays, and dance and song, folk drama is often studied as a part of ritual and/or myth. Traditional plays, such as the British **mummers' play**, the Mexican **pastorela**, the Spanish **Corpus Christi** play, even the American **minstrel show**, have been studied in great depth by folklore and ritual scholars.

Three very useful essays on folk drama are Roger D. Abrahams' "Folk Drama" (pp. 351-362), in *Folklore and Folklife*, edited by Richard M. Dorson; Robert C. Toll's "Folklore on the American Stage" (pp. 247-256), in *Handbook of Folklore*, edited by Dorson; and Jan Brunvand's "Folk Dances and Drama," in his *Study of American Folklore* (3rd ed., pp. 350-366). See also Robert Spiller et al.'s "Folk Drama," in their *Literary History of the United States* (4th ed., New York: Macmillan, 1974), with an historic overview of folk drama in Vol. 1 and a brief bibliography in Vol. 2. And, there is a special issue of the *Journal of American Folklore* devoted to folk drama (Vol. 94, 1981); it is edited by Thomas A. Green.

The anthropologist Victor W. Turner studied ritual theater. In *From Ritual to Theatre: The Human Seriousness of Play* (New York: Performing Arts Journal Publications, 1982) he looked at the relationship between ritual and drama, while a later work, *The Anthropology of Performance* (New York: PAJ Publications, 1986), is concerned with both ritualistic and aesthetic drama--carnivals, social dramas, film, etc.

There are many, many studies of particular types of folk dramas and/or the folk drama of one culture. British folk drama has been widely studied. Roger D. Abrahams, in his article cited directly above, says that Robert Withington's *English Pageantry: An Historical Outline* (2 vols., London: Benjamin Blom, 1963) "is central to the understanding of the varieties of festival dramatic forms." (p. 362) It includes a section on aspects of folk mumming, a chronological overview of pageantry up to the beginning of the twentieth century, and a final discussion of folk pageantry as a survival form. Alex Helm's *Cheshire Folk Drama* (Ibnstock [ENG]: Guizer, 1968) and his *Staffordshire Folk Drama* (Ibnstock [ENG]: Guizer, 1984) are typical of several overviews of British folk drama. The English mummers' play has been studied extensively. R.J.E. Tiddy's *The Mummers' Play* (Oxford: Clarendon, 1923) is probably the most famous; Alan Brody's *The English Mummers and Their Plays; Traces of Ancient Mystery* (Philadelphia: University of Pennsylvania, 1970) is a newer one. Other studies of the English mummers' play are Alex Helm's *The English Mummers' Play* (London and Totowa, NJ: D.S. Brewer and Rowman & Littlefield for the Folk Lore Society, 1980) and Edmund Kerchever Chambers' *The English Folk-play* (Oxford: Clarendon, 1933) which discusses the mummers' play--its origins and variants--the plough plays, the Revesby play, and the Morris dance. Chambers' 2-volume *The Medieval Stage* (Oxford: Clarendon, 1967 [1903]) covers minstrelsy and folk drama (village festivals, festival plays, the May-game), the sword dance, the mummers' play, and New Year's customs as well as religious drama. Violet Alford's *Sword Dance and Drama* (Philadelphia, PA: Dufours, 1965 [1962]) relates the sword dance, a ritual dance, to drama or dramatic events in Europe and England; it contains a separate chapter on English folk drama, the mummers' play, and the plough play. Cecil

Sharp has covered ritual dance in his *The Morris Book...* (London: Novello, 1912-1924) and *The Sword Dances of Northern England* (London: Novello, 1912) and *The Sword Dances of England* (London: Novello, 1951 [1900]). V.A. Kolve's *The Play Called Corpus Christi* (Stanford, CA: Stanford University Press, 1966) discusses "this homemade" play, which took 15 hours to perform and was "for 200 years the most truly popular drama England had ever known." And finally, David Wiles' *The Early Plays of Robin Hood* (London: D.S. Brewer, 1981) studies the games and plays concerning Robin Hood which, Wiles says, occurred in the fifteenth century when the legendary character also became known in ballads.

Two studies of Irish folk drama are Alan Gailey's *Irish Folk Drama* (Dublin: Mercier Press, 1969) and Henry Glassie's *All Silver and No Brass: An Irish Christmas Mumming* (Bloomington: Indiana University Press, 1975), which includes interviews with Irish men and women about the Christmas mummers and essays on the survival, performance, meaning, and function of the play. Spanish religious drama has been studied in Ricardo Arias' *The Spanish Sacramental Plays* (Boston, MA: Twayne, 1980), focusing on the plays presented for the feast of Corpus Christi. Spanish-American folk drama has been studied by Richard M. Dorson, who covers **los pastores** (episodes from the Bible) in his *American Folklore* (pp. 104-107) and includes a bibliography of Spanish-American folk drama (pp. 293); Arthur Campa looks at the origins of folk drama in "El Origen y la Naturaleza del Drama Folklorico" (*Folklore Americas* 20 [December 1960]: 13-47). John Englekirk provided "Notes on the Repertoire of the Northern Mexican Spanish Folktheater" (in *Southern Folklore Quarterly* 4 [December 1940]: 227-237) and studied the New Mexican passion play in a two-part article in *Western Folklore* (Vol. 25 [1966]: 17-33; 105-121). The Mexican shepherds' play (a still active liturgical folk drama) was studied by Juan B. Rael in his *Sources and Diffusion of the Mexican Shepherds' Plays* (Guadalajara [MEX]: Libreria la Joyita, 1965). Native American ritual drama has been studied extensively by anthropologists: Charlotte J. Frisbie's *Southwestern Indian Ritual Drama* (Prospect Heights, IL: Waveland Press, 1989 [1980]) is a good introductory work in this field.

The early anthropologist, Martha Warren Beckwith, studied "Christmas Mumming in Jamaica," in *Jamaica Folk-Lore* (New York: American

Folk-Lore Society, 1928; reprinted: New York: Kraus, 1969). Herbert Halpert and G.M. Story have edited *Christmas Mumming in Newfoundland: Essays in Anthropology, Folklore, and History* (Toronto: University of Toronto Press for Memorial University of Newfoundland, 1990 [1969]), seminar papers from a 1963 conference by Halpert and Story, John Szwed, and others.

African folk drama has been studied in Janet Beik's *Hausa Theatre in Niger: A Contemporary Oral Art* (New York: Garland, 1987) and Peter Larlham's *Black Theater, Dance, and Ritual in South Africa* (Ann Arbor, MI: UMI Press, 1985), both of which deal in part with contemporary African folk drama. Victor Turner also studied African ritual drama. His *Chihamba, the White Spirit: A Ritual Drama of the Ndembi* (New York: Humanities Press for the Rhodes-Livingstone Institute, 1962) is a medical ritual drama.

Asian folk drama has also been widely studied: Yoshinobu Inoura and Toshio Kawatake looked at *The Traditional Theater of Japan* (New York: Weatherhill, 1981), covering ancient and medieval drama and some contemporary drama. Indian folk drama has also been intensively studied. Balawanta Garagi's *Folk Theater of India* (Seattle: University of Washington Press, 1966) is an overview as is Kapila Vatsyayan's *Traditional Indian Theatre: Multiple Streams* (New Delhi: National Book Trust, 1980). John Stratton Hawley and Shrivatsa Goswami studied *At Play with Krishna: Pilgrimage Dramas from Brindavan* (Princeton, NJ: Princeton University Press, 1981). Jagdish C. Mathur has looked at *Drama in Rural India* (New York: Indian Council for Cultural Relations, 1964) and E.R. Sarachchandra has studied *The Folk Drama of Ceylon* (2nd ed., Colombo: Dept. of Cultural Affairs, 1966).

Be sure to consult the section on Dance, in Chapter 4, as many of the ritual dances (e.g., the Morris and sword dances) are included in that section.

Bibliography--Folk Drama

1882.   Acuña, René. *El Teatro Popular en Hispanoamérica: Una Bibliografía Anotada.* Mexico: Universidad Nacional Autónoma de Mexico, Instituto de Investigaciones Filólogicas, Centro de Estudios Literarios, 1979. 114p. LC 80-132031; ISBN 968-58-2530-0.

There are 380 annotated entries, mostly in Spanish, on Spanish and Hispanic folk drama, including reference works, play texts, religious works, etc. Covers catalogs, bibliographies, regional works, then specific types of American and Spanish-American folk dramas. There is only an author index.

1883. Penninger, Frieda Elaine. *English Drama to 1660 (Excluding Shakespeare): A Guide to Information Sources*. Detroit, MI: Gale Research, 1976. 370p. LC 73-16988; ISBN 0-8103-1223-9. (American literature, English literature, and world literatures in English; v. 5)

There is a section on general works (bibliographies, histories, text collections, etc.) and sections on specific dramatists. See especially, the section called "Folklore and the folk play" (pp. 96-100).

1884. Stratman, Carl Joseph. *Bibliography of Medieval Drama*. 2 vols. 2nd ed., rev. and enl. New York: Ungar, 1972 [1954]. LC 78-163141; ISBN 0-8044-32724.

Covers liturgical and religious drama, mystery and miracle plays, Everyman plays, etc. There is a separate section on **folk drama**. There are 9,000 entries in all. Indexed. This work has been updated by the *Bibliography of Medieval Drama, 1969-1972*, compiled and edited by Maria Spaeth Murphy and Jane Hoy and the *Bibliography of Medieval Drama, 1973-1976*, compiled by Maria Spaeth Murphy et al. (both, Emporia, KS: School of Graduate and Professional Studies of the Emporia State University, 1986), and by the *Bibliography of Medieval Drama, 1977-1980*, compiled by Carole Ferguson and Jane Hoy (Emporia, KS: Emporia State University, 1988).

1885. Whalon, Marion K. *Performing Arts Research: A Guide to Information Sources.* Detroit, MI: Gale Research, 1976. 280p. LC 75-13828; ISBN 0-8103-1364-2. (Performing arts information guide series; v. 1)

There are a few entries cited for **folk drama** as well as some general folklore bibliographies, but mostly this work deals with contemporary theater, dance, costume, film, etc.

Classification--Folk Drama

1886. Halpert, Herbert. "A Typology of Mumming," in *Christmas Mumming in Newfoundland: Essays in Anthropology, Folklore, and History.* 2nd ed. Halpert and G.M. Story. Published for Memorial University of Newfoundland. Toronto: University of Toronto Press, 1990 [1969]. 246p. LC 89-94547; ISBN 0-8020-6767-0 (c); 0-8027-0655 (p).

This is a classification of mumming into two grouped pairs: A) the informal visit and the visit with the formal performance and B) the informal outdoor behavior and the formal outdoor movement. See also E.C. Cawte's *English Ritual Drama: A Geographical Index* (no. 1888), in which the author provides a typology based on the central action of St George mumming plays.

Guide--Folk Drama

1887. Sampson, Henry T. *Blacks in Blackface: A Source Book on Early Black Musical Shows.* Metuchen, NJ: Scarecrow Press, 1980. 552p. LC 80-15048; ISBN 0-8108-1318-1.

Contains a historical overview of black minstrel shows and musical comedies from 1900-1941, giving synopses of shows, alphabetically arranged by title. Also includes brief biographies of "blackface" actors and a partial list of black musical shows. There is an index.

Index--Folk Drama

1888.   Cawte, E.C., et al. *English Ritual Drama: A Geographical Index.*
London: The Folk-Lore Society, 1967. 132p. LC 72-498101.
(Folk-Lore Society Publications, 127)

Gives geographical distributions of the ceremonial dances and
associated customs of English traditional drama, with emphasis on the St.
George mumming play. Appendix I is a table of locations of the play
texts in English counties, Wales, Scotland, Ireland, Canada, the Leeward
Islands, and the United States. Appendix II includes examples of the
texts. A very comprehensive bibliography can be found on pp. 94-132.

Play Texts--Folk Drama

Note: This is a highly select listing of play texts; they are
arranged geographically. Many of the studies cited in the
introduction to this section also include whole or partial play
texts.

Africa

1889.   Bame, Kwabena N. *Come to Laugh: African Traditional Theatre
in Ghana.* New York: L. Barber, 1985. 190p. LC 84-6259; ISBN
0-936508-078 (c); 0-936508-086 (p).

The focus is on one type of African folk drama--comic plays
staged by concert parties (itinerant theater troupes). Eight Ghanian concert
parties are synopsized and transcribed, two completely.

The Americas
North America

1890.   Campa, Arthur L. *"Los Comanches": A New Mexican Folk
Drama.* Albuquerque: University of New Mexico Press, 1942.
43p. (*University of New Mexico Bulletin,* 376; Language series;
v. 7, 1)

This Spanish dance drama, enacted primarily during the harvest season and revived every year, is considered more religious than seasonal. It deals with the history of early colonization and the struggle of the Comanches. The central theme is the kidnapping of the Christ child from a New Mexican village during the Christmas season and what ensues. The play text, from a 1864 manuscript, is entirely in Spanish. A bibliography is appended.

1891.   Campa, Arthur L. *Spanish Religious Folktheatre in the Southwest* (2nd cycle). Albuquerque: University of New Mexico Press, 1934. 157p. (*University of New Mexico Bulletin*; v. 5, 2)

_____. *Spanish Religious Folktheatre in the Spanish Southwest*. Albuquerque: University of New Mexico Press, 1934. 71p. (*University of New Mexico Bulletin*; v. 5, 1)

These two volumes include texts of many religious plays based on the old and new testaments, all in Spanish.

1892.   Engle, Gary D., ed. *This Grotesque Essence: Plays from the American Minstrel Stage*. Baton Rouge: Louisiana State University Press, 1978. 299p. LC 77-16617; ISBN 0-8071-0370-5.

The editor, in his introduction, calls American minstrelsy "a democratic art"; there are 22 plays ("afterpieces") and a brief annotated bibliography. For a good historical overview of American minstrelsy, also see Robert Toll's *Blacking Up: The Minstrel Show in Nineteenth-Century America* (New York: Oxford University Press, 1977 [1974]).

1893.   Radin, Paul. *The Road of Life and Death: A Ritual Drama of the American Indians*. New York: Pantheon, 1945. 345p. LC 46-923.

This is an explanation and text of the Winnebago medicine rite in drama format, done in five parts: the ritual of tears, the ritual of purification, the ritual of expectation, the ritual of rewards, and the ritual of life, death, and rebirth.

Canada

1894. Halpert, Herbert, and G.M. Story, eds. *Christmas Mumming in Newfoundland: Essays in Anthropology, Folklore, and History.* 2nd ed. Published for Memorial University of Newfoundland. Toronto: University of Toronto Press, 1990 [1969]. 246p. LC 89-94547; ISBN 0-8027-0655.

Includes three printed texts. See also Antoinette Taylor's "An English Christmas Party" (no. 1905) and Marie Campbell's "Survivals of Old Folk Drama in the Kentucky Mountains" (*Journal of American Folklore* 51 [1938]: 10-24) a text of a mummers' play performed in America.

West Indies

1895. Beckwith, Martha Warren. "Christmas Mumming in Jamaica," in *Jamaica Folk-Lore.* New York: American Folk-Lore Society, 1928. (Memoirs of the American Folk-Lore Society; v. 21). Reprinted: New York: Kraus, 1969.

This gives full texts and variants, along with songs, verses, and descriptions of how each should be produced.

South and Central America

Note: See the bibliography (no. 1882) and the play texts compiled by Arthur Campa listed above (nos. 1890, 1891).

1896. Barber, George C., ed. and trans. *The Shepherds' Play of the Prodigal Son (Coloquio de Pastores del Hijo Pródigo): A Folk Drama of Old Mexico.* Berkeley: University of California Press, 1953. 167p. (Folklore studies, 2)

The introduction covers religious folk drama in Spanish Mexico, variations and distribution of religious folk drama, origin, language style and translations and contextual information about actual performers and performances, with a text of the play. Includes notes and a bibliography.

1897.   Cole, M.R., ed. and trans. *Los Pastores; A Mexican Play of the Nativity*. Boston, MA: Published for the American Folk-Lore Society by Houghton Mifflin, 1907. 234p. LC 07-11974. (Memoirs of the American Folk-Lore Society; v. 9). Reprinted: New York: Kraus, 1969.

This is the full text with notes of "an old religious play of Mexican origin."

1898.   Rael, Juan B., coll.; Michael J. Doudoroff, ed. *'Moros y Cristianos' in Zacatecas: Text of a Mexican Folk Play*. Lawrence, KS: Amadeo Concha Press, 1981. 43p. LC 81-1558; ISBN 0-839448-00-9.

The introduction to the text discusses this "generally humorless, crudely written, verbose and bombastic, historically inaccurate, culturally anachronistic, stereotype-laden" play about the Moors and the Christians. The play or pageant was performed at **Moros y Cristianos** fiestas. Aside from a history of the play, a contextual study, and the full text, there is a useful selected, annotated bibliography.

1899.   Robe, Stanley L., ed. and intro. *Coloquios de Pastores from Jalisco, Mexico*. Berkeley: University of California Press, 1954. 158p. (Folklore studies, 4)

This "Christmas play...still presented yearly in the small towns and rural communities...is an expression of sincere religious devotion." Robe discusses Spanish and European origins, describes and analyzes performances--casting, costume, verse, music, etc., and gives two full-text versions of the play. There is an appendix of music, notes, and a bibliography.

Asia

Note: John Stratton Hawley's and Shrivasta Goswami's *At Play with Krishna*... (Princeton, NJ: Princeton University Press, 1981), mentioned in the headnote to this section, also includes some play dialogue.

1900.   Cho, Oh Kon. *Korean Puppet Theatre: Kkoktu Kaksi.* East Lansing, MI: Asian Studies Center, Michigan State University, 1979. 188p. LC 79-623953. (Asian Studies Center, East Asian series; Occasional paper, 6)

The author gives an historical account and discusses the genre and elements of production. There are three full-length play texts given with a glossary and bibliography.

1901.   Gamble, Sidney D. *Chinese Village Plays from the Ting Hsien Region.* Amsterdam: Philo Press, 1970. 782p. LC 72-134043; ISBN 90-6022400-0.

Includes texts of 48 Chinese rural plays as staged by villagers from Ting Hsien, a province in northern China; each is introduced and explained and has extensive notes.

Europe

Note: Folk drama texts, such as Leopold Schmidt's *Le Théâtre Populaire Europeen* (Paris: Maisonneuve et Larose, 1965), which excerpts 30 traditional plays, are in non-English languages.

Europe--Great Britain

Note: Several of the studies listed in the headnote to this section include full play texts or fragments. See, for example, Alan Gailey's *Irish Folk Drama*, with texts mostly of mummers' plays, Alan Brody's *The English Mummers and Their Plays*, with texts in the appendix, R.J.E. Tiddy's *The Mummers' Play*, which includes a large section, "The Plays" (pp. 140-257), with several short play texts, and E.K. Chambers' *The English Folkplay* which includes several texts within the study of mummers' plays.

1902.   Baskervill, Charles. *The Elizabethan Jig and Related Song Drama.* New York: Dover, 1965 [1929]. 642p. LC 65-12255.

Jigs were "an afterpiece in the form of a brief farce which was sung and accompanied by dancing." Part II contains the texts in ballad format for the most part.

1903.   Helm, Alex. *The Chapbook Mummers' Plays: A Study of the Printed Versions of North-West of England.* Ibnstock [ENG]: Guizer Press, 1969. 54p. LC 73-478286; ISBN 0-90206-500-9.

Includes texts and notes on dating of the plays, illustrations used with the printed texts, sources, and the end product. There is also a checklist of these mummers' plays, which were printed in chapbook format.

1904.   Helm, Alex. *The English Mummers' Play.* London and Totowa, NJ: Published by D.S. Brewer and Rowman & Littlefield for the Folk-Lore Society, 1980. 116p. ISBN 0-85991-067-9 (UK): 0-8476-7014-7 (US).

There is a lengthy discussion on the wooing ceremonies, sword dance ceremonies, hero-combat ceremonies, and "abnormal" texts that appeared abroad. Appendix I includes the chapbook texts, and Appendix II is an explanation of these texts. A long bibliography (pp. 101-112) is noteworthy. There is an index. See also *Six Mummers' Acts,* by Helm and E.C. Cawte (Ibnstock: Guizer, 1968).

1905.   Taylor, Antoinette. "An English Christmas Party." *Journal of American Folklore* 22 (1909): 389-394.

Play text, collected from a man who had taken part in a mummers' play 35 years earlier, is printed in two parts.

FOLK RITUAL
Folk Games

There has been a large amount of scholarly work done on the subject of play and games.

Jan Brunvand's "Folk Games," in his *Study of American Folklore* (3rd ed., pp. 378-397), is a good place to start. Also useful are several journal articles on games, especially Elliott Orvig's "Folk Games and Game Theory" (*Folklore Forum* 1 [1968]: 8-15) and Alan Dundes' "On Game Morphology: A Study of the Structure of Non-Verbal Folklore" (no. 1916). See also Don Yoder's "Children's Games: Folk-Cultural Questionnaire, No. 16" (*Pennsylvania Folklife* 18 [1970]) and the special issue on games in *Keystone Folklore Quarterly* (Vol. 11 [1966]). As beginning works, the studies of Brian Sutton-Smith, an expert on children's game and play, should be consulted, especially his books of essays, *The Folkgames of Children* (Austin: published for the American Folklore Society by the University of Texas, 1972); it combines essays that provide an historical, anthropological, psychological, and "united" approach to the study of children's and adolescents' games. Other works by Sutton-Smith include two compilations of articles from leading folklore and anthropology journals: *A Children's Games Anthology: Studies in Folklore and Anthropology* (New York: Arno, 1976) which describes games from all over the world, and his *The Games of the Americas: A Book of Readings* (New York: Arno, 1976), with readings about play and games in Central and South America (Part I) and in North America (Part II).

There are also many full-length studies of games. Two classic works are Johan Huizinga's *Homo Ludens: A Study of the Play Element in Culture* (Boston, MA: Beacon Press, 1950), in which the author discusses the nature and significance of play as a cultural phenomenon, and Roger Caillois' *Man, Play, and Games* (New York: Free Press of Glencoe, 1961). Elliot Avedon and Brian Sutton-Smith's *The Study of Games* (New

York: John Wiley, 1971) is divided into the following large sections with readings and a bibliography for each: history and origins of games (which has three articles on the folklore of games), the usage of games, and structure and function. And Amanda Dargan's and Steven Zeitlin's *City Play* (New Brunswick, NJ: Rutgers University Press, 1990) is an impressive overview of play in urban society with chapters on "incorporation," about block games mostly, on "transformation," about pretend with toys and dress-up, and on "control," about turf; there is an afterword by Barbara Kirschenblatt-Gimblett and a selected bibliography.

Anthropological studies of play are particularly numerous: David F. Lancy and B. Allan Tindall edited *The Anthropological Study of Play: Problems and Prospects: Proceedings of the 1st Annual Meeting of the Association for the Anthropological Study of Play* (Cornwall, NY: Leisure Press, 1976) with essays on theoretical approaches in the study of play and ethnographic studies of children's games and acculturating societies, etc. The proceedings from the 2nd annual meeting of the Association for the Anthropological Study of Play (in memory of B. Allan Tindall) was titled *Studies in the Anthropology of Play* (West Point, NY: Leisure Press, 1977), edited by Phillip Stevens, Jr. The 1977 proceedings, *Play: Anthropological Perspectives*, with essays linked around the theoretical contributions to the study of play, play and cultural values, and the play-world of children, was edited by Michael Salter (West Point, NY: Leisure Press, 1978). Helen B. Schwartzman edited the 1978 annual proceedings, *Play and Culture* (West Point, NY: Leisure Press, 1980) with articles on play theory, the ritual dimensions of play, linguistic play, children's play, and an article by Charles Adams, "Distinctive Features of Play and Games: A Folk Model from South Africa." The proceedings from 1979, *Play as Context*, with essays on play and ritual, was edited by Alyce Taylor Cheska (West Point, NY: Leisure Press, 1981).

Other issues of proceedings of the Association for the Anthropological Study of Play include Bernard Mergen's *Cultural Dimensions of Play, Games, and Sport* (Champaign, IL: Human Kinetics Publishers, 1986) with essays grouped around descriptions of play, theories of play, games, and sports and Kendall Blanchard's *The Many Faces of Play* (Champaign, IL: Human Kinetics, 1986) which has a chapter on play in celebration and ritual. See also Jacques Ehrmann's *Game, Play, Literature* (Boston, MA: Beacon, 1971), with several articles of interest to the folklorist, Brian

Sutton-Smith's and Diana Kelly-Byrne's *The Masks of Play* (New York: Leisure Press, 1984) which has articles on festival play, adult recreation and games, child's play, and the theory of human play, and Helen B. Schwartzman's *Transformations: The Anthropology of Children's Play* (New York: Plenum Press, 1978) which is ethnographic in focus, covering children's play in Asia, Oceania, Central and South America, North America, Africa, the Near East, and Europe.

There are several histories of play and games, notably Brian Sutton-Smith's *A History of Children's Play: New Zealand, 1840-1950* (Philadelphia: University of Pennsylvania Press, 1981) and B.G. Rosenberg's and Brian Sutton-Smith's "Sixty Years of Historical Change in the Game Preference of American Children" (*Journal of American Folklore* 74 [1961]:17-46; also in *The Folkgames of Children*, no. 1969). Also, there are several studies of play and games as practiced by one group of people, such as Cary Goodman's *Choosing Sides: Playground and Street Life on the Lower East Side* (New York: Schocken, 1979), a fascinating book, which discusses organized play among Jewish youth on the streets and school playgrounds of the lower East Side of New York.

Finally, there is the Association for the Anthropological Study of Play, which publishes a quarterly newsletter. It is available from its editor, Brian Sutton-Smith, from the Graduate School of Education, University of Pennsylvania.

This section of folk games includes a subsection on **String Games**, a specialized aspect of folk games. The section on **Play-party Games** is included in the chapter on folk music and dance, Chapter 4. Other relevant sections of this work should be searched in conjunction with a study on folk games, notably **Children's Rhymes** in Chapter 3, **Children's Oral Lore**, also in Chapter 3, and **Folk Toys** in Chapter 7.

This section covers folk games in general; it is followed by a brief section on **String Games.**

Bibliographies--Folk Games

1906. Avedon, Elliot M., and Brian Sutton-Smith. "Selected References," in *The Study of Games*. New York: John Wiley, 1971. 530p. 217-223. 530p. Reprinted: Huntington, NY: R.E. Krieger, 1979. LC 79-21194; ISBN 0-8957-4045-2.

This bibliography, a part of a section on folklore sources in games, contains general references on children's games, references on children's games in specific cultures, games with music, and games with string.

1907. Brewster, Paul G. "A Partial List of Books and Articles on Games." *Southern Folklore Quarterly* 34 (1970): 353-364.

Brewster omits American books and articles as well as books and articles on string figures and tricks which, he says, "in the strict sense of the word, can hardly be classed as games." The arrangement is by country (**Africa** to **Vietnam**) and includes specialized studies and ethnological works especially.

1908. Daiken, Leslie H. "Children's Games: A Bibliography." *Folklore* 61 (1950): 218-222.

This bibliography covers books about ancient and medieval games, Oriental and primitive games, and English and Scottish games with a separate listing of Irish periodicals and references. Sources and titles are international in scope. The listing is chronological within the topics named above.

1909. Mergen, Bernard. "Games and Toys," in *Handbook of American Popular Culture*, 2 vols., ed. M. Thomas Inge. Rev. and enl. ed. This section is in Vol. 1. Westport, CT: Greenwood, 1989. pp. 497-524. LC 88-39032; ISBN 0-313-25406-0 (set).

This is a bibliographic essay, discussing historical works, reference works, research collections, history and criticism, and anthologies. An appended bibliography includes books, articles, and periodicals.

1910. Mergen, Bernard. *Play and Playthings: A Reference Guide.* Westport, CT: Greenwood, 1982. 281p. LC 82-6139; ISBN 0-313-22136-7. (Series in American popular culture)

This is the major bibliographic work on games and play. It is divided into two sections: Part I covers the history of children at play in the United States; Part II is a bibliographic guide which covers, in bibliographic essay format, books and articles on the history of childhood and play, source material for historical study, autobiographies, books and articles on games and play in child development, on playgrounds, on toys, on museums, and on the material aspects of play. Of particular interest, is a section of material on the anthropology and folklore of play (pp. 204-211). The appendix includes a list of research collections and a list of the most useful books on children's play.

1911. Scheffler, Lillian. "The Study of Traditional Games in Mexico: Bibliographical Analysis and Current Research," in *Anthropological Study of Play: Problems and Prospects*, ed. David F. Lancy and B. Allan Tindall. Cornwall, NY: Leisure Press, 1976. pp. 58-66. LC 80-492497.

This bibliographic essay discusses studies of games played in Mexico: children's games, games of physical skill, and games of chance, with a section on the current research.

1912. Schwartzman, Helen B. "Works on Play: A Bibliography," in *Studies in the Anthropology of Play: Papers in Memory of B. Allan Tindall*, ed. Phillip Stevens, Jr. West Point, NY: Leisure Press, 1977. pp. 250-265. LC 86-11225; ISBN 0-918438-098.

The works are divided into evolutionary and developmental studies, socialization/enculturation studies, psychoanalytic studies, communication studies, works about children's verbal play, ecological and ethnological studies, cognitive studies, and experimental studies. There is also a section of geographical studies from Africa, Central and South America, North America, Asia, Europe, the Near East, and Oceania. Schwartman also has a bibliographical essay in this work, "Research on Children's Play: An Overview and Some Predictions" (pp. 105-115), in which she examines "anthropological, sociological and psychological studies of children's play." A full bibliography is appended.

Classification--Folk Play

1913.   Browne, Ray B. "Southern California Jump-Rope Rhymes: A Study in Variants." *Western Folklore* 14 (1955): 3-22.

Browne lists 41 jump-rope rhymes and variants, but also classifies four distinct types of jumping: 1) a single child turns a jump rope over her own head; 2) two persons turn a single rope between them while one or more children jump; 3) two persons turn two ropes between them concurrently; and 4) one person holds a short rope and spins around.

1914.   Buckley, Bruce. "Jump Rope Rhymes--Suggestions for Classification and Study." *Keystone Folklore Quarterly* 11 (1966): 99-111.

Although this is concerned with rhymes, Buckley also classifies jump rope games into plain jumps, endurance jumps, call in/call out jumps, speed jumps, and action jumps.

1915.   Caillois, Roger. "The Classification of Games," in *Play Orbit*, ed. Jasia Reichardt. London: Studio International, 1969. pp. 77-83.

Caillois divides games into several "fundamental categories": **agnon** (competition), **alea** (chance); **mimicry** (simulation), and **clinx** (vertigo), with two elements: **paidia** (tumult, agitation) to **ludus** (patience). The same scheme was proposed in an earlier article, "The Structure and Classification of Games," *Diogenes* 12 (Winter 1955): 62-75. For more of Caillois' theories, see his *Man, Play, and Games* (New York: Free Press of Glencoe, 1961).

1916.   Dundes, Alan. "On Game Morphology: A Study of the Structure of Non-Verbal Folklore." *New York Folklore Quarterly* 20 (1964): 276-288.

In an attempt to arouse fellow folklorists' concern for non-verbal folklore and using the theories of folktale morphology of V.I. Propp (*Morphology of the Folktale*, Bloomington: Indiana University Press, 1958), Dundes classifies games by structural units.

1917.   Georges, Robert A. "The Relevance of Models for Analyses of Traditional Play Activities." *Southern Folklore Quarterly* 33 (1969): 1-23.

Georges proposes a contextual-behavioral approach, with three models representing interactions that occur during "traditional play activities."

1918.   Hawthorne, Ruth. "Classifying Jump-Rope Games." *Keystone Folklore Quarterly* 11 (1966): 113-126.

Hawthorne suggests four classification schemes based on: 1) positions or actions of the rope; 2) positions or action of the jumper; 3) pattern of the verse; and 4) purpose of the rhyme or game. She then classifies 31 games and rhymes using the above schemes.

Dictionaries--Folk Games

1919.   Gomme, Alice B. *The Traditional Games of England, Scotland, and Ireland; With Tunes, Singing-Rhymes, and Methods of*

Playing According to the Variants Extant and Recorded in Different Parts of the Kingdom. 2 vols. London: D. Nutt, 1894-1898. Part I of *Dictionary of British Folk-Lore*, ed. Laurence Gomme. Reprinted: New York: Dover, 1964. LC 63-21811.

Over 600 games are arranged in alphabetical order, with extensive directions on how to play, with variants and verses. Vol. 2 contains addenda and a "Memoir on the Study of Children's Games." (See also no. 1964.)

1920.   Maclagan, Robert Craig, comp. *The Games & Diversions of Argyleshire.* London: Published for the Folk-Lore Society by D. Nutt, 1901. 270p. (Publications of the Folk-Lore Society, 47)

All entries, some of which are games, some not (e.g., **activity, general, auguries, ball games, balancing, blindfold games,** etc.), are arranged alphabetically. For each game, the compiler gives instructions and variant games. An appendix includes the verses. There is an index.

1921.   Pick, J.B. *Dictionary of Games.* New York: Philosophical Library, 1952. 318p.

Includes mostly contemporary games, but there is a section on "outdoor tag and tug games," older tag games, work games, and toy games, with games listed alphabetically within each section. Gives instructions on how to play the games and tells who plays them. There is an index.

Index--Folk Games

1922.   "Index of Toys and Games," in *Play Orbit*, ed. Jasia Reichardt. London: Studio International, 1969. pp. 18-39.

This is an index of sound toys, optical or "philosophical" toys, theatrical toys, outdoor toys, balls and ball games, table and other indoor games, spinning toys, simple movement toys, dolls and dolls' houses, toy soldiers, and toy animals.

Annotated Collections and Descriptions--Folk Games

Note: A subsection on **String Games** follows; **Play-party Games** are listed in Chapter 4. The listings under **Folk Games-- Dictionaries** (nos. 1919-1921) also include annotated descriptions of games.

General/International

1923. Daiken, Leslie. *Children's Games Throughout the Year*. London: Batsford, 1949. 216p. Reprinted: New York: Arno, 1976. LC 75-35067; ISBN 0-405-07918-4. (Studies in games and play)

The games are arranged by month (January-December), with games listed and fully described that might be played in those months. The scope is international and there is an index of names and games.

1924. Grunfeld, Frederic V., ed. *Games of the World: How to Make Them, How to Play Them, How They Came to Be*. New York: Holt, Reinhart & Winston, 1975. 280p. LC 75-13812; ISBN 0-03-015261-5.

Includes board and table games, street and playground games, field and forest games, party and festival games, and puzzles, tricks, and stunts. For each game cited, the editor gives a brief history of the game, explains how it is played, notes materials and tools needed to make the game, and tells how to construct it. The book has wonderful, clear diagrams, and many full-color photographs. Indexed.

1925. Hunt, Sarah E. *Games and Sports the World Around*. 3rd ed. New York: Ronald Press, 1964. 271p. LC 64-18466.The 1st and

2nd eds. (1941, 1950) were compiled by Sarah Hunt and Ethel Cain under the title *Games the World Around: 400 Folk Games*.

The third edition is arranged by country: Africa, Asia, Australia and New Zealand, Europe, etc. For each game listed, the name of the game in English and the native language is given, as well as the ages it is played by, the number of players, place, supplies needed, type of activity, appeal, and description. There is an index of game titles, index by age level, index by playing area (indoors, outdoors, etc.), and by type of activity. The first and second editions had an introduction on "folklore in the play pattern of mankind"; the format of the three editions in presentation of the games is similar, but the games included vary.

1926. Millen, Nina. *Children's Games from Many Lands*. New and rev. ed. New York: Friendship Press, 1965 [1941]. 192p. LC 65-24039.

Games are described and arranged by country: Africa, Asia, Europe, Latin America, North America, Oceania. Information given for each game includes English- and native-language game name, number of players required, the age of the players, and what type of game it is. Indexed by name of game.

1927. Vinton, Iris. *The Folkways Omnibus of Children's Games*. Harrisburg, PA: Stackpole Books, 1970. 320p. LC 71-110479; ISBN 0-8117-06880.

The sections in this work are: games shared by the world's peoples (hand games, American ball games, etc.); games for certain seasons (sun myths transformed into games, myth and play based on seasonal changes); old cultures in traditional games (sliding and hurling, kites, traditional ball games, festival games); geography and climates as molders of play; games of travel; games as magic and symbol; making believe; celebrating special days and events; and games for urbanites. Many games are listed within each section. For each, the author tells where the game originated, how it was played, and by whom. There is a guide to games, a guide to lands and people, and a bibliography.

1928.   Abrahams, Roger D. "There's a Black Girl in the Ring," in *Two Penny Ballads and Four Dollar Whiskey*, ed. Kenneth S. Goldstein and Robert H. Byington. Hatboro, PA: Published for the Pennsylvania Folklore Society by the Folklore Associates, 1966. pp. 121-135. LC 64-24802.

Describes eight games played by black children in Philadelphia and gives accompanying words and music. See also Abrahams' *Jump-Rope Rhymes, A Dictionary*, in the section on rhymes (no. 699).

1929.   Babcock, W.H. "Games of Washington Children." *American Anthropologist* 1 (1888): 243-284.

Ring games, archway games, games of mimicry, jumping games, rigamaroles and jingles, catches and riddles, games of hands and feet, games with toys, games of transposition, games of search, games of chase, and child-stealing games are given with directions on how to play them and accompanying verse or rhyme where appropriate.

1930.   Brewster, Paul G. *American Nonsinging Games*. Norman: University of Oklahoma Press, 1953. 218p. LC 53-5476.

Games are arranged alphabetically within the following types of games: guessing games, forfeit games, hiding, chasing, ball, elimination, jumping and hopping games, practical jokes, paper and pencil games, games of dexterity, courtship games, stick games, games of little girls, and miscellaneous games. Brewster tells the source of each game and how to play it, gives comparisons to others, and tells how the game is played in other countries. The bibliography (pp. 187-198) is comprehensive, and there is an index of rhymes.

1931. Brewster, Paul G., et al., eds. "Children's Games and Rhymes," in *The Frank C. Brown Collection of North Carolina Folklore*. Vol. 1. Durham, NC: Duke University Press, 1952. pp. 29-219.

Included are ball games, hiding games, jumping and hopping games, practical jokes, bottle games, dramatization games, guessing games, forfeit and penalty games, games of chance, games of dexterity, imitative games, courtship and marriage games, teasing games, tug-of-war and similar games, games of smaller children, eliminating games, dancing games, and miscellaneous games. For each game described, the source is given and a verse if needed. The bibliography (pp. 207-214) is quite complete; the index can be found on page 215.

1932. Bronner, Simon J. "Nonsinging Games," in his *American Children's Folklore*. Little Rock, AK: August House, 1988. pp. 175-198. LC 88-23469; ISBN 0-8748-3068-0.

Includes descriptions and instructions on hiding and blindfolding games, chasing and tagging games, stepping and approaching games, team play, and street and sidewalk play.

1933. Butler, Francelia, and Gail Haley. *The Skip Rope Book*. New York: Dial Press, 1963. unpaged. LC 63-10035.

Includes 46 rhymes with brief explanations of actions for most of the skip ropes.

1934. Culin, Stewart. *Games of the North American Indians*. Washington, DC: 24th Annual Report of the Bureau of American Ethnology to the Secretary of the Smithsonian Institution, 1902-03. 846p. Reprinted: New York: AMS, 1973. LC 73-8094; ISBN 0-404-11201-3.

Culin's paper includes games of chance, games of dexterity, minor amusements, unclassified games, and games derived from Europeans. An appendix includes information on the running race. Within each section, games are arranged by tribe, listed alphabetically. A tabular index to tribes and games is also given as well as a general index, including games and tribes. This is an old but important work.

1935. Culin, Stewart. "Street Games of Boys in Brooklyn." *Journal of American Folklore* 4 (1891): 221-237.

Forty games are listed and described, some with diagrams and accompanying verses. Informants are also described.

1936. Evans, Patricia. *Rimbles; A Book of Children's Classic Games, Rhymes, Songs, and Sayings.* Garden City, NJ: Doubleday, 1961. 157p. LC 61-9504.

These games were collected from children in San Francisco between 1945 and 1960. There are descriptions of games of hopscotch, jump rope, and jacks. Each game includes instructions on how to play it and the accompanying rhyme. Indexed by game name and by first line of rhyme. Evans also wrote *Hopscotch* (San Francisco, CA: Porpoise Bookshop, 1955), a guidebook to the sidewalk game.

1937. Ferretti, Fred. *The Great American Marble Book.* New York: Workman, 1973. 158p. LC 74-156778; ISBN 0-911104-27-5.

More guide than compendium, this work begins with an historical overview with a discussion of marble games played in various countries and a study of the types of marbles made from various substances (e.g., **aggies**, from agate, marble, or limestone; **alleys**, from alabaster, etc.). Also included is a lexicon of "mibology," a chapter on "opinions and techniques," a list of games, with descriptions, some diagrams and lots of black-and-white photos, a list of tournaments, with information on regulations, scoring, officials names, penalties, and additional rules, a list of marble champions, arranged by city (Pittsburgh, PA, had the most up to 1973!) and state, and a list of national records since 1949. Not indexed.

1938.   Ferretti, Fred. *The Great American Book of Sidewalk, Stoop, Dirt, Curb, and Alley Games.* New York: Workman, 1975. 240p. LC 75-7291; ISBN 0-911104-59-3 (p).

Includes a good introduction on sidewalk and alley games and variants. Includes 60 games played on sidewalks and stoops, on dirt, on curbs, and in alleys. Each game is described with instructions on how to play. There is an index of games. Great black-and-white photos. See also Rosellen Brown's *Street Games* (New York: Doubleday, 1974) and Amanda Dargan's and Steven Zeitlin's *City Games* (New Brunswick, NJ: Rutgers University Press, 1990).

1939.   Jones, Bessie, and Bess Lomax Hawes. *Step It Down; Games, Plays, Songs, and Stories from the Afro-American Heritage.* New York: Harper, 1972. 233p. LC 71-83598; ISBN 0-06-011783-4. Reprinted: Athens: University of Georgia Press, 1987. LC 87-5945; ISBN 0-8203-0960-5 (p)

Includes baby's games and plays, clapping plays, jumps and skips, skipping plays, home amusements, outdoor games, and stories told by Bessie Jones, a black southern woman. Tunes, words, and contextual information are given with annotations to the games. Each game is described in full with instructions on how it is played and who traditionally plays it. There is a selected bibliography, an index, and a discography. A terrific book.

1940.   Langstaff, John, and Carol Langstaff. *Shimmy Shimmy Coke-Ca-Pop! A Collection of City Children's Street Games and Rhymes.* New York: Doubleday, 1973. 95p. LC 72-92227; ISBN 0-385-05769-5.

These games are collected from Irish, Puerto Rican, Italian, American, Portuguese, Jewish, Syrian, and Chinese children in the Boston area. Included are descriptions of name-calling, ball-bouncing, sidewalk drawing, jump-rope, and action games, follow-the-leader, hand-clapping games, and dramatic play. Verses and some directions for playing are given. No index but it has a good table of contents and wonderful photos of children at play.

1941. Milberg, Alan. *Street Games*. New York: McGraw-Hill, 1976. 302p. LC 74-22605; ISBN 0-87749-734-6.

Covers historical and current games and gives variants of games such as tag, street hockey, hide and seek, mumbly peg, jacks, etc. It is a little difficult to use, although there is an index of game titles. Includes terrific pictures of city kids at play.

1942. Newell, William Wells. *Games and Songs of American Children*. New York: Harper, 1883. 289p. Reprinted: New York: Dover, 1963. LC 63-3347.

This is a classic study of games. Almost 200 games are listed and described within broad subject areas: playing at work, love games, guessing games, games of chase, ball games, and similar sports, etc. For each game, Newell tells how it is played, gives the source of the game, and gives rhymes and tunes where appropriate. Games are easily accessed in the table of contents and the index. An appendix includes collections of children's games, comparisons of variants, and references.

1943. Roberts, Warren. "Children's Games and Game Rhymes." *Hoosier Folklore* 8 (1949): 7-34.

There are 400 game versions listed here that were collected mostly by Roberts' students from children all over the U.S and Canada. There are descriptions and rhymes for chasing games, games involving forfeits, guessing games, circle games, games played with hands, and miscellaneous games. Comparative references are included as are the sources of the games.

1944. Skolnik, Peter. *Jump Rope!* New York: Workman, 1974. 157p. LC 75-8811; ISBN 0-911104-47-X.

Includes rope lore and history, a glossary of jump-rope rhymes, a section on jump-rope technique with information on the basic steps and on "fancy footwork," and detailed step-by-step instructions for many simple and advanced jump-rope plays with illustrations. There is a section of over 250 rhymes, divided into 13 categories, from classics to call-in rhymes, etc.

1945.   Solomon, Jack, and Olivia Solomon. *Zickary Zan: Childhood Folklore.* University: University of Alabama Press, 1980. 180p. LC 79-1117; ISBN 0-8173-0012-0.

The first section of this book includes folk play (pp. 11-43): games, jump rope rhymes, counting-out rhymes, taunts, riddles, nonsense verse and parodies, and autograph albums, all collected from children in Alabama. Games are described and sources are given. Concludes with a bibliographic essay.

1946.   Wagonvoord, James. *Hangin' Out: City Kids, City Games.* Philadelphia, PA: Lippincott, 1974. 120p. LC 73-16293; ISBN 0-397-01028-1.

Explains various street games: "skillzies," jump-rope games, tops, "ringolevio," hopscotch, etc., gives verse for each, directions, and lots of black-and-white photos of kids in action.

1947.   Walker, J.R. "Sioux Games." *Journal of American Folklore* 18, 19 (1905-06): 227-290; 29-36. Reprinted in *The Games of the Americas*, ed. Brian Sutton-Smith. New York: Arno, 1976. LC 75-35081; ISBN 0-4050-7929-x.

There are 22 Sioux games explained, with directions on how to play them, who plays them, and the sources if known.

1948.   Welsch, Roger. "Nebraska Finger Games." *Western Folklore* 25 (1966): 173-194.

Arranged into noise-makers, activity games, "punchliners," visual and tactical sensation games, games of competition, lyric games, naming games, games of deception, and ritual games. There are 53 games, illustrated and explained, all with variants given.

1949. Wieand, Paul R. *Outdoor Games of the Pennsylvania Germans.* Plymouth Meeting, PA: Mrs. C. Naaman Keyser, 1950. 34p. (Homecraft course; v. 28)

Twenty-six games are described with methods of play given and some verses with an additional section called "short games or stunts," also with rhymes. There is no index or bibliography.

Canada

1950. Fowke, Edith. *Sally Go Round the Sun: Three Hundred Songs, Rhymes, and Games of Canadian Children.* Garden City, NY: Doubleday, 1978 [1969]. 160p. LC 77-87873.

There are singing games, skipping rhymes, ball-bouncing and clapping songs and games, foot and finger plays, counting-out rhymes, taunts and teases, etc. The bulk of this work is the rhymes (see no. 718) and the songs (see no. 1224), but there is a section called "How to Play Games," in the back with a brief paragraph for each game.

West Indies

1951. Beckwith, Martha Warren. "Folk-Games of Jamaica," in *Jamaica Folk-Lore.* New York: G.E. Steckert for the American Folk-Lore Society, 1928. (Memoirs of the American Folk-Lore Society; v. 21. pp. 5-95). Published originally by Vassar College, 1922 as Publications of the Folk-Lore Foundation; v. 1. The 1928 version has a 20-page addendum. Reprinted: New York: Kraus, 1969.

Lists and describes 73 games in all with texts, music, and variants. Gives place source as well as extensive notes. There is an index to the original edition.

1952. Parsons, Elsie Clews. "Ring Games and Jingles in Barbados." *Journal of American Folklore* 43 (1930): 326-329.

Gives texts and movements for 13 games.

Asia

1953. Anima, Nid. *Filipino Ethnic Games.* Quezon City: Omar, 1977. 112p. LC 80-106024.

The following games are described: Muslim games, Mangya games, other tribal games, Panasinese games, Iocano games, board games, insect games, coin games, courtship games, funeral games, fiesta games, and Easter games. For the games listed within these sections, the author tells how the game is played, who plays it, where it is played and its origin. There is no bibliography or index, and the quality of the photographic illustrations is very poor.

1954. Culin, Stewart. *Chinese Games with Dice and Dominoes.* Washington, GPO, 1895. Extract from Smithsonian Institute Report, 1893. Facsimile reproduction: Seattle, WA: The Shorey Bookstore, 1972. ISBN 0-8466-6017-2 (p).

Culin treats games with dice and games with dominoes separately. For each game, he gives the name, history of the game, and describes how to play it. Included are some diagrams but no index.

1955. Culin, Stewart. *Games of the Orient: Korea, China, Japan.* Rutland, VT: Charles E. Tuttle, 1958 [1895, as *Korean Games, with Notes on the Corresponding Games of China and Japan*]. 177p. LC 58-11074.

This work is "intended not only as a survey of the games of Korea, but as a practical introduction to the study of the games of the world." There are 97 games listed, described, and pictured. Included are a general index and indexes to Korean, Japanese, and Chinese names.

1956.   Haas, Mary R. "Thai Word Games," in *Language in Culture and Society; A Reader in Linguistics and Anthropology*, ed. Dell Hymes. New York: Harper & Row, 1964. pp. 301-304. LC 64-15151.

Thai word games are explained and described. Of particular interest is her bibliography, "Children's Games and Speech Play" (pp. 303-304).

1957.   Hummel, Siegbert, and Paul G. Brewster. *Games of the Tibetans.* Helsinki: Suomalainen Tiedeakatemia, 1963. 33p. LC 64-57061. (*FF Communications*, 187)

This includes a study and description of dice games, swinging games, board games, children's games, and riddles with an extensive section of notes.

1958.   Lopez, Mellie Leandicho. *A Study of Philippine Games.* Quezon City: University of the Philippines Press, 1980. 500p. LC 81-184568.

This is really a study, introduced by Alan Dundes, but it includes 128 "pre games" (counting-out rhymes, finger games), ordinary games, jokes and trickster games, and formula games collected in the field. For each game, the author gives number of players, setting, props needed, informant, place played, directions, and an annotation. There is an index and a great bibliography. This is an impressive study and collection.

*Eurasia--*Russia and *Eastern Europe*

1959.   Sebeok, Thomas A., and Paul G. Brewster. *Games.* Vol. 6 of
        Studies in Cheremis Folklore. Bloomington: Indiana University
        Press, 1958. 123p. LC 58-63056. (Indiana University
        Publications. Folklore series, 11)

        This work is divided into "it" games, individual competitions,
team play, games played by partners, rhythmic and dramatic games,
practical jokes, and unclassified or unidentified games. There are 97
games in all; for each, the game is explained with information on how to
play, a commentary, and comparative data (to other games throughout the
world and to other collections) given. There is a finder list and a
bibliography.

Europe

1960.   Brady, Eilís. *All In! All In!: A Selection of Dublin Children's
        Traditional Street-Games with Rhymes and Music.* Dublin:
        University College Belfield, 1975. 195p.

        The games and verses are listed within the following categories:
taking notice (games to encourage children to take notice), words at will
(chants), pure devilment, make believe (playing house), simple pleasures,
dexterity, picking sides, ball games, skipping, portraits of life, from kerb
to kerb, good vs. evil, strength, guessing games, chasing, marbles, bets.
Very clear game directions are provided; words and actions are explained;
verses, variant verses, and tunes are also given. There is a classified index
and an index of first lines.

Europe--Great Britain

1961.   Brewster, Paul G. "Games and Sports in Shakespeare." *Folklore
        Forum* 17 (1954). 26p. Reprinted: Helsinki: Suomalainen
        Tiedeakatemia, 1959. (*FF Communications,* 177)

The 50 games are arranged alphabetically, from **archery** to **wrestling**. Origins of the games are given, along with the play title in which it is included and simple descriptions. Brewster also wrote "Games and Sports in Sixteenth- and Seventeenth-Century English Literature" (*Western Folklore* 6 [1947]: 143-156) which covers much of the same material.

1962.   Douglas, Norman. *London Street Games*. 2nd ed., rev. and enl. London: Chatto & Windus, 1931 [1916]. 102p. Reprinted: Detroit, MI: Singing Tree, 1968. LC 68-30189.

Includes a description of "about a thousand of the outdoor games they play down our way." Written in text format, the index, however, will provide access to specific games. Some verses are also given.

1963.   Ford, Robert. *Children's Rhymes, Children's Games, Children's Songs, Children's Stories: A Book for Bairns and Big Folk*. 2nd ed. Paisley: Alexander Gardner, 1904. 287p. Reprinted: Detroit, MI: Singing Tree, 1968. LC 67-16003.

Some games are described, especially counting-out games, with verses.

1964.   Gomme, Alice B. *The Traditional Games of England, Scotland, and Ireland; With Tunes, Singing-Rhymes, and Methods of Playing According to the Variants Extant and Recorded in Different Parts of the Kingdom*. 2 vols. London: D. Nutt, 1894-1898. Part 1 of *Dictionary of British Folk-Lore*, ed. Laurence Gomme. Reprinted: New York: Dover, 1964. LC 63-21811.

Listed also under dictionaries (no. 1919), this is the standard collection of children's games. Arranged in dictionary format from **accroshay** to **would you know how doth the peasant**, Gomme gives the source for each, a verse, if needed, and a description of the game.

Addenda material in Vol. 2 include extra entries and a "Memoir on the Study of Children's Games" (pp. 458-531).

1965. Opie, Iona, and Peter Opie. *Children's Games in Street and Playground: Chosing, Catching, Seeking....* London: Oxford University Press, 1969. 371p. LC 76-437542.

This work is concerned "solely with the games that children, aged about 6-12, play of their own accord when out of doors, and usually out of sight." Excludes party games, team games, and sports. Almost 2,500 games were taken from about 10,000 children from England, Scotland, and East Wales. Included are starting-in games, chasing games, catching games, seeking games, hunting games, racing games, duelling games, exerting games, daring games, guessing games, acting games, and pretending games. The source, variants, and rhymes are given for each. There is an index of games and game rhymes.

1966. Ritchie, James T.R. *Golden City.* Edinburgh: Oliver & Boyd, 1965. 182p. LC 66-2941.

These games, collected by a school teacher in Edinburgh, are included in the following broad sections: "playing in the green, choosing sides and counting-out rhymes--chasie, tig, and hide-&-seek; booles, knifie, and such-like; single and double ballie; peevers; skipping; singing games." Tunes are included; there is an index of first lines but no general index.

1967. Strutt, Joseph. *The Sports and Pastimes of the People of England from the Earliest Period, Including the Rural and Domestic Recreations, May Games, Mummeries, Shows, Pageants, Processions and Pompous Spectacles.* 1801. Reprint of a "much enlarged and corrected" edition by J. Charles Fox: New York: Augustus M. Kelley, 1970. 322p. Preface by Norris McWhirter and Ross McWhirter. A variant title (to 1810 ed.) is *Glig-Gamena Angel Deod. Or, the Sports and Pastimes...*

A major hodgepodge, divided into "earlier amusements, rural exercises practiced by persons of rank--hunting, banking and horse racing, rural exercises generally practiced: archery, rowing, skating, games with balls, etc.; pastimes usually exercised in towns, cities or places adjoining them: plays (Miracle plays, Mystery plays, etc.), minstrels, puppets, jugglers, dancing, tumbling, balancing, bowling, etc.; domestic amusements of various kinds; and pastimes appropriate to particular seasons: holiday games; and games popular with children" (pp. 379-404). There is an index.

Oceania

1968.   Armstrong, Alan. *Maori Games and Hakas: Instructions, Words, and Actions.* Wellington: A.H. & A.W. Reed, 1964. 182p. LC 66-87708.

Covers games, old and new: hand games, stick games, and string figures as well as Maori music and the musical dance with emphasis on the **haka** dance, "an expression of the passion, vigour and identity of the race." (p.119) Pictures, diagrams, and a glossary complete this book, but unfortunately there is no index.

1969.   Sutton-Smith, Brian. *The Folkgames of Children.* Austin: Published for the American Folklore Society at the University of Texas Press, 1972. 559p. LC 74-23980; ISBN 0-292-72405-5. (Publications of the American Folklore Society; Bibliographical and special series; v. 24)

The first part of this work is a description of the games of New Zealand children, which are arranged and classified into singing games, dialogue games, informal games, leader games, chasing games, rhythmic games, games of chance, teasing activities, parlor games, games of skill and additional naming games. The games are listed into two groups for each section above, those played from 1870-1920 and those played from 1920-1952. The second part is a long essay on historical change in game preferences of American children. Also included are discussions of anthropological approaches, psychological approaches, and unified approaches to game theory. An earlier version of this work is Sutton-Smith's *The Games of New Zealand Children* (Berkeley: University of California Press, 1959; Folklore studies; v. 12).

String Games

Annotated Collections and Descriptions--String Figures

1970. Anderson, Johannes. *Maori String Games.* Wellington: The Board of Maori Ethnological Research, 1927. 173p. Reprinted: New York: AMS Press, 1979. LC 75-35223; ISBN 0-404-14402-0.

There are 36 string games and 12 string tricks presented, each with photographs to show how to start and explanations. The origin and source are given as well as other variant games and an explanation of what the string movements represent symbolically. There is a bibliography and an index.

1971. Dickey, Lyle A. *String Figures from Hawaii, Including Some from New Hebrides and Gilbert Islands.* Honolulu: Bernice P. Bishop Museum, 1928. 169p. (Bernice P. Bishop Museum Bulletin, 54). Reprinted: New York: Kraus, 1985. LC 85-87; ISBN 0-5270-2160-1 (p).

Covers Hawaiian figures made by one player or two play players and Hawaiian slip tricks as well as New Hebrides string tricks. There are illustrations of hands and string and clear instructions. Concludes with a bibliography.

1972. Haddon, Kathleen. *Artists in String; String Figures: Their Regional Distribution and Social Significance.* New York: Dutton, 1930. 174p. Reprinted: New York: AMS, 1979. LC 75-32823; ISBN 0-404-14127-7.

An early, seminal international study of string figures, 41 games are grouped by ethnic group (Alaska, Eskimo, Navaho Indians, etc.), described, analyzed, and pictured. There is a long bibliography and an index. See also Alfred C. Haddon's "A Few American String Figures and Tricks," reprinted in Brian Sutton-Smith's *The Games of the Americas*, Part I, which describes and explains 12 string games.

1973.   Haddon, Kathleen. *String Games for Beginners*. Enl. and rev. Cambridge [ENG]: N. Heffer & Sons, 1942. 40p. LC 43-2423.

This pamphlet has descriptions of 28 string figures from various native cultures with instructions on how to learn them.

1974.   Hrabalová, Olga, and Paul Brewster G. "A Czechoslovak Cat's Cradle Series." *Ceskoslovenska Ethnografie* 5 (1957): 176-183.

This work describes at some length several variants of cat's cradle as played in Czechoslovakia and gives instructions. There is an excellent bibliography on string figures.

1975.   Jayne, Caroline Furness. *String Figures and How to Make Them: A Study of Cat's Cradle in Many Lands*. New York: Dover, 1962 [1906]. 407p. LC 62-51880.

These string figures are arranged by their opening movements, known as the first position and/or Opening A: figures beginning with Opening A; figures which do not being with Opening A; and tricks and catches. There are also sections on tricks and catches and on Eskimo and Indian games from Alaska. There is an index, a geographic distribution, and a bibliography. See also Kathleen Haddon's *Cat's Cradles from Many Lands* (New York: Longmans, Green, 1911).

1976.   Maude, H.C., and H.E. Maude. *String-Figures from the Gilbert Islands*. Wellington, NZ: Polynesian Society, 1958. 161p. (Memoirs of the Polynesian Society, 13)

Games are divided into the following classifications: figures with magic co-religious significance; figures which are stationary and of fixed design; figures which progress from pattern to pattern; three-dimensional figures; figures which slide back and forth with the pulling or pressing of a string; figures which are made by two persons; catches; trick figures; and string-games. A diagram and instructions are given. There is also an analysis of objects represented by Gilbertese figures. There is a list of references but no index.

Chapter VII

MATERIAL CULTURE

"Culture, defined simply, is what you need to know to be one of the folk. Material culture is what the folk have made with what they know." (Kyvig, no. 156) **Material culture** is a very broad term that covers all aspects of folk craft, food, architecture, etc. It has been defined as artifact study, but the best studies of material culture include contextual descriptions also. For working purposes, Thomas Schlereth's definition will suffice: Material culture is "the study through artifacts (and other pertinent historical evidence) of the belief systems--the values, ideas, attitudes, and assumptions--of a particular community or society, usually across time." (*Material Culture Studies in America*, p.3).

This chapter is burdensomely diverse and long. *The MLA International Bibliography* (the outline on which this work is based) divides **Material Culture** into three separate divisions: **folk art** (including folk painting and sculpture); **folk craft** (including architecture, ceramics, costume, furniture, household items, toys, weaving); and **technology** (including agriculture, fishing, glass blowing, metal work, and textiles). To avoid mass confusion, I have adhered to this format with some minor changes, although I disagree with the classification scheme somewhat (for example, I personally do not consider **folk architecture** to be a craft, nor do I consider what is now called **foodways** to be a craft). In many places, an art or craft form overlaps into several categories, and I have placed it in the category that appears first in the title. This chapter ends with a section on folk museums and their collections which the *MLA International Bibliography* does not cover in its section on Material Culture.

MATERIAL CULTURE
General

There are several "spokespersons" for **material culture**, notably Henry Glassie, Simon Bronner, Michael Owen Jones, Ian Quimby, and Thomas Schlereth, Don Yoder, and Fred B. Kniffen. Their works (much of which is collected essays and some bibliographical work) provide an excellent introduction to this subject.

Henry Glassie's *Pattern in the Material Folk Culture of the Eastern United States* (Philadelphia: University of Pennsylvania Press, 1968) is a seminal work which deals with folk and popular artifacts. An extensively revised version of this work, "Artifacts: Folk, Popular, Imaginary and Real," can be found in Marshall Fishwick's and Ray Browne's *Icons of Popular Culture* (Bowling Green, OH: Bowling Green University Press, 1970). Also on the general subject of material culture, Glassie has written, "Folkloristic Study of the American Artifact: Objects and Objectives," in Richard M. Dorson's *Handbook of American Folklore* (pp. 376-383), which discusses the relationship between folklore, folklife, material culture, and artifact study. A more difficult introductory essay by Glassie is "Structure of Function, Folklore, and Artifact" (*Semiotica* 7 [1973]: 313-351). Other works by Glassie are covered below under **Folk Architecture** (nos. 2161, 2162).

Simon J. Bronner has also written widely on the subject and has been one of its chief bibliographers (see nos. 1978, 1996, 1997). *American Material Culture and Folklife: A Prologue and Dialogue* (Ann Arbor, MI: UMI Research Press, 1985) is a book of essays edited by Bronner with articles on folk artifacts, folk houses, and folklife and the museum. His *Grasping Things: Folk Material Culture and Mass Society in America* (Lexington: University Press of Kentucky, 1986) "analyzes expressions of middle-class culture and episodes from American community history," mostly in Indiana and Pennsylvania. Bronner also wrote the essay, "Folk Objects," in *Folk Groups and Folklore Genres* (pp. 199-223), edited by Elliott Oring.

The term **folklife** (discussed at the beginning of Chapter 1) more often than not includes material culture. Of the link between them, Bronner has written, in *American Material Culture and Folklife*:

> Material culture is made up of tangible things crafted, shaped, altered, and used across time and across space. It is inherently personal and social, mental and physical. It is art, architecture, food, clothing, and furnishing. But more so, it is the weave of these objects in the everyday life of individuals and communities. It is the migration and settlement, custom and practice, production and consumption that is American history and culture. It is the gestures and processes that extend ideas and feelings into three-dimensional forms. (p.3)

A classic in the field of folklife and artifact study is *Forms upon the Frontier; Folklife and Folk Arts in the United States*, edited by Austin and Alta Fife and Henry H. Glassie (Logan: Utah State University Press, 1969), with essays on architecture, arts and crafts (pottery, gravestone carvings, and aspen tree doodling), folk medicine, and folk life, customs, and ethnic groups; Warren Roberts' *Viewpoints on Folklife: Looking at the Overlooked* (Ann Arbor, MI: UMI Press, 1988) is a series of essays published in the 1970s and 1980s that deals with many aspects of folklife and traditional material culture: folk arts and crafts, folk architecture, agricultural tools, etc. Don Yoder's *American Folklife* (Austin: University of Texas Press, 1976) covers artifact study, fieldwork, and documentation.

Ian Quimby's *Material Culture and the Study of American Life* (New York: Published for the Winterthur Museum by Norton, 1978) includes essays by noted American studies scholars and folklorists on artifacts, vernacular architecture, historical preservation, and folklife museums. Thomas J. Schlereth has edited two collections of essays, *Artifacts and the American Past* (1980) and *Material Culture Studies in America* (1982) (both published by the American Association for State and Local History, Nashville, TN). The latter is a collection of previously printed essays with a statement of history, of theory (including Henry Glassie's article, "Folk Art"), of method, and of practice and field work. *Artifacts and the American Past* includes articles on graphics as artifacts, historical sites as artifacts, and landscapes as artifacts. (See also no. 1986.)

Although these are some of the main studies of material culture, several other works on specific aspects of material culture are available. Robert Blair St. George's *Material Life in America, 1601-1860* (Boston, MA: Northeastern University Press, 1988) is an important new historical overview with essays on the method and meaning of material culture and artifact study, new world cultures, the production and control of property, the landscape, ritual space (e.g., meetinghouses, courthouses, cemeteries, etc.), and the environment (e.g., agriculture and architecture). Other less general works on material culture include *Contextual Studies of Material Culture*, edited by David W. Zimmerly (Ottawa: National Museums of Canada, 1978), with five articles that survey the field of material culture from an anthropological point of view (e.g., contextual studies of North American and Eskimo Indian artifacts--kayaks and tipis) and Richard A. Gould's and Michael B. Schifffer's *Modern Material Culture: The Archaeology of Us* (New York: Academic Press, 1981) which looks at the subject from still another viewpoint. Edith Mayo has edited a book of essays, *American Material Culture: The Shape of Things Around Us* (Bowling Green, OH: Bowling Green State University Popular Press, 1984), many of which deal with the concept of material culture as a form of nonverbal communication.

Regional studies include Richard C. Poulsen's *The Pure Experience of Order: Essays on the Symbolic in the Folk Material Culture of Western America* (Albuquerque: University of New Mexico Press, 1982) which includes essays on western fence symbols, the handclasp motif in Mormon folk burial, the symbolic meaning of making molasses in the desert, etc., as well as an essay on repetition in folk artifacts and folk architecture, and Janet C. Gilmore's *The World of the Oregon Fishboat: A Study in Maritime Folklife* (Ann Arbor, MI: UMI Research Press, 1986).

Fred B. Kniffen is the chief proponent of **cultural geography**, a discipline that studies groups of people and analyzes the material details of the landscape, for example, the American prairie: its early Indian inhabitants, their artifacts and dwellings, crops, farming techniques, farm dwellings and outbuildings. Kniffen has written widely on the subject of cultural geography, but a good starting point might well be his "Material Culture in the Geographical Interpretation of the Landscape," in *The Human Mirror*, ed. Miles Richardson (Baton Rouge, LA: LSU Press,

1974, pp. 252- 267).

UMI Research Press (Ann Arbor, Michigan) is producing an American Material Culture and Folklife series, which covers all aspects of material culture and artifact study. Aside from Simon Bronner's *American Material Culture and Folklife* and Janet Gilmore's *The World of the Oregon Fishboat: A Study in Maritime Folklife* (mentioned above), this series also includes several works on folk art and folk crafts mentioned in the next sections, Michael Owen Jones' *Exploring Folk Art: Twenty Years of Thought on Craft, Work, and Aesthetics* (1987), John Vlach's and Simon Bronner's *Folk Art and Art Worlds: Essays...* (1986), Verni Greenfield's *Making Do or Making Art: A Study of American Recycling* (1986), C. Kurt Dewhurst's *Grand Ledge Folk Pottery: Traditions at Work* (1986), Claudine Weatherford's *The Art of Queena Stovall: Images of Country Life* (1986), Joseph W. Glass' *The Pennsylvania Culture Region: A View from the Barn* (1986), and Beauveau Borie's *Farming and Folk Society: Threshing among the Pennsylvania Germans* (1986).

Several early articles in the *Journal of American Folklore* dealt with the relationship between material studies and folklore. Don Yoder's "Folklife Studies Movement" (*Pennsylvania Folklife* 13 [1963]: 43-56) and Norbert Riedl's "Folklore and the Study of Material Aspects of Folk Culture" (*Journal of American Folklore* 79 [1966]: 557-563) both discussed the lack of study on material culture. "On the whole," wrote Riedl, "the gross neglect of the material aspect of American folk culture is a truism which cannot be denied." (p. 558) American folklore journals "responded," however, with a raft of special issues on material culture through the 1970s, beginning with, "Material Culture in the South," in *Southern Folklore Quarterly* (Vol. 39 [December 1975]). *Keystone Folklore* (Vol. 21 [1976-77]) focused on material culture as did the *Mississippi Folklore Register* (Vol. 12 [Fall 1978]). *Southern Folklore Quarterly* (Vol. 42 [1978]) had a special issue on "Afro-American Material Culture," edited by William Ferris, with articles on Afro-American craftsmen emphasizing pottery, basketry, and woodcarving. Simon Bronner and Stephen Poyser edited a special issue of *Folklore Forum* (Vol. 12 [1979]), titled "Approaches to the Study of Material Aspects of American Folk Culture," with an introduction to "object oriented folklore research" by the editors, articles on vernacular architecture by Dell Upton, Elizabeth Mosby, and Thomas Adler, and one on Swedish folk houses. The journal *American*

Quarterly, which covers American studies, has done two special issues on American material culture (Vols. 26 [1974] and 35 [1983]), both with articles and substantial bibliographies. (See no. 1978.) And, *Canadian Folklore. Folklore Canadien* (Vol. 4 [1972], nos. 1 and 2) did a special issue on Material Culture, "People and Things: Folk Material Culture in Canada," edited by Jean-Francois Blanchette, with essays in French and English on different types of Canadian artifacts. Journals which focus on all aspects of material culture include *The American Quarterly* (published by the American Studies Association, 1949--); *The Clarion: America's Folk Art Magazine* (published by the Museum of American Folk Art; 1975--); *The Journal of American Culture* (published by Popular Culture Association, 1978--); *The Journal of Early Southern Decorative Arts* (1975--); *The Journal of Popular Culture* (published by the Popular Culture Association, 1967--); *Material Culture: The Journal of Pioneer America Society* (formerly *Pioneer America*, 1968-1984; 1984--): *Pennsylvania Folklife* (1949); and *Winterthur Portfolio* (1964--; renamed and issued with the subtitle, *A Journal of American Material Culture*, with vol. 14, 1979).

And finally, there are many articles and essays on the study of folk material culture, its relationship to other disciplines, and collection methodology. A seminal article is Jules David Prown's "Mind in Matter: An Introduction to Material Culture Theory and Method" (*Winterthur Portfolio* 17 [1982]: 1-20; reprinted in R.B. St. George's *Material Life in America, 1600-1860*, cited above, pp. 17-38) which considers the question of what is material culture and then covers theoretical background and the methodology of material culture as well as the investigation of external evidence. Prown also makes some observations on the categories of artifacts and concludes with a selective bibliography of general works, theoretical works, and cultural works. Thomas Schlereth's "Material Culture Studies and Social History Research" (*Journal of Social History* 16 [1983]: 111-143) is a fine example of a study of the place of material culture in social history research.

Bibliographies--Material Culture-General

1977. Blanchette, Jean-Francois, et al. "A Bibliography of Material Culture in Canada, 1965-1982." *Canadian Folklore. Folklore Canadien* 14 (1982): 107-146.

Includes alphabetical listings of works in French and English within sections: bibliographies, general works and specialized studies on folk art, craftsmen and technology, furniture, textiles and clothing, food, and architecture. Exhibition catalogs are included. There is no index.

1978. Bronner, Simon J. "'Visible Proofs': Material Culture Study in American Folkloristics." *American Quarterly* 35 (1983): 316-338.

This is a bibliographic essay, which organizes material culture studies into the "core concerns of various researchers," moving from "older, more conventional standpoints" to "newer perspectives in the discipline." (pp. 318-319) Bronner titles his categories "object and text," "setting and region," "group and network," "individual and personality," "event and action," "idea and thought," "new objects," and "remaining concerns."

1979. Eubanks, Sharon Y. *A Bibliography of Books, Pamphlets, and Films Listed in The Living Historical Farm Bulletin from December 1970 through May 1976.* Washington, DC: Association for Living Historical Farms and Agricultural Museums, 1976. 73p. LC 78-309833.

This slim work might well serve as an excellent basic bibliographic introduction to the field of material culture, though it is now out of date. Over 830 books and articles are listed with one-line annotations within the following sections: arts and crafts, crops and livestock, earth and water, gardens and orchards, hearth and homes, money and records, odds and ends, places and people.

1980. Glassie, Henry. "Bibliography," in *Pattern in the Material Folk Culture of the Eastern United States.* Philadelphia, PA:

University of Pennsylvania Press, 1969. 316p. pp. 243-316. LC 68-9739.

Although Glassie's book focuses on folk architecture, it is concerned with establishing broad cultural patterns within folklore. The bibliography, an author listing of books and articles, covers all aspects of cultural material and folklife.

1981.   Gritzner, Janet, and Charles Gritzner. "Selected Bibliography of Studies Relating to Rural Settlement and American Material Folk Culture," in *Forgotten Places and Things: Archeological Perspectives on American History*, comp. and ed. Albert E. Ward. Albuquerque, NM: Center for Anthropological Studies, 1984. 358p. LC 84-159419; ISBN 0-932752-07-1 (p).

The bibliography is appended to an article titled "Cultural Geography and Historical Archeology: A Call for Cooperation Along a Rich Interdisciplinary Interface." The bibliographic listing includes books and articles about rural settlements, farmsteads, and agricultural practices, house types, construction materials and building techniques, and barns and other outbuildings.

1982.   Hamp, Stephen K. "Special Bibliography/Meaning in Material Culture: Bibliographical References Towards an Analytical Approach to Artifacts." *Living Historical Farms Bulletin* 9 (May 1980): 9-13.

The intent of Hamp's bibliography is to "address the subject of cultural meaning in objects, instead of merely descriptive information on isolated subjects." This author listing of almost 70 articles and books then is an "attempt to bring about some of the analytical, rather than descriptive, literature."

1983.   Johnson, Mary. "Women and the Material Universe: A Bibliographic Essay," in *American Material Culture: The Shape of Things Around Us*, ed. Edith Mayo. Bowling Green, OH:

Bowling Green State University Popular Press, 1984. pp. 218-255. LC 84-71338; ISBN 0-87972-303-3 (c); 0-8792-304-1 (p).

This is a useful listing of books and articles concerned with "the relevance of the object to women's experiences" (e.g., foodways and cookery, textiles and the manufacturing process). Also included are historical studies and works on research methods, studies concerned with the aesthetic qualities of artifacts women use, general studies of women at work, and cultural analyses.

1984.   Landrum, Larry N. *American Popular Culture: A Guide to Information Sources.* Detroit, MI: Gale Research, 1982. 435p. LC 82-11902; ISBN 0-8103-1260-3. (Gale information guide library; American information guide studies; v. 12)

There are sections of this bibliography of popular culture materials that cover aspects of material culture: sections on "Aspects of Everyday Life" (pp. 33-64); "Material Culture" (pp. 93-210); "Architecture" (pp. 111-116); "Games" (pp. 123-128). Included are books and article entries, each with a very brief annotation. There is a name index and a separate subject index.

1985.   Lornell, Kip. "Bibliography: Black Material Folk Culture." *Southern Folklore Quarterly* 42 (1978): 287-294. Reprinted in William Ferris' *Afro-American Folk Art and Crafts* (no. 2001).

This is part of a special issue on black material folk culture. The annotated bibliography is divided into sections: architecture, arts--clay; arts--miscellaneous; arts--painting; arts--wood; crafts--clay; crafts--miscellaneous; crafts--stone; medicine; and tools and technology.

1986.   Schlereth, Thomas J., ed. *Material Culture: A Research Guide.* Lawrence: University of Kansas Press, 1985. 224p. LC 85-15643; ISBN 0-7006-0274-7 (c); 0-7006-0275-5 (p).

Chapters 2-6 are bibliographic essays which were included in *American Quarterly* 35 (1983) (cited above and directly below). Schlereth has written an introduction, "Material Culture and Cultural Research" and included an essay on "Social History Scholarship and Material Culture Research." There is "A Guide to General Research Sources" (pp. 197-206) which includes a "bibliography of bibliographies" and a list of serial publications that publish material culture studies. There is a great deal of material in this volume, but it is sometimes hard to get at.

1987.   Schlereth, Thomas J., ed. "Material Culture Bibliographies," in a special issue of *American Quarterly* 35 (1983): 236-338, titled "American Studies and Students of American Things."

These are a series of bibliographic essays on different aspects of American material culture and an introduction by Schlereth. Bibliographic essays are on such subjects as American cultural landscape, vernacular architecture, American decorative household furnishings, technology and material culture, and folklore and material culture.

1988.   Wertheim, Arthur Frank, ed. *American Popular Culture: A Historical Bibliography.* Santa Barbara, CA: ABC-Clio Information Services, 1984. 246p. LC 82-24285; ISBN 0-87436-049-8. (Clio bibliography series, 14)

This is a superb bibliography, mostly of journal articles from many disciplines, on all aspects of American popular culture. There are 2,719 entries in this critically annotated bibliography, with several inclusions for the researcher of material culture. "Arts and Architecture" are included under the section, **Popular Arts**, and "Decorative Arts," "Interior Design," and "Material Culture," are listed under the section, **Architecture**. There is a separate section, **Folk Culture** (pp. 91-110), that includes "Folk Art, Architecture, and Artifacts," and one on **Customs, Behavior, and Attitudes,** with subsections on fashion, rituals, celebrations, and foodways. To help the researcher, there is a very detailed subject index. Because the journals searched for this work are so diverse and from so many disciplines, this is a wonderful place to turn up articles that might not ordinarily be available to the folklorist. This was compiled from a database, so hopefully it will be updated frequently.

Classification--Material Culture-General

1989.   Fleming, E. McClung. "Artifact Study: A Proposed Model." *Winterthur Portfolio* 9 (1974): 153-173.

Fleming presents a model developed within the context of the study of early American decorative arts, utilizing a five-fold classification of the basic properties of an artifact and a set of four operations to be performed on these properties. In this article, Fleming then applies that classification scheme to an early American cupboard.

1990.   Marchese, Ronald. "Material Culture and Artifact Classification." *Journal of American Culture* 3 (Winter 1980): 605-618. Reprinted in Edith Mayo's *American Material Culture: The Shape of Things Around Us* (Bowling Green, OH: Bowling Green State University Press, 1984), pp. 11-24.

This paper "examines the interrelationship between archaeological classification and behavioral history as seen through the material record." Calling classification "the means by which artifactural material is categorized and subjected to manipulation," Marchese discusses three types of categories, stating that we "must not be satisfied with simple classifications since each artifact provides an infinite series of sense impressions, mental processes and attitudes. The function of artifact classification is to discover these processes." (p. 23)

Encyclopedia--Material Culture-General

1991.   Wilson, Charles Reagan, and William Ferris, eds. *Encyclopedia of Southern Culture.* Sponsored by the Center for the Study of Southern Culture at the University of Mississippi. Chapel Hill: University of North Carolina Press, 1989. 1,634p. LC 89-17054;

ISBN 0-8078-1823-6.; Reprinted in 4 paperback vols.: New York: Anchor Books, 1991.

This large work includes large sections on many aspects of material culture, including **agriculture, arts and architecture,** and **folklife,** edited by Ferris, with articles on **aesthetics, Afro-American art, arts and crafts, basketmaking, cemeteries, folk painting, folk sculpture, foodways, grave markers, house types,** etc. There is a general index.

I. FOLK ART
General

Although the term **folk art** is often used generically to denote both **folk art** *and* **folk craft,** the *MLA International Bibliography* separates the two, a format which will be adhered to in this work. This section on works dealing with general aspects of folk art therefore includes those works that either use the term "folk art" in the title (though many of these use the term comprehensively) or are, in the compiler's determination, more art than craft. Painting and sculpture are also included as subheadings of **Folk Art.** Researchers should, of course, also look at the **Folk Crafts -- General** section (nos. 2111-2133) for general works on the subject. Also, although there are several major bibliographic works on folk art (see Bronner, nos. 1996, 1997; Ehresmann, no. 2000; and Sokol, nos. 2011, 2012), many of the bibliographies in Chapter 1, listed under **Folklore-- General,** have sections on folk art. Particularly useful is the annual, *Internationale Volkskündliche Bibliographie* (no. 8), with sections on popular culture and folk art, and Robert Wildhaber's bibliography (no. 64) which covers a wider range of folklife materials than most bibliographies by early American folklore bibliographers.

Two basic introductory essays on the subject are Jan Brunvand's "Folk Crafts and Art" (3rd ed., pp. 425-443), in his *Study of American Folklore*, and Henry Glassie's "Folk Art" (pp. 253-280), in Richard M. Dorson's *Folklore and Folklife*, both with excellent bibliographies. Several texts and articles will serve as additional introductory material and help to clarify a prominent theme evident in several articles--the establishment of a clear definition of folk art, distinguishing it from folk craft, decorative arts, and material on antiques. The introductory essays in Henry Glassie's catalog, *The Spirit of Folk Art: The Girard Collection at the Museum of International Folk Art* (New York: Harry Abrams, 1989; no. 2048), on the relationship between folk art, fine art and popular art, are excellent introductions to this subject. Burt Feintuch's article, "A Contextual and Cognitive Approach to Folk Art and Folk Crafts" (*New York Folklore* 2 [1976]: 69-78), discusses the problem of separating art from craft and determining what qualities of art and/or craft make it folkloric. "What is Folk Art? A Symposium" (*Antiques* 57 [1950]: 350-362; reprinted in Jack Ericson's *Folk Art in America: Painting and Sculpture*, New York: Mayflower, 1979) is an informative group of essays written by decorative art specialists, antique dealers, and folklorists. Another article that probes for a definition of folk art is Joshua C. Taylor's "The Folk and the Masses," in his *America as Art*, published for the National Collection of Fine Arts by the Smithsonian Institution, 1976 (pp. 217-262). And Robert C. Bishop's and Jean Lipman's *Young America: A Folk-art History* (New York: Hudson Hills, 1986) serves as a general history of American folk art.

There are several writers concentrating on **folk art** at the present time: Michael Owen Jones, John Michael Vlach, Simon Bronner, and Ian Quimby, whose works serve as fine introductions to this subject. Michael Owen Jones has written extensively on style and aesthetics in folk art, beginning with his dissertation, "Chairmaking in Appalachia: A Study in Style and Creative Imagination in American Folk Art" (Indiana University, 1969) and continuing with several articles in the 1970s: "The Concept of Aesthetic in the Traditional Arts" (*Western Folklore* 30 [1971]: 77-104), and "'For Myself I Like a Decent Plain-Made Chair': the Concept of Taste and the Traditional Arts in America" (*Western Folklore* 31 [1972]: 27-52), which discusses isolating a "folk aesthetic." Jones wrote *The Study of Folk Art: Reflections on Images* in 1974 (Folklore Preprint Series, Vol. 1, 9; Bloomington, Indiana: Folklore Publications Group). He edited and wrote the introduction to "Works of Art: Art as Work and the Art of Working," a special issue of *Western Folklore* (Vol. 33 [1974]: 172-221), essays on folk art in the city. Much of this material was compiled into his *The Hand Made Object and Its Maker* (Berkeley: University of California Press, 1975) which was recently revised and printed under the title *Craftsman of the Cumberlands: Tradition &*

Creativity (Lexington: University Press of Kentucky, 1989). And finally, in 1987, Michael Owen Jones wrote *Exploring Folk Art: Twenty Years of Thought on Craft, Work, and Aesthetics* (Ann Arbor, MI: UMI Research Press, 1987) which includes articles on "making things," the sensory experience of folk art, art at work, and method and concept; it also has a superb bibliography (pp. 205-214).

John Michael Vlach and Simon J. Bronner edited *Folk Art and Art Worlds* (Ann Arbor, MI: UMI Research Press, 1986), articles on folk painting, folk art in context, and collection, with an afterword by Henry Glassie on "The Idea of Folk Art." And Ian Quimby and Scott T. Swank edited *Perspectives on American Folk Art* (New York: Published for the Winterthur Museum by W.W. Norton, 1980) with 11 articles on aspects of folk art and an introduction.

Folk art, especially American folk art, has been covered very thoroughly in book and article format. Because of the sheer numbers of them, I have had to omit all general surveys of folk art, such as Marcel Griaule's *Folk Art of Black Africa* (Paris: Editions du Chène; New York: Tudor, 1950) or Cynthia Rubin's *Southern Folk Art* (Birmingham, AL: Oxmoor House, 1985). There are literally thousands of these books, all readily available in university and public libraries. Although they may well be useful to the researcher with the aid of a good index, space simply forbids their being included here. I have included selected exhibition catalogs and also catalogs or descriptions of museums and private collections; I have excluded, for the most part, journal articles.

General works on **Folk Art** are covered first, followed by subsections on **Folk Painting** and **Folk Sculpture**.

Bibliographies--Folk Art-General

> Note: Be sure to consult the bibliographies for **Folk Painting** (nos. 2073, 2074) and **Folk Sculpture** (no. 2102), and various sections of **Folk Craft** also.

1992.   Ames, Kenneth L. "American Decorative Arts/Household Furnishings." *American Quarterly* 35 (1983): 280-303.

This is an excellent bibliographic essay covering orientations in decorative arts study; Ames looks at previous studies and uses American furniture as a case study. See also 2111, Ames' full-length bibliography on decorative arts and household objects.

1993.   Bailey, Joyce Waddell. *Handbook of Latin American Art= Manual de Arte Latinoamericano: A Bibliographic Compilation*. 2 vols. Santa Barbara, CA: ABC-Clio Information Services, 1984. LC 83-26656; ISBN 0-87436-386-1 (set).

Vol. 1, general references of the nineteenth and twentieth centuries, is in two parts, covering North America and South America. Vol. 2 covers the art of the colonial period: art and architecture, painting, and popular art are included. This is a difficult book to use as there is no general index.

1994.   Biebuyck, Daniel P. *The Arts of Central Africa: An Annotated Bibliography*. Boston, MA: G.K. Hall, 1987. 300p. LC 86-29555; ISBN 0-8161-8601-4. (Reference publications in art history)

The bibliography, following a lengthy introduction, covers classifications of languages, general ethnographies, travelogs, general studies on African art (handbooks, surveys, comparative studies, exhibition catalogs, museum guides, etc.), and general studies on Zairian art. Then the work is divided by place: Northwestern Zaire, East/Central Zaire, etc. There is a separate author index, an ethnic group index, and a subject index, with entries for architecture, artifacts, beadwork, beliefs, body adornment, charms, circumcision rites, furniture, jewelry, and sculpture, etc.

1995.   Boicourt, Eva. "American Folk Art: A Selected Bibliography." *American Bookseller* 8 (December 1984): 30-32.

This bibliography excludes how-to books but includes books on quilts, coverlets, and samplers, books on Native American folk art, and books on regional folk art (other than Pennsylvania Dutch). There are brief annotations and "essential" books are starred.

1996.   Bronner, Simon J., ed. *American Folk Art: A Guide to Sources.* New York: Garland, 1984. 313p. LC 83-49308; ISBN 0-8240-9006-3. (Garland reference library of the humanities; v. 464)

In the preface, Bronner calls this "a guide for students and scholars through the burgeoning field of folk art study." (ix) This is a series of bibliographic essays on such subjects as background and history, art criticism and aesthetic philosophy, the various genres (painting, sculpture, furniture, textiles, ceramics, metal), biographies of artists, regional and local art, ethnic and religious art, Afro-American folk art, workers and trades, symbol and image and theme, and collections and museums, as well as public art, and folk art and the elderly, etc. There is an introduction to each chapter, the essay, and then a selection of annotated citations of American books, articles, and films. Included also are 30 pages of photographs and separate author and subject indexes. Bronner and his essayists/bibliographers have amassed a huge amount of material which will be hard to keep updated.

1997.   Bronner, Simon J. *A Critical Bibliography of American Folk Art.* Bloomington, IN: Folklore Publications Group, 1978. 112p. LC 78-113721. (FPG monograph series; v. 3)

There are 704 items in this bibliography which covers various aspects of American folk art, excluding decorative crafts: painting, drawing, sculpture, and carving.

1998.   Burt, Eugene C. *An Annotated Bibliography of the Visual Arts of East Africa.* Bloomington: Indiana University Press, 1980. 371p. LC 80-7805; ISBN 0-253-17225-x. (Traditional arts of Africa)

This excellent bibliography is arranged by locale--East Africa (general), Kenya, Tanzania, Makonde Group, Uganda--and then arranged alphabetically by author within these groupings. There are 2,028 entries, some annotated. Included also are a variety of indexes: a culture index, author index, and a subject index, with such subject entries as architecture, basketry, body decoration, circumcision and initiation, clothes/dance/games, masks/material culture, pottery/ painting, sculpture, ritual objects, sculpture, textiles, woodcarving, etc.

1999.   Creswell, K.A.C. *A Bibliography of the Architecture, Arts, and Crafts of Islam to the 1st Jan. 1960.* Cairo: American University at Cairo Press. Distributed in London by the Oxford University Press, 1961. 1,330p.+index. LC 62-3352. Supplement, published in 1973, covers January 1960-January 1972.

This is an unannotated listing in two parts: Part I covers **architecture**, and Part II covers **arts and crafts**, including ceramics, costumes, painting textiles (carpets, cotton embroidery, silk, etc.), woodworking. Both parts are arranged by country: Spain, North Africa, India, Persia, Turkey, Egypt, Arabia, Syria, and Sicily. There is an author index.

2000.   Ehresmann, Donald L. *Applied and Decorative Arts: A Bibliographic Guide to Basic Reference Works, Histories, and Handbooks.* Littleton, CO: Libraries Unlimited, 1977. 232p. LC 76-55416; ISBN 0-87287-136-3.

This is a classified bibliography arranged within subject chapters, such as applied, general arts, folk art (American folk art, European folk art, Oriental folk art, etc.); arms and armor; ceramics, with a section on American pottery and stoneware; clocks, watches; costumes; enamels; furniture; glass; ivory; jewelry; metalwork; musical instruments; textiles; and toys and dolls). Ehresmann lists basic texts in the field and annotates them briefly and descriptively. There is an author index and a separate subject index.

2001. Ferris, William, ed. *Afro-American Folk Art and Crafts*. Boston, MA: G.K. Hall, 1983. 440p. LC 82-11752; ISBN 0-8161-9045-3. (Perspectives on the Black world). Reprinted: Jackson: University Press of Mississippi, 1986. LC 86-3458; ISBN 0-8780-5306-9 (p).

There are *three* bibliographies included in this book of essays: 1) "Folklore and Art History" by Simon J. Bronner and Christopher Lornell (pp. 353-404), an annotated bibliography; 2) "Black Artisans and Craftsmen--Colonial Era through 1900: A Select Historical Bibliography" by Clarence Mohr (pp. 405-418); and 3) "Films" by Ellen Slack (pp. 419-429).

2002. Garrett, Wendell D., and Jane N. Garrett. "The Arts in Early America: Historical Needs and Opportunities for Study. Bibliography," in *The Arts in Early American History*, by Walter Muir Whitehill. Chapel Hill: Published for the Institute of Early American History and Culture at Williamsburg by the University of North Carolina Press, 1965. 170p. pp. 35-151. LC 65-63132.

The bibliography is annotated and divided into sections on general works; architecture and architects (by locale); topography; painting, painters, catalogs of portrait collections; sculpture and carving; graphic arts; crafts; furniture (general books, cabinetmakers, regional studies); silver and silversmiths; pewter; woodenware; pottery; wall decorations; textiles, etc.

2003. Gaskin, L.J.P., comp. *A Bibliography of African Art*. London: International African Institute, 1965. 120p. LC 66-70409. (International African Institute, B series)

Divided in two parts. Part I covers 4,826 general works: encyclopedias, ethnographical works, books and articles on African and primitive art, technology, crafts, the artist, and African art today; Part II is a regional classification, arranged by country, and subdivided by subject: figures and masks, buildings and furniture, clothing and adornment, rock art, techniques, utensils/tools/ weapons, and catalogs and guides to museums, exhibitions, collections, and periodicals. There are author, geographical and ethnic, and subject indexes.

2004.   Hanson, Louise, and F. Allan Hanson. *The Art of Oceania: A Bibliography*. Boston, MA: G.K. Hall, 1984. 539p. LC 84-10778; ISBN 0-8161-8645-6. (Reference publication in art history)

There are 6,650 entries arranged regionally (Polynesia, Micronesia, Melanesia, Australia, etc.), and subdivided by type of art. Each entry includes a very brief one-sentence annotation. There is a comprehensive index.

2005.   Igoe, Lynn Moody, and James Igoe. *250 Years of Afro-American Art: An Annotated Bibliography*. New York: Bowker, 1981. 1,266p. LC 81-12226; ISBN 0-8352-1376-5.

This massive work is divided into three parts: a basic bibliography, subject bibliography, and artist bibliography. The basic bibliography is an annotated bibliography of books, exhibition catalogs, and periodical and newspaper articles that refer to more than one artist or to Afro-American art in general, arranged alphabetically by author, issuing organization, or title. The subject bibliography is arranged alphabetically by subject and includes many entries that are folk art related: architecture, crafts--traditional (a large section), folk art, pottery, grave decoration, quiltmaking, weaving, wood carving. There is no index, but there are two appendixes: the first is artwork by anonymous artists, and the second is artwork by groups. Within the subject bibliography, there is a section on art galleries and museums, arranged by state, and giving type of artwork that each one specializes in.

2006.   Karpel, Bernard, ed. *Arts in America: A Bibliography*. 4 vols. Washington, DC: Published for the Archive of American Art by the Smithsonian Institution, 1979. LC 79-15321; ISBN 0-87474-578-0.

Vol. 1 is the most useful one for the folk arts as it includes bibliographies on the art of Native Americans, architecture, decorative arts (ceramics, costume, glass, jewelry, textiles, furniture, and American decorative crafts and other catalogs), design, and sculpture; Vol. 2 covers fine art; Vol. 3 covers photography, film, theater, and dance, and includes a section on serials, dissertations, theses, and visual resources. An author and subject index comprise Vol. 4. Each section has been prepared by an expert in the field or a team of contributors.

2007.   Martin, Charles E. "Kentucky's Traditional Arts and Crafts: A Bibliography." *Kentucky Folklore Record* 31 (1985): 1-94.

There are 733 items listed alphabetically by author or anonymous title as well as a subject index, chronological index (by year), and a chronological ordering of main articles by subject.

2008.   Mayer, L.A. *Bibliography of Jewish Art*. Jerusalem: Magnes Press, Hebrew University, 1967. 374p. LC 68-2647.

This is an international, classed list of over 3,000 entries with one-sentence descriptive annotations. The index includes entries concerned with amulets, applied arts, architects, ceremonial arts, pottery, embroidery, textiles, etc.

2009.   Riccardi, Saro John, comp. *Pennsylvania Dutch Folk Art and Architecture; A Selective Annotated Bibliography*. New York: New York Public Library, 1942. 15p. LC 42-5314. Reprinted from *The Bulletin of the New York Public Library* (June 1942, pp. 471-483).

The bibliography includes 138 annotated entries and a subject index.

2010.   Smith, Robert C., and Elizabeth Wilder. *A Guide to the Art of Latin America*. Washington, DC: U.S.G.P.O., 1948. 480p.

Reprinted: New York: Arno, 1971. LC 74-151054; ISBN 0-405-03421-0. (Hispanic Foundation, Library of Congress, Latin America series, 21)

An introduction discusses the arts in various Latin American countries, first giving general works, then arranging them chronologically from the Colonial period to the present time. Within this framework, the books and articles are subdivided into subject areas: architecture, minor arts, painting, graphic arts, and sculpture. Titles are given in the original language (most are Spanish) with brief annotations given in English. There is a comprehensive index. An earlier work, also from the Library of Congress' Hispanic Foundation, is *Fine and Folk Arts of the Other American Republics: A Bibliography of Publications in English* (Washington, DC: Library of Congress, Archive of Hispanic Culture, 1942). Not seen.

2011. Sokol, David M. *American Architecture and Art: A Guide to Information Sources*. Detroit, MI: Gale Research, 1976. 341p. LC 73-17563; ISBN 0-8103-1255-7. (American studies information guide series; v. 2)

This is divided into general reference sources (bibliographies, directories, dictionaries, encyclopedias, general histories) and subject sources (aesthetics, taste; American architecture; and American decorative arts--furniture, metalwork, ceramics, textiles; American painting, etc). Included are separate author index, short-title index, and subject index.

2012. Sokol, David M. *American Decorative Arts and Old World Influences: A Guide to Information Sources*. Detroit, MI: Gale Research, 1980. 294p. LC 80-18249; ISBN 0-8103-1465-7. (Art and architecture information guide series; v. 14)

Includes bibliographies, general dictionaries, encyclopedias, and histories of decorative art; period surveys and studies; general and period surveys of the decorative arts of individual countries and regions (Africa, Canada, China...). Subject surveys of decorative arts, general works on American decorative arts, American ceramics, American furniture,

American glass, American textiles, quilts, samplers, weavings and industrial textiles, are also included. There is also an author index, title index,
and subject index.

2013.   *Tribal and Ethnic Art.* Santa Barbara, CA: ABC-Clio Press,
        1982. 99p. LC 82-152085; ISBN 0-903450-60-7. (Modern art
        bibliographical series; v.1)

        Over 900 entries are drawn from ARTbibliographies, MODERN
database of abstracts, dissertations, exhibition catalogs published before
1977, and journals. Arrangement is by subject: general (includes
collections and Shamanism), Africa (ceramics, collections, masks, etc.),
the Americas (basketry, beadwork, ceramics, costume, textiles, etc.), and
other regions (Australian aborigine, Eskimo, Indian, Indonesian, Lapp,
Malaysia, Nepal, the Philippines and Oceania, Sri Lanka, Taiwan). An
addendum is appended, and there is a separate author and subject index.
The annotations range from very short to quite substantial.

2014.   Western, Dominique Coulet, comp. *A Bibliography of the Arts
        of Africa.* Waltham, MA: African Studies Association, Brandeis
        University, 1975. 123p. LC 75-330472.

        There are three main divisions: art, architecture, and oral
literature. Art and architecture are subdivided into general works and then
geographically, subdivided by tribe and culture. The oral literature section
is divided into music and dance. The bibliographic entries are not
annotated. There is an author index but no subject index, which might
make it less useful.

Catalogs--Folk Art-General

2015.   Tinkham, Sandra Shaffer, ed. *The Consolidated Catalog to the
        Index of American Design.* Cambridge [ENG]: Chadwyck-Healy;
        Teaneck, NJ: Somerset House, 1980. 800p. LC 79-22293; ISBN
        0-914146-95-5.

This is really a guide to *The Index of American Design* (see no. 2029 for an explanation of the *Index*...) which is now published in microfiche format. This work, mirroring the larger one which indexes well over 15,000 drawings of the work of 800 artists from 35 states, is arranged in ten parts: 1) textiles, costumes and jewelry; 2) art and design of utopian and religious communities; 3) architecture and naive art; 4) tools, hardware, and firearms; 5) domestic utensils; 6) furniture and decorative accessories; 7) wood carvings and weathervanes; 8) ceramics and glass; 9) silver, copper, pewter, and tableware; and 10) toys and miscellaneous items. Includes also a subject index.

Dictionary Catalogs--Folk Art-General

2016. New York Public Library. Art and Architecture Division. *Bibliographic Guide to Art and Architecture, 1975--*. Boston, MA: G.K. Hall, 1977--. Annual. Supplement to the Division's *Dictionary Catalog*.

This impressive work is a list of publications cataloged during the previous year by the Research Libraries of the New York Public Library and the Library of Congress, which serves as an annual supplement to the original *Dictionary Catalog of the Art and Architecture Division of the Research Library of the New York Public Library* (Boston, MA: G.K. Hall, 1975). There are many folkloric entries, especially under the heading **Folk Art**, but there are also entries for **decorative and applied arts, architecture, ceramics, costume, folk painting, pottery,** and **textile arts.**

2017. *The Winterthur Museum Libraries Collection of Printed Books and Periodicals.* 9 vols. Wilmington, DE: Scholarly Resources, 1974, with the cooperation of the Henry Francis DuPont Winterthur Museum, 1974. LC 73-88753; ISBN 0-8420-1725-9.

This is a reproduction of the card catalog of the Winterthur Museum, with many entries for **Folk Art**. Vols. 8 and 9 contain cards for the Rare Book Collection, and Vol. 9 includes auction catalogs and the

Edward Deming Andrews Memorial Shaker Collection, a collection of many works on Shaker furniture and customs.

Dictionaries and Encyclopedias--Folk Art-General

2018.   Fleming, John, and Hugh Honour. *Dictionary of the Decorative Arts*. New York: Harper & Row, 1977. 896p. LC 76-50163; ISBN 0-06-011936-5.

This deals primarily with European, Canadian, and American furniture and furnishings from the Middle Ages and Colonial Period to the present. The authors include "objects that have played a part in the development of the decorative arts in the West" (e.g., Chinese and Japanese ceramics). Includes also bibliographic notes.

2019.   Osborne, Harold, ed. *The Oxford Companion to the Decorative Arts*. Oxford: Clarendon Press, 1975. 865p. LC 75-331784; ISBN 0-19-866113-4

This is intended as an introduction to "those arts which are made to serve a practical purpose but are nevertheless prized for the quality of their workmanship and the beauty of their appearance." Included are traditional crafts, like ceramics, textiles, costumes, woodworking, metalworking, etc. The arrangement is encyclopedic with several long surveys; for example, the entry for **Africa**, which covers wood, iron, bronze, ivory, pottery, textiles, basketry, carving and paintings done by traditional African craftsmen, is very long.

2020.   Stoutenburgh, John L. *Dictionary of Arts and Crafts*. New York: Philosophical Library, 1956. 259p. LC 56-13756. (Mid-century reference library)

Although this is a "popular" work, it contains useful information and provides some basic information on folk art and crafts.

2021. Hemphill, Herbert W., and Julia Weissman. *Twentieth- century American Folk Art and Artists.* New York: Dutton, 1974. 237p. LC 74-12934; ISBN 0-5282-2473-4.

This is "a broad survey of the wealth and variety of American folk art produced since 1900." The work is arranged chronologically with an index to artists and a bibliography. There are 385 paintings and objects photographed in color and black and white.

2022. Johannsen, Christina B., and John P. Ferguson, eds. *Iroquois Arts: A Directory of A People and Their Work.* Warnerville, NY: Association for the Advancement of Native North American Arts and Crafts; distributed: Schoharie, NY: Schoharie Museum of the Iroquois Indian. 1983. 406p.

Not seen.

2023. Johnson, Jay, and William C. Ketchum, Jr. *American Folk Art of the Twentieth Century.* New York: Rizzoli, 1983. 342p. LC 83-42933; ISBN 0-8478-0503-4.

There are 118 artists introduced in this work, many of whom are painters, but there are also sculptors, potters, stone, and textile workers. The arrangement is alphabetic by artist, most of whom are contemporary folk artists with many works dating from 1970. There is a biographical sketch for each artist with an explanation of his or her media and special techniques. There are 230 works pictured, all in color, and described. The introduction is by Robert Bishop; there is a large, though not very up to date bibliography of 150 items and an index. A beautiful book.

Guides and Handbooks--Folk Art-General

2024.   Andrews, Ruth, ed. *How to Know American Folk Art: Eleven Experts Discuss Many Aspects of the Field.* New York: Dutton, 1977. 204p. LC 77-72039; ISBN 0-525-474609.

This is a basic introductory guide to identification of the following folk art forms: early New England gravestones, the wildfowl decoy, redware and stoneware folk pottery, folk art of Spanish New Mexico, American painting, American country furniture, American quilts, Pennsylvania-German folk art, American folk sculpture, and American folk art in the twentieth century. Each section is written by a subject expert. There are black-and-white illustrations with a center section of color plates. Index.

2025.   Bishop, Robert, et al. *Folk Art: Paintings, Sculpture, & Country Objects.* New York: Alfred A. Knopf/Random House, 1983. 478p. LC 82-48945; ISBN 0-394-71493-8. (Knopf collectors' guides to American antiques)

This is part of a series of guide books on American folk art published by Knopf. An introductory section includes a definition of folk art, tells how to identify folk art, discusses folk painting, folk sculpture, and country household objects, and tells how to evaluate folk art. The 370 items--paintings, sculptures, and household objects--are pictured and described in detail. There is a glossary, a list of public collections, a bibliography, a price guide, a checklist of artists and craftsmen, and an index.

2026.   Nöel Hume, Ivor. *A Guide to Artifacts of Colonial America.* New York: Alfred A. Knopf, 1970. 323p.+index. LC 76-79314.

The author, the director of the Department of Archaeology at Williamsburg, discusses artifacts, which are listed alphabetically: armor, bayonets, beads, bells, bottles, bricks and brickwork, buttons, ceramics.... The descriptions are intended to help identify objects. There is an abundance of drawings and an index.

2027.   Pokropek, Marian. *A Guide to Folk Art and Folklore in Poland.*
        Warsaw: Arkady, 1980. 269p. LC 81-141017; ISBN 8-3213-
        3014-2.

        Contains information about "the most important extant
monuments of folk culture." Includes paintings, architecture, sculpture,
graphic arts, ceramics, weaving, metal work, and wood work. The
arrangement is geographical. Maps are included.

Indexes--Folk Art-General

2028.   *Art Index.* New York: H.W. Wilson, 1929--. Issued quarterly;
        cumulated annually.

        Lists articles, books, publications, collections, and exhibition
catalogs. The latest annual had entries to folk art bibliographies, and
entries for American, Austrian, Chinese, Indian, and Mexican folk art.
There are also entries for folk art museums and collections, folk crafts,
etc.

2029.   Christensen, Erwin Ottomar. *The Index of American Design.*
        New York: Macmillan, for the National Gallery of Art,
        Smithsonian Institution, 1950. 229p. LC 50-10215.

        The Index of American Design, consisting of 17,000 drawings
and 5,000 photographs, is "a repository of the skill of craftsmen as it
stands, the largest and most nearly comprehensive collection of its kind."
It was begun in 1935 as part of the WPA Federal Art Project, under the
direction of Holger Cahill, its aim being "to compile and eventually to
publish a visual survey of the objects of the decorative, folk, and popular
arts made in America." This publication is taken from the files of the
Index (now housed in the National Gallery of Art), and includes
illustrations and photos from all over the world, representing a cross
section of American decorative and popular arts from about 1700-1900.
There are 378 items pictured and discussed as well as a subject list and
a selected bibliography and index. In 1950, when this was published, the
Index was considered the "largest and most comprehensive collection of

its kind in the world." And Jan Brunvand wrote about this particular book, "More broadly considered, the most important single picture-book on American folk art is *The Index of American Design*" (1st ed., *Study of American Folklore*, p. 285) Several other works have been based on the Index. See Hornung's work below (no. 2030) and Tinkham (no. 2015).

2030.   Hornung, Clarence P. *Treasury of American Design; A Pictorial Survey of Popular Folk Arts Based upon Watercolor Renderings in the Index of American Design, at the National Gallery of Art.* 2 vols. New York: Abrams, 1977 [1972]. 846p. ISBN 0-8109-0516-7.

Over 2,900 items, pictured and described, are grouped by objects. Book I covers objects that are "on land and sea" (ship's figures, tavern signs, carriages, etc., and Book II covers objects that are found "in the home and around the house" (food, children's toys, etc.). Included also are a listing of state projects in the folk arts, a general index, and an index of artists. This is a beautiful set of books, the most comprehensive description of the Index.

2031.   Meyer, George H., ed. *Folk Artists Biographical Index*. Detroit, MI: Gale Research, 1987. 496p. LC 86-15029; ISBN 0-8103-2145-9.

This work, the subtitle tells us, is "a guide to over 200 published sources of information on approximately 9,000 American artists from the seventeenth century to the present." Aside from the biographical information for each folk artist, there is an art locator, a bibliography of sources, and many indexes--ethnic, geographical, media, and type of work-- as well as a directory of almost 300 institutions where the artists are located. Very comprehensive.

Exhibition Catalogs and Guides to Collections--Folk Art-General

Note: This is a **selection** of what is available and in print, selected for regional or historical importance. These are

848

catalogs of exhibitions or guides to museum collections of general folk art. If the collection or exhibition included or includes mostly folk paintings or folk crafts, then those catalogs will be listed under those sections, following this one. Also, Elizabeth Mosby Adler's article, "Directions in the Study of American Folk Art" (*New York Folklore* 1 [1975]: 31-44), is an excellent, comprehensive compilation of museum exhibits of folk art from 1924 through the mid-1970s. These are arranged geographically.

The Americas
North America

2032.   Ames, Kenneth L. *Beyond Necessity: Art in the Folk Tradition: An Exhibition from the Collections of Winterthur Museum at the Brandywine River Museum, Chadds Ford, Pa.* Winterthur, DE: Published for the Winterthur Museum by W. W. Norton, 1977. 131p. LC 77-84854; ISBN 0-912724-05-6.

This catalog includes a long introductory text, a catalog of 225 objects, most of which are illustrated, and an annotated bibliography.

2033.   [Bishop, Robert]. *American Folk Art: Expressions of a New Spirit.* New York: Museum of American Folk Art, 1983. 146p. ISBN 0-912161-83-1.

This catalog is from a traveling exhibition (mainly to Europe and London) of about 130 works from the museum's permanent collection. Objects are pictured and described. A brief bibliography is appended.

2034.   Bivens, John, Jr., and Paula Welshimer. *Moravian Decorative Arts in North Carolina: An Introduction to the Old Salem Collection.* Winston-Salem, NC: Old Salem Inc., 1981. 111p. LC 81-186794.

This covers separately Moravian furniture, pottery, textiles, metalwork, prints, and paintings, and includes an overview of the

Moravians and Moravian decorative art. Most of these items, which are in the Old Salem Collection, were produced locally between 1775-1840. Each section is arranged chronologically and includes many photographs, some in color. There is a glossary and notes, but no index or bibliography.

2035.   Cahill, Holger. *American Folk Art; The Art of the Common Man in America, 1750-1900.* New York: Museum of Modern Art, 1932. 52p. text+172 black-and-white photographs. LC 32-34218. Reprinted: Williamsburg, VA: Abby Aldrich Rockefeller Folk Art Collection, 1968.

Cahill's introduction discusses different types of American folk art in this catalog to one of the first major exhibits of American folk arts in the United States. One hundred seventy-five items are discussed and shown, of which 122 are paintings of different media on several different surfaces; the balance of the works are metal and wood sculptures, with a few plaster ornaments. Appended is a bibliography of books and publications.

2036.   Cannon, Hal, ed. *Utah Folk Art: A Catalog of Material Culture.* Provo, UT: Brigham Young University Press, 1980. 149p. LC 80-13920.

The works here are cataloged and described within the following sections: Indian art, frontier art, ranch, house, craft, women, carving, symbol, painting, and death. Each section includes an essay, relating it to Utah crafts (e.g., **Death:** gravestone imagery, etc.). There are 156 items pictured in all.

2037.   Center for Southern Folklore. *Folk Arts and Crafts: The Deep South.*

A description of one of the Smithsonian's circulating exhibitions available from the Center for Southern Folklore, 1216 Peabody Ave., P.O.Box 4080, Memphis, TN.

2038. Chase, Judith Wragg. *Afro-American Art and Craft*. New York: Van Nostrand Reinhold, 1971. 142p. LC 76-163485.

Although this is primarily a study, it is based on the collection at the Old Slave Market Museum, in Charleston, South Carolina. Covered is West African art and craft, urban craft and craftsmen, plantation craft and craftsmen, pioneer art and artists, and Depression and contemporary black art and craft.

2039. *Circles of Tradition: Folk Arts in Minnesota*. St. Paul: Published for the University of Minnesota Art Museum by the Minnesota Historical Society Press, 1989. 162p. LC 88-37753; ISBN 0-87351-239-1.

Introductory matter includes essays on Minnesota folk art, Norwegian-American arts and crafts, Ojibway ritual design, the Mexican-Corrida tradition, and a Latvian mitten knitter. The catalog includes 109 items and a Minnesota folk art survey. Concludes with a selected bibliography and index.

2040. Deacon, Deborah A. "The Art & Artifacts Collection of the Schomburg Center for Research in Black Culture: A Preliminary Catalogue." *Bulletin of Research in the Humanities* 84 (1981): 145-261.

This is a history and a full catalog of this marvelous collection which includes African arts and artifacts (paintings, sculpture, prints, and drawings). The artifacts are listed by place and tribe from which they came; the art works are listed alphabetically by painter, sculptor, etc. The listings are all annotated with long descriptions and, when appropriate, biographical information about the artist is given. Many photographs enhance this terrific reference work.

2041. Dewhurst, C. Kurt, et al. *Artists in Aprons: Folk Art by American Women*. New York: E.P. Dutton for the Museum of

American Folk Art, 1979. 202p. LC 78-55945; ISBN 0-525-05857-5 (c); ISBN 0-525-47503-6 (p).

The catalog covers all types of folk art done by American women, including needlework, paintings and *frakturs*, and sculpture, old and new. Included are brief biographies of the women artists and craftspersons. There is a very complete bibliography which covers books and articles about women and society and about the various art forms.

2042. Dewhurst, C. Kurt, et al. *Religious Folk Art in America: Reflections of Faith.* New York: E.P. Dutton in association with the Museum of American Folk Art, 1983. 163p. LC 83-71103; ISBN 0-525-93300-x (c); 0-525-48071-4 (p).

A scholarly introduction on the relationship between religion and folk art prefaces this exhibition of 216 items, all described: paintings, icons, quilts, samplers, crucifixes, etc. Although this exhibition and catalog are described "as merely an overview of America's rich heritage of religious material folk culture," this is a thorough overview of American religious folk material in all media. There is also a comprehensive bibliography covering all aspects of folk art and religion in society.

2043. Dickens, Roy S., Jr. *Of Sky and Earth: Art of the Early Southeastern Indians.* Atlanta: Georgia Department of Archives and History, 1982. 96p. LC 83-11582; ISBN 0-87049-388-4.

This catalog of an exhibit held at the High Museum, Atlanta, in 1982, describes 161 items and pictures many of them in color and black and white.

2044. Doty, Robert. *American Folk Art in Ohio Collections.* Akron, OH: Akron Art Institute; distributed by Dodd, Mead, 1976. [95p]. LC 76-54374; ISBN 0-396-07360-3.

The catalog includes mourning pictures, baptismal certificates, clocks, portraits, ceramics, scrimshaw, pots, carving, etc., all dated, with name of artist, if known, the size of the painting or object, lender, and full description. Arranged chronologically.

2045. Ewing, Douglas C. *Pleasing the Spirits: A Catalogue of a Collection of American Indian Art.* New York: Ghylen Press, 1982. 401p. LC 82-82130.

The author divides this anonymously-owned collection into four categories: ritual and medicine, warfare and the horse, clothing and personal adornment, and domestic life. There are 479 items described and illustrated. An index is included.

2046. Fife, Austin, et al., eds. *Forms Upon The Frontier; Folklife and Folk Arts in the United States.* Logan, Utah: Utah State University Press, 1969. 189p. (Monograph series; v. 16, 2)

Although this is basically a book of essays on Utah architecture, arts and crafts, medicine, recipes, folklife, customs, and ethnic groups, there is a catalog of an exhibit included. The items listed and described are tools, folk arts, house types, farms and ranches, rural mail boxes, barbed wire, rawhides, braiding, gravestones, and furniture.

2047. Garvan, Beatrice B., and Charles F. Hummel. *The Pennsylvania Germans: A Celebration of Their Arts, 1683-1850.* Philadelphia, PA: Philadelphia Museum of Art, 1982. 196p. LC 82-61416; ISBN 0-87633-048-0.

The exhibition, co-sponsored by the Philadelphia Museum of Art and Winterthur Museum, includes portraits, furniture, bowls, bottles, *frakturs*, manuscripts, roof tiles, saddles, textiles, paintings, weaving, dishes, silverware, musical instruments, baskets, and bee sheps. There are 333 items included; 132 are photographed in color. Note: a "more scholarly" edition of this work was published as *Pennsylvania German Art, 1683-1850*, published for the Philadelphia Museum of Art and the

Winterthur Museum by the University of Chicago Press, 1984. It is double the size (365p.) but covers the same categories. Descriptions of items are fuller; fiche are included in a pocket.

2048. Glassie, Henry. *The Spirit of Folk Art: The Girard Collection at the Museum of International Folk Art.* New York: Harry N. Abrams in association with the Museum of New Mexico, Santa Fe, 1989. 241p. LC 88-21854; ISBN 0-8109-1522-7; 0-89013-193-7.

The foreword is by A. Stanley Marcus. The catalog is a collection really of several essays--on the spirit of folk art, on folk art in the Girard Collection, on the difference between "folk," "art," and "folk art," and on the relationship between folk art, fine art, and popular art. The Girard collection houses over 100,000 works, 274 of which are pictured in full color, with a brief description, throughout the book. There are bibliographic notes, chapter bibliographies, and an index. This is not so much a collection catalog as a full-scale study of folk art, using pieces from this wonderful collection as examples. A stunning book.

2049. Grave, Alexandra. *Three Centuries of Connecticut Folk Art.* [New Haven]: Art Resources of Connecticut, 1971. 104p. LC 79-124402.

There are 293 pieces in this exhibition of Connecticut craftsmen, past and present, divided into the following sections: gravestones, stenciled and painted decorations, pottery, early Connecticut decoration, tavern and trade signs, weathervanes, portraits, paintings and drawings, "women's work," decoys, scrimshaw, toys, bone, and "fantasies."

2050. Jasper, Pat, and Kay Turner. *Art Among Us=Arte Entre Nosotros: Mexican American Folk Art of San Antonio.* San Antonio, TX: San Antonio Museum Association, 1986. 103p. LC 86-60762.

Essays are in Spanish and English, and 50 figures are described throughout the text. Includes bibliography.

2051. Kleeblatt, Norman L., and Gerard C. Wertkin, comps. *The Jewish Heritage in American Folk Art.* New York: Universe Books, 1984. 124p. LC 84-40352; ISBN 0-87663-449-8 (c); 0-87663-858-2 (p).

This book catalogs 128 items of folk art from the Jewish Museum in New York, all greatly described with many full-color illustrations. There are also interesting articles on "Aspects of Jewish History and Folk Art Perspective" and on "Jewish Folk Art in America: Traditional Forms and Cultural Adaptations." A bibliography and glossary conclude this catalog.

2052. Lipman, Jean, and Alice Winchester. *The Flowering of American Folk Art, 1776-1876.* New York: Viking Press in cooperation with the Whitney Museum of Art, 1974. 288p. LC 73-6081; ISBN 0-670-32120-6.

This was a major traveling exhibit that appeared at the Whitney Museum of American Art (New York), the Virginia Museum of Fine Arts (Richmond), and at the Fine Arts Museum of San Francisco, at the de Young Memorial Museum, in 1974. There are essays that work to define American folk art and a listing of exhibitions, publications, collectors, and collections. Over 400 items are shown, including pictures which are painted, drawn and stitched, sculpture in wood, metal, stone and bone, decorations for home and highway, and furnishings. There is a biographical index of authors and an excellent basic bibliography arranged by genre.

2053. Little, Nina Fletcher. *The Abby Aldrich Rockefeller Folk Art Collection: A Descriptive Catalogue.* Williamsburg, VA: Colonial Williamsburg Foundation, 1957. 402p. LC 57-6251.

This catalog of a major folk art collection includes 424 pieces: paintings in oil (by far the bulk of the collection), watercolor and pastel paintings, paintings on glass, *frakturs*, and needlework and painted textiles. Each work is illustrated in color, with the title, a date and artist's name, if known, the size, medium, and a brief note. Appendix material includes notes on conservation and on the artists represented in the collection. There is a bibliography and index. See also Beatrix T. Rumford's *The Abby Aldrich Rockefeller Folk Art Collection, a Gallery Guide* (Williamsburg, VA: Colonial Williamsburg Foundation, 1975), a pamphlet that contains a brief history of the museum and a guide to items in the permanent collection.

2054.   Little, Nina Fletcher. *American Folk Art from the Abby Aldrich Rockefeller Folk Art Collection*. Williamsburg, VA: Colonial Williamsburg Foundation, 1966. 47p. LC 66-23513.

This exhibition, co-sponsored with the American Folklore Association, included 55 items, many paintings, but also wood carvings, jugs, weathervanes, etc. (See also nos. 2053, 2078, 2079.)

2055.   Little, Nina Fletcher. *Little By Little; Six Decades of Collecting American Decorative Arts*. New York: E.P. Dutton, 1984. 291p. LC 84-70630; ISBN 0-525-24265-1.

This is sort of an autobiographical account of the collecting and collections of Nina and Bert Little, covering especially paintings (portraits, interiors, landscapes, and family records), folk carvings (decorative and useful), furniture and textiles, and toys. There are 366 plates, notes, a selected bibliography, and an index.

2056.   Livingston, Jane, and John Beardsley. *Black Folk Art in America, 1930-1980*. Jackson, MI: University Press of Mississippi and the Center for the Study of Southern Culture for the Corcoran Gallery of Art, Washington, DC, 1982. 186p. LC 81-24072; ISBN 0-87805-158-9.

This exhibition of the work of 20 black American craftsmen was shown at the Corcoran, the J.B. Speed Museum (Louisville, KY) in 1982, the Brooklyn Museum, the Craft and Folk Art Museum (Los Angeles), and the Institute for the Arts, Rice University (Houston) in 1983. There are introductory essays on the origins and manifestations of early American folk art and one called, "Spiritual Epics: The Voyage and Vision in Black Folk Art" as well as biographical profiles on the artists, arranged alphabetically, from **Jesse Aaron** to **Joseph Yoakum**. There is a catalog of 391 items, a listing by title of each object and its owner, with 150 illustrations, and a selected bibliography in two parts: general texts and works about the 20 artists.

2057.   Milwaukee Art Museum. *American Folk Art: The Herbert Waide Hemphill, Jr. Collection*. Milwaukee, WI: Milwaukee Art Museum, 1981. 112p. LC 81-83157.

This work includes an interview with Hemphill, an overview of the collection, an essay on twentieth century folk art, and a catalog of 105 items arranged chronologically from the eighteenth century through 1979. There is a selected bibliography.

2058.   Montgomery, Charles F., and Patricia E. Kane, gen. eds. *American Art: 1750-1800: Towards Independence*. Boston. MA: Published for Yale University Art Gallery, New Haven, CT, and the Victoria and Albert Museum, London, by the New York Graphic Society, 1976. 320p. LC 75-24591; ISBN 0-8212-0692-3.

This is a major catalog which includes essays on American art and American culture by J.H. Plumb, Neil Harris, and Frank H. Sommers as well as one on "Regional Preferences and Characteristics in American Decorative Arts: 1750-1800" by C.F. Montgomery, and a catalog including 240 plates of paintings, furniture, glassware, textiles, etc., all of which are intertwined with the text. There is also a substantial bibliography.

2059. The Museum of Early Southern Decorative Arts. *A Collection of Southern Furniture, Paintings, Ceramics, Textiles, and Metalwork.* Winston-Salem, NC: Old Salem Foundation, 1979. 96p. LC 78-61989.

Frank L. Horton's introduction about the southern craftsman is followed by a room-by-room description of MESDA.

2060. Museum of International Folk Art. *The Idea of Folk Art; The Bartlett Collection.* Santa Fe, NM: Museum of New Mexico Press, 1963. 20p. LC 63-20792.

This exhibition of the collection of Florence Dibwell Bartlett was held at New Mexico's Museum of International Folk Art in 1963. In the catalog, written by James Taylor Forrest, there is some introductory matter on folk art as traditional, rural, universal, and useful as well as a descriptive catalog of 134 items: paintings, silver pendants, embroidered silk pieces, a ceremonial dress from the American Indians, wedding dresses from Serbia, Mongolian plates, pottery jugs from eastern Europe, and carriage ornaments, flat irons, jewelry, furniture, *retablos*, etc., from the U.S.

2061. Nosanow, Barbara Shissler. *More Than Land or Sky: Art from Appalachia.* Washington, DC: Published for the National Museum of American Art by the Smithsonian Institution Press, 1981. 127p. LC 81-13566.

This is a catalog of an exhibition of Appalachian art held at the Smithsonian in 1981-1982. The artwork is arranged and listed by artist following a long introduction.

2062. Pike, Martha V., and Janice Gray Armstrong. *A Time to Mourn: Expressions of Grief in Nineteenth Century America.* Stony Brook, NY: The Museums at Stony Brook, 1980. 192p. LC 80-15105.

These are "tangible expressions of grief." An introduction treats custom and change, the cemetery, the funeral, and aspects of mourning. The catalog of 244 items includes paintings, samplers, mourning pictures, mourning rings, lockets, spoons, hearse designs, letters, funeral bills, etc. See Schorsch (no. 2064).

2063.　Polley, Robert L., gen. ed. *America's Folk Art; Treasures of American Folk Arts and Crafts in Distinguished Museums and Collections.* New York: Putnam, 1968. 189p. LC 68-31615.

This work covers separately woodcraft, wrought iron and cast iron work, common metal work, toys, country furniture, needlework and textiles, glassware, pottery, porcelain, the decorative arts, folk painting, guns, and western crafts. Situates work in museums and collections.

2064.　Schorsch, Anita. *Mourning Becomes America: Mourning Arts in the New Nation.* Clinton, NJ: Main Street Press for the William Penn Memorial Museum [Harrisburg, PA], 1976. unpaged. LC 76-4645.

This a collection of mourning art, mainly stitched or painted. There is a long introduction to the field of mourning art and an annotated catalog of 259 pieces including paintings of mourning pictures and artifacts--dishes, plates, jugs, and reliefs. Seventy-five of them are pictured and described. See also Pike and Armstrong (no. 2062).

2065.　Shalkop, Robert L. *The Folk Art of a New Mexican Village.* Colorado Springs: The Taylor Museum of the Colorado Springs Fine Art Center, 1969. 48p. LC 76-7657.

This catalog serves as an introduction to mostly Spanish religious art including church and chapel architecture, sculpture, and painting. There is a catalog of the Museum's holdings in folk art.

2066.   Vlach, John Michael. *The Afro-American Tradition in Decorative Arts*. Cleveland, OH: Cleveland Museum of Art, 1978. 175p. LC 77-19326; ISBN 0-910386-39-0. Reprinted, with a new preface: Athens: University of Georgia Press, 1990. LC 89-205742; ISBN 0-8203-1232-0 (c); 0-8203-1233-9 (p).

This catalog was compiled for a travelling exhibition, which began at the Cleveland Museum in 1978 and travelled to other museums into 1979. There are 99 items cataloged and described, all photographed either in black and white or color. The folk art genres covered include basketry, musical instruments, woodcarving, quilting, pottery, boat building, blacksmithing, architecture, and graveyard decoration, each section having running descriptions of artifacts. There are notes and an extensive bibliography appended.

2067.   Walker Art Center. *American Indian Art: Form and Tradition*. Minneapolis, MN: Walker Arts Center, 1972. 154p. LC 72-90701.

This exhibit was held from October-December 1972. There are many introductory essays in the catalog: "Of Traditions and Esthetics" by Martin Friedman, "Rock Art" by David Gebhard, "Men and Nature in Pueblo Architecture" by Vincent Scully, "Indian Art in the Southwest" by Frederick J. Dockstader, etc. The catalog describes the 862 items in the exhibit, many pictured throughout the book. Also included are maps and a bibliography.

2068.   Welsh, Peter C. *American Folk Art: The Art and Spirit of A People;...*. Washington, DC: Smithsonian Institution Press, 1965. unpaged. LC 66-61813. (Smithsonian publication, 4165)

This is an introduction to and a catalog of 147 items from the Eleanor and Mabel Van Alstyne collection. Included also are 64 plates and a bibliography.

Canada

2069. Field, Richard Henning. *Spirit of Nova Scotia: Traditional Decorative Folk Art, 1780-1930.* Toronto: Dundeen Press, 1985. 211p. LC 86-170437; ISBN 1-55002-064-4 (c); 1-55002-004-8 (p).

The catalog covers textiles, sculptures, paintings, watercolors, and drawings, with a section on decorated utilitarian objects. Each section includes an essay. The 295 items are pictured, mostly in black and white. There is a map of Nova Scotia and a selected bibliography.

South and Central America

2070. Burnaby Art Gallery. *The Folk Art of Latin America: A Tripartite Exhibition.* Burnaby [CAN]: Burnaby Art Gallery, 1973. [56p.]. LC 75-309716.

This exhibit originated at three different Canadian centers: Burnaby Art Gallery exhibited the art of Peru; the Fine Arts Gallery, University of British Columbia, exhibited the art work of Mexico and Guatemala; and the Simon Fraser Gallery, Vancouver, showed Ecuadorian and jungle crafts. Separate essays cover the folk art of Guatemala, Ecuador, and Peru. All 42 objects exhibited at all three art centers are photographed and described. And there is a bibliography.

Asia

2071. Ecke Tseng, Yu-ho. *Chinese Folk Art in American Collections, Early 15th through Early 20th Centuries.* New York: China Institute in America, 1976. 99p. LC 76-20011.

The catalog is compiled from an exhibit held in California and Hawaii in 1977-78 and covers such crafts as basketry and other woven objects, cotton textiles, cotton fabrics dyed in the design, cotton embroidery, cotton appliqué, wood utensils, lacquered utensils, gourds, pewter and silverware, wooden statues, woodblock prints, religious and secular objects, folk painting, tile engravings, and paper crafts. Over 135 items are pictured in black and white photos. There are separate bibliographies of Chinese and English articles and books and Japanese books.

2072. University of Texas Art Museum. *Himalaya: An Exhibit of the Arts and Crafts of Tibet and Nepal. December 6-January 5, 1964*. Austin: University of Texas for the University Art Museum, 1964. 26p. LC 65-64871.

This catalog is a running text on the art of Tibet and Nepal with examples and black-and-white photographs taken from the exhibition.

FOLK ART
Folk Painting

This section is confined to reference materials about folk painting. Covered specifically are naive and folk painting, *fraktur* of the Pennsylvania Germans, folk wall paintings (stencilling, murals, etc.), and *retablos*, the painted board, relief-panel or print, representing a saint or holy person, found mainly in the American southwest.

There were some new theories concerning folk painting published at the end of the 1980s. John Michael Vlach, in *Plain Painters: Making Sense of American Folk Art* (Washington, DC: Smithsonian Institution Press, 1988), complains that most folk painting portraits are elitist, "the opposite of the folk experience," so that what is needed is a "reevaluation of folk art thinking...a useful, accurate interpretation of folk art," one that involves sorting out the problem of terminology, folk art being alternately termed **primitive, naive**, or **amateur art**, and also simply **folk painting**, a term which, he says, "embodies an internal contradiction as they are not expressions of folk culture." Vlach would label these works **plain painting**, "a work like fine art but simpler, less ostentatious; it is a plain version of what potentially could have been quite elaborate or complex under different circumstances." (xi-xv) Another definitional study is Roger Manley's exhibition catalog *Signs and Wonders: Outsider Art Inside*

862

North Carolina (no. 2096), in which he defines the "outsider" in his title as "outside of [the] sanctioned mainstream of the art world; the art has been created by ordinary individuals who are not part of the art world and who, initially at least, often have no concept of themselves as artists or of their creations as art"; outsider artists, then, are those whose work is "marked by an intensity of creation." (ix)

Again, there are many, many surveys of folk painting, which have been excluded because of space limitations. There are a great number of general surveys of folk painting, such as Mary Black's and Jean Lipman's *American Folk Painting* (New York: Clarkson Potter, 1979), which surveys portrait painting, landscape painting, and illumination. There are also full-length studies of several folk painters, such as Jean Lipman's and Alice Winchester's *Primitive Painters in America, 1750-1950* (New York: Dodd, Mead, 1950; reprinted: New York: Books for Libraries, 1971) and Ramona Lampell's *O, Appalachia: Artists of the Southern Mountains* (New York: Stewart, Tabori & Chang, 1989; distributed by Workman), both of these containing biographical sketches of historical (in the first work) and contemporary (in the latter work) painters, and full-length studies of one folk artist such Jane Kallir's *Grandma Moses, The Artist Behind the Myth* (no. 2090), Otto Kallir's *Grandma Moses* (New York: Harry N. Abrams, 1973), and Leon Arkus' *John Kane, Painter* (Pittsburgh, PA: University of Pittsburgh Press, 1971), with a catalogue raisonné of Kane's work. There are also surveys of the paintings of one culture such as Dorothy Dunn's *American Indian Painting of the Southwest and Plains Areas* (Albuquerque: University of New Mexico Press, 1968), and surveys of types of paintings such as Don Yoder's *Pennsylvania German Fraktur and Color Drawings* (Lancaster, PA: Landis Valley Associates, 1969) or José Espinosa's *Saints in the Valleys: Christian Sacred Images in the History, Life and Folk Art of Spanish New Mexico* (Albuquerque: University of New Mexico Press, 1967 [1960]) or Nina Fletcher Little's *American Decorative Wall Painting, 1700-1850* (New York: Dutton, 1972 [1952]).

Bibliographies--Folk Painting

Note: Be sure to consult also the bibliographies listed under **Folk Art--General** (nos. 1992-2014).

2073.   Boyd, E. "The Literature of Santos." *Southwest Review* 35 (1950): 128-40; reprinted: Dallas, TX: SMU Press, 1950.

Santo is a generic term used in the southwest to denote any representation of saints or holy persons. There are two types of **santos**: the *retablo*, mentioned above, a two-dimensional representation, such as a board painting or print, and the *bulto*, a sculpture. This is a bibliographical essay on these religious artifacts, which begins with a brief history of the art form.

2074.   Leeds, Wendy. "Fraktur: An Annotated Bibliography." *Pennsylvania Folklife* 25 (Spring 1976): 35-46.

Glassie defines *fraktur* as "a combination of medieval calligraphy and traditional Pennsylvania motifs, such as the tulip and pomegranate, *distelfink*, and parrot. Although influenced by German copybooks, *fraktur* is traceable to the folk art of southwestern Germany, Switzerland, and Alsace." (*Pattern in the Material Folk Culture of the Eastern United States*, p. 43.) This brief work includes an introduction to the bibliography which is arranged alphabetically by author or anonymous title and is annotated.

Classification--Folk Painting

2075.   Borneman, Henry S. *Pennsylvania German Illuminated Manuscripts; A Classification of Fraktur-Schriften and An Inquiry into Their History and Art.* Norristown, PA: Pennsylvania German Society, 1937. 59p. LC 38-4824. (Proceedings of the Pennsylvania German Society; v. 46). Reprinted: New York: Dover, 1973. LC 72-95047; ISBN 0-4862-2926-2.

This is really an overview of specimen texts taken from the following categories of manuscripts: rewards of merit, primers, birth certificates, baptismal certificates, wedding certificates, family records, house blessings, and spiritual labyrinths. Examples of texts and designs are given and a description of the implements and materials used, with a brief history of the Ephrata cloister and the folk art of the Pennsylvania Germans. Includes 38 plates in black and white and color.

Dictionaries and Encyclopedias--Folk Painting

2076. Bihalji-Merin, Oto, and Nebojsa-Bato Tomasevíc. *World Encyclopedia of Naive Art.* Belgrade: Scala; distributed in the U.S. by Harper & Row, 1985. 735p. LC 84-51455; ISBN 0-935748-62-8.

There is a long introduction (pp. 1-84), "A Hundred Years of Naive Art," which is followed by an alphabetical listing of naive artists of the world, from Argentina to Zaire (pp. 85-637). This is followed by historical surveys of naive art in Africa, Argentina, Australia, Belgium, Brazil, Canada, China, Czechoslovakia, France, Bali, Israel, Italy, Japan, Mexico, the Netherlands, Nicaragua, Poland, Romania, Switzerland, the USA, the USSR, Venezuela, and Yugoslavia. There is a list of artists arranged according to country and a list of important exhibitions of naive art and museums and galleries that show or have shown primitive art, also arranged by country. This work is lavishly illustrated, with a full color photograph of at least one work by every artist mentioned. There is a long bibliography (pp. 711-716, in small print) but unfortunately there is no index which would have been useful with such a massive work.

Dictionary Catalog--Folk Painting

2077. Weiser, Frederick S., and Howell J. Heaney, comps. *The Pennsylvania German Fraktur of the Free Library of Philadelphia: An Illustrated Catalogue.* 2 vols. Breinigsville and Philadelphia, PA: Free Library of Philadelphia and the Pennsylvania German Society, 1976. LC 76-13357; ISBN 0-911122-32-x. (Publications of the Pennsylvania German Society; vols. 10, 11)

This catalogs 1,021 *frakturs* located in the Free Library of Philadelphia, many of which are exquisitely illustrated with photographic examples (the color is particularly clear and beautiful). Indexes are included in Vol. 2. See Connor and Roberts below (no. 2080).

Exhibition Catalogs and Guides to Collections--Folk Painting

Note: This is a sampling of catalogs that are in print. Other than Kallir's (no. 2089), they all deal with American folk painting.

2078.   Abby Aldrich Rockefeller Folk Art Center. *American Folk Paintings: Paintings and Drawings Other than Portraits from the Abby Aldrich Rockefeller Folk Art Center.* New York: New York Graphic Society in Association with Colonial Williamsburg, 1988. 449p. LC 87-26156; ISBN 0-8212-1620-1. (Abby Aldrich Rockefeller Folk Art Center, series, 2)

The introductory essay by Carolyn J. Weekley is concerned with a definition of folk art. The catalog, prepared by Beatrix Rumford, groups the paintings and drawings by subject--sea and landscapes, still lifes, portraits, family records (*frakturs*), mourning pictures, etc., and further divides them into works whose artists are identifiable and anonymous works. Each work is described, with the painter's name given, if known, along with the site painted, materials or medium used, and a long annotation. To conclude, there is a short title list and an index. The bibliography lists exhibitions and publications.

2079.   Abby Aldrich Rockefeller Folk Art Center. *American Folk Portraits: Paintings and Drawings from the Abby Aldrich Rockefeller Folk Art Center.* Boston, MA: New York Graphic Society Books, 1981. 295p. LC 81-4990; ISBN 0-8212-1100-5. (Abby Aldrich Rockefeller Folk Art Center, series, 1)

Edited by Beatrix Rumford with introductions by Donald R. Walters and Carolyn J. Weekley. This work catalogs 298 portraits, describing all of them and illustrating many of them in full color. There is a bibliography and index.

2080. Connor, Paul, and Jill Roberts, comps. *Pennsylvania German Fraktur and Printed Broadsides: A Guide to the Collections in the Library of Congress.* Washington, DC: Library of Congress, 1988. 48p. LC 88-600044; ISBN 0-8444-0600-7. (Publications of the American Folklife Center, 16)

This is a guide to 168 manuscripts and prints found in the Library of Congress' collections. There is an introduction by Don Yoder--a historical overview and analysis of the function of *fraktur* to the Pennsylvania Germans. Includes black-and-white and color plates. (See also no. 2077.)

2081. Fawcett, David M., and Lee A. Callander. *Native American Painting: Selections from the Museum of the American Indian.* New York: Museum of the American Indian, 1982. 95p. LC 82-60422; ISBN 0-934490-40-6 (p).

Seventy-one paintings are shown and described from this collection along with a list of all the paintings and drawings belonging to this collection. Arrangement is by tribe.

2082. [Garbisch, Edgar William]. *American Naive Painting of the 18th and 19th Centuries: 111 Masterpieces from the Collections of Edgar William and Bernice Chrysler Garbisch.* New York: American Federation of the Arts, 1969. 159p. LC 72-85150.

This exhibition travelled from 1968-1970, from the prairie to West Point, New York. There are 112 full-page black-and-white and color plates with notes on the articles as well as a full catalog.

2083. [Garbisch, Edgar William]. "American Primitive Painting. Collection of Edgar William and Bernice Chrysler Garbisch." *Art in America* 42 (May 1954): 87-170.

This is a special issue of *Art in America*. The foreword is by the Garbisches, with essays on folk painting, portraits, landscapes, and still lives. Paintings from the collection are shown throughout the whole issue.

2084.   [Garbisch, Edgar William]. *101 American Primitive Watercolors and Pastels from the Collection of Edgar William and Bernice Chrysler Garbisch*. Washington: National Gallery of Art, 1966. 143p. LC 66-61970.

This is an exhibition catalog of a small part of the Garbisch collection, which numbers in toto about 1,000 pieces, of which 101 are shown here: portraits, landscapes, and *frakturs*. They are briefly described and identified.

2085.   Hirschl & Adler Galleries. *Plain and Fancy, a Survey of American Folk Art*. New York: Hirschl and Adler, 1970. 72p. LC 73-18930.

There are 94 paintings described and pictured in black and white, arranged alphabetically by painters. Paintings from the American School of painting and a few pieces of sculpture of anonymous artists are included in the second half of the catalog.

2086.   Hougland, Willard. *Santos: A Primitive American Art*. New York: Lynton R. Kistler, 1946. 49p. LC 48-5699.

This is a sampling of the collection of the Taylor Museum, Colorado Springs, CO, with an introduction to history, background and techniques of *santos*. There are 64 black-and-white plates of sculpture and paintings. See also Robert L. Shalkop's *Wooden Saints: The Santos of New Mexico...* (Feldafing: Bucheim, 1967), a study of works from the Taylor Museum, as well as no. 2099.

2087. Jones, Agnes Halsey, and Louis C. Jones. *New-Found Folk Art of the Young Republic*. Cooperstown, NY: New York State Historical Association, 1960. 35p. LC 77-377482.

This is an exhibition catalog of 81 of the 175 new paintings that were given to the Fennimore Museum at Cooperstown by three people, including Jean Lipman. There is a short introduction to American folk art and a catalog of the paintings, described, analyzed, and pictured in black and white.

2088. Joyaux, Alain, and Richard J. Wattenmaker. *American Naive Paintings: Eighteenth- and Nineteenth-Century: The Edgar William & Bernice Chrysler Garbisch Collection*. Flint, MI: Flint Institute of Arts, 1981. 95p. LC 81-70934; ISBN 0-9386-04-4.

This exhibit catalog includes descriptions and black-and-white and color illustrations of the 111 paintings exhibited in Michigan. There is an artist index.

2089. Kallir, Jane. *The Folk Art Tradition: Naive Painting in Europe and the United States*. New York: Viking, 1982. 100p. LC 81-16057; ISBN 0-670-32325-X.

This catalog of an exhibition held at the Galerie St. Etienne (New York) contains essays on religious folk art, folk painting and painters in the United States (e.g., Grandma Moses), folk art in modern times, French naive art, American nonacademic painters (e.g., John Kane, Horace Pippin), and a modern peasant revival in Yugoslavia. There are 71 black-and-white and 29 color plates, as well as a notes section and bibliography.

2090. Kallir, Jane. *Grandma Moses, the Artist Behind the Myth*. New York: Distributed by Clarkson Potter in association with Galerie St. Etienne, NY, 1982. 160p. LC 82-7683; ISBN 0-517-54748-1 (c) (Clarkson Potter); 0-910810-21-4 (p) (St. Etienne).

Most of this is comprised on essays on the "making of a legend," the status of folk art in the U.S., Moses' development of style, and artistic growth. There is a biographical chronology, many photos of her work, notes, and an index.

2091.   Kallir, Jane. *John Kane, Modern America's First Folk Painter.* New York: Galerie St. Etienne, 1984. [47p.]. ISBN 0-910810-24-9.

There is an essay by Kallir and 32 of the paintings that were in this exhibit are illustrated and described. See also Leon Arkus' oral autobiographical account of Kane in his *John Kane, Painter* (Pittsburgh, PA: University of Pittsburgh Press, 1971), which includes a *catalogue raisonné* of Kane's work.

2092.   Kennedy Galleries. "American Naive and Folk Art of the Nineteenth Century." *Kennedy Quarterly* 13 (1974): 1-64, 178-224.

This is a catalog of 202 items, all pictured, with notes on the works at the back of the journal.

2093.   Kennedy Galleries. "American Primitives: Primitive, Folk and Naive Art from the Eighteenth, Nineteenth, and Twentieth Century." *Kennedy Quarterly* 9 (1969): 156-228. Followed by: *Kennedy Quarterly* 11 (1972): 132-192, and *Kennedy Quarterly* 12 (1973): 1-64.

These three issues of *Kennedy Quarterly* include exhibition catalogs of three exhibits with the same name. In 1969, 233 paintings, *frakturs*, and portraits were pictured and described; in 1972, 148 were pictured and described, and, in 1973, 51 additional items were pictured with notes presented separately in the back of the journal.

2094.   Kennedy Galleries. "Eighteenth and Nineteenth Century Naive
        Art." *Kennedy Quarterly* 16 (1978): 1-64.

There are 52 paintings and three weathervanes described and
pictured. See also the catalog for the Kennedy Galleries' exhibit on "Two
Hundred Years of American Portraits" (*Kennedy Quarterly* 9 [1970]: 232-
292), which includes many American primitive portraits.

2095.   Lipman, Jean, and Tom Armstrong, eds. *American Folk Painters
        of Three Centuries.* New York: Hudson Hills Press, in
        association with the Whitney Museum of American Art, 1980.
        233p. LC 79-21212; ISBN 0-933920-05-9 (c); 0-933920-06-7
        (p).

This catalog of an exhibition held in 1980 is arranged by century
with essays about different folk art genres and a leading essay by Lipman
on "American Folk Art: Six Decades of Discovery." There are many
full-color plates and a bibliography.

2096.   Manley, Roger. *Signs and Wonders: Outsider Art Inside North
        Carolina.* Raleigh: North Carolina Museum of Art, 1989. 135p.
        LC 89-60598; ISBN 0-88259-957-7.

Manley, as explained in the headnote to this section, uses the
term "outsider" to mean those artists who are not mainstream artists. This
exhibit catalog is arranged by artists with listings and photographs of their
work. Included also is biographical information, a select bibliography, and
an exhibition checklist.

2097.   National Gallery of Art. *American Naive Paintings from the
        National Gallery of Art.* Washington, DC: Published for the
        International Exhibition Foundation [by the] National Gallery of
        Art, 1985. 90p. LC 85-4874; ISBN 0-89468-083-8.

This exhibit began at the Museum of American Folk Art in New
York and travelled for two years. The foreword is by J. Carter Brown and

the introduction is by Mary Black. There are 60 items pictured in full color and briefly described with additional notes on the artists.

2098. New York State Historical Association. *Folk Art's Many Faces: Portraits in the New York State Historical Association.* Cooperstown, NY: New York State Historical Association, 1987. 224p. LC 87-61301; ISBN 0-917334-14-0 (c); 0-917334-159 (p).

This is the first published catalog of the New York State Historical Association's renowned collection of American folk art. The foreword by Louis and Agnes Halsey Jones serves as an introduction to American folk art at the Fenimore House in Cooperstown. In all there are 158 items pictured, divided into those by identified artists and those by unidentified artists. The pictures of all the artists are illustrated, and biographical information is provided for known artists. Pictures are described and any marks or inscriptions are noted, as is the condition of the work, its provenance, and where it has been exhibited. There is an index.

2099. *Santos: An Exhibition of the Religious Folk Art of New Mexico.* Fort Worth, TX: Amon Carter Museum of Western Art, 1964. 30p. LC 64-20043.

An introductory essay by George Kubler discusses Spanish-American religious art, sources of New Mexican art, and the *bultos* and *retablos* in this exhibit. Eleven plates are included. See also *Santos: An Exhibition of Holy Images Predominantly from New Mexico and South America...* (Fullerton, CA: The Gallery, 1974) and no. 2086 for further exhibition catalogs of *santos*.

2100. Woodward, Richard B., comp. *American Folk Painting: Selections from the Collection of Mr. and Mrs. William E. Wiltshire III.* Richmond, VA: Virginia Museum, 1977. 110p. LC 77-24971; ISBN 0-917046-03-x (c); 0-917046-02-1 (p).

Catalog entries are arranged chronologically. All 51 paintings are pictured in color and there are extensive notes describing them.

FOLK ART
Folk Sculpture

It is very difficult to differentiate **folk sculpture** from wood carving and whittling, so no attempt has been made here to do so, though most likely these are crafts more than folk art. I have eliminated tombstone carving from this section (see **Gravestone Art**, nos. 2276-2283) and wooden toy-carving and carved toys are included in the section on **Folk toys** (see nos. 2386-2401). This section also excludes how-to books such as E.J. Tangerman's *Whittling and Woodcarving* (New York: McGraw Hill, 1936) and Ben Hunt's *The Whittling Book* (New York: Macmillan, 1944). However, Tangerman's *Design and Figure Carving* (New York: Dover, 1964 [1940]) is a good introductory work to carving. In it, the author discusses design principles, methods of carving, and the tools used; there are, in particular, two chapters on the folk carving of animals, birds, and the human figure.

There has been relatively little written on folk sculpture other than surveys and some work on religious folk sculpture. Charles Briggs' *The Wood Carvers of Cordova, New Mexico: Social Dimensions of an Artistic Revival* (Knoxville: University of Tennessee Press, 1980) is a scholarly study concerned with religious sculpture that covers the history, work being done presently, and some of the symbolism of image carving. Norma Lalibere's and Maureen Jones' *Wooden Images* (New York: Reinhold, 1966) is a study of wooden carved images, most religious, that is international in scope and covers flat wooden images, relief images, sculptured images, and assembled images.

As is the case in most of the folk arts and crafts, there are great number of surveys of various types of folk sculpture which have been eliminated here due to lack of space. There are general surveys, most of which are usually focused on one country, such as Robert Bishop's *American Folk Sculpture* (New York: Dutton, 1974) or Marian and Charles Klamkins' *Wood Carvings: North American Folk Sculpture* (New York: Hawthorn

873

Books, 1974) which covers figure heads, ship carvings, patriotic symbols, parade carvings, trade signs and shop figures, Indian carvings, carousel carvings, weathervanes and whirligigs, toys, dolls, small animal figures, butter molds, and other household objects, bird and fish decoys, and whimsical carvings. Terence Barrow's *Maori Wood Sculpture of New Zealand* (Rutland, VT: Charles E. Tuttle, 1970), covering classic wood sculpture and religious, domestic, and personal carvings, and Kalyan Dasgupta's *Woodcarving of Eastern India* (Calcutta: Firma KLM, 1990) are just two examples of the study of the woodcarving of other cultures.

There are surveys dealing with specific types of carved pieces: **cigar store figures** (e.g., Frederick Fried's *Artists in Wood; American Carvers of Cigar-Store Indians, Show Figures, and Circus Wagons*, New York: Clarkson Potter, 1970), **decoys** (e.g., Adele Earnest's *The Art of the Decoy*, New York: Clarkson Potter, 1965), **ivory and jade carvings** (e.g., S. Howard Hansford's *Chinese Carved Jades*, Greenwich, CT: New York Graphic Society, 1968), *netsuke*--Japanese miniature sculptures usually done in wood, ivory and lacquer, which are toggles, small fobs attached by cords to cases for personal seals and medicines, tobacco pouches, and to other portable objects (e.g., Richard Barker's and Lawrence Smith's *Netsuke: The Miniature Sculpture of Japan*, London: British Museum Publications, 1976), **carved masks** (e.g., Leon Underwood's *Masks of West Africa*, London: A. Tiranti, 1948), **scrimshaw**--decorations carved into ivory, bone, coconut shells, or walrus tusks by sailors (e.g., William Gilkerson's *The Scrimshander: The Nautical Ivory Worker and His Art of Scrimshaw, Historical and Contemporary*, San Francisco: The Troubador Press, 1978 [1975]), **ship-carving** (e.g., M.V. Brewington's *Shipcarvers of North America*, New York: Dover, 1972), and **carved weathervanes** (e.g., Robert Bishop's and Patricia Coblentz's *A Gallery of American Weathervanes and Whirligigs*, New York: Dutton, 1981).

A *Decoy Collector's Guide*, edited and published by Hal Sorenson, Davenport, IA, was published quarterly from 1963-1965, and as an annual in 1966/67 and in 1968; *North American Decoys* has been published quarterly, by Hillcrest Publications, Heber City, UT, since 1967.

Bibliography--Folk Sculpture

2101.   Cole, Herbert M., and Robert Farris Thompson. *Bibliography of Yoruba Sculpture*. New York: The Museum of Primitive Art, 1964. 11p. LC 65-2531. (Primitive art bibliographies, 3)

This listing of 279 items dealing with Yoruba sculpture and sculpture-related problems is divided into two parts: sources on Yoruba sculpture and general handbooks and exhibition catalogs. A subject index is included.

Guides and Handbooks--Folk Sculpture

Note: These differ from the surveys in that they are intended for identification purposes.

2102.   Bushell, Raymond. *Collectors' Netsuke*. New York: Walker/ Weatherhill, 1971. 199p. LC 70-139687; ISBN 0-8027-2446-9.

Netsuke are discussed, pictured, described, and arranged chronologically.

2103.   Ueda, Reikichi. *The Netsuke Handbook*. Adapted from the Japanese by R. Bushell. Rutland, VT: Charles E. Tuttle, 1961. 325p. LC 61-8739; ISBN 0-8048-0424-9.

This work discusses the origins and development of this art form, types of *netsuke*, *netsuke* materials (wood, ivory and horn, metal and porcelain, lacquer, etc.), *netsuke* subjects and designs, *netsuke* artists, and regional characteristics (discussed by area). Includes also a section on the literature on *netsuke* and *netsuke* collections, a section of reminiscences of a carver, an index of *netsuke* carvers, a general bibliography, a glossary, and an index.

2104.   Flower, Milton E. *Wilhelm Schimmel and Aaron Mountz: Wood Carvers.* Williamsburg, VA: Abby Aldrich Rockefeller Folk Art Collection, 1965. 24p. LC 89-832253.

This is a catalog of the work of two nineteenth-century Pennsylvania-German folk artists whose sculptures of parrots, birds, roosters, dogs and poodles, squirrels, and lions are pictured and discussed. There are 83 pieces in all.

2105.   Hemphill, Herbert W., ed. *Folk Sculpture USA.* Brooklyn, NY: Brooklyn Museum of Art, 1976. 96p. LC 75-37338; ISBN 0-87213-035-57.

The text introduces the topic of "folk sculpture without the folk," the artist as collector, and American folk sculpture, "with some considerations of its ethnic heritage." The exhibition pieces are illustrated throughout the text with short descriptive paragraphs. There is also a catalog of the exhibit which consisted of 98 pieces.

2106.   Johnsgard, Paul A., ed. *The Bird Decoy: An American Art Form.* Lincoln: University of Nebraska Press, 1976. 190p. LC 76-2072; ISBN 0-8032-0887-1.

Several people prepared the text material which covers the history and techniques of decoy making, the aesthetics of wildfowl decoys, decoys for the folk art collection, decoys of functional objects, decoys from the viewpoint of a naturalist, and Atlantic Coast waterfowl decoys. The catalog includes illustrations and descriptions of 207 decoys with the type of bird carved, the carver's name, the dimensions, place and date, lender's name, references to other exhibitions, and a long note.

2107.   Museum of American Folk Art. *Wood Sculpture of New York State.* New York: Museum of American Folk Art, 1975. 20p. LC 76-371251.

Covers cigar figures and trade signs, circus and carousel carvings, ship figureheads, decoys, whirligigs and toys, and weathervanes. In all, 139 items are listed, described, and a few are pictured.

2108.   Newark Museum. *American Folk Sculpture: The Work of Eighteenth and Nineteenth Century Craftsmen.* Newark, NJ: The Newark Museum, 1931. 108p. LC 37-15658.

There are 192 pieces listed, most of which are wood carving, but there are also some stone carvings and some plaster ornaments as well as some metal work. There are extensive notes on the types of crafts exhibited; very few pictures.

2109.   Radin, Paul, and Elinore Marvel, selectors. *African Folktales & Sculpture.* New York: Bollingen Foundation, by Pantheon Books, 1964 [1952, Bollingen Foundation]. 357p. text; plates separate. LC 64-23669. (Bollingen series, 32)

The section "African Negro Sculpture" is introduced by James Johnson Sweeney, then director of the Museum of Primitive Art, New York. Included are 187pp. of plates of beauifully photographed pieces of sculpture followed by a descriptive catalog. A very handsome work.

2110.   Zhuravleva, L.S., ed. *Carved and Painted Woodwork by Russian Craftsmen at the Smolensk Museum of Art History and Architecture.* Moscow: Sovetskaya Publications, 1985. 227p. LC 85-195396.

The text is in Russian but there is an English summary. There are 236 items pictured and cataloged in the back of the book with extensive notes. See also Olga Kruglova's *Traditional Russian Carved and Painted Woodwork From the Collection of the State Museum of History and Art in the Zagorsk Reservation* (Moscow, 1981) which describes 163 carved pieces.

MATERIAL CULTURE
Folk Craft--General

As Jan Brunvand has noted in his chapter, "Folk Crafts and Art," in his *The Study of American Folklore* (3rd ed., pp. 424-443), it is very difficult to determine where "a utilitarian **craft** leave[s] off and...**art** begin[s]." **Folk crafts**, Brunvand goes on, "are usually thought of as amateur labor resulting in traditional homemade objects that are primarily functional. But these items may also be made by professional or semiprofessional artisans well aware of their creative abilities, and often the artifacts are decorative as well as useful." (p. 424)

There is an abundance of introductory material on folk crafts and craftspersons. One could well begin with Warren E. Roberts' "Folk Crafts" (pp. 233-252), in *Folklore and Folklife: An Introduction*, edited by Richard M. Dorson as well as John Michael Vlach's "Folk Craftsmen" (pp. 301-305), in *The Handbook of Folklore*, also edited by Dorson. The chapter noted above by Brunvand on "Folk Crafts and Art" is also an excellent place to begin a study.

There are several full-length studies which focus on craftspersons: J. Geraint Jenkins' *Traditional Country Craftsmen* (London: Routledge & Kegan Paul, 1965), Bruce Nickerson's *A Study of United States Folk Crafts--Artists* (Washington, DC: National Endowment for the Arts, 1977), and Ian Quimby's *The Craftsman in Early America* (New York: W.W. Norton, for the Winterthur Museum, 1984) are all good introductions to crafts and their makers. Also concerned with craftspersons is *Local Color: A Sense of Place in Folk Art*, edited by William Ferris (Developed for the Center for Southern Folklore; published, New York: McGraw-Hill, 1982), biographical sketches of nine southern artisans. A similar work is Ramona and Millard Lampell's *O, Appalachia: Artists of the Southern Mountains....* (New York: Stewart, Tabori & Chang; distributed by Workman, 1989), with biographies of 20 artisans. *Afro-American Folk Art and Crafts*, edited by William Ferris (no. 2001), includes essays on quiltmakers, sculptors, instrument makers, basketmakers, and southern folk potters. Charles F. Hummell's *With Hammer in Hand: The Dominy Craftsmen of East Hampton, New York* (Charlottesville: Published for the Henry Francis du Pont Winterthur Museum by the University of Virginia Press, 1968) is a full-length study of the Dominy family of craftsmen on Long Island and Michael Owen Jones' *Craftsman of the Cumberlands: Tradition & Creativity* (Lexington: University Press of Kentucky, 1989), "an extensive revision of *The Hand Made Object and Its Maker* (Berkeley: University of California Press, 1975), is really a long contextual biographical sketch of a chairmaker in Kentucky. Frances Louise Goodrich's *Mountain Spun*, a study of the Allandstand Cottage Industry, an early twentieth-century handicraft revival project, has recently been reprinted (Knoxville: University of Tennessee Press, 1989 [1931]); it provides a wonderful insight into the craftsmen of the North Carolina mountains at the beginning of the century and their work.

Finally, there are traditional and ethnic crafts that have not been included as separate sections here. *Classic Crafts: A Practical Compendium of Traditional Skills*, edited by Martina Margretts (New York: Simon and Schuster, 1989), for example, includes several of the crafts covered in the chapter--quilting, weaving, toy making, and basketry--but also discusses and analyzes several of those crafts that have been omitted (primarily for lack of materials): textile crafts, such as handblock printing, dyeing, knitting (Aran knits, for example, are a traditional craft), tassling and braiding, and smocking; papercrafts, such as hand papermaking, paper marbling, calligraphy, woodengraving; kitchen crafts, such as festival bread, dried flowers, preserve making, smoking fish, candlemaking; and decorative crafts, such as gilding, leatherwork, stained glass, wreathmaking, and jewelrymaking (though this is mentioned in the section on metalwork). A similar work is Nicholas Barnard's *Living with Folk Art: Ethnic Styles From Around the World* (Boston, MA: Little, Brown, 1991), an overview of all aspects of folk craft in the twentieth century--ceramics, masks, basketware, carvings, and textiles.

Noteworthy is an annual, *Studies in Traditional American Crafts* (Oneida, NY: Madison Country Historical Society), edited by John Braunlein. Vol. 1 (1978), *Fourteenth Annual Traditional Crafts Days: September 9 and 10, 1978*, includes essays on wilderness architecture, snowshoe making, and ice fishing; Vol. 3 (1980) is a study of an Adirondack pack basketmaker, by Henry Glassie; Vol. 4 (1981) includes a study of chain carving by Simon Bronner and an essay on wooden wheel making by Jennifer Esle; and Vol. 5 (1982), by Laurie Northrup, is on early American stencilling.

As before, surveys of folk crafts have been excluded here. Most of these general surveys are limited to an overview of the crafts of one people, such as René Gardi's *African Crafts and Craftsmen* (New York: Van Nostrand Rinehold, 1969), Yuzuru Okada's *Japanese Handicrafts* (Tokyo: Japan Travel Bureau, 1962 [1941]), or Neelima Dahiya's *Arts and Crafts in Northern India* (New Delhi: B.R. Publishing, 1986). There are many surveys of American folk crafts. Some of the classics are Allen Eaton's *Handicrafts of New England* (New York: Harper, 1940) and his *Handicrafts of the Southern Highlands* (New York: Russell Sage Foundation, 1937; reprinted: New York: Dover, 1973) as well as Erwin Christensen's *American Crafts and Folk Arts* (Washington: R. B. Luce, 1964). June Sprigg's *By Shaker Hands* (New York: Knopf, 1975) is one of many works on all aspects of Shaker crafts.

As noted earlier at the beginning of this chapter, to avoid confusion, this chapter on Material Culture will adhere for the most part to the categorization worked out in the *MLA International Bibliography*. A section on general folk crafts will be followed by sections on **architecture** (which, as also noted earlier, the compiler does not agree is a craft form), **ceramics, costume, food craft, household items** (basketry, all forms of needlework: quilts, samplers, etc.), **rugs and carpets**, and **weaving**.

Be sure to consult the sections on **Material Culture** (nos. 1977-1991) and **Folk Art--General** (nos. 1992-2072) as many of the works listed in those section embrace aspects of folk craft.

Bibliographies--Folk Crafts-General

2111.   Ames, Kenneth L., and Gerald W.R. Ward, eds. *Decorative Arts and Household Furnishings Used in America, 1650-1920: An Annotated Bibliography*. Charlottesville: University Press of Virginia for the Winterthur Museum, 1989. 392p. LC 89-20010; ISBN 0-912724-19-6.

This is a compilation of bibliographic essays by different people on types of and themes concerned with folk art and crafts. Covers architecture, ceramics and glass, furniture, metals, textiles (floor coverings, needlework, quilts, and textiles), time pieces, household activities and systems (e.g., kitchen artifacts), and artisan and culture (craftsmen), and the arts and crafts movement in America. Each of these sections contains guides to basic references, an overview of the research being done on that topic, a survey of the art form, and an annotated bibliography. Concludes with an author/title index. A handsome book.

2112. Chicorel, Marietta, ed. *Chicorel Index to the Crafts*. 4 vols. New York: Chicorel Publishers, 1974-1977. LC 74-195924.

Arranged by type of craft (e.g., **basketry, costume**), craftsman (e.g., **embroiderer**), and product (e.g.,**rugs and carpets**). Within each large section, there are subdivisions, with one for the **folk** aspect of each craft listed (e.g., **folk weaving**). The listing is by title with a separate section for reference books. There is also a list of museums and collections and a glossary of technical terms but no author index or general subject index.

2113. Christensen, Edwin Ottomar. *Arts and Crafts, a Bibliography for Craftsmen*. Washington, DC: National Gallery of Art, Index of American Design, in collaboration with the Federal Security Agency, Office of Education, 1949. 80p. LC 49-4188.

This now outdated work "includes publications in a number of craft fields which give information on the making as well as the designing of craft products." Covers from **basketry**, *block printing and engraving, bronze work*, and **ceramics** to **weaving**, *wood carving, wood finishing, wood turning, woodworking*, and *wood workers in crafts and their tools*. Each section is arranged alphabetically by author. Annotated.

2114. Franklin, Linda Campbell, ed. *Antiques and Collectibles: A Bibliography of Works in English, 16th Century to 1976*. Metuchen, NJ: Scarecrow, 1978. 1,091p. LC 77-25026; ISBN 0-8108-1092-1.

This is a listing only of 10,783 works (mostly books) about "collectible" items. There is a section on **Folk Art** (pp. 601-610) but also applicable are sections on applied and decorative art, furniture, ceramics, glass, silver and gold, woodwork, metalwork, ivory, jade, lacquer and enamel, costume, textiles and textile art, games and toys, animals and agriculture (tools), and household objects. Also included is a general bibliography and a subject index. This is a formidable work which could use continuous updating.

2115.   Martin, Charles E. "Kentucky's Traditional Arts and Crafts." *Kentucky Folklore Record* 31 (1985): 1-94.

This is an unannotated listing of 773 books, articles, exhibition catalogs, etc., dealing with crafts in Kentucky. There is a subject index, a chronological index (1902-1985), and a chronological ordering of main articles (e.g., **basketmaking** [1914]...).

2116.   Mohr, Clarence. "Black Artisans and Craftsmen--Colonial Era through 1900: A Select Historical Bibliography," in *Afro-American Folk Art and Crafts*, ed. William Ferris. Boston, MA: G.K. Hall, 1983. pp. 405-418.

Included in this annotated bibliography are documentary collections, secondary works, studies of slavery, and state and local studies. See also Ellen Slack's annotated bibliography of films about crafts and craftsmen in this study, pp. 419-426.

2117.   Sink, Susan. *Traditional Crafts and Craftsmanship in America: A Selected Bibliography*. Washington, DC: Library of Congress, American Folklife Center, 1983. 84p. LC 84-127666. (Publication of the American Folklife Center, 11)

This is a reprint, with additions, of a bibliography in *Traditional Craftsmanship in America: A Diagnostic Report* (Washington, DC: National Council for the Traditional Arts, 1983). The reprinted bibliography contains approximately 1,000 references to traditional crafts and craftsmanship in America. This is an alphabetical listing of mostly printed items, with a few unpublished theses and dissertations. The general index contains large subject entries (e.g., **basketry**, *black arts and crafts, blacksmithing*, etc.). The introductory material includes definitions and parameters and there is a section on trends in publishing on the crafts. Although the entries are not annotated, this is probably the best bibliographic source in the field which hopefully will be updated periodically.

Dictionaries and Encyclopedias--Folk Crafts-General

2118. Boger, Louise Ade, and H. Batterson Boger, comps. and eds. *The Dictionary of Antiques and the Decorative Arts.* New York: Scribner, 1967 [1957]. 622p. LC 67-18131; ISBN 0-6841-1003-2.

The subtitle reads "A Book of Reference for Glass, Furniture, Ceramics, Silver, Periods, Styles, Technical Terms, etc." The scope of this work is international, and access is made easier by means of a classified list of subjects and terms. Types of crafts are subdivided by country, and processes and methods are given for each. There is a bibliography.

2119. Laye Andrew, H.E. *The Arco Encyclopedia of Crafts.* New York: Arco, 1982 [1978]. 432p. LC 78-2841; ISBN 0-6680-4630-9.

The arrangement of this work is alphabetical by type of craft, tool, technique, etc. (e.g., **assemblages, castings, god's eyes, corn dollies,** etc.). The articles are quite long and comprehensive, with emphasis on contemporary crafts as practiced throughout the world. For example, the article on **beads** talks about materials used and where and how sewn beads are used in Nigeria, with examples of the technique used; string beads, where and how they're done, etc. The work is well illustrated with black-and-white photos of finished projects and drawings of directions. The appendixes include a piece on the structure of the craft process, a brief bibliography, a conversion and translation chart (i.e., metric conversion, translations of artists' colors, etc.), a list of suppliers in America and Britain with addresses, information on A-V material on crafts, and a list of museums of interest.

2120.   Stoutenburgh, John Leeds, ed. *Dictionary of Arts and Crafts.* New York: Philosophical Library, 1956. 259p. LC 56-13756. (Mid-century reference library)

This dictionary "tries to clarify terms which are used by others rather freely and are taken for granted." All aspects of craft--methodology, materials used, and products--are included. Cross referenced, but there is no index or bibliography.

2121.   Torbet, Laura, ed. *The Encyclopedia of Crafts.* 3 vols. New York: Scribner, 1980. LC 80-13431; ISBN 0-684-16409-4 (set).

On the whole, this includes brief entries on all aspects of folk craft terms, materials and genres, from **acanthus** and **accordion pleating** to **weaving** with a few substantial articles. The illustrations are skimpy, the scope is international, and there is no appendix, index, or bibliography.

Directories/Guides to Collections--Folk Crafts-General

2122.   Georgia Council for the Arts & Humanities. Appalachian Crafts Project. *Georgia Crafts Appalachia.* Gainesville, GA: GCAH Crafts Program, 1979. 168p. A 43-page supplement was published in 1980, but was not seen.

This is the product of a survey of Georgia craftspersons to determine the following basic demographic information: the degree of involvement with the craft, sources of supplies used, method of studio operation, and merchandising approaches used. The product is an alphabetic listing of craftspersons, with addresses and art forms, a list of organizations of craftspersons, a list of suppliers, an index by craft, and a calendar (January-December) of fairs and festivals that show crafts, a list of exhibits, and a list of acquisitions opportunities: galleries and annual exhibitions.

2123.   Stapleton, Constance. *Crafts of America: Guide to the Finest Traditional Crafts Made in the United States: How They Are Made, Who Makes Them, Where to Buy Them.* New York: Harper & Row, 1988. 341p. LC 87-45671; ISBN 0-06-096079-5.

This is a marvelously useful book for the collector and the researcher. It is an alphabetic listing of minor and major crafts: baskets, blankets, boxes, carving, chairs, dolls, embroidery, leatherwork, furniture, etc., each subdivided by types (e.g., **furniture**: Adirondack, Chinese, Chippendale, country, etc.). The author describes each craft, gives some history, and then focuses on contemporary craftsmen, for whom she gives addresses, catalog information, prices, etc. There is a state by state listing of additional resources of people who sell traditional American crafts and an index. Informative and useful, one would hope this is planned as an annual or biennial.

Guide--Folk Crafts-General

2124.   Seymour, John. *The Forgotten Arts.* New York: Knopf, 1984. 192p. LC 84-47646; ISBN 0-394-53956-7.

This guide covers woodland crafts (besom, crib, bark basketmaking), building crafts (thatching), crafts of the field (hedge-laying), workshop crafts (blacksmithing), textiles, and homecrafts. There is a page or two on each product, telling how it is done and how to identify it. Concludes with an index but no bibliography.

Indexes--Folk Crafts-General

2125.   Salz, Kay, comp. and ed. *Craft Films: An Index of International Films on Crafts.* New York: Neal-Schuman, 1979. 156p. LC 79-14780; ISBN 0-918212-08-1.

A useful book, this is a "nonevaluative general listing of 16mm films on crafts." (intro.) Films are arranged alphabetically by title, each entry including film title, release date, running time, language used, director, distributor, producer, and description of film. The appendix includes a listing of videotapes, a distribution index, an index of artists and craftspeople, and a subject index of crafts, subdivided by country. See also Ellen Slack's 1983 filmography (cited in Mohr above, no. 2116).

Catalogs of Exhibitions and Guides to Collections--Folk Crafts-General

> Note: This is a selection of catalogs of exhibitions and annotated descriptions of private and public museum collections. This only covers general folk crafts; catalogs for exhibitions of specific crafts are covered elsewhere, as are catalogs for folk art collections and exhibitions.

2126. *Doing It Right and Passing It On: Northern Louisiana Crafts.* Alexandria, LA: Alexandria Museum/Visual Arts Center, 1981. 49p.

Following an essay on northern Louisiana and on the craftsmen of the area, there is a catalog of 78 pieces--household crafts, toys, working crafts, and others.

2127. Herbert F. Johnson Museum of Art. *The Handwrought Object, 1776-1976.* Ithaca, NY: Herbert F. Johnson Museum of Art, Cornell University, 1976. 55p. LC 76-1614.

The purpose of this exhibition was to compare two periods--the settler and rural homesteader period of the late eighteenth and early nineteenth century and the present. In all, 342 artifacts of wood, fiber, and other materials are listed and described.

2128. Hufford, Mary, et al. *The Grand Generation: Memory, Mastery, Legacy.* Washington, DC: Smithsonian Institution Press, 1987.

Distributed by the University of Washington Press. 127p. LC 87-28532; ISBN 0-295-96610-6 (c); 0-295-96611-4 (p).

This catalog of a travelling show of the folk crafts by the elderly includes an introduction by Barbara Kirshenblatt-Gimblett, and essays on traditional culture and the stages of life, on memory, the living past, legacies, etc. There is a checklist of the items exhibited arranged by artist, notes, a bibliography, and wonderful photographs of the craftspersons involved.

2129. Katzenberg, Dena S. *Blue Traditions; Indigo Dyed Textiles and Related Cobalt Glazed Ceramics from the 17th through the 19th Century.* Baltimore, MD: Baltimore Museum of Art, 1973. 203p. LC 73-91962.

This is a catalog of an exhibit held in 1973-1974. The introduction deals with the use of indigo (which is extracted from the plant) material in the Indies, England and France, and also textiles of the seventeenth throughout the nineteenth centuries from Europe, America, and the Far East, printed, woven and embroidered textiles, and related ceramics. The catalog is divided into textiles (of which there are 119 pieces, arranged by country) and ceramics (of which there are 64 pieces, arranged by country). A selected bibliography is also included.

2130. *Made By Hand--Mississippi Folk Art.* Jackson: Mississippi Department of Archives and History, 1980. 120p. LC 79-620054.

There are six essays by William Ferris, John Michael Vlach, Georgeanna Greer, Roland Freeman, William Wiggins, Jr., Kenneth York, and Robert J. Balter and a catalog of 222 items, with a list of Mississippi craftsmen from 1850 on.

2131. Peate, Iorwerth C. *Guide to the Collection Illustrating Welsh Folk Crafts and Industries.* Cardiff: National Museum of Wales, 1935. 75p.+16p. LC 36-15070.

In two parts; the first is a descriptive account of crafts and industry, listed by trade (e.g., **smith, wig-maker, wood-turner**, etc.). The second is a descriptive catalog of 22 items from the craft collection at the National Museum of Wales, arranged within the same sections. A brief bibliography is included.

2132.   Sprigg, June. *Shaker Design.* New York: Whitney Museum of American Art in association with W.W. Norton, 1986. 228p. LC 85-26317; ISBN 0-393-02338-9 (c); 0-87427-047-2 (p).

There are 114 items in this exhibit, which originated at the Whitney and was also at the Corcoran in 1986-1987. Items pictured include furniture, household objects, tools and equipment, textiles and textile equipment, and graphics. Also included is a selected bibliography and an index. Ms. Sprigg has also curated and written catalogs for several other exhibits of Shaker crafts, notably *The Gift of Inspiration: Art of the Shakers, 1830-1880* (New York: Hirschl & Adler Galleries, 1979), *Simple Gifts: A Loan Exhibit of Shaker Craftsmanship Primarily from Hancock Shaker Village* (Storrs, CT: Benton Museum of Art, University of Connecticut, 1978), and *Shakers: Masterworks of Utilitarian Design....* (Katonah, NY: Katonah Gallery, 1983). (See also no. 2133.)

2133.   Whitney Museum of American Art. *Shaker Handicrafts.* New York: Whitney Museum of American Art, 1935. 15p.

This very early exhibition of Shaker crafts was held in 1934-1935 at the Whitney. Introduced by Edward Deming Andrews, the catalog describes and locates 53 items--furniture, baskets, clocks, books and manuscripts, prints, and inspirational drawings.

FOLK CRAFTS
Folk Architecture

"There is a substantial record of publication in American folk architecture." (Marshall [no. 2146], i) A good starting point might be

Warren E. Roberts' "Folk Architecture" (pp. 281-293), in *Folklore and Folklife*, ed. by Richard M. Dorson, and Jan Brunvand's "Folk Architecture" (3rd ed., pp. 413-423), in his *Study of American Folklore* as well as Arthur Lawton's "The Ground Rules of Folk Architecture" (*Pennsylvania Folklife* 23 [Autumn 1973]: 13-19) and Warren E. Roberts' "Function in Folk Architecture" (*Folklore Forum* 8 [1971]: 10-13). A new overview of vernacular architecture is *Vernacular Architecture: Paradigms of Environmental Response*, edited by Mete Turan (Aldershot [ENG]: Avebury, 1990).

Fred Kniffen, the cultural geographer, has also studied folk housing, and his article, "Folk Housing: Key to Diffusion" (*Association of American Geographers Annual* 55 [1965]: 549-570) is useful as is Kniffen's and Henry Glassie's "Building in Wood in the Eastern United States: A Time-Place Perspective" (*Geographical Review* 56 [1966]: 40-66). Two other works that deal tangentially with landscape and aspects of folk architecture are W.G. Hoskins' *English Landscape* (London: BBC Publications, 1973), a broad discussion of the English landscape and what is found there: hedgerows, deserted medieval villages, roads, bridges, fields, churches, etc., and John R. Stilgoe's *Common Landscapes of America, 1580-1845: An Analysis* (New Haven, CT: Yale University Press, 1982) which is concerned with landscape (wilderness, roads, etc.), planting, national design, agriculture (lore, farmland, farm houses, fences, woodlots, etc.), community (graveyards, rural churches, camp meetings, schoolhouses, fairs, etc.), and artifices (furnaces, sawmills, factories, etc.).

There are essay collections on vernacular architecture. Dell Upton's and John Michael Vlach's *Common Places: Readings in American Vernacular Architecture* (Athens: University of Georgia Press, 1986) includes articles by Kniffen, Vlach, Glassie, Roberts, Ken Ames, Dell Upton, Fred Peterson and others grouped under the following subject headings: definitions and demonstration, construction, function, history, design, and intention. Another group of essays is Camille Wells' *Perspectives in Vernacular Architecture* (Annapolis: Vernacular Architecture Forum, 1982), "the first publication of Vernacular Architecture Forum to present the results of architectural research, field work, and analysis." There, papers from a 1980 conference are gathered on barns, house types, grist mill construction, farm buildings, Baptist church houses, and one-room schools in the U.S., Great Britain, and Canada. *Perspectives in*

Vernacular Architecture, II (Columbia: University of Missouri Press, 1986), also compiled by Wells, contains essays on methods for understanding buildings, buildings in their geographical contexts, types of vernacular buildings, elements and forms of vernacular buildings, and buildings in their social contexts; it also contains a list of Vernacular Architectural Forum Conferences held between 1982-1984. *Perspectives in Vernacular Architecture, III*, edited by Thomas Carter and Bernard L. Herman, was published in 1989 (Columbia: Published for the Publications for the Vernacular Architecture Forum by the University of Missouri Press, 1989).

An enormous amount of material is available on American homes. There are surveys of American homes, such as Lee Pennock Huntington's *Americans at Home: Four Hundred Years of American Houses* (New York: Coward, McCann & Geoghegan, 1981), and social histories, such as David P. Handlin's *The American Home: Architecture and Society, 1815-1915* (Boston, MA: Little, Brown, 1979). There are studies of various types of houses. Terry G. Jordan's *American Log Buildings: An Old World Heritage* (Chapel Hill: University of North Carolina Press, 1985) discusses log construction in American culture and log construction in America and Europe. C.A. Weslager's *The Log Cabin in America; From Pioneer Days to the Present* (New Brunswick, NJ: Rutgers University Press, 1969) is concerned with the log cabin in the American colonies, the west, and Europe. Donald A. Hutslar's *The Log Architecture of Ohio* ([Columbus]: Ohio Historical Society, 1977) is a regional study of various aspects of log construction. There are many books on barns and barn construction, some of which are included in the section on **Agriculture/Farming** in this chapter. A typical one is Alfred Shoemaker's *The Pennsylvania Barn* (Lancaster, PA: Pennsylvania Folklore Center, 1955).

Regional studies of vernacular architecture are abundant, a sampling of which are John M. Coggeshall's and Jo Anne Mast's *Vernacular Architecture in Southern Illinois: The Ethnic Heritage* (Carbondale: Southern Illinois University Press, 1988), Howard Wight Marshall's *Folk Architecture in Little Dixie: A Regional Culture in Missouri* (Columbia: University of Missouri Press, 1981), a fascinating book on the history, land, and politics of "Little Dixie"--the construction of houses and barns, William Lynwood Montell's and Michael Lynn Morse's *Kentucky Folk*

Architecture (Lexington: University Press of Kentucky, 1976) which covers folklife and the cultural landscape, folk house construction and barns and cribs with a section of house and barn plans, and Doug Swaim's *Carolina Dwelling: Towards Preservation of Place: In Celebration of North Carolina Vernacular Landscape* ([Raleigh]: North Carolina State University, 1978), with essays on North Carolina folk housing, coastal vernacular, the I-House, and North Carolina porch, tobacco barns, farmhouses, churches, court house squares, and pre-1940 mountain houses. Another book on southern folk architecture is Eugene M. Wilson's *The Alabama Folk Houses* (Montgomery: Alabama Historical Commission, 1975).

Francis Edward Abernethy's *Built in Texas* (Waco, TX: E-Heart Press, 1979; Publications of the Texas Folklore Society, 42) deals with methods and materials, style and form, barns and outbuildings, gates and fences, wells, and restoration and preservation. Roger L. Welsch's *Sod Walls; The Story of the Nebraska Sod House* (Broken Bow, NE: Purcells, 1968) is a classic study of one type of folk house. And finally, *Navajo Architecture: Forms, History, Distributions* by Stephen C. Jett and Virginia E. Spencer (Tucson: University of Arizona Press, 1981) covers indigenous Native American architecture. *Shaker Architecture*, compiled by Herbert Schiffer (Exton, PA: Schiffer Publications, 1979), is an overview of Shaker architecture; the arrangement is by place (e.g., Mt. Lebanon, NY, Hancock, MA, Enfield, CT, Sabbathday Lake, ME, etc.) with a brief history of each settlement's buildings.

There are several books that take an anthropological view of architecture. One example of this type is Enrico Guidoni's *Primitive Architecture* (New York: Abrams, 1978), with chapters on architecture and territory, architecture and clan, architecture and lineage, and architecture, myth, and power; the appendix includes short paragraphs on the primitive peoples of the Arctic and subarctic regions, the Lapps, the peoples of North Africa, etc.

And finally, there are several books on international folk architecture. *La Maison Traditionelle au Quebec*, by Michel Lessard and Gilles Vilandre (Montreal: Editions de l'Hommes, 1974), is a study of traditional architecture in Canada; Olive Cook's *The English House through Seven Centuries* (Harmondsworth [ENG]: Penguin, 1984, [1968]) and R.W.

Brunskill's *Houses* (London: Collins, 1982) and his *Traditional Farm Buildings of Britain* (London: Victor Gollancz, 1987 [1982]) which covers barns where grain is processed, animal barns, granaries, bird accommodations, and farmsteads, are typical of several books about British vernacular architecture. There are several books about Irish folk architecture, such as Alan Gailey's *Rural Houses of the North of Ireland* (Edinburgh: John Donald, 1984), which concentrates on vernacular housing, the environment, construction, wall material, the roof, heath and chimney, the farmhouse, the farmyard, preservation, and conservation. And Gwyn Meiron-Jones' *The Vernacular Architecture of Brittany: An Essay in Historical Geography* (Edinburgh: J. Donald, 1982) is concerned with the architecture of northwest France.

There are several journals that cover folk architecture; *Vernacular Architecture* is probably the main one, but *Material Culture* (formerly *Pioneer America*), *Folk Life*, and *Ulster Folk Life* also have articles on folk architecture fairly frequently. The organization Vernacular Architecture Forum has published a newsletter from 1978 on.

For the most part, works specifically about barns and other farm outbuildings are included in the section on **Agriculture/Farming** (nos. 2433-2444).

Bibliographies--Folk Architecture

2134.   Camp, J.C. "Architectural Theory for Folklife Study: A Bibliographic Guide." *New York Folklore* 2 (1976): 29-41.

This difficult bibliography is intended for the folklife scholar to enable him "to confront the work of the architectural community on its own terms--recognizing the motivations from which this community has proceeded and the standards by which it is evaluated." This is a list of books and articles "pertinent to an understanding of architectural theory as a tool in folklife scholarship." So although these books are not about folk architecture, they are for the folklore scholar. Camp's listing is divided into four groups: **General Works**--historical overviews, origins, historical documents, visionary writings, and bibliographies; **Classification**--typology, structure, style, theme, motif, cognitive and cultural; **Analysis**--aesthetic, semiotic, epistemological, ecological, historical; and **Relation of Architectural Theory to**: technology, math, homopathology, natural science, design, art, psychology, philosophy, and religion.

2135. Caspar, Dale E. *Vernacular Architecture, 1982-1988: A Bibliography.* Monticello, IL: Vance Bibliographies, 1989. 5p. (Architecture series, Bibliography A-2150)

Not seen.

2136. Coppa & Avery Consultants. *Log Cabin Architecture: A Bibliographic Overview.* Monticello, IL: Vance Bibliographies, 1981. 10p. LC 81-157721. (Architectural series, A-490). A 6-page updated version appeared in 1986. (Architecture series, Bibliography A-1622)

Covers listings for log cabin architecture with subtopics on regional log cabin architecture, history of log cabins, and log cabin construction. This is an author listing; there is no index.

2137. Cuthbert, John A., et al. *Vernacular Architecture in America: A Selective Bibliography.* Boston, MA: G.K. Hall, 1985. 145p. LC 84-22569; ISBN 0-8160-0436-0.

This computer-generated list of 638 books and articles focuses more narrowly than Marshall (see no. 2146) on "modern literature pertaining to architecture of the American folk tradition." The arrangement is alphabetic by author with a comprehensive index. Also worthwhile is an excellent introduction on vernacular architecture which mentions specific important works. See also Dale E. Casper's 5-page *Vernacular Architecture, 1982-1988: A Bibliography* (Monticello, IL: Vance Bibliographies, 1989; series A-2150).

2138.   Ehresmann, Donald L. *Architecture: A Bibliographic Guide to Basic Reference Works, Histories, and Handbooks*. Littleton, CO: Libraries Unlimited, 1984. 338p. LC 83-19600; ISBN 0-87287-394-3.

Although this reference work covers all architecture, there is material in here about primitive and vernacular architecture. In all, there are 1,359 works listed: general reference works (bibliographies, library catalogs, indexes and directories, dictionaries and encyclopedias), general histories and handbooks (historical surveys, works on building technology, city design), books and articles on primitive and historic architecture, and architectural periods arranged chronologically and by geographical area (European, New World, etc). Annotations are brief. There is an author/title index and a subject index.

2139.   Garrett, Wendell D., and Jane N. Garrett. "The Arts in Early America: Historical Needs and Opportunity for Study: A Bibliography," in *The Arts in Early American History*, by Walter Muir Whitehill. Chapel Hill: Published for the Institute of Early American History and Culture at Williamsburg, Va., by the University of North Carolina Press, 1965. 170p. pp. 47-81. LC 65-63132.

The section on "Architecture" (pp. 47-81) is an annotated bibliography of general works, of works about specific architects, and of works concerning architecture in French Canada and the Maritime Provinces, and in New England, the Mid-Atlantic states, the south, the old northwest, and the Spanish southwest.

2140.   Hall, Robert de Zouche. *A Bibliography on Vernacular Architecture*. Newton Abbot [ENG]: David & Charles, 1972. 191p. LC 73-157612; ISBN 0-7153-56534.

Defining **vernacular architecture** as "the study of houses and other buildings, which, in their form and materials, represent the unselfconscious tradition of a region rather than ideas of architectural style," Hall lists articles and books under the following headings: general works--on the nature of vernacular buildings, methodological studies and dictionaries, general surveys of houses (restricted for the most part to the British Isles), treatises on the design of farm houses and buildings, studies of particular features/materials/building techniques, conservation and building repair; regional and local studies; rural buildings; town buildings; early and primitive buildings; and construction and materials. Annotations, when they occur, are brief one-liners. There is an index of authors only, no subject index.

2141. Harmon, Robert B. *Southern Colonial Architecture in America: A Brief Style Guide.* Monticello, IL: Vance Bibliographies, 1982. 15p. LC 82-227594; ISBN 0-8806-6237-9 (p) (Architecture series, Bibliography A-827)

This bibliography, concerned with styles of southern colonial architecture, is not an identification guide. Includes general surveys, article, and books on southern architecture. There is also a brief annotated guide for further study.

2142. Harmon, Robert B. *Vernacular Architecture in England: A Selected Bibliography.* Monticello, IL: Vance Bibliographies, 1980. 12p. LC 80-132735. (Architecture series, Bibliography A-303)

Not seen.

2143. Hitchcock, Henry Russell. *American Architectural Books: A List of Books, Portfolios, and Pamphlets on Architecture and Related Subjects Published in America before 1895.* New, expanded ed. New York: Da Capo, 1976 [1946, 1961]. 150p. LC 75-25672; LC 0-306-70742-x. (Da Capo Press series in architecture and decorative art)

An alphabetic listing by author of 1,461 items, some with annotations. The subject index and short title index were compiled by William H. Jordy.

2144.   Jakle, John A., et al. *American Common Houses: A Selected Bibliography of Vernacular Architecture*. Monticello, IL: Vance Bibliographies, 1981. 28p. LC 81-185562. (Architectural series, Bibliography A-574).

Lists books and articles under the following headings: 1) house types and characteristics universal to the United States during successive building periods; 2) house types and characteristics in different regions of the United States--the northeast, midwest, west, south; 3) house types and characteristics in Canada; and 4) architectural planbooks, builders' guides, and sales catalogs.

2145.   Jakle, John A., et al. *Past Landscapes: A Bibliography for Historical Preservationists*. Rev. ed. Monticello, IL: Vance Bibliographies, 1980 [1974]. 68p. LC 80-132831. (Architecture series, Bibliography A-314)

This listing of books, articles, dissertations, and theses uses the following headings: 1) general surveys; 2) methodology; 3) historical preservation as landscape management; 4) the rural scene: rural settlement patterns, rural house types--both by area, barn types, farmsteads, fence types and boundary lines, rural roads and bridges, rural churches and cemeteries; 5) the village and small town scene: village and town settlement patterns, court house spaces, fairs, and markets; and 6) urban scenes: urban settlement patterns, urban house types, urban churches, and cemeteries.

2146.   Marshall, Howard Wight. With the assistance of Cheryl Gorn and Marsha Maguire. *American Folk Architecture: A Selected Bibliography*. Washington, DC: Library of Congress, American Folklife Center, 1981. 79p. LC 81-603154. (Publication of the American Folklife Center, 8)

Following a brief introduction, the bibliography, which for the most part is unannotated, is grouped into five "arbitrary and awkward" categories: 1) theory and general works, 2) antecedents to American buildings, 3) regional works by region (New England, mid-Atlantic, the south, the midwest, and the west), 4) museums and historic preservation, and 5) field documentation. Within each section, books and articles are arranged alphabetically by author. A list of pertinent journals is included. Coverage is comprehensive up to about 1980. The lack of an index might hamper use by beginners.

2147.   Mekkawi, Mod, comp. and ed. *Bibliography on Traditional Architecture in Africa*. Washington, DC: Mekkawi, 1979. 117p. LC 79-100026.

This was compiled as a "guide for study and research in the field of folk architecture in Africa"and includes over 1,600 citations of books, articles, reviews and notes written between 1880 and 1979 covering building types in Africa--dwellings, granaries, mosques, rock-churches, rock shelters, walls, and fortifications--as well as related subjects--mural painting and decoration, furniture, tombs, sepulchral monuments, and the environment. The listing is alphabetic and, unfortunately, there is no index.

2148.   Roos, Frank John. *Bibliography of Early American Architecture; Writings on Architecture Constructed Before 1860 in Eastern and Central United States*. Urbana: University of Illinois Press, 1968 [1943, titled, *Writings on Early American Architecture*]. 389p. LC 68-24624; ISBN 0-252-72680-4.

This book contains 4,377 entries which are organized under general references, then by period (Colonial and early Republic), then geographically (New England, mid-Atlantic, etc.), subdivided by state. There is also a section on architects, now out of date. The index is comprehensive but is not especially effective for subject searching in vernacular architecture (though the material is there).

2149.   Smith, John F. *A Critical Bibliography of Building Conservation: Historic Towns, Buildings, Their Furnishings and Fittings*. London: Mansell, 1978. 207p. LC 78-322175; ISBN 0-7201-0707-5.

Over 2,200 books and articles are grouped in categories such as history, philosophy, and attitudes to conservation, legislation, towns and villages, buildings, etc.

2150. Sokol, David M. *American Architecture and Art: A Guide to Information Sources.* Detroit, MI: Gale Research, 1976. 341p. LC 73-17563; ISBN 0-8103-1255-7. (American studies information guide series; v. 2)

There is a section on **American Architecture** (pp. 23-86) with brief annotations of books and articles as well as general histories and surveys, regional, state, and city surveys, studies of specific architectural forms (i.e., barns), urban architecture and city planning, and aesthetics, taste, and style. Sokol also includes period surveys of American architecture from the seventeenth to the twentieth century and works on individual architects. There are separate author, short title, and subject indexes.

2151. Upton, Dell. "Ordinary Buildings: A Bibliographical Essay on American Vernacular Architecture." *American Studies International* 19 (Winter 1981): 57-75.

Vernacular architecture, which Upton defines as "buildings of all places, all eras, and all types," is, he says, "the most aggressively interdisciplinary of the American studies today." (pp. 57, 58) Upton discusses early studies of vernacular architecture, building technology resources, books which typify a diffusion of vernacular form and technologies, acculturation studies, books which deal with the problem of "how architecture is thought," and books on popular architecture. Concludes with a section on "Research--recording vernacular architecture and cataloging it."

2152. Upton, Dell. "The Power of Things: Recent Studies in American Vernacular Architecture." *American Quarterly* 35 (1983): 263-279.

This is part of a special issue on "American Studies and Students of American Things," edited by Thomas J.Schlereth. In this bibliographic essay, Upton covers object-oriented studies, socially-oriented studies, culturally-oriented studies, and symbolically-oriented studies.

2153. Vance, Mary. *Vernacular Architecture: A Bibliography*. Monticello, IL: Vance Bibliographies, 1983. 8p. LC 83-196532; ISBN 0-8806-6620-x (p). (Architecture series, Bibliography A-1030)

This is a good basic bibliography, an author listing that includes books and articles on traditional structures and folk architecture from all over the world.

2154. "Vernacular Architecture Bibliography." *Vernacular Architecture Newsletter*.

There is a bibliography compiled by Dell Upton and others in every issue.

2155. Weaver, William Woys. "Pennsylvania German Architecture: Bibliography in European Backgrounds." *Pennsylvania Folklife* 24 (Spring 1975): 36-40.

Preceded by a brief historical overview of the studies of Pennsylvania-German folk architecture, the bibliography is an unannotated alphabetical author listing of German- and English-language books, although German titles are translated.

2156. White, Anthony G. *Shaker Architecture: A Brief Bibliography*. Monticello, IL: Vance Bibliographies, 1986. 4p. LC 88-129706; ISBN 1-5559-0034-8 (p). (Architecture series, Bibliography A-1684)

Not seen.

2157.	Wodehouse, Lawrence. *Indigenous Architecture Worldwide: A Guide to Information Sources.* Detroit, MI: Gale Research, 1980. 392p. LC 79-26580; ISBN 0-8103-1450-9. (Architecture information guide series; v. 12)

This book is divided into two parts, the first being an annotated bibliography of articles and books, arranged by country (Africa, the Americas, Asia, Australia, etc.). The second part of the book is devoted to the vernacular revival of the nineteenth century and modern architecture of twentieth. Part II also includes a selection of general reference books on British, European, and American architecture in the English language. The appendix deals with the use of the *National Geographic Magazine* as a research tool in locating visual (and, to a limited extent, written) material on indigenous architecture. There are separate author, title and subject indexes and a geographical and building location index. Wodehouse, an architectural historian, has also written two bibliographies on American architects (Gale Research, 1976 and 1977) and one on British architects (Gale Research, 1978).

2158.	Wrightson, Priscilla. *The Small English House: A Catalogue of Books.* London: B. Weinreb Architectural Books, 1977. 148p. LC 77-374984.

There are 665 annotated items.

Classification and Typologies--Folk Architecture

2159.	Bastian, Robert W. "Indiana Folk Architecture: A Lower Midwestern Index." *Pioneer America* 9 (1977): 113-136.

This is really a classification of folk dwellings in rural Indiana. The author classifies houses (the upright-and-wing house, the four-over-four house, the I-house, the one-and-a-half-story house, etc.) and barns (the single-level, three-bay barn, the transverse-crib, and broken-gable barn, etc.).

2160. Gailey, Alan. *Rural Houses of the North of Ireland.* Edinburgh: J. Donald, 1984. 289p. LC 85-2702; ISBN 0-85976-098-7.

This text and survey of Irish rural homes includes a classification of vernacular house types.

2161. Glassie, Henry. *Folk Housing in Middle Virginia: A Structural Analysis of Historic Artifacts.* Knoxville: University of Tennessee Press, 1975. 231p. LC 75-11653; ISBN 0-87049-173-3.

Although this is a scholarly text, Glassie sets out a useful typology of house types and subtypes.

2162. Glassie, Henry. "The Types of the Southern Mountain Cabin," in *The Study of American Folklore*, ed. Jan H. Brunvand, 3rd ed. New York: W.W. Norton, 1986. pp. 529-562. LC 85-2960; ISBN 0-393-95495-1.

Glassie maintains that there are two Southern mountain types of cabins: the square (from Britain) and the rectangular (from west Britain and Ireland). The log construction has its roots in Germany.

Guides and Handbooks--Folk Architecture

2163. Blumenson, John J.G. *Identifying American Architecture: A Pictorial Guide to Styles and Terms, 1600-1945.* 2nd rev. ed. New York: W.W. Norton, 1981 [1977, American Association for State and Local History]. 120p. LC 80-28103; ISBN 0-393-01428-2 (c); 0-910050-50-3 (p).

The author includes "vernacular" styles as well as Dutch Colonial, federal, Greek revival, etc. Also, there is a pictorial glossary of terms concerning orders (e.g., Doric order), roofs, roof details, porches, porticoes, entrances, doors, windows, bricks, wall finishes, etc.

2164.   Brunskill, R.W. *Illustrated Handbook of Vernacular Architecture*. 3rd ed., rev. and exp. London: Faber & Faber, 1987 [1971, 1978]. 256p. LC 86-11560; ISBN 0-571-13916-7 (p).

In the introduction, Brunskill talks about types of vernacular architecture, then separately he discusses walling (construction and material), roofing (shape, construction, and materials), plans, farm buildings, architectural details, urban vernacular and minor industrial buildings, makes comparisons, and forms conclusions. Although confined to vernacular architecture in the British Isles, there are many useful illustrations, diagrams, and photos. Several appendixes will also prove interesting, especially the one on how to study vernacular architecture. There is a bibliography, a glossary, and a comprehensive index.

2165.   Foley, Mary Mix. *The American House*. New York: Harper & Row, 1980. 299p. LC 79-1662; ISBN 0-06-011296-4.

Arranged chronologically, Foley covers medieval-inspired homes (Dutch traditional, log traditional and pioneer house, and German, French and Spanish traditional), houses of the classical period, the Victorian age, American Revolution, and the modern house. Many vernacular house types are included. Indexed.

2166.   Gottfried, Herbert, and Jan Jennings. *American Vernacular Design, 1870-1940: An Illustrated Glossary*. New York: Van Nostrand, 1985. 270p. LC 84-17240; ISBN 0-442-23067-0 (c); 0-442-22739-6 (p).

Although called a glossary, this work is really a guide to identification of architectural **elements** (structure, cladding material, roofs, towers, turrets, chimneys, gables, windows, etc.) and **types** (roofs--gabled, hipped, mansard, gambrel, etc.). Included also are a bibliography and an index. Many drawings and labels help make this easy to use.

2167.   McAlester, Virginia, and Lee McAlester. *A Field Guide to American Houses*. New York: A.A. Knopf, 1984. 525p. LC 82-48740; ISBN 0-394-51032-1 (c); 0-394-73969-8 (p).

The purpose of this book is to supply identifying features with principal subtypes, variants, and details. The authors cite the occurrence of each style (arranged in chronological order from Colonial houses to the American house since 1946), providing commentary on the origins and history of the style. There is a separate section on **Folk houses** (pp. 62-101), which covers Native American, pre-railroad, and national styles. There are many illustrations and photos and an excellent pictorial key. A bibliography, glossary, and index are included.

2168.   Pillsbury, Richard, and Andrew Kardos. *A Field Guide to the Folk Architecture of the Northeastern United States*. Hanover, NH: Dartmouth College, Dept. of Geography, 1970. 99p. LC 72-18762. (Geography publications at Dartmouth, 8)

This is a geographical guide to house types. All types of homes found in one geographical area are discussed: New England--Garrison, saltbox, gable front, etc.; folk architecture of Pennsylvania--log house, one-room deep house, barns, etc.; folk architecture of the Chesapeake, etc. The introduction discusses the relationship between region and style. Appendixes include lists of areas to visit, a glossary of terms, and a brief bibliography.

2169.   Pratt, Dorothy, and Richard Pratt. *A Guide to Early American Homes*. 2 vols. Vol. 1: North; Vol. 2: South. New York: McGraw-Hill, 1956. LC 56-10867.

Arranged by state, from east to west, and then by town or city. The compilers give dates, histories, and descriptions of prominent homes. Some vernacular house types are included. There is an index of homes and places.

2170. Rifkind, Carole. *A Field Guide to American Architecture*. New York: New American Library, 1980. 322p. LC 79-29651; ISBN 0-453-00375-3 (c); 0-452-25224-5 (p).

Covers residential, ecclesiastic, civic, commercial, and utilitarian buildings and homes. Each section is arranged chronologically with many drawings, plans, and photos. Some are vernacular buildings and homes. The final section includes a classed bibliography of recommended reading and a list of architectural periodicals.

Exhibition Catalog--Folk Architecture

2171. Rudofsky, Bernard. *Architecture Without Architects: A Short Introduction to Non-Pedigreed Architecture*. New York: Doubleday, 1964. 156p. LC 64-8755. Reprinted: Albuquerque: University of New Mexico Press, 1987. LC 87-10778; ISBN 0-8263-1004-4 (p)

The catalog of this exhibit, held at the Museum of Modern Art in 1964-65, includes a descriptive text and 156 photographs of vernacular "homes" of the past world, including town structures, rural structures, and classical vernacular structures.

FOLK CRAFT
Ceramics/Pottery

There is a great deal of literature on folk pottery. Introductory material includes Elmer Lewis Smith's book *Pottery; A Utilitarian Folk Craft* (Lebanon, PA: Applied Arts Publishers, 1972) or *Regional Aspects of American Folk Pottery* (York, PA: The Historical Society of York, 1974), an exhibition catalog. Also useful might be Michael Owen Jones' "The Well Wrought Pot: Folk Art and Folklore as Art" (*Folklore Forum* 12 [1974]: 82-87) and *Ceramics in America*, edited by Ian Quimby (Published for the Winterthur Museum by the University Press of Virginia, Charlottesville, VA, 1973), proceedings of the eighteenth annual Winterthur Conference with essays on the cultural dimensions of pottery (e.g., ceramics as social documents), ceramic production in various parts of the U.S., types of ceramics (e.g., Straffordshire, salt-glazed stoneware, etc.), collections of pottery, use of ceramics in America, and on the significance of Spanish ceramics. Georgeanna Greer's *American Stonewares: the Art and Craft of Utilitarian Potters* (Exton, PA: Schiffer, 1981) is another basic introductory work.

An early history of pottery is Edwin Atlee Barber's *Pottery and Porcelain of the United States; An Historical Review of American Ceramic Art...: To Which Is Appended a Chapter on the Pottery of Mexico* (New York: Feingold & Lewis, 1976 [1893]. A newer history of ceramics is Elaine Levin's *The History of American Ceramics, 1607 to the Present: From Pipkins and Bean Pots to Contemporary Forms* (New York: Harry Abrams, 1988). M.L. Branin's *The Early Makers of Handcrafted Earthenware and Stoneware in Central and Southern New Jersey* (Rutherford, NJ: Fairleigh Dickinson University Press, 1988) and William Ketchum, Jr.'s *Potters and Potteries of New York State, 1650-1900* (2nd ed., Syracuse, NY: Syracuse University Press, 1987 [1983]) are typical of many regional historical overviews of pottery, most of which list, by place, the pottery, the potters who worked there, and what was produced. Other histories of American pottery include Harold F. Guilland's *Early American Folk Pottery* (New York: Chilton, 1971) and Albert Hastings Pitkin's early work, *Early American Folk Pottery* (Hartford, CT: Lockwood, 1918), a history primarily of Bennington pottery. Susan Myers' *Handcraft to Industry: Philadelphia Ceramics in the First Half of the Nineteenth Century* (Washington, DC: Smithsonian Institution Press, 1980) is a study of the move from traditional pottery to machine-made pottery. Myers' earlier work, "A Survey of Pottery Manufacture in the Mid-Atlantic Northeast United States" (*Northeast Historical Archaeology* 6 [1977]: 1-13), is a brief history of traditional pottery in the mid-Atlantic and northeastern part of the U.S. in the eighteenth and nineteenth centuries. Potters are discussed by area (e.g., New England, New York) and then by century.

Much of the writing on pottery and ceramics focuses on specific regional potters and potteries. One such work, an early classic, is John Ramsay's *American Potters and Pottery* (Clinton, MA: Hale, Cushman & Flint, 1939) which defines pottery, includes essays on potters and pottery of several regions of the U.S., has a history of earthenware and porcelain, discusses pottery types, and contains a regional checklist of American potters, a 128-item bibliography, and 35 pages of potters' marks. Regional studies include another classic work, John Spargo's *The Potters and Potteries of Bennington* (Boston, MA: Houghton Mifflin, 1926; reprinted: New York: Dover, 1972), a history and study of 16 potters, the pottery, and the Bennington styles. Cornelius Osgood's *The Jug and Related Stoneware of Bennington* (Rutland, VT: Charles E. Tuttle, 1971) is a study of specific types of Bennington pottery. Donald Webster's *Early Canadian Pottery* (Toronto: McClelland & Stewart, 1971) discusses the pottery of Quebec, Ontario, and the Maritimes.

There are many works on southern potters and potteries, the south being an area where folk potters still "work their trade." For North Carolina potters and potteries, see Charles Zug's *Turners and Burners: The Folk Potters of North Carolina* (Chapel Hill: University of North Carolina Press, 1986), John Bivins' *The Moravian Potters in North Carolina* (Chapel Hill: Published for Old Salem, Inc., Winston-Salem, by the University of North Carolina Press, 1972), and Jean Crawford's *Jugtown Pottery: History and Design* (Winston-Salem, NC: F. Blair, 1964); folk potters in Georgia are chronicled in Ralph Rinzler's and Robert Sayer's *The Meaders Family, North Georgia Potters* (Washington, DC: Smithsonian Institution Press, 1980). See also John Burrison's exhibition catalog of the Meaders family pottery (no. 2198), his *Brothers in Clay: The Story of Georgia Folk Pottery* (Athens: University of Georgia Press, 1983), and his dissertation, "Georgia Jug Makers: A History of Southern Folk Pottery" (unpublished dissertation, University of Pennsylvania, 1973). Alvin H. Rice's and John B. Stoudt's *The Shenandoah Pottery* (Berryville, VA: Virginia Book Co., 1974 [1929]) covers Virginia pottery as does William E. Wiltshire's *Folk Pottery of the Shenandoah Valley* (New York: Dutton, 1975). Southwestern potters and potteries have been discussed in Georgeanna H. Greer's and Harding Black's *The Meyer Family: Master Potters of Texas* (San Antonio, TX: Published for the San Antonio Museum Association by Trinity University Press, 1971) and C. Kurt Dewhurst's *Traditions at Work: Grand Ledge Folk Pottery* (Ann Arbor, MI: UMI Research, 1986). Ruth L. Bunzel's *The Pueblo Potter; A Study of Creative Imagination in Primitive Art* (New York: Columbia University Press, 1929) is an older work on regional pottery.

And finally, there has been some work done on foreign potters, especially Japanese ceramists and ceramics. One such study is Brian Moeran's *Lost Innocence: Folk Craft Potters of Onta, Japan* (Berkeley: University of California Press, 1984), about a group of potters who live in a small community in southern Japan and make Onta ware, "a kind of stoneware pottery that is generally referred to as 'folk art' or 'folk craft'."

As has been the case previously in this chapter, surveys of ceramics have been excluded. There have been numerous surveys of the pottery of one group of people such as Sarah Peabody Turnbaugh's *Domestic Pottery of the Northeastern United States, 1625-1850* (Orlando, FL: Academic Press, 1985) or Gertrude Litto's *South American Folk Pottery* (New York: Watson-Guptill, 1976), Roy Andrew Miller's *Japanese Ceramics* (New York: Crown, 1962), and Dawn Rooney's *Khmer Ceramics* (Singapore: Oxford University Press, 1984). There have also been surveys of different types of ceramics, such as Edwin Atlee Barber's *Lead Glazed Pottery* (New York: Doubleday, Page, 1907) and his *Tulip Ware of the Pennsylvania-German Potters* (Philadelphia, PA: Patterson and White, 1903; reprinted: New York: Dover, 1970), or William Ketchum, Jr.'s *American Country Pottery: Yellowware and Spongeware* (New York: Knopf, 1987), a study and identification guide of a specific type of glazed pottery, or Donald Blake Webster's *Decorated Stoneware Pottery of North America* (Rutland, VT: Charles E. Tuttle, 1971), dealing with decorative motifs and techniques.

There is a journal called *Ceramics Monthly* (1953--) and one published bi-monthly, *Ceramics Review* (1973--).

Bibliographies--Ceramics/Pottery

2172.   Campbell, James E. *Pottery and Ceramics: A Guide to Information Sources*. Detroit, MI: Gale Research, 1978. 241p. LC 74-11545; ISBN 0-8103-1274-3. (Art and architecture information guide series; v. 7)

    This annotated bibliography, intended to update Solon (no. 2176), includes journal articles and books, mainly in English, listed under reference works, general histories, dictionaries and encyclopedias, then chronologically (from ancient and pre-Columbian ceramics to the twentieth century) and by location (U.S., Canada, and Mexico, etc.). There are also references on marks, technical aspects, ceramic materials and processes, as well as a list of ceramics periodicals, organizations and societies, and museum collections in the U.S. There are separate author, title, and subject indexes.

2173.   Farrington, William. *Prehistoric and Historic Pottery of the Southwest: A Bibliography*. Santa Fe, NM: Sunstone Press, 1975. 24p. LC 75-315622; ISBN 0-913270-45-8.

The unannotated entries (limited mainly to New Mexico and Arizona) are divided into three sections: **general** books and articles about the history, archaeology, anthropology and culture of Southwestern Indians; works dealing with **prehistoric** pottery (before the advent of Europeans, ca. 1600); and **historic** works, covering pottery after the Spanish conquest (seventeenth century to date).

2174.   Oppelt, Norman T. *Southwestern Pottery: An Annotated Bibliography and List of Types and Wares*. 2nd ed., rev. and expanded. Metuchen, NJ: Scarecrow, 1988 [1976]. 325p. LC 88-6424; ISBN 0-8108-2119-2.

This is a listing of 965 entries, dealing with prehistoric or historic pottery or related topics. The annotations are long and often contain an abstract or, at least, a description of the contents. There is also a list of types and wares with articles cited beneath and a comprehensive index.

2175.   Schwartz, Stuart C., comp. *North Carolina Pottery: A Bibliography*. Charlotte, NC: Mint Museum of History, 1978. 23p.

This was published in honor of "Raised in the Mud," a pottery "celebration" sponsored by the Sandhill Arts Council and the Sandhill Regional Library System, Robbins, NC. The bibliography covers general introductory material to American ceramics, entries on American art pottery, pottery of the South (general references, by state: Georgia potters, Kentucky potters...), pottery of North Carolina: general references, by area or type (Seagrove area, Sanford area, Catawba Valley, Union County, the Moravian potters, Buncombe County, contemporary potters, Cherokee Indian potters), and related ceramic studies, bibliographies, newsletters and maps. Also included is a listing of significant collections of North Carolina ceramics. For each section, the compiler includes general references, books and articles, exhibition catalogs, and brochures, pamphlets, and sales catalogs.

2176.   Solon, Louis Marc Emmanuel. *Ceramic Literature: an Analytical Index to the Works Published in All Languages on the History and the Technology of the Ceramic Art; Also to the Catalogues of Public Museums, Private Collections, and of Auction Sales...and to the Most Important Price-Lists of the Ancient and Modern Manufactories of Pottery and Porcelain.* London: Griffin, 1910. 660p. Reprinted: Leipig: Zentralantiquariat, 1986.

Not seen.

2177.   Strong, Susan R. *History of American Ceramics: An Annotated Bibliography.* Metuchen, NJ: Scarecrow, 1983. 184p. LC 83-10046; ISBN 0-8108-1636-9.

There are 629 books listed in the following categories: bibliographies, dictionaries and encyclopedias, marks, general histories, specialized histories, techniques, early books, early museum collections, expositions, manufacturers, historical archeology, antiques, art education, **folk pottery** (pp. 47-49), art pottery, stoneware, dinnerware, porcelain, modern ceramics, regional local histories, individual potteries, individual potters, etc. Each item is fully annotated, and there are separate author, title, and subject indexes for easy access.

2178.   Weidner, Ruth Irwin, comp. *American Ceramics Before 1930: A Bibliography*. Westport, CT: Greenwood, 1982. 279p. LC 82-6117; ISBN 0-313-22831-0. (Art reference collection, 2)

Defining ceramics as the "art and technology of producing materials from fired clay, or products made from fired clay," Weidner emphasizes "decorative ceramics such as fine porcelain, art pottery, dinnerware, and architectural terra cotta." The work is divided by type of research material: books and pamphlets, conference proceedings, catalogs of exhibits, collections and sales, theses and dissertations, federal, state and municipal publications, trade publications and periodical articles (2,325 entries from 232 journals!). The arrangement within each section is alphabetic by author. The appendixes include guides to selected American clayworking, ceramics, china painting, and crockery journals before 1930, and there is an author index and a subject index.

Classification--Ceramics

2179.   Kempton, Willett. *The Folk Classification of Ceramics: A Study of Cognitive Prototypes*. New York: Academic Press, 1981. 237p. LC 81-20643; ISBN 0-12-404080-2.

Defining folk classification as "the referential meaning of terms used by some group of people" and using an interview technique (in Mexico) to identify Mexican vessels, the author was able to elicit categories of Mexican vessels. Prototype models are then illustrated. There is an appendix of Mexican-Spanish terms, a bibliography, and an index.

Dictionaries and Encyclopedias--Ceramics

2180.   Boger, Louise Ade. *The Dictionary of World Pottery and Porcelain*. New York: Scribner, 1971. 533p. LC 72-123829; ISBN 0-684-10031-2.

The alphabetic format gives "an account of the meaning and significance of the names and terms most frequently encountered in the study of pottery and porcelain over a span of almost 7000 years." Covered are international types of pottery, techniques, and marks. There are drawings and photos.

2181.   Charles, Bernard H. *Pottery and Porcelain: A Dictionary of Terms.* Newton Abbot [ENG]: David & Charles, 1974. 320p. LC 74-183188; ISBN 0-7153-6123-6. Reprinted: New York: Hippocrene Books, 1983. ISBN 0-8825-4278-8.

Not seen.

2182.   Fournier, Robert. *Illustrated Dictionary of Pottery Form.* New York: Van Nostrand, 1981. 256p. LC 80-36664; ISBN 0-442-26112-8.

Arranged alphabetically, this work is basically concerned with form but also covers ceramic products, styles, aspects of ornamentation, aesthetic terms (**asymmetry**), and pot parts (**base**). Some entries are very full (e.g., the ones for **handle** and **plate**), but most are short. A bibliography precedes the dictionary. Includes photographs and silhouettes of forms. See also Rhodes (no. 2183).

2183.   Hamer, Frank, and Janet Hamer. *The Potter's Dictionary of Materials and Techniques.* New, rev. ed. New York: Watson-Guptill, 1986 [1975]. 374p. LC 86-7783; ISBN 0-8230-4211-1.

This work, intended for the "individual and workshop potter, teacher, and student," includes entries on all aspects of pottery-making, techniques, ornamentation and decoration, firing and products. The entries range in length, there is much cross referencing, and lots of photographs and drawings, chemical compounds, tables, etc. (There are 42 tables in the numerous appendixes!) There is a bibliography, expanded from the first edition, which includes books on all aspects of ceramics, on glazes, minerals, raw materials, kilns, and on historical and contemporary ceramics, plus a set of publications on health and safety and a list of periodicals dealing with ceramics. Appendixes cover suppliers of materials, equipment, kilns, cones, etc., in America, Great Britain, and West Germany.

2184. Honey, William Bowyer. *European Ceramic Art from the End of the Middle Ages to About 1815.* 2 vols. London: Faber & Faber, 1949-52. LC 49-6149.

Vol. 1 is an illustrated historical survey of European ceramics, but Vol. 2 is a dictionary, which includes potters, potteries, technical terms, etc.

2185. Savage, George, and Harold Newman. *An Illustrated Dictionary of Ceramics; Defining 3,054 Terms Relating to Wares, Material, Processes....* New York: Van Nostrand, 1974. 319p. LC 73-17999; ISBN 0-442-27364-9.

This is a dictionary of "terms--nouns, verbs, adjectives, and descriptive names and phrases--encountered in the world of ceramics" related to wares, materials, processes, styles, patterns, and shapes, old and new. Much of this relates to "high" art pieces and technologies, and entries are brief, but there is some applicable material here.

Directory--Ceramics

2186. Ketchum, William C. *Early Potters and Potteries of New York State.* New York: Funk & Wagnalls, 1970. 278p. LC 71-100537.

Potteries are arranged and discussed by place: Manhattan, Long Island, Hudson Valley, Upper Hudson Valley, Mohawk Valley, Southern Tier, etc. Appended is a list of New York potters and their marks.

Glossary--Ceramics

2187. Barber, Edwin Atlee. *The Ceramic Collectors' Glossary.* London: Walpole Society, 1914. 119p. Reprinted: New York: Da

Capo, 1967. LC 67-27448. (Da Capo series in architecture and decorative arts; v. 7)

This glossary covers technical information, products, types of pottery, decorative topics (e.g., **sgraffito**) in alphabetical order from **aftabek** ("a Persian vessel used to hold water for washing hands") to **yellow ware**. Basic and useful work, lacking, however, an index and bibliography.

Guides and Handbooks--Ceramics

2188.   Barry, John W. *American Indian Pottery: An Identification and Value Guide*. Rev. ed. Florence, AL: Books Americana, 1984 [1981]. 214p. LC 84-175194; ISBN 0-89689-047-3.

Pictured are 28 basic styles and shapes of prehistoric, historic, and modern pieces of Indian pottery. Over 625 pots are shown and described, and there is a table of general characteristics of contemporary Pueblo potters. Included are a glossary, a bibliography, a listing of private and public pottery collections, a pricing guide to about 600 of the pieces shown, and an index.

2189.   Brown, Roxanna M. *The Ceramics of South-East Asia: Their Dating and Identification*. 2nd ed. Singapore: Oxford University Press, 1988 [1977]. 130p.+63 plates. LC 88-22454; ISBN 0-19-5-58889-8.

The pottery forms, techniques, kilns, and products of the Vietnamese, the Khmer, the Thai, and the Burmese are covered. There are a bibliography and index as well as many plates.

2190.   Denker, Ellen, and Bert Denker. *The Main Street Pocket Guide to North American Pottery and Porcelain*. Pittstown, NJ: Main Street Press, 1985. 256p. LC 85-18799; ISBN 0-915590-79-4 (p).

Divided into redware, stoneware, yellow ware, and whiteware, and subdivided by type (e.g., **redware:** plain utilitarian, sgraffito decoration, New England slip decoration, New Jersey slip decoration, Shenandoah Valley decoration, etc.), For each section, the Denkers give a general introduction and then the potteries from the areas which produce those types of pottery, giving dates of activity, place, and a description of the pieces. There is a selected bibliography and an index.

2191.   Ketchum, William C., Jr. *Pottery and Porcelain.* New York: A.A. Knopf, 1983. 478p. LC 82-48946; ISBN 0-394-71494-6 (p). (Knopf collector's guide to American antiques)

The introductory matter includes a definition of American pottery, hints for identifying it, a brief history of the American ceramics industry, and information on how to date pottery by shape, on how pottery and porcelain objects are made, and on the typical parts of a ceramic object. Over 367 items are pictured and described--crocks, jars, bottles, cups, plates, bowls, kitchenware, etc. There is a list of plates by decorative technique (porcelain, redware, stoneware), a list of potters and porcelain marks and manufacturers, and a glossary, bibliography, price guide, and index.

2192.   Ketchum, William C., Jr. *The Pottery and Porcelain Collector's Handbook: A Guide to Early American Ceramics from Maine to California.* New York: Funk & Wagnalls, 1971. 204p. LC 71-137487.

This work is divided into redware, stoneware, brownware and yellowware, whiteware, and porcelain. Each section has an introduction on the techniques of manufacture and the potteries that produce them; kilns and factories are discussed by region, then by state. For example, **redware** is divided into Eastern redware potters (Mass., Conn., etc.), southern kilns (Md., Del, Va., NC, etc); midwestern redware shops; western earthenware factories, etc. Exact locations of factories, kilns, and shops are given for each, with the name of the founder and approximate date of founding. Illustrations are sparse and in black and white. Appendix material includes a list of early American potters by state, giving locality, name of pottery, period of activity, and type of ware produced. There is a general index and no bibliography, though references are mentioned throughout the text. Not as easy to use as no. 2191 by the same author.

2193. Rhodes, Daniel. *Pottery Form*. Radnor, PA: Chilton, 1976. 243p. LC 76-301; ISBN 0-8019-5935-7.

Forms of pottery, defined by technique (e.g., cylindrical forms and thrown off the hump and duplicate forms), are discussed, as well as forms that are defined by their product (e.g., jars and vases, bottles, bowls, pitchers, plates, pots, cups and mugs, teapots). Also covered are techniques, such as methods of trimming, ornamentation, and decoration (e.g., glazes), and parts (e.g., feet, lids, handles, etc.). The author, a working potter, says that this book, along with his two other works, *Clay and Glazes for the Potter* (Radnor, PA: Pittman, 1974) and *Kilns* (Radnor, PA: Chilton, 1981 [1968]), form a "trilogy."

Guides to Marks and Decorations--Ceramics/Pottery

2194. Chaffers, William. *Marks & Monograms on European and Oriental Pottery and Porcelain, with Historical Notices of Each Manufactory; Over 5,000 Potters' Marks and Illustrations*. 15th rev. ed. 2 vols. London: William Reeves, 1965 [1908]. 1,089p. LC 66-38182.

The new edition has been edited by Frederick Litchfield and R.L. Holson. This is the standard work on marks in English. The arrangement is chronological and follows a history of marks. The index to both volumes is in Vol. 2. A one-volume abridgement of this work is the *Collector's Handbook of Marks and Monograms on Pottery and Porcelain* (rev. and enl. by Frederick Litchfield, 40th ed., London: Reeves, 1968). A supplement to the 13th ed. of Chaffers' *Marks and Monograms...* is titled *New Keramic Gallery, Containing 700 Illustrations of Rare, Curious, and Choice Examples of Pottery and Porcelain* (2 vols., 3rd ed., rev. and ed. by H.M. Cundall; London: Reeves, 1926).

2195.   Cushion, John Patrick, and William Bowyer Honey. *Handbook of Pottery and Porcelain Marks*. 4th ed., rev. and exp. London: Faber & Faber, 1980 [1956]. 272p. LC 81-145719; ISBN 0-571-04922-2.

Arrangement is by country (Austria-Switzerland), subdivided by town. Given are the approximate date and type of ware and the mark. An appendix includes an index of names and dates of manufacturers, retailers, wholesalers, and others in Great Britain. There is also a general index.

2196.   Godden, Geoffrey A. *Encyclopaedia of British Pottery and Porcelain Marks*. London: Jenkins; New York: Crown, 1964. 765p. LC 64-22014.

There are over 4,000 British china marks arranged alphabetically by the name of the manufacturer or potter. An abridgement of this work is Godden's *The Handbook of British Pottery and Porcelain Marks* (New York: Praeger, 1968) which has, in addition to the marks, a short description of many techniques: basalt, bisque, blue and white, creamware, Delft, ironstone, Jackfield, Jasper, lustre, porcelain, pottery, printing, redware, salt glaze, slip ware, stoneware and terra cotta. The china marks are similarly arranged alphabetically by name of manufacturer or potter. Bibliography and index are also included.

Catalogs of Exhibitions and Guides to Collections--Ceramics/Pottery

Note: This is a particularly limited sampling of exhibition catalogs and collection guides; shows and collections of ceramics are very popular.

2197.   Bensch, Christopher. *The Blue and the Gray: Oneida County Stoneware*. Utica, NY: Munson-Williams-Proctor Institute, 1987. 80p. LC 87-1542; ISBN 0-915895-05-6.

There are 171 ceramic pieces listed, described, and photographed in black and white. Bensch's introduction covers pottery, stoneware, glazes, decorations, etc. There is a bibliography also.

2198.　Burrison, John A. *The Meaders Family of Mossy Creek: Eighty Years of North Georgia Folk Pottery.* Atlanta: Georgia State University, 1976. 32p.

Mossy Creek is one of eight former jug towns, or pottery communities, in Georgia. The catalog to this retrospective exhibit begins with short essays on appreciating Georgia folk pottery, on making pottery at Mossy Greek, on the Mossy Creek community, on the history of early pottery, and on the Meaders family. The catalog list includes 117 pieces, non-Meaders wares as well as early and late Meaders' blackwares: decorative pieces, art wares, miniatures, and playthings, etc.

2199.　Dibble, Charles Ryder. *The John R. Fox Collection of Korean Ceramics at Syracuse University.* Syracuse, NY: The Art School, 1965. 107p.

Many of these lovely pieces are pictured, and all are cataloged. There is a glossary and a bibliography.

2200.　Koyama, Fujio, ed. *Japanese Ceramics from Ancient to Modern Times.* Oakland, CA: Oakland Art Museum, 1961. 70p. LC 79-244670.

This catalog is arranged by type of pottery: *jomon* and *yayoi* pottery, sueware, ash glaze pottery of the Heian period, etc. Some porcelain is included also. There is a full section on folk ceramics and the folk art movement in Japan. All 171 items are illustrated and described. Includes bibliography.

2201.　Leith-Ross, Sylvia. *Nigerian Pottery.* Ibadan, Nigeria: Ibadan University Press for the Department of Antiquities, Lagos, 1970. 200p. LC 70-24406.

The works are divided among ten groups inhabiting Nigeria. Within each section, the pots are arranged alphabetically (e.g., **anagute** pots, **argas pots**, etc.). Various potting and firing techniques are discussed in the appendix. There is a glossary, an index, and maps.

2202.   Museum of the American Indian, Heye Foundation. *Naked Clay; 3000 Years of Unadorned Pottery of the American Indian.* New York: New York Museum of the American Indian, 1972. 76p.

Includes an essay by Frederick J. Dockstader, curator of the exhibit and director of the museum and an essay by Lewis Krevolin on the technology of American Indian pottery. The 90 pieces in the show range from ca. the first century to the present and come from South and North America. There is an excellent, comprehensive bibliography.

2203.   Wilkinson, Charles. *Iranian Ceramics.* New York: Distributed by Harry N. Abrams, 1963. 145p. LC 63-25239. (An Asia House gallery publication)

There is a brief introduction to this exhibition shown in the galleries at Asia House, but the bulk of the catalog is a series of plates of the 101 items shown, cataloged, and described. Included also is a bibliography.

2204.   Willett, E. Henry, and Joey Brackner. *The Traditional Pottery of Alabama.* Montgomery, AL: Montgomery Museum of Fine Arts, 1983. 70p. LC 83-11409; ISBN 0-89280-020-8 (p).

The catalog to this exhibition, held in 1983-1984, includes essays on traditional pottery of Alabama and its forms, on ceramic grave markers, the glazes and decorations used, the potters and potteries of Alabama, and the decline of traditional pottery in Alabama. The 92 pieces in the show are cataloged and described and 53 are pictured. There is a selected bibliography.

2205.   Willetts, William. *Ceramic Art of Southeast Asia.* Singapore: Southeast Asia Ceramics Society, 1971. 194p. LC 74-942878.

All 352 items in the exhibition--dishes, bowls, plates, etc.--are shown and described.

2206. Young, Carol, et al., eds. *Vietnamese Ceramics*. Singapore: Oxford University Press and Southeast Asia Ceramic Society, 1982. 181p. LC 82-941262.

Not seen.

2207. Zug, Charles G., III. *The Traditional Pottery of North Carolina*. Chapel Hill: University of North Carolina, Ackland Art Museum, 1981. 66p. LC 80-70884.

In his introduction, Zug talks about the earlier work of the traditional North Carolina potters and the decline and current revival of the craft. The catalog lists 238 pieces of pottery; each one is described, dated, located, etc. Twenty are photographed.

FOLK CRAFT
Folk Costume

The *MLA International Bibliography*, from which this work takes its format, considers **folk costume** a folk craft, so it will be included in the Folk Craft section here.

Don Yoder has defined **folk costume** as "the standardized dress of a religious sect, sub-group, or order, which serves as a badge of group identity, both to the group itself and to the outside world," such as Hasidic costume or sectarian costumes (e.g., Quaker bonnets or Amish traditional dress). (*Forms Upon the Frontier*, p. 41). However, often it is difficult to differentiate **folk costume** (sometimes called **traditional costume**) from **national dress**, **regional** or **ethnic dress** or, even, **costume**.

Don Yoder's two articles, "Folk Costume," in *Folklore and Folklife* (pp.

295-323), edited by Richard M. Dorson, and his "Sectarian Costume Research in the United States" (pp. 41-75), in *Forms Upon the Frontier; Folklife and Folk Arts in the United States*, edited by Austin Fife et al. (Logan: Utah State University, 1969), are good starting points when beginning a study of folk costume. Jan Brunvand also has written an introductory article, "Folk Costumes," in his *The Study of American Folklore* (3rd ed., pp. 444-453).

There are some scholarly narrative texts on folk costume such as Petr Bogatyrev's *The Functions of Folk Costume in Moravian Slovakia* (The Hague: Mouton, 1971) and Carmen Espinosa's *Shawls, Crinolines, Filigree: The Dress and Adornment of the Women of New Mexico, 1739 to 1900* (El Paso: University of Texas at El Paso, 1970). Two works on religious sect garb are Melvin Gingerich's *Mennonite Attire through Four Centuries* (Breinigsville, PA; The Pennsylvania-German Society, 1970) and Amelia Mott Gummere's earlier work *The Quaker; A Study in Costume* (New York: Benjamin Blom, 1968 [1901]).

Much of the writing on folk and ethnic costume is historical surveys. Wolfgang Bruhn's and Max Tilke's *A Pictorial History of Costume; A Survey of Costume of all Periods and Peoples from Antiquity to Modern Times Including National Costume in Europe and Non-European Countries* (New York: Praeger, 1955 [1943]) is a fascinating work, covering many countries and periods. Mary Evans' *Costume Throughout the Ages* (New York: Rizzoli: 1982 [1930]), Douglas Gorsline's familiar *What People Wore; A Visual History of Dress from Ancient Times to Twentieth-Century America* (London: Batsford; New York: Viking, 1952), Alice Morse Earle's early work, *Two Centuries of Costume in America...* (2 vols. in 1, New York: Macmillan, 1910), Alfred Rubens' handsome *A History of Jewish Costume* (London: Peter Owen, 1981), Margot Lister's *Costume: An Illustrated Survey, from Ancient Times to the Twentieth Century* (London: Barrie & Jenkins, 1977 [1967]), and Millia Davenport's *The Book of Costume* (2 vols., New York: Crown, 1948, 1966) are a few more of the many historical surveys of costume available.

There are many, many general surveys of costume. There are surveys of folk and regional costumes of the world such as Angela Bradshaw's *World Costumes* (London: Black, 1973), John Gilbert's *National Costumes of the World* (London: Hamlyn, 1972), Frances Haire's *The*

Folk Costume Book (New York: A.S. Barnes, 1934 [1926]), Robert Harrold's *Folk Costumes of the World in Colour* (London: Blandford, 1978), E. Lepag-Medvey and André Varagnac's *Costumes Nationaux* (Paris: Hyperion, 1939), and Ruth Turner Wilcox's *Folk and Festival Costume of the World* (New York: Scribner, 1965). There are also numerous regional studies such as Ruth Turner Wilcox's *Five Centuries of American Costume* (New York: Scribner, 1963), Chloe Sayer's *Costumes of Mexico* (Austin: University of Texas Press, 1985), Lilla Fox's *Folk Costume of Western Europe* (London: Chatto, 1969) and *Folk Costume of Southern Europe* (London: Chatto, Boyd & Oliver, 1972), Kathleen Mann's two-volume *Peasant Costume in Europe* (London: Black, 1950), D.W. Pettigrew's *Peasant Costume of the Black Forest* (London: Black, 1937), and F.W.S. van Thienen's and J. Duyvetter's *Traditional Dutch Costumes* (Amsterdam, 1968 [1962]).

There are many surveys on Eastern European costume, notably the many-volume *Atlas of Polish Folk Costume* (Leiblin, 1949-1970), Vadim Ryndin's and V. Kozlinsky's 5-volume *Russki Kostium [Russian Costume]* (Moscow, 1960), Karel Smirous' and B. Sotková's *National Costumes of Czechoslovakia* (Prague: Artia, 1985), and M.G. Veleva's and E. Lepavtsova's *Bulgarian Folk Costumes and Bulgarian National Dress* (Sophia: Bulgarian Academy of Sciences, 1982) as well as Lilla Fox's *Folk Costume of Eastern Europe* (Boston, MA: Plays, 1977).

British costume is represented by M. Ellis' *Welsh Costume and Customs* ([Aberyswyth]: National Library of Wales, 1961 [1951]), Ilid Anthony's *Costumes of The Welsh People* (St. Fagans: Welsh Folk Museum, 1975), and H.F. McClintock's *Old Irish and Highland Dress* (rev. ed., Dundalk: Dundalgan Press, 1950 [1943]).

Finally, the Oceanic area is represented by Sidney M. Mead's *Traditional Maori Clothing* (Wellington [NZ]: Reed, 1969).

A journal, *Dress: Journal of the Costume Society of America*, has been published as an annual since 1975 by the Costume Institute.

Bibliographies--Folk Costume

Note: See also 2213.

2208. Anthony, Pegaret, and Janet Arnold. *Costume: A General Bibliography*. Rev. and enl. London: Costume Society, Department of Textiles, Victoria and Albert Museum, 1974 [1966]. 42p. LC 76-357498; ISBN 0-9034-0706-X.

The original edition has 400 books and articles published since 1900, with listings of bibliographies, encyclopedias, glossaries, and dictionaries, and a section of works on social background; then the arrangement is by country, subdivided by century. The second edition adds books and articles on Oriental, ceremonial, legal, and academic dress and costume as well as works on occupational costume, regional costume and traditional dress, and books and articles on printed and woven textiles, embroideries, and lace.

2209. Brooklyn Public Library. *A Reading and Reference List on Costume*. Brooklyn, NY: Brooklyn Public Library, 1909. 64p. LC 10-4602.

This useful historical document contains bibliographies, a list of periodicals (e.g., *Godey's Lady's Book*) and general works, followed by a classified listing of books and articles by country or subjects (e.g., **Abyssinia, Arab countries, foot-wear, peasant costume**) with one-line descriptive annotations. There is no index. A similar older bibliography is the Detroit Public Library's *Costume: A List of Books* (Detroit, MI: Detroit Public Library, 1928).

2210. Eicher, Joanne Bubolz. *African Dress; A Select and Annotated Bibliography of Subsaharan Countries*. East Lansing: Michigan State University Press, 1973 [1969]. 134p. LC 73-731220. Updated: *Africa Dress II: A Selected and Annotated Bibliography*, by Ila M. Pokornowski et al. E. Lansing: African Studies Center, Michigan State University Press, 1985. 316p. LC 86-102600. Not seen.

There are 1,025 English-language publications arranged by large geographical area (West Africa, Central Africa, South Central Africa, East Africa, Southern Africa) and listed with a brief annotation when the contents were not obvious from the title. There is an author index.

2211. Snowden, J. *European Folk Dress; A Guide to 555 Books and Other Sources of Information*. London: The Costume Society, Victoria and Albert Museum, 1973. 60p. LC 74-181305.

This bibliography of books and periodical articles lists general works, then arranges them by culture area (Austro-Hungarian Empire to Southern Europe), subdivided by country. Annotations are brief and describe contents.

Catalog--Folk Costume

2212. Lipperheide, Franz Joseph. *Katalog der Freiherrlich von Lipperheide'schen Kostumbibliothek*. 2 vols. Berlin: F. Lipperheide, 1896-1905. Reprinted: New York: Hacker Art Books, 1963. 1,495p. LC 65-27140.

In German but a standard work on costume before the twentieth century. The books are arranged first chronologically, then geographically: Germany (by province), Austria, Switzerland, Holland and Belgium, Denmark, Sweden, Spain, Portugal, Russia and Poland, Turkey, Asia, Africa, and America. There are separate listings for decoration, for aesthetics, etc.; then there are listings for almanacs, handbooks, bibliographies, catalogs, etc. The indexes--subject and name--take up nearly 100 pages.

Dictionary Catalog--Costume

2213. Hiler, Hilaire, and Meyer Hiler, comps. *Bibliography of Costume; A Dictionary Catalog of about Eight Thousand Books and Periodicals*. Ed. Helen Grant Cushing and Adah V. Morris. New

York: H.W. Wilson, 1939. 911p. LC 39-4340. Reprinted: New York: B. Blom, 1967. LC 66-12285.

This large work includes approximately 8,400 items, including "books, periodicals, and portfolios of plates dealing with dress, jewelry, and decoration of the body, in general and for special occasions, of all countries, times and peoples." The introduction differentiates between costume and dress, cites theories dealing with the psychology of dress, and includes customs and beliefs concerned with costume. There is also a discussion of general works, periodicals, encyclopedias, museums, and special museum collections. The dictionary catalog has many entries for **folk costume**, arranged by country (e.g., **France--folk costume**). Old but useful.

Encyclopedias--Folk Costume

2214.   Kybalova, Ludmila, et al. Trans. Claudia Rosoux. *The Pictorial Encyclopedia of Fashion*. New York: Crown, 1968. 604p. ISBN 0-6000-3068-7.

Not seen, but Don Yoder calls this "the best recent one-volume historical survey of clothing, from ancient Egypt to the twentieth century." ("Folk Costume," in *Folklore and Folklife*, ed. Richard M. Dorson, p. 322).

2215.   Planché, James Robinson. *A Cyclopaedia of Costume; or, Dictionary of Dress*. 2 vols. London: Chatto and Windus, 1930 [1876-79]. 971p. LC 30-63.

This is a classic work. Vol. 1 is an alphabetical listing of terms, pieces of clothing, textiles, etc. Vol. 2 is a history of costume from 53 B.C. through the eighteenth century with additional entries for theatrical, allegorical, and fanciful costume. There is an index.

2215A. Racinet, Albert. *The Historical Encyclopedia of Costumes.* New York: Facts on File, 1988 [1888]. 320p. LC 88-11186; ISBN 0-8160-1976-2.

This is a handsome new translation and abridgement of a 6-volume work. Section IV contains information on "Traditional Costumes of the 1880s" from Eastern and Northern Europe. For each country or region, there is a page of text with a facing page of full-colored paintings of the period. Indexed.

2216. Yarwood, Doreen. *The Encyclopaedia of World Costume.* New York: Scribner, 1978. 471p. LC 78-3726; ISBN 0-684-15805-1.

"Related subjects are discussed together in one larger entity," so that **cloak**, for example, is covered chronologically and internationally. Although intended for use in the English-speaking world, this also includes articles on Polish, Scandinavian, Spanish dress, etc. The bibliography (pp. 454-494) is very comprehensive and lists separately encyclopedias and dictionaries, general histories, books about costumes in the ancient world, costumes in Britain, Europe, the Americas, Asia, Polynesia, types of clothing, textiles, etc. Also included is an index and a section of British museums with collections of costumes.

Index--Folk Costume

2217. Monro, Isabel Stevenson, and Dorothy E. Cook, eds. *Costume Index: A Subject Index to Plates and to Illustrated Text.* New York: H.W. Wilson, 1937. 338p. LC 37-7142; Supplemented: Isabel Stevenson Monro and Kate M. Monro. New York: H.W. Wilson, 1957. 210p.

The arrangement is alphabetical by type of costume (e.g., **Biblical costumes**). Entries for folk costumes are found under European subdivisions. A list of books indexed is included.

2218. Haffenreffer Museum of Anthropology. *Costume as Communication: Ethnographic Costumes and Textiles from Middle America and the Central Andes of South America in the Collection at the Haffenreffer Museum of Anthropology, Brown University*, ed. Margaret Blum Schevill. Bristol, RI: The Museum, 1986. 138p. LC 86-26958; ISBN 0-9120-8904-4. (Studies in anthropology and material culture; v. 4)

The Haffenreffer Museum at Brown University has a substantial collection of textiles and costumes from Latin American countries. This catalog describes 422 pieces of clothing, some of which are illustrated in black and white and a few in color. The introduction covers the topic of costume as communication and cloth and costume in Middle America as well as a history of weaving.

FOLK CRAFT
Folk Food

Folk food is considered a craft in the *MLA International Bibliography*, so it will be included as a craft here.

Jan Brunvand says,

> Folk foods are the only traditional product to be quickly and wholly consumed, usually in a short time after preparation.... The study of folk foods, therefore, should include the entire process of traditional food handling and consumption: what is eaten, how and when it is eaten, food preparation and preservation, seasoning and serving food, ethnic and regional foods, religious food taboos and other requirements, food terms and beliefs, kitchens and cookware, table manners, and so forth." ("Folk Foods," in Brunvand's *The Study of American Folklore*, 3rd ed., p. 454)

A good place to start a study of folk food might well be Brunvand's article cited above (pp. 454-470) or Don Yoder's "Food Cookery," (pp. 325-350) in *Folklore and Folklife*, edited by Richard M. Dorson. There have been several special issues on foodways in folklore journals: *Keystone Folklore* (Vol. 16, 1971) had a special food issue, edited by Jay Anderson with an overview essay by Anderson on "The Study of Contemporary Foodways in American Folklife Research"; Michael Owen Jones edited a special issue of *Western Folklore* (January 1981) on "Foodways and Eating Habits: Directions for Research," with 13 articles organized in three parts: the sensory domain, the social dimensions, and resources and methods, republished as *Foodways and Eating Habits: Directions for Research* (Los Angeles: California Folklore Society, 1983), edited by Michael Owen Jones et al.; and there was a special issue in *Journal of American Culture* (Vol. 2, Fall 1979), "Focus on Food and Foodways," edited by Kay Mussell and Linda Keller Brown (pp. 329-571), with articles on ethnic foodways, food as metaphor, and a bibliography by Charles Camp (no. 2220). The Foodways Section of the American Folklore Society has published a newsletter since 1977, *The Digest: A Newsletter for the Interdisciplinary Study of Food* (available from the Dept. of Folklore and Folklife, 415 Logan Hall, University of Pennsylvania, Philadelphia, 19104).

There are several fine scholarly texts on folk food from both the disciplines of folklore and anthropology. Peter and Jane Benes have edited the proceedings from "Foodways in the Northeast: The Dublin Seminar for New England Folklife," held in 1982 and published by Boston University in 1984 (no. 2221). The proceedings of the Centenary Conference of the Folklore Society [England], *Folklore Studies in the Twentieth Century*, edited by Venetia Newall (Woodbridge [ENG]: Brewer; Totowa, NJ: Rowman & Littlefield, 1980), includes a useful article on folk food: "Perspectives in the Study of Eating Behavior," by Michael Owen Jones (pp. 260-265). The proceedings of the 3rd International Conference on Ethnological Food Research held in Cardiff, Wales, in 1977 was published as *Food in Perspective*, edited by Alexander Fenton and Trefor M. Owen (Edinburgh: J. Donald, 1981). Theodore and Lin Humphrey have edited *"We Gather Together": Food and Festival in American Life* (Ann Arbor, MI: UMI, 1988), with essays on family and friends, ritual and renewal, regional specialties, and food and festive performances. There is an afterword by Michael Owen Jones on "Discovering the Symbolism of Food Customs and Events" and a notable selected bibliography by Jones and Theodore H.C. Humphrey. Another full-length folklore study of food is Roger Welsch's and Susan Rosowski's *Cather's Kitchens: Foodways in Literature and Life* (Lincoln: University of Nebraska Press, 1987). Charles Camp has written widely on foodways, beginning with his Ph.D. dissertation, "America Eats: Toward a Social Definition of American Folkways" (University of Pennsylvania, 1978), a study of a research project conducted by the USDA's Commission on Food Habits between 1935-1943 called "America Eats"; a recent work of Camp on folk food is *American Foodways: What, When, Why, and How We Eat in America* (Little Rock, AK: August House, 1989), an introduction to the meaning of food, with a section on foodways and American folklife (tales and legends, folk songs, rhymes, customs, etc.), and others on the food event, and on research in foodways.

There are several scholarly cultural studies of ethnic food: Linda Keller Brown and Kay Mussell have edited *Ethnic and Regional Foodways in the United States: The Performance of Group Identity* (Knoxville: University of Tennessee Press, 1984), essays on the meaning of shared foodways with implications of foodways research for public policy. Margaret Visser's wonderfully interesting book, *Much Depends on Dinner: The Extraordinary History and Mythology, Allure and Obsessions, Perils and Taboos, of an Ordinary Meal* (New York: Grove Press, 1987) is a cultural study of various foods: corn, salt, butter, chicken, rice, etc., which explains how earlier cultures and today's populations use these foods daily. A newer work by Visser is *The Rituals of Dinner: The Origins, Evolution, Eccentricity and Meaning of Table Manners* (New York: Grove Weidenfeld, 1991) continues this strain of inquiry. *'Twixt the Cup and the Lip; Psychological and Socio-cultural Habits Affecting Food Habits*, by Margaret Cussler and Mary L. de Give (Washington, DC: Consortium Press, 1972), includes theories of food ideas and attitudes, a discussion of the transmission of foodways, and some thoughts on tradition in foodways, which they define as food which appears emotion centered. Carol A. Bryant et al.'s *The Cultural Feast: An Introduction to Food and Society* (St. Paul, MN: West Publishing, 1985) includes some information on religious and health beliefs and food. Paul Fieldhouse's *Food & Nutrition: Customs & Culture* (London: Croom Helm, 1986) discusses cultural perspectives on nutrition, food ideology, social functions of food, food taboos, food superstitions, food and religion, and cultism and food. Margaret Arnott has edited *Gastronomy: The Anthropology of Food and Food Habits* (The Hague: Mouton, 1975) with papers by anthropologists and food specialists from the Ninth International Congress of Anthropology and Ethnographical Sciences. Three other anthropological studies include Marvin Harris' *[Good to Eat]*. *The Sacred Cow and the Abominable Pig: Riddles of Food and Culture* (New York: Simon & Schuster, 1987) which "explains the diversity of the world's gastronomic customs, demonstrating that what appears at first glance to be irrational food tastes turns out really to have been shaped by practical, or economic, or political necessity," Peter Farb's and George Armelagos' *Consuming Passions: The Anthropology of Eating* (Boston, MA: Houghton Mifflin, 1980) which discusses eating as cultural adaptation, and *Food and Evolution: Toward A Theory of Human Food Habits*, edited by Marvin Harris and Eric B. Ross (Philadelphia, PA: Temple University Press, 1987). There are also several anthropological regional studies, one example of which is K.C. Chang's *Food in Chinese Culture: Anthropological and Historical Perspectives* (New Haven, CT: Yale University Press, 1977).

There have also been many historical studies and surveys of food and food habits, some examples of which are Stephen Mennell's *All Manners of Food: Eating and Taste in England and France from the Middle Ages to the Present* (London: Basil Blackwell, 1985), Waverley Root's and Richard de Rochement's *Eating in America: A History* (New York: Ecco Press, 1981 [1976]), Richard J. Hooker's *Food and Drink in America: A History* (Indianapolis, IN: Bobbs-Merrill, 1981), Alexander Fenton's and Eszter Kisban's *Food in Change: Eating Habits from the Middle Ages to the Present Day* (Edinburgh: J. Donald, 1986), and Harvey Levenstein's *Revolution at the Table: The Transformation of the American Diet* (New York: Oxford University Press, 1988) which deals chronologically with changes in food habits from the late 1800s to the present. Maguelonne Toussaint-Samat's *Histoire Naturelle & Morale de la Nourriture* (Paris: Bordas, 1987) is an historical account which deals with types of food, food concerns, food production, and food symbolism, customs, traditions, etc.

Aside from these general histories, there are several regional historical surveys of food and foodways. Sanborn Brown's *Wines & Beers of Old New England* (Hanover, NH: University Presses of New England, 1978) is mostly historical; Nicholas P. Hardeman's *Shucks, Shocks, and Hominy Blocks: Corn as a Way of Life in Pioneer America* (Baton Rouge: Louisiana State University Press, 1981) is a cultural history of corn in Louisiana; and Eugene N. Anderson's *The Food of China* (New Haven, CT: Yale University Press, 1988) is both an historical overview and a regional study of Chinese food as it is used today in different regions of China and for different purposes (i.e., for medicine).

And finally, there are works on food that defy categorization, such as *Plain Southern Eating From the Reminiscences of A.L. Tommie Bass, Herbalist*, compiled and edited by John K. Crellin (Durham, NC: Duke University Press, 1981), which includes "recipes" with many reminiscences of food, eating, and cooking all sorts of southern foods.

A great deal of current scholarly research is readily available on the topic of folk food; indeed, it is clearly a "hot" topic of research. A good example of this is a bibliographic essay in the Sunday *New York Times Book Review* (September 24, 1989: 36) by food writer Betty Fussell, "Reading Food: There's a Mythological Construct in My Soup," which is concerned with the many recent works on food by university presses. Fussell cites, among others, *Chicken Foot Soup and Other Recipes from the Pine Barrens*, ed. Arlene Ridgway (New Brunswick, NJ: Rutgers University Press, 1980), *Food and Evolution: Toward a Theory of Human Food Habits*, edited by Marvin Harris and Eric B. Ross (cited above), Claude Levi-Strauss' *The Raw and the Cooked* (New York: Octagon, 1979), Virginia K. Bartlett's *Pickles and Pretzels: Pennsylvania's World of Food* (Pittsburgh: University of Pittsburgh Press, 1980), Kathy Starr's *The Soul of Southern Cooking* (Jackson: University Press of Mississippi, 1989), Barbara Ketcham Wheaton's *Savoring the Past: The French Kitchen and Table from 1300 to 1789* (Philadelphia: University of Pennsylvania Press, 1983), Juanita Tiger Kavena's *Hopi Cookery* (Tucson: University of Arizona Press, 1980), Julia Floyd Smith's *Slavery and Rice Culture in Low Country Georgia, 1750-1860* (Knoxville: University of Tennessee Press, 1985), Carolyn J. Niethammer's *The Tumbleweed Gourmet: Cooking with Wild Southwestern Plants* (Austin: University of Texas Press, 1985), *Bacon, Beans, and Galantines: Food and Foodways on the Western Mining Frontier* by Joseph R. Conlin (Las Vegas: University of Nevada Press, 1986), and Susan Puckett's *A Cook's Tour of Iowa* (Ames: University of Iowa Press, 1988) as well as several books already mentioned above or in the bibliography below.

I have opted to divide this section on folk foods into two parts: 1) works on **food habits**, those concerned with the cultural aspects of food, food use, and food traditions and 2) those works that focus on the **culinary** aspect of folk food, sometimes called **folk cookery, ethnocuisine**, or **ethnogastronomy**. The division is sometimes tenuous, so both sections should be consulted.

FOODWAYS

Bibliographies--Foodways

2219. Brown, Linda Keller, and Kay Mussell, eds. "Selected Ethnic Bibliography," in *Ethnic and Regional Foodways in the United States: The Performance of Group Identity.* Knoxville: University of Tennessee Press, 1984. pp. 259-263. LC 83-16715; ISBN 0-87049-418-X.

This is an especially useful bibliography on ethnic foodways, arranged alphabetically. No annotations.

2220. Camp, Charles. "Food in American Culture: A Bibliographic Essay." *Journal of American Culture* 2 (1979): 559-570.

Excluding cookbooks, Camp includes only books and articles under the following sections: general tools--bibliographies and guides to the literature and contributions to American foodways research grouped by the following disciplinary orientations: nutrition and health--group studies (ethnic, age, occupational and sex groups); regional studies; history and geography; social studies; folklore and folklife; and popular literature.

2221. Derven, Daphne, et al. "Foodways Bibliography," in *Foodways in the Northeast: The Dublin Seminar for New England Folklife. Annual Proceedings. June 25-27, 1982.* ed. Peter and Jane M. Benes. pp. 130-139. Boston, MA: Boston University Press, 1984. 144p. LC 86-198884.

The general bibliography for the proceedings includes primary and secondary source material and works on diet, food preparation, and cooking in the northeast. It is organized into four sections: general studies; period recipes and instructional books; archeological and anthropological studies; and works on agriculture and utensils. Very complete.

2222. *The Digest: A Newsletter for the Interdisciplinary Study of Food.* Philadelphia: University of Pennsylvania, Department of Folklore and Folklife, 1977--. (See headnote for full address.)

The Fall 1978 issue (Vol.1, no. 3) has a bibliography of relevant doctoral dissertations.

2223. Freedman, Robert L., comp. *Human Food Uses: A Cross-Cultural, Comprehensive Annotated Bibliography.* Westport, CT: Greenwood, 1981. 552p. LC 81-469; ISBN 0-313-22901-5. Supplemented: *Human Food Uses: Supplement....* Westport, CT: Greenwood, 1983. 387p. LC 82-25163; ISBN 0-313-23434-5.

This incredibly comprehensive work deals "with various aspects of food and human culture." The arrangement is alphabetic by author or anonymous title; the entries are gleaned from all countries and all media. There are 9,097 entries in the original work, and the supplement adds 4,024 entries, some annotated briefly, some very fully, some not at all. A key word index serves as a subject index and there are many entries under **folklore**.

2224. Gottlieb, David, and Peter H. Rossi. *A Bibliography and Bibliographic Review of Food and Food Habit Research.*

Chicago, IL: Library Branch, Technical Service Office, Quartermaster Food and Container Institution for the Armed Forces, 1961 [1958]. 111p. (Library bulletin, 4)

"The purposes of this bibliographic review are to provide an overview of the major lines of research on food habits, to summarize their major findings, and point up their implications for research in inducing changes in food habits." (p.1) Although most of the bibliographic essay material is not folkloric, there are some useful entries, especially those in Section V, "Descriptive Studies: Cultural Patterns and Food Consumption," with 306 unannotated entries.

2225.   Newman, Jacqueline M. *Melting Pot: An Annotated Bibliography and Guide to Food and Nutrition Information for Ethnic Groups in America*. New York: Garland, 1986. 194p. LC 86-2140; ISBN 0-8240-4326-x. (Garland reference library of social science; v. 351)

The introduction includes an overview of food habits, ethnic food in America, and a discussion on the difference between "ethnic" and "immigrant" food. The bibliography is divided into sections on black Americans, Hispanic Americans, Chinese Americans, Japanese Americans, other Asian Americans, Indian Americans, Middle Eastern Americans, Americans from the Mediterranean, and mixed ethnic groups. There is also a section on general food habit information. Each section includes an introduction, annotated references, and resources for recipes. Most sections are subdivided (e.g., **Hispanic Americans**: Mexican Americans, Puerto Rican Americans, Cuban Americans, etc.). Included at the end of the work are tables of food compositions and sources that deal with nutritive values, food composition, etc. This is very comprehensive, but, unfortunately, it does not have an index.

2226.   Wilson, Christine S. "Food Custom and Nurture: An Annotated Bibliography on Sociocultural and Biocultural Aspects of Nutrition." *Journal of Nutrition Education* 11 (1979): 213-261.

Supplements the article below (no. 2227). This "bibliography of food habits and factors affecting them" is divided into several sections: sociocultural factors (nutritional anthropology), which includes books and articles on folklore, the social role of food (social status of food, festivals, feasting and fasting, food gifts, ceremonial foods), environmental factors, biological factors, psychological factors, foodways (cuisine, ethnic food classification), implications, and methodology. Annotations are critical. Includes an author index.

2227. Wilson, Christine S. "Food Habits: A Selected Annotated Bibliography." *Journal of Nutrition Education* 5 (1973): 41-70. Also published as a monograph by the Society for Nutrition Education, Washington, DC, 1973.

This is a "handbook of references, 1928-1972, for all concerned with better understanding of man's eating customs." Divided into three parts: cultural and environmental factors (nutritional anthropology--social roles of food, food symbolism, ceremonial foods, feasting, ethnic food classification), food selection (food beliefs, taboos and prejudices, worthy or unusual indigenous foods), and implications. Annotations are often long and critical. There is an author index. Supplemented by no. 2226.

Annotated Collections--Foodways

2228. Ficklin, Ellen. *Watermelon*. Washington, DC: Library of Congress, American Folklife Center, 1984. 64p. ISBN 0-8444-0464-0.

This small work "includes a history and dietary facts, humorous observations, poetry, and a touch of serendipity, to capture something of the good-time feelings that watermelons seem to produce."

2229. Linck, Ernestine Sewell, and Joyce Gibson Roach. *Texas Food Customs*. Fort Worth: Texas Christian University, 1989. 257p. LC 88-20158; ISBN 0-87565-032-5 (c); 0-87565-035-X (p). Published also as *Eats: A Folk History of Texas Foods*.

Divided into two parts, this discusses Texas cooking by region and then covers the state's various seasonal celebrations. There are 150 recipes interwoven in the commentary.

2230.   Mothershead, Alice Bonzi. *Dining Customs Around the World: With Occasional Recipes*. Garrett Park, MD: Garrett Park Press, 1982. 150p. LC 81-85930; ISBN 0-912048-29-8 (p).

The customs are arranged by country, from Afghanistan to Yugoslavia. In each section, the author discusses the customs of eating, what's eaten, how it's eaten, and what is or can be discussed at the table, usually with several recipes from that country. There is an index to food and beverage.

FOLK FOOD
Folk Cookery

Bibliographies--Folk Cookery

2231.   Axford, Lavonne Brady, ed. *English Language Cookbooks, 1600-1973*. Detroit, MI: Gale Research, 1976. 675p. LC 76-23533; ISBN 0-8103-0534-8.

This listing of cookbooks is arranged by title. There is an author index and a separate subject index, which includes entries for states, countries, almanacs, bibliographies, etc.

2232.   Feret, Barbara L. *Gastronomical and Culinary Literature: A Survey and Analysis of Historically Oriented Collections in the U.S.A.* Metuchen, NJ: Scarecrow, 1979. 124p. LC 78-32098; ISBN 0-8108-1204-5.

The literature is arranged chronologically from "before printing" to the present. There is also a bibliographic essay which discusses the collections of culinary literature, an index to these collections, an appendix called "Culinary Bibliographies and Bibliographic Commentary," and a listing of secondary historical texts and references. Included also are an index and a general bibliography.

2233.   Gourley, James Edwin, comp. *Eating Round the World: Foreign Recipe Books and Magazine Articles in English.* New York: privately printed. 1937. 50p. LC 38-9860.

These recipe books are grouped under general books and then by country—**Afghanistan** to the **West Indies**.

2234.   Gourley, James Edwin, comp. *Regional American Cookery, 1884-1934; A List of Books on the Subject.* New York: New York Public Library, 1936. 36p. Reprinted, with additions from the New York Public Library *Bulletin*, June-July 1935. LC 36-10112.

These cookbooks are arranged under general works and by state and region (Cape Cod, New England, high altitude, etc.) and then by author.

2235.   Lowenstein, Eleanor. *Bibliography of American Cookery Books, 1742-1860.* 3rd ed. Worcester, MA: American Antiquarian Society, 1972. 132p. LC 72-81730.

Lowenstein's bibliography is based on Waldo Lincoln's *American Cookery Books, 1742-1860.* The works in this book are arranged chronologically, with a brief statement as to contents and sources in 51 American libraries. There are over 800 titles given. Includes an index of titles.

2236.   McKee, John. *Bibliography of South African Cookery.* Capetown [SA]: University of Capetown, School of Librarianship, 1951. 42p. LC 54-39496. (Bibliographic series 41, 1)

Not seen.

2237.   Patten, Marguerite. *Books for Cooks: A Bibliography of Cookery.* New York: Bowker, 1975. 526p. LC 75-7799; ISBN 0-85935-005-3.

This is an alphabetical listing by author of about 1,700 international cookbooks. A subject index includes entries by country as well as many entries under **folklore**. There is also a title index.

2238.   Simon, André Louis. *Bibliotheca Gastronomica: A Catalogue of Books and Documents on Gastronomy:....* London: The Wine and Food Society, 1953. 196p. LC 54-1542.

An alphabetic author listing of 1,644 books in all languages dealing with food and/or wine. Includes a short title index and a subject index.

2239.   Vicaire, Georges. *Bibliographie Gastronomique: A Bibliography of Books Pertaining to Food and Drink and Related Subjects, from the Beginning of Printing to 1890.* 2nd ed. London: Derek Verschoyle. Academic and Bibliographical Publications, 1954 [1890]. 972p. LC 54-6692.

A classic bibliography on gastronomy arranged alphabetically by author. There is a title index.

2240.   Yoder, Don. "Historical Sources for American Traditional Cookery: Examples from the Pennsylvania-German Culture." *Pennsylvania Folklife* 20 (1970-71): 16-29.

This is really not a bibliography but a paper discussing "problems in cookery research" which suggests "the values and problems in using historical materials in their solutions" and provides a "model for regional archives of traditional cookery in the United States." Yoder discusses various historical texts (e.g., cookbooks, government reprints), manuscript sources (e.g., wills, inventories), and iconographic sources (e.g., books and periodical illustrations from the late nineteenth century, photographs, etc.).

Dictionaries and Encyclopedias--Food Cookery

2241.   Coyle, L. Patrick. *The World Encyclopedia of Food.* New York: Facts on File, 1982. 790p. LC 80-23123; ISBN 0-87196-417-1.

Entries are mainly individual fruits, grains, vegetables, animals, fish, etc. Much of what is covered in this international encyclopedia is folkloric. Includes an index and a selected bibliography.

2242.   FitzGibbon, Theodora. *The Food of the Western World: An Encyclopedia of Food from North America and Europe.* New York: Quadrangle/New York Times, 1976. 529p. LC 74-24279; ISBN 0-8129-0427-3.

This is one of the most international of the dictionaries. It has an entry, for example, for **aardappal**, the Dutch word for potatoes, which explains how Dutch families would gather "around for a meal solely of boiled potatoes." Recipes are included in the entries. There is a comprehensive bibliography. (See also no. 2248.)

2243.   Lang, Jenifer, ed. *Larousse Gastronomique: The New American Edition of the World's Greatest Culinary Encyclopedia.* New York: Crown, 1989. 1,193p. LC 88-1178; ISBN 0-517-57032-7.

This is a rewriting of the famous *Larousse Gastronomique* (no. 2245) "in a completely international English language edition...with corrections." Maintaining the same dictionary format, the main entry words are in the original language with variants given. Includes many, many recipes.

2244.   Mariani, John F. *The Dictionary of American Food and Drink.* New Haven, CT: Ticknor & Fields, 1983. 477p. LC 83-4977; ISBN 0-89919-199-1.

Main entries are specific foods or drink, often accompanied by a representative dish or recipe. Also included are indigenous and "transformed" dishes (cajun foods, for example). Folklore mythology is liberally appended, an example being how the Indians ate acorns.

2245.   Montagné, Prosper. *Larousse Gastronomique; The Encyclopedia of Food, Wine & Cookery.* Trans. Nina Froud, et al. New York: Crown, 1961. 1,101p. LC 61-15788; ISBN 0-517-50333-6.

This is the "granddaddy" of all gastronomical encyclopedias. Included are all types of food--fruits, vegetables, eggs, etc., culinary techniques (e.g., **sauteeing**), entries for countries, plus food-related items (e.g., **frying pan**). Food habits, origins of food, ethnic foods, and many recipes are also included in this comprehensive work. Appended is a very detailed index and a bibliography.

2246.   Root, Waverley. *Food, An Authoritative and Visual History and Dictionary of the Foods of the World.* New York: Simon and Schuster, 1980. 602p. LC 80-14737; ISBN 0-671-22589-8.

This dictionary includes a great deal of information on ethnic foods and food customs. Includes entries for foods, spices, techniques, etc. Some entries--**apple**, for example--are very long. Black-and-white photographs are included. This work is particularly international in scope. A bibliography is included, but no general index.

Index--Food Cookery

2247.   Kleiman, Rhonda A., comp. *American Regional Cookery Index.*
New York: Neal-Schuman, 1989. 221p. LC 88-27283; ISBN 1-
55570-029-2. (Neal-Schuman cookery index series, 2)

Not seen. "Provides quick access to 10,000 recipes from the
different states and regions of the United States."

Cookbooks--Food Cookery

Note: There are many, many cookbooks with traditional and
ethnic recipes. I have excluded most regional cookbooks such as
Ferne Shelton's *Southern Appalachian Mountain Cookbook*
(High Point, NC: Hulcraft, 1964), Mary Ulmer's and Samuel
Beck's *Cherokee Cooklore* (Cherokee, NC: Mary and Goingback
Chiltoskey, 1980), Haydn S. Pearson's *The Countryman's
Cookbook* (New York: McGraw-Hill, 1946), Josephine J.
Dauzvardis' *Popular Lithuanian Recipes* (Chicago, IL:
Lithuanian Catholic Press, 1977), Hanna Goodman's *Jewish
Cooking Around the World* (Philadelphia, PA: Jewish Publication
Society of America, 1973), and Diana Kennedy's *Recipes from
the Regional Cooks of Mexico* (New York: Harper, 1984 [1978]).
Also omitted are folklore journal articles containing regional
recipes, such as Marjorie Sackett's "Folk Recipes in Kansas"
(*Midwest Folklore* 12 [1962]: 81-86), or James Spears' "Favorite
Southern Negro Folk Recipes" (*Kentucky Folklore Record* 16
[1970]: 1-5). The cookbooks listed below are a **sampling** of
those that contain folkloric information and customs as well as
traditional, ethnic, or regional recipes.

2248.   FitzGibbon, Theodora. *A Taste of Scotland: Scottish Traditional
Food.* Boston, MA: Houghton-Mifflin, 1971. 124p. LC 79-
149295; ISBN 0-395-12430-1.

Includes food from all the Celtic countries--Scotland, Ireland,
Wales, and Britain. Recipes are given at random, each taking one or two
pages, with much accompanying history and customs. There are

wonderful historical black-and-white photos of people preparing and eating the food. Index. FitzGibbon has written on international foods (no. 2242) as well as about the foods of Ireland, London, Paris, Rome, the Lake District, Wales, and Yorkshire in separate volumes.

2249.   Heaton, Nell St. John. *Traditional Recipes of the British Isles.* London: Faber & Faber, 1951. 215p. LC 57-16056.

Begins with an introductory section on special days and their customs, food, and table manners. Includes the recipes and food customs of the North counties and the Isle of Man, the southern counties, eastern counties, the Midlands, western counties, Wales and Northern Ireland, Scotland, and "the Isle." There is an index of recipes and a "theme index."

2250.   Kavasch, E. Barrie. *Native Harvests: Recipes and Botanicals of the American Indian.* New York: Random House, 1979 [1977, by the American Indian Archeological Institute, Washington, CT] 1977. 202p. LC 78-21791; ISBN 0-3945-0411-9.

Covers nature's seasonings, Native American soups, vegetables, wild meats, sea harvests, natural breads, wilderness beverages, natural chewing gums, wild medicines, and cosmetics. Gives recipes and descriptions and tells what part of a plant is used and how. There is also a list of harvests by English and Latin name, an index and a bibliography. See also Michael Weiner's *Earth Medicine--Earth Food; Plant Remedies, Drugs, and Natural Food of the North American Indians* (no. 1745) and Carolyn Niethammer's *American Indian Food and Lore* (New York: Macmillan, 1980).

2251.   Lambert, Walter N. *Kinfolks & Custard Pie: Recollections and Recipes from an East Tennessean.* Knoxville: University of Tennessee Press, 1988. 211p. LC 88-14342; ISBN 0-87049-585-2.

Organized around the seasons of the year, this work "emphasizes the dependence of country cooks upon the seasonal availability of many foods, while showing their ingenuity." Recipes, folkways, and memories are abundant. There is a general index of foods, recipes and food-related items. A similar work is *Plain Southern Eating: From the Reminiscences of A.L. Tommie Bass, Herbalist*, compiled and edited by John K. Crellin (Durham, NC: Duke University Press, 1988), with recipes and herb- and food-related reminiscences from Alabama.

2252.   Manos, Sue. "Ethnic Foodways in Oklahoma," in *Festival of American Folklife. 1982*. pp. 30-34. Washington, DC: Smithsonian Institution Press, 1982. 51p.

Included are a Czech recipe for *kolaches*, German *plumma moos* (plum soup), Mexican beef *tamales masa*, Italian corn shucks, Easter bread, Southeast Asian *cha gio* (meat rolls), American Indian fried bread and grape dumplings, black American fried okra and ham, and Anglo-American chicken fried steak. (See entries listed in nos. 2253.)

2253.   Nathan, Joan. *American Folklife Cookbook*. New York: Schocken, 1984. 336p. LC 84-5430; ISBN 0-8052-3914-6.

Interviews and recipes from "traditional cooks" from New Mexico, Appalachia, Pennsylvania, Vermont, California, Texas, Southern Maryland, Martha's Vineyard, etc., are given. A section called "ethnic traditions" covers church bazaars, Passover, Italian Christmas, Norwegian food traditions, and Vietnamese cooking in Maryland. A bibliography, index, and many recipes are provided. See the newer *Smithsonian Folklife Cookbook* by Katherine S. and Thomas M. Kirlin (Washington, DC: Smithsonian Institution Press, 1990).

2254.   Piercy, Caroline B., and Arthur P. Tolve. *The Shaker Cook Book: Recipes and Lore from the Valley of God's Pleasure*. Bowling Green, OH: Gabriel's Horn, 1984. 175p. LC 85-108027; ISBN 0-911861-02-5.

This is a version of Mrs. Piercy's *The Shaker Cook Book; Not By Bread Alone* (New York: Crown, 1953; reissued, 1986). There is a great deal of discussion on where these recipes were taken from, Shaker cooking, utensils, use of herbs, etc. Includes soups, main dishes, sauces, vegetables, salads, breads and desserts, sweetmeats, beverages, preserves/jams/jellies and pickles, and concludes with information on the Shaker Historical Society (of Shaker Heights, OH), a glossary, and an index to recipes. This is one of many Shaker cookbooks.

2255. Pinelands Folklife Project. *Cranberries*. Washington, DC: Library of Congress, American Folklife Center, 1984. 32p.

Traditional recipes are given.

2256. Sokolov, Raymond. *Fading Feast: A Compendium of Disappearing American Regional Foods*. New York: Farrar Straus Giroux, 1981. 276p. LC 81-12564; ISBN 0-374-15213-6.

This is really a text divided into chapters dealing with the regional food of the midwest, the south, and the west, and with "fading" foods, traditional foods that are no longer eaten by the population at large. Recipes abound, and there are some beautiful color photographs of foods. Includes an index.

2257. Solomon, Jack, and Olivia Solomon, comps. *Cracklin Bread and Asfidity: Folk Recipes and Remedies*. University: University of Alabama Press, 1979. 215p. LC 77-13065; ISBN 0-8173-86505.

Alabama folk recipes are given (pp. 1-116) for beverages, breads, doughs, dressings and stuffings, cakes, cookies, candies, other desserts, meats, vegetables, soups, jellies, and condiments.

2258.   Longone, Janice Bluestein, and Daniel T. Longone. *American Cookbooks and Wine Books, 1797-1950*. Ann Arbor, MI: Clements Library and the Wine and Food Library, University of Michigan, 1984. 68p. LC 84-166085.

This catalog includes a brief history of American cookbooks. The grouping is by area and type (i.e., New England, midwest, west, foreign language, and the south) with a section for books dealing with regional and ethnic traditions within each regional section. Included also is an annotated bibliography of 34 books.

FOLK CRAFT
Folk Furniture

There is not a huge body of literature on folk furniture. Michael Owen Jones, however, has written widely on the subject. His unpublished Ph.D. dissertation, "Chairmaking in Appalachia: A Study in Style and Creative Imagination in American Folk Art" (Indiana University, 1970) is a good starting point for study in this subject area as well as his article, "The Study of Traditional Furniture: Review and Preview" (*Keystone Folklore Quarterly* 12 [1967]: 233-245), an excellent overview of the state of study of traditional furniture in America in the mid-1960s, in which Jones calls for an interdisciplinary study of furniture. Jones' *Craftsman of the Cumberlands: Tradition & Creativity* (Lexington: University Press of Kentucky, 1989), "an extensive revision of *The Hand Made Object and Its Maker*" (Berkeley: University of California Press, 1975), is concerned mostly with chair-making, and much of it is an interview with one particular chairmaker from southeast Kentucky.

Surveys of folk furniture have been omitted here, although they are useful for research. Helena Hayward's *World Furniture: An Illustrated History* (New York: McGraw-Hill, 1965) is typical of the general histories: it covers furniture from many countries, from the classical period through the twentieth century, including "primitive furniture." Gislind M. Ritz looked at *The Art of Painted Furniture* (New York: Van Nostrand,

Rinehold, 1971) in Europe and Robert Bishop and Dean Fayles studied *American Painted Furniture, 1660-1880* (New York: Bonanza, 1986 [1972]).

Different types of American furniture have been surveyed. The most written about piece of furniture is the chair, in such works as Michael Owen Jones' work cited above and Charles Muller's and Timothy Rieman's *The Shaker Chair* (Winchester, OH: The Canal Press, 1984), a scholarly and historical overview of the Shaker chair. Other works on chairs are Robert Bishop's *The American Chair: Three Centuries of Style* (New York: Bonanza, 1983 [1972)], Robert Trent's *Hearts and Crowns: Folk Chairs of the Connecticut Coast, 1720-1840* (New Haven, CT: New Haven Colony Historical Society, 1977), and Benno M. Forman's *American Seating Furniture, 1630-1870; An Interpretive Catalog* (New York: W.W. Norton, 1988). Monroe Fabian studied *The Pennsylvania-German Decorated Chest* (New York: Universe Books, 1978) and John Morse edited a book of essays on *Country Cabinetwork and Simple City Furniture* (Charlottesville: University of Virginia Press for the Winterthur Museum, 1970).

Shaker furniture has been the subject of a great deal of study in America, some examples of which are the several works of Faith and Edward Deming Andrews, prominent collectors of Shaker furniture, who have written *Religion in Wood; A Book of Shaker Furniture* (Bloomington: Indiana University Press, 1966), with an introductory essay by Thomas Merton, and *Shaker Furniture; The Craftsmanship of an American Communal Sect* (New Haven, CT: Yale University Press, 1937; reprinted: New York: Dover, 1950). John Kassay's *The Book of Shaker Furniture* (Amherst, MA: University of Massachusetts Press, 1980) and Charles Muller's, Jerry Grant's *Shaker Furniture Makers* (Hanover: Published for the Hancock Shaker Village, Pittsfield, MA, by the University Press of New England, 1989), and Timothy Rieman's *The Shaker Chair* (mentioned above) are three more recent examples of the study of Shaker furniture.

There are overviews of the traditional furniture of many countries. As just one example--of English-language works on the indigenous furniture of Asia--see George N. Kates' *Chinese Household Furniture* (New York: Harper, 1948), Michel Beurdeley's more recent *Chinese Furniture*

(Tokyo: Kodansha, 1979), an historical overview as well as Edward R. Wright's study of Korean furniture in his *Korean Furniture: Elegance and Tradition* (Tokyo: Kodansha International, 1984) and Yoon Bok Cha et al's *Korean Furniture and Culture* (Seoul: Shinkwang, 1988).

Bibliography--Folk Furniture

2259.   Semowich, Charles J., comp. *American Furniture Craftsmen Working Prior to 1920: An Annotated Bibliography*. Westport, CT: Greenwood, 1984. 381p. LC 84-4459; ISBN 0-313-23275-x.

In all, there are 2,052 entries, all briefly annotated, divided into sections on works about individual craftsmen, groups of craftsmen, general books, and trade catalogs. An appendix includes a listing of American furniture periodicals and a list of manuscript collections. There is also a craftsmen biographical index, an author/title index, and a subject index with many entries for folk furniture and folk art.

Classification--Folk Furniture

2260.   Jones, Michael Owen. "'They Made Them for the Lasting Part': A 'Folk' Typology of Traditional Furniture Makers." *Southern Folklore Quarterly* 35 (1971): 44-61.

Jones proposes a local typology, distinguishing among chairmakers according to occupational specialization, motivation, and relative emphasis on either the technical or the aesthetic aspect of the craft.

Dictionaries--Folk Furniture

2261.   Boyce, Charles, ed. *Dictionary of Furniture*. New York: Facts on File Publications, 1985. 331p. LC 83-20753; ISBN 0-8160-1042-0.

The author claims in the preface that this "is certainly the most comprehensive listing in a single volume of terms that refer to furniture--its style, manufacture, and makers--in all countries and cultures." Covers all types of furniture and styles as well as designers and makers and decorations, etc.

2262.   Gloag, John. *A Short Dictionary of Furniture*. Rev. and enl. London: Allen & Unwin, 1969 [1952]. 813p. LC 79-389777; ISBN 04-7490093-8.

Although this dictionary, containing over 2,600 entries, is mostly concerned with classical furniture styles, several entries, such as **painted furniture**, **regional furniture**, and **rocking chair** might be of interest to folklorists.

Guides and Handbooks--Folk Furniture

2263.   Johnson, Axel Petrus, and Marta K. Sironen, comps. *Manual of the Furniture Arts and Crafts*. Grand Rapids, MI: A.P. Johnson, 1928. 899p. LC 28-18389.

This old but still useful guide includes an historical overview of furniture and sections on origins and identification of designs, technical descriptions of furniture--periods and styles, on furniture woods with a key for identification of common furniture woods by means of characteristics seen on longitudinal surfaces, a section on veneers and plywoods, and on furniture machinery. At the end there is a section on furniture in American museums, biographies of furniture craftsmen, architects, and artisans, and a long bibliography (pp. 685-745). Ends with a glossary, a subject index, and a general index.

2264.   Ketchum, William C., Jr. *Chests, Cupboards, Desks & Other Pieces*. New York: A.A. Knopf, 1982. 476p. LC 82-47847; ISBN 0-394-71270-6 (p). (Knopf collectors' guides to American antiques)

The introduction includes information on identifying furniture, a survey of American furniture styles, parts of furniture, and hardware. Then the author describes 334 pieces of furniture (dry sinks, washstands, commodes, sideboards, desks and secretaries, cupboards, cabinets, highboys, etc). Each one is pictured. Includes a price list and index.

2265. Kirk, John T. *American Furniture & the British Tradition to 1830*. New York: Knopf, 1982. 397p. LC 82-15201; ISBN 0-394-40038-0.

This includes essays relating to British and American furniture and a visual survey of British and American furniture and chests, boxes, etc. In all, there are 1,508 pieces photographed in black and white and described with tables, notes, and indexes.

2266. Kovel, Ralph M., and Terry H. Kovel. *American Country Furniture, 1780-1875*. 2nd ed. New York: Crown, 1985 [1965]. 248p. ISBN 0-5175-4668-X (p).

This guide covers chairs, chests, cradles, desks, washstands, Pennsylvania furniture, Shaker furniture, furniture construction, and tools. There are many illustrations as well as a glossary of accessories and terms, an index, and a bibliography.

2267. Meader, Robert F.W. *Illustrated Guide to Shaker Furniture*. New York: Dover, 1972. 128p. LC 74-164732; ISBN 0-486-22819-3.

Covers chairs and footstools, tables and desks, case pieces, miscellaneous pieces, pegs and pegboards, clocks, and "decadent and doubtful" pieces. Also includes a Shaker chair catalog issued in 1871 at Mt. Lebanon, NY.

2268. Naeve, Milo M. *Identifying American Furniture: A Pictorial Guide to Styles and Terms, Colonial to Contemporary*. 2nd ed., rev. and exp. Nashville, TN: The American Association for State and Local History, 1989 [1981]. 87p. LC 89-14923; ISBN 0-910050-961.

The author describes pieces of furniture in the classic styles (Queen Anne, Chippendale, etc.) but also in the vernacular, national, and Shaker styles. All are illustrated with photographs.

2269. Raycraft, Donald R. *Early American Folk & Country Antiques.* Rutland, VT: Charles E. Tuttle, 1971. 148p. LC 70-142778; ISBN 0-8048-0961-5.

This has an introductory section "on collecting," followed by identification guides to country antiques, country furniture, country kitchen antiques, and early artificial lighting fixtures. Many illustrations are included, with an index and bibliography.

2270. Schwartz, Marvin D. *Chairs, Tables, Sofas & Beds.* New York: A.A. Knopf, 1982. 478p. LC 82-47846; ISBN 0-394-71269-2 (p). (Knopf collector's guides to American antiques)

There is introductory material on how to identify American furniture, furniture styles, parts of furniture, and joinery construction. Then 347 items are pictured and described (chairs, sofas, stools, beds, and tables). There is also a checklist for identifying styles, a list of plates by style, an upholstery guide, a list of public collections, glossary, bibliography, price guide, and index.

Exhibition Catalogs and Guides to Collections--Folk Furniture

Note: This is a select list of regional exhibitions. Many other exhibition catalogs are available.

2271. Emerich, A.D., comp. *Shaker; Furniture and Objects from the Faith and Edward Deming Andrews Collection;....* Washington:

Published for the Renwick Gallery of the National Collection of Fine Arts of the Smithsonian Institution, 1973. 88p. LC 73-14614.

This exhibition of the Andrews collection was held in 1973-1974 to commemorate the "Bicentenary of the American Shakers." The catalog includes several essays, including one by Edward Deming Andrews on "The Shakers in New England," another by Janet Malcolm on "The Modern Spirit in Shaker Design," and an interview with Faith Andrews by Emerich. Forty items from the collection are pictured and described. Another catalog of a Shaker furniture exhibition is *True Gospel Simplicity: Shaker Furniture* (Concord: New Hampshire Historical Society, 1974).

2272.   Green, Henry D. *Furniture of the Georgia Piedmont Before 1830*. Atlanta, GA: High Museum of Art, 1976. 143p. LC 76-20949.

An excellent introduction covers the people and culture of early Piedmont Georgia, woods used, forms and styles of the furniture, decoration, and cabinetmakers. The catalog includes 185 pieces: huntboards and sideboards, tables, cellarets, medicine boxes, chests of drawers, desks, corner cupboards, chairs, and beds. Each entry includes the place and date built, wood used, dimensions, a brief note, and where the piece is now if known.

2273.   *Neat Pieces: The Plain-Style Furniture of 19th-Century Georgia*. Atlanta, GA: Atlanta Historical Society, 1983. 204p. LC 83-50809.

This introduction states that there is a dearth of scholarly work on "furniture that best conveys impressions of the everyday life of representative Georgians of the nineteenth century." (p. 11) The catalog is divided into sections: Georgians at home, picturing and describing 20 items used at home (bureaus, tables, secretaries, paintings, chairs, etc.), with pictures of homes and inhabitants interspersed; furniture for sleeping, furniture for sitting, furniture related to food and drink, furniture for textile storage, furniture related to reading, writing, and record keeping, and multipurpose tables and small stands. There is also a preliminary list of nineteenth-century Georgia furniture makers, arranged alphabetically by name.

2274. *North Carolina Furniture, 1700-1900.* Raleigh: North Carolina Museum of History. Department of Cultural Resources, 1977. 74p. LC 77-14718.

This catalog "documents the evolution of furniture in North Carolina from 1700 until 1900 when it centered in and around High Point, known today as the 'Furniture Capital of the World'." An introduction relates that most of the craftsmen were also farmers, that most communities "of any size" had cabinet makers, that they used local wood, that they trained apprentices, that they were aware of pervading national tastes, and that North Carolina furniture is characterized by its unadorned style and high quality. The catalog is arranged by style: Colonial style (1710-1810), Federal style (1790-1830), and Victorian style (1830-1900), with a section on the common chair (1710-1870). There is an introduction for each section and a description and photograph of all 71 catalog pieces. Each is given a date and place, information on the wood used, and dimensions, with a long note and the collections it is in. There is a glossary.

2275. *Thomas Day, Cabinetmaker: An Exhibition at the North Carolina Museum of History.* Raleigh: North Carolina Museum of History. Department of Cultural Resources, 1975. 75p.

Thomas Day, a free black, worked in Milton, NC, from the 1820s until about 1859. (p. 7) This catalog of his furniture, which pictures one or two per page and includes a photograph and a description for each, includes tables, bureaus, washstands, rockers, sofas, wardrobes, chairs, cradles, sideboards, etc. Also given is the museum or private collection where the piece is permanently housed. There is also a section of his architectural woodwork.

FOLK CRAFT
Gravestone Art

There is quite a bit of contemporary scholarly writing on tombstone carving. A fascinating comparative study is Gian Carlo Susini's *The Roman Stonecutter: An Introduction to Latin Epigraphy* (Oxford: Blackwell, 1973), with many examples of Roman funerary carvings and epigraphs. *Cemeteries and Gravemarkers: Voices of American Culture*, edited by Richard E. Meyer (Ann Arbor, MI: UMI Research Press, 1989), covers icon and epitaph (e.g., Victorian children's gravemarkers), origins and influences (e.g., the French influence on New Orleans gravestones), ethnicity and regionalism (e.g., Afro-American sections of Newport's [RI] common burial ground), and business and pleasure. See also as a general introduction "The Cemetery as a Cultural Text" (*Kentucky Folklore Record* 26 [1980]: 103-13) by Ricardas Vidutis and Virginia Loewe, a semiotic approach to grave markers and a survey of motifs and design of cemetery markers in a small town in Indiana.

Much of the scholarly work on tombstone carving has been done on New England gravestones. Peter Benes' *The Masks of Orthodoxy: Folk Gravestone Carving in Plymouth, Massachusetts, 1689-1885* (Amherst: University of Massachusetts Press, 1971) looks at the history of the northeast through gravestone cutting; Benes' thesis is that gravestone markers in Plymouth County were "motivated by conscious intent." Allan I. Ludwig's *Graven Images; New England Stonecarving and Its Symbols, 1650-1815* (Middletown, CT: Wesleyan University Press, 1966) and Harriette Merrifield Forbes' *Gravestones of Early New England, and the Men Who Made Them, 1653-1800* (Boston, MA: Houghton Mifflin, 1927; reprinted: New York: Da Capo, 1967) are historical studies of cutters and gravestones in New England each with a list of New England stonecutters. Dickran and Ann Tashjian's *Memorials for Children of Change; The Art of Early New England Stonecarving* (Middletown, CT: Wesleyan University Press, 1974) deals with the Puritan religion and the Puritan attitude towards art, literature, etc. It includes 161 epitaphs with figures of their headstones and a good bibliography on the subject.

Studies of gravestone carving in other regions of America include: Preston Barba's *Pennsylvania German Tombstones; A Study in Folk Art* (no. 2279) which lists and discusses the symbols found on Pennsylvania-

German headstones: the sun, the heart, the tree of life, each with its inscription, and a description of the whole stone; Terry G. Jordan's *Texas Graveyards: A Cultural Legacy* (Austin: University of Texas Press, 1982), a study of graveyards as artifacts, with chapters on a typical southern folk cemetery in Texas, traditional southern grave markers, a Mexican graveyard in Texas, and a Texas-German graveyard (the bibliography, pp. 135-143, is noteworthy); Diana Williams Combs' *Early Gravestone Art in Georgia and South Carolina* (Athens: University of Georgia Press, 1986), a study of English and native iconic tombstones in two southern states executed by English or New England stone carvers and the changes that occurred in the iconography of gravestones from the late eighteenth to the early nineteenth century. Klaus Wust's *Folk Art in Stone, Southwest Virginia* (Edinburg, VA: Shenandoah History, 1970) is another study of southern gravestones, especially concerned with motifs, carvers, lettering, and graveyards. Other regional works include Richard F. Welch's *Memento Mori: The Gravestones of Early Long Island, 1680-1810* (Syosset, NY: Friends for Long Island's Heritage, 1983), a chronological study of the work of Long Island gravestone carvers, what influenced their work and the origins, traditions and symbols of Long Island gravestones, Dorothy Mellett's *Gravestone Art in Rockland County, New York* (Tappan, NY: Hudson Valley Press, 1991), and Carol Foss Swinehart's *Gravestone Art: The Tombstone Cutters of Early Fairfield County, Ohio, and Their Art* (Lancaster, OH: Fairfield County Chapter Ohio Genealogical Society, 1984). Two studies of Canadian gravestone carving are Deborah E. Trask's *Life How Short, Eternity How Long: Gravestone Carving and Carvers in Nova Scotia* (Halifax, NS: Nova Scotia Museum, 1978), a historical account, covering primitive carvings, German and Scottish stones, and iconographic motifs and materials used (iron, bronze, granite), and Carole Hanks' *Early Ontario Gravestones* (Toronto: McGraw-Hill Ryerson, 1974) on material, techniques, craftsmen, shapes, epitaphs, and motifs of the gravestones of the past and today.

There are several British gravestone studies: Pamela Burgess' *Churchyards* (London: SPCK, 1980) covers gravestones, carvers, and carving, and Dane Love's *Scottish Kirkyards* (London: Robert Hale, 1989) is a study of Scottish tombstones, cemeteries, and funeral customs.

An important journal for gravestones is *Markers: The Annual Journal of the Association for Gravestone Studies* (Worcester, MA), which began with the 1979/80 edition. And the journal *AFFWord* (1971--) often includes articles on cemeteries, and gravestone markers and their decoration.

Bibliography--Gravestone Art

2276. Buckeye, Nancy. "Bibliography: Puritan Gravestone Art," in *Puritan Gravestone Art*. The Dublin Seminar for New England Folklife. Annual Proceedings, 1976. Boston, MA: Boston University, 1976. Vol. 1 of the Dublin Seminar for New England Folklife: Annual Proceedings. pp. 130-142.

This includes a bibliographic essay, "Early American Gravestone Studies: The Structure of the Literature" (pp. 130-136) and a "Bibliography of Gravestone Studies" (pp. 137-142). Listings only. This was *updated* by "Bibliography of Gravestone Studies," *Puritan Gravestone Art II*. The Dublin Seminar for New England Folklife. Annual Proceedings, 1978. Boston, MA: Boston University Press, 1978. pp. 149-159; it is also a listing of titles.

2277. Meyer, Richard E. "Bibliography," in *Cemeteries and Gravemarkers: Voices of American Culture*, ed. Richard E. Meyer. Ann Arbor, MI: UMI Research Press, 1989. pp. 329-339. LC 88-30119; ISBN 0-8357-1903-0. (American material culture and folklife)

Citing the fact that a bibliography is not available on this subject, Meyer compiled this unannotated one. It is arranged by subjects: regional/subregional studies, the cemetery and social values, visual symbolism, epitaphs, ethnicity, the cemetery as landscape, the rural cemetery movement, non-American material, guidebooks, and general/correlative books on death and culture.

2278. Zaniello, Thomas A. "American Gravestones: An Annotated Bibliography." *Folklore Forum* 9 (1976): 115-137.

The thesis of this article is that, while the study of American gravestones used to be the concern only of the folklorist, as of the mid-1970s it had become an interdisciplinary concern. The bibliography is divided into the following sections: 1) studies in cultural theory, history, esthetics, and iconography; 2) regional studies of graven imagery; New England, mid-Atlantic, south, midwest, and west; 3) geographical and sociological aspects of cemeteries; 4) stonework, sculpture, and decoration; 5) epitaphs; and 6) methods of field study. There are about 75 entries, each with long, critical annotations.

Guides--Gravestone Art

2279. Barba, Preston A. *Pennsylvania German Tombstones; A Study in Folk Art*. Allentown, PA: Schlechters for the Pennsylvania German Folklore Society, 1954. 232p. (Proceedings of the Pennsylvania German Society; v. 18)

Although the first part is a study of the motifs "that underlie and characterize German peasant art...with special reference to that on their tombstones," the second part of this work contains drawings of Pennsylvania German tombstones with the epitaphs, notes, and site notations.

2280. Duval, Francis Y., and Ivan B. Rigby. *Early American Gravestone Art in Photographs*. New York: Dover, 1978. 133p. LC 78-54867; ISBN 0-486-23689-7.

This is a set of black-and-white photographs of mostly New England gravestones with extensive notes for each. There is also a list of colonial and American seventeenth-, eighteenth-, and nineteenth-century stonecarvers from Connecticut, Maine, Massachusetts, New Hampshire, New Jersey, New York, Ohio, Rhode Island, Vermont, and Virginia, and a list of select burial grounds from the same states. Appended is an alphabetical list of gravestone motifs (**anchors-wreaths**).

2281.　George, Diana Hume, and Malcolm A. Nelson. *Epitaph and Icon: A Field Guide to the Old Burying Grounds of Cape Cod, Martha's Vineyard, and Nantucket*. Orleans, MA: Parnassas Imprints, 1983. 128p. LC 82-62903; ISBN 0-9401-6021-8 (c); 0-9401-6017-X (p).

Following an introduction to epitaphs and iconography, the compilers arrange this work geographically: Cape Cod--Sandwich, Barnstable, etc., Martha's Vineyard, and Nantucket. There are many photographs of headstones and tombstones, notes on the photographs, rubbings, and data collections. There are many references and an index but no separate bibliography.

2282.　Smith, Elmer L. *Early American Grave Stone Designs; A Pictorial Presentation*. Lebanon, PA: Applied Arts Publications, 1972. 32p.

This includes rubbings of stones with some drawings of motifs and some photographs. Covers mostly New Jersey, Pennsylvania, Maryland, and Virginia.

2283.　Wasserman, Emily. *Gravestone Designs: Rubbings and Photographs from Early New York & New Jersey*. New York: Dover, 1972. 33p.+135 plates+16p. appended matter. LC 79-1774493; ISBN 0-486-22873-8.

The introduction is concerned with the origins and purposes of early gravestones, the art of the stonecutter, sources for imagery, and epitaphs, inscriptions, lettering, calligraphy and iconography. There are 65 plates of rubbings of motifs and many photos of cemeteries. An appendix includes extensive notes; there is a bibliography and lists of towns covered, stonecutters, and unillustrated stones by cutters.

FOLK CRAFT
Household Items

The *MLA International Bibliography* has a section under folk craft called **household items** which includes works on **baskets, clocks, carpets and rugs**, and some **needlecraft**. I have included all needlecraft together here, even though some might not be considered household items (i.e., **lace**); **weaving** is considered as a separate craft by the *MLA International Bibliography* and although many weaving products (i.e., **coverlets**) are really household items, I have opted to keep works on all aspects of weaving together (nos. 2402-2427). The *MLA International Bibliography* lists **textiles** under the Technology section of Material Culture, even though the textiles referred to are not necessarily machine made. I have, therefore, included titles about textiles under that section, and it should be consulted also (nos. 2459-2491). Finally, glassware and ceramics, which might well be considered part of household items, are listed separately by the *MLA International Bibliography* and so are listed elsewhere here (nos. 2172-2207 and nos. 2445-2449).

HOUSEHOLD ITEMS
Baskets

There are comparatively few books available about basketry or basketmaking. A classic work is Otis Tufton Mason's two-volume *Indian Basketry: Studies in Textile Art Without Machinery* (New York: Doubleday, 1954; originally published in 1902 as *Aboriginal American Basketry*). Vol. 1 defines basketry, discusses materials, basket making, ornamentation, and uses; Vol. 2 is about ethnic varieties. A new, full-length contextual study is Rosemary O. Joyce's *A Bearer of Tradition: Dwight Stump, Basketmaker* (Athens: University of Georgia Press, 1989), a biographical and technical study of one basketmaker with a listing of traditional basketmakers (weavers, plaiters, coilers) at the end. See also Ed Rossbach's *Baskets as Textile Art* (New York: Van Nostrand, 1973) and *The Basketmaker's Art: Contemporary Baskets and Their Makers*, edited by Rob Pulleyn (Asheville, NC: Lark Books, 1986). There are also several how-to books, some of which are quite informational, such as Virginia Harvey's *The Techniques of Basketry* (3rd ed., Seattle: University of Washington Press, 1986), and several on collecting (see **Guides and Handbooks**). I have not found a comprehensive bibliography on the subject.

A few surveys of basketry have been published, notably John E. McGuire's *Old New England Splint Baskets and How to Make Them* (West Chester, PA: Schiffer Publishing Co., 1985), Guy Reinert's *Pennsylvania German Splint and Straw Baskets* (Plymouth Meeting, PA: Mrs. C. Naaman Keyser, 1946), Sue H. Stephenson's *Basketry of the Appalachian Mountains* (New York: Van Nostrand, 1977), and Gloria Roth Teleki's *The Baskets of Rural America* (New York: Dutton, 1975) which talks about technical and historical aspects of baskets made by American Indians, the New Englanders, the Shakers, and the Afro-Americans, and Gulla baskets. Don and Carol Raycraft's *Country Baskets* (Des Moines, IA: Wallace-Homestead Books, 1976) is an overview of early American baskets. And, Jeannette Lasansky's *Willow, Oak & Rye: Basket Traditions in Pennsylvania* (Lewisburg, PA: Union County Oral Traditions Projects, 1978) is a study of traditional basketmaking in northern Pennsylvania. Alastair Heseltine's *Baskets and Basketmaking* (Aylesbury: Shire, 1982) is concerned with British traditional baskets and Wendy Arbeit's *Baskets in Polynesia* (Honolulu: University of Hawaii Press, 1990) is concerned with Polynesian basketry.

I have tried to omit how-to books on basketmaking, though they often provide a great deal of information. Two recent examples of these are Lyn Siler's *Handmade Baskets* (New York: Sterling, 1991) which includes directions for 28 baskets and Hisak Sekijima's *Basketry: Projects from Baskets to Grass Slippers* (Tokyo: Kodansha International, 1991 [1986]), a handsome book with several sets of instructions for basketry projects.

Classification--Baskets

2284. Balfet, Hélène. "Basketry: A Proposed Classification." *Papers on California Archaeology* 47 (April, 1957): 1-21+. University of California Archeological Survey, Department of Anthropology, Berkeley, CA.

Balfet proposes that baskets be categorized according to standards (relatively fixed elements that make up the foundation of the basket) and threads (moving elements that hold the standards by intertwining among them). She then further classifies basket styles into four principal types: 1) bound lattice work basketry; 2) coiled basketry; 3) twined basketry; and 4) woven basketry. There are many pages of explanatory illustrations. See also 2284A below.

Guides and Handbooks--Baskets

2284A. Adovasio, J.M. *Basketry Technology: A Guide to Identification and Analysis.* Chicago, IL: Aldine, 1977. 182p. LC 77-70388. (Aldine manuals on archeology)

This work first classifies baskets into major groups and subclasses. Then it analyses and describes, with drawings, twined basketry, coiled basketry, plaited basketry, and miscellaneous basketry configurations. Indexed.

2285. Irwin, John Rice. *Baskets and Basket Makers in Southern Appalachia.* Exton, PA: Schiffer, 1982. 191p. LC 81-86386; ISBN 0-91683-860-9 (c); 0-91683-361-7 (p)

Covers types and styles of Appalachian baskets, basket materials, and basket-related items. Many photos.

2286. Ketchum, William C., Jr. *American Basketry and Woodenware: A Collector's Guide.* New York: Macmillan, 1974. 228p. LC 73-6486; ISBN 0-02-562970-0.

Both woodenware and basketry of American Indians and settlers from the seventeenth century on are included. Ketchum covers splint basketry, splint household basketry, farm and market baskets, fishermen's basketry, willow basketry, farm baskets, and miscellaneous materials. Each section includes descriptions of baskets and their uses; some are photographed. An appendix includes a list of early American basketmakers, arranged by state, then city, with dates given. There is a bibliography of books and articles and a general index.

2287. Larason, Lew. *The Basket Collectors* [sic] *Book*. Chalfont, PA: Scorpio Publications, 1978. 155p. LC 78-55928.

This is arranged into sections on splint baskets, straw baskets, and small baskets, and preceded by an introduction on the baskets of the American Indians and the Shakers and the baskets indigenous to Nantucket Island.

2288. Miles, Charles, and Pierre Bovis. *American Indian and Eskimo Basketry: A Key to Identification*. San Francisco, CA: Pierre Bovis, 1969. 144p. LC 70-9044.

There is a general discussion on techniques--plaiting, wicker work, twining, coiling and sewing--and then on types of baskets made by specific tribes. The author also shows common utility baskets with illustrations and guides to identification. This may be difficult to use for identification purposes.

2289. Schiffer, Nancy. *Baskets*. Exton, PA: Schiffer Publications, 1984. 176p. LC 84-51185; ISBN 0-88740-018-3.

There is a discussion of makers, tools, and materials, but this guide is especially good for identifying splint, wicker, and coil baskets. There are many plates, a bibliography, and an index.

2290. Teleki, Gloria Roth. *Collecting Traditional American Basketry*. New York: E.P. Dutton, 1979. 131p. LC 78-73091; ISBN 0-525-08262-x (c); 0-525-47553-2 (p).

Covered are native peoples' baskets, baskets of communities (e.g., Shakers, Pennsylvania Germans, Nantucket), southern baskets, baskets of Hawaii, Alaska, and Puerto Rico. Gives advice on collecting today (e.g., prices, how to build a collection, care, and display, etc.). Includes notes, selected bibliography, and an index.

2291. Wright, Dorothy. *Complete Book of Baskets and Basketry*. New York: Scribners, 1977. 192p. LC 77-92088; ISBN 0-684-15644-x.

Materials and basketmaking techniques are discussed with many examples of American baskets. There are also sections on care and repair and on design. Also included are a glossary of terms, a bibliography, and an index.

Exhibition Catalogs--Baskets

2292. Fallon, Carol. *The Art of the Indian Basket in North America*. Lawrence: University of Kansas Museum of Art, 1975. 56p. LC 75-21766. (Miscellaneous publication of the Museum of Art, 99)

This is a catalog of an exhibition held in 1975, which includes an introduction to Indian baskets and a catalog of 66 baskets, with many photos of women making the baskets and photos of the baskets themselves. In addition, there is a section on techniques of construction and a section on embroidery techniques as well as a map showing the locations of the tribes included in the catalog. Includes also a good bibliography. See also two other catalogs of Native American basketry: *Indian Basketry of Western North America, From the Collection of the Bowers Museum, Santa Ana, California* (Los Angeles, Brooke House, 1977) and *Baskets Red Willow and Birchbark* (Rapid City, SD: Sioux Indian Museum and Crafts Center, 1990), and exhibition catalog.

2293. Jones, Suzi, ed. *Pacific Basket Makers, A Living Tradition: Catalog of the 1981 Pacific Basketmaker's Symposium and Exhibition*. Fairbanks, AL: Published for the Consortium for Pacific Arts and Culture, Honolulu, Hawaii, by the University of Alaska Museum, 1983. 80p. LC 84-622413; ISBN 0-8348-0916-5 (p).

Aside from the catalog of objects, mostly pictured in black and white at the end of this book, this work is noteworthy for the symposium's papers, including a survey of Pacific basketmakers, Barre Toelken's "The Basket Imperative," Roger Rose's essay on some perspectives on North American and Pacific basketry, and Steven F. Arvizu's article on "Cultural Preservation and Pluralism: Strategies and Policies for Survival in the Pacific and the United States."

2294.   Rosengarten, Dale. *Row Upon Row: Sea Grass Baskets of the South Carolina Lowcountry*. Columbia: McKissick Museum, University of South Carolina, 1986. 64p. LC 86-61725; ISBN 0-9389-8302-4 (p).

Not seen.

HOUSEHOLD ITEMS
Carpets and Rugs

There are several works on rag and hooked rugs and many on Oriental carpets. For an overview of rugmaking in the folk tradition, see Lydia Le Baron Walker's *Homecraft Rugs; Their Historic Background, Romance of Stitchery and Method of Making* (New York: Frederick Stokes, 1929) and Ella Shannon Bowles' *Handmade Rugs* (Boston: Little, Brown, 1927). A wonderful newer book on rag rugs as a craft is Geraldine Niva Johnson's *Weaving Rag Rugs: A Woman's Craft in Western Maryland* (Knoxville: University of Tennessee Press, 1985) which studies the craft historically and contextually. Much of it is interviews with contemporary weavers; the bibliography is particularly good. Joel and Kate Kopp's *American Hooked and Sewn Rugs: Folk Art Underfoot* (New York: Dutton, 1975) deals with bed rugs, yarn-sewn rugs, embroidered, braided, and hooked rugs from the nineteenth and twentieth centuries. Two interesting works that discuss rug-making design and techniques are Mary Allard's *Rug Making: Techniques and Design* (Philadelphia, PA: Chilton, 1963) and Peter Collingwood's *The Techniques of Rug Weaving* (New York: Watson-Guptill, 1968).

There are many, many historical overviews and surveys of rugs and carpets. The standard history of worldwide, handwoven and machine-made rugs and carpets that are not Oriental is Cornelia Bateman Faraday's *European and American Carpets and Rugs; A History of the Hand-Woven Decorative Floor Coverings..., With More than 400 Illustrations of Antique and Modern European American Carpets and Rugs* (Grand Rapids, MI: Dean-Hicks, 1929). Some examples of surveys of American rugs and carpets are Nina Fletcher Little's *Floor Coverings in New England Before 1850* (Sturbridge, MA: Old Sturbridge Village, 1972 [1967]) which covers Turkish carpets, floor cloths, home woven carpets, and small homemade rugs. Helene von Rosentiel's *American Rugs and Carpets from the Seventeenth Century to Modern Times* (New York: Morrow, 1978) discusses rag rugs, floor cloths, knitted and crocheted rugs, braided, hooked and embroidered rugs, and embroidered carpets. Estelle Ries' *American Rugs* (Cleveland, OH: World, 1950) covers rag, braided, knitted and tufted, hooked, and embroidered rugs. There are several surveys of hooked rugs: William Winthrop Kent's *The Hooked Rug: A Record of Its Origin, Modern Development...* (Detroit, MI: Book Tower, 1971 [1930]) is a classic history and survey of American and Canadian hooked rugs with information on how they are made, collecting, and care. Stella Hay Rex's *Choice Hooked Rugs* (Englewood Cliffs, NJ: Prentice-Hall, 1972 [1953]) covers the same territory. The American Folklife Center has published a small look at *Rag Rugs* (Washington, DC: American Folklife Center, 1980).

There is an abundance of work on all types of Asian, Oriental, and Indian carpets. E. Gans-Ruedin has published several overviews, all stunning books, notably *The Splendor of Persian Carpets* (New York: Rizzoli, 1978), *Indian Carpets* (New York: Rizzoli, 1984), *The Great Book of Oriental Carpets* (New York: Harper and Row, 1983), and *Caucasian Carpets* (New York: Rizzoli, 1986). Fabio Formenton's *Oriental Rugs and Carpets* (New York: McGraw Hill, 1972) and Ulrich Schürmann's *Oriental Carpets* (rev. and exp., London: Octopus, 1979 [1966]) cover the whole range of Oriental carpets. Kurt Erdmann's *Oriental Carpets: An Essay on Their History* (New York: Universe, 1962) and his *Seven Hundred Years of Oriental Carpets* (Berkeley: University of California Press, 1970) are both historical overviews. Nathaniel Harris' *Rugs and Carpets of the Orient* (London: Hamlyn, 1977) is another historical overview and a study of motifs, designs, and decorations with notes on collecting, care, and repairing. Carl Hopf's *Old Persian Carpets and Their Artistic Values* (Munich: F. Bruchmann, 1913) is a classic work on Persian carpets. Michael Craig Hillmann's *Persian Carpets* (Austin: University of Texas Press, 1984) provides an identification and classification guide. Raoul Kazal Tschebill's *Carpets of the Caucasus* (Near Eastern Rug Center, 1970) includes mostly plates, but also technical descriptions. Hallvard Kuløy's study, *Tibetan Rugs* (Bangkok: White Orchard Press, 1982), is a study of rugs used for sitting and sleeping--in monasteries and for ritual and ceremonial purposes--saddlery rugs, and floor rugs. Ulrich Schürmann covers eighteenth- and nineteenth-century Turkoman rugs from Turkestan, East Turkey, and Afghanistan in *Central-Asian Rugs* (Frankfurt: Osterrieth, 1970). *Turkmen, Tribal Carpets and Traditions*, edited by Louise W. Mackie and Jon Thompson (Washington, DC: Textile Museum, 1980), is another work on Turkish carpets and Kamaladevi Chattopadhyaya studies Indian rugs in *Carpets and Floor Coverings of India* (Bombay: Taraporevala, 1969). Chinese carpets are considered by Charles I. Rostov and Jia Guanyan's in *Chinese Carpets* (New York: Harry N. Abrams, 1983) and by Murray L. Eiland in *Chinese and Exotic Rugs* (Boston, MA: New York Graphic Society, 1979). Kilims, a form of rug from Asia, are covered in Yanni Petsopoulos' *Kilims: Flat-woven Tapestry Rugs* (New York: Rizzoli, 1979), which describes and pictures 444 kilims from Anatolia, Caucasus, and Persia.

This section covers works on all types of rugs and carpets, including woven rugs. As before, how-to books, such as Joan Moshimer's *The Complete Book of Rug Hooking* (New York: Dover, 1989 [1975, as *Complete Rug Hooker: A Guide to the Craft*]), have been omitted, though they contain useful information on the craft.

Atlas--Carpets and Rugs

2295.   Black, David, ed. *The Macmillan Atlas of Rugs & Carpets*. New York: Macmillan, 1985. 255p. LC 85-5154; ISBN 0-02-511120-5.

Covers carpet production and design, the history of carpets (mostly Oriental), and carpets from different areas: Turkey, the Caucasus,

Persia, Turkoman, East Turkestan, Tibet, China, India, Morocco, Europe, and North America (with a section on Navajo weaving). There is also information on the decoration, buying, and care of carpets as well as a glossary, a selected bibliography, and an index. Included also are many full-color photographs, maps, and extensive notes.

Dictionaries and Encyclopedias--Carpets and Rugs

2296.	Neff, Ivan C., and Carol V. Maggs. *Dictionary of Oriental Rugs: With a Monograph on Identification by Weave*. New York: Van Nostrand Reinhold, 1979 [1977]. 238p. LC 79-3941; ISBN 0-442-20617-8.

From **Abadeh** to **Persia**, this very thorough dictionary covers manufacture, history, and design of each type of rug. The plates include a photograph of the whole rug and a close-up. References and bibliography complete the work.

Guides and Handbooks--Carpets and Rugs

2297.	Bishop, Robert Charles, et al. *Quilts, Coverlets, Rugs & Samplers*. New York: Knopf, 1982. 476p. LC 82-47848; ISBN 0-394-71271-4. (The Knopf collectors' guides to American antiques)

Tells how to identify rug types. The section on rugs is subdivided. Rugs are pictured and described and dimensions, locality, and period are noted. A commentary on each rug includes hints for collectors, some prices, etc. A bibliography, glossary, and price guide conclude this very comprehensive work.

2298.	Dedera, Don. *Navajo Rugs: How to Find, Evaluate, Buy, and Care for Them*. Flagstaff, AZ: Northland, 1975. 114p. LC 74-31617; ISBN 0-87358-138-5 (p).

This hard-to-use guide covers rugs and their history, Navajo artistry, identification of blankets for all purposes, and contemporary work. There is information on where to buy Navajo rugs and a buyer's guide, with notes on "fakes and frauds," and a section on the care of Navajo rugs. Includes numerous illustrations, a bibliography, and an index. See also Gilbert S. Maxwell's *Navajo Rugs: Past, Present and Future* (rev. ed., Santa Fe, NM: Heritage Art, 1984 [1963]).

2299.   Eiland, Murray L. *Oriental Rugs: A Comprehensive Guide*. Rev. and expanded ed. Boston, MA: New York Graphic Society, 1976 [1973]. 214p. LC 76-12189; ISBN 0-8212-0643-5.

Covers the history and development of Oriental rugs, elements of design, notes on dyes, and a section of construction. The guide itself is to Persian, Turkish and Turkoman rugs, and rugs of the Caucasus. There are many black-and-white illustrations with 32 color plates and maps.

2300.   Ford, P.R.J. *The Oriental Carpet: A History and Guide to Traditional Motifs, Patterns, and Symbols*. New York: Harry N. Abrams, 1981. 352p. LC 80-28851; ISBN 0-8109-1405-0.

This is a guide on how to identify an Oriental carpet by its designs (border designs, universal designs, geometric designs, and floral designs), fineness of weave, and design condition. Also includes a rug classification based on structure and color. Includes information on values, dating, knot construction, sizes and carpet names, a pronunciation guide and maps, a guide to symbolism of motifs and patterns, an index of carpet origins, a general index, and a bibliography.

2301.   Gans-Ruedin, E. Trans. Valerie Howard. *The Connoisseur's Guide to Oriental Carpets*. Rutland, VT: Charles E. Tuttle, 1971. 430p. LC 70-157255; ISBN 0-8048-0988-7.

More up to date than Lewis' *The Practical Book of Oriental Rugs* (no. 2303) and covers the same material. Includes characteristics of carpets (materials, dyeing, weaving, knitting), types of rugs (the Kilim, Soumah, etc.), washing directions, and a glossary. There is a section on buying and caring for these carpets and a classification by country: Turkey, Caucasus, Iran-Azerbaijan, Kalar Dasht, Varamen, Arak/Seraband and Lilihan, Kirman/Yazd and Afshar, Kamodan, Kuristan, Isfahan, etc. Includes a bibliography and index. This is a beautiful book, easy to use, because only one type of rug is described per page with a facing page photograph.

2302.　Jacobsen, Charles W. *Oriental Rugs: A Complete Guide.* Rutland, VT: Charles E. Tuttle, 1962. 479p. LC 62-14117.

Introductory matter covers designs, materials and methods, dyes, chemical treatment of rugs, the difference between European and American markets, Oriental rugs vs. domestic rugs, used rug sales, care of rugs, and books about rugs. The guide itself is arranged alphabetically by type of rug--Caucasian, Persian, etc. For each, the author gives the availability, where it is made, the general characteristics, miscellaneous information, and a concluding note. The black-and-white and color plates are separate.

2302A.　Ketchum, William C. *Hooked Rugs: A Historical and Collector's Guide: How to Make Your Own.* New York: Harcourt Brace Jovanovich, 1976. 164p. LC 76-13880; ISBN 0-1514-2168-4.

Not seen. See also Joan Moshimer's *The Complete Rug Hooker: A Guide to the Craft* (Boston, MA: Graphic Society, 1975), also not seen.

2303.　Lewis, George Griffin. *The Practical Book of Oriental Rugs.* New, rev. ed. Philadelphia, PA: Lippincott, 1945 [1911]. 317p. LC 45-37887.

This is meant as a guide to identifying and classifying Oriental carpets. Part I covers dealers and auctions, antiques, care and the material of rugs, dyes, weaving and weavers, designs and their symbolism, and identification. Part II is a classification of Persian, Turkish, Caucasian,

Turkoman, Beluchistan, Chinese, and Ghileem rugs, and a classification based on their intended use--prayer rugs, hearth, grave, dowry or wedding rugs, mosque rugs, bath rugs, pillows, saddle bags, floor coverings, runners, and hangings. There is also a section on "famous rugs," a listing of museum collections, a 17-page glossary, a bibliography, and an index. A useful book.

Index--Carpets and Rugs

2303A. The Textile Museum. Arthur D. Jenkins Library. *Rug and Textile Arts: A Periodical Index, 1890-1982: Arthur D. Jenkins Library.* Boston, MA: G.K. Hall, 1983. 472p. ISBN 0-8161-0426-3.

This is a dictionary catalog of articles about textiles and rugs found in over 300 periodicals housed in the library of the Textile Museum [Washington, DC]. The museum itself, founded in 1925, houses over 10,000 textiles and 1,000 rugs. (Note: A recent library index said the museum now houses about 14,000 textiles.)

Exhibition Catalogs and Guides to Collections--Carpets and Rugs

2304. Der Manuelian, Lucy, and Murray L. Eiland. *Weavers, Merchants, and Kings: The Inscribed Rugs of Armenia.* Fort Worth, TX: Kimball Art Museum, 1984. 211p. LC 84-848115; ISBN 0-912804-18-1 (c); 0-912804-17-3 (p).

There is an introduction to rug weaving in Armenia and some discussion of motifs and inscriptions of these handwoven rugs. The catalog lists and describes 68 rugs, giving names, dates, material, motifs and designs, analyses of the patterns, and technical descriptions. Illustrations are in full color. There is a bibliography and index.

2305. Dimand, Maurice S. *Oriental Rugs in the Metropolitan Museum of Art.* New York: Metropolitan Museum of Art. Distributed by the New York Graphic Society, 1973. 353p. LC 73-2846; ISBN 0-87099-124-8.

This catalogs the rugs from Persia, India, Ottoman Turkey, Spain, the Caucasus, Western Turkestan, China, and Chinese Turkestan. There are 236 rugs listed and cataloged with brief descriptions; most are pictured in black and white. Includes a bibliography.

2306. Dimand, Maurice S. *Peasant and Nomad Rugs of Asia.* New York: Asia House, 1961. 82p.

Introduction covers the history, decoration, techniques, and a variety of Asian rugs. The catalog (of an exhibition held at Asia House) describes 32 rugs, most of which are pictured. Includes a bibliography.

2307. Ellis, Charles Grant. *Oriental Carpets in the Philadelphia Museum of Art.* Philadelphia, PA: Philadelphia Museum of Art. Distributed by the University of Pennsylvania, 1988. 304p. LC 87-32713; ISBN 0-8122-7959-x (University of Pennsylvania); 0-87633-070-7 (p).

This is an overview of the carpet collection in the Philadelphia Museum of Art which includes carpets from Turkey, Egypt, Syria, Persia, India, Spain, Russia, and China. Seventy-six carpets are described and pictured, with long descriptions of motifs and technical analyses.

2308. Museum of American Folk Art. *Hooked Rugs in the Folk Art Tradition.* New York: Museum of American Folk Art, 1974. 41p. LC 74-16921.

This catalog discusses yarn-sewn rugs, shirred and thummed rugs, and hooked rugs. There are 65 listed, described, and pictured.

2309. Roberts, Ernest. *Treasures from Near Eastern Looms.* Brunswick, ME: Bowdoin College Museum of E.H. Roberts Art, 1981. 80p. LC 81-68474; ISBN 0-916606-02-3 (p).

The exhibit was held at Bowdoin College and at the Textile Museum, Washington, DC, in 1981-1982. The catalog includes 73 rugs and carpets, all described and pictured. There is a glossary and bibliography.

2310.   Spuhler, Friedrich. *Oriental Carpets in the Museum of Islamic Art, Berlin.* Trans. Robert Pinner. Washington, DC: Smithsonian Institution Press, 1987. 332p. LC 87-43094; ISBN 0-87474-884-4.

There are 208 carpets from Turkey, Egypt, and Persia described, dated, and pictured in black and white and color.

2311.   Textile Museum. *Prayer Rugs.* Washington, DC: Textile Museum, 1974. 139p. LC 74-15703.

The introduction by Richard Ettinghauser covers the early history of prayer rugs, their use, and iconography, and there is an essay by Maurice S. Dimand on prayer rug-weaving sites. The 53 catalog entries are from Turkey, the Ottoman Empire, Mughal India, Persia, the Caucasus, and Turkoman. Each work is pictured, described, and located, and there is additional information on size, warp and weft, the pile, colors, condition, and where it has been published or shown before.

2312.   *Turkoman Rugs.* Cambridge, MA: Fogg Art Museum, Harvard University, 1966. 63p. LC 66-11620.

This catalog has an introduction by Joseph V. McMullan, a map of the area from which these rugs come, and a catalog of 52 rugs, pillow faces, and saddle bag faces, all described and illustrated mostly in black and white.

HOUSEHOLD ITEMS
Clocks

There is virtually no material on clockmaking in the folk tradition; most of the emphasis in this subject area is on antique clocks. The standard work in the field, according to Sheehy, is Frederick James Britten's *Britten's Old Clocks and Watches and Their Makers* (9th ed., rev. and enl. by Cecil Clutton et al., London: Methuen, 1982), a chronological historical survey of clocks and watches, especially in Europe and England, with a listing of clock makers, their dates, and where they worked; it includes an extensive bibliography. See also H.A. Lloyd's *Old Clocks* (4th ed., rev. and enl., London: Benn; New York: Dover, 1970). E.J. Tyler's *The Craft of the Clockmaker* (New York: Crown, 1973) discusses early sixteenth- and seventeenth-century clocks, especially the longcase clock, tools and techniques of early clockmakers, the watch, and the nineteenth-century clock.

Surveys of American clockmaking and clockmakers include Carl William Drepperd's *American Clocks and Clockmakers* (enl. ed., Boston, MA: Branford, 1958 [1947]), a history of the American clock, with a list of American clockmakers, a glossary, and bibliography. George H. Eckhardt's *Pennsylvania Clocks and Clockmakers; An Epic of Early American Science, Industry, and Craftsmanship* (New York: Bonanza Books, 1955) is an historical overview as well as a discussion of types of clocks with a list of clockmakers inside and just outside Philadelphia. See also Brooks Palmer's *A Treasury of American Clocks* (New York: Macmillan, 1967) and *The Book of American Clocks* (New York: Macmillan, 1950). Eric Bruton's *The Longcase Clock* (New York: Praeger, 1968) is a study of one type of clock.

Bibliography--Clocks

2313. Baillie, Granville Hugh. *Clocks and Watches; An Historical Bibliography.* London: N.A.G. Press, 1951. 414p. LC 53-357.

This annotated bibliography is a listing of books, articles, manuscripts, and pamphlets, arranged chronologically from 1344-1799. In his introduction, Baillie cites 11 earlier bibliographies in book or serial form, and he notes which London libraries have good collections on clocks. The listing is annotated with evaluative and historical comments on content and, sometimes, biographical information about the author. He also cites accessibility (or lack of it) of earlier works. There are separate author and subject indexes.

Dictionaries--Clocks

2314.   *The Country Life International Dictionary of Clocks.* Alan Smith, consulting ed. New York: Putnam, 1979. 350p. LC 78-65713; ISBN 0-319-12338-5.

Not seen.

2315.   Lloyd, Herbert Alan. *Collector's Dictionary of Clocks.* New York: A.S. Barnes, 1965. 214p. LC 65-24840.

This is an alphabetic arrangement with many illustrations. Much of this goes beyond folk artistry, but there is some folk material, for example, a section on grandfather (longcase) clocks. There is a separate dictionary of horological terms in English, French, German, and Italian.

Guide--Clocks

2316.   Distin, William H., and Robert Bishop. *The American Clock; A Comprehensive Pictorial Survey, 1723-1900, With a Listing of 6153 Clockmakers.* New York: E.P. Dutton, 1976. 359p. LC 76-20201; ISBN 0-525-05310-7. Reprinted: New York: Bonanza, 1983. LC 83-6058; ISBN 0-5174-1359-0.

Although it calls itself a survey, this work is really an identification guide; clocks are arranged by type of clock and then arranged chronologically within that section.

HOUSEHOLD ITEMS
Needlework

This section on needlework includes a group of works on all aspects of needlework even though some needleworked items are not household items. **Embroidery, lacework, quilts,** and **samplers** will be covered separately below, within the needlework section. **Textiles** and **weaving** are covered separately from needlework (nos. 2459-2491 and 2402-2427).

NEEDLEWORK
General

A fine introduction to needlework is Susan Burrows Swan's *Plain & Fancy: American Women and their Needlework, 1750-1850* (New York: Holt, 1977) on the relationship of women to needlework--plain needlework, done by wives and children, and fancy needlework, done by craftsmen. Other historical overviews include Betty Ring's *Needlework: An Historical Survey* (new and expanded ed., Pittstown, NJ: The Main Street Press, 1984) with essays from *The Magazine Antiques* on English embroidery, canvas work, schoolgirl embroidery (samplers), bed coverings, and carpets; Therl Hughes' *English Domestic Needlework, 1660-1860* (London: Abbey Fine Arts Press, 1961), which covers wool work, embroidery, bed hangings and pillows, quilting, patchwork, samplers, etc.; and G. Saville Seligman's and Talbot Hughes' *Domestic Needlework: Its Origins and Customs Throughout the Centuries* (London: Country Life, 1926). Margaret H. Swain's *Historical Needlework; A Study of Influences in Scotland and Northern England* (London: Barrie and Jenkins, 1970) is another study of historical British needlework. For the history of American needlework, see Georgiana Brown Harbeson's *American Needlework; The History of Decorative Stitchery and Embroidery from the Late 16th to the 20th Century* (New York: Bonanza, 1965 [1938]) and Margaret Schiffer's *Historical Needlework of Pennsylvania* (New York: Scribner, 1968).

Surveys or overviews of the art of needlework include Virginia Churchill Bath's *Needlework in America: History, Designs, and Techniques* (New York: Viking, 1979) which covers North American Indian needlework, surface embroidery, bed rugs, thread-counted embroidery, patchwork, appliqué and quilting, rug hooking, white embroidery, and lace and Denise Longhurst's *Vanishing American Needle Arts* (New York: Putnam,

973

1983) on lace, cutwork, embroidery, netting, smocking, tatting, etc. Adolph S. Cavallo's *Needlework* (New York: Cooper-Hewitt Museum, 1979) is both an international historical overview and a study of techniques and types of needlework from the West, Western Asia, the Near East, and the indigenous peoples of Africa and America, with a section on the study and collecting of needlework, technical notes, stitch diagrams, a bibliography, and a list of some public collections of needlework. Popular craftsperson Erica Wilson wrote *Needleplay* (New York: Scribner, 1975) and *More Needleplay* (New York: Scribner, 1979).

See also the journal *Needle Arts* (1970--).

Dictionaries and Encyclopedias--Needlework-General

2317.   de Dillmont, Thérèse. *The Encyclopedia of Needlework.* English ed. Mulhouse (Alsace): Brustlein, 1890. 578p. LC 07-2314.

The preface includes verbal and pictorial descriptions of all aspects of needlework with discussions of theory and patterns. There are chapters on plain sewing, mending, single and cut open work, net and damask stitches, white embroidery, flat stitch and gold embroidery, tapestry and linen embroidery, knitting, crochet work, tatting, macramé, netting, Irish lace, and miscellaneous fancy work. Appendixes cover information on threads, cottons, braids, etc.

2318.   Ryan, Mildred Graves. *The Complete Encyclopedia of Stitchery.* Garden City, NY: Doubleday, 1979. 689p. LC 77-16942; ISBN 0-385-12385-x.

This easy to use work includes separate sections for crocheting, embroidery, knitting, macramé, rugmaking, sewing, and tatting. Each section covers basic techniques, equipment used, stitches, patterns, and types of each craft (e.g., **rugmaking** includes sections on braided, crocheted, embroidered, hooked, knitted, and knotted rugs). There is a bibliography for each type of stitchery.

Handbook--Needlework-General

2319.   Lane, Rose Wilder. *Woman's Day Book of American Needlework*. New York: A Fireside Book published by Simon and
Schuster, 1963. 208p. LC 63-17731; ISBN 0-671-22786-6.

Lane (the daughter of Laura Ingalls Wilder) embraces a broad
definition of needlework. Included are chapters on embroidery, crewel
work, cross-stitch, needlepoint, patchwork, appliqué, quilting, hooking,
crochet, knitting, weaving, candlewicking, and rugmaking. For each
section, there is "a historical commentary," a few pages of instructions on
how to do the specific craft, and then directions for one piece. The work
is lavishly illustrated.

Pattern Book--Needlework-General

2320.   Landsman, Anne Cheek. *Needlework Designs from the American
Indians: Traditional Patterns of the Southeastern Tribes*. South
Brunswick, NJ: A.S. Barnes, 1977. 122p. LC 76-10871; ISBN
0-498-01804-0.

Covers basic stitches and then includes 122 patterns.

Exhibition Catalogs and Guides to Collections--Needlework-General

2321.   Ring, Betty. *Let Virtue Be a Guide To Thee: Needlework in the
Education of Rhode Island Women, 1730-1830*. Providence:
Rhode Island Historical Society, 1983. 276p. LC 83-62244.

Introductory essays cover female education and the needlework
of various areas: Newport, Providence, Bristol, Warren, and Warwick.
There are 121 pieces scattered throughout the text and fully described.
One appendix covers the components of schoolgirl embroideries (textiles,
patterns, and verses) another deals with the framing and glazing of
needlework, and a third, an overview of the schoolgirl, includes
demographics of 200 young women (e.g., whether they're married or
unmarried, etc.). Concludes with a bibliography and an index.

2322.   Swan, Susan Burrows. *A Winterthur Guide to American Needlework*. New York: Crown Publishers; a Winterthur Book, Rutledge Books, 1976. 144p. LC 76-10602; ISBN 0-517-52785-5.

There are 117 representative examples of American needlework in the Henry Francis DuPont Winterthur Museum: samplers, canvas work, crewelwork, embroidery, silk work, quilts, knitting, white work as well as uncommon needlework forms: hatchments and coats of arms, bed rugs, sailors' embroidery, etc. One hundred are illustrated in black and white. A bibliography is appended.

NEEDLEWORK
Embroidery (Crewelwork, Needlepoint)

The *MLA International Bibliography* puts **embroidery** under **Folk Art**, however, it is considered here as part of needlework because most of the sources on needlework include embroidery.

There are several overviews of embroidery, crewelwork, or needlepoint. Hope Hanley's *Needlepoint* (New York: Scribner, 1964) and Mildred J. Davis' *The Art of Crewel Embroidery* (New York: Crown, 1962) are general surveys as are Erica Wilson's *Crewel Embroidery* (New York: Scribner, 1962) and her *Embroidery Book* (New York: Scribner, 1962). Muriel Baker's *Stumpwork: The Art of Raised Embroidery* (New York: Scribner, 1978) is an example of an overview of one type of embroidery.

There has been a great deal of work on eastern European embroidery, examples of which are Blazena Szenczi's *Croatian Folk Embroidery* (Zagreb: Hrvatske, 1974), Nina T. Klimova's *Folk Embroidery of the U.S.S.R.* (New York: Van Nostrand, 1981), Mary Gostelow's *Embroidery of All Russia* (New York: Scribner, 1977), and A. Patrik's *Embroidery of Ourha* (Erevan: "Sovetakan Grogh," 1985), a study of Armenian embroidery. Muriel Lewis Baker's *Blue and White: The Cotton Embroideries of Rural China* (New York: Scribner, 1977) is a study of an Asian traditional craft. Embroidery of the western countries has been looked at in Mary Eirwen Jones' *A History of Western Embroidery*

(London: Studio Vista; New York: Watson-Guptill, 1969); Pamela Warner's *Embroidery: A History* (London: Batsford, 1991) is a more current historical overview of the craft. Victorian needlework is the subject of Freda Parker's handsome *Victorian Embroidery* (New York: Crescent Books, 1990) which looks at beadwork, samplers, Berlin woolwork, surface embroidery, whitework, ribbonwork, crewelwork, smocking, and pincushions. And American embroidery work has been studied by Hope Hanley, in her *Needlepoint in America* (New York: Scribner, 1969), and by Catherine Hedlund, in her *A Primer of New England Crewel Embroidery* (2nd ed., Sturbridge, MA: Old Sturbridge Village, 1967 [1963]).

Several journals deal with embroidery, *Embroidery* (1932--), *Needle Arts* (1970--), *Needlepoint Bulletin* (1973--), *Needlepoint Plus* (1974--), and *Stumpwork Chronicle* (1979--).

Samplers, which are embroidered, are considered separately (nos. 2380-2384).

Encyclopedia--Embroidery

2323.   Swift, Gay. *The Larousse Encyclopedia of Embroidery Techniques*. New York: Larousse, 1984. 240p. LC 84-47852; ISBN 0-88332-365-6.

This encyclopedia, arranged alphabetically, has entries that range in length from fairly brief to fairly long. Covered are entries concerning fabrics, fibers, stitches, products, techniques, etc. Heavily illustrated in black and white, there is also an extensive bibliography and a list of collections in prominent museums. See also the earlier dictionary, Mary H. Thomas' *Dictionary of Embroidery Stitches* (New York: Morrow, 1935).

Handbook--Embroidery

2324. Baker, Muriel Lewis. *A Handbook of American Crewel Embroidery*. Rutland, VT: Charles E. Tuttle, 1966. 67p. LC 66-16722; ISBN 0-8048-0230-0.

This work describes the stitches and design elements used and explains how they are done. There is also some discussion of historical work. Bibliography is included. Lewis also compiled *The ABC's of Canvas Embroidery* (Old Sturbridge, MA: Old Sturbridge Village, 1968) and *The XYZ's of Canvas Embroidery* (Old Sturbridge, MA: Old Sturbridge Village, 1971).

Pattern Books--Embroidery

2325. Davis, Mildred J. *Early American Embroidery Designs*. New York: Crown, 1969. 159p. LC 68-9099.

Shown are designs for embroidered bed furnishings, apparel, accessories, and pictorial needlework. Motifs with patterns are given. There is a bibliography.

2326. Davis, Mildred J., ed. *Embroidery Designs, 1780-1820; From the Manuscript Collection, The Textile Resource and Research Center, The Valentine Museum, Richmond, Virginia*. New York: Crown, 1971. 94p. LC 72-151024.

Designs are presented mostly in black-and-white photographs, with a few in color. There is a brief introduction to each one and a discussion of what designs might be appropriate for specific items (e.g., aprons, bed covers, etc.).

2327. Hawley, W.M. *Chinese Folk Design, A Collection of Cut-Paper Designs Used for Embroidery, Together with 160 Chinese Art Symbols and Their Meanings*. New York: Dover, 1971 [1949]. 319p. LC 77-179790; ISBN 0-486-22633-6.

The meaning of each cutout design is given (e.g., **Dragon chasing the pearl**: symbols of the Emperor, eternity, beneficial forces of nature).

2328.   Kluger, Phyllis. *A Needlepoint Gallery of the Patterns from the Past*. New York: A.A. Knopf, 1975. 191p. LC 75-8234; ISBN 0-394-49110-6.

The designs are from the art of ancient Minoa, Egypt, the Near East, Greece and Rome, and from the Byzantine Empire, the Middle Ages, Islam, the Renaissance, and the seventeenth through the nineteenth century. There is a separate section for designs inspired by American folk art (pp. 173-191).

2329.   Ruryk, Nancy R., comp. and ed. for the Ukrainian Women's Association of Canada. *Ukrainian Embroidery Design and Stitches*. Winnipeg [CAN]: Trident, 1958. 130p. LC 67-118670.

Embroidery stitches are shown and described, with examples of drawn thread work (e.g., hemstitches, decorative spider stitch, etc.). There is also a section on decorated household linens, ecclesiastical vestments, altar cloth embroidery, and some weaving patterns. The embroidered fabrics are shown on specific pieces of apparel. Unfortunately, the photos are of very poor quality.

Exhibition Catalogs and Guides to Collections--Embroidery

2330.   Brett, Katharine B. *English Embroidery; Sixteenth to Eighteenth Century Collections of the Royal Ontario Museum*. Toronto: Royal Ontario Museum, 1972. 92p. LC 72-190533.

The collection includes Tudor embroidery, samplers, crewelwork, eighteenth-century canvas work, eighteenth century silk embroideries, quilting, and white work. The compiler also gives information on embroidery equipment and on stitch identification with samples of each. There is a selected bibliography.

2331. Manushina, T., ed. *Early Russian Embroidery in the Zagorsk Museum Collection*. Moscow: Sov Rossiia, 1983. 293p. LC 84-158954.

This covers ecclesiastical and ornamental embroidery from the fifteenth-seventeenth centuries, pieced work in silver and gold, colored silk work, and pearl work. There are over 200 pieces in this collection, of which 105, "of high artistic quality," are described and 105 are pictured in full color. Text is in Russian, with English summaries and an English glossary. Includes a bibliography.

2332. Ring, Betty. *American Needlework Treasures: Samplers and Silk Embroideries from the Collection of Betty Ring*. New York: E.P. Dutton in association with the Museum of American Folk Art, 1987. 112p. LC 87-70264; ISBN 0-525-24514-6 (c); 0-525-48290-3 (p).

Included are silk embroideries from eight eastern seaboard states and Canada, all described and many pictured with notes. Concludes with a bibliography and index.

2333. Wace, A.J.B. *Mediterranean and Near Eastern Embroideries from the Collection of Mrs. F.H. Cook*. 2 vols. London: Halton, 1935. LC 35-8202.

Vol. 1 is a text on the colors and patterns of the embroidery of Algiers, Morocco, the Greek Islands, Turkey, the Caucasus, Persia, Turkestan, and India, with a catalog of works arranged by country and maps. Vol. 2 consists entirely of 132 plates.

2334. Wardle, Patricia. *Guide to English Embroidery*. London: Her Majesty's Stationery Office, 1970. 40p.+57 plates. LC 77-198094; ISBN 0-11-2900305.

This is really a guide to embroidery in the Victoria and Albert Museum. It includes a brief history of English embroidery through the middle of the twentieth century. Ninety-three pieces are described and some are pictured in black and white. There is also a useful bibliography of books and articles.

NEEDLEWORK
Lace

There is not much material on lacemaking as a folk craft. Maria Mies' *The Lace Makers of Narsapur* (Westport, CT: Lawrence Hill, 1982) is a fascinating study of Indian housewives who have been producing lace for the world market. Pat Earnshaw's *Lace in Fashion: From the Sixteenth to the Twentieth Centuries* (London: Batsford, 1985) is a history of lace, with one chapter on "peasant laces," which will be of interest to the folklorist.

Most of the studies of lace are historical overviews. Alfred von Henneberg's *The Art & Craft of Old Lace* (New York: Weyhe, 1931) is a basic descriptive survey of old lace, a discussion of its essential characteristics with some directions on lacemaking technique and an essay on the development of style. Two earlier histories of lace and lace making are Mrs. Bury Palliser's *History of Lace* (no. 2335) and Emily Jackson's *A History of Hand-Made Lace...* (no. 2339). L. Paulis' *Technique and Designs of Cluny Lace* (Carlton, Bedford [ENG]: Ruth Bean, 1984) is a methodological and design study of French lace and lacemakers. Emily Noyes Vanderpoel's *American Lace & Lace Makers* (New Haven, CT: Yale University Press, 1924) is a study of lacemaking in the United States. And Anne Kraatz' *Lace: History and Fashion* (New York: Rizzoli, 1989) is a more current history of lace as used in clothing.

There is a journal, *Lace and Crafts*, which has been published since 1987; it was formerly known as *Lace Crafts Quarterly*.

Bibliographies--Lace

2335. Palliser, Mrs. Bury. *History of Lace*. "Entirely revised, rewritten and enlarged." London: Sampson, Low, 1910 [1870]. 536p.

Reprint of the third edition (1875): Detroit, MI: Tower Books, 1971. LC 75-78219.

This is a classic history of lace, arranged by country and city: Italy, Venice, Milan, Florence, Spain, Portugal, Flanders, Brussels, etc. The appendix includes a listing of pattern books for lace and embroidery, arranged chronologically. Updated by Strange, no. 2336.

2336.   Strange, Edward F. "Early Pattern Books of Lace, Embroidery and Needlework." *Transactions of the Bibliographical Society* 7 (1902-1904): 209-246.

This is a bibliographical essay and a list of 94 early lace pattern books, intended mainly to print those books not listed in *History of Lace*, by Mrs. Bury Palliser (no. 2335).

2337.   Whiting, Gertrude. *A Lace Guide for Makers and Collectors; With a Bibliography and Five-Language Nomenclature.* New York: E.P. Dutton, 1920. 415p. LC 20-2109.

The bibliography (pp. 243-402) lists 1,958 international works with some annotations.

Dictionaries and Encyclopedias--Lace

2338.   Clifford, C.R. *The Lace Dictionary: Including Historic and Commercial Terms, Technical Terms, Native and Foreign.* New York: Clifford & Lawton, 1913. 156p. Reprinted: Detroit, MI: Gale Research, 1981. LC 81-6613; ISBN 0-8103-4311-8.

Lace is defined as "open work fabric" and divided into eight main varieties: drawn-work, darned-work, cut-work, needle-point, bobbin-work, knotted-work, crochet work, and machine lace. The dictionary has very brief definitions. Entries include towns where lace is made, names of lace (e.g., **Alençon point**), tools and equipment used, and techniques (e.g., **appliqué**).

2339. Jackson, Emily. *A History of Hand-Made Lace: Dealing with the Origin of Lace, the Growth of the Great Lace Centres, the Mode of Manufacture, the Methods of Distinguishing and Care of Various Kinds of Lace*. London: Gill; New York: Scribner, 1900. 245p.

A dictionary is on pp. 107-206 of this work which is a standard history of lace making.

Guides and Handbooks--Lace

2340. Bath, Virginia Churchill. *Lace: History and Guide*. Chicago, IL: Henry Regnery, 1974. 320p. LC 73-20671; ISBN 0-8902-8926-1.

There is a brief history followed by sections on needle lace, bobbin lace, and mixed lace. Each section begins with an overview of the art form, and includes information on techniques, patterns, and designs, and many examples of finished pieces. Each section includes some contemporary work, and "how-to" information. The guide ends with a list of suppliers in England and America, a bibliography of old pattern books and general works, and a comprehensive index.

2341. Blum, Clara M. *Old World Lace; or, A Guide for the Lace Lover*. New York: E.P. Dutton, 1920. 85p. LC 21-1529.

Covers lace of Italy, Flanders, France, Spain, England, and Ireland. Includes a glossary.

2342. Whiting, Gertrude. *A Lace Guide for Makers and Collectors; With a Bibliography and Five-Language Nomenclature*. New York: E.P. Dutton, 1920. 415p. LC 20-2109.

The "guide part" of this work includes "Rules for Making" (pp. 69-242), directions, patterns, photographs of works-in-progress, and finished pieces. There is also a section called "explanations and nomenclature" (pp. 38-68), a glossary of terms in English, French, Italian, Spanish, and German.

NEEDLEWORK
Quilts

There is probably more written about quilting than any other craft--folk or otherwise. The emphasis is on traditionally-made American quilts, especially Amish quilts. Also plentiful are pattern books and manuals, a sample of which are included below.

Two early historical studies of quilts are Florence Peto's *American Quilts and Coverlets: A History of a Charming Native Art* (New York: Chanticleer, 1949) and *Historic Quilts* (New York: American Historical Co., 1939), both chronological studies of American quilts with instruction manuals. Much material has been written since the 1970s. A basic introductory text to all types of quilts is Patsy and Myron Orlofsky's *Quilts in America* (New York: McGraw-Hill, 1974) which is a history of the quilt and the craft, an explanation of the tools and equipment needed, an overview of types of quilts, and a discussion of patterns and pattern names; there are sections on identifying signs and initials, on knowing the age of a quilt, on its care, and on where to see them (listed by state). Another work dealing with contemporary quilts and quiltmaking is Ann-Sargent Wooster's *Quiltmaking; The Modern Approach to a Traditional Craft* (New York: Galahad, 1975 [1972]).

Several studies of quiltmaking are based on interviews with quilters. One such work is *The Quilters: Women and Domestic Art* by Patricia Cooper and Norma Bradley (New York: Doubleday, 1977) which is a sociological account of quilts and their makers, with many interviews with women quilters in Texas and New Mexico and a study of their environment; it also contains a useful quilt index. Another book of particular interest to folklorists is Nancy Callahan's *The Freedom Quilting Bee* (Tuscaloosa: University of Alabama Press, 1987), a history of the Freedom Quilting Bee, which was formed in 1965 by black women in Wilcox County, Alabama, as a means of economic survival; much of the text is transcript material from interviews done with the quilters. Another work, also based

984

on interviews with quilters, is Jeannette Lasansky's *Pieced by Mother: Over 100 Years of Quiltmaking Traditions* (Lewisburg, PA: Oral Traditions Project, 1987); the quilts discussed are arranged chronologically, then by pattern and motif. Linda Otto Lipsett's *Remember Me: Women & Their Friendship Quilts* (San Francisco, CA: The Quilt Digest Press, 1985) covers several quilters from Vermont to California and their quilts in great depth.

There are many, many general surveys of American quilts, such as Erica Wilson's *...Quilts of America* (Birmingham, AL: Oxmoor House, 1979), which discusses the motifs and designs of quilts and gives methods of making and patterns. Carleton L. Safford and Robert Bishop wrote *America's Quilts and Coverlets* (New York: Dutton, 1972), followed by Bishop's and Patricia Coblentz's *New Discoveries in American Quilts* (New York: Dutton, 1975) "just to document as many as possible of the beautiful quilts that have been brought to my attention since 1972"; it covers the bed-rug, linsey-woolsey, whole-cloth, pieced quilt, Amish quilt, log-cabin patterns, candlewick spread, stencil spread, and crazy quilt.

There are also many surveys of specific types of quilts. Jonathan Holstein's *The Pieced Quilt: An American Design Tradition* (Greenwich, CT: New York Graphic Society, 1973) is an historical overview of pieced quilts and quilt makers. Averill Colby's *Patchwork Quilts* (London: Batsford, 1965) is a classic study of materials, tools and equipment, patterns, designs, colors, and finishes of the patchwork quilt. Carrie A. Hall's and Rose G. Kretsinger's *The Romance of the Patchwork Quilt in America* (Caldwell, ID: Caxton, 1935) is a classic study in three parts covering history, with reproductions of patches, quilts of colonial ancestry, and modern designs. And Lenice Ingram Bacon's *American Patchwork Quilts* (New York: Morrow, 1973) is an historical overview with some information on making, collecting, and caring for patchwork quilts; a newer regional work on patchwork quilts is Margaret Rolfe's *Patchwork Quilts in Australia* (Richmond, VA: Greenhouse, 1987).

There have been many surveys of regional quilts, such as Mary Washington Clarke's *Kentucky Quilts and Their Makers* (Lexington: University Press of Kentucky, 1976), which covers types of historical and contemporary quilts as well as some quilting customs. Alfred Allan

Lewis' *The Mountain Artisans Quilting Book* (New York: Macmillan, 1973) documented the work of the cooperative of Appalachian mountain artisans, begun by Sharon Rockefeller, and covered European and American origins and specific regional quilts: crazy quilts, diamond tufted quilts, fence rail quilts, log cabin quilts, and Sunbonnet Sue quilts. Suzanne Yabsley's *Texas Quilts, Texas Women* (College Station; Texas A & M University Press, 1984) is an overview of quilts and quilters in Texas but also serves as a directory to quilts in Texas museums. John Rice Irwin's *A People and Their Quilts* (Exton, PA: Schiffer, 1983) is a survey of southern Appalachian people and their quilts, taken also from interviews. Bets Ramsay's and Merikay Waldvogel's *The Quilts of Tennessee: Images of Domestic Life Prior to 1930* (Nashville, TN: Rutledge, 1986) is a fascinating and impressive work. Thirty "quilt days" were held throughout the state, when quilters brought their quilts and agreed to be interviewed. The result is a description and catalog of 1,425 quilts, many wonderfully photographed with their makers. Also included is a list of museums in Tennessee and a bibliography. A similar attempt to document the quilts of one state is *North Carolina Quilts*, by Ellen Fickling Eanes et al., ed. by Ruth Haislip Roberson (Chapel Hill: University of North Carolina Press, 1988); 10,000 quilts were brought to 75 "quilt documentation days" in places throughout the state, 100 of which are pictured, with information about many different types of quilts. (See Oshins, no. 2347 for a listing of other state quilt documentation projects.)

Also available in quantity are books which picture and describe in great detail a number of quilts. Two recent examples of this are Susanna Pfeffer's *Quilt Masterpieces* (New York: Park Lane, 1988), a close analysis of 48 quilts, and *America's Quilts Created by the Country's Best Quilters* (New York: Gallery Books, 1990) which highlights contemporary American quilts and their makers. Both these works are handsome coffee table type books.

There are many studies of Mennonite and Amish quilts, notably Robert Bishop's and Elizabeth Safanda's *A Gallery of Amish Quilts: Design Diversity from a Plain People* (New York: Dutton, 1976), M.K. Graeff's *Pennsylvania German Quilts* (New York: Mrs. Naaman Keyser, 1946), Phyllis Haders' *Sunshine & Shadow: The Amish and Their Quilts* (new ed., Pittstown, NJ: Main Street Press, 1984 [1976]), Rachel T. Pellman's and Joanne Rauch's *Amish Quilts: Quilts Among the Plain People* (Lancaster, PA: Good Books, 1981) which describes the quilts and gives the patterns, Rachel and Kenneth Pellman's *Amish Crib Quilts* (Intercourse, PA: Good Books, 1985), arranged by season, and their *The World of Amish Quilts* (Intercourse, PA: Good Books, 1984), David Pottinger's *Quilts from the Indiana Amish: A Regional Collection* (New York: Dutton, 1983) which pictures full-size and crib quilts in many brilliant colors, and Judy Schroeder Tomlonson's *Mennonite Quilts and Pieces* (Intercourse, PA: Good Books, 1985) which covers quilts and quilters and the quilting community and includes many, many beautiful colored plates as do most of the above books. The most handsome book on Amish quilting is Robert Hughes' *Amish: The Art of the Quilt* (New York: A.A. Knopf, 1990), a text written in conjunction with a splendid exhibition of Amish quilts.

Mary Conroy's *300 Years of Canada's Quilts* (Toronto: Griffin Press, 1976) includes a survey of Canadian quilts, 15 tracing patterns, and a list of where to see quilts in Canada. Elizabeth Hake's *English Quilting Old & New* (London: Batsford, 1937) is an early historical study and overview of British quilts.

Finally, it might be noted that the popularity of quilting is evident in the many journals that focus just on the art and craft of quilting: *American Quilter* (1985--), *Canada Quilts* (1975--), *Quilter* (1979--), *Quilt Digest* (1983--), *Quilter's Newsletter Magazine* (1969), *Quilting International* (1987--), *Quiltmaker* (1982--), and *Traditional Quilter* (1989--) are some of the quilting journals that can be found on library shelves. Also available is an annual publication, *Uncoverings* (1980--), the papers of the American Quilt Study Group, Mill Valley, CA, which publishes scholarly papers and special presentations on quilting.

Bibliographies--Quilts

Note: See also no. 2346.

2343.   Makowski, Colleen L. *Quilting, 1915-1983: An Annotated Bibliography*. Metuchen, NJ: Scarecrow, 1985. 157p. LC 85-2497; ISBN 0-8108-1813-2.

This bibliography contains 715 entries for books, exhibit catalogs, and periodical articles, nonprint media, museum collections, and periodicals.

2344. Roach, Susan, and Lorre M. Weidlich, comps. "Bibliography of American Quilt Making." *Folklore Feminists' Communication* 3 (Spring 1974): 17-28.

The compilers hope "to encourage interest in and respect for the women's art of quilt-making, to show the bulk and continuity of the material already available on the art, and to promote needed folklore study in the area of quilting...." The bibliography is in two sections: 1) an annotated listing of books and periodical articles (scholarly and popular books dealing with quilt making, scholarly articles, and a sampling of popular magazine articles) and 2) an unannotated listing of supplementary articles, exhibit catalogs, collections, historical works, works on techniques, etc. Each section is alphabetical by author.

Directories--Quilts

2345. Burke, Lisa M., and M. Ellen Mason, eds. *Quilter's Quest: A Quilter's Resource Directory*. Albuquerque, NM: New Mexico Quilter's Association, 1982. 119p. LC 86-122739.

Not seen.

2346. Dee, Anne Patterson. *Quilter's Sourcebook: The Super Guide to Quilts, Quilters, & Quilting*. Lombard, IL: Wallace-Homestead, 1987. 200p. LC 86-50646; ISBN 0-87069-491-X (p).

Includes listings of: 1) mail order sources for patterns, suppliers, and publishers, arranged alphabetically by state; 2) 289 quilt and quilt-oriented shops, arranged alphabetically by state; 3) handmade quilts and quilt-related gift items, also by state; 4) guilds, groups, and associations ("more than 75% of the existing quilting and quilt study groups have been formed since 1980"), quilters' newsletters and magazines in the U.S., Europe, Australia, and the Orient); 5) workshops, lectures, and professional quilters; 6) museums with permanent quilt collections, arranged by state; and 7) books, publications, and periodical articles (564 in all). Indexed. A treasure trove.

2347.   Oshins, Lisa Turner. *Quilt Collections: A Directory for the United States and Canada.* Washington, DC: Acropolis Books, 1987. 255p. LC 87-17455; ISBN 0-87491-845-6 (c); 0-87491-844-8 (p).

The arrangement is geographical by state and province. The compiler tells what each state's collecting strengths are, gives institutions, addresses, phones, hours, describes collections and special quilt services, public services, publications, etc. Also included are a list of quilt associations, a glossary, a list of participating institutions, a filmography, a list of quilt documentation projects in the U.S. and Canada, a section on conservation, and a selected bibliography. This is an excellent resource for quilters, admirers, and collectors, and, one hopes, it will be updated often.

Guides--Quilts

2348.   Bishop, Robert C., et al. *Quilts, Coverlets, Rugs & Samplers.* New York: Knopf, 1982. New York: A.A. Knopf, 1982. 476p. LC 82-47848; ISBN 0-394-71271-4 (p). (The Knopf collectors' guides to American antiques)

Introduction explains how to identify textiles and differentiates among quilt types, coverlet types, bedcovers, rug types, and sampler types. There are separate sections for quilts, coverlets, other bedcovers, rugs, and samplers, and this is subdivided into types (e.g., **quilts**--those with central motifs, log cabin quilts, crazy quilts, etc.). The dimensions of each piece are given, and it is dated and located geographically; includes also extensive commentaries on each piece discussed and sometimes gives hints for the collector. There is a price guide directory in the back, as well as a quilt pattern guide, quilt stitches guide, coverlet pattern guide, sampler and needlework stitches guide. Also included is a bibliography, glossary, and an index. Very comprehensive.

2349.   Haders, Phyllis. *The Warner Collector's Guide to American Quilts*. New York: Warner Books, 1981. 255p. LC 80-25304; ISBN 0-44697636-9.

This is a visual identification guide to American quilts, classified by technique (e.g., pieced quilts, appliquéd quilts, white work). Very easy to use; most quilts are pictured, categorized, located, and described, with sources given, and a price range.

Handbooks, Manuals, Primers--Quilting

Note: These are a sample of the existing quilting manuals. See also pattern books below.

2350.   Heard, Audrey, and Beverly Pryor. *The Complete Guide to Quilting*. Des Moines, IA: Creative Home Library, 1974. 285p. LC 74-14643; ISBN 0-696-25800-5.

Covers the basics (drafting, estimating yardage, cutting pieces, quilting, and finishing) and supplies information on how to make pieced patchwork quilts, appliqué quilts, needlework quilts, and quilted wall hangings. There are 200 patterns and diagrams, 100 color plates, and detailed directions on how to make ten quilts. Contains a brief bibliography and index.

2351.   Hinson, Dolores A. *Quilting Manual*. New York: Hearthside Press, 1974 [1966]. 192p. Reprinted: New York: Dover, 1980. LC 79-55841; ISBN 0-486-23924-1.

Includes a short history of European and American crazy quilts, tied quilts, and pieced quilts, a dictionary of quilting terms, a list of quilt names and their etymologies, a classification of pieced quilts, a list of quilting customs and superstitions, and directions on how to piece, sew, and quilt a top quilt. Includes an index of quilt names and a general index.

2352.   Ickis, Marguerite. *The Standard Book of Quilt Making and Collecting*. New York: Dover, 1959 [1949]. 276p. LC 62-222; ISBN 0-486-20582-7.

Includes advice and directions on all aspects of planning and making a quilt with information on collecting quilts and descriptions of famous American quilts, with directions on how to draft their patterns. There is an index of quilt designs.

2353.   James, Michael. *The Quiltmaker's Handbook*. Englewood Cliffs, NJ: Prentice-Hall, 1978. 147p. LC 77-15592; ISBN 0-13-749416-5 (c); 0-13-749408-4 (p). A sequel, *The Second Quiltmaker's Handbook* was published in 1981 by Prentice-Hall. Not seen.

Gives a history of quilting, discusses materials, and the planning, making, and care of quilts. There is a bibliography of historical works, on quilt how-to books, catalogs, periodical articles, and an index.

2354.   McClun, Diana, and Laura Nownes. *Quilts Galore!: Quiltmaking Styles and Techniques*. San Francisco, CA: The Quilt Digest Press, 1990. 166p+templates. ISBN 0-91327-211-2.

Talks about identifying features and gives plans and detailed instructions for drafting and making the following types of quilts: appliqué, crazy, trapunto, whole cloth, stenciled, and medallion. McClun and Nownes are also the authors of *Quilts! Quilts!! Quilts !!!: The Complete Guide to Quiltmaking* (San Francisco, CA: The Quilt Digest Press, 1988).

Pattern Books--Quilts

Note: Many general survey books and handbooks (see above) also include patterns.

2355.   Grafton, Carol Belanger. *Early American Patchwork Patterns: Full-size Templates & Instructions....* New York: Dover, 1980. 58p. LC 79-53932; ISBN 0-486-23082-2.

Grafton's *Traditional Patchwork Patterns* (New York: Dover, 1980 [1974]) contains patterns and instructions for cutting, sewing, blocking, and finishing 12 more quilts.

2356.   Johnson, Mary Elizabeth. *Prize Country Quilts: Designs, Patterns, Projects.* Birmingham, AL: Oxmoor House, 1977. 230p. LC 76-40858; ISBN 0-8487-0444-4.

This includes a portfolio of quilting techniques and prizewinning quilt patterns.

2357.   Khin, Yvonne M. *The Collector's Dictionary of Quilt Names & Patterns.* Washington, DC: Acropolis Books, 1988 [1980]. 489p. LC 80-14246; ISBN 0-8749-1408-6 (c); 0-8749-1409-4 (p).

Includes several types of quilting patterns: those arranged into squares, rectangles, diamonds, circles, and hexagons, and appliquéd types. There is also a section on the origin of quilt names and a list of quilting terms and types of quilts. Indexed by pattern names.

2358.   McKim, Ruby S. *One Hundred and One Patchwork Patterns: Quilt Name Stories, Cutting Designs....* New York: Dover, 1962. 124p. LC 63-1453; ISBN 0-486- 20773-0.

Tells how to cut, piece, sew together, and quilt the material. The patterns, arranged alphabetically by quilt name, are of original quilt designs.

Note: This is a highly selected list; there are thousands of these exhibits each year--in galleries, small museums, and in major museums throughout the world.

2359. Albacete, M.J., et al. *Ohio Quilts, A Living Tradition.* Canton, OH: The Canton Art Institute, 1981. 59p. LC 81-71429.

There are 77 old and new quilts pictured, among them appliqué, linsey-woolsey, stuff-work, and piece work, arranged chronologically from 1835/46 through 1981. There is a separate section for Amish quilts, collected from 1883-1929, and a separate section for contemporary quilts of the 1980s. Also included are instructions on how to make an Ohio Star Quilt.

2360. Allen, Gloria Seaman. *First Flowerings: Early Virginia Quilts.* Washington, DC: D.A.R. Museum, 1987. 46p. LC 87-404702.

Twenty-two quilts are pictured and described with biographical information on the quilters as well as dates, pattern information, etc. The catalog concludes with many tables containing information on the settings of the quilts, the quilters, the quilt owners, and the use of the quilts (e.g., number of quilt records and owners, percentage of men with quilts, percentage of women with quilts, number of slave owners, percentage of quilt owners with slaves, etc.).

2361. Betterton, Shiela. *Quilts and Coverlets from the American Museum in Britain.* [Bath]: The American Museum in Britain, 1978. 128p. LC 79-309112; ISBN 0-950497142.

Includes plain quilts, pieced quilts, appliquéd quilts, crazy quilts, patchwork quilts, candlewick coverlets, stencilled and embroidered bedcovers, etc. Most are illustrated in full color (many are shown on the bed) and there is information for each on the sources, the type of quilt it is and its physical qualities. An index and a bibliography are included.

2362. *Black Belt to Hill Country: Alabama Quilts from the Robert and Helen Cargo Collection.* Birmingham, AL: Museum of Art, 1982. 111p.

The catalog includes an introduction and short essays on quilting women and their quilts. Forty-four pieces are cataloged, pictured, and described. Includes bibliography.

2363. Bordes, Marilynn Johnson. *12 Great Quilts from the American Wing.* New York: Metropolitan Museum of Art, 1974. 36p. LC 74-180367.

Twelve quilts are pictured (some in color, some in detail) and described. Motifs are explained, and the works are ascribed to a quilter and a place. Selected bibliography.

2363A. Bowman, Doris M. *The Smithsonian Treasury of American Quilts.* New York: Random House, 1991. 96p. LC 91-18638; ISBN 0-517-05952-5.

Eighty-eight quilts--of all types--from the Smithsonian are described and pictured.

2364. Bresenhan, Karoline Patterson, and Nancy O'Bryant Puentes. *Lone Stars: A Legacy of Texas Quilts, 1836-1936.* Austin: University of Texas Press, 1986. 156p. LC 85-31589; ISBN 0-292-74641-5 (c); 0-292-74649-0 (p).

The official catalog from the Texas Sesquicentennial Quilt Association's traveling exhibit. This is part of the "Great Texas Quilt Round Up," a state project "to identify and document the state's quilts." The quilts are arranged chronologically from 1825 on, giving patterns, county made, makers, owners, colors, motifs, etc. Pictured are whole quilts and details and some quilters at their work. A comprehensive work, it concludes with a selected reading list.

2365.   Burnham, Dorothy K. *Pieced Quilts of Ontario*. Toronto: Royal Ontario Museum, 1975. 64p. ISBN 0-88854-175-9.

This work shows the completed quilt, and then details of the pattern for it, so it can also serve as a pattern guide.

2366.   Carlisle, Lilian Baker. *Pieced Work and Appliqué Quilts at the Shelburne Museum*. Shelburne, VT: Shelburne Museum, 1957. 95p. LC 57-14118. (Pamphlet series, 2)

Discusses and catalogs separately pieced work and appliqué work. Pictures only one quilt on a page, describes it, and includes a black-and-white photograph.

2367.   Cohen, John, coll. *Mountain Artisans; An Exhibition of Patchwork and Quilting, Appalachia*. Providence: Rhode Island Museum of Art and the Rhode Island School of Design, 1970. unpaged. LC 78-22316.

The introduction to the catalog by Eleanor Fayerweather curator of the costume center at the Providence Museum of Art is a brief history of Mountain Artisans, begun by Sharon Rockefeller "to preserve the traditional patterns and handskills unique to the Appalachian culture." The catalog includes 21 items, many illustrated and described.

2368.   Curtis, Phillip H. "American Quilts in the Newark Museum Collection." *The Museum*. new series. Summer-Fall, 1973.

All are cataloged by pattern or type of quilt (e.g., pieced quilts, linsey-woolsey type, etc.). Each one is described, several in great depth, and some are pictured. A listing of all pieces held by the museum is included with basic information on their origins. Also included is a bibliography of books and other museum catalogs. See also Margaret E. White's *Quilts and Counterpanes in the Newark Museum* (Newark Museum, 1948).

2369.   Denver Art Museum. *Quilts and Coverlets*. Denver, CO: Denver Art Museum, 1974. 160p. LC 74-7687; ISBN 0-914738-02-X.

Covers pieced quilts, crazy quilts, appliqué quilts, and overshot, doubleweave, and Jacquard coverlets. Over 140 are pictured, a few in color. There is a bibliography.

2370.   Fox, Sandi. *Quilts in Utah: A Reflection of the Western Experience*. Salt Lake City, UT: Salt Lake Art Center, 1981. 48p. LC 81-52754.

This exhibition catalog, with an introduction, includes 20 quilts from Utah and other western states, most selected in a juried competition. Each is pictured in full color with explanatory notes at the back. There is a reference list.

2371.   Holstein, Jonathan. *American Pieced Quilts*. Lausanne: Editiones de Massons S.A., 1972. 94p. ISBN 0-670-12004-9.

This exhibit, shown at the Renwick Gallery, 1972-1973, was circulated by the Smithsonian Institution's Traveling Exhibition Service from 1972-74. The introduction to the catalog was written by Holstein; 84 quilts are described and photographed. Bibliography.

2372.   Jones, Stella M. *Hawaiian Quilts*. 2nd rev. ed. Honolulu: Daughters of Hawaii, 1973 [1930]. 78p. LC 73-88714.

This is the catalog of an exhibition of Hawaiian quilts held in 1973 with a reprint of an earlier monograph. The quilts described and pictured are mostly from the nineteenth century with a few very early ones.

2373.   Katzenberg, Dena S. *Baltimore Album Quilts*. Baltimore: The Baltimore Museum of Art, 1981. 124p. LC 81-67526; ISBN 0-912298-52-9.

An album quilt is "a collection of squares laid out in a grid pattern in horizontal and vertical rows; the squares are composed of appliquéd or pieced work, or a combination of both, made from a whole range of materials...." There are 24 quilts pictured, fully described, and dated with information on techniques, borders, etc. There is a bibliography.

2374. Macneal, Patricia Miner, and Maude Southwell Wahlman. *Quilts from Appalachia.* University Park, PA: Pennsylvania State University Press for the Palmer Museum of Art, 1988. 68p. ISBN 0-911209-37-9.

Introductory matter includes a study of the region today, a history of the settlement of the area, a study of the textile traditions and of the quilts and quilters of the Appalachian mountains. The catalog is arranged by quilters; each quilt is described and pictured, and biographical information is given about the quilter. There is a bibliography.

2375. Milwaukee Public Museum. *Dressing the Bed: Quilts and Coverlets from the Collections of the Milwaukee Public Museum.* Milwaukee, WI: Milwaukee Public Museum, 1985. 64p. LC 85-230174; ISBN 0-89326-116-5 (p).

This is an exhibition catalog of quilts and coverlets taken from the museum's eight collections. There are 35 quilts and coverlets described, pictured, analyzed, dated, and ascribed to a quilter or weaver. There is also a glossary, a checklist of quilts and coverlets in the permanent collections of the Milwaukee Public Museum, and a bibliography.

2376. Mississippi Department of Archives and History. *Something to Keep You Warm: The Roland Freeman Collection of Black American Quilts from the Mississippi Heartland.* Jackson, MI: Mississippi Department of Archives and History, 1981. 46p. LC 81-620010; ISBN 0-938896-31-8.

There are introductory essays on "slave quilting on ante-Bellum plantations," and on the "aesthetics of Afro-American quilts." Twenty-five quilts, from this exhibition of 50, are pictured in full color and biographical information on the quilters is supplied.

2377. University of Kansas. Museum of Art. *150 Years of American Quilts*. Lawrence KS: University of Kansas Art Museum, 1973. 136p. LC 73-622705. (Miscellaneous publications of the Museum of Art, 90)

There are 131 patchwork, appliqué, stuffed, and combined technique quilts described and pictured in black and white. Includes a bibliography.

2378. University of Nebraska. *Quilts from Nebraska Collections*. Lincoln: University of Nebraska, Sheldon Memorial Art Gallery, 1974. 75p. LC 75-621730.

There are 55 quilts pictured, dated, and described, with biographical information on the quilter given, name of owner, and an analysis of techniques and colors.

2379. University of North Carolina. *North Carolina Country Quilts: Regional Variations*. Chapel Hill: University of North Carolina, Ackland Art Museum, 1979. 56p. LC 79-120125.

The arrangement of these 16 quilts is mainly by county; each is pictured in black and white and described.

NEEDLEWORK
Samplers

Samplers are considered to be schoolgirl embroideries. Typically, samplers were done by young girls and they contained the alphabet, a verse, some figures or motifs, etc. One scholarly study of samplers is Toni Flores Fratto's *Samplers: The Historical Ethnography of an American Popular Art* (Philadelphia: University of Pennsylvania Press, 1971) which sets samplers and their makers in a cultural context in terms of sex, age, class, geographical location, and education, and analyzes their contents (design and verses) based on a study of several sampler makers. Anne Sebba's *Samplers: Five Centuries of a Gentle Craft* (New York: Thames & Hudson, 1979) is another historical study.

Averill Colby's *Samplers: Yesterday and Today* (London: B.T. Batsford, 1964) is considered the classic study of samplers. Another overview of samplers is Cecile Dreeman's *Samplers for Today* (New York: Van Nostrand, 1972). Ethel Stanwood Bolton and Eva Johnston Coe studied *American Samplers* (New York: Weathervane, 1973); it also includes a register of early nineteenth-century samplers, arranged chronologically, and an anthology of verses. Mary Eirwen Jones' *British Samplers* (Oxford: Pen-in-Hand Press, 1948) includes a history of the evolution of British samplers and a study of stitches, patterns, color schemes, maps, and a section on alphabetic samplers. Jane Toller's *British Samplers: A Concise History* (Chichester: Phillimore, 1980) is a newer history of British samplers. Marcus Huish's *Samplers & Tapestry Embroideries* (2nd ed., New York: Dover, 1970 [1900]) is a study of mostly British samplers, needlework, and embroidery.

Bibliography--Samplers

2380.   Fratto, Toni Flores. "Bibliography of Samplers," in "'Remember Me': The Sources of American Sampler Verses." *New York Folklore* 2 (1976): 205-222.

The bibliography section of this article (pp. 221-222) includes works about samplers.

Guide--Samplers

2381.   Krueger, Glee F. *New England Samplers to 1840*. Sturbridge, MA: Old Sturbridge Village, 1978. 227p. LC 79-107906. (Old Sturbridge Village booklet series)

Defines samplers and analyzes their elements: fabrics, stitches, threads, designs, etc., then discusses them chronologically from the mid-eighteenth through the mid-nineteenth century. There are 93 shown, dated, described, and located in a collection. Also included is a list of New England schools and/or teachers offering needlework courses between 1706-1804. There are notes and an extensive bibliography. The index is to embroiderers and teachers. See also Robert Bishop's *Quilts, Coverlets, Rugs & Samplers* (New York: Knopf, 1982), an identification and price guide.

Exhibition Catalogs and Guides to Collections--Samplers

2382.   Cooper-Hewitt Museum. *Embroidered Samplers in the Collection of the Cooper-Hewitt Museum*. New York: The Museum. 1984. 32p. LC 83-13735; ISBN 0-910503-43-5.

The international collection of samplers at the Cooper-Hewitt Museum (New York City) includes 1,000 samplers from two donors, Mrs. Henry E. Coe (given in 1941) and Gertrude M. Oppenheimer (given in 1980). There are 18 shown throughout the text. Includes also a selected bibliography.

2383.   Krueger, Glee F. *A Gallery of American Samplers: The Theodore H. Kapnek Collection*. New York: E.P. Dutton, in association with the Museum of American Folk Art, 1978. 96p. LC 78-59876; ISBN 0-525-11130-1. Reprinted: New York: Bonanza, 1984. LC 84-14458; ISBN 0-517-45592-7.

There is a good introduction to the subject of samplers, followed by a catalog of 125 samplers pictured and described in appended notes. Includes a bibliography.

2384. Ring, Betty. *American Needlework Treasures: Samplers and Silk Embroideries from the Collection of Betty Ring*. New York: E.P. Dutton, in association with the Museum of American Folk Art, 1987. 112p. LC 87-70264; ISBN 0-525-24514-6 (c); 0-525-48290-3 (p).

Samplers are from eight eastern seaboard and southern states, England, and Scotland.

FOLK CRAFT
Stenciling

Laurie Northrup has written a short study of stenciling, *Recovering Early American Stenciling: Walls, Floors, Fabrics* (Oneida, NY: Madison County Historical Society, 1982). There is no real reference material on stenciling, other than general surveys, such as Janet Waring's *Early American Stencils on Walls and Furniture* (New York: Dover, 1968 [1937]), which covers walls and furniture stenciling separately and then describes stenciled pieces by state. There is one section on stenciled floors, and the section on stenciled furniture covers fine furniture, Pennsylvania-German furniture, and the Hitchcock chair; also covered is composition and techniques of stenciling, stenciling on tin and velvet, and the work of two artisans--William Eaton and George Lord.

Pattern Books and Designs--Stencils

2385. Bowers, Edward H. *A Treasury of Stencil Designs for Artists and Craftsmen*. New York: Dover, 1976. 60p. LC 75-46105; ISBN 0-486-23307-3.

A listing of black-and-white stencil patterns taken from "stencils used to decorate the interior of Pennsylvania Railroad passenger coaches between 1924-1934, when the company, in the face of increasing competition from bus and cars, was seeking an inexpensive means for making its services more attractive to the broader public."

2386.   Tuer, Andrew W., coll. *Japanese Stencil Designs; One Hundred Outstanding Examples Collected and Introduced by Andrew W. Tuer.* New York: Dover, 1967 [1892]. unpaged. LC 67-196999; ISBN 0-486-21811-2.

Includes 100 facsimile illustrations of the art of the Japanese stencil-cutter. There is a brief explanation of the art of stencil cutting, its uses, the tools, and procedures used. Each stencil is numbered, named, and described.

FOLK CRAFT
Toys

Antonia Fraser, in her *A History of Toys* (London: Weidenfeld & Nicolson; New York: Delacorte, 1966), says that "nowhere is the universality of toys more apparent than in the history of folk toys, not only studied vertically through history, but also horizontally across the world." (p. 39) For a good general introduction on folk toys, see Mac E. Barrick's "Folk Toys" (*Pennsylvania Folklife* 29 [Autumn 1979]: 27-34) and Wendy Lavitt's "America's Folk Toys" (*The Clarion* [Winter 1980/1981]: 42-47). Other introductory materials include Brian Sutton-Smith's *Toys as Culture* (New York: Gardner, 1986) which discusses the toy in the family (the history of toys), the toy as technology (including a section on the anthropology of games), and the toy as education, etc., and Daniel Foley's *Toys Through the Ages: Playthings Filled with History, Folklore, Romance & Nostalgia* (Philadelphia, PA: Chilton, 1962).

There is an abundance of survey material on folk toys. International surveys include William Accorsi's *Toy Sculpture* (New York: Reinhold, 1968), an international sampling of small wooden, often kinetic, toys from the past and the present, some carved, some constructed from found objects. Gabriel Channan and Hazel Francis's *Toys and Games of Children of the World* (Paris: UNESCO, 1984) is concerned with the cultural significance of toys and games; it includes a separate section on folk toys. Emanuel Hercik's *Folk Toys: Les Jouets Populaires* (Prague: Orbis, 1952) is both a history of toys and a catalog of 175 toys from Czechoslovakia, Russia, Poland, England, France, and Germany. Antonia

Fraser's *A History of Toys* (cited above) covers ancient and primitive toys through the 1920s and includes a small section on folk toys. Constance E. King's *Antique Toys and Dolls* (New York: Rizzoli, 1979) covers toy houses, tin toys, optical toys, dolls, soft toys, board games, and jig saw puzzles. Florence and Robert Pettit concentrate on Mexican toys in their *Mexican Folk Toys: Festival Decorations and Ritual Objects* (New York: Hastings House, 1978). There are several studies of Asian folk toys: Tekiho Nisizawa's *Japanese Folk-Toys* (Tokyo: Japanese Tourist Bureau, 1939) gives an historical sketch of Japanese folk toys and a classification: **engi** toys (luck-bringing toys), historical and legendary toys, children's playthings, and miscellaneous toys. Other books on Asian toys include Misako Shishido's *The Folk Toys of Japan* (Tokyo: Japan Publications Trading Co., 1963) (see no. 2394), Kiyoshi Sonobe's and Kazuya Sakamoto's *Japanese Toys* (Rutland, VT: Charles E. Tuttle, 1965), Ann E. Grinham's *Japanese Games and Toys* (Tokyo: Hitachi, 1973) which lists and discusses 28 games and toys, Yuan Tien's *Chinese Folk Toys and Ornaments* (Beijing: Foreign Languages Press, 1980), and Ajit Mookerjee's *Folk Toys of India* (Calcutta: Oxford Book & Stationery Co., 1956). Leslie Daiken's *Children's Toys Throughout the Ages* (London: Batsford, 1953) covers mostly British toys: toys that teach, toys that move, dolls, war toys, toy animals, etc. *Les Jouets Populaires* by Raymond Humbert (Paris: Messidor, Temps Actuels, 1983) covers animal dolls, dolls, cars, soldiers, marionettes, circus animals, clowns, and musical toys in paper and wood and includes an excellent bibliography of books and journals and a list of museums which either have significant toy collections or exhibit toys.

There are several studies of folk dolls, two examples of which are Wendy Lavitt's *American Folk Dolls* (New York: A.A. Knopf, 1982) which is concerned with cloth, corn, wooden, apple/nut and bean, black, and Indian dolls and Tokube Yamada's *Japanese Dolls* (Tokyo: Japan Travel Bureau, 1964), an historical survey of painted wooden dolls, dolls in clothes, clay dolls, folk dolls, dolls used for festivals, and puppets.

This section covers folk toys only; **games** are covered in Chapter 6.

Bibliographies--Folk Toys

2387.   Jean-Leó, and Christian Macoir. *Jouets, Jeux, Livres d'Enfants.*
[Toys, Games, Children's Books: A Bibliographic Guide for
Collectors and Researchers, Comprising Numerous Original
Articles, with 65 illustrations]. Brussels: Le Grenier du
Collectionneur, 1974. 202p. LC 75-515035. (Bibliotheque des
Collectionneurs; v. 1)

There are entries for automata, music boxes, playing cards, circus
animals, games (pp. 108-190), children's games (pp. 191-287), and toys
(pp. 288-499). The entries are international, and the annotations are brief.
Includes a subject and author index.

2388.   Renson, Roland, and B. Van Reusel. "Toy Bibliography."
Association for the Anthropological Study of Play. Newsletter 4
(Spring 1978): 17-18.

This unannotated bibliography lists 19 mostly European books
and articles.

Classification--Folk Toys

2389.   Barrick, Mac E. "Folk Toys." *Pennsylvania Folklife* 29 (Autumn
1979): 27-34.

Barrick defines a **folk toy** as "an object made by the folk for use
in play." (p. 27) Barrick proposes a two-part classification system for
folk toys based on "contrastive features": imitative toys and abstract toys,
which are then subdivided into further categories.

Encyclopedia--Folk Toys

2390.   King, Constance Eileen. *The Encyclopedia of Toys.* New York:
Crown, 1978. 272p. LC 78-6851; ISBN 0-517-53027-9.

Divided into miniature living, toys purely for pleasure, wheeled toys and children's transport, metal toys, board and table games, tops, and pastimes. Very little on folk toys. Bibliography.

Guides and Handbooks--Folk Toys

2391. Hertz, Louis H. *Handbook of Old American Toys.* Wethersfield, CT: Mark Haber, 1947. 119p. LC 47-12372.

Covers classification and identification of old American toys, materials, and terminology, with separate chapters for tin toys, iron toys, clockwork toys, wooden toys, steam toys, banks, canons, cap pistols, bombs, musical and bell toys, electric toys, clockwork track trains; toy household equipment; games; friction toys, wheel toys, steel toys, and dolls. Indexed.

2392. Ketchum, William C., Jr. *Toys & Games.* Washington, DC: Smithsonian Institution, for the Cooper-Hewitt Museum, 1981. 127p. LC 80-70088. (The Smithsonian illustrated library of antiques)

Covers the "earliest toys" (including Greek and Roman toys), wonder playthings (including folk art toys), dolls, doll houses and playthings (ethnic and British and American toys), rag dolls, tin and cast-iron toys, soldiers, paper play objects, etc. Includes also a glossary, a bibliography, a list of some published collections, and an index.

2393. Page, Linda Garland, and Hilton Smith, eds. *The Foxfire Book of Toys and Games: Reminiscences and Instructions from Appalachia.* New York: E.P. Dutton/A Foxfire Press Book, 1985. 267p. LC 85-10373; ISBN 0-525-24353-4 (c); 0-525-48181-8 (p).

Includes dolls and playhouses, toys and instructions. For toys, the authors give instructions on how to make them with reminiscences added.

2394. Shishido, Misako. *The Folk Toys of Japan*. Rutland, VT: Japan Publications Trading Co., 1963. 71p. LC 63-22034.

Each page covers one toy, with explanatory text on one page and illustration on the facing page. The author tells where the toy is made, its use (e.g., for festivals), and beliefs associated with the toy. A glossary is included. Ann Grinham's *Japanese Games and Toys* (Tokyo: Hitachi, 1973) lists 28 games and toys; each is pictured in full color and explained in English.

2395. Whitton, Blair. *Toys*. New York: A.A. Knopf, 1984. 478p. LC 84-47637; ISBN 0-394-71526-8 (p). (The Knopf collectors' guides to American antiques)

Introductory material covers how to identify old toys, their history, and the materials and techniques used in creating manufactured and mechanical toys. There are 351 toys, categorized into games and educational toys, animals and figures, dolls' houses, banks, mechanical toys, toys on wheels, horse-drawn toys, cars, trucks and buses, boats and planes, rocking horses, and riding toys. Each is described and pictured, with details on materials, marks and dimensions, maker, locality and period and hints for collecting. Concluding information includes how to evaluate toys, where to look for them, lists of major toy manufacturers, organizations for collections, public collections (arranged by region of the country), a glossary, and price guide for each piece discussed. There is a bibliography and an index.

Exhibition Catalogs and Guides to Collections--Folk Toys

2396. Girard, Alexander H. *El Encanto de un Pueblo: The Magic of a People; Folk Art and Toys from the Collection of the Girard Foundation*. New York: Viking, 1968. 73p. LC 68-15482.

This is a sampling of folk art and toys from the collection of the Girard Foundation. There are 68 items shown in color: dolls, horses, carts, battleships, toy animals, religious, and secular sculptures--all from Mexico, New Mexico, and South America. No bibliography.

2397.   Longenecker, Martha, ed. *First Collections: Dolls and Folk Toys of the World*. La Jolla, CA: Diego: Mingei International Museum of World Folk Art, 1987 [1978]. 158p. ISBN 0-914155-05-9.

There is an introduction to folk dolls and toys, with commentary on dolls and toys throughout the Western world and Indian and Japanese games and toys. The illustrations are mostly magnificent full-color photographs. Bibliography.

2398.   Murray, Patrick. *Toys*. London: Studio Vista, 1968. 160p. LC 71-460446; ISBN 0-289-37050-7.

This work is based on the toy collection at the Museum of Childhood, Edinburgh [Scotland], and includes paper toys, metal toys, modelled toys, surprise toys, momentum toys and yoyos, trains, toy soldiers, go-carts, rocking horses, etc., some old, some new, some folk toys, some not.

2399.   Reichardt, Jasia, ed. *Play Orbit*. London and New York: A Studio International Publication, 1969. 186p. LC 81-154004.

This was written to coordinate with an exhibit held in Wales and London in 1969-1970, "an exhibit of toys and games, and playable by people who are not professionally involved with the design of playthings." (p.7) It includes essays on a variety of toys and objects (e.g., Hans Christian Andersen's Christmas paper decorations).

2400.   Winn, Robert K. *V.J.M. y J.: Viva Jesus María y José: A Celebration of the Birth of Jesus: Mexican Folk Art and Toys from the Collection of Robert K. Winn*. San Antonio, TX: Trinity University Press, 1977. 103p. LC 77-589457; ISBN 0-911536-68-x.

There is an introductory essay to this collection of toys and religious objects used to celebrate Christmas with many pictured in color. Concludes with a glossary and bibliography.

2401.   Wyle, Edith, curator. *Traditional Toys of Japan*. Los Angeles, CA: Craft and Folk Art Museum, 1979. 46p. LC 79-52387.

Describes and pictures Fukushiman dolls, Okinawan dolls, Darumas dolls, **tengu** (long-nosed goblins), **oni** (ogres), animals, whistles, puppets, and Mikaru dolls, made out of papier maché, fiber, wood, and clay and all painted. Folk toys in Japan are more than children's playthings; they are objects of art and are part of religious rites. There is a bibliography.

FOLK CRAFT
Weaving

The Art of the Weaver, edited by Anita Schorsch (New York: Universe Books, 1978), is a good group of essays from *The Magazine Antiques* with which to begin a study of weaving. Eliza Calvert Hall's *A Book of Hand-woven Coverlets* (Boston: Little Brown, 1912) is still a classic study. There have been several regional studies of weaving, such as Guy F. Reinert's *Pennsylvania German Coverlets* (Kutztown, PA: Kutztown Publishers, 1947), a history and study of weaving with a list of Pennsylvania-German coverlet weavers and Lou Tate's *Kentucky Coverlets* (Louisville: Commercial Litho Co., 1938). Sadye Tune Wilson's and Doris Finch's *Of Coverlets: The Legacies, The Weavers* (Nashville, TN: Tunstede Press, 1983) is a study of the woven coverlets collected by the Tennessee Textile History Project, which aimed to "investigate the state of early handwoven textiles of Tennessee" and "to document and analyze a wide sample of early handwoven coverlets and bedding in Tennessee."

Many of the regional studies of American weaving have concentrated on the weaving of Native Americans, especially that of the Navajo. Such works include George Wharton James' *Indian Blankets and Their Makers* (New York: Dover, 1974 [1914]), a list of Navajo weaving styles, intermixed with descriptions of rites and ceremonies in which these blankets are worn or used, with a classification of Navajo weaving products, Alice Kaufman's and Christopher Selser's *The Navajo Weaving Tradition: 1650 to the Present* (New York: E.P. Dutton, 1985), a beautifully illustrated survey of the craft and techniques of Navajo blankets and rugs, and Charles Avery Amsden's *Navajo Weaving: Its Technique and History* (Salt Lake City, UT: Peregrine Smith, 1975 [1934]). Bertha Pauline Dutton looked at contemporary Navajo weaving in *Navajo Weaving Today* (rev. ed., Santa Fe: Museum of New Mexico Press, 1975 [1964]). Two newer works on Navajo weaving include Kate Peck Kent's *Navajo Weaving: Three Centuries of Changes* (Seattle: University of Washington Press, 1985), a catalog of the School of American Research Collection (Santa Fe, NM), and Harriet and Seymour Koenig's *Navajo Weaving, Navajo Ways* (Katonah, NY: Katonah, Gallery, 1986), also an exhibition catalog. Cheryl Samuel has studied *The Chilkat Dancing Blanket* (Seattle, WA: Pacific Search Press, 1982), a rich tapestry robe worked by Native Americans, so named for the people who made it in historic times, which is only used for ceremonial dancing. See also the works by Fox and Mera below (nos. 2409 and 2413).

Since weaving is often considered part of **textiles**, that section should be searched also (see nos. 2459-2491).

Bibliographies--Weaving

2402.   Axford, Lavonne B. *Weaving, Spinning, and Dyeing*. Littleton, CO: Libraries Unlimited, 1975. 148p. LC 75-16436; ISBN 0-87287-080-4.

Not seen.

2403.   Gamer, Nora. "The Joy of Weaving: A Handweaving Bibliography." *Choice* 14 (September 1977): 795-805.

This is a bibliographic essay which covers both "art" books and "how-to" books and appends a list of the cited works.

Classification--Weaving

2404.   Reath, Nancy. *The Weaves of Hand-Loom Fabrics; A Classification with Historical Notes.* Philadelphia: Pennsylvania Museum, 1927. 64p. LC 28-3052.

Reath classifies hand-loomed weaves into simple weaves, compound weaves, and velvet weaves, with many subtypes (e.g., **simple weaves:** simple cloth, simple twill, simple satin, plaited weave, and knitted and crocheted weaves). There are many explanatory illustrations. Indexed.

Dictionary--Weaving

2405.   Zielinski, Stanislaw A. *Encyclopaedia of Hand-Weaving.* New York: Funk & Wagnalls, 1959. 190p. LC 59-11308.

Actually, this is more of an elaborate glossary than an encyclopedia. British and American handweaving terminology is arranged alphabetically. Included in the entries are information about the origins of the weave, many draft patterns, cross references, and illustrations.

Directory--Weavers

2406.   Heisey, John W. *A Checklist of American Coverlet Weavers.* Williamsburg, VA: Williamsburg Foundation, 1978. 149p. LC 77-15968; ISBN 0-87935-048-2. (Available from the Abby Aldrich Rockefeller Folk Art Center, Drawer C., Williamsburg, VA 23185.)

This is an alphabetic listing of weavers with the dates and places of birth and where they worked as well as a pictorial survey of weaving trademarks and a listing of where to see coverlets. Also includes a bibliography and index.

Note: See also no. 2413.

2407. Bishop, Robert C., et al. *Quilts, Coverlets, Rugs & Samplers.* New York: A.A. Knopf, 1982. 476p. LC 82-47848; ISBN 0-394-71271-4 (p). (The Knopf collectors' guides to American antiques)

Tells how to identify coverlet types and explains how they are made. Also presents some coverlets, describes them, gives dimensions, locality and period made, etc. A price guide is included at the end.

2408. Davison, Mildred, and Christa C. Mayer-Thurman. *Coverlets; A Handbook on the Collection of Woven Coverlets in the Art Institute of Chicago.* Chicago, IL: Art Institute of Chicago, 1973. 228p. LC 73-82570.

Although this is a catalog of the museum's coverlet collection (see no. 2425), it is really a guidebook. Part I, "The Hand-loom Woven Coverlet," illustrates and describes the handwoven coverlets (overshot, summer and winter, multiple shaft, double cloth, and Beiderwand), and dates and locates them. Part II, "Coverlets Woven on Mechanized Pattern Control Looms," covers coverlets woven on mechanized looms from New York, Pennsylvania, New Jersey, Maryland, Ohio, Indiana, Illinois, Iowa, and Maine, on drawn-looms, hand-looms with Jacquard attachments, and on power looms. There is also an extensive bibliography of books and periodical articles.

2409. Mera, H.P. *Spanish-American Blanketry: Its Relationship to Aboriginal Weaving in the Southwest.* Santa Fe, NM: School of American Research Press, 1987. 80p. LC 87-12879; ISBN 0-93345-2-21-7.

This is basically an overview of Spanish-American weaving, but there are 24 plates in full color with explanations and descriptions intended to serve as identification guides.

2410.   Atwater, Mary Meigs. *The Shuttle-Craft Book of American Hand-Weaving; Being an Account of the Rise, Development, Eclipse, and Modern Revival of a National Popular Art, Together with Information of Interest and Value to Collectors, Technical Notes for the Use of Weavers, and a Large Collection of Historical Patterns.* Rev. ed. New York: Macmillan, 1951 [1928]. 341p. LC 51-1000.

This is the standard text on all aspects of weaving. Contains a history of the craft and the literature of handweaving and lists of collections and collectors. But there is a large section devoted to the practice of handweaving: spinning, dyeing, the loom: its tie-up, dressing, weaving on the loom, etc., draft-writing and notation, with many draft patterns given: double-weave, double-face twill, damask, summer and winter weave, double-weave, and linen weave.

2411.   Black, Mary E. *The Key to Weaving: A Text Book on Hand-weaving for the Beginning Weaver.* 2nd ed., rev. New York: Macmillan, 1980 [1945]. 698p. LC 79-26177; ISBN 0-02-511170-1. The 1957 edition was titled *New Key to Weaving.*

This basic text covers the loom and how to warp it, weaves-- plain weaves, twills, overshot, crackle weave, summer- and-winter weaves, tartan weaves, tapestry weaves, information on the theory of weaving and technique--how to read and understand drafts, weaving on paper, fabric analysis, etc., and general information on fibers and color. Appendixes include "articles to weave" and "ready reference tables." Each chapter includes a bibliography, and there is a glossary and a comprehensive index at the back of the book.

2412.   Cyrus-Zetterstrom, Ulla. *Manual of Swedish Handweaving.* Trans. Alice Blomquist. Newton Centre, MA: Charles Branford, 1977 [1950]. 186p. LC 78-341217; ISBN 0-8231-5019-4.

Contains a theory of fabric structures and weaves: tabby, twills, overshot, etc., an analysis of weave structure and calculations of the set of warp and weft and of warp width and length yarn calculations. There is also a section on weaving equipment and another on the techniques for preparing the warp for the loom, dressing it, etc.

2413. Fox, Nancy, ed. *Navajo Weaving Handbook*. Santa Fe: Museum of New Mexico, 1977. 78p. LC 77-74888; ISBN 0-89013-092-2. (A Museum of New Mexico guidebook)

This contains an introductory history on Navajo weaving and a primer of Navajo textiles, with information on how to weave a Navajo rug and restore a Navajo blanket. It also discusses how to tell a genuine Navajo rug and gives a map of the rug-weaving regions of Navajoland. Contains exquisite photographs of rugs and weavings and a bibliography.

2414. Mattera, Joanne. *Navajo Techniques for Today's Weaver*. New York: Watson-Guptill, 1975. 160p. LC 75-12648; ISBN 0-8230-3153-5.

Contains a history of Navajo weaving as well as information on Navajo weaving material, how the loom is made and used, weaving techniques, loom variations, warps and yarns, and finishing techniques. Details of work projects are pictured with many diagrams. There is a glossary, a list of suppliers, a bibliography, and an index.

2415. Oelsner, Gustaf H. *A Handbook of Weaves*. Rev. ed. New York: Macmillan, 1915 [1875]. 402p. LC 15-25573.

Discusses drawing in drafts, drafting weaves, and the characteristics of the weaves themselves: plain weaves, twill weaves, satin weaves, derivative weaves, basket weaves, and undulating twills and textures, diversified weaves, crepe weaves, etc. Includes many diagrams and an index.

2416.   Plath, Iona. *The Craft of Handweaving*. New York: Scribner, 1972 [1964, with the title, *Handweaving*]. 128p. LC 74-39006; ISBN 0-684-12742-3 (p).

Discusses how to weave from patterns, gives a cotton yarn yardage table, and then covers woven upholstery, curtains, pillows, decorative fabrics, rugs, place mats, fashion fabrics, yarns, and stoles, giving instructions for several pieces within each category and a detail of the project. Ends with a glossary of weaving terms, a list of suppliers of yarns and looms, and an index.

2417.   Thorpe, Heather G. *A Handweaver's Workbook*. New York: Macmillan, 1956. 179p. LC 56-7668.

Part I covers four-harness looms--assembly and processes; Part II includes "some weaves of four-harness looms" ("weaves are not the same as weaving drafts but are the particular methods of threading the warp which introduces new principles into the construction of the woven fabric or into the forming of patterns"). (vii) Ends with a glossary, bibliography, and index.

2418.   Tod, Osma Gallinger. *The Joy of Hand Weaving*. 2nd ed. New York: Bonanza Books, 1964. 326p. Reprinted: New York: Dover, 1977. 326p. LC 76-42959; ISBN 0-486-23458-4.

In Part I of this classic work, the author deals with simple or plain weaving, covers its history, and explains plain weave (with several simple projects), rug weaving, Indian weaving, color, two-harness loom weaving, warp preparation, and two-harness methods and weave designs; Part II covers the fundamentals of pattern weaving and the four-harness loom weaves: twill, overshot, and diamond patterns, as well as color, notation, etc. A bibliography and glossary complete this guide.

Draft/Pattern Books--Weaving

2419. Atwater, Mary Meigs. *A Book of Patterns for Hand-Weaving, Designs for the John Landes Drawings in the Pennsylvania Museum.* 4 vols. in 1. Cambridge. MA: Shuttle-Craft Guild, 1925-26. LC 25-22562.

Gives 95 patterns and threading drafts and shows illustrations of finished pieces. Atwater also prepared *Shuttle-Craft Drafts for Weaving Coverlet Patterns* (Basin, MT: The Shuttle-Craft Shop, nd) which was not seen.

2420. Davison, Marguerite P. *A Handweaver's Pattern Book.* Rev. ed. Swarthmore, PA: M.P. Davis, 1950 [1944]. 217p. LC 50-7736.

Includes drafts for four-harness weave patterns--for twills, bird's eye and rose path patterns, modified twills, twill combinations, grouped warp threads, M's and O's, canvas weaves, texture weaves, huck-a-buck weaves, barley corn weaves, overshot weaves, etc. For each one, there is a draft and a photograph of a finished piece given. Includes also bibliography and index.

2421. Hargrove, John, and Rita J. Adrosko. *The Weavers* [sic] *Draft Book and Clothiers Assistant.* Worcester, MA: American Antiquarian Society, 1979. Reprint of 1792 ed. 18p. LC 79-110297; ISBN 0-912296-17-8.

This is a facsimile of a late nineteenth-century draft book with 52 weaving drafts and an "approved receipt for sizing cotton warps and for dyeing cotton or linen."

Exhibition Catalogs and Guides to Collections--Weaving

2422. Baltimore Museum of Art. *The Great American Cover-Up: Counterpanes of the Eighteenth and Nineteenth Centuries.* Baltimore, MD: Baltimore Art Museum, 1971. 48p. LC 76-31369.

The introduction by Dena S. Katzenberg covers designs, patterns, weaves, and types of coverlet blankets. The rest is a catalog of 89 coverlets with brief descriptions and some black-and-white photographs. There is a bibliography.

2423. Burnham, Dorothy K. *The Comfortable Arts: Traditional Spinning and Weaving in Canada*. Ottawa: National Gallery of Canada, 1981. 238p. ISBN 0-88884-474-3.

There are 162 pieces pictured in black and white, each with the name of the weaver, the place made, and a long description. Included are rugs, fabrics, wall hangings, sweaters and bonnets, blankets, coverlets, dresses, and band woven pieces. Some patterns and drafts are included as well as some pictures of the weavers. A bibliography concludes the catalog.

2424. Burnham, Harold B., and Dorothy K. Burnham. *"Keep Me Warm One Night": Early Handweaving in Eastern Canada*. Toronto: University of Toronto Press, in cooperation with the Royal Ontario Museum, 1972. 387p. LC 72-83388; ISBN 0-8020-1896-3.

The Textile Department of the Royal Ontario Museum began "to record material that was still in existence together with the history of individual pieces in the hope that the bits of information would fit together to form a homogenous whole." (intro.) Many pieces, pictured and described, are grouped into basic weaves, costumes, carpets, and a variety of coverlets. Tools and equipment are also pictured.

2425. Davison, Mildred, and Christa C. Mayer-Thurman. *Coverlets; A Handbook on the Collection of Woven Coverlets in the Art Institute of Chicago*. Chicago, IL: Art Institute of Chicago, 1973. 228p. LC 73-82570.

See entry no. 2408. Includes a history of coverlet weaving and two sections: 1) hand-loom woven coverlets and 2) coverlets woven on mechanized pattern-controlled looms. Also included is an alphabetical list of weavers and a bibliography. Over 150 coverlets from the collection are photographed and described.

2426. Elvehjem Art Center. *American Coverlets of the Nineteenth Century from the Helen Louise Allen Textile Collection.* Madison, WI: Elvehjem Art Center, University of Wisconsin, 1974. 95p. LC 75-622430.

This is a catalog of coverlets of simple and compound weaves, hand woven and machine woven. In all, 38 coverlets are described and pictured. There is a concluding section on coverlet drafts and patterns.

2427. Shaeffer, Margaret W. *Made in New York State: Handwoven Coverlets, 1820-1860.* Watertown, NY: Jefferson County Historical Society, 1985. 71p. LC 84-25062.

There are two introductory essays on handweave coverlets and American coverlet looms followed by 24 plates of coverlets, dated, analyzed, located, and described. There is also a list of New York state coverlet weavers and a bibliography.

III. TECHNOLOGY

The *MLA International Bibliography* includes in its section on Technology the following subsections: **Agriculture, Glass Blowing, Metalcraft,** and **Textiles.**

General

The most substantial history of technology is Charles Singer et al.'s 8-volume *A History of Technology* (Oxford: Clarendon Press, 1954-1984), arranged chronologically from very early times through the twentieth century. International in scope, it contains many entries of interest for the folklorist. Vol. 8 has "consolidated indexes": an index of names, an index of place names, and an index of subjects. David Shuldmer's "The Art of Sheet Metal Work" (*Southwest Folklore* 4 [1980]: 37-41) is a rare example of a study of one aspect of technology.

Bibliographies--Technology-General

Note: Richard S. Thill, in "A Bibliography of Materials Relevant to Folklore and Technology" (*Keystone Folklore* 18 [Winter 1973]: 197-199; reprinted: *Tennessee Folklore Society Bulletin* 40 [March 1974]: 8-9), proposed to write a bibliography of "scholarly books, articles, and papers presented at professional meetings." There were to be two parts to this bibliography: 1) lists and annotations of works which discuss the "folklore of technology, investigations of beliefs, anecdotes, and attitudes centering on man's relationship to the machines which he has created" and 2) "discussions reporting the use of computers and card sorters to organize folklore materials for analysis or storage." I do not think it was ever published.

2428. "Current Bibliography in the History of Technology." *Technology and Culture*, 1969--.

This is an annual bibliography, running about two years late (i.e., the bibliography for 1984 was published in 1986). The one for 1984, which is 131 pages, is divided into chronological divisions and into 11 classifications, including architecture and building construction, agricultural and food technology, etc. The entries are briefly annotated, and each annual bibliography includes an author and a subject index.

2429. Ferguson, Eugene. *Bibliography of the History of Technology*. Cambridge, MA: Society for the History of Technology, 1968. 347p. LC 68-21559. (Society for the History of Technology monograph series; v. 5)

This bibliography includes general works, encyclopedias, histories, and library lists, as well as material on early source books and manuscripts, encyclopedias, compendia, and technology, and on specific subject fields: glass, ceramics, textiles, hand tools, crafts and craftsmen, and musical instruments, etc. There is a comprehensive index.

2430.   Hindle, Brooke. *Technology in Early America: Needs and Opportunities for Study.* Chapel Hill: University of North Carolina Press for the Institute of Early American History and Culture, Williamsburg, VA, 1966. 145p. LC 66-25357. (Needs and opportunities for study, 5)

This book contains an essay, "The Exhilaration of Early American Technology" (pp. 3-28) and a "Bibliography of Early American Technology" by Hindle, a bibliographic essay based on the following subjects: sources, surveys and studies, agriculture and food processing, mining and metals, canals and railroads, roads, bridges, building, manufacturing: crafts and craftsmen, tools, woodwork, metalwork, clocks, instruments, glass, pottery, and textiles, among others. Also included in this work is a section on technology in American history and a "Directory of Artifact Collections" by Lucius F. Ellsworth. A book of essays on the use of lumber and wood in America in the nineteenth century was also written by Brooke Hindle, *America's Wooden Age* (Tarrytown, NY: Sleepy Hollow Restorations, 1975).

2431.   Josephson, Aksel G.S. *A List of Books on the History of Industry and Industrial Arts.* Chicago, IL: The John Crerar Library, 1915: Reprinted: Detroit, MI: Gale Research, 1966. 486p. LC 67-14030.

Although this bibliography is obviously out of date, it is interesting historically and contains some items pertinent to folk culture, for example, a listing of books on the history of agriculture and rural economics (listed by country), history of agricultural implements and farm buildings, history of domestic science, fashion and costume, history of ceramics, history of the textile industry (by country), history of clocks and clock-making, history of smithcraft and metal work, history of building and architecture, etc. The scope is international; there are no annotations, but full citations are given, and there is a general index.

2432.   Rittenhouse, Jack D. *Carriage Hundred; A Bibliography on Horse-Drawn Transportation*. Houston, TX: Stagecoach Press, 1961. 49p. LC 61-9110.

This charming book covers works about carriages, their construction and care, driving, and related subjects (ponies, blacksmithing, etc.) from the seventeenth century to the present. Although most entries are English language, there are a few foreign language entries. There is no index. The author has also compiled an annotated bibliography on *American Horse-Drawn Vehicles* (New York: Bonanza, 1948), a bibliography, with illustrations of 183 different types of American horse-drawn vehicles.

TECHNOLOGY
Agriculture

Most of the material in this section is concerned with farming and related aspects of farming, such as farm buildings, farm machinery and tools. Farming predominates this section probably because, as George Shannon said in his introduction to Beauveau Borie's *Farming and Folk Society: Threshing Among the Pennsylvania Germans* (Ann Arbor, MI: UMI Research Press, 1986), "In many ways farming represents a kind of craft tradition with strands of continuity reaching deep into the past." (preface)

For background reading, there are several histories of farming, one good example of which is John Schlebecker's *Whereby We Thrive: A History of American Farming, 1607-1972* (Ames: Iowa State University Press, 1986 [1975]), covering farming methods and tools, crop growing, use of the land, harvesting and processing, etc. Michael Chibnik's *Farm Work and Fieldwork: American Agriculture in Anthropological Perspective* (Ithaca, NY: Cornell University Press, 1987) is a book of essays that "examine the causes and consequences of changing agricultural technology, economic conditions and government programs" and provide "an interview of current anthropological research in rural America." Two previously cited works deserve noting here as introductory studies to agriculture: John Stilgoe's *Common Landscape of America, 1580-1845* (New Haven, CT: Yale University Press, 1982) which looks historically at, among other things, landscape and agriculture (including lore, farmsteads, farmhouses, farmland, fencing, cowpers, woodlots, etc.) and W.G. Hoskins' *English Landscapes* (London: BBC Publications, 1973), covering also the rural landscape and farm buildings.

There are several books about farming that are specifically related to folklore. *Folk and Farm: Essays in Honour of A.T. Lucas* (Dublin: Royal Society of Antiquaries of Ireland, 1976), edited by Caoimhín Ó Danachair (Kevin Danaher), has essays on fieldwork, ploughing, traditional house types, Irish trade banners, the tinkers' trade and tools, food, religion among the farmfolk, the Irish wheel, and an essay by I.C. Peate on "Some Thoughts on the Study of Folk Life." Amos Long, Jr., studied the Pennsylvania-German farm in his *The Pennsylvania German Family Farm* (Breinigsville, PA: Publications of the Pennsylvania German Society; v. 6, 1972), subtitled "A Regional Architectural and Folk Cultural Study of an American Agricultural Community"; it is a study of the farm family, the farmstead, outbuildings, fences, etc. George Carey's "A Folklorist, Not a Farmer, a Commentary" (pp. 289-294), in *Agricultural Literature: Proud Heritage, Future Promise*, edited by Alan Fusonie and Leila Moran (Washington, DC: Graduate School Press, 1977), is concerned with the relationship of folklore, farming, and collecting techniques. Beauveau Borie's *Farming and Folk Society: Threshing Among the Pennsylvania Germans* (cited above) studies the Pennsylvania-German farm as an artifact of Pennsylvania-German culture, especially the function of threshing with a **dreschfleggel** (threshing flail); it contains a very substantial bibliography (pp. 111-136) covering farming, folklore, and the Pennsylvania Germans.

Other folklorists have studied specific farms in depth. An example of this is Henry Glassie's "The Wedderspoon Farm" (*New York Folklore Quarterly* 22 [1966]: 165-187), "an attempt to leave a folk architectural study--in this case the study of one central New York farm--in context." (p. 165) Glassie describes the house and outbuildings through interviews with Mr. Wedderspoon and visually depicts the changes of the farm layout from 1858-1890. Aspects of farm work have also been described, such as Darrell D. Henning's "Maple Sugaring: History of a Folk Technology" (*Keystone Folklore Quarterly* 11 [1966]: 239-274), which gives the early history of maple sugaring, some information about the sugar maple tree, maple technology, tapping, collecting receptacles, gathering and storage, and evaporating processes.

Two examples of material on British farming and folklife, about which there is an abundance of material, are George Ewart Evans' *The Pattern Under the Plough: Aspects of Folk-Life of East Anglia* (London: Faber & Faber, 1966) and Emyr Estyn Evans' *Irish Folk Ways* (no. 1489) which covers farms, farm houses, furniture, etc., farmyards and fences, farm machinery and tools, cars and carts, and boats and fishing as well as Irish rural customs.

The barn is the farm building/artifact most often studied by folklorists and others. Many of the books on barns are slick, beautifully photographed surveys of different types of barns, such as Eric Arthur's and Dudley Witney's *The Barn; A Vanishing Landmark in North America* (Toronto: McClelland & Stewart, 1972; Boston, MA: New York Graphic Society, 1974) which is a historic overview of the barns in North America: Dutch barns, Pennsylvania barns, connecting barns, circular, and polygonal barns, the decorated arts in barns, and the barn in detail. Eric Sloane, the popular folklorist and illustrator, has done two of his typical books on barns: *An Age of Barns* (New York: Henry Holt, 1990 [1962]) and *American Barns and Covered Bridges* (New York: W. Funk, 1954), in which he labels his illustrations with some descriptive text. Charles Klamkin's *Barns; Their History, Preservation, and Restoration* (New York: Hawthorn, 1973) details how barns were built, describes the transition from general to specialized barns, and shows how three barn owners restored their barns. There have been many studies of regional barns: Thomas C. Hubka's *Big House, Little House, Back House, Barn: The Connected Farm Buildings of New England* (Hanover, NH: University Press of New England, 1984) talks about the New England connected farm buildings, especially in the context of the land and the people; John Fitchen's *The New World Dutch Barn: A Study of Its Characteristics, Its Structural System, and Its Probable Erectional Procedures* (Syracuse, NY: Syracuse University Press, 1968) describes Dutch barns in central New York State and provides a checklist of barns seen and photographs of many of them; Henry Glassie's "The Variation of Concept Within

Tradition: Barn Buildings in Otsego Co., New York," in *Man and Cultural Heritage: Papers in Honor of Fred B. Kniffen*, edited by H.J. Walker and W.G. Haag (Baton Rouge: Louisiana State University Press, 1974; reprinted by New York State Historical Assn., Cooperstown, NY, 1974) is a survey of the barns in Otsego County, with data collected from 2,193 barns, 149 of which were carefully studied. It includes also interviews with farmers and carpenters, a simple formal typology, and descriptive accounts of masonry and frame technology. Henry Glassie also wrote about "The Old Barns of Appalachia" (*Mountain Life and Work* 40 [Summer 1965]: 21-30). Probably the Pennsylvania barn has been the most studied. A good cultural study is Joseph W. Glass' *The Pennsylvania Culture Region: A View from the Barn* (Ann Arbor, MI: UMI Research, 1986). Other works about Pennsylvania barns include Alfred L. Shoemaker's *The Pennsylvania Barn* (Lancaster, PA: Franklin Dutch Folklore Center, 1955) and Charles H. Dornbusch's *Pennsylvania German Barns* (Allentown, PA: Pennsylvania German Folklore Society, 21, 1959), both about the Pennsylvania-German barn. However, Robert F. Ensminger's "A Search for the Origin of the Pennsylvania Barn" (*Pennsylvania Folklife* 30 [Winter 1980-81]: 50-71) and Henry Glassie's "The Pennsylvania Barn in the South" (*Pennsylvania Folklife* 15 [1965-66]: 8-19, 12-25) look at all types of Pennsylvania barns. R.W. Brunskill has written a survey of British farm buildings, *Traditional Farm Buildings of Britain* (London: Gollancz, 1987 [1982]); Eurwyn Williams's *Traditional Farm Buildings in North-east Wales, 1500-1900* (Cardiff: National Museum of Wales, Welsh Folk Museum, 1982) is a historical overview of Welsh farm structures. A fascinating detailed study of British barns is Walter William Horn's and Ernest Born's *The Barns of the Abbey of Beaulieu at its Granges of Great Coxwell & Beaulieu-St. Leonards* (Berkeley: University of California Press, 1965), a study of timbered medieval barns of the Abbey of Beaulieu in Berkshire and in Hampshire, England. And, finally, there have been several studies of hex signs, notably John Joseph Stoudt's *The Decorated Barns of Eastern Pennsylvania* (Allentown, PA: Schlechter, PA., 1945), Elmer L. Smith's *Hex Signs and Other Barn Decorations* (Manheim, PA: Photo Arts, 1982 [1965]), and August C. Mohr's "Origin and Significance of Pennsylvania Dutch Barn Symbols," in Alan Dundes' *Study of Folklore* (pp. 373-399). See also Don Yoder's *Hex Signs: Pennsylvania Dutch Barn Symbols and Their Meaning* (New York: E.P. Dutton, 1989).

There have also been a great many studies of farm implements and machinery as artifacts. Several surveys and histories of farm tools are available: R. Douglas Hurt's *American Farm Tools: From Hand-Power to Steam-Power* (Manhattan, KS: Sunflower University Press, 1982) and Michael Partridge's *Farm Tools Through the Ages* (New York: Graphic Society, 1973) cover farm implements of the United States, and Philip Wright's *Old Farm Implements* (London: Adam & Charles Black, 1961) is concerned with British farm tools. Percy Blandford's *Old Farm Tools and Machinery: An Illustrated History* (London: David & Charles, 1976) is a general survey of both tools and machinery. Suzanne Beedell's *Windmills* (New York: Scribner, 1979) covers the origins, history, and working mechanics of windmills, milling, millwrighting, and millstones in Denmark, Holland, France, and America. And Albert Sandklef, like Beauveau Borie (in Borie's *Farming and Folk Society: Threshing Among the Pennsylvania Germans*, mentioned above), has also studied the thresher in his book, *Singing Flails; A Study in Threshing-Floor Constructions, Flail-Threshing Traditions and the Magic Guarding of the House* (Helsinki: Suomalainan Tiedeakatemia, 1949, *FF Communications*, 136). Finally, Henry T. Mercer's *Ancient Carpenters' Tools...* (5th ed., Doylestown, PA: Horizon Press for the Bucks County Historical Society, 1975 [1929]) is a study of tools used in America in the last two centuries.

Bibliographies--Agriculture

2433. Bush, E.A.R. *Agriculture: A Bibliographical Guide.* 2 vols. London: Macdonald, 1974. LC 75-312274; ISBN 0-3560-4505-6.

Not seen.

2434. Carlson, Alvar W. "Bibliography on Barns in the United States." *Pioneer America* 10 (1978): 65-71.

These books and articles are arranged alphabetically by author. There are no annotations.

2435. Dworaczek, Marian. *Sources of Information in Agriculture.* Monticello, IL: Vance Bibliographies, 1982. 25p. LC 82-208689. (Public administration series: P 1032)

There are about 260 items listed (no annotations) and categorized into general bibliographies and guides to the literature, encyclopedias, dictionaries, directories, handbooks and manuals, guides to agriculture, selection aids, data bases, and indexing and abstracting services. There is an author index.

2436. Fusonie, Alan M. *Heritage of American Agriculture: A Bibliography of Pre-1860 Imprints.* Beltsville, MD: National Agriculture Library, 1978 [1977]. LC 75-600876.

Not seen.

2437. Fussell, G.E. *The Old English Farming Books.* 4 vols. London: The Pindar Press, 1947-1984.

The arrangement of these four volumes is chronological (from 1523-1860), and the format is the bibliographical essay, so it is a bit hard to use. However, there are separate indexes and bibliographies in each volume. Another volume was planned.

2438. Noble, Allen G. "The Farm Silo: An Annotated Bibliography." *Journal of Cultural Geography* 1 (Spring/Summer 1981): 118-126.

These books, articles, and agricultural reports deal mostly with innovative silage methods but also cover the building aspects of silos.

2439. Noble, Allen G., and Jean M. Danis. "The Literature on Fences, Walls and Hedges as Cultural Landscape Features," *Pennsylvania Folklife* 33 (1983): 41-47.

There are 66 articles and books arranged alphabetically by author or anonymous title following an introduction.

2440. Schlebecker, John T. *Bibliography of Books and Pamphlets on the History of Agriculture in the United States, 1607-1967.* Santa Barbara, CA: Clio Press, 1969. 183p. LC 69-20449.

This is an author listing, "occasionally annotated" (and very briefly at that), which covers much folklore material. The index is inclusive but has subject entries on topics of interest to folklorists; prominent are articles and books on rural life in America.

2441. Schultz, LeRoy G. *Barns, Stables, and Outbuildings: A World Bibliography in English, 1700-1983.* Jefferson, NC: McFarland, 1986. 150p LC 85-31012; ISBN 0-89950-193-1.

This is a listing only of 334 entries concerned with the barns of England, Scotland, Wales, and Ireland, the barns of Germany and Switzerland, the barns of Sweden, Norway, Finland, and Denmark, the barns of France, the barns of other European countries, and the barns of America. There is an author index and a subject index with many entries for different types of farms and other outbuildings: hop barns, stables, corn cribs and granaries, silos, tobacco barns, etc.

2442. Tucher, Andrea J., comp. *Agriculture in America, 1622-1860: Printed Works in the Collections of the American Philosophical Society, the Historical Society of Pennsylvania, the Library Company of Philadelphia.* New York: Garland, 1984. 212p. LC 83-49300; ISBN 0-8240-8967-7. (Americana to 1860; v. 2)

This is a very useful book. There is an introductory essay, "Reaping Machines in Eden," by Tucher, followed by a bibliography that covers over 2,200 books, articles, and pamphlets dealing with "the history of American agriculture literature before the Civil War." Most deal with farm life and farm cultivation; there is a wide variety of farmers' almanacs and books about produce, farm animals, etc. The analytic index includes addresses, and entries for such typical items as agriculture--by place, botany, cattle, clay, fruit, etc. Also included is a chronology of articles from 1622-1860.

2443. Vance, Mary. *Windmills and Wind Power: A Bibliography*. Monticello, IL: Vance Bibliographies, 1981. 59p. (Bibliography A-518)

There are 514 items listed about windmills. Also included is an author index and a subject index.

Encyclopedia--Agriculture

2444. Schapsmeier, Edward L., and Frederick H. Schapsmeier. *Encyclopedia of American Agricultural History*. Westport, CT: Greenwood, 1975. 467p. LC 74-34563; ISBN 0-8371-7958-0.

This is an alphabetic listing with entries on many aspects of folk culture and agriculture: almanacs, barn dances, barn raisings, etc. There are also several special indexes, which are also useful, that group references together by such topics as almanacs, equipment and implements, food (e.g., **hoecake, grits**), Indians, pioneer and rural life. There is also a general index.

TECHNOLOGY
Glassblowing

There is not a great deal of writing about glass blowing or glassmaking as a folk craft. Jane Shadel Spillman's *Glassmaking, America's First Industry* (Corning, NY: Corning Museum Glass, 1976) is a good basic survey of glassblowing as a craft. Marvin D. Schwartz edited a series of articles about glass in *American Glass, from the Pages of Antiques: Blown and Molded* (Princeton, NJ: Pyne Press, 1974). And there have been several studies done of Stiegel glass, notably Frederick William Hunter's *Stiegel Glass* (Boston, MA: Houghton, 1914; reprinted Dover,

1950). Henry William Stiegel was an eighteenth-century German immigrant who settled in Lancaster County, Pennsylvania, and made beautiful glass objects. This work contains a biographical sketch, a study of his glassmaking, and an analysis of early glassblowing in America. Fritz Kampfer's and Klaus G. Beyer's *Glass: A World History: The Story of 4000 Years of Fine Glass-Making* (trans. and rev., Edmund Launert, London: Studio Vista, 1966; Greenwich, CT: New York Graphic Society, 1967) is a classic chronological history of glass, which discusses all the glassmaking techniques. Two surveys of American glass are Rhea Mansfield Knittle's *Early American Glass* (New York: Century, 1939) and George S. and Helen McKearin's *American Glass* (New York: Crown, 1941), which divides the contents by type of glass (molded, pressed, blown, etc.); it contains a chronological chart of American glass houses, a bibliography, and index. Jean S. Melvin's *American Glass Paperweights and Their Makers* (New York: T. Nelson, 1970 [1949]) takes a look at the craftsmen who made paperweights, explains the process involved, and surveys the products.

Bibliography--Glass

2445. "Checklist of Recently Published Articles and Books on Glass." *Journal of Glass Studies*, 1959--. Corning Museum of Glass. Corning, NY.

The *Journal of Glass Studies* was begun to "serve as a vehicle for international scholarship in the history, art, and early technology of art." The journal is an annual, and each volume contains the "Checklist," with publications which have been added to the Rakow Library of Corning Museum of Glass. The listing is divided into general publications, technological publications (including those on conservation), and historical publications (arranged chronologically).

Classification--Glass

2446. Lee, Ruth Webb. *Early American Pressed Glass: A Classification of Patterns Collectible in Sets....* Wellesley Hills, MA: Lee

Publications, 1946. 666p. Reprinted: Rutland, VT: Charles E. Tuttle, 1985. LC 85-50502; ISBN 0-8048-7004-7.

Although this is basically a survey of American pressed glass, the author also includes a classification of patterns of pressed glass.

Dictionary--Glass

2447.   Newman, Harold. *An Illustrated Dictionary of Glass*. London: Thames & Hudson, 1977. 351p. LC 78-303963; ISBN 0-500-23262-8.

There are over 2,400 entries in this work which is "intended primarily to define terms relating to glass and glassware, such as the constituent elements, the methods of production and decoration, and the styles in various regions and periods, and also to describe some pieces that bear recognized names." There is also an introduction by R.J. Charleston on the history of glassmaking.

Guides--Glass

2448.   Spillman, Jane Shadel. *Glass Tableware, Bowls & Vases*. New York: A.A. Knopf, 1982. 478p. LC 82-47849; ISBN 0-394-71272-2 (p). (The Knopf collectors' guide to American antiques)

The introductory material discusses how to identify glass, gives a brief history of the glass industry and changing decorative styles, tells how glass is made, describes parts of a glass object, and gives the six basic glass types. Then there are 350 pieces of glassware (tumblers, stemware, pitchers, etc.) described, pictured, and placed historically and geographically. Hints for collectors are also given.

2449.   Wilson, Rex L. *Bottles on the Western Frontier*. Tucson: University of Arizona Press, 1981. 144p. LC 81-11703; ISBN 0-8165-0414-8 (c); 0-8165-5076-2 (p).

This is an identification guide to bottles found on the western frontier before 1900. Covered are beer, ale and stout, whiskey, wine, bitters, soda-water, ginger, medicine, toiletry, and culinary bottles. There is a guide to shapes and finishes, bottle marks, and impressed stamps. Includes a bibliography.

TECHNOLOGY
Metalcraft

This section includes work done in all metals--brass, tin iron (cast and wrought), copper, pewter, silver, and gold.

There is not a large body of work on metalwork as a folk craft, and not a distinct bibliography, though general works on folk arts and crafts will have sections on this. As is true with all the arts and crafts, it is difficult to differentiate folk metal craft from national or regional metalwork, or antiques crafted in metal.

There are many surveys of metalcrafts. There are several older studies of iron work, such as James Aston's and Edward B. Story's *Wrought Iron: Its Manufacture, Characteristics, and Applications* (4th ed., Pittsburgh, PA: A.M. Byers, 1956 [1939]). General international surveys of iron work include Fritz Kühn's *Decorative Work in Wrought Iron and Other Metals* (New York: Architectural Book Publishing, 1977 [1967]) which covers vessels, candelabras, religious objects, signs, clocks, light fixtures, furniture, fire grates and tools, and door knockers, and Kühn's *Wrought Iron* (New York: Architectural Book Publishing, 1969) which covers rails, gates, and screens and their ornaments. John Seymour Lindsay's *Iron and Brass Implements of the English and American Home* (rev. ed., Bass River, MA: C. Jacobs, 1974 [1927]) includes a survey of hearth, cooking and other kitchen utensils, and other metalwork, with emphasis on American colonial implements. American ironwork has been covered in Henry J. Kauffman's *Early American Ironware, Cast and Wrought* (Rutland, VT: Charles E. Tuttle, 1966) which is arranged by craftsmen, in Albert H. Sonn's 3-volume *Early American Wrought Iron* (New York: Scribner, 1928), and in Philip B. Wallace's *Colonial Ironwork in Old Philadelphia: The Craftsmanship of the Early Days of the Republic* (New

York: Dover, 1970 [1930]). A regional study of American ironwork is *Southwestern Colonial Ironwork: The Spanish Blacksmithing Tradition from Texas to California* (Santa Fe: The Museum of New Mexico Press, 1980), by Marc Simmons and Frank Turley, on ironworking in Spain, in colonial Mexico, and in the Spanish southwest; it contains a discussion of the smithy, farrier, tool forging, and ironwork in the home. Canadian iron work has been studied by Eric Arthur and Thomas Ritchie, in their *Iron: Cast and Wrought Iron in Canada from the Seventeenth Century to the Present* (Toronto: University of Toronto Press, 1982), a historical survey of fences, railings, grates, gates, kitchen utensils, andirons, iron horses, etc. John Seymour Lindsay studied British wrought iron crafts, arranged chronologically, in his *An Anatomy of English Wrought Iron* (New York: Taplinger, 1965). One of several studies of European ironwork is Arthur Byne's and Mildred Stapley's *Spanish Ironwork* (New York: Hispanic Society of America, 1915), an early study of the craft.

Two studies look at the work of the blacksmith: Jeannette Lasansky's *To Draw, Upset, and Weld: The Work of the Pennsylvania Rural Blacksmith, 1742-1935* (Lewisburg, PA: The Oral Traditions Project, 1980) describes the blacksmiths' work and products, analyzes materials used and forms made, and includes a list of contemporary smiths; Jean-Claude Dupont's *L'Artisan Forgeron* (Quebec: Les Presses de l'Université Laval, 1979) is a full-length study of the techniques, decorative motifs, and work of the forger; it includes a section on "the folklore of work: the forger in oral literature."

For an historical overview of pewter, see John Carl Thomas' *American and British Pewter: An Historical Survey* (New York: Main Street/Universe Books, 1976), essays from *The Magazine Antiques* on old pewter. N. Hudson Moore studied American and English pewter in his *Old Pewter: Brass, Copper & Sheffield Plate* (New York: Frederick Stokes, 1905). American pewter is a popular subject: Henry J. Kauffman's *The American Pewterer: His Techniques and His Products* (Camden, NJ: T. Nelson, 1970) covers all types of pewterware. J.B. Kerfoot's *American Pewter* (Boston, MA: Houghton, 1924) is the classic history of pewter, while Charles F. Montgomery's *A History of American Pewter* (rev. and enl. ed., New York: Dutton, 1978 [1973]) is a more recent historical account, covering church pewter, lighting, drinking vessels, plates, dishes, and utensils.

An historical overview of silver can be found in Jane Bentley Kolter's *Early American Silver and Its Makers: From The Magazine Antiques* (New York: Mayflower Books, 1979), essays on silver and silversmiths. Another historical overview is Seymour Wyler's *The Book of Old Silver: English, American, Foreign* (New York: Crown, 1937) which looks at silver products: tea services, condiment sets, etc., then English provincial silver, and hallmarks from many countries. Early American silver has been studied by Clara Louise Avery, in her *Early American Silver* (New York: Russell & Russell, 1968 [1930]). George Barton Cutten looked at *The Silversmiths of Virgina, Together with Watchmakers and Jewelers, from 1694-1850* (Richmond, VA: The Dietz Press, 1952). There have been many, many studies of British silver, such as G. Bernard and Therle Hughes' *Three Centuries of English Domestic Silver, 1500-1820* (New York: Praeger, 1968), which is arranged by type of silverware: candlesticks, salts, pomanders, etc., and Edward Wenham's *Domestic Silver of Great Britain and Ireland* (London: Oxford University Press, 1931). Two works on American jewelry made from silver are Margery Bedinger's *Indian Silver: Navajo and Pueblo Jewelers* (Albuquerque: University of New Mexico Press, 1973) which has a 10-page bibliography on Native American jewelry, and Mary L. Davis' and Greta Pack's *Mexican Jewelry* (Austin: University of Texas Press, 1963). H. Ling Roth studied Asian silvermaking in his *Oriental Silverwork, Malay and Chinese* (Kuala Lampur: University of Malaysia Press, 1966).

The crafting of American tinware is the subject of a book by Shirley Spaulding De Voe, *The Tinsmiths of Connecticut* (Middletown, CT: Published for the Connecticut Historical Society by Wesleyan University Press, 1968). Elmer L. Smith edited *Tinware Yesterday and Today* (Lebanon, PA: Applied Arts, 1975), which discusses candle molds, hand lanterns, weathervanes, lamps, cookie cutters, and other objects crafted from tin. Jeannette Lasansky's *To Cut, Piece and Solder: The Work of the Rural Pennsylvania Tinsmith, 1778-1908* (University Park: Pennsylvania State University Press, 1982) surveys the work of nineteenth-century tinsmiths, gives an account of the objects they made, and analyzes the forms, decorative motifs, and material of tinwork.

Henry J. Kauffman studied copper and work in allied metals in his *American Copper & Brass* (Camden, NJ: T. Nelson, 1968) and in his

Early American Copper, Tin, and Brass (New York: Medill-McBride, 1950).

European metal craft, especially goldwork, has been widely studied. Most are historical surveys, such as Cyril Bunt's *The Goldsmiths of Italy* (London: Martin Hopkinson, 1926; reprinted: New York: Garland, 1979) and Jacques Helft's *French Master Goldsmiths and Silversmiths from the Seventeenth to the Nineteenth Century* (New York: French & European Publications, 1966). Alexander von Solodkoff's *Russian Gold and Silverwork, 17th-19th Century* (New York: Rizzoli, 1981) is an exquisite book covering all types of gold and silver, cloisonné work, and marks.

Dictionaries and Encyclopedias--Metalcraft

2450.   Clayton, Michael. *The Collector's Dictionary of The Silver and Gold of Great Britain and North America.* 2nd ed. Woodbridge [Suffolk]: Antique Collector's Club, 1985 [1971]. 481p. LC 85-139608; ISBN 0-9074-6257-x.

This alphabetical listing includes artisans, important pieces, silver and gold products (**altar candlesticks**, etc.) and processes (**design, decoration, color**). There are many black-and-white photos and a bibliography.

2451.   Cotterell, Howard Herschel. *Old Pewter, Its Makers and Marks in England, Scotland and Ireland.* London: Batsford, 1963 [1929]; Rutland, VT: Charles E. Tuttle, 1963 [1929, Scribner]. 432p. LC 63-4599; ISBN 0-8048-0443-5.

This is an alphabetical listing of pewter makers and their marks and an alphabetical list of initialled marks, with illustrations of anonymous marks. There are several indexes besides a general index (e.g., an index to devices and an index to hallmarks).

2452.   French, Hollis. *A Silver Collectors' Glossary and a List of Early American Silversmiths and Their Marks.* New York: Da Capo,

1967. 164p. LC 67-27454. (Da Capo Press series in architecture and decorative art; v. 9)

This is an alphabetical listing by artisans, giving place of work, his mark, and approximate years working. There is a glossary of terms but no index or bibliography.

2453. Höver, Otto. Trans. Ann C. Weaver. *Wrought Iron; Encyclopedia of Ironwork.* 2nd ed. New York: Universe, 1962 [1927]. unpaged. 320 plates. LC 62-12006.

This is a chronological study, international in scope, with many plates.

Guides--Metalcraft

2454. Kovel, Ralph M., and Terry H. Kovel. *A Directory of American Silver, Pewter, and Silver Plate.* New York: Crown, 1961. 352p. LC 60-8620.

Part I covers silver spoons, cups and bowls, teapots, and coffeepots, Part II covers pewter products, and Part III is concerned with silverplate products. There is also an alphabetical listing of artisans in each section with their marks and a comprehensive bibliography.

Exhibition Catalogs and Guides to Collections--Metalcraft

2455. Buhler, Kathryn C. *American Silver, 1655-1825, in the Museum of Fine Arts, Boston.* 2 vols. Greenwich, CT: New York Graphic Society, 1972. 708p. LC 75-190547; ISBN 0-87846-064-0.

Vol. 1 covers the silver work from Massachusetts only and lists the craftsmen chronologically. Vol. 2 continues Massachusetts and discusses the silversmiths of New Hampshire, Connecticut, Rhode Island, New York, and Philadelphia. There is an index.

2456.   De Kolb, Eric. *Ashanti Goldweights and Senufo Bronzes.* New York: Gallery d'Hautbarr, 1969. 83p. LC 68-3925.

There are 477 goldweights, used by the Ashanti to measure gold dust and gold nuggets, drawn and described; in many cases, proverbs are appended. Also included are some symbolic designs with the interpretations that are still known among contemporary Ashanti.

2457.   Flynt, Henry N., and Martha Gandy Fales. *The Heritage Foundation Collection of Silver; With Biographical Sketches of New England Silversmiths, 1625-1825.* Old Deerfield, MA: The Heritage Foundation, 1968. 391p. LC 67-26102.

This catalog contains essays on silver making in six New England states. There are 118 objects from the collection pictured and discussed in a running text. Also included are biographical sketches of New England silversmiths and their marks, arranged alphabetically by artisan. There is an index and a long bibliography.

2458.   Plass, Margaret Webster. *African Miniatures: Goldweights of the Ashanti.* New York: Praeger, 1967. 26p. LC 67-29603.

This exhibit of Ashanti goldweights was part of a larger exhibition, "Metals of Africa," held at the University of Pennsylvania Museum (Philadelphia) in 1964. There are 166 goldweights, representing humans, mammals, insects, and flora--all pictured.

TECHNOLOGY
Textiles

Although the word **textile** comes from the Latin, *texere*: to weave, the *MLA International Bibliography* considers **weaving** a folk craft and covers **textiles** as part of the section on Technology. Included here therefore are titles about textiles or textile arts or fabrics.

An excellent introduction to textiles as a craft is Leslie J. Clarke's *The Craftsman in Textiles* (New York: Praeger, 1968), a survey of the following textile crafts: dyeing and finishing, carpets, embroidery, lace, and needlework, with a discussion of tools, raw materials, methods, and design of each one; there is also a chapter on the craftsman in society. Also relevant is *Ethnographic Textiles of the Western Hemisphere; A Roundtable on Museum Textiles, 1976 Proceedings,* edited by Irene Emery and Patricia Fiske (Washington, DC: The Textile Museum, 1977), which covers ethnographic textiles of the western hemisphere, South America, Central America and Mexico, the American southwest, and other parts of North America with one section of papers on the European influences on western hemisphere ethnographic textiles. Ethel Lewis' *The Romance of Textiles: The Story of Design in Weaving* (New York: Macmillan, 1953 [1937]) is an early but still viable historical overview and survey of fabrics and textiles with sections on American weaves and patterns and on "contemporary" fabrics and fibers. Two newer histories of textiles are Judith R. Weissman's and Wendy Lavitt's *Labors of Love: America's Textiles and Needlework, 1650-1930* (New York: Knopf, 1981) and *The Illustrated History of Textiles,* edited by Madeleine Ginsburg (New York: Portland House, 1991), a history and collector's guide to carpets, embroidery, knitting, lace, and tapestries.

There is an abundance of survey material on textiles from many countries. African textiles are covered in Esther Warner Dendel's *African Fabric Crafts: Sources of American Design and Technique* (New York: Taplinger, 1974), an overview of traditional and contemporary African crafts--appliqué and embroidery work, African looping, braiding, plaiting, etc. Joanne Bubolz Eicher studied *Nigerian Handicrafted Textiles* (Ile-Ife [Nigeria]: University of Ife Press, 1976) and discusses the general setting and the fibers, fabrics, dyes, etc., as well as the woven textile and dyed textile crafts and products. Asian textiles are often studied. R.B. Serjeant covered *Islamic Textiles* (Beirut: Librairie du Liban, 1972) and includes a history and technical discussion of the textiles of Syria, Egypt, Sicily, Armenia, etc. Marie Jeanne Adams studied Indonesian textiles, in her *System and Meaning in East Sumba Textile Design; A Study in Traditional Indonesian Art* (New Haven, CT: Yale University, Southeast Asia Studies, 1969) as did Warda Warming and Michael Gaworski in their *The World of Indonesian Textiles* (Tokyo: Kodansha International, 1981), dealing with warp ikat, weaving and woven patterns, and batik.

Also useful is Garrett and Bronwen Solyom's *Textiles of the Indonesian Archipelago* (Honolulu: University of Hawaii Press, 1973). (See also no. 2487.) Indonesian textiles were also studied by John R. and Robyn Maxwell in their *Textiles of Indonesia* (Victoria: Indonesia Art Society in Association with the National Gallery of Victoria, 1976). Japanese textiles have been considered in Seiroku Noma's *Japanese Costume and Textile Arts* (New York: Weatherhill, 1974). Cyril Bunt covered *Persian Fabrics* (Leigh-on-Sea [ENG]: F. Lewis, 1963) and Ludmila Kybalová studied *Coptic Textiles* (London: Hamlyn, 1967), while W.F. Volbach and Ernst Kuehnel considered *Late Antique Coptic and Islamic Textiles of Egypt* (New York: E. Weyhe, 1927). Indian textiles were surveyed by Rustam J. Mehta in *Masterpieces of Indian Textiles: Hand spun--Hand woven-- Traditional* (Bombay: D.B. Taraporevala, 1970), a study of India's traditional textile crafts and fabrics: silks and brocades, cotton, Indian shawls, embroidery, saris, and Indian rugs and carpets.

Textile Folk Art, by Antonia Vaclavik and Jaroslav Orel (London: Spring Books, 1955), is concerned with the textiles of Czechoslovakia and other Eastern European countries. Magda Gabor looked at *Hungarian Textiles* (Leigh-on-Sea [ENG]: F. Lewis, 1961) and Nevana Geliazkova studied *Bulgarian Textiles* (Leigh-on-Sea [ENG]: F. Lewis, 1958).

There have been a great many surveys of early American textiles: Catherine Fennelly's *Textiles in New England, 1790-1840* (Sturbridge, MA: Old Sturbridge Village, 1961) and Nancy Dick Bogdonoff's *Handwoven Textiles of Early New England: The Legacies of a Rural People, 1640-1880* (Harrisburg, PA: Stackpole Books, 1975) are good examples. Both cover bedding--coverlets and bedticking material--table linens, furniture accessories, and curtains. And Frances Little's *Early American Textiles* (New York: Century, 1931) is an early study of silk, spun and woven work, embroidery, and cotton printing. There have been several regional studies of American textile arts, such as Nancy Fox's *Pueblo Weaving and Textile Arts* (Santa Fe: Museum of New Mexico Press, 1978) and Beverly Gordon's *Shaker Textile Arts* (Hanover, NH: University of New England in cooperation with the Merrimack Valley Textile Museum and Shaker Community, 1980) which discusses production of textiles, household textiles, clothing and personal accessories, and fancywork. See also Montgomery below (no. 2471). There are several studies of Canadian textiles among which is Gerald L.

Pocius' *Textile Traditions of Eastern Newfoundland* (Ottawa: National Museums of Canada, 1979). And finally, Central and South American textiles are covered in Raoul d'Harcourt's *Textiles of Ancient Peru and Their Techniques* (Seattle: University of Washington Press, 1974 [1962]) and Alan R. Sawyer's *Tiahuanaco Tapestry Design* (New York: Museum of Primitive Art, 1963).

> Note: the section on **Weaving** (nos. 2402-2427) should obviously be consulted, as there is great overlap between weaving and textiles.

Bibliographies--Textiles

2459.   Gordon, Beverly. *Domestic American Textiles: A Bibliographic Sourcebook*. Pittsburgh, PA: Center for the History of American Needlework, 1978. 217p. LC 78-108861.

This is an annotated bibliography of 574 books, periodical articles, and exhibition catalogs, covering all aspects of textiles, including, for example, quilts and coverlets. There is a listing of popular magazines and scholarly periodicals that deal with Gordon's definition of textiles and an index.

2460.   Green, Judith Strupp, and Linda L. Fisk. "A Bibliography of Mexican Ethnographic Fabrics: Textiles and Costume," in *Ethnographic Textiles of the Western Hemisphere*; Irene Emory Roundtable on Museum Textiles, 1976 Proceedings, eds. Irene Emery and Patricia Fiske. pp. 172-237. Washington, DC: The Textile Museum, 1977. 535p. LC 77-81899.

This is a listing of general works, followed by works arranged geographically by culture area. Unfortunately, there is no index.

2461.   Pang, Hilda Delgado. "A Preliminary Bibliography on Guatemalan Ethnographic Textiles," in *Ethnographic Textiles of the Western Hemisphere*; Irene Emory Roundtable on Museum

Textiles, 1976 Proceedings, eds., Irene Emery and Patricia Fiske. pp. 94-105. Washington, DC: The Textile Museum, 1977. 535p. LC 77-81899.

This is an unannotated listing, like no. 2460, of articles and books on Guatemalan textiles and weaving and Central American crafts and customs.

2462.   Ralston, Valerie H. *Textile Reference Sources: A Selective Bibliography.* Storrs: University of Connecticut Library, 1973. 47p. LC 75-621194. (Reference bibliography series, 1)

This bibliography includes guides to the literature (general references, encyclopedias, indexes, and abstracts), dictionaries, and a selected bibliography of general works on textiles. There is a subject index.

2463.   Seiler-Baldinger, Annemarie. "General Introduction to Literature on South American Ethnographic Textiles Since 1950," in *Ethnographic Textiles of the Western Hemisphere; Irene Emory Roundtable on Museum Textiles, 1976 Proceedings,* eds. Irene Emery and Patricia Fiske. pp. 17-35. Washington, DC: The Textile Museum, 1977. 535p. LC 77-81899.

This is another listing (see nos. 2460 and 2461) of books and articles about all aspects of South American textiles, arranged chronologically.

2464.   Wright, Helena E. *The Merrimack Valley Textile Museum: A Guide to the Manuscript Collections.* New York: Garland, 1983. 378p. LC 82-49169; ISBN 0-8240-9172-8. (Garland reference library of the humanities; v. 395)

Included are books, articles, inventories, legal papers, tax valuations, wills, records, time and payroll books, lists of tenants, and lists of materials, etc., dealing with the organization and administration of the textile business, information on sales, on machinery, production, labor, associations, cotton mills, woolen mills, flax, jute and silk mills, raw material dealers, dyeing and finishing, water power, researchers, and inventors, etc. Indexed.

Classification--Textiles

2465. Emery, Irene. *The Primary Structures of Fabrics: An Illustrated Classification.* Washington, DC: Textile Museum, 1966. 339p. LC 65-19743.

Part I deals with components of fabrics, structures of material, and content and structural make-up. Part II is the classification of felted fibers and interwoven fibers. Part III covers structures and accessories to fabrics: accessory stitches, fabrics, objects. There are many illustrations throughout with a bibliography for each section and an explanation of terms. The general bibliography (pp. 260-308) is quite comprehensive.

2466. Reath, Nancy Andrews, and Eleanor B. Sachs. *Persian Textiles and Their Technique from the Sixth to the Eighteenth Centuries, Including a System for General Textile Classification.* New Haven, CT: Yale University for the Pennsylvania Museum of Art; London: Oxford University Press, 1937. 133p. LC 37-14436.

Not seen.

Dictionaries and Encyclopedias--Textiles

2467. Burnham, Dorothy K. *Warp & Weft: A Dictionary of Textile Terms.* New York: Scribner's, 1981 [1976, Toronto: R.O.M., as *Warp & Weft: A Textile Terminology*]. 216p. LC 81-9350; ISBN 0-684-17332-8.

This work was "adapted and expanded" from *The Vocabulary of Technical Terms* (Lyons: Centre d'Etudes des Textiles Anciens, 1964) and includes **textile** terms only, "textile" being defined by Burnham in its narrowest sense as "woven fabric." The current work is a tidy dictionary of patterns (e.g., **basket-weave**), descriptive terms (e.g., **braided**), and types of weaves (e.g., **band weaving**). Words are given in French, German, Italian, Portuguese, Spanish, and Swedish, with a brief definition and lots of cross referencing. Appendix material includes a table of weaves, a list of specialized French terms, notes, and a long bibliography. There is unfortunately no index.

2468. *Encyclopedia of Textiles.* By the editors of *American Fabrics and Fashions Magazine.* 3rd ed. Englewood Cliffs, NJ: Prentice-Hall, 1980 [1959]. 636p. LC 79-26497; ISBN 0-13-276576-4.

Subtitled: "An Illustrated and Authoritative Source Book on Textiles. Presenting a Complete and Practical Coverage of the Entire Field--Its History and Origins, Its Art and Design, Its Natural Man-made Fibers, Its Manufacturing and Finishing Processes, Colors, and Dyes, Textile Printing, Specialty End Uses, and a Dictionary of Text Terms." The text is divided into eight sections: the textile fibers: man-made, cotton, wool, specialty fiber, silk, etc.; history and origins; textile design (including collections across the U.S.): textiles in the Americas, especially Peruvian and North American textiles; manufacturing processes: spinning, weaving, knitting, lace-making, ribbon-making, felts and non-woven fabrics; fabric finishing: processes, colors and dyes and their processes; printing textiles, and a list of U.S. textile schools; specialty uses of textiles: curtains and drapes, sheets and quilts, rugs and carpets, industrial fabrics; and textile definitions: a 90-page dictionary of textile terms. Index.

2469. Flemming, Ernst; trans. and ed. Renate Jaques. *Encyclopedia of Textiles; Decorative Fabrics from Antiquity to the Beginning of the 19th Century, Including the Far East and Peru.* New York: Praeger, 1958. 304p.

This is a translation of Flemming's *Das Textilwerk* [1927], "with revisions and new material." There is a 38-page introduction, which is a history of textile production from ancient Egypt to the nineteenth century, followed by many plates with some text material. Very hard to use as there is no index or order to the plates.

2470. Grayson, Martin, ed. *Encyclopedia of Textiles, Fibers, and Nonwoven Fabrics*. New York: John Wiley, 1984. 581p. LC 84-13213; ISBN 0-471-81461-X. (Encyclopedia reprint series)

Textiles are covered on pp. 459-498; nonwoven textiles on pp. 252-305. There are long articles on such topics as a survey of textiles and on finishing, which are fairly technical. There is a general index.

2471. Montgomery, Florence M. *Textiles in America, 1650-1870: A Dictionary Based on Original Documents: Prints and Paintings, Commercial Records, American Merchants' Papers, Shopkeepers' Advertisements, and Pattern Books with Original Swatches of Cloth*. New York: W.W. Norton, 1984. 412p. LC 83-25339; ISBN 0-393-01703-6. (A Winterthur Book)

A long (140-page) introduction covers furnishing practices in England and America, bed hangings, window curtains, upholstery, and textiles for the period room in America. The dictionary goes from adatais (an imported fine muslin or cotton) to zanella ("serge made with cotton warp and worsted fillings, used for linings and umbrella covers"). There is no index but the bibliography (pp. 379-412) is extensive.

2472. Wingate, Isabel B. *Fairchild's Dictionary of Textiles*. 6th ed. New York: Fairchild, 1979 [1915, 1920, 1924, 1959, 1967]. 691p. LC 78-73964; ISBN 0-87005-198-9.

This is a dictionary of terms intended to help the user identify fiber-based products. The entries are brief, covering all aspects of textiles and fibers and their products.

2473.   Bach, Pieter, ed. *Textile, Costume, and Doll Collections, in the United States and Canada*. Lopez, WA: R.L. Shep, 1981. 69p. LC 81-9022; ISBN 0-914046-01-2 (p).

Divided into three sections, textiles, costumes, and dolls are covered separately; each includes an alphabetical list of collections, arranged by state, with name, city, address given. Canada follows U.S. holdings and is arranged alphabetically by province. Not indexed.

2474.   Lubell, Cecil, ed. *Textile Collections of the World*. 3 vols. New York: Van Nostrand Reinhold, 1976, 1977. Vol. 1: LC 75-30412; ISBN 0-442-24896-2 (336p.); Vol. 2: LC 74-31999; ISBN 0-442-24895-4 (240p.); Vol. 3: LC 77-1628; ISBN 0-442-24894-6 (238p.).

Vol. 1: United States and Canada; divided into U.S. and Canadian collections, arranged alphabetically by city, state, or city and province. Lots of information is given, including addresses of collections, phone numbers, curators' names, holdings, etc. Also includes an essay on U.S. and Canadian textile traditions and fabrics of the North American Indians. Includes an index.
Vol. 2: United Kingdom and Ireland. Guide to 42 textile collections, listed alphabetically by city with size of each and an evaluation of each one's major holdings. There is an essay on textile design evolution in Great Britain, a color section, and a textile design index.
Vol. 3: France. Includes an overview of French textiles and French textile collections. Museum and private collections are given with information as above. It concludes with an essay on textile traditions of France and an index.

Handbook--Textiles

2475.   Birrell, Verla. *The Textile Arts, A Handbook of Fabric Structure and Design Processes: Ancient and Modern Weaving, Braiding,*

Printing, and Other Textile Techniques. New York: Harper, 1959. 514p. LC 58-8363.

Part I covers **weaving**: history, textile fibers and yarns and their uses, simple looms; belt looms and belt weaves, rug looms and rug-making techniques, mechanically-operated looms, basic weaves. Part II covers **non-weaving structural processes**: non-woven fabrics and embroidery and needlework; and Part III covers **nonstructural ornamentation**: dyes and dyeing processes, textile painting processes, and textile stamping and printing processes. There is also a glossary, an index, and references.

Exhibition Catalogs and Guides to Collections--Textiles

2476. Blomberg, Nancy J. *Navajo Textiles: The William Randolph Hearst Collection.* Tucson, AZ: University of Arizona Press, 1988. 257p. LC 88-4794; ISBN 0-8165-1078-4.

In three parts: "from blanket to rug" (historical development of Navajo textiles); "from weaver to consumer to weaver" (the marketing of raw textiles), and "from collector to curator," which is the catalog of 270 items: *serapes,* ponchos, chief-style blankets, women's garments, children's and saddle blankets, banded blankets, pictorials, eyedazzlers, transitional blankets and rugs, and rugs. Each item is pictured, almost all in full color, dated, the size of the piece is given along with a fiber count, and a description of the color, yarn used, ply and spin of both warp and weft, a note on the selvage quality, a provenance, and a critical note. An appendix includes material on the economical history of the Hearst collection and a list of the complete Hearst collection by accession number. There is a bibliography and an index. See also Jon Erickson's *Navajo Textiles from the Read Mullan Collection* (Phoenix, AZ: The Heard Museum, 1976).

2477. *Catalogue of the Exhibition of Japanese Country Textiles.* Toronto: Royal Ontario Museum, Governors of the University of Toronto, 1965. 40p.

There is an introductory essay by Barbara Stephen on Japanese folk art with some information on equipment and fibers. The catalog is divided into sections: striped and banded materials (23 items), **Kasuri** and **Egasuri** (50 items), stencilled and painted cottons (42 items), and clothing (18 items).

2478.   Cavallo, Adolph S. *Textiles, Isabella Stewart Gardner Museum.* Boston, MA: Published by the Trustees, 1986. 223p. LC 85-518363; ISBN 0-914660-09-8 (c); 0-914660-10-1 (p).

Much of this collection would be considered "high art" (e.g., tapestries, lace, etc.), however, some of the woven textiles and Eastern textiles (woven, embroidered, and printed) could be considered traditional. In all 199 pieces are described and pictured, and there is a checklist at the end.

2479.   Gehret, Ellen J., and Alan G. Keyser. *The Homespun Textile Tradition of the Pennsylvania Germans.* Harrisburg: Pennsylvania Historical and Museum Commission, 1976. 62p. LC 75-31049.

This is "an exhibition of the work of spinners, weavers and dyers of the Pennsylvania Museum of Landis Valley." A short introduction precedes this catalog with 98 black-and-white plates. A bibliography is included.

2480.   Gilfoy, Peggy Stoltz. *Fabrics in Celebration from the Collection.* Indianapolis: Indianapolis Museum of Art, 1983. 391p. LC 82-84075; ISBN 0-936260-02-2 (c); 0-936260-10-6 (p).

The catalog includes information about this extensive collection, its history, conservation practices, and notes on technical analysis of the textiles. The catalog itself lists 168 items from Indonesia, India, China, Japan, Eastern Islam, Western Islam, Europe and America, and Africa. Each item is described with materials used, techniques used, and thread count.

2481.　Katzenberg, Dena S. *"And Eagles Sweep Across the Sky": Indian Textiles of the North American West.* Baltimore, MD: Baltimore Museum of Art, 1977. 151p. LC 77-83121.

The exhibit's thrust was the textiles from the southwestern portion of the country. The exhibition pieces are presented as examples of the textual material, which is concerned with both the history of the Indians and their textile crafts and the aesthetics of the work. The arrangement is by tribe of Indians and/or location. There is a select bibliography but no index.

2482.　Mera, H.P., and Joe Ben Wheat. *The Alfred I. Barton Collection of Southwestern Textiles.* Rev. ed. Coral Gables, FL: Lowe Art Museum and University of Miami, 1978 [1949]. 104p.

The catalog of this exhibit of Pueblo, Navajo, and Rio Grande textiles includes for each entry an accession number, title, date, and a description, including the size, warp and weft count, color, and dye and materials. Three essays on the history, uses, and techniques of Pueblo, Navajo, and Rio Grande textiles precede the catalog, and there is a bibliography.

2483.　Museum of Contemporary Art. *Contemporary African Fabrics: An Exhibition of Contemporary African Fabrics from the Girard Foundation.* Chicago, IL: Museum of Contemporary Art, 1975. 16p.

Introduction explains how fabrics are important aspects of African culture. The pieces of fabric come from all parts of Africa. A few are pictured in black and white.

2484.　Rowe, Ann Pollard. *A Century of Change in Guatemalan Textiles.* New York: Center for Inter-American Relations, 1981. 151p. LC 81-70077; ISBN 0-295-95908-8 (p).

The introduction covers historical background, textile history, modern costume repertory, the loom, descriptive approaches, and changes. Various villages and their textiles are described, and there is a three-page bibliography on Guatemalan art, craft, and textiles.

2485. Ryan, Judith. *Tribal and Traditional Textiles.* Melbourne: National Gallery of Victoria, 1978. 51p. LC 80-480651; ISBN 0-7241-0047-4.

This is a catalog of a traveling exhibit. The introduction covers tribal and traditional textiles. The arrangement of the textiles is by country--China, Japan, Indonesia, Central Asia, Afghanistan, Kuristan, Pakistan, Turkey, and Peru, and the work of the Uzbeck and the Navajo Indian as well as European folk textiles, folk embroidery, and needlework from the Greek Islands and Italy. There are 90 pieces of all types of textiles pictured and described. Bibliography.

2486. Santa Fe. New Mexico. Museum of International Folk Art. *Spanish Textile Tradition of New Mexico and Colorado.* Santa Fe: University of New Mexico Press, 1979. 264p. LC 78-68065; ISBN 0-89013-112-0 (c); 0-89013-113-9 (p). (Series in southwestern culture)

This was part of a project to gather data on Spanish woven materials in museums throughout the U.S. In 1969, a list of museum holdings, of 1,100 textile pieces from 36 collections, was completed. In 1975, the staff of the Museum of International Folk Art analyzed and recorded 700 textiles and analyzed in addition 1,000 Rio Grande blankets, 500 Mexican textiles, and 250 of other types. The introduction to this work describes the area from which the weaving came and gives a brief history of Spanish textile production in the southwest. The catalog consists of a variety of the recorded and analyzed textiles: bands and stripes, Mexican serapes, Saltillo designs, weft Ikat weavings, and embroidered work with many black-and-white and full-color plates, each with extensive notes. There is also a list of the public collections and brief essays on treadle loom fabric structure, dyes, etc., as well as a glossary, index, and a substantial bibliography.

1047

2487.   Solyom, Bronwen, and Garrett Solyom. *Fabric Traditions of Indonesia*. Pullman, WA: Washington State University Press, for the Museum of Art, 1984. 60p. LC 84-22091; ISBN 0-87422-019-X.

The catalog covers bark-cloth, beaded and shell work, warp stripes and warp Ikat, exotic silks, and batiks, and there is a selection of ceremonial shirts and objects pictured and described throughout this lovely catalog. Bibliography.

2488.   Start, Laura Emily. *The McDougall Collection of Indian Textiles from Guatemala and Mexico*. Oxford; Oxford University Press, 1948. LC 50-148. 114p.+16p. plates. (Occasional papers on technology, 2)

Describes a collection found at Pitt Rivers Museum, Oxford University. Describes separately Guatemalan and Mexican textiles. Ms. Start has cataloged many collections of ethnic textiles in England, one example of which is *Burmese Textiles from the Shan and Cachin Districts* (Halifax [ENG]: F. King for the Bankfield Museum, 1917).

2489.   Van Stan, Ina. *The Fabrics of Peru*. Leigh-on-Sea [ENG]: F. Lewis, 1966. 16p. LC 67-79078. (World's heritage of woven fabrics)

Catalogs and describes 60 pieces of Peruvian fabrics.

2490.   Weibel, Adèle Coulin. *Two Thousand Years of Textiles; The Figured Textiles of Europe and the Near East*. New York: Hacker Art Books, 1972 [1952, Detroit Institute of Art]. 169p.+ 331 plates. LC 77-143367; ISBN 0-87817-086-3.

Includes introduction, catalog, and plates.

2491.   Wheeler, Monroe, ed. *Textiles and Ornaments of India: A Selection of Designs*. New York: Museum of Modern Art, 1956. 95p. LC 56-8578; ISBN 0-4050-1564-X.

There are introductory essays on the role of Indian fabrics in Indian life and on Indian textiles in historical perspective. Also included are 60 pages of plates with descriptions and a full bibliography.

MATERIAL CULTURE
Folk Museums and Living Historical Farms

This section includes works about **folk museums, artifact collections,** and **living historical farms** or **museums.** For background reading, start out with Warren Roberts' "Folk Architecture in Context: The Folk Museum" (*Pioneer America Society Proceedings* 1 [1973]), J. Geraint Jenkins' "The Use of Artifacts and Folk Art in the Folk Museum," in *Folklore and Folklife*, edited by Richard M. Dorson (pp. 497-516), Willard B. Moore's "Folklore Research and Museums" (pp. 402-410), in the *Handbook of American Folklore*, edited by Richard M. Dorson, and from the same book, Ormond H. Loomis' "Organizing a Folklore Museum" (pp. 499-506). Another article by Willard B. Moore, "Folklife Museums: Resource Sites for Teaching" (*Indiana English Journal* 11 [Winter, 1976-77]: 3-10) traces the history of folk museums from the founding of the first one in Sweden in 1891 to the mid-twentieth century. Moore's article calls for the use of these "total environments" as resource sites for all levels of education.

Folklife and Museums: Selected Readings (Nashville, TN: American Association for State and Local History, 1987), edited by Patricia Hall and Charlie Seemann, includes 14 articles and a bibliography (no. 2496) on this subject. Edward P. Alexander's *Museums in Motion: An Introduction to the History and Functions of Museums* (Nashville, TN: AASLH, 1979) describes open-air museums in the section on the history of the museum. Howard Wight Marshall's "Folklife and the Rise of American Folk Museums" (*Journal of American Folklore* 90 [1977]: 391-413) is a useful overview that discusses this "conscious new movement and points out the usefulness of these museums in folk life research, public education and recreation, and the selected preservation of the built environment" (p.391) and relates American living museums to the European ones. Marshall also relates material culture to the museum, in "Material Culture and the Museum," in *Association for Living Historical Farms and Agricultural Museums Annual* (v. 3 [1977]: 35-38). George Stocking, Jr., edited *Objects and Others: Essays on Museums and Material Culture* (Madison: University of Wisconsin Press, 1985), scholarly essays primarily on ethnological collections. Linda Place's "The Object as Subject: The Role of Museums and Material Culture Collections in American Studies" (*American Quarterly* 26 [1974]: 281-294) discusses the use of the museum for material culture research and includes a bibliography on the museum and the university.

Jay Anderson's *Time Machines: The World of Living History* (Nashville, TN: American Association of State and Local History, 1984) is a good introduction to the concept of living history museums. Citing the historical museum movement as a "particular way in which people have chosen to slip away from the modern world," Anderson notes three groups of "time travellers": 1) those who use simulation as a mode of interpreting reality (in living museums); 2) those who use simulation as a research tool (at architectural and historical sites); and 3) history buffs who like to recreate time past. Specific studies of living historical farms (sometimes called open-air museums) include Thomas Morain's "In the American Grain: The Popularity of Living History Farms" (*Journal of American Culture* 2 [1979]: 550-577), in which Morain says that in 1975, the Association for Living Historical Farms and Agricultural Museums (based at the Smithsonian) identified 32 operating historical sites. They appeal, says Morain, "to a public who vaguely realize that individuals have lost not only control of the technology which provides the essentials of life but also their faith in that technology to insure that abundance is the ultimate destiny of everyone. Behind the current popularity of the farms may be the quiet desperation of those who have begun to suspect that the world of their grandchildren may focus less on abundance and more on survival." (p. 556) John T. Schlebecker, who has written widely on living historical museums, describes them and their appeal in *Living Historical Farms: A Walk into the Past* (Smithsonian Institution, 1968; reproduced in *Early American Life* 2 [1971]: 8-31, 54-59), and in *The Past in Action: Living Historical Farms* (Washington, DC: Smithsonian

Institution, 1967). Another study of the function of this type of museum is David Percy's *Living Historical Farms, The Working Museum* (Accokeek, MD: The Accokeek Foundation, 1981).

A good overview of the relationship between anthropology and museums is Cornelius Osgood's *Anthropology in Museums of the* [sic] *Canada and [the] United States* (Milwaukee, WI: Milwaukee Public Museum, 1979), which talks about the history, functions, organization and administration of the museum as well as museum buildings, services, exhibitions, collections, cataloging practices, preservation, and conservation. There is a list of museums on pp. 7 and 8.

And finally, Ormond H. Loomis' *Cultural Conservation: The Protection of Cultural Heritage in the United States* (a study by the American Folklife Center, Library of Congress, carried out in cooperation with the National Park Service, 1983) is a report to the 96th Congress, which commissioned a "report...on preserving and conserving the intangible elements of our cultural heritage such as arts, skills, folklife, and folkways." The report gives recommendations for federal protection of cultural heritage in the U.S., includes principles and concepts of cultural conservation and a survey of existing state and federal efforts and agencies. Appendixes include a review of significant legislation, activities, events relative to cultural conservation in the U.S. and an excellent bibliography (pp. 109-123). A somewhat similar later work is *The Conservation of Culture: Folklorists and the Public Sector* (Lexington: University Press of Kentucky, 1988), edited by Burt Feintuch, papers from a conference on "Folklife and the Public Sector: Assessment and Prognosis," held in 1985, which are about public sector programs rather than museum conservation programs.

Bibliographies--Folk Museums and Museum Work

2492.   de Borhegyi, Stephan Francis, et al. *A Bibliography of Museums and Museum Work, 1900-1960.* Milwaukee, WI: Milwaukee Public Museum, 1960. 72p. Supplemented in 1961. 102p. LC 70-288295. (Milwaukee Public Museum publications in museology, 11)

Books and articles are divided into several subject areas: general works, training, exhibits, museum categories, foreign museums, and **folk and regional museums**, which contains 18 articles and books.

2493. Loomis, Ormond. "Sources on Folk Museums and Living Historical Farms." *Folklore Forum.* 1977. 59p. LC 80-126830. (Bibliographical and special series, 16)

Books and articles, briefly annotated, are listed within the following categories: the field (perspective, identity, activity); methods and techniques (administration, conservation and restoration, research and collation, cataloging and archiving, interpretations, exhibition education programs); descriptive works (Europe--surveys, then by country, North America, Africa, Asia and Oceania, South America); bibliographies; and indexes. There are separate indexes of authors and museums.

2494. Rath, Frederick L., Jr., and Merrilyn Rogers O'Connell. *Guide to Historic Preservation, Historical Agencies, and Museum Practices: A Selective Bibliography.* Cooperstown: New York State Historical Association, 1970. 369p. LC 76-138977.

This includes works on general reference, preservation principals and practices, administration, the study and care of the collection (includes documentation of collections by type), and research methods and sources. There is some material on folk museum work. Also has sources for folk studies. There is an index.

2495. Rath, Frederick L., Jr., and Merrilyn Rogers O'Connell, eds. *A Bibliography on Historical Organization Practices.* 6 vols. Nashville, TN: American Association for State and Local History, 1975-1984.

This is a series of works, edited by Rath and O'Connell: Vol. 1: *Historical Preservation*, 1975, by Rath and McConnell; Vol. 2: *Care and Conservation of Collections*, 1977, by R.S. Reese; Vol. 3: *Interpretation of Collections*; Vol. 4: *Documentation of Collections*, 1979, by R.S.

Reese; Vol. 5: *Administration of Collections*; and Vol. 6: *Research*, 1984, by Rath and McConnell.

2496.   Seemann, Charles, and Patricia Hall. " Folklife and Museums: A Selected Bibliography," in *Folklife and Museums: Selected Readings*, ed. Patricia Hall and Charlie Seemann. Nashville, TN: American Association for State and Local History, 1987. pp. 183-190.

The purpose of this unannotated bibliography is "to supply readers and students with a comprehensive selection of sources for further reading about folklife and museums."

Catalogs--Folk Museum Publications

Note: Many anthropological and folk museums publish occasional papers, monographs, or annuals. As an example, Vol. 1 of *The Occasional Papers of the Rhodes-Livingston Museum* (printed by Manchester University on behalf of the Institute for African Studies, 1974) has articles on African material culture, dances, music, rites and ceremonies, and folk medicine.

2497.   Wasserman, Paul, and Esther Herman, eds. *Catalog of Museum Publications & Media: A Directory and Index of Publications and Audiovisuals Available from U.S. and Canadian Institutions.* 2nd ed. Detroit, MI: Gale Research, 1980 [1973]. 1,044p. LC 79-22633; ISBN 0-8103-0388-4.

Lists publications by museum, arranged alphabetically. Gives address and phone number and lists books, booklets and monographs, catalogs, pamphlets, leaflets, portfolios, videotape programs, films, facsimiles, slides, etc. There is a title and key word index, periodicals index, subject index, and geographic index. Complemented by no. 2498.

2498.   World Museum Publications. *A Directory of Art and Cultural Museums, Their Publications and Audio-Visual Materials*. New York: Bowker, 1982. 711p. LC 82-640913; ISBN 0-8352-1444-3.

This is similar to Wasserman's and Herman's tome (no. 2497) but is international in scope. The work lists museum publications by institution and includes a geographical guide to museums, arranged by country, subdivided by museums and listed alphabetically within that. There is an author index to periodical articles, a title index to other publications, a title index to A-V material, and a key to publishers and distributors.

Source Books and Resources--Folklife Museums

2499.   Anderson, Jay. *The Living History Sourcebook*. Nashville, TN: American Association for State and Local History, 1985. 469p. LC 85-19945; ISBN 0-910050-75-9 (p).

Includes museums, events, books, articles, magazines, films, games, etc.

Classification and Cataloging--Folk Museum Collections

2500.   Chenhall, Robert G. *Museum Cataloging in the Computer Age*. Nashville, TN: American Association for State and Local History, 1975. 261p. LC 74-16439; ISBN 0-910050-12-0.

Covers computers and their use in museum documentation and collection, records management, and creating the museum catalog. Lists computer networks. Outdated now.

2501.   Chenhall, Robert G. *Nomenclature for Museum Cataloging: A System for Classifying Man-Made Objects*. Nashville, TN: American Association for State and Local History, 1978. 512p. LC 77-20097; ISBN 0-910050-30-9.

Chenhall creates a lexicon based on the assumption that "Every man-made object was originally created to fulfill some function or purpose" and "that original function is the only common denominator that is present in all of the artifacts of man." Categories are defined: 1) structure, 2) building-furnishings, 3) personal artifacts, 4) tools and equipment, 5) communication artifacts, 6) transportation artifacts, 7) art objects, 8) recreational artifacts, 9) societal artifacts, 10) packages and containers, and 11) unclassified artifacts. The bulk of the book consists of a hierarchical listing of major artifacts categories, classification terms, and object names within the 11 categories listed above. There is an alphabetical listing of object names and a bibliography and index.

2502. Higgs, J.W.Y. *Folk Life Collection and Classification: Handbook for Museum Curators*. Part C: Permanent Collections, Archeology & Ethnology, Section 6. London: Museums Association, 1963. 58p. LC 65-82566.

Higgs firmly believes that "folk life, in as far as it has an accepted place in a museum classification, is properly a subdivision of ethnography." Although this includes the classification scheme used by the Museum of English Rural Life, this work is highly theoretical.

Handbooks--Folk Museum and Living Farm Administration

Note: See also no. 2502.

2503. Mukherji, Shyam Chand. *Folklore Museum*. Calcutta: Indian Publications, 1969. 56p. LC 72-902681. (Indian publications folklore series, 14)

The bulk of this work is a practical manual on folk museum services, on preservation and conservation practices, and on classification systems. Talks specifically about museum material and data collections, museum buildings, displays, documentation, organization, and general administrative strategies. There is a brief index and a 62-item bibliography.

2504.   Schlebecker, John T., and Gale E. Peterson, *Living Historical Farms Handbook*. Washington, DC: Smithsonian Institution Press, 1972. 91p. LC 72-601475. (Smithsonian studies in history and technology, 16)

Schlebecker defines living historical farms as those in which "men farm as they once did during some specific time in the past." The information in this handbook, he says, will be useful in getting people started in creating these museums or for keeping them going. Included is a chronology of the living historical farm movement with specific information on starting a living historical farm, on capital and overhead and on income as well as a state directory of historical farms and museums. The Lincoln Boyhood Memorial, Upper Canada Village, Old Sturbridge Village and the Farmers' Museum, Cooperstown, are described. There is also a directory of persons interested in living historical farms (now out of date) and an index.

Directories--Museums and Living Farms-General
Worldwide/International

2505.   Hudson, Kenneth, and Ann Nicholls. *The Directory of Museums & Living Displays*. 3rd ed. New York: Stockton Press, 1985 [1975,1981]. 1,047p. LC 85-9967; ISBN 0-94-3818-17-6.

Museums and living displays are arranged alphabetically by country, then by state or province, and in the U.S., by city. Given is basic information at the heading of each country: GNP per capita (in U.S. dollars), population, number of museums, and a basic introduction. For each museum, full address is given and a sentence about the holdings. There is no subject index which will make it difficult to look up a particular type of museum.

2506.   Jackson, Virginia, editor-in-chief. *Art Museums of the World*. 2 vols. New York: Greenwood, 1987. 1,681p. LC 85-5578; ISBN 0-313-21322-4 (set).

This is really a book of essays, individually authored, concerning the museums in different countries. Each essay has an individual bibliography. Vol. 2 contains a general bibliography and an index that serves as a subject guide. There are several folk collections listed, such as Dresden's Folk Art Museum.

2507. *Museums of the World.* 3rd rev. ed. New York and Munich: K.G. Saur, 1981. 623p. LC 81-198337; ISBN 3-598-10118-X. (Handbook of international documentation and information; v. 16)

Over 18,000 museums in over 150 countries are arranged by country, then city. Given are the address, type of museum, date of founding, and information on the basic collection. There is a name index (persons, places, collections) and a subject index with a huge entry for **folklore** by country as well as separate entries under **food, baskets,** etc.

The Americas
North America

2508. *American Art Directory, 1991-92.* 53nd ed. New York: Bowker, 1991. 782p. LC 99-1016; ISBN 0-8352-2896-7.

Lists museums and collections by state and province. Includes many indexes, especially a detailed subject index that will lead the user to many folk art collections--general (e.g., **folk art**) and specific (e.g., **furniture museums**).

2509. American Association of Museums and the Smithsonian Institution. *Official Museum Directory, United States, Canada, 1987.* Wilmette, IL: National Register Publishing Co., 1987. 1,120p. LC 79-144808; ISBN 0-87217-951-6. Supersedes *Museums Directory of the United States and Canada* (1961-1965).

The bulk of this work includes listings of institutions by state and alphabetical listings of museums but also includes a listing of institutional directors and department heads, and institutions by category. Includes also information on state humanities programs and committees, regional arts organizations. A subject index includes entries for archeological museums, arts and crafts museums, costume museums, folk art museums, furniture museums, historical houses and historical buildings, preservation projects, textile museums, etc. The listing for each museum includes location information, funding data, congressional district or governing authority, personnel, collections, activities, publications, etc.

2510. Bartis, Peter T. *Rhode Island Folklife Resources.* Washington, DC: Library of Congress, American Folklife Center, 1983. 567p. LC 82-600313.

This is an alphabetical listing of museums, societies, farms, historical homes, etc., that house traditional artifacts or share programs about Rhode Island folklife.

2511. Bartis, Peter T., et al., comps. *Folklife Resources in New Jersey.* Washington, DC: Library of Congress, American Folklife Center, 1985. 91p. LC 84-24158.

Identifies and locates archives, museums, farms, historical societies, etc., holding New Jersey folklife materials.

2512. Chase, Daryl, ed. *Selected Living Historical Farms, Villages, and Agricultural Museums in the United States and Canada.* Washington, DC: Association for Living Historical Farms and Agricultural Museums, Smithsonian Institution, 1973. 64p.

This details 32 living historical farms and villages, gives a history of each, the location, dates and hours it is open, if an admission fee is charged, and the name of a contact person. The arrangement is east to west (Massachusetts to Hawaii). There are lots of mainly black-and-white photos of the farms and villages.

2513.   Faison, Samson Lane. *The Art Museums of New England.* 2nd
ed. Boston, MA: David Godine, 1982 [1958]. 463p. LC 80-
83952; ISBN 0-8792-3372-9 (c); 0-8792-3373-7 (p).

The museums are arranged by state: Connecticut, Maine,
Massachusetts, New Hampshire, Rhode Island, and Vermont. There are
long descriptions of the museums and the collections, especially the
Shelburne Museum. Also included is a selected list of historical houses
and buildings, historical societies, and museums of local interest. There
is an index, but no separate entry for **folk-art,** though there are entries for
furniture, etc.

2514.   Fein, Cheri. *New York--Open to the Public: A Comprehensive
Guide to Museums, Collections, Exhibition Spaces, Historic
Houses, Botanical Gardens, and Zoos.* New: York: Stewart,
Tabori & Chang, 1982. 221p. LC 81-21468; ISBN 0-941434-
00-1.

This is an alphabetical listing of museums, farms, etc., with
descriptions of sites, times open, admission information, access (how to
get there), whether picture taking is allowed, and research facilities.
Indexed by boroughs and by category of museum. Wonderful photos by
Joseph Kugielski.

2515.   Folwell, Betsy, and Peggy Ann Ingalls. *Cultural Resources in
New York's North Country.* Blue Mountain Lake, NY: The
Adirondack Museum, 1980. 188p. LC 81-176164.

Museums are arranged by county, then alphabetically by
institution. The information given for each is the address, hours, a
description of the collection, state programs and services, any fees, and
then a statement of purpose. The index is helpful for the folklorist, as it
lists **African art, blacksmith shop/tools, folk art, Indian art,** etc.

2516.   Gutek, Gerald Lee, and Patricia Gutek. *Experiencing America's Past: A Travel Guide to Museum Villages.* New York: John Wiley, 1986. 263p. LC 85-29565; ISBN 0-471-82892-0.

Museum farms/villages are arranged into geographical regions: New England, mid-Atlantic, the south and southeast, and the midwest, etc., and then by state. Each entry lists facts about the village, identifies and categorizes it, gives address, phone, hours, dates open, and indicates restaurants, shops, etc., gives fee and indicates where to stay. An additional text describes the site and gives historical background. An appendix includes a brief history of the Shakers. There is an index.

2517.   Lestz, Gerry. *Farm Museum Directory: A Guide Through America's Farm Past.* 2nd ed. Lancaster, PA: Stemgas Publishing Co., 1988. 47p.

Arranged by state and Canadian province. Given is a description of each museum, its location, contact person, and hours and dates open.

2518.   Rath, Frederick L., ed. *New York State Historical Society and Its Museums; An Informal Guide.* Cooperstown: New York State Historical Society, 1975 [1968].

Covers mostly the buildings and museums of Cooperstown: the Farmers' Museum, Village Crossroads, Fenimore House, and the Carriage and Harness Museum.

2519.   Sherman, Lila. *Art Museums of America: A Guide to Collections in the United States and Canada.* New York: William Morrow, 1980. 416p. LC 79-20022; ISBN 0-688-03570-1.

Museums are arranged alphabetically by state or province, then by city. For each museum, the compiler gives the address, a history of it and a description of the museum's holdings. There is a section called "Where to find special collections" that lists by broad subject; large museums are listed under **general**, but there are also separate entries for **African art**, **Afro-American folk art**, etc. There is a general index also.

2520. Spaeth, Eloise. *American Art Museums: An Introduction to Looking*. 3rd ed. New York: Harper & Row, 1975. 483p. LC 74-1857; ISBN 0-06-013978-1.

Arranged by state, there are several museums of folk art and artifact museums included and discussed, including the Renwick, Winterthur, the Amon Carter Museum of Western Art, Shelburne Museum, the Abby Aldrich Rockefeller Folk Art Collection, etc. There are long descriptions of each. Unfortunately, there is no subject guide, though there is a general index.

2521. Truesdell, Bill. *Directory of Unique Museums*. Phoenix, AZ: Oryx, 1985. 165p. LC 85-42726; ISBN 0-89774-197-8.

Includes American and Canadian museums, arranged by state and province. A subject index has entries for **agriculture, arts and crafts, American Indians, coverlets and quilts, furniture making and woodworking, glass, toys, textiles,** etc. There is a museum name index.

2522. Wynar, Lubomyr, and Lois Buttlar. *Guide to Ethnic Museums, Libraries, and Archives in the United States*. Kent, OH: Program for the Study of Ethnic Publications, School of Library Science, Kent State University, 1978. 378p. LC 78-624077.

The arrangement is by ethnic group, **Afro-American, Albanian-American** to **Welsh-American, Yugoslavian-American.** Museums, archives, and art galleries are intermixed. For museums, the authors list for each: address/phone, personnel--director/ curator, founding date, admission fee, scope of collection, holdings, and comments. Needs updating. See also Wynar's and Pat Kleeburger's *Slavic Ethnic Libraries, Museums, and Archives in the United States* (no. 190) and Paul Wasserman's and Alice E. Kennington's *Ethnic Information Sources of the United States* (no. 188).

2523.	Zook, Nicholas. *Museum Villages, USA.* Barre, MA: Barre Publishers, 1971. 136p. LC 71-111102; ISBN 0-8271-7008-4 (c); 0-8271-7002-5 (p).

The arrangement is by type of museum: Indian villages, museums dealing with first settlements and Colonial towns, life in the new republic, the western migration, gold and silver rush, Lincoln and the Civil War, wild west, religion, iron, and lumber as well as farm villages. Included is a directory of museum villages arranged by state with one- or two-line descriptions. Many black-and-white photos are used for illustrations.

Canada

2524.	Canadian Museum Association. *Official Directory of Canadian Museums and Related Institutions: Répertoire Officiel des Musées Canadiens et Institutions Connexes.* Ottawa: Canadian Museums Assn., 1987 [1978]. 276p. ISBN 0-919106-21-8.

Museums are listed alphabetically and by institutional category within provinces and municipalities.

2525.	Selick, Marsha. *Directory of Ontario Museums, Art Galleries, Archives & Related Institutions.* Toronto: Ontario Museum Association, 1982. 53p. LC 83-1730; ISBN 0-920402-04-6.

There is an alphabetical listing of the galleries, museums, and archives as well as a subject listing and a geographical listing. The entries have addresses, phone numbers, directors' names, descriptions and an indication of the "governing authority" for each one. Includes historic and/or restored communities and villages.

Asia

2526.	Japanese National Committee. *Museums in Japan.* Tokyo: Maruzen, 1980. 279p. LC 81-160806.

There are 240 major museums arranged geographically from north to south, then arranged in alphabetical order, with location given, a brief history, and information on exhibits and collections, publications, administration, etc. The work indexes art museums but not by subject, though the table of contents indicates whether each a museum is a folklife museum.

2527. Roberts, Laurance P. *Roberts' Guide to Japanese Museums of Art and Archaeology*. Rev. and updated. Tokyo: Simul Press, 1987. 283p. ISBN 4-3775-0737-0.

Over 350 museums are arranged in alphabetical order, with addresses, telephone numbers, directors' names, fees, and a description of the collection with comments. There is a glossary as well as several indexes: Japanese name, branch museums and other collections, types of collections, prefectures. Many folk art and material culture museums are included.

Europe

Note: See the *Handbuch der Museen [Handbook of Museums]*. *Bundesrepublik Deutschland, Deutsche Demokratische Republik, Österreich, Schweiz, Liechtenstein* (Munich: K.G. Saur, 1981) for a comprehensive listing of over 5,000 museums in Europe. Others are available. See also Hobbie (no. 2534).

2528. Welle-Strand, Erling. *Museums in Norway*. Oslo: The Royal Ministry of Foreign Affairs, 1974. 48p. LC 75-310450; ISBN 82-7177-003-9.

Contains information about more than 320 museums of all kinds, including some living historical farms and folk museums. Museums are grouped according to subject field, then listed by county. Each annotation includes a brief description of the museum and gives address and phone. There is an index of museums, a map of Norway, and a map of each county with the appropriate towns marked.

2529.   Hudson, Kenneth, and Ann Nicholls. *The Cambridge Guide to the Museums of Britain and Ireland.* Cambridge and New York: Cambridge University Press, 1987. 435p. LC 86-34343; ISBN 0-521-32272-3.

This is an alphabetical listing by country and city. Gives name of each museum, phone and address, hours, director, a brief history, and a synopsis of the collection. There are many maps of the various countries and counties and one of London. Included is an index of museum names and a subject index, which includes entries for **folklore, folk art, folk life, basket-making,** etc.

2530.   *Museums and Galleries in Great Britain and Ireland. An Annual.* London: Index Publishers, 1955--. LC 58-46943.

Museums are listed in alphabetical order by city and town. There is a subject index and a complete alphabetical listing of all museums. Many listings are shown under **folk art.**

Directories to Different Types of Specific Collections--Folk Museums and Living Farms

Note: many guides to specific types of collections are included in various sections within this chapter.

2531.   Bach, Pieter, ed. *Textile, Costume, and Doll Collections, in the United States and Canada.* Lopez, WA: R.L. Shep, 1981. 69p. (See no. 2473 for full citation.)

Textile, costume, and doll collections are listed separately by state in the U.S. and by province in Canada.

2532.   Bartis, Peter T., comp. *Maritime Folklife Resources: A Directory and Index.* With the assistance of Mary Hufford. Washington,

DC: Library of Congress, American Folklife Center, 1980. 129p. (Publications of the American Folklife Center, 5)

This is an alphabetical listing of 172 museums, historical societies, archives, and libraries that hold maritime resources and artifacts.

2533. Ellsworth, Lucius F. "A Directory of Artifact Collections," in Brooke Hindle's *Technology in Early America*. Chapel Hill: University of North Carolina Press, 1966. pp. 95-126.

This has an introduction, a section on writing on artifact collections, and the directory itself which is based on the following arrangement: 1) raw material production (mining and quarrying, lumbering, farming, whaling, etc.); 2) manufacturing (process related artifacts--metals, textiles, glass, tanning, food preparation; product-related artifacts: heating, lighting); 3) tools and instruments (tools of the craftsmen, culinary tools, machine tools, clocks and watches, etc.); 4) Power (animal, wind, power, etc.); 5) transportation (water vehicles, land vehicles and railroad); and 6) communications (printing and bookbinding, photography, etc.). Museums and other institutions are listed with their holding collections.

2534. Hobbie, Margaret, comp. *Museums, Sites, and Collections of Germanic Culture in North America: An Annotated Directory of German Immigrant Culture in the United States and Canada.* Westport, CT: Greenwood, 1980. 155p. LC 79-6822; ISBN 0-313-22060-3.

This is an attempt to "make material culture, and other nonbibliographic sources, more readily available to students of German-American and German-Canadian history, through a descriptive listing of locations where such materials can be found." (pref.) The introduction includes an overview of German-American history from 1787. It then lists 271 collections, alphabetically by name of organization, giving address, phone, head, number of staff, collection holdings, dates covered, organization, hours, fee, and whether it is a lending institution or not. There is also a list of sites from the National Register and a selected list of European sources, listed alphabetically by institution. Appendix material includes a list of cultural attachés in Washington and Ottawa, and there is a name index, general index, and a bibliography. There is a particularly good list of European folklife museums included.

2535. Hunter, John E. *Inventory of Ethnological Collections in Museums of the United States and Canada*. 2nd ed., rev. and enl. Milwaukee, WI: Milwaukee Public Museum, 1967. 120p.

Collections are cited in museums, which are arranged alphabetically by name (e.g., Alaska State Museum, American Museum of Natural History, etc.). Ethnological collections are listed by culture area also. The facility is described and discussed and suggested research topics are given. An appendix includes a culture area outline, and there is an index.

2536. Lubell, Cecil, ed. *Textile Collections of the World*. 3 vols. New York: Van Nostrand, 1976, 1977. (See no. 2474 for full citation.)

Covers United States and Canada in Vol. 1, United Kingdom/ Ireland in Vol. 2, and France in Vol. 3.

2537. Minter-Dowd, Christine. *Finders' Guide to Decorative Arts in the Smithsonian Institution*. Washington, DC: Smithsonian Institution Press, 1984. 213p. LC 82-600320; ISBN 0-87474-636-1 (c); 0-87474-637-x (p).

Describes the collections in the Archives of American Art, Cooper-Hewitt Museum, the Freer, the Hirshhorn, the National Museum of American Art (the Renwick), and the Smithsonian Institution Archives, especially the furnishings collection. There is a detailed index.

2538. Polley, Robert L., ed. *America's Folk Art; Treasures of American Folk Arts and Crafts in Distinguished Museums and*

Collections. New York: Published by Putnam in association with County Beautiful Foundation, 1968. 189p. LC 68-31615.

Discusses many objects and tells where they are found: woodcrafts; carvings: wood and scrimshaw; wrought and cast iron; the common metals: copper, brass, tin, pewter; lighting devices; weathervanes; toys, country furniture; needlework and textiles; glassware; pottery and porcelain; the decorative arts; folk painting; and wagons, guns and western gear. An appendix includes a listing of 42 museums and a description of their collections.

2539.	Schlebecker, John T. *Agricultural Implements and Machines in the Collection of the National Museum of History and Technology*. Washington, DC: Smithsonian Institution Press, 1972. 57p. LC 72-194474. (Smithsonian studies in history and technology, 17)

There is an introduction and an essay on the use of farm machinery in America, followed by a catalog of implements, machines, models, and sketches. For all 414 items described, the author gives the date, a physical description, a statement on its use and the source, if known. Indexed.

2540.	University of Pennsylvania. Museum. *Guides to the Collections. The University Museum. University of Pennsylvania.* Philadelphia: University of Pennsylvania Press, 1965--.

This is a series of separate guides to various collections: *The Near East, North America, Middle America and South America, The Mediterranean World, Africa, Oceania and Austronesia,* and *China.*

Descriptions of Various Folk Museums, Artifact Collections, and Living Historical Farms

Note: There are many descriptions of archaeological, anthropological, and ethnographic collections and museums. For example, the Instituto Nacional de Antropologia, Cordoba, Mexico, publishes pamphlets describing their collections (e.g., on yokes, axes and palmas, on Mayan ceramics, etc.). The Mexican National Museum of Anthropology, Mexico City, has been described in a beautiful work, *National Museum of Anthropology*, by Pedro Vasquez (London: Hamlyn, 1968) and in the *Newsweek* publication (part of the Great Museums of the World series), *National Museum of Anthropology: Mexico City* (London: Hamlyn, 1971). The British Museum has a 2-volume set, *Handbook to the Ethnographic Collections* (1910) and there are published catalogs of the great Peabody Museum at Harvard (see no. 106).

Included below is a **sampling** of just a few of the works that are available which describe specific folk museum collections.

The Americas
North America

2541.   Cumming, Albert Lowell, ed. "Restoration Villages." *Art in America* 43 (May, 1955).

This is a special issue on restoration villages, with separate articles on folk art in the Shelburne Museum, restoration in Colonial Williamsburg, demonstration crafts at Old Sturbridge, The Farmers' Museum at Cooperstown, Old Deerfield, and Mystic Seaport.

2542.   Glassie, Henry. *The Spirit of Folk Art: The Girard Collection at the Museum of International Folk Art.* New York: Harry Abrams in association with the Museum of New Mexico, Santa Fe, 1989. (See no. 2048 for full citation.)

Discusses the collection of 100,000 items. See also *Celebrate! The Story of the Museum of International Folk Art*, edited by Richard Polese (Santa Fe: Museum of New Mexico Press, 1979), an older description of the collection.

2543. Henry Ford Museum Staff. *Greenfield Village and the Henry Ford Museum.* New York: Crown, 1972. 7p. LC 78-189980.

Discusses the museum's galleries, the folk art collection, special exhibitions, the educational activities, the museum's research library, and the Ford archives. Also reproduces many photos of the village and the museum and its holdings.

2544. Hill, Ralph Nading, and Lilian Baker Carlisle. *The Story of the Shelburne Museum.* 2nd ed. Shelburne, VT: Shelburne Museum, 1960 [1955]. 113p. LC 59-15285.

Talks about the folk art collection, the school, and the types of collections (pewter, glass, ceramics, doll and toy), the "hat and fragrance" collection (quilts, samplers, textiles, etc.), the outbuildings (cottages, the jail, the Shaker building, the barn, country store, etc.). No index or bibliography. The Shelburne Museum has also published pamphlets describing individual collections (e.g., H.R. Bradley Smith's *Blacksmiths' and Farrier's Tools at the Shelburne Museum* or David Webster's and William Kehoe's *Decoys at the Shelburne Museum*).

2545. Jones, Louis C. *The Farmers' Museum.* Cooperstown: New York State Historical Association, 1948. 48p. LC 48-7667.

Describes the museum and its surroundings. See also Rath's *New York State Historical Society and Its Museums* (no. 2518).

2546. Lynes, Russell. *More Than Meets the Eye: The History and Collections of Cooper-Hewitt Museum, the Smithsonian Institution's National Museum of Design.* Washington, DC: Smithsonian Institution, 1981. 159p. LC 81-68216.

The Smithsonian's Cooper-Hewitt Museum (in New York City) includes textiles, wall coverings, and decorative arts: furniture and woodwork, ceramics, glass, metalwork, etc.

2547.   Marshall, Howard Wight. "Folklife and the Rise of American Folk Museums." *Journal of American Folklore* 90 (1977): 391-413. Reprinted in *Folklife and Museums: Selected Readings*, ed. Patricia Hall and Charlie Seemann (Nashville, TN: American Association of State and Local History, 1987).

Marshall cites and describes several folk life museums in depth: Pioneer Homestead, Cherokee, NC; Black Creek Pioneer Village, Toronto; Old World Wisconsin, Madison; Westville Village, Lumpkin, GA; The Clayville Rural Life Center, Springfield, IL; Louisiana State University Rural Life Museum, Baton Rouge. Marshall has also described The Conner Prairie Pioneer Settlement, in a pamphlet, *The Conner Prairie Concept* (Noblesville, IN: Conner Prairie Settlement, 1975).

2548.   Sloane, Eric. *A Museum of Early American Tools*. New York: Ballantine/Random House, 1973 [1964]. 108p. LC 64-13741.

Sloane draws items from his own collection that form this museum. Included are axes, hatchets, hammers, adzes, wedges, splitting tools, chisels, molds, saws, plows, jacks, etc. Each one is described and placed in a historical perspective.

Eurasia--**Russia** and *Eastern Europe*

2549.   Foçsa, Gheorghe. *The Village Museum in Bucharest*. 2nd ed. Bucharest: Meridiane Publishing House, 1967. 62p. LC 72-211408.

Describes and pictures in black-and-white photos many objects in the museum. Text is in English.

2550.   Foçsa, Marcela. *Folk Art Museum of the Socialist Republic of Romania, Bucharest*. Bucharest: Meridiane Publishing House, 1967. 25p.+59 plates.

This museum was begun as a joint museum of ethnography and folk art in 1906 and became the Folk Art Museum of the Socialist Republic of Romania in 1953. The collection includes 40,000 items: pottery, wood objects, metal objects, objects made of bone or horn, musical instruments, fabrics, national costumes, icons, painted glass, and Easter eggs.

Europe

2551. Michelsen, Peter. *Frilands Museet: The Danish Museum Village at Sorgenfri; A History of Open-Air Museum and Its Old Buildings.* Copenhagen: The National Museum of Denmark, 1973. 237p. ISBN 87-480-7711-9.

Gives the history of the village and a page-by-page guided tour of the houses and buildings. Includes many color illustrations.

2552. Rasmussen, Holger, ed. *Dansk Folkemuseum and Frilands-museet: History & Activities.* Copenhagen: Nationalmuseet, 1966. 266p. LC 67-77574.

Articles by Rasmussen in English are concerned with the origin and development of the Danish Folk Museum; there are articles by others on the costume and textile collections, recording of furniture, on popular amusements, on the research and study of material culture in Denmark, and on the Danish open-air museums. See also Axel Olrik's *Dansk Folkemidesamling (DFS): The National Collection of Folklore in Copenhagen* (Helsinki: Finnish Academy of Science, 1910 [*FF Communications*, 1]; reprinted, 1959) which describes the collection and its use.

2553. Thompson, G.B. *The Ulster Folk Museum.* Cultra Manor: Ulster Folk Museum, 1968. 13p.

Not seen.

2554. Peate, Iorwerth C. *Amgueddfeydd Gwerin: Folk Museums.* Cardiff: University of Wales Press, 1948. 63p.

Written in Welsh with English translation, this mostly compares the Nordiska Museen and the Northern Museum but also discusses the function of a museum, the creation of the folk museum, its development, and the movement and development of the Welsh Folk Museum.

Chapter VIII

FOLKLORE AND FOLKLIFE
SOCIETIES AND JOURNALS

SOCIETIES/ASSOCIATIONS

Directories--Societies/Associations

2555. Hickerson, Kathryn W., and Kathleen Condon. *Folklife and Ethnomusicology Societies in America.* Washington, DC: Library of Congress, Archive of Folk Culture, 1982. 14p.

This lists associations by state giving addresses only. The American Folklore Society is found under the District of Columbia, where its main offices are. An appended sheet lists several additional sources where associations might be located.

2556. Weber, Sol. *Folk Music & Dance Societies and Related Organizations (Folklore, Storytelling, etc.).* Astoria, NY: the author, 1982. (Sol Weber, 25-14 37th St., Astoria, NY 11103.)

Not seen. Listed in no. 2555.

2557. Wynar, Lubomyr R., et al. *Encyclopedic Directory of Ethnic Organizations in the United States*. Littleton, CO: Libraries Unlimited, 1975. 414p. LC 75-28150; ISBN 0-87287-120-7.

This work, now outdated but perhaps still useful, lists "1,475 ethnic organizations under 73 headings" by ethnic group (**Albanian-American** to **Yugoslav-American**). Given is the name of the organization, the place, phone, etc. as well as director and staff, membership information, convention information, date founded, etc.

JOURNALS/PERIODICALS/SERIALS

The pamphlet *Folklore/Folklife* says there are over 250 folklore and folklife journals, and no. 2558 lists about 280 American and Canadian folklife and ethnomusicology journals, excluding those that deal with crafts, such as *Warp and Weft* or *Quilt World*. Jan Brunvand lists 84 in *The Study of American Folklore* (3rd ed., pp. xvii-xix). And Alan Dundes lists 16 "leading American folklore journals" and 25 non-American journals in *The Study of Folklore* (pp. 479-481). Robinson's work on music and dance journals (no. 2561) is the most useful work for a list of serials dealing with most aspects of ethnomusicology. There is a good basic list of material culture journals in "A Selected Listing of Serial Literature in Material Culture Research," in *Material Culture: A Research Guide*, edited by Thomas J. Schlereth (no. 1986). However, the most comprehensive listing of international journals in all subject areas is *Ulrich's International Periodicals Directory* (no. 2562).

Directories--Journals/Periodicals/Serials

2558. Griffin, William J. "The *TFS Bulletin* and Other Folklore Serials in the United States." *Tennessee Folklore Society Bulletin* 25 (1959): 91-96.

Presents a list of about 80 periodicals "devoted specifically to some aspect of folklore and published in the United States." (p. 92) Many of these journals are still being published.

2559.   Hickerson, Joseph. "Journals and Magazines," in *Folk Song U.S.A.*, ed. John Lomax et al. 2nd ed. New York: New American Library, 1957. pp. 505-520.

Lists 132 magazines and periodicals dealing with folk music.

2560.   Hickerson, Kathryn W., and Kathleen Condon. *Folklife and Ethnomusicology Serial Publications in North America.* Washington, DC: Library of Congress, Archive of Folk Culture, 1982. 16p. Reprinted 9/83.

Lists almost 300 American and Canadian folklife and ethnomusicology journals alphabetically by title, giving addresses.

2561.   Robinson, Doris. *Music and Dance Periodicals: An International Directory & Guidebook.* Voorheesville, NY: Peri Press, 1989. 382p. LC 89-15180; ISBN 0-9617844-4-x.

Cites 1,862 periodicals dealing with music and dance. Arranged by subject and indexed.

2562.   *Ulrich's International Periodicals Directory, 1991-92.* 30th ed. 3 vols. New Providence, NJ: Bowker, 1991. LC 32-16320; ISBN 0-8352-3126-7.

This calls itself (and rightfully so) "the premier serials reference source." Now in its 30th edition and compiled and updated on a database (the directory and periodic updates are available on a database and on CD-ROM), the first two volumes are a classified listing of 118,500 serials from all over the world arranged into 696 subject headings; each entry is briefly described and includes publishing information, beginning, and name changes. The third volume is a title index. Among the subjects that might be useful for folklore/folklife scholars are: agriculture, archaeology, architecture, art, arts and handicrafts, ceramics/glass/pottery, clothing trade, dance, ethnic interests, **folklore** (pp. 1916-1936), gardening and horticulture, history, instruments, jewelry/clocks/watches, museums and art galleries, music, pharmacy and pharmacology, religion and theology, sound recordings and reproduction, sports and games, and textile industries and fabrics.

2563. **Wynar, Lubomyr R., and Anna T. Wynar.** *Encyclopedic Directory of Ethnic Newspapers and Periodicals in the United States.* 2nd ed. Littleton, CO: Libraries Unlimited, 1976 [1972]. 248p. LC 76-23317; ISBN 0-87287-154-1.

The goal of this work is "to identify the newspapers and periodicals published by various ethnic groups in the U.S. and to describe their content and bibliographical features. There are 977 newspapers and journals listed, arranged by ethnic and multi-ethnic groups (e.g. **Afro-American** to **Yugoslavia).** Each entry is annotated and includes statistical analyses. Indexed.

Indexes--Journals/Periodicals/Serials

Note: Most journals are indexed in each issue and annually, usually in December. However, some journals index cumulatively, a major time-saving tool. Listed below are those folklore journals that have been cumulatively indexed. They are listed alphabetically by journal title.

2564. *Devil's Box.* "Cumulative Index to Articles Published in the Devil's Box: 1968-1980." *Devil's Box* 15 (March 1981): 48-64.

Lists "articles of major interest" from issues of *Devil's Box* and from its *Newsletter.*

2565. *Folklore.* Bonser, Wilfrid, comp. *A Bibliography of Folklore, As Contained in the First Eighty Years of the Publications of the Folklore Society.* London: Published for the Folk-Lore Society by W. Glaisher, 1961. 126p. LC 62-53502. (Publications of the Folk-Lore Society; v. 121)

Bonser, Wilfred, comp. *A Bibliography for 1958-1967: Being a Subject Index Vols. 69-78 of the Journal Folklore.* London: Published for the Folk-Lore Society by W. Glaisher, 1969. 54p. LC 76-375037. (Publications of the Folklore Society; v. 130)

Both editions serve as indexes to journals listed in *Folk-Lore Record* (1878-1882), *Folk-Lore Journal* (1883-1889), *Folk-Lore* (1890-1957), and *Folklore* (1958--). The articles are indexed according to an "outline of folklore," in effect, a subject listing. The supplement includes 832 annotated entries. Both include an author index, geographical index, "foreign country, race, and tribe" index, and a subject index.

2566. *Folklore Fellows Communications. FF Communications: An Index to Volumes I-LXXXI, nos. 1-195, 1910-1964.* Helsinki: Suomalainen Tiedeakatemia, 1963. 19p.

This supersedes the index following no. 137 which indexes numbers 1-137 (1910-1949). The most comprehensive one lists articles by volume and number and includes an author index only.

2567. *Folklore Forum.* Lowe, Virginia Polioudakis. "Index to *Folklore Forum*, Vols. 1-10 (1968-1977)." *Folklore Forum* 12 (1979): 1-96.

This lists by broad subject area. The subject index lists articles alphabetically by author.

2568. *Hoosier Folklore Bulletin* and *Hoosier Folklore.* Posen, I. Sheldon, et al. "Index to *Hoosier Folklore Bulletin* (1942-1945) and *Hoosier Folklore* (1946-1950)." *Folklore Forum* 10 (1973). 83p. (Bibliographic and special series, 10)

This journal became *Midwest Folklore* (1951-1964), *Indiana Folklore* (1968-1980), and *Indiana Folklore and Oral History* (1985--). The introduction cites the *Hoosier Folklore Bulletin* as "among the first of many state and regional folklore journals which have flourished and faded in North America." (p. vii) Includes subject, author and title index, song-title index, song first-line index, children's rhymes first-line index, tale-type index, legend type-index, and motif-index.

2569. *Journal of American Folklore.*
Index to Volumes 1-40 (1888-1927). New York: Stechert, 1930. 106p. (Memoirs of the American Folklore Society; v. 14)

Coffin, Tristram P. *An Analytical Index to the Journal of American Folklore. Vols. 1-67, 68, 69, 70.* Philadelphia: American Folklore Society, 1958. 384p. (Bibliographic and special series; v. 7)

Jackson, Bruce, et al., eds. and comps. *The Centennial Index: One Hundred Years of the Journal of American Folklore.* Washington, DC: American Folklore Society, 1988. 502p. Published concurrently in the *Journal of American Folklore* 101 (1988).

The first index is a classified index with titles, authors, and broad subject areas. The Coffin index has eight separate indexes: index of titles of articles, notes, etc.; index of authors of articles, notes, etc.; index of authors of book reviewed; index to news and notices (awards, archives, publications, etc.); index to subjects and areas in folklore (this makes up the bulk of the book); index to nationalities and ethnic groups; index to songs and rimes [sic] by titles and first significant lines; and index to tales--types, incidents, characters, objects. The Centennial index is based on "a three-level hierarchy of genre classification which defines every item in the Journal according to (1) a general generic designation, (2) a more specific designation, and (3) an even more specific, subgeneric designation." Over 9,500 articles, reviews, notes, obituaries, queries, and announcements are indexed. The serial listing is arranged chronologically. And there are author, subject, and title indexes as well.

2570. *Journal of the Folklore Institute.* Murdoh, Alice Morrison. "Analytical Index to the *Journal of the Folklore Institute,*

Volumes 1-15." *Journal of the Folklore Institute* 18 (1961): 157-273.

Includes separate author index, title index, and subject index to articles contained in this prestigious journal.

2571. *Kentucky Folklore Record.* Clarke, Kenneth, and Mary Clarke. *Kentucky Folklore Record Ten-Year Index, 1955-64....* Bowling Green, KY: Kentucky Folklore Society, 1966. 44p. (Kentucky folklore series, 2)

Barrick, Mac E. "The Complete and Official Index to the First Fifteen Volumes." *Kentucky Folklore Record.* Supplement 15 (1970). 55p.

Clarke, Mary, and Charles S. Guthrie. *Twenty-Year Index to the Kentucky Folklore Record, 1955-1974.* Bowling Green, KY: Western Kentucky University, 1974. 32p. (Kentucky folklore series, 6)

Collins, Camilla, et al. "*Kentucky Folklore Record*: Comprehensive Index." *Kentucky Folklore Record* 33 (1987): 1-112.

The last work supersedes the previous ones. *Kentucky Folklore Record* was merged with *Southern Folklore Quarterly* in 1989, the title of which was then shortened to *Southern Folklore*. Articles are listed alphabetically by author's name with separate sections for book reviews and notes, records and film reviews, and comments.

2572. *North Carolina Folklore.* Buermann, Theodore Barry. "An Analytical Index to North Carolina Folklore, Volumes 1-8." *North Carolina Folklore* 9 (December 1961): 1-59.

Includes an author/contributor index, title index, verse/title/first-line index, geographical index, subject index, and word index.

2573.   **Pennsylvania Folklife.** Fryer, Judith E. *25 Year Index to Pennsylvania Folklife, Volumes 1-25, 1949-1976.* Collegeville, PA: Pennsylvania Folklife Society, 1980. 94p.

This originally was called *The Pennsylvania Dutchman* and *The Dutchman* (1949-1957). Includes a subject index and a surname index, compiled by Bernadine T. Collins, to genealogy and immigration articles.

2574.   **Pioneer America: The Journal of Historical American Material Culture.** Newton, M.B., Jr., and F. Amber Washburn. "Cumulative Index." *Pioneer America* 11 (June 1979): 7-94.

Pioneer America became *Material Culture* with Vol. 16 (1984). The cumulative index of vols. 1-10 is an alphabetical classified (author, title, subject) listing of 3,000 entries.

2575.   **Tennessee Folklore Society Bulletin.** Griffin, William J. "Indexes to the First Thirty Volumes of *The Tennessee Folklore Society Bulletin.*" *Tennessee Folklore Society Bulletin* 31 (1965): 68-97.

Adair, Dan, et al. "Geographical Index." *Tennessee Folklore Society Bulletin* 52 (1986): 77-107.

The 1965 work includes author, title, and subject indexes; the 1986 work indexes by county.

2576.   **Texas Folklore Society. Publications.** Bratcher, James T. *Analytical Index to Publications of the Texas Folklore Society. Volumes 1-36.* Dallas: Southern Methodist University Press, 1973. 322p. LC 72-97597; ISBN 0-87074-135-7.

Part I includes specialized indexes: tale-type, motif-, and ballad numbers; Part II, tale synopses; and Part III, an alphabetical index to personal names and places, names of ethnic groups, food, plants, titles and first-lines of songs, proverbs and proverbial expressions, "subjects of a folkloristic, cultural, or historical bearing," and some organizations, etc.

2577. **Western Folklore** and **California Folklore Quarterly.** Perkal, Joan Ruman. *Western Folklore and California Folklore Quarterly: Twenty-five Year Index.* Berkeley: University of California Press, 1969.

This was listed in *Handbook of American Folklore*, edited by Richard M. Dorson, on p. 542. There is a note on p. 256 of the 25th anniversary issue of *Western Folklore* (October 1966) that says that Ms. Perkal's index would be ready in late 1967, but I never saw it or verified it.

AUTHOR INDEX

This is a listing of authors, editors, curators, and compilers of articles and books in the entries only. (Only the first and second authors, editors, or compilers are given.) Numbers refer to entry number.

Ball, John, 223, 246
Ballesteros, Octavio A., 411
Baltimore Museum of Art, 2422
Balys, Jonas, 541, 836
Bambra, Audrey, 1344
Bame, Kwabena N., 1889
Banc, C., 572
Banerji, Projesh, 1390
Banks, Mary MacLeod, 1803, 1804
Barakat, Robert A., 414
Barba, Preston A., 2279
Barbeau, Marius, 1029-1032, 1386
Barber, Edwin Atlee, 2187
Barber, George C., 1896
Barbour, Frances M., 395
Baring-Gould, Ceil, 737
Baring-Gould, Sabine, 1082, 1083
Baring-Gould, William S., 737
Barker, Mark, 580
Barrère, Albert, 269
Barrett, William Alexander, 1084
Barrick, Mac E., 465, 2389, 2571
Barry, John W., 2188
Barry, Phillips, 939, 1145
Bartis, Peter T., 146, 173-176,
    1590, 2510, 2511, 2532
Bartlett, John, 376
Bartók, Béla, 837-839, 1055-1060
Barton, Nancy, 1851
Barton, William E., 1250
Başgöz, Ilhan, 489
Baskervill, Charles, 1902
Baskin, Wade, 1458, 1634
Bassett, Fletcher S., 113, 1592
Bastian, Robert W., 2159
Bastien, Joseph W., 1747
Bath, Virginia Churchill, 2340
Bauer, Helen, 1792
Baughman, Ernest W., 535
Baumgartner, Anne S., 613
Bayard, Samuel P., 840

Beamer, Nona, 1115
Beardsley, John, 2056
Beaumont, Cyril W., 1335, 1338
Beck, Horace P., 743, 1593
Beckwith, Martha Warren, 410,
    475, 639, 1895, 1951
Belden, Henry M., 955, 1152
Bellingham, Susan, 1336
Ben-Amos, Dan, 134
Bender, Harold Stauffer, 1613
Benes, Jane, 2211
Benes, Peter, 2211
Benjamin, Steven M., 26, 1614
Bensch, Christopher, 2197
Bereczki, Gábor, 1066
Bergen, Fanny D., 1494, 1553,
    1577, 1582
Berger, Abraham, 1606
Berk, Fred, 1360
Bernard, Henry, 1065
Bernardo, Gabriel Adriano, 77
Bernstein, Ignatz, 371
Bernstein, Ira G., 1362
Berrey, Lester V., 270
Betterton, Shiela, 2361
Beyerl, Paul, 1583
Bhagwat, Durga, 481
Bhuriya, Mahipala, 1048
Bianchini, Francisco, 1718
Bianco, Carla, 88
Biebuyck, Daniel P., 1994
Bierhorst, John, 675
Bihalji-Merin, Oto, 2076
Billings, Anna Hunt, 653
Binder, Pearl, 1669
Birrell, Verla, 2475
Bishop, Robert Charles, 2025,
    2033, 2297, 2316, 2348, 2407
Bivens, John, Jr., 2034
Black, David, 2295
Black, George Fraser, 344

Chaffers, William, 2194
Chamberlain, Mary, 1714
Chambers, Robert, 690, 722, 1187, 1806
Chambers, Wicke, 1776
Champion, Selwyn Gurney, 378
Chapman, Robert L., 271
Chappell, W., 1087, 1195
Charles, Bernard H., 2181
Chase, Daryl, 2512
Chase, Gilbert, 794
Chase, Harrison V., 1777
Chase, Judith Wragg, 2038
Chase, Richard, 945, 1205, 1206
Chase, William D., 1777
Chenhall, Robert G., 2500, 2501
Chickering, Geraldine Jencks, 1158
Chicoine, Marie, 1861
Chicorel, Marietta, 2112
Child, Francis, James, 1188
Child, Heather, 1670
Childers, J. Wesley, 555
Cho, Oh Kon, 1900
Ch'oe, Sang-Su, 1796
Chòe, In-hak, 545
Christensen, Erwin Ottomar, 2029, 2113
Christensen, Nerthus, 802
Christensen, Reidar Th., 590
Christenson, Donald Edwin, 1243
Christian, Donna, 325
Chuks-Orji, Ogonna, 336
Chun, Malcolm Naea, 1716
Cirese, Alberto M., 89
Cirlot, Juan Eduardo, 1658
Clark, Joseph D., 1467, 1554, 1596
Clarke, Kenneth Wendell, 192, 530, 2571
Clarke, Mary Washington, 2571
Clayton, Michael, 2450
Clayton, Robert J., 907

Clements, William M. 27, 569
Cleveland Public Library, 104, 105, 817, 1138, 1244
Clifford, C.R., 2338
Cobos, Rubén, 397
Cochran, Robert, 124
Cooley, Marguerite, 228
Coe, Linda C., 177
Coffin, Tristram Potter, 136, 600, 841, 1125, 1126, 1778, 1835, 2569
Cohen, Daniel, 1537
Cohen, David Steven, 28, 1514
Cohen, Hennig, 600, 1778
Cohen, John, 2367
Colcord, Joanna C., 946
Cole, Herbert M., 2101
Cole, M.R., 1897
Cole, William, 1088
Coleman, Arthur, 641
Coleman, Satis N., 947
Colles, Dorothy, 1670
Collin de Plancy, Jacques Albin-Simon, 1515
Collins, Camilla, 604A, 2571
Collins, Vere, 443
Colombo, John Robert, 685
Comber, Leon, 1797
Combs, Josiah H., 948, 1016
Condon, Kathleen, 251, 925, 2555, 2560
Conklin, Harold C., 523
Conklin, Nancy F., 247
Connor, Paul, 2080
Conway, David, 1755
Cook, Dorothy E., 2217
Cooley, Marguerite, 228
Coon, Nelson, 1568
Cooper, B. Lee, 862, 1274
Cooper, J.C., 1659
Cooper-Hewitt Museum, 2384

Eliade, Mircea, 621, 1630
Eliot, Alexander, 621
Ellis, Charles Grant, 2307
Ellis, Peter Berresford, 650
Ellsworth, Lucius F., 2533
Elmore, Francis H., 1730
Elschek, Oskár, 804
Elscheková, Alicia, 843
Elvehjem Art Center, 2426
Elwell-Sutton, Laurence P., 416
Emboden, William A., 1574
Emeneau, M.B., 477
Emerich, A.D., 2271
Emery, Irene, 2465
Emezi, Herbert O., 758
Emrich, Duncan, 140, 196, 679, 1872
Engle, Gary D., 1892
Enright, D.J., 1877
Epstein, Elaine J., 331
Erdeley, Stephen, 844
Erskine, William Hugh, 1794
Esdaile, Arundell J.K., 642
Eubanks, Sharon Y., 1979
Evans, Emyr Estyn, 1489
Evans, Patricia H., 710, 1936
Ewing, Douglas C., 2045

Faison, Samson Lane, 2513
Falassi, Alessandro, 91
Falconer, Charles M., 125
Fales, Martha Gandy, 2457
Fallon, Carol, 2292
Fancy, Margaret, 834
Farmer, John Stephen, 274
Farr, Sidney Saylor, 33
Farrington, William, 2173
Fawcett, David M., 2081
Fay, George Emory, 1784
Feather, Rebecca, 255
Fein, Cheri, 2514

Feintuch, Burt, 767
Fenton, Ann D., 897
Feret, Barbara L., 2232
Ferguson, Charles A., 359
Ferguson, Eugene, 2429
Ferguson, George Wells, 1671
Ferguson, John P., 2022
Ferretti, Fred, 1937, 1938
Ferris, William R., 34, 102, 112, 768, 866, 1991, 2001, 2116
Fertig, Barbara C., 175
Fetros, John G., 1538
Ficklin, Ellen, 2228
Field, John, 355
Field, Richard Henning, 2069
Fielding, William John, 1873
Fife, Alta S., 231, 956
Fife, Austin E., 231, 956, 1874, 2046
Fine, Elizabeth C., 149
Fingerhut, Bruce, 1852
Fink, Paul M., 275
Finnegan, Ruth, 668
Fischer, Andreas, 330
Fish, Lydia, 601
Fisher, Miles Mark, 957
Fiske, Linda L., 2460
FitzGibbon, Theodora, 2242, 2248
Flake, Chad J., 1620
Flanagan, Cathleen C., 35, 771
Flanagan, John T., 35, 200, 771
Flanders, Helen Hartness, 958-960, 1154-1156
Fleckner, John A., 166
Fleming, E. McClung, 1989
Fleming, John, 2018
Flemming, Ernst, 2469
Flexner, Stuart Berg, 306
Flood, Jessie B., 1381
Flower, Milton E., 2104
Floyd, Samuel A., Jr., 769, 770

Flynt, Henry N., 2457
Foçsa, Gheorghe, 2549
Foçsa, Marcela, 2550
Fogel, Edwin M., 398, 1468
Fogg Art Museum, 2312
Foley, John Miles, 256
Foley, Mary Mix, 2165
Folk Dance Federation of California, 1348
Folk Lore Council of Australia, 1116
Folwell, Betsy, 2515
Foner, Philip S., 961
Forbes, Fred R., Jr., 1323
Forcucci, Samuel L., 962
Ford, P.R.J., 2300
Ford, Robert, 723, 1227, 1963
Founounkidis, E., 827
Fournier, Robert, 2182
Fowke, Edith, 70, 717, 718, 792, 927, 963, 1035-1037, 1223, 1224, 1950
Fowler, David C., 1119
Fox, Grace I., 1349
Fox, Nancy, 2413
Fox, Sandi, 2370
Frances, John de, see De Frances, John
François, Raymond E., 936A
Frank, Lawrence, 276
Frankel, Barbara, 1469
Franklin, Ben, 399
Franklin, Linda Campbell, 2114
Franklyn, Julian, 335
Franks, Bob, 1366
Fraser, Amy Stewart, 724
Fratto, Toni Flores, 2380
Freedman, Robert L., 1679, 2223
Freeman, Roland L., 2376
Freeman, William, 277
French, Hollis, 2452

Frewin, Anthony, 1766
Friedman, Albert B., 1140
Frisbie, Charlotte J., 772
Frost, Helen, 1367
Fry, Donald K., 643
Frye, Ellen, 1071
Fryer, Judith, 2573
Furay hah, Anis, 417
Fuson, Harvey H., 1157
Fusonie, Alan M., 2436
Fussell, G.E., 2437

Gable, J. Harris, 1199
Gaffney, Sean, 435
Gailey, Alan, 2160
Gainer, Patrick W., 964
Galbreath, Robert, 1503
Gallacher, Stuart A., 216
Galpin, Francis W., 1432
Gamble, Sidney D., 1901
Gamer, Nora, 2403
Gans-Ruedin, E., 2301
Garbisch, Edgar William, 2082-2084
Gardner, Emelyn Elizabeth, 1158
Gargan, William, 1320A
Garrett, Jane N., 2002, 2139
Garrett, Wendell D., 2002, 2139
Garriott, Edward B., 1599
Garvan, Beatrice B., 2047
Gaskell, George Arthur, 1631, 1661
Gaskin, L.J.P., 2003
Gaster, Theodor Herzl, 1826
Gaultier, André Pascal, 1455
Gehret, Ellen J., 2479
Gennep, Arnold van, see van Gennep, Arnold
George, Diana Hume, 2281
Georges, Robert A., 36, 150, 167, 1917

Georgia Council for the Arts and
Humanities, 2122
Gettings, Fred, 1516
Gibb, H.A.R., 1646
Gibbons, Roy W., 1422
Gilbert, Cecile, 1350
Gilbert, Elizabeth Rees, 1854
Gilbert, Russell W., 680
Gilfoy, Peggy Stoltz, 2480
Gillespie, Angus K., 1672
Gillespie, George T., 651
Gillis, Frank J., 749, 910, 1526
Gillmor, Frances, 191
Gilmore, Melvin R., 1731
Girard, Alexander H., 2396
Glass, Paul, 965
Glassie, Henry, 157, 1980, 2048,
2161, 2162, 2542
Glazer, Joe, 927
Glazier, Jack, 460
Glazier, Phyllis Gorfain, 460
Gloag, John 2262
Gluski, Jerzy, 379
Godden, Geoffrey A., 2196
Godrich, John, 1240, 1291
Goehring, Eleanor E., 37
Goldin, Hyman E., 278
Goldsmith, Judith, 1866
Goldstein, Kenneth S., 151, 1928
Gomme, Alice B., 702, 1228, 1229,
1919, 1964
Gomme, George Laurence, 119
Gonzáles, Dolores, 1209
Goodland, Roger, 1759
Goody, Jack, 1876
Gordon, Beverly, 2459
Gordon, Edmund I., 418
Gordon, Lesley, 1585
Goren, David, 1286
Gorham, Rex, 73
Görög, Veronika, 510

Goss, Michael, 1504
Gottfried, Herbert, 2166
Gottlieb, David, 2224
Goulden, Joseph C., 607
Gourlay, Kenneth, 809
Gourley, James Edwin, 2233, 2234
Gowing, Gene, 1368
Grafton, Carol Belanger, 2355
Granger, Byrd Howell, 591
Grave, Alexandra, 2049
Graves, Robert, 1189
Gray, John, 759
Gray, Michael H., 1263
Gray, Roland Palmer, 966
Grayson, Martin, 2470
Green, Archie, 598
Green, Bennett W., 279
Green, Henry D., 2272
Green, Jonathon, 280
Green, Judith Strupp, 2460
Green, Rayna, 38
Greene, Ellin, 508
Greene, Hank, 1369
Greenleaf, Elizabeth Bristol, 474,
1168
Greenway, John, 967
Gregor, Walter, 725
Gregory, Ruth W., 1765, 1767,
1768
Greig, Gavin, 1090
Grider, Sylvia Ann, 258
Grieve, Maude, 1720
Griffin, William J., 2558, 2575
Grigson, Geoffrey, 1141
Grimal, Pierre, 622
Grimé, William, 1732
Grimes, Ronald L., 1760
Gritzner, Charles, 1981
Gritzner, Janet, 1981
Grose, Francis, 281
Grunfield, Frederic V., 1924

Gruntvig, Sven, 1176
Guadalupi, Gianni, 1563
Gubernatis, Angelo de, *see* De Gubernatis, Angelo
Gudde, Erwin G., 350
Guédon, Marie Françoise, 793
Guerrero, Margarita, 1536
Guershoon, Andrew, 429
Gullen, F. Doreen, 726
Gummere, Francis B., 1190
Gupta, Shakti M., 1569
Gureau, Elba Farabegoli, 1403
Gutch, Patricia, 2516
Gutch, John Matthew, 1200
Gutek, Gerald Lee, 2516
Guthrie, Charles Snow, 468, 2571

Haas, Mary R., 1956
Habenstein, Robert, 1878
Haders, Phyllis, 2349
Haddon, Kathleen, 1972, 1973
Haffenreffer Museum of Anthropology, 2218
Haga, Hideo, 1795
Hague, Eleanor, 1041
Haining, Peter, 1517, 1531
Hale, Horatio, 1763
Haley, Gail, 1933
Hall, J. Tillman, 1351
Hall, Joseph S., 282
Hall, Patricia, 2496
Hall, Robert de Zouche, 2140
Hall, Trevor H., 1505
Halliwell-Phillipps, James O., 283, 664, 727
Halpert, Herbert, 259, 1485, 1886, 1894
Hamer, Frank, 2183
Hamer, Fred, 1091
Hamer, Janet, 2183
Hamilton, Goldy M., 1210

Hamp, Stephen K., 1982
Hanayama, Shinsho, 1625
Hand, Wayland, 250, 602, 1470, 1680, 1697
Handoo, Jawaharlal, 80, 517
Handy, W.C., 1297
Hangen, Eva C., 1662
Hanks, Patrick, 345
Hansen, Terrence Leslie, 536
Hanson, F. Allan, 2004
Hanson, Louise, 2004
Haque, Abu Saeed Zahural, 39
Harder, Kelsie B., 351
Hargrove, John, 2421
Haring, Lee, 531
Harkins, William E., 92, 520
Harlow, Frederick Pease, 968
Harmon, Robert B., 2141, 2142
Harper, Howard V., 1824
Harries, Lyndon, 673
Harris, Jane A., 1352
Harris, Sheldon, 1290
Harrison, Frank Llewellyn, 750
Harrison, Ira E., 1677, 1681
Harrold, Robert, 1398
Hart, Donn V., 487, 1867
Hart, Henry Hersch, 421
Hart, Mary L., 1283
Hartley, Kenneth R., 1231
Hartley, William G., 161
Hartman, Tom, 1837
Hassell, James Woodrow, 432
Ha, Tae-hung, 1052
Hatch, Jane M., 1779
Hatfield, Diana, *see* Diana Callahan
Hatton, J.L., 1073
Hattori, Ryutaro, 1050
Hauk, Richard Boyd, 587
Hautala, Juoko, 238
Havlice, Patricia Pate, 1275

1094

Martin, Laura C., 1587, 1588
Martin, Mark, 1813
Marvel, Elinore, 2109
Mason, M. Ellen, 2345
Mason, Michael, 1318
Massé, Henri, 1486
Mather, J.Y., 329
Mathews, Mitford M., 288
Mattera, Joanne, 2414
Mattfeld, Julius, 753
Maude, H.C., 1976
Maude, H.E., 1976
Mawhinney, Paul C., 868
Mayer, Fanny Hagin, 519
Mayer, L.A., 2008
Mayer-Thurman, Christa C., 2408, 2425
Mayo, Edith, 1983, 1990
Mayo, Margot, 1374
Mead, Rita H., 785
Meader, Robert F.W., 2267
Mechling, Jack, 1672
Meckler, Alan M., 183
Megas, Georgios A. 1801
Mekkawi, Mod, 2147
Melton, J. Gordon, 1507, 1644
Meltzer, David, 1869, 1879
Memsink, Onno, 1426
Mencken, H.L., 290
Mera, H.P., 2409, 2482
Mercatante, Anthony S., 611, 617, 628, 1548, 1589
Mercer, Paul, 896
Meredith, John, 1118
Mergen, Bernard, 1909, 1910
Merin, Jennifer, 1849
Merriam, Alan P., 201, 749, 786, 869
Metford, J.C.J., 1639
Metropolitan Museum of Art, 1427
Meyer, George H., 2031

Meyer, Richard E., 2277
Meyers, Rick, 1375
Meynen, Emil, 1616
Michelson, Peter, 2551
Mieder, Wolfgang, 360-368, 382, 401A
Migita, C.L., 1051
Milberg, Alan, 1941
Milburn, George, 991
Miles, Charles, 2288
Miles, Clement A., 1840
Millen, Nina, 1926
Miller, Amy Bess, 1735
Miller, Julia E., 94
Miller, Richard Alan, 1576
Miller, Terry E., 787
Milligan, Jean C., 1411
Mills, Alan, 1037
Millspaugh, Charles F., 1736
Milne, Jean, 1785
Milton, Donald, 857
Milwaukee Art Museum, 2057
Milwaukee Public Museum, 2375
Minary, Ruth, see Moorman, Ruth
Minneapolis Public Library, 12, 1202, 1342
Minter-Dowd, Christine, 2537
Mintz, Jerome R., 1656
Mississippi Department of Archives and History, 2376
Mitchell, Faith, 1737
Mitchell, P.M., 645
Mittlefehldt, Pamela J., 49
Modern Language Association of America, 657
Modoi, Evelyn, 1045
Moe, John F., 1846
Moerman, Daniel E., 1685, 1738, 1739
Mohr, Clarence, 2116
Moll, Otto, 369

Molloy, J.L., 1073
Mondloch, Margaret, 1682
Monro, Isabel Stevenson, 2217
Montagné, Prosper, 2245
Montell, William Lynwood, 1880
Montgomerie, Norah, 738
Montgomerie, William, 738
Montgomery, Charles F., 2058
Montgomery, Florence M., 2471
Montreynaud, Florence, 383
Moore, Chauncey O., 1162
Moore, Ethel, 1162
Moore, Mafori, 1870
Moore, Michael, 1740
Moorman, Charles, 661
Moorman, Ruth, 661
Morgenstern, Julius, 1865
Morris, Alton Chester, 992
Morris, Frank, 1565
Morris, John W., 1272
Morris, Mary, 291, 292
Morris, Ruth, 1565
Morris, William, 291, 292
Morrison, James E., 1376
Morthland, John, 1307
Morton, Julia F., 1741
Mothershead, Alice Bonzi, 2230
Moylan, Terry, 1401
Mukherji, Shyam Chand, 2503
Munro, Ailie, 1095
Murdock, George Peter, 50
Murdoh, Alice, 1570
Murphy, Edward, 1377
Murray, Patrick, 2398
Museum of American Folk Art, 2107, 2308
Museum of Contemporary Art, 2483
Museum of Early Southern Decorative Arts, 2059

Museum of International Folk Art, 2060, 2486
Museum of the American Indian, Heye Foundation, 2202
Mussell, Kay, 2219
Mynatt, Constance V., 1356

Naeve, Milo M., 2268
Nathan, Joan, 2253
National Folk Festival Association, 1856
National Gallery of Art, 2097
Neff, Ivan C., 2296
Nelson, Malcolm A., 2281
Nettl, Bruno, 754, 885
Neuburg, Victor E., 663
Neuland, Lena, 547
New York Public Library, 818, 825, 1339, 2016
New York State Historical Association, 2098
New York Times Oral History Program, 184
Newall, Venetia J., 1501, 1518, 1559
Newark Museum, 2108
Newell, William Wells, 713, 1213, 1942
Newman, Harold, 2185, 2447
Newman, Jacqueline M., 2225
Newman, Joyce Joines, 2377
Newman-Sanders, C.W., 1412
Newton, M.B., Jr., 2574
Nha-Trang, Công-Huyên-Tôn-Nữ, 85
Nicholls, Ann, 2505, 2529
Nicholson, John, 293
Nicolson, Alexander, 498
Nigg, Joe, 1560
Niles, John Jacob, 1144
Niles, Susan A., 516

Nketia, J.H. Kwabena, 933
Noble, Allen G., 2438, 2439
Nöel Hume, Ivor, 2026
Nolsøe, Mortan, 1132
Norman, Howard, 681
North, Gail, 1241
North Carolina Museum of History, 2274, 2275
Northall, G.F., 294, 691, 728
Northcote, Lady Rosalind Lucy, 1758
Northcote, Thomas W., 15
Nosanow, Barbara Shissler, 2061
Nowlin, William, 917
Nownes, Laura, 2354
Noy, Dov, 237
Nugent, Donald, 1508
Nyembezi, C.L. Sibusiso, 389
Nygeres, Anton, N. 548

O Boyle Seán, 1075
O'Brien, Art, 1402
O'Connell, Merrilyn Rogers, 2494, 2495
Ó Danachair, Caoimhín, see Danaher, Kevin D.
Odum, Howard W., 993, 944
Oelsner, Gustaf H., 2415
Ofori, Patrick E., 1611
Ohrbach, Barbara C., 697
O'Keefe, J.G., 1402
Olatunji, Michael Babatunde, 1431
Olderr, Steven, 1665
O'Leary, Timothy, 50
Oliver, Paul, 1293
O'Lochainn, Colm, 1180
Olney, Marguerite, 1155
Olrik, Axel, 1177
Olschki, Leo S., 1509
Opie, Iona, 729, 730, 735, 736, 739, 1230, 1456, 1965

Opie, Peter, 729, 730, 735, 736, 739, 1230, 1965
Opoku, A.A., 1773
Oppelt, Norman T., 2174
O'Rahilly, Thomas Francis, 436
Ord, John, 1096
Oring, Elliott, 142
O'Rourke, Brian, 1076
Orso, Ethelyn G., 575
Orton, Harold, 326
O'Ruadháin, Micheál, 1556
Osborne, Harold, 2019
Osborne, Jerry, 1308, 1309
Osgood, Bob, 1378, 1379
Oshins, Lisa Turner, 2347
Oster, Harry, 1298
Ó Súilleabháin, Seán, 120, 159, 551, 1490, 1881
O'Sullivan, Sean, see
   Ó Súilleabháin, Seán
Owen, Trefor M. 1815
Owens, William A., 995, 1214
Owomoyela, Oyekan, 390

Page, Linda Garland, 2393
Page, Michael, 1541
Page, Ralph, 1380, 1384
Pagter, Carl R., 608
Palliser, Mrs. Bury, 2335
Palmer, A. Smyth, 295
Palmer, Arthur Hudson, 955, 1152
Palmer, Geoffrey, 1816
Palmer, Robin, 1564
Palmer, Roy, 930, 1097, 1110, 1193
Pang, Hilda Delgado, 2461
Paredes, Américo, 230, 605, 996
Paris, Ferdinand, 1722
Park, Thomas Choorbai, 1044
Parks, Vernon, 228
Parler, Mary Celestia, 1477
Parmar, Shyam, 87

Schwann, W., 873
Schwartz, Alvin, 577
Schwartz, Marvin D., 2270
Schwartz, Stuart C., 2175
Schwartzman, Helen B., 1912
Schwarzbaum, Haim, 1608
Schwendener, Norma, 1388
Scott, Charles T., 478
Scott, John Anthony, 1164
Scott, Sir Walter, 1197
Scottish Official Board of Highland
  Dancing, 1415
Scully, Virginia, 1742
Seal, Graham, 100, 185
Sealock, Richard B., 333
Sears, Minnie Earl, 899
Sebeok, Thomas A., 431, 458, 548,
  1056, 1959
Seeger, Anthony, 911
Seeger, Charles, 855
Seeger, Peggy, 1094
Seeger, Pete, 1010
Seeger, Ruth Porter Crawford, 1011
Seeman, Charles, 2496
Seeman, Erich, 1174
Seiler-Baldinger, Annemarie, 2463
Sein, Maung Than, 479
Selick, Marsha, 2525
Semowich, Charles J., 2259
Sen Gupta, Sankar, 87
Sendrey, Alfred, 813
Senior, Doreen H., 1034
Seymour, John, 2124
Shaeffer, Margaret W., 2427
Shalkop, Robert L, 2065
Shambaugh, Cynthia, 1511
Shankle, George Earlie, 340
Shannon, George, 508, 509
Shapiro, Nat, 1276
Sharma, Sue, 1320A

Sharp, Cecil James, 1012-1014,
  1102-1106, 1229, 1416-1418
Shaw, Lloyd, 1357, 1383
Shaw, Margaret Fay, 1107
Shay, Frank, 1015, 1594
Shearin, Hubert G., 1016
Shemanski, Frances, 1850, 1858
Shepard, Leslie, 1520
Sheppard, H. Fleetwood, 1083
Sherman, Lila, 2519
Shields, Hugh, 805
Shirley, Kay, 1299
Shipley, Joseph T., 299
Shishido, Misako, 2394
Shoemaker, Henry Wharton, 1017
Shuldham-Shaw, Patrick, 1108
Shumway, Gary, 161
Silber, Fred, 932
Silber, Irwin, 932, 1018
Silverman, Jerry, 1300
Simmons, Merle Edwin, 11-14, 795
Simon, André Louis, 2238
Simon, James E., 1683
Simpson, Claude Mitchell, 1198
Simpson, J.A., 447
Sinclair, Marjorie, 693
Singer, Isidore, 1637
Singer, Samuel, 384
Sink, Susan, 2117
Sironen, Marta K., 2263
Skelton, Robin, 1525
Skolnik, Peter, 1944
Skowronski, JoAnn, 1267
Slack, Ellen, 102
Slaveikoff, Pencho, 1065
Slaven, Neil, 1292
Slavens, Thomas P., 1604
Sloane, Eric, 1598, 2548
Slocombe, Marie, 242
Smeets, René, 1674
Smith, Alan, 2314

Tubach, Frederic C., 566
Tucci, Giuseppe, 1054
Tucher, Andrea J., 2442
Tudor, Dean, 1273, 1277, 1278
Tuer, Andrew W., 2386
Tuft, Harry M., 891
Tuleja, Tad, 1764
Tully, Marjorie F., 61
Turner, Harold W., 1613
Turner, Ian, 733
Turner, Kay, 2050
Turner, Lorenzo Dow, 303
Turner, Patricia, 876, 900, 1247
Turville-Petre, Gabriel, 637
Tyler, Varro E., 1707

Udall, Lee, 1848
Ueda, Reikichi, 2103
Ullom, Judith C., 62
Underwood, Charlotte, 1371
Underwood, Peter, 1523
Unger, Claude W., 1696
United States. Library of Congress, 790, 819, 877, 878, 920, 1238, 1286, 1304, 1330
United States. Library of Congress, American Folklife Center, 1238
United States. Library of Congress, Archive of American Folk Song, 917, 919
United States. Library of Congress, Archive of Folk Culture, 740, 789, 921, 1421
United States. Library of Congress, Archive of Folk Song, 1421, 1621
United States. Library of Congress. Music Division, 918
United States. Library of Congress, Rare Book Division, 667

United States. National Archives Publications Commission, 187
United States. National Historical Publications and Records Commission, 186
United States. National Library of Medicine, 1687
University of California. Department of Music, Archive of California Folk Music, 893
University of California at Los Angeles. Music Library, 1444
University of Detroit. Computerized Folklore Archives, 219
University of Kansas. Museum of Art, 2377
University of Nebraska, 2378
University of North Carolina, 2379
University of Pennsylvania. Museum, 2540
University of Texas Art Museum, 2072
Upton, Dell, 2151, 2152
Urdang, Laurence, 311, 1771
Urlin, Ethel L., 1830

Vance, Mary, 2153, 2443
Van Cleef, Frank C., 1385
Van den Bark, Melvin, 270
van Gennep, Arnold, 97, 1487, 1762
Ven Reusel, B., 2388
Van Stan, Ina, 2489
Vargyas, Lajos, 1172
Varley, Douglas H., 761
Vaughan Williams Memorial Library, 243
Vaughan Williams, Ralph, 1110, 1111
Vaughn, Henry Halford, 449

TITLE INDEX

These are titles that are listed in the entries only. The numbers refer to entry numbers. For the most part, beginning articles (e.g., *A*, *An*, and *The*) and subtitles have been omitted but are retained in the main entries. Titles are listed under their most **common** spelling (e.g., *folk song, folk-song*, and *folksong* are listed under *folk song; folklore* and *folk-lore* are listed under *folklore*).

1133

Games of the Orient, 1955

Games of the Tibetans, 1957

Games of the World, 1924

"Games of Washington Children," 1929

Garden Flower Folklore, 1587

Gardener's Magic and Folklore, 1581

Garland of Country Song, 1083

Garland of Green Mountain Song, 958

Garners Gay: English Folk Songs..., 1091

Gastronomical and Culinary Literature, 2232

Gazetteer of Scottish and Irish Ghosts, 1523

General Ethnological Concepts, 107

"General Introduction to Literature on South American Ethnographic Textiles since 1950," 2463

Gennett Records of Old Time Tunes, 1306

Geography of Witchcraft, 1522

"The George Korson Folklore Archive," 227

George Pullen Jackson Collection of Southern Hymnody, 1236

Georgia Crafts Appalachia, 2122

Geraniums for the Iroquois: A Field Guide to American Indian Medicinal Plants, 1739

German and German-American Folklore Collections, 219

German Festivals & Customs, 1800

German Proverbs and Proverbial Phrases, 433

Get Your Ass in the Water and Swim Like Me: Narrative Poetry from Black Oral Tradition, 744

Ghosts Along the Cumberland, 1880

Gift to Be Simple: Songs, Dances and Rituals of the American Shakers, 1249

Glass Tableware, Bowls & Vases, 2448

Glossary of Greek Birds, 1562

Glossary of Hausa Music..., 881

Gods and Symbols of Ancient Egypt, 1664

Golden City, 1966

"Gombo Zhèbes": Little Dictionary of Creole Proverbs, 400

Gospel Music Encyclopedia, 1241

Graffiti, 580

Grampian Collection of Scottish Country Dances, 1410

Grand Generation, 2128

Grandma Moses, 2090

Gravestone Designs, 2283

Great American Book of Sidewalk, Stoop, Dirt, Curb, and Alley Games, 1938

Great American Cover-Up: Counterpanes..., 2422

Great American Marble Book, 1937

Greek Calendar Customs, 1801

Greek Popular Musical Instruments, 1429

Green Magic: Flowers, Plants, & Herbs in Lore & Legend, 1587

Greenfield Village and the Henry Ford Museum, 2543

Greig-Duncan Folk Song Collection, 1108

"The Growth of Folklore Courses," 249

Guide for Collectors of Folklore in Utah, 147

Lore and Language of School-children, 730

Lore & Legends of Flowers, 1584

Louisiana French Folk Songs, 1026

Luganda Proverbs, 393

Lumbering Songs from the Northern Woods, 963

Lumberjack Lingo, 301

Lytell Geste of Robin Hode..., 1200

McDougall Collection of Indian Textiles from Guatemala and Mexico, 2488

Macmillan Atlas of Rugs and Carpets, 2295

Made by Hand--Mississippi Folk Art, 2130

Made in New York State: Hand-woven Coverlets, 1820-1860, 2427

"Madstones in North Carolina," 1596

Magic Garden: The Myth and Folklore of Flowers, Plants, Trees, and Herbs, 1589

Magic Herbs for Arthritis, Rheumatism, and Related Ailments, 1721

Magic Medicines of the Indians, 1708

Magic of Herbs, 1755

Magic Symbols of the World, 1669

Magic, Witchcraft, and Paganism in America, 1507

Magic World: American Indian Songs and Poems, 676

Magical & Ritual Use of Herbs, 1576

Magical Medicine, 1680

Main Street Pocket Guide to North American Pottery and Porcelain, 2190

Maine Folklife Index, 182

Maine Woods Songster, 939

Malagasy Tale Index, 531

Man and Beast in American Comic Legend, 1544

Man, Myth, & Magic, 1513

Management of Oral History Sound Archives, 168

Manual of Swedish Handweaving, 2412

Manual of the Furniture Arts and Crafts, 2263

Manual of the Writings in Middle English, 1050-1500, 654

Manuel de Folklore Français Contemporain, 97, 1762

"Manuscripts of Indiana Folklore in the Indiana University Folklore Archive," 206

Maori Games and Hakas, 1968

Maori String Games, 1970

The Marble Threshing Floor: A Collection of Greek Folk Songs, 1071

Maritime Folklife Resources, 176, 1590, 2532

Marks & Monograms on European and Oriental Pottery and Porcelain..., 2194

Marrow Bones; English Folk Songs..., 1098

Master Book of Herbalism, 1583

Material Culture: A Research Guide, 1986

"Material Culture and Artifact Classification," 1990

1162

1166

SUBJECT INDEX

This subject index is based on the key words in the titles of the entries. Also included are types of references (e.g., bibliographies, indexes, etc.), geographical areas, and subject areas that form the outline of this work as well as a few other entries that will make subject searching easier for the beginning user. Numbers are entry numbers and not page numbers.

Aaron Mountz, wood carver, exibition catalog, 2105

Abby Aldrich Rockefeller Folk Art Collection, 2053, 2054, 2078, 2079

Abstracts, *see also* Indexes: folk music, 815; folklore and folklife, 101

Africa/African--general, *see also* Ashanti, Cameroun, Central Africa, East Africa, Fulani, Hausa, Jabo, Kru, Kxatla, Lugana, Mbeere, Morocco, Nigeria, Ovambo, Sierra Leone, South Africa, Swahili, Tongo, Yoruba, West Africa, Zulu: bibliography--general, 19; calendar and festival rites, 1772,

1773; ceramics, 2201; folk architecture, 1999, 2014, 2141; folk art, 1994, 1998, 1999, 2003, 2014; folk costume, 2210; folk craft, 1995, 1997, 2003; folk dance, 757-760, 1332; folk drama, 1889; folk food, 2236; folk medicine, 1680, 1691, 1756; folk music, 511, 757-761, 846, 869, 881, 904, 910, 933, 934; folk poetry, 511, 671-674; folk sculpture, 2101, 2109; folk tales, 519, 511, 529-533, 2109; folklore/folklife--general, 8, 17-21; herbals and herb lore, 1725-1727, 1756; metalcraft, 2457, 2458; mythology, 638; oral narratives, 511, 2014; personal

America/American cont'd.
2332; fieldwork manuals, 145-148; folk architecture, 1993, 2009, 2011, 2137, 2139, 2141, 2143, 2144, 2146, 2148, 2150-2152, 2156, 2159, 2161-2163, 2165-2170; folk costume, 2473, 2531; folk dance, 772, 1330, 1331, 1361-1385, 1421, 1423, 1424; folk art-general, 1992, 1995, 1996, 1997, 2001, 2002, 2005-2007, 2009, 2011, 2012, 2015; folk drama, 1890-1893; folk festivals, 1852-1861; folk food, 2219-2221, 2225, 2229, 2232, 2234, 2234, 2240, 2242-2245, 2250-2254, 2256-2258; folk furniture, 1992, 2059, 2259, 2263-2275; folk medicine, 1685-1692, 1708, 1728-1745; folk museums, 2497, 2498, 2508-2523, 2532-2235, 2537, 2538, 2540-2548; folk music, 762-791, 816-826, 831-842, 850, 851, 858, 871, 873, 875-890, 893, 897-901, 905, 922, 924-926, 935-1028, 1147, 1149, 1153, 1231-1238, 1243-1247; folk poetry, 675-685; folk speech, 261, 264, 265, 267, 271, 273-279, 281, 284, 285, 287, 290, 298, 300-307, 309, 310; folk tales, 534, 535; folk toys, 2391, 2393; folklore/folklife--general, 17, 22-69, 102, 106, 109, 110, 112, 117; games, 707, 708, 710-715, 1928-1949; glass, 2446, 2449; graffiti, 331, 332; gravestone art, 2276-2283; herbals, 1728-1745; humor, 577; linguistic atlases, 313-325;

material culture--general, 1978, 1981, 1982, 1984-1989; metal-craft, 2059, 2450, 2452, 2454-2456; names and naming, 333, 334, 339-343, 349-352; needle-work--general, 2319-2322; occupational folklore, 600; play-party games, 1202-1222; popular culture--general, 1984, 1988; popular music, 1262-1264, 1267, 1269-1319; proverbs, 358, 395-410; quilts, 2347-2379; religious beliefs, 1611-1619, 1642-1644; riddles, 463, 473; rites--general, 1763, 1764; samplers, 2332, 2380, 2381; technology, 2430; textiles, 2129, 2459, 2471, 2473, 2476, 2479, 2481, 2482, 2486, 2531; weaving, 2406, 2409, 2413, 2426, 2427
American Folklife Center, see U.S. Library of Congress, American Folklife Center
American Folklore Society, 157
American Indian folklore, see Native American folklore
American primitive painting, see Naive painting
Amish folklore, 69, 1614, 1615, 1619
Andes, herbals, 1747
Andrew Lang, 125
Anglo-American ballads, 1128, 1137, 1140-1145
Anglo-American folk songs, 927, 929, 930, 932
Anglo-American folklore, see America/American and English/England
Animals and mythic animals (1534-1555), see also Birdlore:

Animals cont'd.
annotated collections, 1553-1555; bibliographies, 1534, 1535; dictionaries, 1536-1542, 1557; gazetteer, 1543; guides, 1544-1550; lexicons, 1551, 1552
Anne and Frank Warner [Folksong] Collection [Syracuse, NY], 1022
Annotated collections: ballads, 1140-1201; childbirth rites, 1864-1869; children's verse, 704-733; Christmas and Easter customs, 1834-1844; courtship and marriage rites, 1871-1875; customs, beliefs, and superstitions, 1460-1502; death rites, 1877-1881; epics, 695-696; erotic humor, 580-586; family narratives, 595-599; folk drama, see Play texts; folk games, 1923-1976; folk medicine beliefs and remedies, 1690-1717; folk music, 929-1115; folk poetry, 668-693; folk speech, see Dictionaries, etymologies; folk music, 927-1115; foodways, 2228-2230; jokes and humor; 570-577; mythical beast tales, 1553-1555; mythology, see Dictionaries, mythology; occupational legends; nursery rhymes, 737-739; plant and flowerlore, 1581-1591; play-party games, 1203-1230; popular music (blue grass, blues, country), 1281, 1297-1302, 1319; play-party games, 1203-1230; proverbs, see also Dictionaries, proverbs, 376-454; religious beliefs, 1655; religious music (gospels, hymns, and spirituals), 1248-1261; riddles, 460-502; rites, general, 1763, 1764; singing games, 1203-1230; stonelore, 1596; weatherlore, 1599-1601; witchcraft, 1526-1528; toasts, 742-747; urban legends, 606-609

Appalachia/Appalachian: archives, 229, 905; baskets, 2285; folk art-general, 2061; folk dance, 1365; folk games, 2393; folk medicine, 1728; folk music, 875, 905, 1002, 1012-1014; folk toys, 2392; folklore/folklife--general, 25, 33, 56; humor, 573; linguistic atlas, 375; musical instruments, 1423, 1427; quilts, 2367, 2374

Arabia/Arabian: proverbs, 359, 412-420

Archer Taylor, 360

Architecture, see Folk architecture

Archive of California Folk Music, 893

Archive of Folk Culture, see U.S. Library of Congress, Archive of Folk Culture

Archive of Folk Song, see U.S. Library of Congress, Archive of Folk Song

Archive of Ohio Folklore and Music [Miami University], 223

Archives and archiving, 165-244

Archives--Guides to collections, 170-190, 821-828

Archives--Guides to songs in collections, 829, 830

Archives--Guides to sound recordings collections, 172

Archives--Guides to specific collections, 191-244

Archives of Appalachia, 229, 905
Archiving, *see* Archives and archiving
Argentina/Argentinian: calendar and festival rites, 783
Arizona: archive, 191; legend, 591
Arkansas, *see also* Ozarks: customs, beliefs, superstitions: 1477; family narratives, 596; folk medicine, 1744
Armenia/Armenian carpets, 2307
Art Institute of Chicago, 2425
Arthurian romance, 655-662
Artifact collections, *see also* Folk museums and Living history farms, 2532
Artifacts, 1990, 2040
Arts and crafts, *see* Folk art--general, folk crafts--general
Ashanti: metalcrafts, 2456, 2458; proverbs, 391
Asia/Asian--general, *see also* individual countries: calendar and festival rites, 1786-1798; carpets and rugs, 2295, 2296, 2299-2306, 2309-2311; ceramics, 2189, 2199, 2200, 2203, 2205, 2206; childbirth rites, 1867; customs, beliefs, superstitions, 1486; folk costume, 1389; folk architecture, 1999; folk art--general, 1999, 2071, 2072; folk crafts--general, 1999; folk dance, 797, 799, 800, 1389, 1390; folk drama, 1900, 1901; folk games, 1953-1958; folk medicine, 1710, 1711, 1749-1754; folk music, 797-801, 2521, 2526; folk poetry, 686-689; folk toys, 2492; folklore/folklife--general, 75-87; musical instruments, 1426, 1428,

1434; needlework, 2327; plantlore and flowerlore, 1569; proverbs, 359, 412-428; religious beliefs and rites, 1603, 1625-1628, 1645-1651, 1845; riddles, 477-491; stencilling, 2386; symbolism, 1664, 1668; textiles, 2477, 2488, 2490, 2491; weaving, 2466
Atlantic states: linguistic atlas, 320
Atlas, 2295
Australia/Australian, *see also* Oceania: archive, 185; children's rhymes, 733; folk dance, 1399; folk medicine, 1717; folk songs, 1113, 1116-1118; folklore/folklife--general, 100, 112; mythology, 623-626; oral narratives, 559; railwaymen lore, 604; superstitions, 1717
Autograph verse, 709, 734

Bagpipe music, 894
Balkans: folk music, 1065
Ballads, *see also* Broadside ballads (1119-1202): bibliography, 25, 771, 1119-1123; annotated collections, 959, 985, 986, 989, 990, 1001, 1079, 1087, 1114, 1140-1198; catalog, 832; classification, 527, 1124-1137; indexes, 896, 914; Robin Hood ballads, 1199-1201
Baltic proverbs, 373
Baltimore: quilts, 2373
Banjo performers, 907
Barbados: folk games, 1952
Baskets (2284-2294): classification, 2284; guides, 2284A-2291; exhibition catalogs, 2292-2294

Beliefs, *see* Customs, beliefs, and superstitions

Bibliography: archives and archiving, 165; ballads, 1119-1123, children's rhymes, 697; customs, beliefs, and superstitions, 1445-1448; ceramics, 2172-2178; Christmas customs, 1833; clocks, 2313; discographies, 861, 862, 1263; embroidery, 2335; epics, 694; erotic humor, 578; ethno-musicology, *see* Folk music; fables, 503, 504; fieldwork, 144; folk architecture, 2134-2158; folk art--general, 1992-2015; folk costume, 2208-2212; folk crafts--general, 2111-2117; folk dance, 1320A-1330; folk drama, 1882-1885; folk food, 2219-2227; 2231-2240; folk furniture, 2259; folk games, 1906-1912; folk medicine, 1675-1683; folk music, 242, 756-810; folk narratives--folk tales, 507-521; folk museums, 2492-2498; folk painting, 2073, 2074; folk religion, 1602-1629; folk sculpture, 2101; folk speech, 261-265; folk toys, 2378, 2388; folklore and folklife--general, 1-100; folktales, 507-521; graffiti, 331; gravestone art, 2276-2278; history and study of folklore, general, 121-133; lace, 2335; legends, 587-589; material culture--general, 1977-1989; living history museums, 2493, 2496; musical instruments, 761, 1421, 1802; mythology, 610-634; names and naming, 333, 334; needlework--general, 2335;

occupational folklore, 598; oral literature, 256, 257, 258, 259; popular music--general, 1262, 1268; popular music--bluegrass, 1279, 1304; popular music--blues, 1282-1286; popular music--country, 1303, 1304; popular music--folk rock, 1320; proverbs, 357-370; quilts, 2343, 2344; religious folk music, 1231-1238; riddles, 455-487; rites--general; 1759, 1769; rites--calendar and festival rites, 1765; rites--death, 1876; Robin Hood ballads, 1199; romances, 641-644; samplers, 2380; street cries, 740; supernatural beliefs--animals and mythical beasts, 1534-1535; supernatural beliefs, birdlore, 1556; supernatural beliefs--plantlore, 1566; supernatural beliefs--witchcraft, 1503-1511; technology--general, 2428-2431; technology--agriculture, 2433-2443; technology--textiles, 2459-2464; urban legends, 604A, 605; weaving, 2402, 2403

Biography: architects, 2263; folk artists, 2031, 2056; folk musicians, 769, 997, 1269, 1272, 1280, 1282, 1290, 1312-1314; furniture craftsmen, 2259, 2263

Birdlore (1556-1562): bibliography, 1556; dictionary, 1557; guides, 1550, 1558-1560; lexicons, 1561, 1562

Birth rites and customs, *see* Childbirth rites

Black, *see* Afro-American

Bluegrass music: annotated collection, 1281; bibliography, 1279; guide, 889, 1280, 1442, 1443

Blues: annotated collections, 1297-1302; bibliographies, 1282-1286; classification, 1287; concordance, 1288; dictionaries, 1289, 1290; discographies, 1240, 1291-1296, 1300

Bohemia/Bohemian: riddles, 492

Boontling, 267

Boston Public Library: folk music, dictionary catalog, 816

Brazil: folklore/folklife--general, 73; folktales, 515; popular music, 1266

Britain/British, *see* England, Great Britain

Broadside ballads, *see also* Ballads, 198, 664-667, 832, 891

Brooklyn [NY]: folk games, 1935

Bucharest: folk museum, 2550

Buddhism: bibliography, 1625, 1627; dictionaries, 1648, 1649

Bulgaria/Bulgarian: folk dance, 1391; riddles, 479

Cajun music, *see also* Popular music: 936A, 1007

Calendar and festival rites (1765-1824), *see also* Religious calendar and festival rites (Jewish festival rites and Christmas and Easter festival rites and folk festivals): bibliography, 1765; guides, 1493, 1766-1822

California: archives, 192-194; children's rhymes, 1913; folk dance, 1363; folk games, 1913; folk medicine, 1703; folk music, 893; 1018; folk speech, 267; jump-rope rhymes, 1913; linguistic atlas, 315; names and naming, 350; proverbs, 404

Cameroun: folklore/folklife--general, 8

Canada/Canadian, *see also* Labrador, the Maritimes, Newfoundland, Nova Scotia, Ontario, Quebec, Waterloo: animals and mythic beasts, 1550; archives, 175, 178, 181, 234, 235; ballads, 1168-1170; calendar and festival rites, 1777; children's rhymes, 716-718; customs, beliefs, superstitions, 1484, 1485; decorative arts, 2069; folk art--general, 2069; folk costumes, 2473, 2536; folk dance, 1336, 1386; folk drama, 1886, 1894; folk festivals, 1856; folk games, 713, 1386, 1950; folk museums, 2497, 2509, 2519, 2524, 2525, 2535; folk music, 35, 792-794, 822, 834, 848, 874, 896, 923, 1029-1039A, 1422; folklore/ folklife--general, 36, 70, 71; folklore dissertations, 254; folklore studies in colleges and universities, 245; folktales, 514; material culture, 1777; names and naming, 333, 343, 351; proverbs, 408; quilts, 2347, 2368; riddles, 475; rites--general, 1763; singing games, 1223, 1224; textiles, 2473, 2536; weaving, 2423, 2424

Canadian Indian: folk music, 793; rites, 1763

Cape Cod graveyard art, 2281
Caribbean: folk medicine, 1680; religious music, 1232
Carpets and rugs (2295-2312): atlas, 2295; dictionary, 2296; guides, 2297-2303; exhibition catalog, 2304-2312
Catalogs, *see also* Dictionary catalogs and exhibition catalogs: ballads, 664, 665; broadsides, 664-667, chapbooks, 665; folk art, 2015; folk costumes, 2213; folk museums, 2497, 2498, 2499; musical instruments, 1422-1428; proverbs, 371; sagas, 647
Catskills: folk songs, 944
Cattle industry, 22
Central African folk art, 1996
Central America, *see* individual countries and Latin America, South and Central America
Central west [America] folk songs, 998
Ceramics (2172-2207): bibliographies, 2172-2178; classification, 2179; dictionaries, 2180-2185; directory, 2186; glossary, 2187; guides, 2194-2196, exhibition catalogs, 2059, 2129, 2197-2207
Chapbooks: bibliography, 663; catalog, 665; proverbs, 431; folktales, 548
Cheremis: folk games, 1959; folk songs, 1066
Chicano: folk dance, 1324; folk medicine, 1703; folk music, 41; folklore--general, 41
Child Ballads, 1188; abridgement, 1196; classification of ballad tunes, 1127; tunes, 1186

Childbirth rites and customs, 1469, 1866-1869
Children's folk songs, *see also* Children's rhymes: 913, 1011, 1203-1230, 1942, 1950, 1963
Children's folklore, *see also* Autograph verse, Children's rhymes, Games, Nursery rhymes: bibliography, 10, 20, 62, 255-269, 509
Children's rhymes, *see also* Autograph verse, Games, Nursery rhymes: annotated collections, 704-733, 1227, 1943, 1943, 1950, 1963; bibliographies, 5, 697, 698; classification, 1913, 1914; dictionaries, 699-702; guide, 703
China/Chinese: calendar and festival rites, 1787, 1789; erotic humor, 583; folk art--general, 2071, 2327; folk dance, 798; folk drama, 1901; folk games, 1954, 1955; folk medicine, 1710, 1711; folk music, 798, 1044, 1045; folk poetry, 686; folktales, 538, 539; herbals, 1750-1759; mythology, 625, 627; needlework, 2327; riddles, 480; proverbs, 359, 421-423; symbols, 1668
Christian festival rites, *see also* Christmas and Easter, 1831, 1832
Christian guides, 1660, 1670, 1671
Christian traditions: bibliographies, 1602, 1639-1641
Christmas, *see also* Mumming: annotated collections, 1834-1838, 1840-1842, 1844; bibliography, 1833

2505-2530; journals/periodicals, 2558-2563; quilters, 2345-2347; sea lore, 1590; societies/associations, 2555-2557; weavers, 2406

Discographies, *see also* Indexes to sound recordings: folk dance, 1340; folk music, 34, 51, 63, 67, 766, 798, 800, 861-878, 1240, 1263; religious music--general, 1233, 1239, 1240, 1247; religious music--gospel music, 1233, 1240, 1241, 1271, 1291; popular music--general, 1263, 1266, 1271-1273, 1274; popular music--blues, 1271, 1291-1296, 1300; popular music--country, 1271, 1272, 1305-1311

Dissertations, *see* Ph.D. dissertations

District of Columbia, *see* Washington, D.C.

Doctoral dissertations, *see* Ph.D. dissertations

Dominican Republic: folktales, 536

Drama, ritual, *see* Folk play texts

Dulcimers, 1431

Dutch proverbs, 437

East Africa: folk architecture, 1998; folk art--general, 1998; folk crafts--general, 1998; folk songs, 934

East Asia: folk medicine, 1749

East United States: linguistic atlas, 319; material culture, 1980

Easter, 1839, 1843

Eastern Carolina University Folklore Archive, 222

Eastern Europe, *see* Eurasia--general and Armenia,

Balkans, Bohemia, Bucharest, Bulgaria, Cheremis, Czechoslovakia, Hungary, Latvia, Lithuania, Romania, Russia, Serbo-Croatia, Turkey, Ukraine, Yugoslavia

Eastern Orthodox Church traditions, 1640, 1641

Education and folklore, 121

Egypt/Egyptian mythology, 628, 1664

Embroidery (2323-2334): encyclopedia, 2323; handbook, 2324; pattern books, 2325-2329; exhibition catalogs, 2330-2334

Encyclopedias, *see* Dictionaries and encyclopedias

England/English, *see also* Great Britain: archives, 242, 243; ballads, 664, 1190, 1199-1201; broadsides, 656, 666; calendar and festival rites, 1810, 1821; children's rhymes, 702, 725-732; customs, beliefs, superstitions, 1453, 1459, 1493, 1494, 1497, 1499, 1502; folk architecture, 2142; folk dance, 1335, 1407-1409, 1413, 1414, 1416-1418; folk drama, 1883, 1888, 1903-1905; folk food, 2248, 2258; folk games, 1919, 1920, 1962, 1964, 1965; folk music, 1082-1085, 1088, 1090-1093, 1098-1100, 1102-1106, 1109-1112; folk speech, 272, 277, 280, 281, 283, 293, 294, 299, 308; folktales, 534, 535, 561, 593, 1485; linguistic atlases, 326-330; metalcraft, 2451; needlework, 2330, 2334; occupational lore, 601; proverbs, 357, 441, 443,

1183

Europe/European cont'd.
instruments, 1425, 1429, 1430, 1432, 1433, 1444; proverbs, 373, 432-440; religious beliefs, 1603; riddles, 494-496; singing games, 1226; textiles, 2490; weaving, 2412

Exhibition catalogs: ceramics, 2197-2207; embroidery, 2330-2334; folk architecture, 2171; folk art--general, 2032-2072; folk costume, 2218; folk crafts--general, 2126-2133; folk food, 2258; folk furniture, 2271-2275; folk painting, 2078-2100; folk sculpture, 2104-2110; folk toys, 2396-2401; metalcraft, 2455-2458; musical instruments, 1444; needlework--general, 2321, 2322; nursery rhymes, 736; quilts, 2359-2379; rites, 1761; samplers, 2382-2384; textiles, 2476-2491; weaving, 2422-2427

Fables (503-506): bibliographies, 503, 504; classification, 527; dictionaries, 505, 506; guide, 620

Fairylore (1529-1533): classification, 1530; dictionaries, 1529-1531; guides, 1532, 1533

Family narratives/legends: 595-597; fieldwork manuals, 145, 146

Farmers' almanacs, *see* Almanac, Weatherlore

Farmers' Museum (Cooperstown, NY), 2545

Farms and farm buildings: bibliographies, 2434, 2437, 2438, 2441, 2443

Festival rites, *see* Calendar and festival rites, Folk festivals

Fiddling: bibliography, 764

Fieldwork (144-164): bibliographies, 52, 144; guides and manuals, 145-164, 883-892

Fife Collection of Western American Folksong and Folklore [Utah], 231

Filmographies, 56, 102, 103, 879, 880

Finland/Finnish: archives, 238; epic poetry, 696; proverbs, 373; research, 92A; riddles, 495

Flanders Ballad Collection, 914

Florence E. Brunnings [Folk Music] Collection, 829

Florida folk songs, 992

Folk architecture (2134-2171): bibliographies, 25, 41, 1993, 2009, 2014, 2134-2158; classification and typologies, 2559-2162; dictionary catalog, 2016; guide, 2163-2179; exhibition catalog, 2016

Folk art--general (1902-2072), *see also* Folk architecture, Folk painting, Folk crafts, Folk sculpture: bibliographies, 35, 56, 1992-2015, 2073; catalogs, 2015, 2086, 2093; dictionaries and encyclopedias, 2018-2020, 2042, 2065; dictionary catalog, 2016; directories, 2021-2023; exhibition catalogs, 2032-2072; guides and handbooks, 2024-2027; indexes, 2028-2031

Folk artists: biographical index, 2031; directory, 2021-2023

Folk belief systems (Chapter V), *see* Customs, beliefs, and superstitions, Folk medicine, Folk religion, Supernatural beliefs, Symbols

Folk cookery, *see* Folk food

Folk costume (2208-2218): bibliographies, 5, 2208-2212; catalog, 2213; directories to collections, 2473, 2531; encyclopedias, 2214-2216; exhibition catalog, 2218; guide, 1389, 1864; index, 2217

Folk crafts--general (2111-2133), *see also* Baskets, Carpets and rugs, Ceramics, Clocks, Embroidery, Folk architecture, Folk art-general, Folk costume, Folk furniture, Folk sculpture, Folk toys, Glassblowing, Gravestone art, Lace, Needlework, Quilts, Samplers, Stencilling, Textiles, Weaving: bibliographies, 8, 25, 41, 61, 1995, 1999, 2001, 2009, 2111-2117; dictionaries, 2020, 2118-2121; directories, 2122, 2123; exhibition catalogs, 2038, 2072, 2126-2137; guide, 2124; index, 2125

Folk culture--general, *see also* Folklife, Folklore and folklife: bibliographies, 37, 53, 59, 60; curriculum, 247; encyclopedias, 112, 1991; fieldwork manual, 157; handbooks, 163

Folk dance (1321-1440), *see also* Clogging, Contra dance, Dance--ritual, Folk drama, Round dance, Square dance: bibliographies, 25, 26, 34, 757-761; 772, 796-800; 1320A-1330, 1340; classification, 1331-1333; dictionary, 1334; dictionary cata-logs, 1335-1339; discography, 1340; filmography, 879; guide to periodicals, 926; indexes, 814, 1341-1343; instructional guides and manuals, 1344-1420, 1772

Folk dance festivals: directory, 1849

Folk drama (1882-1905): bibliographies, 8, 25, 41, 1882-1885, classification, 1886; guide, 1887; indexes, 1888; play texts, 1889-1906

Folk epics, *see* Epics

Folk festivals (1846-1863): classification, 1846; guides and handbooks, 1847, 1848; directories, 1849-1863

Folk food (2219-2258), *see also* Folk medicine, Foodways, Plantlore: annotated collections, 2228-2230; bibliographies, 8, 37, 38, 56, 61, 2219-2227, 2231-2240; cookbooks, 2248-2257; dictionaries and encyclopedias, 2241-2246; exhibition catalog, 2258

Folk furniture (2259-2775): bibliography, 37, 1992, 2259; classification, 2260; dictionaries, 2261, 2262; exhibition catalogs, 2271-2275; guides, 2263-2270

Folk games (1906-1976), *see also* Play-party games, Singing games: annotated collections, 1216, 1227, 1923-1976; bibliographies, 25, 37, 41, 1906-1912; classification, 1913-1918; guides, 702, 707, 708, 710, 712-

Folk schools: bibliography, 25, 50, 131

Folk sculpture (2101-2110), *see also* Folk art--general: bibliography, 2101; exhibition catalogs, 2104-2110; guides and handbooks, 2025, 2102, 2103

Folk song, *see* Folk music

Folk speech play--general (261-330), *see also* Graffiti, Names and naming, Proverbs, Riddles, Slang: bibliographies, 8, 41, 54, 55, 261-265; dictionaries and etymologies, 266-308; guides and manuals, 309-312; linguistic and word atlases, 313-330

Folk tales, *see* Folktales

Folk toys (2387-2401), *see also* Folk games: bibliographies, 1909, 1910, 2387-2388; classification, 2389; encyclopedias, 2390; exhibition catalogs, 2396-2401; guides, 2391-2395; index, 1922

Folk verse, *see* Autograph verse, Children's rhymes, Mother Goose/nursery rhymes

Folklife--general, *see* Folklore/folklife--general

Folklife archives and guides to collections: 173-182

Folklife fieldwork: manual, 146, 155

Folklife resources, *see also* Folk museums and living historical farms: bibliography, 2496; classification, 2502; catalog, 2502; directories, 2510-2518, 2526, 2528, 2529, 2532, 2535; guides, 173-175, 177-180

Folklore and American literature, 45

Folklore and education (245-255), *see also* Folklore curriculum, Folklore methodology, Folklore study in colleges and universities, Teachers' manuals, Theses and dissertations: bibliography, 121

Folklore and folklife--general (Chapter I): abstracts, 101; bibliographies, 1-100, 1602; dictionaries and encyclopedias, 107-112, 1663; dictionary catalogs, 104-106; guides and handbooks, 113-120; indexes, 102, 103; indexes to media, 35, 36

Folklore Archive of Chico State College, 192

Folklore Archive of the Finnish Literary Society, 238

Folklore associations, *see* Folklore societies

Folklore curriculum, 247, 252

Folklore genres, 134, 142

Folklore journals: directories, 2558-2563; indexes, 924-926, 1278, 1341, 2303A, 2564-2577

Folklore methodology: bibliography, 130

Folklore societies: bibliographies, 2555-2557

Folklore study in colleges and universities, 245, 248-252

Folktales--general, *see also* Motif- and tale-type indexes: bibliographies, 34, 36, 37, 54-56, 61, 72, 507-521; classification, 522-559; dictionaries and encyclopedias, 560-562; indexes, 563-567

Foodways (2219-2230), *see also* Folk food: annotated collections, 2228-2230; bibliographies, 2219-2227

Folk furniture (2259-2775): bibliographies, 37, 1992, 2259; classification, 2260; dictionaries, 2261, 2262; exhibition catalogs, 2271-2275; guides, 2263-2270

Forecastle songs, *see* Sea songs

Fort Hays Kansas State College Folklore Collection, 210

France/French: animal lore, 1555; customs, beliefs, supersitions, 1455, 1487; folk costumes, 1487; folk dance, 1407; folk music, 1067; folk songs, 1067; folklore/folklife--general, 98; plantlore, 1573; proverbs, 432; rites--general, 1762

Frakturs: bibliography, 2074; classification, 2075; dictionary catalog, 2077; guide to collections, 2078, 2080

Free Library of Philadelphia, 2080

Fulani proverbs, 394

Furniture, *see* Folk furniture

Games, *see* Folk games

[Garbisch] Edgar William and Bernice Chrysler Garbisch collections: exhibition catalogs, 2082-2085

Gazetteers: animals and mythic places, 1543; customs, beliefs, superstitions, 1459; ghosts, 1522, 1523; mythical places, 1565

George Korson Folklore Archive (Kings' College, Wilkes-Barre, PA), 227

George Pullen Jackson Collection

of Southern Hymnody, 1236

Georgia, *see also* Sea Islands: ceramics, 2198; folk furniture, 2272, 2273

German culture: bibliography, 53

German-American culture: bibliography, 26; directory, 2543

Germanic folk literature, 560

Germany/German: calendar and festival customs, 1800; epic literature, 651; folklore/folklife--general, 21; folktales, 562; legends, 653; proverbs, 373, 433; sagas, 562

Ghana: calendar and festival rites, 1773; folk drama, 1889; folk songs, 993

Ghosts: encyclopedia, 1514, 1517; gazetteer, 1523

Girard Foundation (Santa Fe, NM): 2048, 2486

Glass (2445-2449): bibliography, 2445; classification, 2446; dictionary, 2447; guides, 2448, 2449

Glossaries: animals and mythic beasts, 1551, 1552; birdlore, 1561, 1562; ceramics, 2187; folk music, 881

Gold and goldweights, *see* metalcraft

Gospel music: bibliographies, 1232, 1233; catalogs, 1246; dictionary, 1289; discographies, 1233, 1240, 1241, 1271, 1291

Graffiti: bibliography, 331; collection, 580; dictionary, 332

Grandma Moses: exhibition catalog, 2090

Gravestone art: bibliographies, 2276-2278; guides, 2279-2283

1189

Great Britain/British--general, *see also* England, Scotland, Wales:
agriculture, 2433; archives, 828; ballads, 1125, 1133, 1134, 1139, 1183-1201; birdlore, 1561; calendar and festival rites, 1803-1822; ceramics, 2195, 2196; children's rhymes, 722-732; customs, beliefs, superstitions, 1453, 1456, 1457, 1459, 1493-1502; fieldwork, 152, 155; folk architecture, 2142, 2158, 2160, 2164; folk crafts, 2131; folk dance, 1335, 1338, 1406-1419; folk drama, 1883, 1902-1905; folk food, 2248, 2249; folk games, 1919, 1920, 1961-1967; folk museums, 2529, 2530, 2554; folk music, 806-807, 820, 828, 845, 863, 870, 895, 898, 1082-1112; folk poetry, 690-692; folk speech, 272, 293, 294; folklore/folklife--general, 2, 15 98, 99; linguistic atlases, 326-328, 330; metalcraft, 2451; names and naming, 345, 346, 354-356; needlework, 2330, 2334; proverbs, 441-451; riddles, 487-501; singing games, 1227-1230

Greece/Greek: birdlore, 1562; calendar and festival rites, 1801; folk music, 1068-1071; folklore/folklife--general, 94, 96; humor, 575; musical instruments, 1429

Greek and Roman myths, *see* Classical mythology

Greenfield Village and Henry Ford Museum, 2543

Guatemalan textiles, 2461, 2484, 2488

Guides and handbooks: animals and mythic beasts, 1544-1550; archives, 166-244; baskets, 2284A-2291; birdlore, 1558-1560; calendar and festival rites, 1766-1823; carpets, 2297-2303; children's rhymes, 699; ceramics, 2188-2196; clocks, 2316; customs, beliefs and superstitions, 1492; embroidery, 2324; fairylore, 1532, 1534; folk art--general, 2024; folk crafts--general, 2124; folk dance, 1344-1420; folk drama, 1887; folk furniture, 2263-2270; folk museums, 2502-2504; folk music, 886-892; folk sculpture, 2102, 2103; folk speech, 309, 310; folklore/folklife--general, 113-120; lace, 2340-2342; metalcraft, 2454; musical instruments, 1441-1443; mythology, 620-640; needlework, 2319; plantlore and flowerlore, 1574-1576; puberty rites, 1870; quilts, 2348-2354; religious calendar and festival rites, 1824, 1844; rites--general, 1762; romances, 653, 654, 662; samplers, 2381; textiles, 2475; weaving, 2407-2421; witches, 1524, 1525, 1532

Guides to collections, *see* Exhibition catalogs

Gulf states: linguistic atlas, 323

Gypsy customs: dictionary, 1458

Haffenreffer Museum of Anthropology, 2218

Haitian folk songs, 1040

Hall Collection [Lexington, KY], 2104

Indexes, *see also* Abstracts, Classification: ballads, 1125, 1127-1131, 1133, 1134, 1137; carpets and rugs, 2302A; films and videotapes, 102, 103; folk art--general, 2028-2031; folk costume, 2214-2216; folk crafts--general, 2125; folk dance, 1202, 1341-1343; folk food, 2247; folk games, 1922; folk medicine, 1687-1689; folk music--general, 814, 815; folk music collections, 829-834, 887; folk speech, 311, 312; folklore/folklife--general, 16, 102, 103; folktales, 16; legends, 563, 564; motif- and type-indexes, 524-553; journals/periodicals, 2464-2577; mythology, 559, 560; popular music, 1275, 1276; proverbs, 375; religious music, 1243-1246; singing games, 1202, 1342; songs (in printed sources), 893-901; sound recordings, 902-923
India/Indian: calendar and festival rites, 179; folk architecture, 1999; folk art--general, 1999; folk costume, 1389; folk craft--general, 1999; folk dance, 797, 1389, 1390; folk music, 797, 1046-1049; folk poetry, 687-689; folklore/folklife--general, 80, 81, 87; folktales, 540-542; musical instruments, 1434; mythology, 629-633; plantlore and flowerlore, 1569; proverbs, 424, 425; riddles, 481, 482; textiles, 2491
Indian folklore, *see* Native American folklore
Indiana: archives, 202-209; ballads, 1147; folk architecture, 2159;

folk festival, 1852; folk medicine, 1707; folk music, 909-912, 1147; folklore/folklife--general, 66; humor, 571; names and naming, 349; play-party games, 1221; proverbs, 396; riddles, 466
Indiana University Archives, 203-208
Indiana University Research Center in Anthropology, Folklore and Linguistics, 202
Indians, North American, *see* Native American folklore
Indigenous architecture, *see* Folk architecture
Indonesia/Indonesian: folklore/folklife--general, 77; riddles, 483; textiles, 2482
Instructional guides, *see* Guides and handbooks
International folklore: agriculture, 2444; ballads, 1140-1144; birdlore, 1560; calendar and festival rites, 1767-1771; carpets, 2295, 2296, 2299; ceramics, 2176, 2180, 2181, 2183, 2185, 2195; childbirth rites, 1866; children's rhymes, 704, 705; Christmas customs, 1844; courtship and marriage rites, 1875; customs, beliefs, superstitions, 1460, 1461; death rites, 1878; decorative arts, 2018, 2019; folk architecture, 2157; folk art--general, 1999, 2008, 2013, 2016, 2018-2020, 2028; folk costumes, 2213, 2216; folk dances, 1321, 1323, 1325, 1328, 1334, 1339, 1340, 1344-1360; folk food, 2223, 2230, 2233, 2237-2239, 2241, 2242, 2245, 2246; folk

International folklore cont'd.

furniture, 2261; folk games, 1923-1927; folk medicine, 1690, 1718-1724; folk museums, 2497, 2505, 2507, 2536; folk music, 748-756, 814, 815, 829-831, 844, 845, 847, 849-852, 854, 855, 864, 867, 868, 873, 880, 882, 885, 886, 897, 902, 903, 926-933; folk painting, 2076; folk poetry, 668-670; folk sculpture, 2108; folk toys, 2392, 2397; folklore/folklife--general, 1-16, 103, 171, 108; folktales, 563-565; ghostlore, 1522; lace, 2341; legends, 594; musical instruments, 1424-1425, 1427, 1430, 1433, 1435; metalwork, 2453; motif- and type- indexes, 524-528; myths, 610-622; needlework, 2333; proverbs, 37, 361-364, 367-370, 372, 375-384; riddles, 459; samplers, 2383; sealore, 1592; supernatural beliefs, 1506; textiles, 2467, 2468, 2474, 2480, 2485

Iowa: customs, beliefs, superstitions, 1482; folk festivals, 1852; play-party games, 1215

Iranian ceramics, 2203

Ireland: archives, 239; ballads, 1131, 1136, 1179-1182; birdlore, 1556; calendar and festival rites, 1802; children's rhymes, 702, 720, 721, 1960; customs, beliefs, superstitions, 1446, 1453, 1456, 1488-1490, 1501; death rites, 1881; fieldwork, 159; folk architecture, 2160; folk dances, 1072, 1400-1402, 1408; folk food, 2248; folk games, 702, 720, 1919, 1960, 1964; folk music, 803, 805, 806, 870, 872, 1072-1076, 1088, 1092, 1178, 2529, 2530, 2553; folklore/ folklife--general, 90; folktales, 550, 551; ghosts, 1523; metalcraft, 2451; mythology, 650; names and naming, 353, 355; proverbs, 435, 436; riddles, 496; singing games, 1226

Irish Folklore Commission, 239

Iron work, see Metalcraft

Isabella Stewart Gardner Museum [Boston, MA], 2478

Islam: proverbs, 417

Islamic religious beliefs: bibliography, 1628; dictionaries/ encyclopedias, 1646, 1647

Israel: archive, 237

Italy/Italian: customs, beliefs, superstitions, 1403, 1447, 1491, 1492; folk architecture, 1999; folk art--general, 1999; folk costume, 1403; folk craft--general, 1999; folk dance, 1403; folk medicine, 1713; folk music, 1077, 1078; folklore/folklife--general, 88, 89, 91, 95; folktales, 552

Jabo [Nigeria] proverbs, 387

Jamaica/Jamaican: folk drama, 1895; folk games, 1950; riddles, 476

Japan/Japanese: calendar and festival rites, 1792-1795, 1823; ceramics, 2200; children's rhymes, 719; folk dance, 800; folk games, 1955; folk museums, 2526, 2527; folk music, 800, 1046, 1050, 1051; folk

Japan/Japanese cont'd.
toys, 2394, 2401; folklore/folklife--general, 75, 78, 83; folktales, 543, 544; musical instruments, 1426, 1428; mythology, 624, 626; proverbs, 412, 413, 426-428; riddles, 484, 488; stencils, 2386; textiles, 2472
Java: folklore/folklife--general, 79
J.D. Robb Collection of Folk Music, 915
Jewish folklore: festival rites and customs, 1825-1829, 1865; folk art, 2008, 2051; folk music, 811-813; folklore--general, 1602, 1605-1609, 1635-1638, 1655-1657; folktales, 525
Jigs, 1402, 1411
Joan O'Bryant Collection of Folk Music [Wichita, KS], 831
John G. White Collection [Cleveland, OH]: 104, 105, 224, 817, 1138
John Henry: bibliography, 589
John Kane: exhibition catalog, 2092
Johns Island [GA], 942
Jokes and anecdotes (568-586), see also Humor: annotated collections, 570-577, 580-586; bibliography, 578; classification, 568, 569, 579
Journals, see Folklore journals
Julius Krohn: bibliography, 130
Jump rope rhymes: annotated collections, 699, 701, 703, 705, 706, 709, 710, 712, 715, 716, 710, 724, 732, 733, 1933, 1944; classification, 1913, 1914, 1918

Kansas: archive, 210; customs, beliefs, superstitions, 1475; folk

music, 831; play-party games, 1215, 1219; quilts, 2377
Kentucky: archive, 211-213; ballads, 1157, 1166; beliefs, customs, superstitions, 1483; deathlore, 1880; folk art--general, 2007; folk crafts--general, 2007; folk festivals, 1852; folk songs, 990, 1004, 1016, 1019, 1028; folk speech, 265; folklore/folklife--general, 67; riddles, 468
King Arthur, see Arthurian romances
Korea/Korean: calendar and festival rites, 1796; ceramics, 2199; erotic humor, 584; folk dance, 799; folk drama, 1900; folk games, 1955; folk music, 799, 1044, 1052, 1053; folktales, 545; proverbs, 413
Kru proverbs, 386
Kxatla riddles, 462

Labor songs, see Work songs
Labrador: ballads, 1169; folk music, 874, 1169
Lace and lacework (2335-2342): bibliographies, 2335-2337; dictionaries, 2338, 2339; guides, 2340-2342
Lang, Andrew, see Andrew Lang
Latin American folklore, see also individual countries and South and Central America: 72, 1327
Latvian folktales, 547
Lebanese proverbs, 417
Ledbetter, Huddie (Leadbelly), 988
Legends (587-594), see also Family narratives, Occupational lore, Urban folklore: annotated

1194

Mbeere riddles, 460

Media: indexes to, 102, 103, 905, 2497, 2498

Meine Library of Folklore and Humor (University of Illinois), 200

Melanesian folktales, 537

Memorial Library of Newfoundland, 923

Mennonite customs and beliefs, 1613, 1617

Mennonite music, 1039, 1242

Metalcraft (2450-2458): dictionary, 2450-2454; exhibition catalog, 2059, 2455-2458

Metropolitan Museum of Art, 1424, 1427, 2304, 2363

Mexican-American folk art, 2050

Mexico/Mexican: archive, 215-219; calendar and festival rites, 1784; ceramics, 2179; childbirth customs and rites, 1709 1868; folk art--general, 2405; folk dance, 1324, 1364, 1387, 1388; folk drama, 1896- 1898; folk games, 1911; folk medicine, 1566, 1729, 1868; folk music, 1018; folk toys, 2405; legends, 1388; plantlore and flowerlore, 1709; proverbs, 411; spiritualism, 1709; textiles, 2488

Michigan, see also Greenfield Village: ballads, 1158; folk festivals, 1780, 1852; folk music, 963

Michigan State University Folklore Archive, 215, 216

Micronesian folktales, 557

Middle and South Atlantic States: linguistic atlas, 321

Middle East: folklore/folklife--

general, 76

Midwest: folk festivals, 1852; linguistic atlas, 313

Milwaukee Public Museum, 2375

Miners' folk songs, 977, 1090

Minnesota: folk art--general, 2039; folk festival, 1852: folk music, 963; folklore/folklife--general, 49

Mississippi: archive, 220; children's rhymes, 709; folk art--general 2130; folk crafts--general, 2130; folk medicine, 1731, 1744; folk music, 866, 970; folklore/folklife--general, 34, 39

Mississippi John Hurt: bibliography, 1228

Missouri, see also St. Louis: ballads, 1146; folk festivals, 1852; folk music, 791, 1146; play-party games, 1203, 1210, 1222

Mongolian riddles, 486

Monsters, see Animals and mythic beasts

Moravian folk art, 2034

Moravian hymns, 1248

Mormon folklore: bibliography, 65, 1620-1622

Morocco: proverbs, 420

Morphology, see Classification

Morris dance, 1418

Mother Goose, see Nursery rhymes

Motif-indexes, see also Classification: 527, 529, 530, 534, 535, 541, 543, 547, 549, 550, 552, 555-558, 648, 649

Multicultural folklore, see International folklore

1196

Mummers' plays and mumming: classification, 1886; indexes, 1888; texts, 1894, 1895, 1903-1905

Murder ballads, 1148

Museum of American Folk Art, 2033, 2041

Museum of Early Southern Decorative Art, 2034, 2059

Museum of International Folk Art, 2048, 2486, 2542

Museum of Modern Art, 2035

Museum of the American Indian, 2081

Museums, *see* Folk museums

Music, *see* Folk music

Musical instruments (1421-1444): bibliographies, 25, 761, 802, 1421; catalogs, 1422-1428; classification, 1429-1437; dictionaries, 1438, 1439; directory, 1440; exhibition catalogs, 907, 1444; filmography, 879; guides and handbooks, 889, 890, 1280, 1441-1443; indexes, 894

Musical notation, *see* Classification-folk music

Mysticism: bibliography, 1629

Mythical beasts, *see* Animals and mythic beasts

Mythical places: dictionaries, 1563, 1564; gazetteer, 1565

Mythology--general (610-640), *see also* Asian mythology, Egyptian mythology, Hindu mythology: annotated collection, 610; bibliographies, 4, 72, 610-612, 1602; classification, 527; dictionaries, 108, 613-619, 1531, 1631, 1663; guides, 620-622;

indexes, 559, 560, 563, 564, 623

Naive folk art/naive folk painting, *see also* Folk painting: dictionary, 2076; exhibition catalogs, 2081-2084, 2087-2089, 2092-2094, 2097, 2098

Names and naming: bibliographies, 25, 333, 334; dictionaries, 335-356

Nantucket: gravestone art, 2281

National dress, *see* Folk costume

National Museum of Canada, 234

Native American folklore: archives, 166, 822, 823; baskets, 2287, 2288, 2290, 2092-2094, 2481; calendar and festival rites, 1775, 1780; carpets and rugs, 2298, 2481; ceramics, 2188, 2202; folk art, 2022, 2043, 2045, 2067; folk dance, 1772; folk food, 2250; folk games, 1934, 1947; folk medicine, 1705, 1708, 1745; folk painting, 2081; folk play, 1893; folklore--general, 27, 30, 32, 38, 50, 62; folktales, 513; herbal medicine guide, 1730, 1731, 1733, 1739, 1742, 1743, 1745; index to sound recordings, 912; needlework, 2391; poetry, 675-679, 682, 683, 685; rites, 1763; textiles, 2476, 2481, 2482, 2485, 2489; weaving, 2413, 2421

Near East: textiles, 2490

Nebraska: customs, beliefs, superstitions, 1465, 1481, 1525; folk games, 1948; folk medicine, 1694; folk music, 8998; play-party games, 1215; proverbs, 403; quilts, 2378

Needlework--general (2317-2322), see also Embroidery (crewelwork, needlepoint), lace, quilts, samplers): dictionaries, 2317, 2318; exhibition catalogs, 2321, 2322; handbook, 2319; pattern book, 2320

Negro, see Afro-American

Nepal/Nepalese: calendar and festival rites, 1790; folk arts--general, 2072; folk crafts--general, 2072

Netsuke: guide, 2102, 2103

New Brunswick: folk songs, 1039A

New England, see also individual states: ballads, 1155; folk dance, 1031, 1386; folk games, 1031, 1386; folk music, 980, 1031; folk museums, 2513; folk speech, 284; gravestone art, 2281; linguistic atlas, 318; metalcraft, 2456

New Guinea folk music, 808

New Jersey: archives, 174, 2511; folk museums, 2511; folklore/folklife--general, 28; gravestone art, 2283

New Mexico: folk art--general, 2048, 2064, 2065; folk drama, 1890; folk music archives, 915, 1003; folk museums, 2542; folk painting, 2099, 2396; folk poetry, 677; folk toys, 2396; folklore/folklife--general, 61; index to sound recordings, 915; riddles, 467; singing games, 1209; textiles, 2542

New York [city]: folk museums, 2514; urban folklore; 609

New York [state]: archives, 221; autograph verse, 734; ceramics, 2186, 2197; folk dance, 1337, 1339; folk games, 1935; folk museums, 2514, 2515, 2518; folk music, 944, 963, 1020; folk painting, 2098; folk sculpture, 2106; gravestone art, 2283; musical instruments, 1424, 1427; weaving, 2427

New York Public Library, 818, 1337, 1339, 2016

New York State Historical Association, 2098, 2518, 2545

New Zealand: folk games, 1968-1970, 1976; folk music, 1114

Newark Museum, 2368

Newfoundland: ballads, 1168; folk drama, 1886, 1894; folk music, 874, 896, 923, 1038, 1168

Nigeria/Nigerian: ceramics, 2201; folk music, 758

Norse mythology (634-637), see also Iceland/Icelandic, Romances and sagas: bibliography, 634; dictionary, 635; guides, 636, 637

North Africa/African: folk architecture, art, and crafts, 1999; folk medicine, 1726

North America, see America/American and United States

North Carolina: archive, 222; ballads, 955; ceramics, 2175, 2207; children's rhymes, 707; customs, beliefs, superstitions, 463, 1467; folk art--general, 2034, 2059; folk furniture, 2274, 2275; folk games, 707 1931; folk medicine, 1688, 1697; folk music, 955, 1152; folk painting, 2096; folk speech, 307; folklore/folklife--general, 31; proverbs, 407; quilts, 2379; riddles, 473

Northeast Archive of Folklore and Oral History, 214

Northeast [England]: coal miners' lore, 601

Northwest [America], *see also* Pacific Northwest: proverbs, 401, 469

Northwestern University Laboratory of Comparative Musicology, 201

Norway/Norwegian, *see also* Norse mythology, Romances and sagas: folk dance, 1404; folk music, 1079; folktales, 553; legends, 590

Nova Scotia: ballads, 1170; customs, beliefs, superstitions, 1484; decorative arts--general, 2069; folk art--general, 2069; folk music, 1033, 1034, 1170

Nursery rhymes (735-739): annotated collections, 737-739; dictionary, 735; exhibition catalogs, 736

Occult: bibliographies, 1503, 1506; dictionaries, 1516, 1519

Occupational lore (598-604), *see also* Urban folklore: annotated collections, 599-604; bibliography, 598; dictionaries, 289, 301, 302

Oceania--general, *see also* Australia, Hawaii, Melanesia, New Guinea, Malta, Hawaii, Samoa, New Zealand: calendar and festival rites, 1823; children's rhymes, 733; customs, beliefs, superstitions, 1452; folk art--general, 809, 2004; folk dance, 1420; folk games, 1968-1971, 1976; folk medicine, 1715-1717;

folk music, 808, 809, 1113-1118; folk poetry, 693; folklore/folklife--general, 100; mythology, 639, 640; proverbs, 452-454; quilts, 2322; religious beliefs, 1011, 1603; riddles, 472, 502

Oceanic mythology, 639, 640

Ohio, *see also* Cleveland Public Library: archives, 223, 224; ballads, 1138, 1153, 1162; customs, beliefs, superstitions, 1479; folk art--general, 2044, 2046; folk festivals, 1852; folk medicine, 1701; folk music, 1138, 1153, 1162, 1243, 1244; folklore/folklife--general, 47; play-party songs, 1204; quilts, 2359

Oil industry: folklore, 599

Oklahoma: folk food, 2252; folk medicine, 1744

Old Slave Market Museum [Charleston, SC], 2038

Ontario: archives, 2524; folk museums, 2524; folk songs, 1036; quilts, 2365

Oral data: collections, 882-885; indexes to, 904, 909-912

Oral folklore, *see also* Ballads, Folk songs, Folktales, Myths, Legends: bibliography, 35, 54, 256, 257

Oral history: archives, 168, 183, 184; bibliography, 33; fieldwork manuals, 153, 160, 161

Oral literature: bibliography, 694

Oregon: archives, 225, 226

Oriental rugs: atlas, 2295; dictionary, 2296; exhibition catalogs, 2304, 2306; guides, 2299-2303

1199

1200

Place names: bibliography, 333; dictionaries, 347-356

Plantlore and flowerlore: annotated collection, 1599; bibliography, 1566; dictionaries/encyclopedias, 1567-1573; guides and handbooks, 1574-1576; lexicons, 1577-1580

Play-party games, *see also* Children's verse, Games: annotated collections, 945, 1203-1230; index, 1202

Play, *see* Folk games

Play texts, 1889-1905

Plays, *see* Folk drama

Poland/Polish: folk art--general, 2027; folk music, 1063; folklore/folklife--general, 2027

Poltergeists: bibliography, 1504

Polynesia/Polynesian: folk dance, 1420; folktales, 557, 558

Popular culture: bibliography, 1984, 1988

Popular music--general, *see also* Bluegrass, Blues, Cajun music, Country and western, Folk rock: bibliographies, 1262-1268; dictionaries, 1269, 1270; discographies, 1263, 1271-1273; handbook; 1274; indexes to printed sources, 1275, 1276; index to reviews, 1277; index to periodicals, 1278

Portuguese folk dance, 1405

Pottery, *see* Ceramics

Preservation: bibliography, 2145, 2149, 2493, 2495

Primitive art: bibliography, 2013

Primitive religion: bibliography, 1613

Protest songs: annotated collections, 927, 966; bibliography, 766

Proverbs (357-454): bibliographies, 8, 96, 357-370; classification, 372-374, 439; dictionaries/collections, 376-454, 1778; indexes, 375

Puberty rites, 1870

Publications of the Folklore Society, 2

Puerto Rico/Puerto Rican: folk music, 796; folktales, 536

Quebec folksongs, 1029, 1030

Quilts (2343-2379): bibliographies, 2343, 2344; directories, 2345-2347; exhibition catalogs, 2359-2379; guides, 2348, 2349; handbooks, 2297, 2350-2354; pattern books, 2355-2379

Railroad folklore, 604

Randall V. Mills Memorial Archive of Northwest Folklore [University of Oregon], 226

Reference collections: bibliography, 126

Regional dialects: bibliographies, 30, 41, 264, 265; dictionaries, 67, 268, 273, 275, 279, 281, 284, 289, 297, 298, 300, 302, 303-305, 307, 313-330

Religious beliefs, *see* Folk religion

Religious calendar and festival rites (1824-1845), *see also* Calendar and festival rites: bibliography, 1765; guides, 1767, 1825-1845

Religious folk art: bibliography, 2073; exhibition catalogs, 2042, 2065, 2086, 2099

Religious folk music, *see also* Afro-American folk music: annotated collections, 1248-1261; bibliographies, 1231-1238; discographies, 1239-1241; encyclopedia, 1241; handbook, 1242; indexes, 1243-1247

Research methods, *see* Archives and archiving, Fieldwork

Rhode Island: archive, 173; folklife resources, 173, 2510; needlework, 2321

Rhymes, *see* Children's rhymes, Folk poetry

Riddles (455-502): annotated collections, 401, 459-502; bibliographies, 8, 37, 455-457; classification, 458

Rites--general (1759-1764), *see also* Calendar and festival rites, Childbirth Rites, Courtship and marriage rites, Death rites, Puberty rites, and Religious calendar and festival rites: annotated collections, 1763, 1764; bibliographies, 1759, 1760; exhibition catalog, 1761; guide, 1762

Rites of passage--general, *see also* Childbirth rites, Courtship and marriage rites, Death rites, and Puberty rites: annotated collections, 1764, 1864-1869

Ritual poetry, 673, 675, 676, 687, 688

Robin Hood ballads (1199-1201): annotated collections, 1143, 1200, 1201; bibliography, 1199

Romances [Spanish], 795

Romances and sagas (641-662), *see also* Arthurian romance: bibliographies, 641-646; catalogs, 647; classification, 527, 549, 648, 649; dictionaries, 562, 650-652; guides and handbooks, 653, 654

Romania/Romanian, *see* Rumania

Round dances: discography, 1340; guides, 1357, 1371, 1382, 1402

Rumania/Rumanian: folk art--general, 2027; folk dance, 1353, 1394; folk museums, 2549; jokes and anecdotes, 572; folk music, 1056; riddles, 494

Russia/Russian: epics, 695; folk medicine, 1712; folk music, 1062, 1064; folk painting and sculpture, 2110; needlework, 2331; proverbs, 429, 430; riddles, 492

Rugs, *see* Carpets and rugs

Sagas, *see* Romances and sagas

Sailors' songs, *see* Sea songs

Samoan proverbs, 454

Samplers (2380-2384): bibliography, 2380; exhibition catalogs, 2332, 2382-2384; guided, 2297, 2381

Santos: bibliography, 2073; exhibition catalogs, 2086, 2099

Scandinavia--general, *see also* individual countries, Romances and sagas: ballads, 1132; folk dance, 1395; mythology, 634, 635; proverbs, 373

Schimmel, Wilhelm, *see* Wilhelm Schimmel

Schomburg Center for Research in Black Culture [New York], 2040

Supernatural beliefs, *see* Animals and mythic beliefs, Birdlore, Fairylore, Ghosts, Magic, Mythical places, Plant and Flowerlore, Sea lore, Stonelore, Weatherlore, and Witchcraft

Superstitions, *see* Customs, beliefs, and superstitions

Swahili: poetry, 673; proverbs, 392

Sweden/Swedish: archives, 240, 241; weaving, 2412

Sword dance, 1409

Symbols and symbolism (1658-1668): dictionaries, 1542, 1557, 1571, 1658-1668; guides, 1575, 1663, 1669-1674

Syrian folk architecture, art, and craft, 1999

Tale type-indexes, *see* Type-indexes

Taylor, Archer, *see* Archer Taylor

Taylor Museum [Colorado Springs, CO], 2086

Teaching of folklore, 245, 249-251

Teaching manuals, *see also* Guides: general, 246, 247; folk dance, 886, 1344, 1347, 1353, 1354, 1356, 1358, 1360, 1370, 1374, 1379, 1389

Technology--general, *see also* Agriculture, Glassblowing, Metalcraft, Textiles: bibliographies, 41, 2428-2431

Tennessee: archive, 228, 229; folk food, 2251; folklore/folklife--general, 37; linguistic atlas, 322; riddles, 471; sound recordings index, 906

Texas: archive, 230; Christmas customs, 1834; folk food, 2230; folk medicine, 1692; folk songs,

975, 995, 996; linguistic atlas, 314, 324; play-party song; quilts, 2364; work songs, 975, 996

Textiles (2459-2491), *see also* weaving: bibliographies, 2459-2464; classification, 2465-2466; dictionaries, 2467-2472; directories, 2473-2474; exhibition catalogs, 2218, 2476-2491; handbook, 2475; periodicals index, 2303A

Texts [folklore], 134-143

Thailand/Thai: folk games, 1956; folk speech, 1956

Theses, *see* Masters' theses

Thomas Day (furniture maker), 2275

Thompson, Stith, *see* Stith Thompson

Tibet/Tibetan: folk arts and crafts--general, 2072; folk games, 1957; folk music, 1054;

Toasts, 742-747

Tobago singing games, 1225

Tongo: calendar and festival rites, 1772; folk dance, 1772; marriage customs, 1772

Toys, *see* Folk toys

Traditional architecture, *see* Folk architecture

Traditional costume, *see* Folk costume

Traditional literature, *see* Fables, Folktales, Jokes and anecdotes, Legends, Mythology, Romances and sagas

Traditions, *see* Customs, beliefs, and superstitions

Tribal art, 2013

Trinidad singing games, 1225

Turkey: folk architecture, folk art and folk crafts, 1999; folk music, 838, 1057; folklore/folklife--general, 86; folktales, 546; musical instruments, 1430; riddles, 489-491

Type-indexes, 524, 525, 528-540, 542-546, 548, 551, 553, 554, 559, 561, 565, 566, 1137

Typologies, *see* Classification

Ukraine/Ukrainian: Christmas rites, 1843; Easter rites, 1843; folklore/folklife--general, 71; needlepoint, 2329

United States. Library of Congress, 195

United States. Library of Congress, Archive of Folk Song, 196-198

United States. Smithsonian Institution, 2537

United States. Smithsonian Institution, Cooper-Hewitt Museum, 2382, 2546

United States. Smithsonian Institution, National Gallery, 2015, 2029, 2030

United States. Smithsonian Institution, National Museum of History and Technology, 2539

University of Arizona Folklore Archive, 191

University of Detroit Computerized Folklore Archives, 219

University of Kentucky Library, 212

University of Mississippi Archive, 220

University of Oregon Archive, 225

University of Pennsylvania University Museum, 2540

University of Texas Folklore Archive, 230

University of Virginia, 232, 833

Uppsala Institute for Philology and Folklore, 240

Urban lore (604A-609), *see also* Toasts, Work songs: annotated collections, 606-609; bibliographies, 30, 604A, 605

Utah: archive, 231; ballads, 1159; customs, beliefs, and superstitions, 1445, 1466, 1620, 1621; fieldwork manual, 147; folk art--general, 2036, 2041; folklore/folklife--general, 2041; material culture--general, 2036; mining lore, 602; quilts, 2370

Vance Randolph, 124

Vaughan Williams Memorial Library, 243, 820

Venezuelan Institute of Folklore, 236

Vermont, *see also* Shelburne Museum: ballads, 1156, 1167; folk medicine, 1700; folk songs, 958-960; sound recordings index, 915

Vernacular architecture, *see also* Folk architecture: bibliographies, 2137, 2140, 2142, 2143, 2151-2153, 2155; classification, 2160; guides, 2163-2166; exhibition catalog, 2171

Vietnam/Vietnamese: ceramics, 2206; folklore/folklife--general, 85

Virginia: archive, 230-232; ballads, 1150, 1151; folk architecture, 2161; folk festivals, 1853; folk music, 232, 842, 901; folk

Virginia cont'd.
speech, 279; hymnals, 1235; popular music, 1271; quilts, 2360

Wales/Welsh: calendar and festival rites, 1815; customs, beliefs, and superstitions, 1406, 1453, 1459, 1494, 1501; folk crafts--general, 2131; folk dance, 1406; folk foods, 2240; folk games, 1965; folk museums, 2554; folk music, 808, 870, 1088, 1101; proverbs, 449; riddles, 494, 497

Washington [DC]: archives, 195-198; children's rhymes, 701; folk festivals, 1853; folk games, 1929

Washington [state]: folklore/folklife--general, 63

Waterloo: folk dance, 1336

Wayne State University Folklore Archive, 218

Weatherlore, 1597-1601, 1781

Weaving (2402-2427), *see also* Textiles: bibliographies, 2402-2403; classification, 2404; dictionary, 2405; directory, 2406; exhibition catalogs, 2422-2427; guides, 2297, 2407-2409; handbooks, 2410-2421

West [America], *see also* individual states, Southwest: folk dance, 1377, 1383; folk medicine, 1740; folk music, 956, 979, 1018; folklore/folklife--general, 22, 23; glass, 2449

West African medicinal plants, 1725

West Indies/West Indian: folk drama, 1895; folk games, 1951, 1952; folk medicine, 1680, 1746; folk music, 1040; folklore/folklife--general, 59, 71; proverbs, 409, 410; religious music, 1040; riddles, 475; singing games, 1225

West Virginia: folk music, 922, 951, 952, 964; singing games, 1207

Western dance, 1377, 1383

Western Kentucky University's Folklore and Folklife Archive, 211, 213

Western music, *see* Country and western music

Western songs, 955

Whaling songs, *see* Sea songs

Wilhelm Schimmel [woodcarver], 2105

Winterthur Museum, 2017, 2032, 2047, 2322

Wisconsin: folk festivals, 1852; quilts, 2375

Witchcraft, *see also* Customs, beliefs, and superstitions, Ghosts, Magic: annotated collection, 1528; bibliographies, 1507, 1508; dictionaries, 1518, 1519; gazetteer, 1522

Women: folk art, 2041; folk music, 763, 936; folklore--general, 3, 33, 38, 59, 247; material culture, 1983; mythology, 619

Work songs: annotated collections, 936, 927, 929, 961, 975, 977, 994, 1010; discography, 871

Worldwide folklore, *see* International folklore

Wrought iron work, *see* Metalcraft